RICHARD SAWYER'S

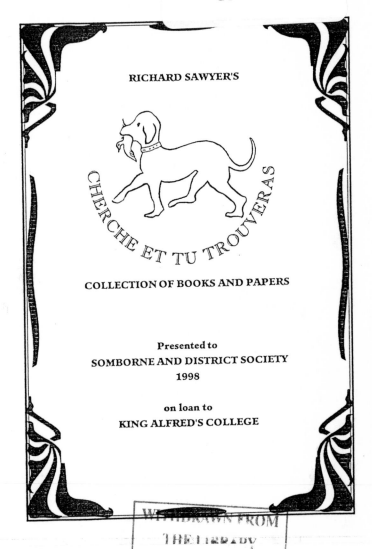

CHERCHE ET TU TROUVERAS

COLLECTION OF BOOKS AND PAPERS

Presented to

SOMBORNE AND DISTRICT SOCIETY
1998

on loan to

KING ALFRED'S COLLEGE

Hampshire Record Series Volume IX

The Cartularies of Southwick Priory

PART 1

edited by

Katharine A. Hanna

Hampshire Record Office for
Hampshire County Council, 1988

ISBN 0 906680 06 9

ISSN 0267-9930

General Editors

C. M. Woolgar : R. C. Dunhill : M. W. Doughty

Graphics Adviser
C. Heywood

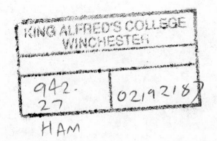
Printed by Hobbs the Printers of Southampton (1009/88)

Three Part Seal Matrix of Southwick Priory
(Photograph by Mr. Robin Lubbock)

PREFACE

The production of this Calendar of the Southwick Priory Cartularies was made possible by the generosity of their owner, the late Mrs E. S. Borthwick-Norton, who entrusted them to the care of the Hampshire Record Office. The present publication comprises a calendar of the first two volumes of the manuscripts, together with a general introduction. A calendar of the third and last volume of the manuscripts will constitute the next publication in the Hampshire Record Series, and this will include a detailed index to the cartularies as a whole.

The task of preparing the calendar has been facilitated by the work done some years ago by Professor Bernard Smith of Swarthmore College, Pennsylvania, with financial assistance provided by the American Philosophical Society and the American Council of Learned Societies. I am most grateful to Professor Smith for readily allowing me to use his transcripts, which included most of Volume I and several items from Volume III.

I owe my return to medieval studies to the interest and help of Professor Paul Harvey, and throughout the present task he has never failed to give me advice and encouragement. I also gratefully acknowledge the help I have received from two friends at Southampton University, Dr Ernest Blake and Dr Brian Golding.

It has been one of the pleasures of working on these documents that I have received such willing and generous help from experts in many fields, from whom I have sought advice. I wish in particular to thank Dr Julian Munby, who has shared with me the fruits of his research on Portchester and has lent me photo-copies of documents, also Mr Roger Davey, Father S. F. Hockey, Dr J. M. Kaye, Mr G. Soffe, Mr D. G. Watts, and Dr David Postles, all of whom have helped me on various points, not all of which can be specified in footnotes to the text.

In connection with the perambulation of the forests, I have received invaluable assistance from Mr Arthur Clarke, Mr David Stagg, Dr Paul Stamper and Mr Edward Yates.

A glance at the Winchester documents calendared here will at once show the debt I owe to the work of Dr Derek Keene. It has been my good fortune that his magnificently comprehensive volume on medieval Winchester was published before I completed this calendar, and the information thus made available has enabled me to identify the precise location of properties held there by Southwick Priory.

In dealing with Portsea Island, I have been greatly assisted in the task of identifying field-names by the work done by Dr John Chapman, and I am particularly grateful to him for allowing me to reproduce here an adaptation of his map of the Common Lands.

During my researches at Winchester and Portsmouth I have received unfailing courtesy and help at the Record Offices, and I am most grateful to Mrs Quail, Mrs Hoad and the staff at Portsmouth, as well as to Miss Dunhill and the staff at Winchester. Mr K. H. Rogers, Wiltshire County Archivist, has been most helpful in dealing with my queries concerning Swindon, and Miss Sheila Thomson, Southampton City Archivist, with those concerning Southampton. I have also received valuable co-operation from the staff of Southampton University Library, especially Mr G. Hampson. For identifying place-names in Normandy I am indebted to the Inspector-General of the Archives de France and also to the Deputy-Keeper of the Archives of the Department of Calvados.

It was Miss Margaret Cash who first suggested that I should undertake this work, and in the initial stages she, as General Editor, generously spared time to advise and to discuss its progress; for the later stages I have been most fortunate in having the support and guidance of Dr Christopher Woolgar, who has also written the description of the manuscripts and of the arrangement of the priory's muniments.

Two special friends have contributed very greatly to the completion of this work. Mr Anthony Light, who has made a most thorough study of the Augustinian priory at Breamore, has not only given me help and encouragement throughout in countless ways, but has also drawn the maps; and Mrs Eileen Leonard has typed—and to a large extent re-typed—the entire manuscript, purely as an act of friendship, with a patience, enthusiasm and care for which no thanks can be adequate.

Finally there is the great debt of gratitude I owe to my family, and in particular to my son, Harold, for his ever-willing assistance. The editing of the cartularies has been a huge task for a part-time researcher working at home. Inevitably the accumulating mountains of paper have tended to overwhelm every available surface. My sons have become used to letting the telephone ring for a very long time, and when eventually I answered I would hear a weary voice saying with resignation, "I suppose you were in the thirteenth century"! Without the forbearance and encouragement of my husband I should never have finished the job. He has many times paused in his own, very different, research to give me practical help and advice, and if I have in some measure achieved my aim of producing a calendar of the text that is not only accurate, but also readable and free from jargon, then much of the literary credit must go to him. The errors—and I know there will be some, though I hope not too many—are mine.

Katharine A. Hanna
Barton-on-Sea, Hampshire
Easter, 1987

Contents

Illustrations

ABBREVIATIONS

Annales monastici	*Annales monastici* ed. H. R. Luard (5 vols., Rolls Series, London, 1864–9)
B.L.	British Library
Beauchamp Cartulary	*The Beauchamp Cartulary* ed. E. Mason (Pipe Roll Society, New Series, 43; 1980)
Beaulieu Cartulary	*The Beaulieu Cartulary* ed. S. F. Hockey (Southampton Record Series, 17; 1974)
Book of Fees	*The Book of Fees* (3 vols., London, 1920–31)
Brocas	M. Burrows *The Family of Brocas of Beaurepaire and Roche Court* (London, 1886)
Cal. Chart. R.	*Calendar of Charter Rolls*
Cal. Close R.	*Calendar of Close Rolls*
Cal. Docs. in France	*Calendar of Documents preserved in France* ed. J. H. Round (London, 1899)
Cal. Fine R.	*Calendar of Fine Rolls*
Cal. Inq. misc.	*Calendar of Inquisitions miscellaneous*
Cal. Inq. p. m.	*Calendar of Inquisitions post mortem*
Cal. Lib. R.	*Calendar of Liberate Rolls*
Cal. Pat. R.	*Calendar of Patent Rolls*
Chapman, "Common Lands of Portsea Island"	J. Chapman, "The Common Lands of Portsea Island" (*The Portsmouth Papers*, 29; 1978)
Chichester Chartulary	*The Chartulary of the High Church of Chichester* ed. W. D. Peckham (Sussex Record Society, 46; 1942–3)
Complete Peerage	G. E. Cokayne *The Complete Peerage* (revised edition, 13 vols., London, 1910–59)
Curia Reg. R.	*Curia Regis Rolls*
D.B.	Domesday Book
DNB	*Dictionary of National Biography*
Fasti	J. le Neve *Fasti Ecclesiae Anglicanae, 1066–1300* ed. D. E. Greenway (in progress, London, 1968–)
Feudal Aids	*Inquisitions and assessments relating to Feudal Aids* (6 vols., London, 1899–1920)
Gallia Christiana	*Gallia Christiana* ed. P. Piolin (16 vols. I–XIII, new edition, Paris, 1870–8; XIV–XVI, Paris, 1856–65)
God's House Cartulary	*The Cartulary of God's House, Southampton* ed. J. M. Kaye (2 vols., Southampton Record Series, 19, 20; 1976)

Gover	J. E. B. Gover, "The Place-Names of Hampshire" (unpublished typescript in H.R.O.)
HBC	*Handbook of British Chronology* ed. F. M. Powicke and E. B. Fryde (2nd edition, Royal Historical Society, London 1961)
Hervey, *History of Colmer and Priors Dean*	T. Hervey, *A history of the united parishes of Colmer and Priors Dean* (Colmer, 1880)
Hoad, "Origins of Portsmouth"	M. Hoad, "The Origins of Portsmouth", *Hampshire Studies presented to Dorothy Dymond* ed. J. Webb, N. Yates, and S. Peacock (Portsmouth, 1981) pp. 1–30
Hockey *Quarr Abbey*	S. F. Hockey, *Quarr Abbey and its lands, 1132–1631* (Leicester, 1970)
H.R.O.	Hampshire Record Office
Itinerary of Henry II	*Court, Household and Itinerary of King Henry II* ed. R. W. Eyton (London, 1878)
Itinerary of Richard I	*The Itinerary of Richard I* ed. L. Landon (Pipe Roll Society, New Series, 13; 1935)
Knights of Edward I	C. Moor, *The Knights of Edward I* (5 vols. Harleian Society, 80–4; 1929–32)
Knowles *Heads of Religious Houses*	*The Heads of Religious Houses of England and Wales, 940–1216* ed. Knowles, Brooke, and London (Cambridge, 1972)
Lancs R.O.	Lancashire Record Office
Langley Cartulary	*The Langley Cartulary* ed. P. R. Coss (Dugdale Society, 32; 1980)
Mansi	*Sacrorum conciliorum nova et amplissima collectio* ed. J. D. Mansi (31 vols., Venice and Florence, 1759–98)
Mason, "The King, the Chamberlain and Southwick Priory"	E. Mason, "The King, the Chamberlain and Southwick Priory" *Bulletin of the Institute of Historical Research* 53 (1980) pp. 1–10
Mason, "The Mauduits and their Chamberlainship of the Exchequer"	E. Mason, "The Mauduits and their Chamberlainship of the Exchequer" *Bulletin of the Institute of Historical Research*, 49 (1976) pp. 1–23
MLWL	*Revised Medieval Latin Word List* ed. R. E. Latham (London, 1965)
Monasticon Anglicanum	W. Dugdale, *Monasticon Anglicanum* ed. J. Caley, H. Ellis and B. Bandinel (6 vols. in 8, London, 1817–30)

Papsturkunden in England	*Papsturkunden in England* ed. W. Holtzmann (3 vols., Berlin and Göttingen, 1930–52)
Pecham Register	*The Register of John Pecham, Archbishop of Canterbury 1279–1292* ed. F. N. Davis and D. Douie (2 vols., Canterbury and York Society, 64–5; 1968–9)
Pontissara Register	*Registrum Johannis de Pontissara Episcopi Wyntoniensis* ed. C. Deedes (2 vols., Canterbury and York Society, 19, 30; 1915, 1924)
Potthast *Regesta Pontificum Romanorum*	*Regesta Pontificum Romanorum inde ab anno post Christum natum MCXCVIII ad annum MCCCIV* ed. A. Potthast (2 vols., Berlin, 1874–5)
Powicke *Loss of Normandy*	Sir M. Powicke *The Loss of Normandy, 1189–1204* (2nd edition, Manchester, 1961)
PR	Pipe Roll: published by the Pipe Roll Society
P.R.O.	Public Record Office
Recueil des Actes de Henri II	*Chartres et Diplômes Relatifs à l'Histoire de France; Recueil des Actes de Henri II, Roi d'Angleterre et Duc de Normandie* ed. L. Delisle and E. Berger (4 vols., Paris 1909–27)
Regesta	*Regesta Regum Anglo-Normannorum, 1066–1154* ed. H. W. C. Davis, C. Johnson, H. A. Cronne, and R. H. C. Davis (4 vols., Oxford, 1913–69)
St Denys Cartulary	*The Cartulary of the Priory of St Denys near Southampton* ed. E. O. Blake (2 vols., Southampton Record Series, 24, 25; 1981)
Selborne Charters	*Calendar of Charters and Documents relating to Selborne and its Priory* ed. W. D. Macray (2 vols., Hampshire Record Society, 4, 9; 1891, 1894)
Sandale Register	*The Registers of John de Sandale and Rigaud de Asserio, Bishops of Winchester, 1316–23* ed. F. J. Baigent (Hampshire Record Society, 8; 1897)
Statutes of the Realm	*Statutes of the realm* ed. A. Luders, T. E. Tomlins, J. Raithby et al. (11 vols., London, 1810–28)

Stubbington Account Roll	Winchester College Muniment
1247	15376(d)
1249	15376(f)
1250	15376(e)
1251	15376(c)
1252	15376(b)
1280–81	15376(a)
1267	15377(d)
1268	15377(c)
1268–69	15377(b)
1270	15377(a)
1269–70	15378
?1281	15379
1287–88	15380
1319–20	15381

Taxatio	*Taxatio ecclesiastica Angliae et Walliae auctoritate P. Nicholai IV circa A.D. 1291* (Record Commission, London, 1802)
VCH	*Victoria County History*
Win. Cath. Cart.	*Chartulary of Winchester Cathedral* ed. A. W. Goodman (Winchester, 1927)
Win. Coll. Cart.	Winchester College Cartulary—part of a cartulary from Southwick Priory in the College muniments (15246)
Woodlock Register	*Registrum Henrici Woodlock* ed. A. W. Goodman (2 vols., Canterbury and York Society, 43–4; 1940–1)
WS I	Winchester Studies I: *Winchester in the Early Middle Ages* ed. M. Biddle (Oxford, 1976)
WS II	Winchester Studies II: D. Keene *Survey of Medieval Winchester* (2 vols., Oxford, 1985)
Wykeham Register	*Wykeham's Register* ed. T. F. Kirby (2 vols. Hampshire Record Society, 11, 13; 1896, 1899)

INTRODUCTION

The Priory and its Surviving Records

Though relatively small in comparison with some of the great English monastic establishments, Southwick Priory was the second-largest of the six Augustinian priories in Hampshire, and larger than any of the six in the neighbouring county of Sussex. With the exception of Christchurch, which had already been a flourishing institution in Saxon times long before being converted into an Augustinian priory, it was the only one of those priories which survived the dissolution of the smaller houses in 1536. Its place in medieval English religious and social life was certainly much more important than might be assumed from the relatively little attention given to it in the published works on those subjects. There are two obvious reasons why it has been neglected. The first is the total destruction of almost the whole of its buildings, so that very little remains to impress the visitor to the site where once they stood.[1] The second, and the most important, is that the wealth of material contained in its cartularies and other records has not been available to scholars. Not only have they not been previously published, but until fairly recently only a nineteenth-century transcript of the third volume of the cartularies has been accessible: it was made by Sir Frederick Madden, and is in the British Library.[2]

The records have, however, survived to a far greater extent than those of many other monastic houses. Almost all of them are now in the care of the Hampshire Record Office. Among them a number of original charters are still in existence. These, however, are relatively few in comparison with the great bulk of material in the main cartularies. In addition to these there are various later copies, which show that interest in those documents continued long after the Dissolution. A few of the copies were made in the sixteenth and seventeenth centuries, probably because they were required as evidence of land-ownership. There is also an eighteenth-century MS (4M53/B7) containing some seventeen entries, two of which are not to be found in the cartularies or elsewhere, and are calendared as Appendix IV in the present work. Seven of the other entries give the names of witnesses not recorded in the copies in the cartularies, and two contain other additions. It seems likely that this MS was copied directly from originals which have now disappeared, and indeed the reason for copying them may well have been that they were already very dilapidated.[3]

Nor is this all. The Hampshire Record Office also has custody of a large number of court rolls, some account rolls, and other miscellaneous but sometimes very illuminating material relating to the priory—only a small proportion of which has been investigated for the purposes of the present study.

Among this material is a MS book[4] of over 350 pages by a certain W. T. Alchin, consisting of a careful inventory and description of the Southwick records, which he made at Southwick, with the permission of their then owner, over a period of some months in 1841. He included at least one item which appears to be no longer in existence, but which would have been of considerable interest: a book containing, amongst other things—such as a list of the donors who contributed a total of £530 to the rebuilding of the priory's church[5]—an inventory made in the time of William Noxton, the last prior, of the contents of the priory, room by room (parlour, cellar, great chamber, chamber over the hall, and kitchen): almost the only mention from any source of the actual buildings, other than the church. Many of the loose charters and other documents are numbered and endorsed in Alchin's careful hand.

Some of the material in the cartularies is also to be found, independently copied from the originals, in Winchester College[6] and in the British Library,[7] and this has been collated with the main cartularies. The Winchester College muniments also include some Southwick manuscripts which do not exist in any other version or copy. Among these the account rolls for Stubbington, in Portsea Island,[8] are of particular importance in that they provide dating evidence for charters, and also information about the working of one of the principal granges and its contribution to the priory's finances.

The Founding of the Priory

The community of Augustinian canons which constituted Southwick Priory was originally founded at Portchester, at some date in the 1120s before the death of William Giffard, Bishop of Winchester, on 25 January 1129.[9] Its site was very close to the royal castle, and was indeed within the area surrounded by the great Roman walls, within which the Norman castle itself had been built. The castle and also the honour of Portchester were at that time held by William de Pont de l'Arche, who had acquired them when he obtained the office of Chamberlain of the Exchequer by paying 1,000 marks to Henry I for licence to marry the daughter and heir of the previous Chamberlain, Robert Mauduit, after Robert's death in 1120.[10] The honour of Portchester included the lands at Southwick to which the priory moved within a quarter of a century of its foundation. Thus most of the lands with which the priory was orginally endowed were held of the king by serjeanty, and could not be alienated without his consent, so that although it was William de Pont de l'Arche who established the priory at Portchester and granted the lands to it,[11] there was an element of justification for later assertions that it was a royal foundation. Its tenure of its existing possessions was, in fact, 'conceded' by Henry I in a charter issued in 1133, of which the authenticity does not seem to be in any doubt, although the original has not survived.[12] This document has often been interpreted as the priory's foundation charter, and its date given as that of the actual foundation: but it does not itself state that it was granted for this purpose.[13]

During Henry I's reign William held a prominent position not only in the financial administration of the state but also as Sheriff of Hampshire, but after the king's death his fortunes fluctuated during the ensuing struggle for the crown. At first he supported Stephen and, since he controlled access to the treasury at Winchester, this support was crucial for Stephen's success in 1135; however by early 1141 he had transferred his allegiance to the Empress Matilda. Fearing an attack on Portchester, he requested reinforcements; but after their arrival their leader, Robert fitz Hildebrand, seduced William's wife and imprisoned him for a time in his own castle. Robert's death provided the opportunity for him to recover something of his former position; this is known from the fact that he witnessed as Chamberlain a charter granted by the empress between 1144 and 1147—apparently his last appearance in royal records.[14] His son and heir, Robert, was not awarded the office of Chamberlain which was recovered by the Mauduits. Nor did he receive the castle and honour of Portchester which were retained by the king, some of the lands being returned to the Mauduits.[15] William's standing and wealth had been dependent on the opportunities afforded to him by the offices and lands he held under the crown; without them, and with no other great estates in Hampshire to bring him wealth and influence, Robert could do little to further the interests of his father's foundation.

During their occupation of the site at Portchester, which was located in the south-east corner of the outer bailey of the castle, the canons erected a church which is still standing, an impressive and beautiful building largely unaltered since the time of its construction; the most recent study of its decoration suggest a date *c.* 1130, and this accords well with the date now established for the priory's foundation.[16] The claustral buildings lay on the south side of the church. An eastern dormitory range running southwards from the south transept, now demolished, had a two-storey reredorter abutting on to the Roman wall of the fort; the garderobe openings on the upper level can still be seen where they were cut through the wall. A western range on the opposite side of the cloister, its western wall almost in line with the west front of the church, did not extend as far as the fort wall, and perhaps was still unfinished when the canons moved to Southwick. There was probably a south range, which might have been expected to contain the refectory, and to have been built after the eastern and before the western range, but it has left no trace on the fort wall, possibly owing to re-surfacing, and any trace of the foundations of its north wall would have been destroyed by later grave-digging. There can therefore be no certainty as to whether it was ever completed, or indeed of its existence.

The church at Portchester remained in the priory's possession until the Dissolution; the priory regularly presented to the vicarage and drew from the church an annual pension of £1. 4s. 0d.[17] The rectory of Portchester (the prior of Southwick being named as rector) was valued for taxation in 1291 at £9. 6s. 8d., while the vicarage was valued at £5.[18] Recent excavations have shown that part at least of the eastern range of buildings was in use for about two centuries after the canons had left; other buildings were probably demolished to serve as a convenient source of stone for repairs to the castle.[19]

The turmoil of the civil war must have made apparent the unsuitability of the Portchester site, and by early 1150 the priory had moved to Southwick. A further reason for the move, and the one stated by Archbishop Theobald when granting indulgence to those who contributed to the expenses of rebuilding, was the canons' need for more space than was available on the original site.[20] That site was of course restricted by the Roman walls of the outer bailey of the castle.[21]

There can be little doubt that the church and conventual buildings which were erected at Southwick were on an even grander scale than those at Portchester. It is all the more ironical that, although Southwick Priory was occupied for over 380 years, compared with little over 20 years' occupancy of the site at Portchester, far less is known about its buildings.

The church was dedicated to St Mary, and the altar which bore her name was regarded with particular reverence and esteem: it attracted pilgrims and offerings; on it were placed charters of gifts, and solemn undertakings were sworn there; benefactors donated land and rent to provide lamps and candles to burn there in perpetuity, and one of the canons had special charge of it (III 682). It is reasonable to suppose that the statue of Our Lady referred to at the time of the Dissolution stood within the church, or possibly in a separate chapel above the priory's gate.[22] The tomb of Lucy de Hommet, wife of William, the Constable of Normandy, lay before a crucifix in the church, and on it a lamp burned by night and candles when Mass was said there daily for her soul (I 71,76). On the north side of the chancel there was an altar dedicated to Saints Katherine and Mary Magdalene (III 427); and another altar on the north side of the nave was dedicated to the Holy Cross (III 225); doubtless there were others. It appears that after 1254 a stone tower surmounted by a lead-covered timber steeple was added to the church, with a peal of seven bells.[23]

Before the church was dedicated in 1181–2, the priory already had a guest-house (I 25); some gifts were specifically directed towards its upkeep (I 140, III 404). There was an almshouse outside the priory's gate, where the poor and sick were cared for, (III 688, 713) as well as the infirmary within the precincts for members of the priory (III 189, 881).

The only remnant of the priory which is still standing is part of one wall of the refectory, and even that is is much altered and patched. It was during work undertaken in 1984 to conserve this wall that bricks were removed which had masked an elaborate lavabo screen of fine workmanship, almost certainly dating from the original building of the priory[24]—an indication of the quality of what has been lost.

It is only by a chance reference that any information can be gleaned from the cartularies about the priory's buildings or its administration. Apart from the prior and sub-prior, mention is made of the sacristan, cellarer, almoner, infirmarian and pittancer. As for the number of canons in the priory, evidence has to be sought elsewhere, and there is none earlier than the late fourteenth century; but the number was probably about thirteen.[25] The account roll for 1386–7 shows that at that time the community consisted of the prior, sub-prior, bailiff, and eleven priests, together with five novices; in 1393–4 the situation was unchanged except that there were three deacons instead of five novices.[26] These numbers probably reflected an increase resulting from the founding in 1369 of William of Wykeham's chantries, which were to be served by five priests (II 111). A century later, however, in 1494, only eleven canons took part in the election of a new prior;[27] but this number appears to have been exceptionally small, for in 1521, on a similar occasion, the number who participated was thirteen.[28] At the Dissolution, the priory consisted of twelve canons in addition to the prior.[29]

The death of William de Pont de l'Arche *c.* 1148 had probably removed an impediment to the move to Southwick; however that may be, the canons took pains to obtain not only the consent and support of William's son, Robert, but also that of the king, the diocesan bishop, the Archbishop of Canterbury, and the pope.[30] A daunting task faced them, in view of the comparatively meagre size of their original endowment. They needed a patron powerful enough not only to protect their interests but to attract benefactors. If Robert de Pont de l'Arche was unable to fulfil the role, the king was the obvious choice, and the circumstances of the original foundation made the adoption of a royal "founder" plausible. Henry II was anxious to strengthen his position by every means at his disposal, and was unlikely to miss the opportunity offered to him by the priory. In terms similar to those of Henry I's genuine charter, he "conceded" to the priory the churches of Portchester and Southwick, confirmed gifts made by William de Pont de l'Arche, and added, ostensibly as a gift of his own, two hides at Fishbourne, Sussex; but it may be that even this gift was no more than a confirmation of one made by Turstin, son of Engelramn, who had held the land of the crown (I 2;III 99,100).

Another genuine charter which the priory obtained from Henry II, probably in 1174, was a notification that the king had taken "his own church of St Mary, Southwick, and his prior and canons" under his protection; henceforth their possessions were to be preserved from harm as if they were royal demesne, and no suit involving their demesne lands was to be heard except by the king himself (I 123). As in the case of the spurious charter of Henry I,[31] the priory later sought to augment their privileges and exemptions by forging a third charter purporting to have been granted by Henry II.[32]

The priory was, however, to discover that having the king as "founder" was not without its disadvantages. It gave him the right to control the election of a new prior and to take the priory's possessions into his hands during a vacancy;[33] it also strengthened his claim to maintenance for royal pensioners—corrodians—whom he sent to Southwick. There is no evidence to suggest that the canons' choice of prior—usually one of their own number—was ever refused, though they had to apply to the king for licence to hold an election.[34]

After the death of Prior John de Clere in 1291, the sheriff took the priory's revenues for the king's use during the ensuing vacancy. The canons thereupon protested that their founder was not the king's progenitor but William de Pont de l'Arche; they also asserted that the king's only role in respect of the vacancy was to send a single representative, when requested by the priory, to reside there at their expense in order to safeguard their property. An inquisition was held on the king's orders; it took place at Southwick, and confirmed the priory's claim.[35] Ten years previously, in 1281, an inquisition held at Fishbourne had already recorded "that neither the king nor any of his progenitors, in the time of vacancy of Southwick Priory, used to have custody there, from the time of the priory's foundation" (III 100). This implies that the jury did not regard Southwick as a royal foundation; and what was implicit in 1281 was made explicit in 1291. Nevertheless it seems that by the end of the following century the local community had ceased to remember the priory's real founder; a series of inquisitions, held after the deaths of successive priors in 1381, 1389 and 1398, all declared that it was a royal foundation (II 32,56,75). In 1381 the king received 20s. 7½d. at the rate of 8¼d. a day for the 30 days' vacancy; in 1389 Richard II waived all claim on account of the priory's poverty; no record survives in the cartularies about the sequel to the inquisition of 1398. As for the obligation to receive royal corrodians, the priory does not appear to have raised objections so long as it only had to provide for one at a time;[36] but when Edward III in 1336 imposed a second pensioner upon their hospitality, they appear to have objected on the ground that they were not a royal foundation, for an inquisition was held on the king's orders to ascertain both the identity of the priory's founder and the extent of its obligation to make provision for royal corrodians. The jury confirmed the priory's claim, and also stated that the founder was "Sir William de Poundelarg' "; whereupon the king conceded that the priory's acceptance of a second pensioner should not be taken as a precedent.[37] Royal corrodians continued to be sent to the priory until the Dissolution.[38]

Royal Benefactors

If the priory sometimes found itself overburdened by royal demands, it nevertheless had reason to be thankful to successive royal benefactors. During Richard I's reign, Eleanor, the Queen Mother, confirmed William de Hommet's gifts to the priory (I 147); the king's niece, Matilda, and her husband, Count Geoffrey de Perche, granted to the canons land at Aldbourne in Wiltshire (I 144); and the king's brother, Count John, gave them Colemore in Hampshire (I 148). After he became king, John granted them Dean, near Colemore, at fee farm (I 162), and in 1214 issued letters patent taking them and their possessions under his protection (I 168). In 1231 Henry III confirmed John's gifts and granted freedom from tallage at Colemore and Dean (III 831). Four years later he bestowed on the priory the right to hold a weekly market and an annual fair lasting for two days.[39] Like his father, Henry visited the priory. He stayed there for a week in 1253, from 24 June to 1 July, during which time he issued a charter taking the priory under his protection.[40] The following year he ordered his bailiffs at Portsmouth to deliver a tun of wine to the priory as his gift.[41]

After passing the Statute of Mortmain in 1279, the good-will of the crown towards the priory was from time to time shown by the granting of licences to receive gifts or make exchanges of land. In 1280 Edward I ordered his steward, Ralph de Sandwyco, to allow both the prior of Southwick and the prior of Portsmouth (God's House) to hold lands in Portsmouth and Kingston, acquired after the publication of the Statute.[42] Nine years later the king licensed an exchange of mills between the priory and Richard de Burhunt.[43] Edward II in 1318 made a valuable concession by allowing the priory to acquire land worth £20 a year, notwithstanding the Statute of Mortmain.[44] He also granted to the canons free warren in all their demesne lands.[45]

The war with France during the reign of Edward III put a severe strain upon the priory, which lay on the route of the king and his entourage when they were making for ports of embarkation, and was obliged to provide hospitality. Its manors were said to have suffered by the passage of those travelling to and from the army, and its property on the coast to have been damaged and burnt in enemy raids. In 1342 the king granted exemption to the priory from payment to him of tenths and tallages for three years owing to the losses it had suffered at the hands of his enemies.[46] Four years later, in June 1346, the priory was excused payment of the annual fee farm due for the land it held from the crown in Colemore and Dean.[47] However, this concession was surrendered, probably because of a gift from the king which was even more profitable. This was the grant of the manor of Crookhorn and Farlington with the advowson of Farlington Church, all of which had been forfeited to the crown on the execution of Hugh le Despenser. The grant was made on account of the depressed condition of the priory brought about by the expenses of hospitality and the losses through enemy action.[48] The following year the prior of Southwick managed to provide £15 as a loan towards the cost of the expedition to France, and received an assurance from the Exchequer of repayment at Michaelmas 1348.[49] But improvement in the priory's financial position, if any, must have been shortlived, as 1348 saw the first onslaught of the Black Death. When Robert Wyvil, Bishop of Salisbury, appropriated the church of Swindon to the priory in 1357, a licence having been obtained from the king, among the reasons given was the fall in the numbers of the priory's tenants and loss of rents as a result of the plague (II 1; III 982,403). Edward III also issued licences for the priory's exchange of lands with William Fifhide in 1356 (III 468), and for the valuable acquisition in 1369 of the manors of Boarhunt Herberd and Herbelyn as the gift of William of Wykeham for the endowment of his chantries (II 112; III 972).

The following reign saw the founding of the Brocas chantry, and Richard II's licence was obtained in 1384 for alienation of land, value c. £20 a year, to the priory by way of endowment (III 421). The next year the prior of Southwick was appointed by the king to supervise work being done at Portchester Castle, to have charge of the expenditure and to render the account. Similar commissions were given to the prior in 1396 and 1398.[50]

Evidence of the cost to the priory of a royal visit is to be found in a surviving account roll, kept by the keeper of the priory's guest-house, for the year 1388–9.[51] Nearly half the annual income of his office appears to have been spent on preparing the apartments for the king and queen, including repairs to the roof, a new door and fastenings, redecoration, and provision of linen sheets and rushes for the floor.

There was another factor which brought the priory into close contact with the crown: that was the proximity of its estates to royal forests which lay on almost every side. Exemptions from forest laws were privileges worth seeking and defending. It is hardly surprising to find the perambulation of the royal forests in Hampshire in 1300 copied into one of the priory's cartularies (II 41–55). The priory's interests were closely involved especially with the Forest of Portchester, or East Bere, but also with Windsor and Woolmer Forests, which lay close to its manors of Moundsmere at Preston Candover and of Priors Dean and Colemore respectively.

In 1274 the prior of Southwick successfully defended his claim to right of pasture in Richard de Portesia's demesne wood within the Forest of Portchester; Richard and others were fined for impounding the prior's beasts on the ground that only the royal foresters had the right to do so (I 105). Edward II, in 1310, responded to a complaint from the prior of Southwick by ordering his officials in the royal Forest of Windsor to desist from demanding the prior's attendance at the Swainmote or imposing other charges on him, because exemption had been granted by King Henry (II 59). The charter shown to Edward was apparently the forged charter purporting to come from Henry I which contained additional privileges and exemptions not found in the genuine charter.[52] It was the inspeximus and confirmation by Henry III in 1269 of this forgery, with other charters, that Edward inspected and confirmed in 1313.[53] The priory also successfully claimed exemption in 1325 after the Keeper of the Forest of Woolmer had demanded that its dogs be expedited and that it should pay heavy fines (II 60).

Early Benefactions from Norman Magnates

The royal connection was probably a factor in attracting to the priory the interest and benefactions of the influential de Hommet family; both Richard de Hommet and his son, William, served the crown as Constables of Normandy.[54] Southwick was conveniently situated for those travelling from Winchester or beyond for embarkation to the continent. Richard apparently had charge of Portchester Castle for a time, and became involved in the settlement of disputes between the priory and its near neighbours, the Boarhunt family.[55] William and his wife, Lucy, were both benefactors of the priory,[56] and by choosing to be buried there, Lucy attracted gifts to the canons not only from her husband for the celebration of her anniversary and for a lamp to burn in perpetuity on her tomb (I 71,76), but also offerings in her memory from her husband's clerk, Robert de Bera (I 39,73–5; III 381); from her liege-man, Ralph de Mesnil (I 81–2); and from her friend, Robert de Novo Burgo (I 78). These gifts brought to the priory lands and rents far off in Ketton, Lincolnshire, and in Cottesmore, Rutland, as well as some more conveniently placed in Boarhunt and Soberton.

The burial of William de Diva at Southwick doubtless prompted his brother, Guy, to give to the canons two marks' worth of land at Hollowell, Northamptonshire (I 132); and William's kinsman, the Earl of Arundel, gave two sesters of wheat a year from his manor of Westbourne, Sussex, for the celebration of William's anniversary at the priory (III 85). Two of the Mesnil family, Ralph and his brother, Henry, were buried at Southwick, and their brother, Jordan, gave to the priory his share of tithes of corn at Maisy in Normandy (III 324). Another gift at Maisy, in this case half an acre, was presented to the canons by Peter de Basevile in gratitude for their care of him during sickness (III 328,58). After the loss of Normandy, the canons sought to retain or recover these rents and tithes, but although the story is incomplete, it seems unlikely that their efforts met with any lasting success (III 325–6, 329–30).

All these transactions belong to the latter part of the twelfth century, by which time it is evident that the priory was involved with members of several notable Norman families as benefactors who sought the benefits of fraternal association with it in life, and the celebration by it of their anniversaries after death.

Gifts of lands and rents at places far from Southwick presented the canons with difficulties over their utilisation or collection. Sometimes the problem was solved by exchanges, as in the case of Lucy de Hommet's gift at Stamford, Lincolnshire, which Southwick Priory gave to the nuns of Stamford Priory in exchange for land which had been given to the nuns at Drayton, near Farlington, only a few miles from Southwick (I 145). Sometimes the priory leased lands for an annual rent, and in the case of Hollowell, Northamptonshire, granted manumission in 1284 to three villein tenants and transferred the land to them at an annual rent of 40s. (III 242–3, II 63). All the property which the priory held at Ketton and Cottesmore was granted by Prior Guy to a local landowner at Stamford in return for the modest rent of a half-mark a year.[57]

Certain gifts to the priory of lands and rents outside Hampshire were the subject of charters copied into the cartularies, but thereafter disappear from the record; perhaps it proved impossible for the priory to take advantage of them, or the undertakings given were never fulfilled. Of such were Engelrann Pincerna's gift of a mark's rent at Eaton Bray, Bedfordshire (I 153); Simon de Wahelle's gift of a similar amount from his mills at Ravenstone, Buckinghamshire (I 40), and Juliana de Berkelay's gift of a tenement in Berkeley, Gloucestershire, which she gave to the priory for the celebration of the anniversary of her father, Robert Pont de l'Arche, son of its founder, after his burial at Southwick (III 199).

There were three gifts outside Hampshire which the priory kept until the Dissolution, and from which it drew a regular income; these were at Fishbourne, not far along the coast in Sussex; at Aldbourne in Wiltshire, and at Clanfield in Oxfordshire.[58]

The Priory's relations with its immediate neighbours

Grants made to the priory outside Hampshire were the exception rather than the norm. By far the greater part of the priory's estates and rents lay within the county, and it was the deliberate policy of the canons to consolidate them so far as possible in fairly clearly defined areas. Even before the move to Southwick there is evidence that the endowment gifts of land there and at neighbouring Applestead were seen as the nucleus for potential expansion. This brought the canons into frequent involvement with successive generations of various branches of the neighbouring family—the Boarhunts or de Burhunts—who appear in the cartularies as benefactors and witnesses, or as litigants in cases concerning exchanges of land or disputes over boundaries and tithes, from the second half of the twelfth century into the second half of the fourteenth.

It would appear that soon after its foundation the priory, while still at Portchester, was engaged in making exchanges of land with Herbert de Burhunt, then head of the family, and from him it received the gift of a chapel and tithes, and the site of a mill. But relations between Herbert and the priory were not entirely amicable. Herbert spent some time in prison at Portchester, probably during the upheaval of the civil war, and during that time he made a vow that on his release he would give to the priory his share of the common of Applestead. However, he failed to keep his promise and subsequently enclosed the land, treating it as his own demesne. Despite an appeal to the custodian of Portchester, then apparently Richard de Hommet, the priory had been unable to make good its claim until Herbert was stricken with mortal illness and hurriedly made amends. Before his death he gave seisin of the disputed land to the prior, with the consent of all his sons; and his heir, Alexander, subsequently added a gift of land for the celebration in the priory of Herbert's anniversary.

Although Alexander and the priory submitted the exchanges of land which had taken place to examination by arbitrators, disputes continued. On one occasion Alexander sought to make the priory responsible for royal service on land he had given to it "as the king was levying Danegeld that year", but the priory objected that there was no precedent for this demand. Agreement was finally reached, Alexander receiving one mark and a palfrey in return for conceding that the priory should hold the land in free alms, quit of all forinsec service (I 121). Another source of contention was the mill which the priory had built on a site given to them by Herbert. In 1165 Alexander sued the canons over flood damage to his land which, he claimed, had resulted from the operation of the priory's sluices. On this occasion arbitration was provided by the steward, constable and justice of the lord of Portchester—presumably still Richard de Hommet—together with neighbours and free men of the shire (I 122, 29). It may have been the difficulty experienced by the prior in reaching a lasting settlement with Alexander that prompted the making of the Final Concord on 18 November 1182 in the King's Court of the Exchequer concerning the same mill and millpond, thereby getting the priory's rights enrolled on the royal record (I 30).

The priory also exchanged lands, apparently before and after 1135, with Henry de Burhunt, who may have been Herbert's brother; certainly Henry's son, Reinelm was a contemporary of Alexander, and possibly his cousin. Again the exchanges led to disputes, and an agreement between Reinelm and the priory was confirmed by Richard de Hommet, possibly in 1164 (I 120). As in the case of Herbert, Henry's soul was to be remembered in the canons' prayers, and Reinelm and his brother, Richard, were received into their fraternity. When the priory's church was dedicated in 1181-2, Reinelm gave the canons two acres outside their main gate next to their newly-built guest-house, and an important source of water from the spring of Offwell with the right to channel it through his fief to the priory (I 25).

The canons continued to make exchanges of land with members of the Boarhunt family until the two manors of Boarhunt Herberd and Boarhunt Herbelyn passed out of the family's possession and in 1369 were granted to the priory by William of Wykeham (I 102, 104, 100, 106; II 163, 176, 145; II 111).

Many of the local landowners who witnessed the Boarhunt charters over some two hundred years were themselves benefactors of the priory. Five generations of the de Bello Alneto or Bellaney family appear in the cartularies, and the name survives in that of Belney Farm, near Southwick. Sir Robert was a frequent witness in the first half of the thirteenth century, and the priory granted him the right to have a private chapel at his home at Belney for the use of his family and descendants under strict conditions which safeguarded the rights and financial interests of the parish church of Southwick (III 668). Sir Robert's son, Sir William, and his grandson, Sir Baldwin, were also closely involved with the priory. Sir Baldwin, who was a minor when his father died in 1262, gave the priory two acres at Portchester; here as elsewhere the family estates lay in close proximity to those of the priory. (III 196).

Sir Baldwin's son, Richard, was the defendant in a long and bitter dispute with the priory, lasting from 1302-29 (II 58; III 451-6), over non-payment of tithes and over wrongful use of the family chapel to the detriment of the parish church. The case went to Winchester, to the Court of Arches, London, and to Canterbury, between 1320 and 1322, and Richard was excommunicated when he failed to obey a judgement ordering him to pay the value of his over-due tithes and the legal expenses of the priory. Richard subsequently submitted and made his peace. But even this was not the end of the matter, because in 1329 another agreement was reached between Richard and the priory "by the intervention and entreaty of mutual friends", whereby Richard promised to pay arrears of the tithes of his mill, together with twelve goats—the arrears of thirteen years—and a hundred doves, which represented seven years' arrears from his dove-cot. This time Richard made a solemn oath in the presence of the prior, canons and witnesses in the chapter house at Southwick that he would in future pay all his tithes (II 71).

The priory's relations with Richard's son, another Baldwin, appear to have been much happier. In 1348 and 1350, Baldwin gave the priory pasture for two hundred and fifty sheep on the family's demesne at East Boarhunt and Paulsgrove, and a cottage-holding with croft in a close belonging to the priory (III 368-70).

The Development of the Hampshire Estates

Apart from the church of Swindon in Wiltshire, all the possessions given to the priory by William de Pont de l'Arche lay in Hampshire. The lands consisted of five hides and one virgate at Preston Candover and a hide each at Southwick, at Applestead which lay adjacent to, and west of, Southwick, and at West Boarhunt (I 2; I 18,19). By the end of the twelfth century the canons had extended considerably their land in the area around Southwick and Boarhunt, stretching from Hipley in the north to Portsdown Hill in the south. Further south over the hill, they had acquired land and salt pans at Portchester, and had a valuable foothold on Portsea Island. They had also acquired houses and land in Winchester. North of Southwick there had been gifts at Soberton (I 33-4,62; III 363, 366) and around Denmead (I 25; III 262, 568), and to the east, the de Cumbrai brothers' gifts at Anmore (I 57-60) and Robert de Henton's at Ludmore (I 128-30).

No less than eighteen charters record the gifts to the priory from Helewise, Lady of Crofton, and her son and heir, Geoffrey Talebot, of land, meadows, grazing and tithes in Crofton and Stubbington in Titchfield (I 41–6, 48–55; III 136–7, 148, 156). Helewise's husband, John Talebot, had been buried at Southwick, and both the widow and heir chose to be buried there and were "accepted into the fraternity". Here is one of the many instances which showed that the priory had already gained a reputation which encouraged leading families of the shire to seek its spiritual aid and the support of its prayers. John's nephew, M. John de Insula, was also a benefactor (I 47) and frequent witness for the priory.

Another virgate at Stubbington in Titchfield was given to the priory by Ralph de Belington (I 15), and a much larger gift of land in Stubbington made by Alfred de Herierd and described in a privilege from Pope Alexander III as consisting of three hides, was probably also in Titchfield, though it may have been in Stubbington in Portsea.[59] Probably before the end of the twelfth century Richard de Hoivilla granted to the priory the tithes of his fulling mill at Funtley near Titchfield (I 36).

The acquisition of Colemore and Dean at the turn of the century has already been noted.[60]

The priory's estates in these areas continued to provide it with revenues until the Dissolution, most of them growing through subsequent gifts, and through purchase and exchange. In the vicinity of Titchfield, however, growth was severely limited by the foundation of a Premonstratensian Abbey there probably in 1232.[61] No manor was established by the priory at Crofton; its lands in that area were administered as part of the manor of West Boarhunt, where the tenants owed suit of court (II 79).

At Portchester also the priory found itself neighbour to the Abbey of Titchfield, which acquired, as part of its original endowment from Bishop Peter des Roches, two-thirds of a manor there; the remaining third being held by the king.[62] An early thirteenth-century rental, which almost certainly deals with the priory's tenants at Portchester, lists twenty holdings with rents totalling £1. 16s. 9d; four of the tenants owed 48 sesters of salt (I 175). In a later rental, which can probably be dated 1248, there were fourteen holdings producing £1. 6s. 0d. rent, and three tenants owed the same quantity of salt (I 193).

Despite the fact that large numbers of charters dealing with the priory's acquisition of land in the first three-quarters of the thirteenth century are copied into the cartularies, the transactions to which they refer were usually on a small scale, often involving only an acre or half-acre, so that the total amount of land involved was far less than the number of charters would at first sight suggest. Most of these charters are undated, and, as the donors or sellers were often humble folk who never featured in royal records, the best hope of identifying the date is the appearance of a notable witness[63] or the naming of a prior.

The main area of new acquisition in the later part of the thirteenth century was at Ellisfield, and it is significant that this gift from Bartholomew Peche was to be the subject of an inquisition to discover whether or not the priory had acquired it before the passing of the Statute of Mortmain. Rival claimants to the land sought to disseise the priory on the grounds that the land had been wrongfully alienated without licence, but the priory produced evidence that the gift had been made in February 1279 (I 104, 108). Ellisfield did not remain permanently in the priory's possession: it was exchanged in 1356 for land in Portsea Island, and a royal licence was then duly obtained authorising the exchange (III 468, 470, 475).

In the fourteenth century the main acquisitions by the priory were at Farlington and Crookhorn, in 1346, the gift of Edward III (I 212); the manors of Boarhunt Herberd and Herbelyn with land at Southwick, Wanstead, Portchester, West Boarhunt and Wymering, the gift in 1369 of Bishop William of Wykeham for the endowment of his chantries (II 111); and the manors of East Hoe and Hannington in 1385, the endowment of Sir Bernard Brocas' chantry (III 427). The foundation of a chantry in the priory for Sir Roger Husee in 1350 seems to have been by way of compensation to him when he gave up his claim to the church and manor of Farlington with Crookhorn, rather than in response to any gift or endowment (III 225).

The flow of charters and gifts recorded in the cartularies dried up in the first half of the fifteenth century. There is a series of charters concerned with the descent of the manor of Hinton Burrant between 1369 and 1425 (II 210-19), and another group dealing with the gift to the priory in 1439 of seventy acres with messuages, cottages and other property in Southwick and Boarhunt from Reginald West, Lord la Warre, together with others. This latter transaction called forth an inquisition to determine whether the gift would be prejudicial to the crown by leaving the donors unable to fulfil their obligations. Having received satisfactory assurances, Henry VI issued on 8 November 1439 a licence for the alienation of the property to the priory, and this date is the latest to appear in the cartularies (II 220-5).

There was another acquisition known to have been made by the priory, that of Sutton Scotney, which it bought in 1482.[64] At the time of the Dissolution, rents there brought in a total of £10. 17s. 11d.[65]

Two areas have been omitted from this survey of the priory's Hampshire estates because they call for separate consideration; they are Portsea Island and Winchester. The priory also held for a time a few rents in Southampton (III 442, 568).

Portsea Island

About 1160, Baldwin de Portesia gave to the priory the church of Portsea, together with lands at Stubbington-in-Portsea and at Buckland (I 6) which became the nucleus of an estate based on a grange at Stubbington. The gift was confirmed by the chief lord, John de Port, by Henry of Blois, Bishop of Winchester, and by Henry II (I 7-9). A further gift from Baldwin involved the payment by the tenant, in addition to an annual rent of 10s. to the priory, of a hawk at Michaelmas to John de Gisors (I 10), who then held the manor of Buckland in which that tenement lay, having apparently acquired it from the de Ports after the issue of Baldwin's earlier charter.[66] It was from John de Gisors himself that the priory later received the site for the erection of a chapel in honour of Thomas Becket (III 116, 61). This and other charters granted by John, and recorded in the Southwick cartularies,[67] provide the chief source of information concerning the origins of Portsmouth, and indicate a developing settlement laid out to a regular plan, and doubtless owing its growth to the vicinity of a sheltered natural harbour.

Apart from his "vill of Portsmouth", John also held Titchfield and Birling in Sussex, but he forfeited all his lands to the crown in 1194, apparently for supporting the rebellion of John against Richard I.[68] Thereafter Portsmouth developed as a royal town with a royal residence, and it was the king who supported the priory's request to the Bishop of Winchester for a cemetery at their chapel of St Thomas, so that the bodies of the dead would not have to be taken along the difficult and dangerous road to the mother church of Portsea. On 12 March 1196 Bishop Godfrey de Lucy gave notice that he had consecrated a cemetery there, as well as altars in the chapel (I 142). This chapel was to become the parish church of Portsmouth, and still forms part of Portsmouth Cathedral.

Throughout the thirteenth century the priory remained closely involved with the developing town and its leading burgesses, receiving numerous gifts of rents and land in the open fields within the liberty of Portsmouth to the north of the town, with an occasional house or shop in the town itself. Over a hundred charters copied into volume III of the cartularies conferred property on the priory by gift, sale, exchange or quitclaim; a further fifty or so involve property passing from one holder to another, before being in most cases acquired by the priory. All these charters provide a wealth of information about Portsmouth and its environs; usually they were witnessed by a group of burgesses whose names recur again and again; frequently the first name is that of the reeve or bailiff and the list ends with "the whole court of Portsmouth". Most of the thirteenth century charters are undated and only an approximate date can be given, but they provide evidence of an organised administration with the borough court used as the forum for land transactions, and of a close-knit group of leading burgesses from which were chosen the reeve and bailiffs, the latter being responsible for the collection of dues payable to the king.

There are far fewer fourteenth century charters in the cartularies concerned with Portsea Island; several that do occur are involved with tenements which carry a rent-charge due to the priory. A particularly interesting group deal with a tenement on the north side of Portsmouth High Street (III 761-3). It changed hands in August 1346, and the new tenant owed a rent of 10s. to the lessor and 8s. to the priory. Two years later, however, both lessee and lessor quitclaimed their rights in respect of the tenement to the priory, and the lessee explained that some time previously the property had been destroyed by enemy action; it was therefore a liability to him and he could not afford to pay the arrears of rent demanded by the priory. He surrendered it in the court of Portsmouth, and his quitclaim, witnessed by the bailiff, received the seal of the commonalty. It seems most unlikely that the priory was able to let it again at a rent of 8s., if indeed they could find any tenant at that time.

By far the largest transaction in which the priory was involved within the liberty of Portsmouth was an exchange of lands with William Fifhide in 1356 (III 470, 475). William's estate can be traced back through three owners to William Stedeham, who was acquiring land from 1314 onwards.[69] In the licence obtained from the king authorising the exchange with the priory, the property is described as a messuage and seventy-six acres.[70] Despite the disastrous losses they had suffered in the enemy raid of 1338 and in the Black Death of 1348-9, the priory evidently thought it worth while to increase its holding in Portsea Island at the expense of its more distant lands at Ellisfield, which it gave in exchange to William Fifhide.

The Rent Roll of the liberty of Portsmouth for the year 1469 shows that the largest single payment was that of Southwick Priory, consisting of 53s. 10d. with 3 lbs. of pepper; next comes God's House, Portsmouth, which paid 50s. and 2 lbs. of pepper; three other religious houses—God's House, Southampton, and the Abbeys of Hyde, Winchester, and Quarr, Isle of Wight—paid only 8s. 2d. between them. The largest payment by a layman was 8s. 7d., owed from Sir Thomas Uvedale's tenement.[71]

In 1526 the priory leased its manor of Stubbington-in-Portsea, with all houses, lands and rents, for £14 a year, out of which it had to pay 54s. 6½d. to the mayor and commonalty of Portsmouth. At the same time the rectories of Portsea and Portsmouth, with all tithes and oblations, were leased to the same tenant for £26. 6s. 8d., of which £4. 13s. 4d. was to be paid in cash, and the remainder in wheat and barley. This was the position at the Dissolution.[72]

Winchester

While still at Portchester, the canons obtained a house and two waste lands in Winchester—a link with the city which was to last until the Dissolution.[73] Although Winchester had declined in status since the Conquest and had suffered considerably during the civil war which followed the death of Henry I, it remained an important political, ecclesiastical and commercial centre, frequently visited by successive kings until the end of Henry III's reign; thereafter less frequently. It was therefore advantageous for the priory to acquire and retain an interest there, placing it in touch with royal officials and with the diocesan bishop, whose favour it would be anxious to cultivate; and incidentally giving it access to the great annual fair on St Giles' Hill, which was to reach its peak in the first decades of the thirteenth century.[74]

By 1219 annual rents totalling £2. 6s. 5d. were due to the priory from twenty-eight tenements in Winchester and on St Giles' Hill; a further tenement with a rent of 6s. was in the hands of the bishop, and there was yet another from which the amount due was left blank in the rental (I 181a).

During the thirteenth century the priory was given other rents and houses in the city and suburbs, and stalls in the fair; the most important gifts came from Walter le Chamberlayn some time between 1256 and 1258 (III 560), and from William Tinctor, *alias* le Tenterer or the Dyer, shortly before his death in 1290 (III 519, 521). Walter's gift was of three houses, 11s. in rent, and six stalls on St Giles' Hill. His sister had married another of Southwick's benefactors, Hugh Raggy, a leading burgess of Portsmouth, and the latter quitclaimed any right he might have to the stalls and half the rent as his wife's dower (III 541). It is not evident from Walter's charters why Southwick Priory should have been the recipient of his gifts, which comprised not only all his possessions in Winchester but any escheat or bequest that might in future accrue to him there, and no gift in return, either material or spiritual, is recorded from the priory.

In the case of William Tinctor, however, various reasons for the choice of the priory as recipient of his benefactions can be deduced: he probably knew the priory and its canons well as his eldest son, William, was a canon there, and he himself chose to be buried at Southwick. In return for his gifts the priory had granted him corrodies of two canons and a servant, and in his will William left individual bequests to the prior and sub-prior, and to each of the canons mentioning Andrew de Winton by name, besides gifts to each altar in the priory's church, and to the chapel of St James, Southwick—the parish church (III 524).

In order to retain control over the property granted to it by William Tinctor, the priory had to have recourse on at least three occasions to the complicated procedure used in the city for recovery of tenements when rents were in arrears. Moreover it successfully negotiated with the Cathedral Priory, which had a claim on the property, and ultimately defeated attempts by the vicar and parish of St Pancras to make good a similar claim. It seems that part at least of that property was still in the hands of Southwick Priory at the Dissolution.[75]

It is not possible to account in detail for all the changes in the numbers and size of the priory's holdings or for the amount of rent it drew from them; doubtless their value fluctuated with the fortunes of the city, being influenced by political upheavals, pestilences and changes in its economic prosperity. Dr Keene has pointed out that in the last two decades of the thirteenth century there was a sharp fall in trade at St Giles' Fair, although the cloth industry continued to flourish and it was some time before there was any sign of a significant decline in the population—that was largely a consequence of the pestilences of 1349 and after, which reduced the number of inhabitants by about a third. From the early fifteenth century to the mid-sixteenth Winchester shrank in wealth and size as shown by the decline of the cloth industry and fall in rents.[76]

In the Taxation of Pope Nicholas IV of 1291, the value of Southwick Priory's Winchester property was assessed at £2. 0s. 0d. a year;[77] a similar assessment was made in a taxation of *c.* 1369–85 (II 230). There is no separate mention of Winchester among the possessions of the priory in the inquisitions post mortem of 1381, 1389 and 1398 (II 32, 56, 75). In the priory's account roll for 1393–4 the Winchester rents amounted to £3. 6s. 8d.,[78] but by 1527–8 they were only £2. 13s. 4d.[79] At the Dissolution the priory was drawing rents totalling £1. 16s. 0d. from six tenements in the city.[80]

The property in Winchester which had in the past belonged to Southwick Priory and to three other religious houses was given to the city in 1554 by Queen Mary in recompense for the expense it had incurred on account of her wedding in the Cathedral to King Philip of Spain, and in view of its poverty and decay.[81]

Churches, chapels, advowsons and tithes given to the priory
From its earliest days the priory depended largely on the revenues it drew from the churches and chapels which it received from its benefactors. Besides those donated by its founder and his son—Portchester, Wymering, Preston Candover, Shalden, Swindon in Wiltshire, and Wanstead[82]—the priory had acquired by 1163 the chapels of Widley, Walesworth, Nutley and Candover Scotland (I 86). Shortly afterwards it was given the church of Portsea and that of Empshott (I 24). The ancient church of St Nicholas at Boarhunt, was the gift of William de Hommet, probably in the 1180s (I 63, 140–1). In 1186 Prior Guy obtained papal confirmation of the priory's possession of its churches and chapels, and the list included, in addition to all these, the church of Portsea and its chapel—the latter being the chapel which the priory had built at Portsmouth in honour of St Thomas Becket—and the chapel of *Stanebiria* in Preston Candover (I 87). The chapel of St James-Without-the-Priory-Gate (now the parish church of Southwick) is first mentioned by this name in a confirmation of *c.* 1185–8 granted by Richard of Ilchester, Bishop of Winchester (I 94). His successor, Godfrey de Lucy (1189–1204), was notified of the gift to the priory of the chapel of St Andrew in the parish of Portsea (III 394). A chapel at Plant is first mentioned in a charter of 1234, although the priory had held land there since 1189 (II 82; I 143).

In 1324, following an investigation into the rights of the priory to the churches and chapels appropriated to it, and to pensions from certain vicars and rectors, those rights were listed and confirmed by Walter Reynolds, Archbishop of Canterbury (III 950). The list of churches included that of Portsmouth (St Thomas') with the chapel of St Mary in the parish of Portsmouth; and the list of pensions, which amounted to £11. 17s. 8d., included 100s. from the vicar of Portsmouth—some indication of of the development of the town over the past century. Another pension was 20s. from the rector of the church of St Andrew, Farlington, which had been granted to the priory *c.* 1215 for the soul of the donor's wife (III 220). But although the grant had been confirmed by Peter des Roches, Bishop of Winchester (III 226), and again by his successor, William Raleigh (III 222), it seems that the priory temporarily lost control of the church, even if it retained a pension from it, as in 1346 the advowson was restored to the priory by Edward III at the same time as he granted to it the manor of Farlington and Crookhorn (I 212).

Farlington was not the only church over which the priory experienced difficulties in establishing its rights. The Mauduits had sought unsuccessfully to recover the church of Shalden, which had been granted to the priory by William de Pont de l'Arche although it was not his to give.[83] The Pont de l'Arche family tried to re-establish control over the church of Swindon,[84] and appears to have had some success in view of subsequent charters acquired by the canons firstly granting and confirming to them a pension from the church, and finally appropriating the church fully to the priory.[85] The chapel granted by Herbert de Burhunt, probably before or soon after the move to Southwick (I 121), is not mentioned again, unless it was in fact the church of St Nicholas at Boarhunt, which was later granted or re-granted to the priory by William de Hommet (I 63, 76). The chapel of Walesworth appears among the priory's possessions in the privilege which Pope Alexander III sent to Prior Walter between October 1162 and June 1163.[86] But Prior Guy (occurs 1185–1210) obtained a charter from Matilda de Bochland and her son, Peter, "giving" the church "so far as it belonged to them", with tithes and certain lands, to the priory (I 115).

But whatever the difficulties they encountered, it is obvious that the canons' efforts to obtain and secure their rights to these churches and chapels were well worthwhile. According to the taxation of Pope Nicholas IV of 1291 the value of the priory's spiritualities in the Winchester diocese amounted to at least £93. 13s. 4d., which includes only the value of those churches of which the prior was named as rector, and the pensions received by the priory.[87] In the taxation of c. 1369–85, the value of the Hampshire churches was given as 133 marks and that of the church of Swindon, Wiltshire, as 20 marks, making a total of £102. The pensions amounted to £10. 12s. 8d; thus the total for all spiritualities was £112. 12s. 8d. This was considerably more than three times the value placed upon the priory's entire temporal possessions. The manors, lands and rents in Hampshire were valued at £27. 19s. 0d., and those possessions in Sussex, Wiltshire, and Oxfordshire at £6. 0s. 0d.: a total for the temporalities of £33. 19s. 0d. (II 230).

When churches were appropriated to the priory it was usual for it to be laid down that the canons should provide adequate maintenance for the vicar who would serve the church.[88] This was usually done by allocating certain land and tithes to the vicarage, but disputes often arose over the respective rights and obligations of the priory and of the vicar; some cases dragged on and were passed from court to court for several years before settlement was reached, sometimes after appeal to the pope (III 669, 485, 687, 785, 511–12, 938–9).

Another source of litigation was the failure of laymen to pay tithes which were claimed by the priory (II 81; 70; 58, 71; III 451–6), and in one case certain parishioners of Southwick were found guilty of conspiring to defraud the priory of oblations donated to that church (II 68, 80).

The Priory's Relations with the Ecclesiastical Hierarchy and with Other Religious Houses
The Papacy

Thirty-five papal privileges, letters and mandates are copied into the cartularies; only two of them are general issues (I 95; III 28), and the remainder are addressed to Southwick Priory or to its prior by name, or are sent to papal delegates for action to be taken in response to complaints made to the pope by the priory, or to allegations made against it.

The two earliest documents were issued by Pope Eugenius III in 1147 and in 1151 or 1152 (I 84–5), and provide evidence for the date of the move to Southwick. Both are privileges extending the pope's protection to the priory and its possessions; the second giving an extended list of property, and including the concession to the priory of the right to accept for burial at Southwick any who had chosen to be buried there, saving the rights of the mother church. The value of this concession may be judged by the considerable numbers who did so choose, and the resulting benefactions to the priory. Similar privileges of protection were issued at the priory's request by Alexander III, Urban III, Gregory IX and Alexander IV (I 86–7; III 21, 7), and there were moreover letters confirming the priory's possession of specific lands and churches.

The church of Swindon was the subject of repeated papal intervention. It had been granted to the priory by its founder, and the grant had been confirmed by his son, Robert de Pont de l'Arche, and by the bishop of Salisbury (I 19, 21–2). But the Pont de l'Arche family sought later to recover the church.[89] In 1177 Alexander III wrote to Prior Philip forbidding him to grant the church to anyone other than the priest serving there, who was to be directly responsible to the priory; the profits of the church being kept entirely for the use of the canons on account of their poverty and need (I 23). It is not clear what lay behind the despatch of this letter, but for one reason or another the priory was not able to retain control of the church of Swindon. It is specifically mentioned as belonging to the priory in letters of Alexander III and Lucius III (III 3; I 91), yet in 1199 Herbert Poore, Bishop of Salisbury, granted to the canons of Southwick a pension of £5 a year from that church—hardly necessary if they had been in full possession of it (I 154). Even this pension was from time to time withheld, and the priory repeatedly pursued its claim for it in the ecclesiastical court at Salisbury and by appeal to the pope (III 18). Eventually, in 1357, Robert Wyvil, Bishop of Salisbury, having obtained a licence from Edward III, appropriated the church to the priory so that the canons would have all the profits over and above the £5 pension (II 1; III 982, 403). More than twenty years later the priory appealed to Urban VI to confirm their possession of the church of Swindon, and in 1397 the pope ordered the Archbishop of Canterbury to enquire into the matter and, if satisfied by the priory's case, to confirm its possession on papal authority (III 31, 415).

Apart from looking to papal support for the safeguarding of its possessions, the priory also sought to bring down the weight of papal censure upon those who failed to pay tithes or attempted to defraud it in other ways. Such appeals, often following long litigation, led to papal mandates appointing delegates to call the parties together, hear and decide the case (III 669, 15). Prior Guy's complaint to Urban III was directed against archdeacons who illegally demanded money for chrism, and when this was refused suspended or excommunicated the priory's clergy; the pope pronounced such suspension or excommunication null and void (I 92).

There were also appeals to the pope on matters affecting the daily life of the canons. These included a request for permission to wear shoes instead of gaiters,[90] and a further request to be allowed to wear caps or fur hoods during divine service in cold weather (III 123). Both requests were granted. Permission was also sought, and obtained, by the canons for the use of a portable altar and for the right to celebrate mass in places that were under interdict, provided this was done privately behind closed doors, and provided that they themselves were not under sentence of excommunication (III 39).

Two papal letters indicate trouble within the priory, but unfortunately neither has been dated with certainty. The first was in response to an appeal from the prior on behalf of canons and lay-brothers who had been excommunicated—some for assault, retention of property, disobedience and conspiracy; some for receiving Holy Orders and celebrating mass while under suspension. The pope authorised the prior to absolve, after due penance, those whose offences were less serious or had been committed in ignorance, and ordered him to send the worst offenders to Rome (III 6). The Pope Alexander who sent this letter can scarcely have been Alexander III (1159–81), whose pontificate occurred when the canons were engaged in building the priory at Southwick; it seems unlikely that this was a time of slackness and grave misdemeanours. It may be that in the mid-thirteenth century, when the pope was Alexander IV (1254–61) the situation was different. Matthew, whose long priorate lasted from 1235 until 1266, had been himself summoned to Rome in 1254, ten months before the death of Pope Innocent IV, to explain, if he could, the appearance of his name in papal letters believed to have been forged.[91] Did he go, and did trouble occur in his absence?

The other papal letter critical of the conduct of the priory was a mandate sent to the Dean of Chichester, ordering him to look into allegations that the prior and canons of Southwick had been illegally making grants from their possessions to clerks and laymen, thereby causing great loss to the priory (III 24). If the Pope Urban who issued that mandate was Urban IV (1261–4), then it would also relate to the priorate of Matthew; but it might have been Urban III (1185–7), and, if so, the criticism may have been due to the fact that Prior Guy found it necessary to lease at a low rent the priory's property in Lincolnshire and Rutland in return for a large lump sum of £26. 13s. 4d. to pay off debts which had been incurred to Jewish money-lenders (I 127).

The Episcopacy

The earliest surviving episcopal register for Winchester is that of Bishop John of Pontoise, 1282–1304, so that there is no help from this source in piecing together the history of the priory before that date. However, from the time of its foundation the priory sought and obtained confirmation of its possessions from the bishops in whose dioceses they lay. Most of them, including both Portchester and Southwick, were in the see of Winchester, but some were in the sees of Salisbury, Chichester and Lincoln.

Episcopal support for the priory was remarkably wide-ranging. The dedication of its church at Southwick was performed not only by the bishops of Winchester and Chichester but also by the bishop of Waterford (I 25), and the church at Portchester was dedicated by the bishop of St David's (III 960). At the time of the move to Southwick, Theobald, Archbishop of Canterbury, granted indulgences to those who came to the aid of the canons faced with the expenses of re-building (III 968); Hilary, Bishop of Chichester (III 967), and Nicholas, Bishop of Llandaff (III 966), issued similar indulgences. The indulgence probably granted by

Pope Alexander III in 1181 on the occasion of the dedication of the priory's church at Southwick[92] was echoed by a similar grant between 1193 and 1205 from Hubert Walter, Archbishop of Canterbury (III 961); in both cases penance was remitted to those who visited the church at the festivals of the Blessed Virgin Mary, in whose honour the church was dedicated. The archbishop expressed the hope that alms of the visitors would help to alleviate the poverty of the canons. Other indulgences were granted by Herlewin, Bishop of Leighlin, in 1204, after consecration of an altar at Southwick (III 964); by William, Bishop of Bath and Wells, in 1254, for benefactors who helped to provide the priory with a steeple and a peal of bells (III 965); by Nicholas, Bishop of Salisbury, in 1293, to those who came to pray at the tomb of John de Clere, the late prior (III 963); and by Gervase, Bishop of Bangor, between 1368 and 1370, after the dedication of a chapel.[93]

John Pecham, Archbishop of Canterbury from 1279 to 1292, visited Southwick Priory twice,[94] and on each occasion found it necessary to take vigorous action in view of the unsatisfactory state of affairs he found there. As a result of his first visit in 1281, he deposed the prior, Andrew de Winton, whom he held responsible for the priory's financial difficulties, and gave detailed instructions to the new prior, John de Clere, for special provision of accommodation, food and clothing for Andrew, who was to attend services regularly and eat with the canons on festal days.[95] Following his second visit, in January 1284, Pecham ordered that Andrew should be deprived of his special privileges;[96] ten months later he wrote to the bishop of Winchester, John of Pontoise, concerning the excommunication of the former prior of Southwick.[97]

John of Pontoise's Register does not contain any injunctions for Southwick Priory; but in 1291, following the election of one of the canons, Robert de Henton, as prior, the bishop sent a letter to the sub-prior and canons warning them that they would have to answer to him for any failure to show the new prior proper obedience;[98] this seems to suggest that some of the canons were not happy with the outcome of the election. In 1299 the bishop sent Brother John of Salisbury, one of Southwick's canons, to the Augustinian Priory of Reigate in Surrey, to receive additional teaching, the cost of six marks a year being paid by Southwick to Reigate.[99] There is no suggestion, however, that this canon was a troublemaker, and although John of Pontoise's successor, Bishop Henry Woodlock, intervened three times to investigate allegations against canons of Southwick and to discipline them when necessary, only one individual is known to have been at fault.[100]

After a visit to Southwick on 13 December 1308, Bishop Henry issued a long list of injunctions evidently designed to tighten discipline within the priory, and to improve the quality of its religious life and the efficiency of the administration of its property.[101] Of the nineteen items in the injunctions, the first four dealt with the stricter observance of the Augustinian rule, which was to be read in the chapter-house each week; and there were instructions concerning the care of infirm brothers. Nine separate disciplinary orders were issued: limiting exeats from the priory to those canons who were licensed to go out for a special purpose, and who were to be accompanied; forbidding visits to the tavern in Southwick, conversation with any female of doubtful reputation, the use of articles of dress other than those of their order, eating or drinking at unaccustomed times and places, and giving away food and drink provided for a canon, except in alms for the poor; hunting was to be limited; sentence of automatic excommunication would befall anyone plotting or stirring up trouble in the priory. The four injunctions addressed specifically to the prior dealt with administrative matters: he was to render account each year, being more careful in the oversight of manors and in the selection of officials; to preserve accounts kept by obedientiars; to seek to free his monastery from debts and obligations to outsiders and to recover property that had been illegally alienated, thus providing for the legitimate needs of the canons; and to refuse manumission to any of the priory's bondmen unless granting it was in the priory's best interests.

With few exceptions these injunctions are very similar to those sent by the same bishop to the Augustinian priory of St Denys, and are hardly an indication of particular laxity or misdemeanours at Southwick. Among the exceptions, the instructions about dress may possibly indicate that the canons had not been content with the concessions they had been granted by the pope[102] and had proceeded to make unauthorised innovations of their own. The bishop did not entirely forbid the canons to engage in hunting, as he recognised that the priory had special liberties from the crown in this respect; but he was concerned to curb it, forbidding frequent participation in it and, especially, indulgence in the revelry that followed it. His threat of excommunication of trouble-makers may have been prompted by the two cases which had already come to his notice.[103] That threat did not prove entirely effective as a deterrent, for by 1343 there were two canons who had been found guilty of acts of violence, and to whom Bishop Orleton granted absolution.[104]

At least one other list of episcopal injunctions to Southwick Priory has survived, though not as might have been expected in the diocesan register; it was issued by Bishop William of Wykeham on 22 August 1397.[105] Initially the pattern followed is familiar, with items enjoining stricter observance of the rule of the Augustinian order and of the constitution of Cardinal Ottobon. To prevent secular persons of both sexes from entering the precincts of the priory, all approaches other than the main gateway were to be blocked. No one was to have access to members of the priory in the outer court, called the Barton, or to go inside the inner gate, except for the purpose of entering the church. No canon was to go out into the vill of Southwick or into the woods and fields belonging to the priory without a suitable companion and authorisation from the prior, thus putting an end to the practice said to have been followed by several canons of wandering in and out without leave, "in an unbecoming and unacceptable fashion".[106] Private meetings and factions, which had in the past caused division and dissension, was strictly prohibited, and anyone found guilty of violence or causing trouble was to be punished by relegation to the last place in the choir and in processions, and could be restored to his usual place by the bishop alone. No canon was to talk with a woman, either inside or outside the priory, except in the presence of three or four reputable persons, lest suspicions be aroused, as had happened in the past.

It appears that the prior and others in authority in the priory had been negligent in checking and punishing offences committed by its members, because the bishop ordered that stricter measures should be taken, without favouritism, according to the nature of the offence and status of the offender; failure to take such measures was to involve suspension from office until the negligence had been purged; in the case of the prior, the bishop himself would prescribe his penance. Another injunction addressed specifically to the prior ordered him to perform his spiritual duties more conscientiously; attending divine services with the canons by day and night, and celebrating mass more frequently; he was to sleep in the dormitory and not in a private room, so as to avoid the spread of rumours and suspicions amongst his fellow canons; if he failed to comply he would be restricted to the confines of the priory for a month.

The last four of the thirteen injunctions were concerned with the administration of the priory and its estates, requiring more careful custody of the common seal of the priory, and more regular provision of accounts, which were to be shown by the bailiffs and other officials once each year to the prior and senior members chosen by the chapter. The final two injunctions occupy nearly a third of the entire document, and show the bishop's extreme concern over the financial state of the priory, which was heavily in debt. A special account-roll drawn up in 1395 in expectation of the bishop's visitation, and purporting to review the priory's finances since 1389, showed average annual receipts amounting to £242. 4s. 0d. and expenditure of £480. 2s. 11¼d., an excess of expenditure over revenue of £237. 18s. 11¼d.; so that it would appear that the priory was spending nearly twice as much as it was obtaining from its resources.[107]

In his injunctions the bishop commented on the great burden of debt owed by the priory to various creditors, and proceeded to order strict retrenchment. This was to start with the prior, who was to give up his own establishment[108] and eat daily in the refectory with the canons, unless the presence of visitors whom he had to make welcome forced him to do otherwise. The amount of each canon's daily food and drink was laid down;[109] twice the standard amount of food being allocated to the prior. The cellarer was to collect food left over from the meal for re-use, and other excess (*fragmenta*) was to be distributed to the poor and not disposed of in any other way. No food and drink was to be taken in private rooms, unless there was a reasonable cause, approved by the prior. Pittances at four festivals were to be allocated as usual, costing two marks a year, but other pittances in cash of 5s. to each canon who was a priest had been surrendered by them as a contribution towards the repayment of the debts.

The rents and profits of two of the priory's manors, Priors Dean and East Hoe, worth £44 a year, were to be allocated to that purpose, together with a further £23 to be taken from other resources. Until the debts were settled the prior was not to provide livery for anyone, and only three horses were to be kept for the priory's use, in addition to a horse provided for the priory's clerk. Finally, the bishop declared that the priory's household had for a long time been too large, placing an excessive burden on it. Henceforth there were to be no more than sixteen domestic servants, including the officials of the church and the custodian of the chapel of the Blessed Mary above the gate.

Any failure to adhere to these regulations for the repayment of the debts was to involve the prior's suspension from the administration of the priory, and the removal and permanent disqualification from office of any other negligent official.

These injunctions show how deeply the bishop cared about both the spiritual and temporal welfare of the priory—in which his father, mother and sister were buried, and his own chantries has been established—and how anxious he was that its reputation should be above suspicion.

Four years later, on 18 August 1401, the bishop again demonstrated his affection and concern for the priory, whose church and buildings had become dilapidated because of extreme poverty. He presented it with 300 marks, and also with a gilded chalice worth ten marks, and a set of silk and gold vestments together with seven copes. Moreover, in his will he bequeathed to it a further 100 marks, to be spent on repairs to the roof of the vault in which his parents were buried, and to the roof of the chancel.

The gifts of 1401 were acknowledged by the then prior, Thomas Curteys, in a document dated 11 January 1402[110] in which the statutes and charter setting up and endowing the bishop's five chantries in the priory were repeated and confirmed, together with the priory's undertaking to carry out faithfully all the conditions laid down, on pain of incurring specific penalties. At the end of that document there are two entries on the subject of the bequest. The first is a receipt, dated 8 April 1407, for £50 received from one of Wykeham's executors as part payment. The second, dated 3 May, acknowledges receipt of the balance of the 100 marks in the form of a pair of silver candlesticks and a silver-gilt basin.

Although Wykeham's injunctions to Southwick Priory do not appear in his register, diocesan registers do provide information about the ordination by bishops of Winchester or their representatives of the priory's canons from acolyte to priest, and the institution of priests and chaplains, on presentation by the priory, to churches appropriated to it, or of which it held the advowson. The bishops of Winchester also played a very important role when a new prior was elected at Southwick. The death or resignation of a prior had to be reported to the bishop, and a licence to hold an election had to be obtained from the king. After the election it was for the bishop to satisfy himself that all had been carried out in due order, and to deal with any objections, before confirming the new prior and notifying the king that he had done so.

The register of Thoman Langton, Bishop of Winchester from 1493 to 1501, provides a step-by-step account of the procedure followed after the resignation of Prior Philip Stanbroke in 1493.[111] No less than eleven documents which passed between the priory, the bishop and the king are copied there. First there is Philip's own testimony that his resignation, which had taken place on 20 April 1494, was entirely voluntary and that he had surrendered his office into the hands of the bishop. This was witnessed by a local magnate, Sir William Uvedale, and by four others, one of whom was Nicholas Mayewe, the bishop's own chancellor. There follows a long account of the election of the new prior, which took place in the chapter-house, after mass at the high altar in the chancel of the priory church. The presiding canon and ten others are named, and the witnesses again included the bishop's chancellor, together with a public notary. John Lawder, the priory's cellarer, was unanimously chosen. The king's letters patent giving assent to the election; the priory's request to the bishop for confirmation, and the bishop's instructions for investigation to see that the election had been properly conducted, are followed by the bishop's notification to the king that he had given confirmation and his request for return of the temporalities to the new prior. Finally the king wrote authorising the bishop to receive John Lawder's oath of fealty due to the crown, and sent a copy, in English, of the oath; and the bishop on 21 June 1494 reported that the oath had been taken in his chapel at Marwell.

Another, even more detailed account of an election is recorded in the case of William Noxton, the last prior of Southwick, elected in 1521; it is to be found in the Register of Bishop Richard Fox.[112] But perhaps the most remarkable instance of episcopal intervention in the life of the priory had taken place two years previously, and was also the work of Bishop Fox. The occasion was a double disaster which had befallen the priory. On 12 November 1512 the steeple of the priory's church had been struck by lightning, and the resulting fire, which burned for three days and three nights, caused great damage, not only destroying the wooden steeple itself together with the bells and a large part of the roof, but also the finely carved timbers of the choir, together with books, vestments and valuable ornaments. The prior had taken immediate steps to repair the damage, and the work of re-building had been completed at a cost of £500. Instead of erecting another wooden steeple, an additional thirty feet of stone-work had been built upon the tower. This was a disastrous mistake, for the structure had been weakened by the fire, and the new super-structure was too massive for it to support. On 24 September 1518 it collapsed bringing down much of the roof and vaulting, and also damaging the cloister. It was at this point, when so much of the priory's church was in ruins and its finances exhausted, that Bishop Fox stepped in to work out a scheme for its recovery.[113]

First, an account was drawn up to ascertain the exact amount of the priory's annual revenues; this was produced and checked on 26 October 1518. Most of the priory's manors and other properties had been granted at farm, and these revenues together with other rents amounted to £309. 9s. 11½d. From this gross total various charges and expenses had to be deducted, amounting to £40. 6s. 0½d.; this left a net amount of £290. 3s. 11d. The annual expenses of the priory, as allowed for item by item by the bishop, came to £209. 0s. 10d.; thus a clear sum of £80. 3s. 1d was made available for the re-building.

To obtain this surplus of revenue over expenditure, the bishop had devised measures which were both drastic and painful. The document in which they were recorded was given the formal assent of the prior and canons, and bears the signature not only of Fox himself but of Thomas Kent, the prior, of Robert Cove, the sub-prior, and of William Noxton, the cellarer. They involved sending away the prior—doubtless a broken man—to Breamore Priory, where he was to stay for three years, receiving a pension of fifty marks a year to cover his expenses and those of one servant and a novice, who were to accompany him. This enabled considerable economy to be made by dismissing the rest of the prior's separate household. The sub-prior was put in charge of the spiritual life of the community, and the cellarer was instructed to oversee the daily management of the priory and its estates in accordance with strict regulations which laid down not only the number of household and farm servants to be employed (twenty-three), but also the wage which each was to receive;[114] the total annual wage bill being limited to £28. 13s. 4d., in addition to food and clothing.[115] The cellarer was also responsible for necessary repairs to property belonging to the priory, but he was not to spend more than £6. 13s. 4d. a year upon them; and hospitality to strangers was not to cost more than £4 a year.

A careful account of all revenues and expenses was to be kept by the cellarer, and he was to include in his reckoning the perquisites of the courts, sales of wood, profits of husbandry, of the dairy and of the priory's sheep. The accounts were to be shown to the bishop each quarter if he was at Winchester or anywhere between Southwick and Winchester, and at the year's end had to be shown to either the bishop or the prior, or to both.

The final item in this remarkable and revealing document dealt with the provision of "Our Ladye stokke box"—evidently an offertory box for the use of pilgrims or those visiting the altar of Our Lady—it was to be made of iron, fitted with three locks, and kept chained to the wall, probably close to the altar or to the statue of the Virgin.[116] The three keys were to be kept by the bishop, the sub-prior and the cellarer. When it was necessary to open the box the bishop would entrust his key to one of his chaplains, who would bring it to Southwick and would be present with the sub-prior and cellarer at the opening of the box and recording of the money taken from it, which was to be used only for the re-building.

There is no means of knowing whether all the provisions laid down by Bishop Fox were adhered to. Before the three years of the prior's enforced withdrawal were at an end, Thomas Kent had died, presumably while at Breamore, on 26 December 1520. It must be assumed that William Noxton, the cellarer, had carried out his heavy responsibilities to the satisfaction of both priory and bishop, as he was elected to be the next prior. There can be little doubt that the re-building took place, but the restored church and cloister were to stand for barely another twenty years before the Dissolution brought far greater destruction, from which there could be no recovery.

Relations with other religious houses
Southwick Priory was one of six Augustinian houses in Hampshire, but apart from Selborne, founded in 1233[117] and the latest of the six, it had no contest with the others over property, as there was no clash of interests. The chapel of Empshott, just two miles south of the site where Selborne Priory was founded, had been given to Southwick before 1181 together with some nearby land (I 113; III 275), and another two acres

there were the gift of Richard of Empshott, who became a canon at Southwick (III 277-8). This property at Empshott caused a dispute over tithes between the two priories; the dispute was resolved in September 1242 and the settlement was sealed by the Official of Winchester, and by the Dean of Oxford acting as papal delegate (III 273). At the same time a careful division of rights over funerals, oblations, bequests and tithes was arranged between the chapel of Empshott and the parish church of Selborne, the latter belonging to Selborne Priory.

The Cistercian Abbey of Quarr on the Isle of Wight was founded probably in 1132,[118] just a few years after the foundation of Portchester Priory. Both Quarr and Southwick received gifts of land from Baldwin of Portsea,[119] and in 1189 the two monasteries reached an agreement over land called *Planta* which had been given to Quarr, but lay just three miles east of Southwick.[120] As this land could not conveniently be cultivated by Quarr, it was granted in perpetuity, with another virgate, to Southwick at an annual rent of 20s. The proviso was made that if Quarr acquired more land in that area Southwick could not claim it by virtue of the agreement. The two houses pledged mutual support in business affairs, and each would celebrate Mass on the death of a member of the other.

Another agreement about lands on grounds of convenience was concluded by Southwick Priory; it was made with the nuns of Stamford Priory in Lincolnshire, and took the form of an exchange (I 145).

In the late twelfth century, after Sir William de Hommet had granted the church of West Boarhunt to Southwick Priory (I 63, 140-1), the abbot of Séez in Normandy renounced his abbey's claim to that church, with the consent of his chapter (I 64). This agreement, said to have been inspired by fraternal charity, also included mutual support for each other's interests, spiritual and temporal, but made no mention of any rent to be paid by Southwick to Séez. However, in 1307, more than a century after the severance of Normandy from England, the Abbey of Séez quitclaimed to Southwick Priory the 20s. annual rent which it used to receive from the priory on account of the church of West Boarhunt (III 102). It seems hardly likely that the priory had been regularly paying this rent year by year. Nevertheless it is evident that after the loss of Normandy the priory did not entirely lose contact with property it had been given there. In 1282 the abbot of Montebourg issued an inspeximus, doubtless at the priory's request, of two charters by which tithes and rents in Normandy had been granted to it (III 325). This was part of the priory's efforts to recover its property (III 326, 330).

Nearer home, the priory was frequently involved with the Premonstratensian Abbey of Titchfield. As in the case of Selborne Priory, Southwick had been given lands and tithes near the site on which the abbey was later founded, and therefore their interests clashed.[121] A long-standing dispute over tithes from land held by the priory in the parish of Titchfield was settled when the priory agreed to pay 5s. a year to the abbey and also certain small tithes to the vicar of the parish church (III 169). The priory was also involved in another dispute with Titchfield Abbey over tithes, though only indirectly, because it possessed the advowson of the church of Walesworth, where the land was part of the original endowment

of the abbey, but the rector claimed the tithes; a settlement of that
dispute, reached in 1241, was sealed not only by the parties directly
interested but also by the priory (III 128). On the whole, however, abbey
and priory appear to have worked well together. Some time between
1259 and 1266 the abbey had quitclaimed to the prior and canons, its
"special friends", all suit of court at Portchester due for land which the
priory held of the abbey's fee there, and at the same time mutual
arrangements were made for the use of the abbey's marlpit at Walesworth
and the priory's at Anmore (III 129). In 1377 the abbey and priory
obtained royal licences for an exchange of rents: Southwick quitclaimed
to Titchfield 6s. 8d. worth of rent in Stubbington-next-Titchfield for land
held from the priory by the abbey, and Titchfield quitclaimed 10s. worth
in Newlands and in Stubbington-next-Portsmouth for land which the
priory held from it (III 974, 127). Obviously a leasing of land in the
interests of convenience and consolidation had taken place, and the final
step was a mutual quitclaim of rents.

The Priory's Income and Expenditure

With the possible exception of St Denys, Southampton, Southwick Priory
was—when it was originally established at Portchester—the earliest foundation of Austin canons in Hampshire. In size and wealth it was far
over-shadowed by Christchurch, a Saxon foundation into which Austin
canons were introduced in 1150; but with that exception it was the largest
and most influential of the six Augustinian priories in the county. It
was never wealthy, and although its geographical situation, its royal
connection, and its status as a place of pilgrimage, brought it advantages
in the form of benefactions and oblations, they also laid upon it a burden
of hospitality that appears often to have proved too heavy for its
resources.[122]

It is very difficult to make any reliable estimate of the priory's income,
or to trace its fluctuations over the period of the priory's existence; the
surviving records are intermittent, often incomplete, and difficult to
interpret. The thirteenth-century rentals in the earliest cartulary (I 175-82,
184-5, 193-6) are for the most part undated, and there is no means of
knowing whether the lists they give are complete; there is no indication
of the value of crops and livestock, or even of the size of the demesne
on the various estates.

At least it can be said that these rentals alone, though providing only
partial evidence of the annual value of the priory's lands, prove without
doubt that the assessment of the value of the temporalities of the priory
within the diocese of Winchester as given in the Taxation of Pope
Nicholas IV in 1290—£27. 17s. 8d.—does not approximate in any way
to the true value of the priory's income, whether gross or even net, at
that time.[123]

This is clear from the account rolls of just one of the priory's
Hampshire estates, Stubbington-in-Portsea. Between 1268 and 1351-2
nine rolls have survived, of which eight record a range of profit of
between £69 and £119 (the ninth, for 1351-2, records only £13 profit
"on account of the pestilence").[124]

The inquisitions post mortem held in 1381, 1389 and 1398 (II 32, 56, 75), following the deaths of three successive priors, likewise cannot be taken as a complete picture of the value of the priory's revenues or as an accurate guide to its financial position. In 1381 the total annual value of eight manors and estates in Hampshire, comprising by far the greater part of the priory's entire temporal property, was said to be £39,[125] of which £1 rent was due to Quarr Abbey.[126] The inquisition ends with the assertion that the prior and his predecessors held no other land, tenements, rent or service—in demesne or in villeinage—in Hampshire. It thus disregards the lands given to the priory as endowment for the Wykeham chantries, which had been founded in 1369; possibly those lands were tacitly regarded as worthless from the point of view of the priory itself, for in the inquisition of 1398 they were explicitly said to be so.[127] By 1398 the Brocas chantry had also been founded (III 427), and the manor of Hannington which had been given for its endowment was similarly declared to be worthless. The manor of East Hoe, given to the priory at the same time as Hannington, was valued at £6, and the total value of the Hampshire property at £45; in 1389 the property had been assessed at £33.

It is to the general account rolls, of which five survive dated between 1358 and 1393-4,[128] that one must turn for real evidence of the priory's annual income. The roll for 1358 shows total receipts of £128, and it also contains evidence that in addition to this total the prior had separate revenues, including the farm of Anmore and 40s. that would otherwise have been accounted with the perquisites of the court, and that from his revenues he paid for wine and also for certain pensions and tenths. Later rolls appear to include these items among the general revenues and expenses, and show a total income that varies from £168 to £456.[129] Nevertheless the priory was failing to keep its expenditure within the limits set by its income.

This was startlingly shown in the roll for 1395, drawn up to explain to the bishop of the priory's financial position over the previous five years.[130] It showed that the priory was in debt to the extent of £238, whereas in 1358 the deficit carried over from the previous year had been £48.

Consecutive rolls exist for the years 1391-2, 1392-3 and 1393-4, and give details of the expenditure which had contributed to the growth of this indebtedness, and which William of Wykeham undertook to prune. Unfortunately no rolls have survived to show how successful his injunctions proved in setting the priory's finances in order.

The expenditure included the provision of linen and furnishings for the prior's hall at an annual cost of between £1 and £2, and livery and wages for the priory's servants at between £20 and £26—both of these items were to be eliminated or severely reduced in accordance with the injunctions. By far the heaviest item of expenditure in 1391-2 had been £66 spent on provisions (of which £13 was spent on wine and ale for the guest house); in the following years this item amounted to £58 and £71 respectively. Expenses of husbandry, including new equipment and repairs to ploughs and carts, cost between £26 and £27 a year, while the annual *rent resolute* (repayments of rent, etc.) comprised of various fixed payments and charges, came to between £18 and £19. Another major item of expenditure was the provision of corrodies for up to ten individuals at a cost of £18 to £21 a year; three of the corrodians had been sent to the priory by the king. Then there were payments of tenths and fifteenths, together with gifts to royal officials and others at a cost of £16 to £18 a year. One very variable item was the cost of repairs to buildings inside the close and outside. In 1391–2 the entire forinsec expenditure of £16 was spent on a new chancel for the church of Swindon, with carriage of timber all the way from the priory's estates at Moundsmere and Hannington, and purchase of a stone window at Salisbury for £1 and of glass for it for the same amount. The item concerning the expenses of the prior and others when travelling on the priory's business, £5–£7, is of interest on account of the places visited and the reasons occasionally given for the journeys. In 1391–2 the prior went to London, Arundel, Winchester, Moundsmere and elsewhere, while Edward Morton travelled with three horses to Northampton for a meeting of the Chapter General of the Order; his return journey cost over £2.[131]

We may conclude that the priory's income was in ordinary circumstances sufficient, but only sufficient, to provide comfortably for its needs. There was probably never a large margin of safety, and negligence, extravagance, or undeserved misfortune, could easily plunge it into debt, which tended to be self-perpetuating. The heavy losses which it suffered through war and pestilence in the middle decades of the fourteenth century were acknowledged by king and bishop, both of whom sought to alleviate the consequent financial distress.[132]

When disaster struck in the shape of lightning and fire in 1512, the priory managed to raise the large sum of £500 for reconstruction, but the second disaster, in 1518, would have spelt ruin if Bishop Fox had not provided a scheme which drastically cut back expenditure so that an annual surplus of £80 could be allocated to the re-building.[133] It must have been an attainable target; the resources were there if carefully husbanded. It was only some thirty-seven years later that the *Valor Ecclesiasticus* reckoned £257 to be the clear annual value of the priory.

The Spiritual and Intellectual Life of the Priory

The surviving records of Southwick Priory—the cartularies, account and court rolls—by their very nature emphasise the temporal rather than the spiritual aspect of its life. They show that it had a recurrent tendency to fall into debt, and that one cause of this was extravagance by the prior's household; but it does not follow that this was the main cause, which is more likely to be found in the various misfortunes which the priory encountered and in the fact that its resources were fairly limited, and also on occasion in the over-commitment of those limited resources to building projects which were intended for the glory of God. If it had not managed to overcome its financial difficulties it would not have survived until the Dissolution. Its very survival in the face of adversity must be reckoned to its credit.

Again, the records provide evidence of wrong-doing, occasionally serious, on the part of individual canons; but there is no reason to suppose that this was typical of the community as a whole. There is no direct evidence as to the spirit in which the daily observances in choir and cloister were performed—with genuine devotion or in a grudging and perfunctory manner. One may reasonably suppose that both elements were present most of the time, and that the preponderance of the one or the other depended on the individuals concerned and the leadership and example of those in authority. It was unfortunately as true in medieval times as today that scandal made news but that the steady performance of service to God, however devoted, would go unrecorded. Even the episcopal records concentrate on the erring individual, the short-comings of those in authority, and the economic problems—such was the diocesan's responsibility—but are silent when all is well.

There are, however, plenty of indications that from its earliest days Southwick Priory acquired a reputation that encouraged many, of both high and low estate, to seek its spiritual aid, both in life and after death. It is highly unlikely that William of Wykeham would have selected it as the place in which to found the elaborate and expensive chantries for his parents, the king and himself, if it had not been a house of more than ordinarily good repute. His own injunctions to Southwick appear designed at least as much to remove any opportunity for scandalous rumour as to correct actual abuses, besides prescribing measures to reduce its indebtedness. Sir Bernard Brocas also chose Southwick Priory in which to establish his chantry in 1385, despite the fact that between 1360 and 1363, during the lifetime of his wife, Mary, widow of Sir John de Burhunt, he had been involved in a bitter dispute with the priory over land. Sir Bernard was not only a close friend and associate of Wykeham, he held office at court and represented Hampshire in Parliament for much of Richard II's reign. It must be an indication of Southwick's standing that a leading magnate should choose to found his chantry there.

Very little evidence remains of the priory's library. There are just sixteen books that are known to have come from Southwick;[134] probably ten of them were copied in the twelfth century or earlier. They include works of the Fathers of the Church, Augustine (in English), Gregory, Bernard and Anselm, and three copies of works by Bede, two of them in English. Two other works in English are an eleventh-century Genealogy and a fourteenth-century Legendary. One would think it probable that Guy, who occurs as prior between 1185 and 1210 and was himself a man of letters, a friend and collaborator of John of Salisbury, encouraged the growth of the library.[135] It was probably he who instigated the making of the earliest cartulary.

The Dissolution

On 7 April 1538 Prior William Noxton, together with twelve canons, signed the deed surrendering the priory to the king.[136] The end can have come as no surprise. Southwick was the only Augustinian priory in Hampshire or Sussex, apart from Christchurch, which had an income of over £200 a year according to the *Valor Ecclesiasticus* of 1535, and so escaped dissolution in 1536.

But in January of that year one of the canons, James Gunwyn, was already writing to Thomas Cromwell with allegations damaging to the priory. He claimed that it was not fulfilling the terms of the Wykeham chantries and had not done so for the past forty years, and he also accused the prior of producing falsified accounts to the King's Commissioners and of being likely to dispose of the priory's plate, money and jewels if he knew of Gunwyn's letter.[137]

Before the end came it appears that a statue of Our Lady which had been the object of pilgrimage to the priory was removed by those sent to clear away relics. On 16 March 1538 a report went to Lord Lisle that "Our Lady of Southwick was taken down",[138] and six days later a letter to Lady Lisle gave the news that "the most part of the saints whereunto pilgrimages and offerings were wont to be made are taken away; Our Lady of Southwick, St Saviour, the Blood of Hayles and others."[139]

The prior made no effort to resist the inevitable. He received a pension of 100 marks or £66. 13s. 4d.,[140] generous when compared with the £18 which had been awarded to the prior of Breamore, but only half the pension of John Draper, head of the much wealthier priory of Christchurch.

The site and buildings of the priory were acquired by John White, who was well placed to secure his bid for them; not only was his patron Wriothesley, later Earl of Southampton, an office-holder and intimate at court, but White had already acquired from the priory in September 1537 a nintey-year lease, at an annual rent of £5, of its outlying demesne and lands around Southwick, from Hipley in the north to pasture on Portsdown Common in the south. Moreover he held for life the office of the priory's bailiff at an annual salary of £5.[141]

The priory church was soon pulled down. White established himself in the other buildings, though he was quick to express himself very dissatisfied with the meagre furnishings he found there.[142] In May 1538 he acquired a lease of the former priory's buildings, apple orchards, gardens and lands at Southwick for £5. 4s. 8d. a year, and in July he leased all the tithes and oblations that had belonged to the priory or the curate of Southwick for an annual payment of £6. 13s. 4d.[143] In March of the following year he paid £251. 13s. 4d. for the grant in fee of the priory site and buildings, with lands and woods around Southwick and pasture for 200 sheep on Portsdown, for all of which he was to pay an annual rent to the crown of £1. 8s. 0d.[144] Most of the remaining property in Hampshire which had belonged to the priory—Hannington, Sutton Scotney, Moundsmere, Denmead Molens, Priors Dean, Colemore, Stubbington and East Hoe—was granted as dower to Anne of Cleves on her marriage to the king, and then passed to Katharine Howard.[145] Farlington with Crookhorn and the advowson of Farlington church were granted in fee to William Pownde in June 1540 on payment of £317. 8s. 4d. and an annual rent of £1. 13s. 0d.[146] One of the earliest of the priory's endowments, Preston Candover with Nutley, passed back into ecclesiastical hands when it was granted in free alms by the king to the Dean and Chapter of Winchester in 1541,[147] and, following the execution of Katharine Howard, Stubbington-in-Portsea, together with the manor of Moundsmere, the rectories of Portsea and Portsmouth, and woodland in Preston Candover and Nutley, were granted to Winchester College as a result of an exchange of lands with the king;[148] a transaction which has fortunately led to the preservation of some of the priory's records among the muniments of the College to this day.

The manuscripts
The principal manuscripts of the Southwick cartularies used in this edition are three volumes in the Hampshire Record Office, 1M54/1-3, deposited by Mrs E. S. Borthwick-Norton.[149] The volumes were rebound in tooled leather on boards and were conserved by the Hampshire Record Office in 1973. All three were previously bound in limp parchment covers, lined with a coarse cloth in lieu of pastedowns, bindings which probably dated from the mid-sixteenth century. The volumes were described at this date as "Leiger of Suthwick" and, on three eighteenth-century labels sewn to the parchment, as "Priory register no. 1", number two and number three. The new binding does not permit a detailed description of the collation to be made, but each of the three volumes is composed of a number of discrete parts.

I. HRO 1M54/1 The volume consists of 58 parchment leaves containing fragments of a cartulary and two rentals and custumals. It has a continuous foliation, dating from the eighteenth century, in the top right corner of each folio and a modern, pencil pagination at the foot of each page. Folios 1-33 come from what was once a most impressive cartulary. The cartulary consists of a number of separate quires, some incomplete and detached from their original context. It is rubricated, with red and green initial letters. Folios 1-33 measure approximately 310×210 mm. They have been pricked for ruling horizontally at 5 mm intervals and there are faint traces of lead rulings. There is also pricking across the top to delineate a margin of 25 mm at the outside edge. In the late twelfth or early thirteenth century the quires of the cartulary would have had a number of blank leaves towards the end of each, onto which later insertions could be made.
1. ff. 1-4 Part of the first quire of a cartulary of late twelfth or early thirteenth century date, written mainly in an accomplished bookhand. ff. 1-3 form a sequence. ff. 1 and 3 are singletons; ff. 2 and 4 are a bifolium, but the contents of f. 4, a continuation of f. 25ᵛ, run in a different sequence from folio 3 and some sections are presumably missing.
2. ff. 5-13 f. 5 continues the sequence from f. 4ᵛ and is in the same hand. The first hand continues to f. 10ʳ and the sequence continues to f. 13ᵛ with some variation in hands. A small piece of parchment, dating from the early thirteenth century, has been inserted between ff. 7 and 8.
3. ff. 14-21 The cartulary returns to the original hand, which continues as far as f. 17ʳ. A series of possibly slightly later entries follows in a variety of business hands. The rubrication is incomplete from f. 19ʳ, and from f. 19ᵛ it was clearly never intended to rubricate. The entries continue in later hands as far as f. 21ᵛ, with a transcript of a document for 30 September 1303 in a contemporary hand.
4. ff. 22-3 A bifolium from the cartulary in the hand of 1.
5. ff. 24-5 A bifolium from the cartulary in the hand of 1. The text of f. 25ᵛ runs onto f. 4ʳ.

6. ff. 26–33 A continuation of the cartulary in a hand of the late twelfth or early thirteenth century, but not the hand of 1. From f. 31 onwards there are additions in progressively later hands, on f. 33^v as late as the mid-fourteenth century.

7. ff. 34–41 Rentals and custumals in a hand of *c.* 1210–40, originally finishing on f. 39^v. There are additions in later hands with a contemporary copy of a court case relating to Portsmouth, *c.* 1332–3, on ff. 40–1. The folios measure 290 × 205 mm. There is no pricking, and the parchment is ruled in lead point to form vertical columns and to form horizontal lines 3 mm apart.

8. ff. 42–55 Rentals and custumals, dated *c.* 1248, in a contemporary hand. From f. 53^v there are additions in successively later hands, up to f. 55^r, late fourteenth century. The folios measure 280 × 210 mm, are ruled in lead point and are pricked for horizontal lines 8 mm apart.

9. ff. 56–7 Mid-fourteenth-century copy of documents about Crookhorn and Farlington.

10. f. 58 Copy, *c.* 1360–90, of documents about the manors of Southwick and West Boarhunt, and about Bernard Brocas.

II. HRO 1M54/2 A volume of 106 parchment folios, measuring 330 × 210 mm.

1. ff. 1–19 A cartulary, probably written in the early 1360s, containing on ff. 1–4 documents about the church of Swindon, 1357–9; followed by, ff. 5–16, copies of royal charters, rubricated on f. 5, but intermittently thereafter; and on ff. 17–19 by other documents in a slightly later hand without rubrication but with the omission of initial letters. The folios are laid out without pricking and are ruled horizontally in lead point to give lines 7 mm apart, with a margin of 45 mm at the outside edge.

2. ff. 20–35, 44^r A list of charters, arranged by place, dated 1366. Under each place the charters are listed in order of *cophinus* (1–13). There are some additions in later hands.

3. ff. 36–43 A list of charters, *c.* 1220–60, *cophinus* by *cophinus* (3–16) for the whole monastery. The list is rubricated, the margin is pricked and there are horizontal rulings in lead point 6 mm apart. The outside margin is 40 mm wide.

4. ff. 44^v–49 A mid-fourteenth-century transcript of a forest parambulation for Hampshire.

5. ff. 50–62^r Copies of further documents, mid-fourteenth century to early fifteenth century.

6. ff. 62^v–66 Cartulary of the manor of Boarhunt, from *cophinus* 16, rubricated at the top of the page, written *c.* 1370.

7. ff. 67–96 A continuation of the same, with rubrication.

8. ff. 97–9 Various additions, the rubrication disappearing.

9. ff. 100–2 A new section, with spaces left for initial capitals at the start of charters, in a hand of the late fourteenth or early fifteenth century.

10. ff. 103–6 Additions from *c.* 1433 onwards, mainly mid-fifteenth century, with the exception of f. 106^v, which is late fourteenth or early fifteenth century.

III. HRO 1M54/3 The volume has 272 parchment leaves, measuring 290 × 215 mm. The margins are pricked and the volume has horizontal rulings in lead point about 5 mm apart in section 1, 6 mm apart and intermittently with rulings in section 2. Section 2 is laid out with 45 mm at the outside edge, 55-60 mm at the bottom, and 15 mm to the headings at the top of the page.

1. ff. 1-13 Part of a cartulary, written in a hand of the late fourteenth century, containing transcripts of papal bulls and one charter of the Bishop of Winchester.

2. ff. 14-119, 136-254 A rubricated cartulary, but without many of the initial letters, dated 1396. There are many earlier memoranda and copies of documents sewn into the volume, some, e.g. f. 74^v, dating from the early thirteenth century. The charters are listed in order of *cophinus* (1-15).

3. ff. 120-35 Two quires from a slightly earlier cartulary. The order of the quires should be ff. 128-35, 120-7.

4. ff. 255-70^r A list of charters, by *cophinus,* in a hand of the late fourteenth century.

5. ff. 270^v-272 Later additions of charters from 1426/7, concluding on f. 272^r with a list of kings and bishops of Winchester, *temp.* Henry VI, with additions into the sixteenth century.

6. A small collection of scraps of paper, removed during binding, mainly place markers, some dating from the early sixteenth century.

Other documents

A fragment of another cartulary is BL MS Harley 317. It is rubricated, with initials in blue, written in a hand of the late fourteenth century, giving on ff. 1-5 transcripts of charters from *cophinus* seven, lands acquired from Bernard Brocas, 1380-6. ff. 5-7 contain additions in a hand of the late fourteenth or early fifteenth century.

A further fragment of a cartulary is in the muniments of Winchester College, written in a number of hands of the late fourteenth and early fifteenth century, containing copies of documents to Portsmouth and Stubbington.

HRO 5M50/1 is a list of the charters in *cophini* one to eleven. The list is on a Chancery fashion roll of five membranes. The first four membranes are in a hand of the early thirteenth century. There are later additions to these membranes and the whole of the fifth membrane is a later addition, in hands of *c.* 1220-60.

The arrangement of the Southwick muniments

Two volumes of the cartulary and a separate roll contain a total of four lists of charters, arranged in *cophini*. A *cophinus* was a wooden box, probably no more than two cubic feet in capacity, typically with a sliding wooden lid, into which charters were placed. Boxes described as *cophini* also occur at the Augustinian priory of Christchurch, and the muniments of the Dean and Chapter of St Paul's were kept in *cophini* or *pixides* within cupboards, by the fifteenth century.[150] Storing muniments in this way was not uncommon. Elsewhere, as at Ramsey Abbey or Norwich Cathedral Priory, the muniments were stored in bags: at the former with

many other documents and books, some in baskets; at the latter, hung
on pegs in large chests.[151] Documents were frequently kept in the treasury
of a monastic house or some other secure place within its confines. At
Southwick there do not seem to have been much above fifty charters to
a box, and sixteen is the greatest box-number recorded, giving a total of
approximately 800 to 900 charters, to which may have to be added
some royal and papal documents and some administrative material. The
Southwick boxes were numbered from the early thirteenth century. No
reference to the boxes appears in the earliest cartulary fragments in
1M54/1. This cartulary does, however, contain individual numbers for
royal, papal and episcopal records, but not for the grants and charters
of others. The earliest list, 5M50/1, excludes royal, papal and episcopal
records, setting out the contents of eleven boxes. The charters appear to
be grouped roughly together by acquisition of property. There are also
some comments on the charters themselves. In *cophinus* two, there was
a charter of William, Count of Aumale, but it was of no use (*sed non
est utile*). The fifth membrane of this roll is an addition of the mid-
thirteenth century, and there are insertions also on the other membranes.
The second list to survive, 1M54/2, ff. 36–43, shows some correlation in
its contents with the earliest list. The *cophini* number sixteen. Box thirteen
contained the royal charters, fourteen the papal bulls, fifteen episcopal
charters, and box sixteen, agreements with other religious houses. There
are also some similarities in the list of 1366, 1M54/2, ff. 20–35, 44^r,
although royal charters had been added in other places and this document
is more of a place index than a list of contents, giving for each place a
list of charters in order of *cophinus*. The latest list, 1M54/3, ff. 255–70,
from the very end of the fourteenth century, shows some variations. The
contents of the boxes do not appear to have remained constant. Box
fifteen now held the royal charters; papal bulls do not appear in this
list. The conclusion to be drawn from these variations is that although
the boxes were numbered (and perhaps the numbers on them were
changed from time to time), the individual items were probably not
marked with a box number, and it is extremely unlikely that they had
individual piece numbers: even where the contents of the boxes are
similar, the order in which they are listed is different, suggesting that
they were noted down as they came to hand out of the box. It would
have been easy for items to migrate from one box to another.

These arrangements are typical of record-keeping in many religious
houses, although there were more sophisticated systems in the larger
monasteries where the quantities of muniments were much more substan-
tial. A series of box marks appears on the deeds of Lewes Priory,
distinguishing papal bulls, royal charters, the documents issued by the
Warenne family, by various bishops, and on a topographical basis.[152] At
the much smaller Cistercian house of Robertsbridge, a complex scheme
of capital letters, Roman numerals and dots had been devised by 1250
to identify individual charters within an arrangement probably founded
on a topographical division, but excluding papal and royal documents.
A similar scheme was employed at Stanley Abbey.[153] The isolation of
royal, papal and archiepiscopal documents also formed part of the
classification at Norwich Cathedral Priory, and the division was more

elaborate at Durham Priory.[154] The *Liber ruber* of Merton College, Oxford, *c.*1288, gives box references to the charters it lists.[155] Although the earliest Southwick cartulary does not give references to *cophini,* its arrangement may have been founded on the existing order of the archive, with separate categories for papal and royal documents. A close relationship between the order of the archive and the order of its transcription into a cartulary was not uncommon.[156] Indeed the Southwick cartulary of 1396 is a transcription of the archive as it was found, arranged box by box.

Notes on the Method of Editing

Rubrics and marginal notes have been omitted, unless they include information which is not given in the text of the charter or entry for which they are provided. Variations in the spelling of names which appear in the rubrics are shown in square brackets in the calendar of the text.

Christian names are translated, where a modern equivalent exists, but surnames are kept in the form given in the MS: for example, Robert Clericus of Southwick, or Robert de Suthewyk', clerk. *Dominus* is rendered "Sir"; *domina,* "Lady"; *vicedominus,* "Vidame"; *magister,* M. (or written in full in front of an initial: M. Henry, but *Magister* H.). Place-names are given in modern spelling, followed, on the first occasion on which the name appears in a particular entry, by the spelling or spellings given in the MS; exceptions are made for Southwick, which occurs so frequently, and for towns such as Winchester with well-known Latin names (unless the spelling is unusual). All places are in Hampshire unless otherwise stated. Unidentified place or field-names are given in the original spelling, and are printed in italics.

When charters or other documents were presented to the priory, they were usually addressed "to God and the Church of St Mary of Southwick and the canons serving God there" (*Deo et ecclesia sancte Marie de Sudwica* (Suthewyk', etc.) *et canonicis ibidem Deo servientibus*), or "to the Church of the Blessed Mary of Southwick and the canons of that place" (*ecclesie beate Marie de Suwic' et canonicis eiusdem loci*). These forms and variants of them have been rendered by "Southwick Priory".

The term GIFT is used to denote a charter which gives title to tangible landed property (*dedi concessi et hac presenti carta mea confirmavi*— and variants), and GRANT for intangible property, i.e., rents, advowsons, etc. "In free alms" is used for *in liberam puram et perpetuam elemosinam* and variants, but a list of those charters in which the word "pure" is omitted has been given as Appendix VI. Use of this list will show that a number of the charters which are *not* included in it—i.e. in which the gift is professed to be made in "pure" alms—specifically state that forinsec service was the responsibility of the donee (e.g. I 43; III 148, 199), and there are even some which require some kind of payment to be made to the donor (e.g. III 219, 267). Evidently the word "pure" was sometimes included mechanically without thought of what it was supposed to mean. The promise "to warrant, acquit and defend a gift in perpetuity against all people" is indicated by "with warranty", but any special conditions are given in full. Similarly, "hold freely" or "hold by hereditary right in perpetuity" are used for the formulas: "to have and hold freely, quietly and wholly", or "freely, well and in peace by hereditary right in perpetuity" (*habendum et tenendum libere quiete et integre,* or *libere bene et in pace iure hereditario imperpetuum*) and variants.

Clauses referring to the seal appended to the document have been omitted, unless it is stated that some special seal has been affixed (cf. III 666). Lists of witnesses are given as fully as in the MS—where they are often incomplete.

In the present work the charters are calendared from the text in the main cartularies in the Hampshire Record Office. Many of them, however, exist in more than one copy; indeed, the majority of those in Volume I reappear in Volume II or III, and the entries in the cartulary in Winchester College are almost all to be found in Volume III, while those in the few folios in the British Library are in Volumes II or III. There also exist a number of later copies; these, together with some surviving originals, are preserved in the Hampshire Record Office, except for one of the originals, which is in the Public Record Office in London, and two which are in Winchester College. The text which is calendared here is that of the charter when it first appears in the main cartularies. Any subsequent copy in those cartularies, together with any copy existing elsewhere, is noted, with particulars of any variants, after the footnotes at the end of the entry. For the sake of consistency, those originals which have survived are dealt with similarly, even though they are intrinsically more important than any copy, including that which is being calendared.

The charters in each of the three volumes have been separately numbered. In volume I, where the folios are not bound in accordance with their numerical sequence (as indicated above p. xliii), the documents as calendared have been numbered consecutively from folio 1 onwards, irrespective of the position of the folios in the bound volume. When a charter reappears after having been calendared previously, a cross-reference is provided: e.g., III 178. Copy of I 31. Folio numbers are included, but their position in relation to the text of the manuscript is necessarily only approximate.

Editorial insertions in the calendared text are indicated by square brackets, as are estimated dates for undated documents.

A few of the documents are in French, and where that is the case the fact is stated in a footnote. All the rest of the text of the cartularies is in Latin.

NOTES TO INTRODUCTION

1. For details of a recent discovery and work on the site see p. xiv.
2. B.L. Add. MSS. 33280.
3. See note on the space left in the copy of III 290. All the entries in 4M53/B7 which also appear in the cartularies are collated with the cartulary copies, and any variants are shown at the end of the cartulary entries.
4. H.R.O. 4M53/Alchin/Suthwyk Record.
5. See below, pp. xxxv–xxxvi.
6. Winchester College Muniments 15246, described as "A portion of the Registers of Southwick Priory containing evidences of lands etc. in Portsmouth and Stubbington". The two entries in this MS which do not appear in the main cartularies are calendared as Appendix III to Part II of the present work. The reason why these records came into the hands of Winchester College is explained on pp. xlii–xliii.
7. B.L. MS Harley 317. The only entry in this fragment of a cartulary which does not appear in the main cartularies is calendared as Appendix II.
8. Winchester College Muniments: ST/A/1, 15376 a–f.
9. The priory's possession of the churches of Portchester and Wymering was confirmed ("given") by Bishop Giffard (I 3, 4).
10. This account is based on the studies by Emma Mason, "The King, the Chamberlain and Southwick Priory"; "The Mauduits and their Chamberlainship of the Exchequer", pp. 2–3, and *The Beauchamp Cartulary* pp. liii–liv.
11. William had probably already helped to found the Priory of Southwark, Surrey, with the active participation of Bishop William Giffard. The date given for that foundation is 1106, but there is some doubt whether the original community was of Augustinian canons or whether they were introduced later (*V C H Surrey* II, p. 107; Mason, "The King, the Chamberlain and Southwick Priory", p. 2, n. 10; D. Knowles and R. N. Hadcock *Medieval Religious Houses* (London, 1953) p. 153; J. C. Dickinson *The Origins of the Austin Canons* (London, 1950) p. 120). Dickinson is inclined to dismiss William Pont de l'Arche's involvement with Southwark on the grounds that Southwark may have been misread as Southwark.
12. I 1. Another version of this charter purporting to have been granted to the priory by Henry I and containing additional privileges has been shown to be a forgery (I 1, n. 3; II 8).

   No charter from William de Pont de l'Arche has survived, and none is copied into the cartularies, although there are several from his son, Robert, which confirm his father's gifts (I 11, 18–20; III 404).

13. The scribe who copied the charter, towards the end of the twelfth century, as the first entry in the earliest of the Southwick cartularies, refers to the king in the rubric as "our founder". Dickinson recognised the role of William de Pont de l'Arche in the foundation of Southwick Priory (*op. cit.*, p. 124), and it has more recently been discussed by Emma Mason (*loc. cit.*, p. 1).

14. *Regesta* iii, no. 277.

15. Mason, "The Mauduits and their Chamberlainship of the Exchequer", p. 3.

16. Alan Borg has written an excellent account of the church ("St Mary's Church", in B. Cuncliffe and others *Excavations at Portchester Castle, iii, Medieval, the Outer Bailey and its Defences* (London, 1977) pp. 105–15). He followed the view then generally held that the date of the priory's foundation at Portchester was 1133, and was therefore concerned with the possibility that the canons took over a church that was already in existence; this argument is now superseded in view of the earlier date established for the foundation.

    The following account of the claustral buildings is based on the report of the excavations given in the same volume (pp. 97–105; see also the plan of the existing church and walls of the fort, showing in addition the probable outline of the claustral buildings and the extent of the excavations which have been carried out: fig. 67, facing p. 98).

17. I. 184; III 950, 926. Account for rolls for 1386–7 and 1391–5 record that the pension of 24s. due from the church of Portchester was not paid because of the poverty of that church (H.R.O. 5M50/43–7).

18. These figures are taken from a taxation of spirituals of the diocese of Winchester, contained in a manuscript volume, written between 1333 and 1345, and printed as Appendix I to *Wykeham's Register* (I, pp. 361–382); the manuscript is said to have belonged to the bishop. The assessments are identical with those given in Pope Nicholas IV's Taxation (from which they are said to have been copied); but in instances where the churches are appropriated to religious houses, this fact is recorded in the Wykeham version, thus showing which churches were held at that time by Southwick Priory, the value at which each was assessed, and the pension from it, if any.

19. B. Cunliffe and others, *op. cit.*, pp. 101, 119–20; figs. 67, 69.

20. See III 968. This indulgence must have been granted before Archbishop Theobald became papal legate, early in 1150, because he does not use that style in the grant; therefore the move to Southwick had taken place before that date. (This has been noted by Emma Mason in "The King, the Chamberlain and Southwick Priory", p. 4.) The other evidence for dating the move comes from two privileges issued by Pope Eugenius III; the first was addressed between July and October 1147 to Anselm as Prior of Portchester, and the second, some time between July 1151 and October 1152, was addressed to him as Prior of Southwick (I 84, 85).

21. A similar reason—lack of space for the necessary buildings—was given when the priory of Barnwell, Cambridgeshire, was moved from its original site (*Customs of the Augustinian Canons at Barnwell* ed. J. W. Clark (Cambridge, 1897) p. xii). That site had also lacked a good supply of fresh water; perhaps a similar lack at Portchester influenced the decision to make the move from there to Southwick, where it was available in plenty.

22. See p. xlii.

23. III 965; H.R.O. 4M53/E10; and also p. xxxv.

24. For a description of the lavabo and a report on its discovery, see G. Soffe, "Southwick Priory and its late Romanesque sculptured lavabo" *Hampshire Field Club and Archaeological Society, Newsletters*, New Series, 3 (Spring 1985) pp. 27-9. This article includes an illustrations of the lavabo by J. Thorn.

25. A foundation charter often stated the number of canons who were to make up the community, but no such charter has survived in the case of Southwick. However, it is known that Mottisfont was founded for a prior and eleven canons; St Denys for twelve or thirteen canons, and Selborne for fourteen; but none of these houses managed to maintain these numbers (Knowles and Hadcock *Medieval Religious Houses* pp. 146, 152-3).

26. H.R.O. 5M50/43, 46.

27. Register of Bishop Thomas Langton, H.R.O. A/1/16, f. 41^v.

28. Register of Bishop Richard Fox, H.R.O. A/1/20, ff. 37-43.

29. *Letters and Papers, Henry VIII*, XIV, i, p. 596. The signatures of the twelve canons, together with that of the prior, are given on the deed of surrender (*8th Report of the Deputy Keeper of the Public Records*, 1847, Appendix II, p. 41).

30. I 20, 2, 3, 5; III 968, 969; I 85.

31. Above n. 12.

32. See III 989.

33. Susan Wood *English Monasteries and their Patrons in the Thirteenth Century* (Oxford, 1955) p. 3.

34. For the procedure followed in electing a new prior, see pp. xxxiv–xxxv.

35. I 200, 201. Custody by the king's escheator during a vacancy could involve a monastery in such heavy losses as to make it worth-while to pay heavily in order to buy the custody out of his hands. Very limited or token custody, such as was claimed by Southwick as their right, was not, however, unusual; for example, Isabel de Forz granted a similar arrangement to Christchurch (Wood, *op. cit.*, pp. 82-6). Although the king agreed to the limited form of custody, it appears that patronal right of presentation to livings during a vacancy was upheld: in 1393-4 two out of three royal corrodians in the priory were clerks who had been sent there by the king following the deaths of the two preceding priors, and had to be maintained until livings were available (H.R.O. 5M50/46). In nominating one of these clerks, Thomas Athelyngton, in 1389, the king's letter to the priory declares that Thomas is to receive a pension there until provided with a benefice, as the priory is bound to provide for one

of the king's clerks by reason of the creation of a new prior (*Cal. Close R., Richard II, 1389–1392* p. 81).

36. There was however the occasion on which Edward II sent a pensioner to the priory in December 1316, and a week later sent another (*Cal. Close R., Edward II, 1313–1318* pp. 437, 447). This is not recorded in the cartularies and the outcome is not known.

37. II 9–11. But see above n. 36.

38. *Letters and Papers, Henry VIII,* II, i, 344; IV, iii, 6751; V, 364 (14).

39. *Cal. Chart. R., I, 1226–1257* p. 199.

40. *Cal. Lib. R., IV, 1251–1260* pp. 141–3; *Cal. Pat. R., Henry III, 1247–1258* p. 202; III 990.

41. *Cal. Lib. R., IV, 1251–1260* p. 144.

42. *Cal. Close R., 1279–1288* p. 17.

43. *Cal. Pat. R., Edward I, 1281–1292* p. 335; III 983.

44. III 977; *Cal. Pat. R., Edward II, 1317–1321* p. 109.

45. *Cal. Chart. R., III, 1300–1326* p. 428.

46. *Cal. Pat. R., Edward III, 1340–1343* p. 579

47. *Cal. Pat. R., Edward III, 1345–1348* p. 125.

48. *Op. cit.,* p. 153; I 212.

49. *Op. cit.,* p. 341.

50. *Cal. Pat. R., Richard II, 1381–1385* p. 551; *1391–1396* p. 700; *1396–1399* p. 373.

51. H.R.O. 5M50/66. The total annual income recorded amounts to £3. 0s. 2½d., derived mostly from oblations received at the chapel of Plant (£1. 14s. 11½d.), together with oblations at the chapel of the guesthouse (7d.) and at Walesworth (1s. 4d.), and the profits of the garden (£1. 3s. 4d.). The total sum expended on items expressly or probably connected with the royal visit was £1. 7s. 3d. out of a total expenditure for the year of at least £2. 6s. 2d. (totals are left blank on the roll and one amount is illegible). The guesthouse keeper appears to have been responsible for the fabric of the building, the furnishings and the garden, and for similar provision at the chapel of Plant, but his account roll does not include any provision of food and drink.

52. I 1, n. 3; II 8.

53. *Cal. Chart. R., II, 1257–1300* p. 124; *III, 1300–1326* p. 209; II 8(d).

54. *Regesta* III, p. xxxvii; *Recueil des Actes de Henri II* Introduction, pp. 429–30, 485–6; R. W. Eyton *Itinerary of Henry II* pp. 233–6.

55. See p. xx.

56. I 63, 65, 66, 70; III 138; Appendix I.

57. I 127; see also p. xxx.

58. III 99, I 2; I 144, III 97; III 286–96, I 158. The annual amounts drawn from Aldbourne and Clanfield were 20s. and 46s. 8d. respectively according to the rental of *c.* 1225–30 (I 182). An inquisition held at Fishbourne in 1281 declared that the true annual value of the priory's property there—a messuage and two hides—was £10, a remarkably large amount compared with later assessments, assuming that the size of the property remained unchanged. In the Taxation of Pope Nicholas IV of 1291, the temporalities in the possession of

Southwick Priory at Fishbourne were assessed at £2. 1s. 4d., at Aldbourne at £1. 3s. 4d., and at Clanfield at £2. 16s. 8d. (*Taxatio* pp. 138, 192, 44). The inquisition post mortem of 1381 recorded annual rents of £2. 0s. 0d. from Fishbourne; £1. 0s. 3d. from Aldbourne; and £2. 16s. 8d. from Clanfield (II 32). Identical amounts were given for the value of the three holdings in the Taxation of *c.* 1369–85 (II 230). In 1538–9 the total rents from Old Fishbourne were £5. 6s. 8d.—13s. 4d. from two customary tenants, and £4. 13s. 4d. from the manor which had been leased at farm for 41 years by the priory on 12 September 1537, just seven months before the Dissolution; from Aldbourne the total rent was £1. 3s. 4d.—the three tenements having been leased at farm, two in 1506 and 1508 respectively, for lives, and the third in 1532 for 30 years; from Clanfield the total rents were £2. 17s. 1½ d., comprised of 3s. 7d. from two rents of assize and £2. 13s. 6½d. from the rents of four customary tenants (P.R.O. SC6/Henry VIII/3340, m. 29).

59. I 17 and n. 2, I 86.
60. Above p. xvi.
61. H. M. Colvin *The White Canons in England* (Oxford, 1951) p. 184.
62. Colvin, *op. cit.*, p. 186.
63. Even then there is also, of course, the problem of distinguishing between father, son and sometimes even grandson of the same name, not to mention possible cousins, any of whom may be witnessing charters at the same time.
64. *VCH Hants* III p. 456.
65. P.R.O. SC6/Henry VIII/3340, m. 25.
66. This is noted by Margaret Hoad in "Origins of Portsmouth", p. 16.
67. I 133, 134; III 191, 206, 208, 214; see also III 716.
68. Hoad, "Origins of Portsmouth", pp. 19–20. *Book of Fees* I, pp. 258, 259, 618. *Pipe Rolls Society, New Series, VI,* (1929), pp. 36, 40. *Red Book of the Exchequer, II,* p. 555.
69. III 908, 907, 915, 341. William was succeeded by his son, Henry. In 1346, after Henry's death, his executors sold his tenements in Portsmouth to Robert Bonyng of Chichester (III 905, 906). In accordance with the terms of Robert's will, his widow and son in 1352 sold all his property within the liberty of Portsmouth to pay his debts. The purchaser was Adam de Lymbergh', vicar of Walberton, Sussex (III 901–911, 916), who granted this property, with other property that he had acquired (III 912), to William Fifhide in January 1356 (III 917); and in December of that year William made the exchange with Southwick Priory (III 474, 475).
70. III 468. The entry in the Calendar of Patent Rolls describes the holding as a messuage and 16 acres (*Cal. Pat. R., Edward III, 1354–1358* p. 474). It seems likely that this is a mistake, as the priory's land at Ellisfield, when acquired in 1279, amounted to 40 acres with 10 acres of woodland (I 104).
71. R. East *Extracts from the Portsmouth Records* (Portsmouth, 1891) p. 493.
72. P.R.O. SC6/Henry VIII/3340, mm. 32–3.

73. Two entries in the Winton Domesday Survey of 1148 deal with property held by the canons of Portchester (*W S I* pp. 115, 133).
74. This account of medieval Winchester is based on the work of Dr Keene (*W S II* i and ii).
75. I 191, 190, 192; II 19; *W S II* 413, p. 747; P.R.O. SC6/Henry VIII/ 3340, m. 36.
76. *W S II* pp. 88–94.
77. *Taxatio* p. 213.
78. H.R.O. 5M50/46.
79. H.R.O. 4M53/D5.
80. The priory had 3s. 4d. rent of assize from the Star Inn (*Sterr Ine*); 19s. 8d. from three customary tenants; 12s. annual rent from a tenement with garden and kitchen which fourteen years previously had been granted at farm for 50 years; and 1s. rent from a plot granted at farm 28 years previously for 40 years (P.R.O. SC6/ Henry VIII/3340, m. 36). The last tenement, held by Thomas Webbe and his wife, was probably part of the property which the priory had recieved from William Tinctor (*W S II* 413, p. 747. For the Star Inn, see 82, pp. 509—11, Fig. 56).

   Dr Keene has estimated that in real terms the value of the priory's property at the Dissolution was perhaps only a sixth of what it had been in 1219 (*W S II* i, p. 201).
81. *W S II* i, p. 206.
82. I 18. This confirmation from Robert de Pont de l'Arche does not mention Wymering Church, although it appears to have been part of the earliest endowment (I 3). Dr Mason has suggested that either the reference to Wymering Church as being held by the priory in the episcopate of William Giffard is a mistake, or, as Wymering was mostly royal demesne, the canons may not have wanted to draw attention to their tenure of it in 1133 when Henry I granted to them his charter, which makes no mention of it (I 1; Mason, "The King, the Chamberlain and Southwick Priory", p. 2).
83. I 31, 111, and notes. See also reference to the church of Shalden in I 83.
84. *Curia Regis R.* III, pp. 65, 192; IV, 33; *Cal. Pat. R., Henry III, 1225–1232* p. 213.
85. I 154, 107. It appears that the priory was unable to take advantage of a licence which was granted by Edward II in 1325 to appropriate the church of Swindon (*Cal. Pat. R., Edward II, 1324–1327* p. 122). The appropriation finally took place in 1357 (II 1; III 413).
86. I 86; see also I 4.
87. The Taxation of Pope Nicholas IV does not distinguish those churches which were appropriated to monasteries, but this is clearly shown in the valuation of the spirituals of the diocese of Winchester said to have been copied from Pope Nicholas' Taxation and contained in a small manuscript volume which, it is believed, belonged to William of Wykeham (*Wykeham Register* I, Appendix I, pp. 361–82). The valuations of the churches and the pensions are identical in both cases. The Wykeham manuscript lists seven churches of which the prior of Southwick is rector: Empshott, Preston

Candover, Portsea with chapel, Portchester, Wymering, Boarhunt and Southwick, and one, Nutley, which was annexed to the priory. The total value of these was £88. 13s. 4d. There were also pensions to Southwick Priory from five churches: Shalden, Portsea, Boarhunt, Widley and Walesworth—totalling £5. The churches of Wanstead and Walesworth were not assessed "because of their poverty" (*propter exilitatem*). The Wykeham manuscript does not, of course, include the church of Swindon, which was listed among the spirituals of the archdeanconry of Berkshire and Wiltshire in Pope Nicholas' Taxation (p. 190). That church was valued at £13. 6s. 8d. and a pension of £5 was recorded as payable to "the monks of Suthewyk".

88. See for example the careful regulations laid down for support of the vicarage at Swindon (II 3).

89. Above p. xxvii.

90. III 38. This concession was probably granted by Gregory IX in 1227 or Gregory X in 1272. The General Chapter of the Augustinian Order in England issued ordinances in 1359 and again in 1374, insisting upon the wearing of gaiters and boots, and forbidding the use of shoes (*Chapters of the Augustinian Canons* ed. H. E. Salter (Canterbury and York Society, 29; 1922) pp. 64, 72. There is no evidence to show whether Southwick Priory claimed exemption on the grounds of its papal dispensation.

91. *Cal. of Papal Letters, I, 1198–1304* p. 303.

92. I 17. See also the indulgence granted between 1182 and 1183 by Seffrid II, Bishop of Chichester, who had taken part in the dedication (III 959).

93. III 962. From November 17–20, 1281, and on 29 January 1284.

94. *Pecham Register* I, pp. xi, xiii.

95. *Registrum Epistolarum Johannis Pecham, archiepiscopi Cantuariensis*) ed. C. T. Martin (3 vols., Rolls Series, London 1882–5) I, p. 292.

96. *Op. cit.*, II, DX, p. 666.

97. *Op. cit.*, II, DCVI, p. 837.

98. *Pontissara Register* I, p. 50.

99. *Op. cit.*, I, p. 589.

100. In the case of Henry Pruet, who was accused of procuring admission to Southwick Priory by simony, the bishop found that there had been a misunderstanding and cleared Henry of any blame (*Woodlock Register* p. 230). Another canon, Richard Spede, had been found guilty of assault and perjury. The bishop sent three letters to the priory concerning the gradual rehabilitation of Spede, after he had done penance for his misdeeds (*op. cit.*, pp. 241, 411, 423). Six weeks before the bishop visited the priory in 1308 he sent orders to the prior that Canon Philip de Wintonia was to be confined within the priory and prevented from having contact, by writing or otherwise, with any secular person before his arrival. Obviously the bishop intended to investigate some complaint against the canon, or suspected some conspiracy, but the outcome is not recorded (*op. cit.*, p. 319).

101. *Op. cit.*, pp. 512–14.

102. Above p. xxix.
103. Above n. 100.
104. Orleton Register, H.R.O. A/1/6, fo. 121ᵛ.
105. H.R.O. 4M53/A7. It is sometimes assumed that, if no injunctions appear in a bishop's register following a visitation, none were issued or required; obviously this is not necessarily the case.
106. *evagandi . . . . indecenter et etiam insolenter.*
107. H.R.O. 5M50/47.
108. *Dimissa aula vestra.*
109. Each canon was to have cooked provisions (*coquina*) worth 1½d. and the usual loaf (*mich'*); but ale was no longer to be supplied in individual allowances of 1¼ gallons, but only in common, at suitable times and places.
110. This document (H.R.O. 4M53/A6), is in the form of a book, made up of four leaves of parchment sewn together to make eight pages. The fragment of a seal, apparently Wykeham's, is appended to it on a green silk cord.
111. H.R.O., A/1/16, ff. 41–4.
112. H.R.O., A/1/20, ff. 37–43.
113. This is not recorded in Fox's Register, but in a separate document (H.R.O. 4M53/E10).
114. The largest annual wage (£2. 13s. 4d.) was allocated to the clerk of the priory, and the same to the roofer (*hellyar*); the cook was to receive £2; the butler, two carters, the bailiff, the baker, the brewer, and the keeper of the Lady Chapel were each to £1. 6s. 8d; the under-cook, three under-carters, a servant to assist the baker and brewer, the porter, the clerk of the church, the swineherd (*hoggard*), the shepherd, and the cowherd were to have £1 each, and a lad to drive the plough and two dairy-maids (wyfs for the dayry) were to have 13s. 4d. each.
115. Provision of food and drink were not to cost more than 1s. 4d. a week for each of the twelve canons (a total of £41. 12s. 0d. a year), and allowances for their pittances and masses amounted to another £12. 6s. 0d. Food and drink for each of the servants was not to cost more than 1s. a week, and was also to be provided at the same rate for the Vicar of Blandford "and his schild", who were entitled to it as corrody—thus the total annual expenditure was not to exceed £65. The servants were to be allowed 5s. each a year for clothing, except the clerk of the priory who was allowed 10s. £8 was allowed for the canons' clothing, but only £3. 8s. 6d. for "convent wages" because 13s. 4d. had been deducted for each of the nine priests who "of their devotion and freewill" had donated that sum to the re-building.
116. For evidence about this statue see p. xlii.

The account rolls of 1391–5 record annual oblations of around £25 received in "the chapel of the Blessed Mary above the gate" (*de devotionibus in oblat' in capella beate Marie supra portam.* H.R.O. 5M50/44–7). It is possible that it was in this chapel that the statue of Our Lady stood, accessible to pilgrims, and that the "stokke box" was intended for their offerings.

117. *Selborne Charters* I, pp. 7–9.
118. S. F. Hockey *Quarr Abbey and its Lands, 1132–1631* (Leicester, 1970) p. 6.
119. *Op. cit.*, pp. 9, 85; I 6–10.
120. I 142. *Planta* is now represented by Plant Farm.
121. See above p. xxii.
122. The inadequacy of the priory's resources to provide for its customary hospitality was one of the reasons given by the bishop of Salisbury for granting it the appropriation of the church of Swindon in 1357 (II 1).
123. *Taxatio* p. 213. For the priory's temporalities outside Hampshire see above, n. 58. It is however worth mentioning that, unlike the estates in Hampshire, two of the outlying estates were actually producing at the time of the Dissolution only that same amount at which they had been valued in 1290: at Clanfield in Oxfordshire the value in 1290 was £2. 16s. 8d., and rents at the time of the Dissolution were £2. 17s. 1½d.; and at Aldbourne in Wiltshire the amount was £1. 3s. 4d. at each date (P.R.O. SC6/Henry VIII/ 3340, m. 29).

    The calculation of value in Pope Nicholas' Taxation appears to have been based, at least in some cases, on the rent at which an estate might be let (Rose Graham *English Ecclesiastical Studies* (London, 1929) p. 294). One source of revenue which was disregarded by the Taxation was the sale of wool—not as important an item for Southwick as for some monasteries, but producing between £14 and £17 annually between 1391 and 1394 (H.R.O. 5M50/44–6).
124. Five earlier rolls, dated between 1247 and 1267, have survived but do not contain any estimate of value. The formula used in 1268 and subsequently is: *Valet hoc anno manerium in omnimodis exitibus deductis necessariis expensis*, or simply *valet manerium hoc anno*. These rolls are to be found among Winchester College Muniments 15376–87.

    The whole subject of the calculation of profit on various small and meduim-sized medieval estates is dealt with by David Postles in his article, "The Perception of Profit before the Leasing of Demesnes" *Agricultural History Review* 34 (1986) pp. 12–28. Dr Postles has used the Stubbington material, and prints a complete list of the statements of *valor* given in all surviving Stubbington rolls between 1268 and *c.* 1405 (*loc. cit.*, p. 28).
125. This figure and those given below are rounded.
126. There was said to be in all 692 acres of arable, 609 acres of pasture and 32 acres of meadow. The total value was made up of rents producing £19, arable, usually reckoned to be worth 2d. an acre, pasture, worth 1d. and meadow worth 4d. Exceptions were at Stubbington-in-Portsea, where arable was worth 3d. an acre, and pasture, 2d. The remainder of the value was made up of sums for underwood, for dovecots, and for closes for which no acreage was given.

127. The bishop did everything possible to ensure that the endowment of the chantries should be adequate for their support, and that it should be used exclusively for that purpose (II 111).

Initially he gave the priory 158 marks (£105. 6s. 8d.) to spend on seed corn and animals for re-stocking the manors, and further 125½ marks (£83. 13s. 4d.) to finance the chantries until the land yielded a profit sufficient for that purpose: 50 marks (£33. 6s. 8d.) for the first year's expenditure, and the remaining 75½ marks (£50. 6s. 8d.) was a reserve fund to be kept in the priory's treasury and replaced each year from the profits of the manors, so that it would always be available for the upkeep of the chantries in accordance with his instructions.

128. H.R.O. 5M50/42-6.

129. This abnormally large figure is to be explained by the inclusion of £173 among the forinsec receipts.

130. H.R.O. 5M50/47.

131. H.R.O. 5M50/44.

132. See above p. xvii.

133. See above pp. xxxv–xxxvi.

134. *Medieval Libraries of Great Britain* ed. N. R. Ker (second edition, London 1964) p. 181.

135. *Letters of John of Salisbury, II, 1163-1180* ed. W. J. Millor and C. N. L. Brooke (Oxford, 1979), p. lviii.

136. *Letters and Papers, Henry VIII* XIII, i(1538), 698, p. 266.

137. *Op. cit.*, X (1536), 138, p. 46.

138. *Op. cit.*, XIII, i(1538), 514, p. 193.

139. *Op. cit.*, 580, p. 214.

140. *Op. cit.*, XIV, i (1539), p. 596. This pension was just double the amount allowed by Bishop Fox to Thomas Kent in 1518 (above p. xxxvi).

141. P.R.O. SC6/Henry VIII/3340, m. 22.

142. *Letters and Papers, Henry VIII* XIII, i(1538), 748, p. 281.

143. P.R.O. SC6/Henry VIII/3340, m. 22. *Letters and Papers, Henry VIII* XIV, i (1539), p. 604.

144. *Letters and Papers, Henry VIII* XIV, i (1539), 651 (37), p. 256.

145. *Op. cit.*, II, 432, p. 154; XVI (1540-41), 1500, p. 716

146. *Op. cit.*, XV (1540) 831 (87), p. 412

147. *Op. cit.*, XVI (1540-41) 878, p. 417.

148. *Op. cit.*, XVIII, Part 1 (1543) 981 (46), p. 533.

149. The volumes were described briefly in G. R. C. Davis *Medieval cartularies of Great Britain: a short catalogue* (London, 1958) pp. 104-5.

150. BL MS Cotton Tiberius D VI; G. Yeo, "Record keeping at St. Paul's cathedral", *Journal of the Society of Archivists* 8 (1986) pp. 36-8.

151. *The charters of Norwich Cathedral Priory* ed. B. Dodwell (2 vols., Pipe Roll Society, new series, 40, 46; 1974-85) i, pp. xi-xl; J. A. Raftis *The estates of Ramsey Abbey* (Toronto, 1957) p. 329.

152. V. H. Galbraith, "Press-marks on the deeds of Lewes Priory", *Sussex Archaeological Collections* 65 (1924) pp. 196-205.

153. Royal Commission on Historical Manuscripts *Report on the muniments of Lord de L'Isle and Dudley* (6 vols., London, 1925-66) i, pp. xiii-xviii.
154. *The charters of Norwich Cathedral Priory* i, pp. xi-xl; R. B. Dobson *Durham Priory 1400-1450* (Cambridge, 1973) pp. 392-3.
155. *Merton muniments* ed. P. S. Allen and H. W. Garrod (Oxford, 1928), p. 29.
156. D. Walker, "The organisation of material in medieval cartularies", In *The study of medieval records* ed. D. A. Bullough and R. L. Storey (Oxford, 1971) pp. 132-50.

MAPS

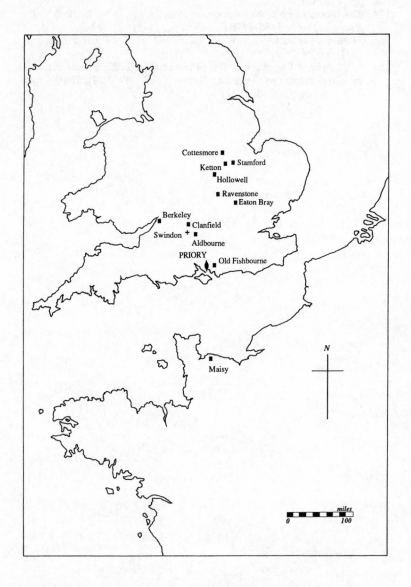

FIG 1. Places outside Hampshire at which grants were made to the Priory

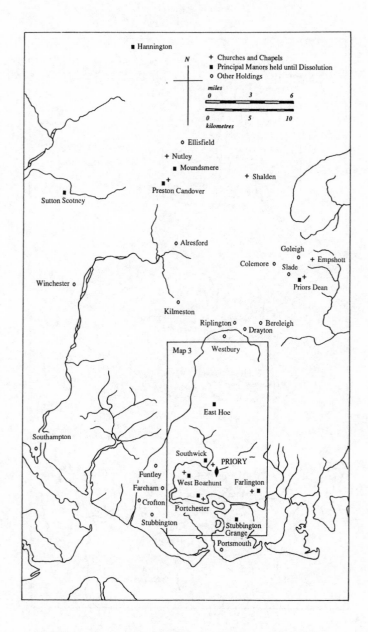

FIG 2. The Priory's outlying possessions in Hampshire
(see also Maps 3 and 4)

FIG 3. The Priory's possessions in the vicinity of Southwick

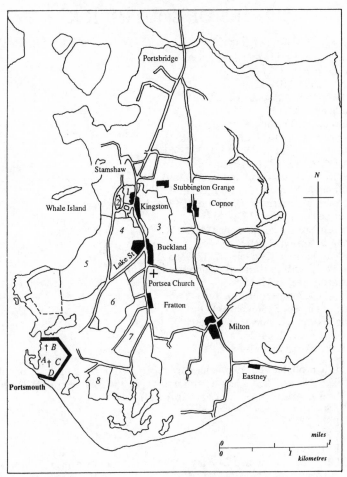

A. St Thomas's Church
B. St Mary's Chapel
C. Kingshall Green
D. God's House

Field Names
1. Pitcroft
2. Balches Croft
3. Beeston, possibly incorporating Easton
4. Meteland
5. Fountain, possibly incorporating Westwood
6. Muryfelde
7. St. Andrew's
8. Hambrook

This map shows the location, as far as it is known, of settlements, churches and fields mentioned in the cartularies. It cannot of course indicate the changes which took place during the four centuries of the priory's involvement there, nor indeed give an accurate picture of the state of development at the Dissolution, as subsequent changes may well have taken place.

The map is based upon that drawn by Dr. John Chapman in his "Common Lands of Portsea Island" (*The Portsmouth Papers*, no. 29, 1978, p. 4). I am most grateful to Dr. Chapman for giving me permission to utilise it here.

FIG 4. Portsea Island

PRIORS OF SOUTHWICK[1]

Anselm, occurs 1147, 1151-2.[2]
Walter, occurs 1162-3, 1165.[3]
Philip, occurs 1177.[4]
Guy, occurs 1185-1210.[5]
Luke, occurs 1219, died 1227.[6]
Walkelin, 1227-35.[7]
Matthew, 1235-66.[8]
Peter de Maupol (Maupudre), 1266-73.[9]
Andrew de Winton (Wynton), 1273-81.[10]
John de Clere, 1281-91.[11]
Robert de Henton (Hempton, Houton), 1291-1315.[12]
Willima de Winton (Wynton), 1315-16.[13]
Nicholas de Cheriton (Cherynton), 1316-34.[14]
John de Gloucestre, 1334-49.[15]
Richard Bromdene (Bramden), 1349-81.[16]
Richard Nowell, 1381-9.[17]
William Hursele (Hurselegh), 1389-98.[18]
Thomas Courteys (Cortays, Curtays), 1398-1432.[19]
Edward Dene, 1432-55.[20]
John Soberton (Soburton), 1456-63.[21]
Philip Stanbroke (Stanebrok), 1463-94.[22]
John Lawder (Lauder), 1494-1504.[23]
Thomas Kent, 1504-20.[24]
William Noxton, 1521-38.[25]

1. It is probable that two names are missing from the early part of this list; Richard Bromdene is referred to as the 17th Prior (II 1) and William Hursele as the 19th (III fo. 14).
2. I 84, 85
3. I 86, 122
4. I 23
5. I 91, 99
6. I 181. Licence issued 24 May 1227 for election of a prior following the death of Luke (*Cal. Pat. R., 1225-32* p. 125).
7. 3 June 1227: royal assent to election of Walkelin, former sacrist, as prior (*ibid.*, p. 127). Licence issued 29 September 1235 for election of a prior after Henry and Matthew, canons of Southwick, brought news to the king of the death of Walkelin (*Cal. Pat. R., 1232-47* p. 118).
8. 17 October 1235: royal assent to election of Matthew, a canon of Southwick, as prior. Mandate to Peter, Bishop of Winchester (*ibid.*, p. 120).
   25 November 1235: mandate to the sheriff of Hants to let Matthew have seisin of the possessions of the priory; writ *de intendendo* to the priory's tenants. 4 March 1266: licence issued for election of a prior, after Walter de Oxonia and Ralph Geyneburg, canons of Southwick, brought news to the king of the death of Matthew (*Cal. Pat. R., 1258-66* p. 565).

12 March 1266: commitment of Southwick Priory to Master William de Clifford, king's clerk, to keep during the king's pleasure and to answer for the issues thereof at the Exchequer; writ *de intendendo* to the priory's tenants (*ibid.*, p. 567).

9. 3 April 1266: royal assent to election of Peter Maupudre, a canon of Southwick, as prior; signification to the bishop of Winchester (*ibid.*, p. 576).

7 April 1266: mandate to Master William de Clifford, escheator this side of Trent, to restore the temporalities of Southwick Priory to Peter Maupudre, whose election as prior has been confirmed by John, Bishop of Winchester (*ibid.*, p. 579).

30 November 1273: licence issued for election of a prior following news of the cession of Peter de Maupol brought to the king by Andrew de Wynton and John Colewyn, canons of Southwick (*Cal. Pat. R., 1272-81* p. 40).

10. 4 December 1273: signification to Nicholas, Bishop of Winchester, of the king's assent to the election of Andrew de Wynton as prior of Southwick; mandate to the sheriff of Hants and writ *de intendendo* to the priory's tenants (*ibid.*, pp. 40-1).

23 November 1281: licence for election of a prior issued by the king following news of the death of Prior Andrew, which was brought to him by John Colewin' and Isaac le Rus, canons of Southwick (*Cal. Pat. R., 1281-92* p. 2).

11. 28 November 1281: signification to the archbishop of Canterbury of the royal assent to the election of John de Clere, a canon of Southwick, as prior (*ibid.*, p. 4).

9 December 1281: mandate to the sheriff of Hants to restore the temporalities of Southwick Priory to John de Clere, the elected prior; writ *de intendendo* to the priory's tenants (*ibid.*, p. 6).

14 December 1291: licence issued for election of a prior, following the death of John de Clere, news of which had been brought to the king by Richard de Suanemere and Isaac le Rus, canons of Southwick (*ibid.*, p. 464).

12. 28 December 1291: signification to the bishop of Winchester of the royal assent to the election of Robert de Hempton, a canon of Southwick, as prior (*ibid.*, p. 463).

5 January 1292: mandate to Malcolm de Harle, the escheator this side of Trent, to restore the temporalitities of Southwick Priory to Robert de Hempton, the elected prior; writ *de intendendo* to the priory's tenants (*ibid.*, p. 466).

13 May 1315: royal licence issued for election of a prior following death of Robert de Honton, formerly Prior of Southwick (*Cal. Pat. R., 1313-17* p. 287).

13. 28 May 1315: royal assent to the election of William de Wynton, a canon of Southwick, as prior (*ibid.*, p. 289).

6 March 1316: licence issued by the king for the election of a prior of Southwick following the death of William de Wynton (*ibid.*, p. 435).

14. 20 March 1316: royal assent to the election of Nicholas de Cherynton, a canon of Southwick, as prior (*ibid.*, p. 439).

20 January 1334: licence for the election of a prior, issued by the king, following the news of the death of Nicholas, which had been brought to him by William le Gayte and John de Merewe, canons of Southwick (*Cal. Pat. R., 1330-4* p. 492).

15. 13 February 1334: signification, to the keeper of the spirituality during the vacancy of the see of Winchester, of the royal assent to the election of John de Gloucestre, one of the canons of Southwick, as prior (*ibid.*, p. 507).

24 September 1334: royal mandate for the restitution of the temporalities of Southwick Priory to John de Gloucestre whose election as prior has been confirmed by the bishop of Winchester and who has done fealty to the king (*Cal. Pat. R.,1334-8* p. 13).

25 September 1334: release to the sub-prior and convent of Southwick of all the issues of the temporalities of the priory, which have been received by them as keepers thereof during the vacancy by royal appointment, and of the account they should render of them (*ibid.*, p. 24).

15 December 1349: licence issued for the election of a prior after news of the death of John de Gloucestre had been brought to the king by Thomas de Chiltelegh and Adam Canoun, canons of Southwick (*Cal. Pat. R., 1348-50* p. 437).

16. 28 December 1349: signification to William, Bishop of Winchester, of the royal assent to the election of Richard de Bramden as Prior of Southwick (*ibid.*, p. 440).

1 January 1350: commission from William Edington, Bishop of Winchester, to Roger de Fulford', Official of Winchester, and John de Wolveleye, canon of Salisbury, to hold an enquiry into the election of Richard de Bromden, canon of Southwick, as prior (*The register of William Edington Bishop of Winchester 1346-1366* ed. S. F. Hockey (2 vols., Hampshire Record Series, 7-8, 1986-7) I 726, p. 109).

4 January 1350: mandate to Henry Sturmy, escheator of Hants, to deliver the temporalities of Southwick Priory to Richard de Bramden whose election as prior has been confirmed by the bishop of Winchester and who has done fealty to the king. Similar mandates to the escheators of Wilts, Sussex and Oxon, and writ *de intendendo* to the priory's tenants (*Cal. Pat. R., 1348-50* p. 433).

28 April 1381, death of Prior Richard Bromden; 4 May, inquisition post mortem (II 32).

17. 25 May 1381: confirmation of Richard Nowell, a canon of Southwick, as prior (*Wykeham Register* I, p. 116).

27 May 1381: mandate for the restitution of the temporalities of Southwick Priory to Richard Nowell (*Cal. Pat. R., 1381-5* p. 15; II 33).

23 September 1389, death of Prior Richard Nowell; 26 October, inquisition post mortem (II 56).

24 September 1389: licence granted by the king for the election of a prior for Southwick Priory in the room of Richard Nowell, deceased (*Cal. Pat. R., 1388-92* p. 115).

18. 19 October 1389: royal assent to the election of William Hurselegh, a canon of Southwick, as prior (*ibid.*, p. 116).

3 November 1389: royal mandates for restoration of the temporalities of Southwick Priory to William Hurslegh (*ibid.*, p. 130).

23 June 1398, death of Prior William Hursele; 24 July, inquisition post mortem (II 75).

28 June 1398: licence granted by the king for the election of a prior for Southwick Priory in the room of William Hurselee, deceased (*Cal. Pat. R., 1396-9* p. 376).

19. 22 July 1398: signification to William, Bishop of Winchester, of royal assent to the election of Thomas Cortays to be prior of Southwick (*ibid.*, p. 377).

2 August 1398: mandate to the escheator of Hants to deliver the temporalities of Southwick Priory to Thomas Cortays, a canon of the house, elected and confirmed as prior; similar mandates to the escheators of Oxon, Sussex and Wilts, and writ *de intendendo* to the priory's tenants (*ibid.*, p. 388).

15 September 1432: royal licence granted to Southwick Priory to elect a prior following the death of Thomas Curtays (*Cal. Pat. R., 1429-36* p. 222).

20. 26 September 1432: royal mandate for delivery of the temporalities of Southwick Priory to Edward Dene, whose election has been confirmed by the bishop of Winchester and who has done fealty to the king (*ibid.*, p. 223).

14 January 1456: royal licence to Southwick Priory to elect a prior in the room of Edward Dene, deceased (*Cal. Pat. R., 1452-61* p. 276).

21. 24 January 1456: royal assent to the election of John Soburton as prior of Southwick (*ibid.*, p. 274).

29 January 1456: mandate from the king for the delivery of the temporalities of Southwick Priory to John Soburton, a canon of the house, now prior (*ibid.*, p. 291).

1 September 1463: royal licence for Southwick Priory to elect a prior in the room of John Soburton, deceased (*Cal. Pat. R., 1461-7* p. 285).

22. 8 September 1463: royal assent to the election of Philip Stanebrok, a canon of Southwick, as prior (*ibid.*, p. 285).

20 September 1463: mandate from the king for the restoration of the temporalities of Southwick Priory to Philip Stanebrok (*ibid.*, p. 290).

16 May 1494: royal licence for the election of a prior for Southwick Priory following the resignation of Philip Stanbroke (*Cal. Pat. R., 1485-94* p. 463).

23. 6 June 1494: royal assent to the election of John Lauder, cellarer of Southwick Priory, as prior (*ibid.*, p. 468).

27 June 1494: mandate from the king for the restoration of the temporalities of Southwick Priory to John Lauder (*ibid.*, p. 468).

16 February 1502: grant to John Lauder, now Prior of Southwick, of the temporalities of the priory during the past vacancy caused by the resignation of Philip Stanbroke, viz. from 1 May to 27 June

1494 (*Cal. Pat. R., 1494–1509* p. 282).

29 August 1504: royal licence granted to the sub-prior and convent of Southwick for the election of a prior in the room of John Laudyr, deceased (*ibid.*, p. 383).

24. 14 September 1504: signification to Richard, Bishop of Winchester, of the royal assent to the election of Thomas Kent, the sub-prior of Southwick, as prior (*ibid.*, p. 384).

26 December 1520, death of Prior Thomas Kent.

7 January 1521: royal licence for the election of a prior for Southwick Priory in the room of Thomas Kent, deceased (*Letters and Papers, Henry VIII* III Part I (1519–23) 1125, p. 416).

25. 1 February 1521: royal assent to the election of William Noxton, cellarer of Southwick Priory, as prior (*ibid.*, 1154, p. 427).

8 February 1521: mandates from the king for the restitution of the temporalities of Southwick Priory to Prior William Noxton (*ibid.*, 1158, p. 432).

7 April 1538: surrender of the priory and all its possessions to the king signed by Prior William Noxton and twelve canons (*Op. cit.*, XIII, Part II, (1538), 698, p. 266; names of the canons recorded, *Op. cit.*, XIV, Part I (1539), p. 596).

The Ruins of Southwick Priory: an undated engraving
(*Photograph by Mrs. Amanda Yale of Hampshire Record Office*)

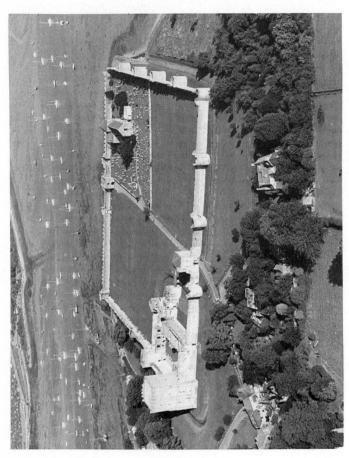

Portchester Castle, showing the Priory's original site and church

(By courtesy of The News, Portsmouth)

SOUTHWICK CARTULARIES—CALENDAR

I 1

Charter of King Henry I, of happy memory, our founder²

[fo. 1] CONCESSION by Henry I³—for the souls of his father and mother, his brother, William, and his ancestors, and for the stability and wellbeing of his realm (*pro statu et incolumitate regni mei*)—to God and the church and canons of Portchester (*Porcestria*), of the church of St Mary, Portchester, with lands, tithes and all appurtenances. Also concession of the gift in alms by William de Pontearch' and his wife, Constance, of the manor of Candover (*Candeura*), comprising 5 hides and 1 virgate, from his demesne; and of 1 hide in Southwick (*Sudwic'*); and of 1 hide in Applestead (*Appelsteda*)⁴ which William bought from Ivo Pantulf for the church's use with the king's consent. The canons will hold these gifts freely, with soke and sake, toll and team, infangentheof, and all liberties, customs and quittances, as William de Pontearch' held them. Witnesses: Henry, Bishop of Winchester; Roger, Bishop of Salisbury (*Sar'*); Bernard, Bishop of St David's (*de Sancto Davio*); Nigel, Bishop-elect of Ely (*Elyense*); Geoffrey, Bishop-elect of Durham (*Dunelm'*); Brient', son of the count; Robert de Ver; Hugh Bigot; Humphrey (*Humfridus*) de Buhun; Aubrey (*Albericus*) de Ver and Richard Basset.

Westbourne [Sussex], for sea crossing
(*apud Burnam in transfretatione mea*).⁵

1 Nigel was nominated Bishop of Ely 28 May, and consecrated 1 October 1133; Geoffrey Rufus was nominated Bishop of Durham 28 May, and consecrated 6 August 1133. Henry I crossed to Normandy on 2 August 1133 (*Regesta* II, p. xxxi).

2 Rubrics are not usually included in this calendar (see Introduction, p. xlvii), but an exception is made here because of the noteworthy last two words—our founder. For an explanation of the confusion that has surrounded the identity of the priory's founder, see Dr Emma Mason's article, "The King, the Chamberlain and Southwick Priory", pp. 5–8. See also Introduction, pp. xii, xv.

3 This charter has been printed for the first time, in full, in Latin, as Appendix 1 to Dr Emma Mason's article (*loc. cit.*, p. 8). It is the sole copy of a genuine royal charter, the original of which no longer exists. The variant, which occurs in the cartulary in the inspeximus of Henry III (II 8), and exists in the original in the Hampshire Record Office (4M53/1), is a forgery, first detected by Mrs. Eleanor Cottrill, former Hampshire County Archivist. The evidence leading to the uncovering of the forgery, and the implications, are fully discussed in Dr. Mason's article (*loc. cit.*, p. 2, note 2).

4 The location of Applestead has been convincingly identified by Mrs. Margaret Hoad from evidence in the cartulary as being immediately west of Southwick. It appears to have been swallowed up by the development of the village of Southwick after the establishment there of the priory (Margaret Hoad, "The Origins of Portsmouth", pp. 11–12).

5 Charters issued by Henry I at Westbourne in 1114 and 1131 were witnessed by William de Pont de l'Arche among others. The king was probably at Westbourne in July 1133, before sailing for Normandy on 2 August (*Regesta* II, pp. 117–20; 252; 266–8).
Copy II 4. Variants: Ponte Arch'; de Sancto Deuuo.

I 2   [January 1155–August 1158][1]

CONCESSION by Henry [II][2]—for the souls of his ancestors and the
stability and wellbeing of his realm—to Southwick Priory, of the churches
of Southwick and Portchester (*Porcestria*) with lands, tithes and all
appurtenances. Also concession of the gift in alms by William de Pontearch, of the manor of Preston Candover (*Candeura*), comprising 5 hides
and 1 virgate from his demesne; and of 1 hide in Southwick; and of 1
hide in Applestead (*Appelsteda*) which William bought from Ivo Pantulf
for the church's use with the consent of Henry [I], the king's grandfather.
The priory will hold these gifts freely, with soke and sake, toll and team,
infangentheof, and all liberties, customs and quittances, as William held
them, as Henry [I]'s charter testifies. Also concession of the gift by
William, of 1 hide in West Boarhunt (*Westburhunta*) with appurtenances,
which Reyner (*Reinerus*) de Evernio had given him for his service.

Moreover Henry [II] has given to the priory 2 hides at Fishbourne
(*Fisseborna*) which Turstin, son of Engelerus, held, and which the priory
will hold for the same service as was owed by Turstin.[3] Witnesses:
Thomas, Chancellor; Roger, Archdeacon of Bayeux (*Baioc'*); Reginald,
Earl of Cornwall; Richard de Hum', Constable; Manass' Biset, Steward
(*dapifer*); Warin, son of Gerald, Chamberlain; Henry de Pomeria; Ralph
de Hast'; Robert de Dunstanvilla.

London (*Lundon*)

1 Thomas Becket was Chancellor from January 1155, but was not elected Archbishop of Canterbury until May 1162. Henry II sailed for Normandy in August
1158 and did not return until Becket had become archbishop (*Itinerary of Henry
II* pp. 40, 58).

2 For the full text, in Latin, of this charter, see Mason, "The King, the
Chamberlain and Southwick Priory", p. 9.

3 The King was in fact confirming the gift made by Turstin (see III 99).
Copy II 5. Variant: Appelstede.

I 3   [1150–*c*. 1152]

CONFIRMATION by Henry, Bishop of Winchester, at the request of
A[nselm], Prior of Southwick, and the priory, of the gift of his prede-
cessor, Bishop William, of the churches of Portchester (*Porcestria*) and
Wymering (*Wimeringis*); and of his own gift of the churches of Candover
(*Candeura*) and Shalden (*Scaldedena*) and all their appurtenances.

1 After the priory's move to Southwick, which had taken place by early 1150
(see above, p. xiii). These churches, confirmed to the priory by Bishop Henry,
are the same as those listed in Pope Eugenius III's confirmation of 1151–2 (I 85).
Bishop William Giffard died *c*. 23 January 1129 so that the foundation of the
priory must have taken place by 1128 at the latest if it was in possession of the
churches of Portchester and Wymering during his episcopate.
Copy III 955. Variant: Wimeringes.

I 4 [1155–71][1]

[fo. 1ᵛ] CONFIRMATION by Henry, Bishop of Winchester, at the request of Walter, Prior of Southwick, and the priory, of the gift by his predecessor, Bishop William, to the priory, of the churches of Portchester (*Porcestria*) and Wymering (*Wimeringis*); and of his own gift of the churches of Candover (*Candeura*), Shalden (*Scaldedena*), and Wanstead (*Wanesteda*), and the chapels of Widley (*Widelega*), Walesworth (*Waleswrd'*),[2] Nutley (*Nutlega*) and Candover Scotland (*Candeura Scudlandi*), and all their appurtenances.

1 The priory was given the chapel of Candover Scotland some time between 1155 and 1163 (I 11); Bishop Henry died in 1171.

2 Walesworth has ceased to exist. It is now represented by Pigeon House Farm, about 1¾ miles south-east of Southwick. I am greatly indebted to Mr. Roger Davey for sharing with me the results of his research on Walesworth, including the suggested site of the chapel (SU 649075; see map 3).
Copy III 946. Variant: Wanstuda.

I 5 [1150–61][1]

CONFIRMATION by Theobald, Archbishop of Canterbury, Primate of England and Papal Legate, of the gift by William de Pontearch' to the priory, of Southwick and other possessions, confirmed by Henry, Bishop of Winchester. Anathema pronounced against anyone causing injury to the canons or their possessions.

1 Archbishop Theobald became papal legate early in 1150 and died in 1161. This confirmation is printed in full, in Latin, as charter no. 307 in A. Saltman, *Theobald, Archbishop of Canterbury* (London, 1956). See also III 968, 969.
Copy III 948.

I 6 [*c.* 1150–71, possibly 1164 or 1166][1]

NOTIFICATION by Baldwin de Porteseia[2] to Henry, Bishop of Winchester, of his gift, in free alms, with warranty—for the salvation of King Henry and Baldwin's lords, Hugh, Henry and John de Port, and of himself, his wife, ancestors, heirs and friends—to Southwick Priory, of his church of Portsea (*Porteseia*), as far as lies within his power as a layman, with tithes, lands and all rights belonging to it; and of ½ hide at Stubbington (*Stubintona*) and ½ virgate at Buckland (*Bocland*), and pasture for 100 sheep, 15 cattle (*animales*) and 20 pigs in his demesne, in common with his men. The priory will hold the church, lands and pasture quit of all exaction and secular service. Witnesses: Ralph, Archdeacon of Winchester; Robert de Clafford; Richard de Wimering'; Robert Clericus; Henry de Mednill', constable of Portchester (*Porc'*); Rein' de Burhu'; Richard, his brother; Richard, son of Daniel; Roger Clericus;

William Aurifaber; William, son of Ansgod; William de Ethinged; Richerius, his son; Ralph Presbyter of Portsea (*Portes'*); Richard Ang'.

1 The move to Southwick had taken place by early 1150 (see above, p. xiii) Bishop Henry died in 1171. See also note to I 9.
2 See III 105, which is a version of I 6 with significant variants and certain dubious additions. See also III 112, possibly Baldwin's earliest grant as it mentions only the church, ½ hide at Stubbington and ½ sester of wheat.
Copy III 109. Variants: Portesia; Bokland; Wymeryng'.
Copy in H.R.O. 4M53/B7, pp. 3–4. Variants: Portesey', Porteseya; John de Porc; Stubynton'; Wymeryng'; Porcestr'; [numbers are written in words, not in Roman numerals; the names of the first 5 witnesses only are given, as in III 109].

I 7   [*c.* 1163–8, possibly 1164 or 1166][1]

CONFIRMATION by John de Port—for the welfare of himself, his wife Matilda, and his sons, and the souls of his father, mother and ancestors— of the gift by Baldwin de Porteseia to Southwick Priory, of his church of Portsea (*Portes'*), with tithes, lands and all rights belonging to it, and ½ hide in Stubbington (*Stubbintona*), as Baldwin's charter testifies.[2] Also confirmation of whatever gift Herbert de Burhun or his son have made to the priory.[3] Witnesses: Ralph, Archdeacon of Winchester; Robert, Archdeacon of Surrey (*Sudr'*); Adel', Prior of St Denis (*Sanctus Dyonis'*); Robert de Clatford; William, son of Ansg'; Richard de Wimering'; Geoffrey de Carit'; Robert de Port'; Herbert Pincerna; William de Bera; William de Liecford.

1 The church of Portsea was not included among the priory's possessions when they were taken under the protection of Pope Alexander III in 1162–3 (I 86), but it did feature in a subsequent confirmation issued by the same pope (I 24). John de Port had died by Michaelmas 1168 (*Complete Peerage* II, p. 319). For possible dates, 1164 or 1166, see I 9, note 1.
2 Possibly III 12, as this charter refers only to the church and ½ hide at Stubbington.
3 See I 29, 30, 103, 121, 122.
Copy III 107. Variants: Portesia; Burhunt'.

I 8   [*c.* 1163–71, possibly 1174 or 1166][1]

[fo. 2] NOTIFICATION by Henry, Bishop of Winchester, to Archdeacon Ralph and all the clergy of Hampshire (*Hantescire*), that he has confirmed the gift by Baldwin de Porteseia to Southwick Priory, of the church of St Mary, Portsea (*Portesia*), with lands, tithes and all things belonging to it; and ½ hide in Stubbington (*Stubinctuna*). Witnesses: Ralph, Archdeacon of Hampshire; Robert, Archdeacon of Surrey (*Surr'*); Robert de Limesi; Robert de Clafford; Peter Medicus; Albert de Summa; William, son of King Stephen.

1 Dated after Pope Alexander III's bull of 1162–3 (I 7, note 1) and before the death of Bishop Henry in 1171—if the last witness is ignored. William, son of King Stephen, died in 1159, but Mrs Hoad has called attention to the suspect inclusion of his name at the end of the list of witnesses (Hoad, "The Origins of Portsmouth", pp. 13–14). For the possible dates 1164 or 1166, see I 9, note 1. See also Baldwin's charters, I 6; III 105, 112.
Copy III 484. Variants: Hamtesir; de Portesia.

I 9 [? 1164 or 1166][1]

CONFIRMATION by Henry [II] of the gift by Baldwin de Portesia to Southwick Priory, of the church of St Mary, Portsea, with all appurtenances. The priory will have and hold it freely, as Baldwin's charter testifies. Witnesses: Richard, Archdeacon of Poitiers (*Pictav'*); John Cumin; William, son of Martin; Jocelin de Baillolio; Alan de Novill'; Ranulf de Broc.

Portchester (*Porces'*).

1 Henry II was at Portchester in 1164 and 1166 (*Itinerary of Henry II* pp. 70, 91). All the witnesses occur in the *Itinerary* at dates covering both 1164 and 1166. There seems no reason to doubt the authenticity of this charter—Henry is described in the contemporary style as King of England, Duke of Normandy and Aquitaine, and Count of Anjou—but see III 105, note 1.
Copy II 6. Variant: Porteseia.
Copy III 800. Variants: Porteseia; Cunin'.

I 10 [*c.* 1164–77][1]

GIFT, in free alms, by Baldwin de Portesia—for the remission of his sins and the souls of his ancestors, and in order that he may be worthily commemorated—to Prior Walter and Southwick Priory, of his body for burial, and the tenement and service of John de Brocheherst. This gift has been made with John's consent; he will pay to the priory an annual rent of 10s. at Michaelmas, and to John de Gizorz, the chief lord, one hawk at Michaelmas. Witnesses: Alexander de Burhunta; Reinavmus; Richard de Wansteda; Richard Presbyter of Wymering (*Wimering'*); Roger Clericus; John de Brocheherst.

1 By 1177 Walter had been succeeded as prior. Probably this grant came after Baldwin's grant to the priory of Portsea church and land at Buckland in *c.* 1164 (I 6). Mrs Hoad has suggested that, as there is no mention in I 6 of John de Gisors as chief lord, and as Brochurst land was in the manor of Buckland (in the area of Balches Croft and Beeston Field, see III 629, 646 and map 4), the de Ports had sold the manor of Buckland to John de Gisors between the dates of Baldwin's grants, i.e. between *c.* 1164 and 1177 (Hoad, "The Origins of Portsmouth", p. 16). The de Portesias retained an interest in part of Brochurst, as, when Hamo de Brochurst gave all his land to the priory shortly before 1247, the canons were responsible for a 5s. annual rent to the lord of Portsea, at that time Andrew de Portesia (III 279).
Copy III 106. Variants: Reinalmus; Brochurste.

I 11　　　　　　　　　　　　　　　　　　　　　　　　　]*c.* 1142–50][1]

NOTIFICATION by Robert de Pontearch to Bishop Jocelin and all the clergy of the bishopric of Salisbury (Sar'), of his concession, in alms, to the canons of Portchester (*Porcestria*), of the church of Swindon (*Swindona*), and confirmation of his father's gift.[2] They are to hold that church with lands, tithes and all appurtenances, particularly the tithes of his demesne. Witnesses: Richard, son of Turst'; William, Richard's brother; Robert de Ulvill'; John de Medehach' and Nicholas, his brother; Adam de Haved; Herbert Tracheveel; Robert, vicar of the same church.

1 Dated between the beginning of Jocelin's episcopate and the canons' move to Southwick. Possibly the notification was made after the death of William de Pontearch, Robert's father, *c.* 1148.
2 There is conflicting evidence concerning the date at which the priory acquired the church of Swindon. Dr Mason has proposed that William de Pont de l'Arche, Robert's father, granted it to the canons shortly before his death *c.* 1148 (Mason, "The King, the Chamberlain and Southwick Priory", p. 4). There is no mention of it among the priory's possessions in Pope Eugenius' confirmatory bulls addressed to Prior Anselm in 1147 or 1151-2 (I 84 and 85). But in I 12, it seems that the canons of Portchester already held the church in the time of Henry I, i.e., before 1135. In I 19, Robert de Pont de l'Arche confirmed it among possessions supposed to have been granted by his father to the canons of Portchester at their foundation. That it was the cause of some dispute and uncertainty may account for the large number of transactions concerned with the priory's possession of the church, before and after the move to Southwick.
See I 19; III 405; I 12, 21, 22, 23.

I 12　　　　　　　　　　　　　　　　　　　　　　　　[after 1152, *c.* 1160][1]

AGREEMENT made before Jocelin, Bishop of Salisbury (*Sar'*), in his synod, in settlement of a dispute between Walter, Prior of Portchester (*Porcestria*), and Robert, priest of Swindon (*Swindon'*). The prior alleged that, in the time of King Henry, Robert, the elder, priest of Swindon, held the church of Swindon and tithes from the demesne of the canons of Portchester, paying them annually 30s.; Robert the elder and many others testified to this. Robert the younger replied that agreement between himself and Robert the elder had been reached in the chapter-house at Salisbury before this bishop, whereby Robert the elder quitclaimed any right he had in that church, and Robert the younger was to provide him with maintenance as long as he lived. Having heard this, the prior and priests came to an amicable agreement, in, and with the consent of, the bishop's council and synod. Robert the younger is to hold the aforesaid church of Swindon and tithes from the canons, paying them 1 mark of silver a year, half at Easter and half at Michaelmas, and providing [fo. 2ᵛ] maintenance for the elder priest as long as he lives.

1 Walter succeeded Prior Anselm after 1152 (I 85). Strictly speaking he should be called Prior of Southwick, as the move from Portchester had taken place by early 1150. If Robert, the elder, was priest at Swindon in the time of Henry I, i.e., before 1135, and was still alive when this agreement was made, it probably belongs to a date not long after 1152. The earliest occurrence of Walter as prior which can be dated is 1162-3 (I 86).

I 13   [1155-63][1]

GIFT by William Escotland [rubric: Escothland], in free alms, to South-wick Priory, of his chapel of Candover (*Candeura*), with full tithes (*cum plenaria decimatione*) in Candover manor, and the tenement which Wlward held and which William gave to the priory for 1 virgate (*pro una virgata*). The chapel and tithe having been handed over to Bishop Henry in his court at Winchester, in the presence of Archdeacons Ralph and Robert, John de Port, and a large gathering of clerics and laymen, agreement was reached, through the mediation of the bishop, between William and Southwick Priory concerning divine office in William's chapel, so that as often as William is resident for three days in the week in the manor; divine services will be celebrated there for him and his family. Witnesses: Archdeacon Ralph; Godfrey Sacerdos; Matthew de Scuris; Walter de Andel'; Geoffrey de Karitate; William de Lecford; Roger Clericus; Richard, son of Daniel; Richard de Wimering.

1 Robert of Inglesham first occurs as Archdeacon of Surrey between 1155 and 59 (*Fasti* II, p. 94). The chapel of Candover Scotland was included among the priory's possessions over which Pope Alexander III extended his protection in 1162-63 (I 86).
Copy III 958. Variants: Escoland; Wulfward; Walter de Andelia.

I 14   [1155-63][1]

NOTIFICATION by John de Port to Bishop Henry and all the clergy of Winchester, of his confirmation of the gift, in perpetual alms, made by his man, William Escotland, to Southwick Priory, of his chapel and 1 virgate. Willim will render service to lay lords for that virgate as for his other lands. Witnesses: Henry, Bishop of Winchester; Archdeacon Ralph; Jordan Fant'.[2] Matthew de Scuris; Alexander de Herierd; Herbert Bucellier.

1 See note to I 13.
2 M. Jordan Fantosme, historian and clerk to Bishop Henry, occurs 1148-74 (*WS I* p. 129).

I 15   [*c.* 1160-80][1]

GIFT, free from all service, by Ralph de Bilenget' [rubric, Bilengetut']
and his wife—for the salvation of their souls, and for the welfare of
themselves and their sons—to Southwick Priory, of 1 virgate at Stubbington (*Stubynctona*)[2], from land which the Earl of Richmond (*Richemonte*)
gave him for service. The donors testified to their gift of the land by
oath on the Gospels at the altar of St Mary's, Southwick (*terram super
altare Sancte Marie de Sudwica per unum textum evangelii optulimus*),
and were received into the fraternity of the priory. Witnesses: John
Clericus;[3] Gilbert Capellanus; Durand; Roger Clericus; Richard, son of
Daniel; Reinelm (*Reinavm'*) de Burhunta; Richard, his brother.

1 Witnesses occur 1165-87.
2 Probably Stubbington in Titchfield. Nearby Crofton was held of the honour of
Richmond (*V C H Hants* p. 226).
3 This witness may be the John Clericus de Insula who witnessed the confirmation
of this gift by Ralph's son, Sampson (III 165), and gave land in Crofton to the
priory *c.* 1173-89 (I 47).
Copy III 164. Variants: Belington'; [to salvation clause add:] for the welfare of
their lords and heirs; [after 1 virgate add:] of *la Hegwode* which Durand Juvenis
held at *Stobynton'*.

I 16   [*c.* 1153-63][1]

GIFT, in free alms, by Matthew de Scuris—for the salvation and welfare
of himself and of his [kindred]—to Southwick Priory, of his chapel of
Widley (*Widelia*), with the full tithe of all things from the demesne of
his manor of Widley; also land called Sheepwash (*Sepewesle*),[2] free from
all lay service. Matthew, with his mother, wife, and sons, placed this
gift of the chapel and land on the altar of St Mary's, Southwick,[3] on
the day of the Purification of St Mary [2 February] in the presence of
these witnesses: Walter de Andel'; Richard de Bera; William de Haliwell;
Richard Grai; Richard Sacerdos of Wymering (*Wim'*); Richard, son of
Daniel; Reinel' de Burhunt'.

1 The chapel of Widley is not included among the priory's possessions confirmed
by Pope Eugenius III in 1151-2 (I 85), but it occurs in Pope Alexander III's
privilege of 1162-3 (I 86). See also III 940.
2 Sheepwash Farm, about 2 miles west-north-west of Southwick.
3 This may mean that they placed the charter itself on the altar (as in III 82), or
simply that they swore to their gift (as in I 15).
Copy III 361. Variants: Widelya; Schepewasch'; Andelia; Richard de labera.

I 17   [*c.* 1153–63][1]

GIFT, in perpetual alms, by Alfred de Herierd', with the consent of his wife and sons—for the remission of his sins, the welfare of his lords and sons, and the souls of his ancestors—to Southwick Priory, of land in Stubbington (*Stubintona*),[2] and of his body [for burial]. The land is assessed at a quarter of a knight's fee [and will be held by the priory] for the service due to the [chief] lords. Witnesses: Henry, the donor's brother (*frater meus*) and Osmund, his uncle; William, son of Roger; Ralph Caballus; Richard and Herbert de la Bere; Sewalus.

1 Alfred de Herierd's gift is included in the list of the priory's possessions recorded in Pope Alexander III's privilege of 1162–3 (I 86), but does not occur in Pope Eugenius III's confirmation of 1151–2 (I 85). It was confirmed by Alfred's lord, Richard de Hommet, Constable of Normandy (I 110), and possibly by Robert de Pontearch' (I 109).
2 There is conflicting evidence in the cartularies concerning the location of Alfred's gift. In the papal privilege of 1162–3 (I 86 and note 2), it is said to be in the same vill as the virgate given by the Lady de Croftuna, which suggests Stubbington in Titchfield (I 41). But in the inquisition held in 1389, after the death of Prior Richard Nowell (II 56), the manor of Stubbington is said to be the gift of Alfred de Heriard and to be held of the king in chief, except for 45 acres in the same manor held of William Fifhyde; the latter gift was definitely in Stubbington in Portsea (III 468–75). See also II 56(v).
Copy III 166. Variant: Stobynton'.

I 18   [*c.* 1155–71][1]

[fo. 3] CONFIRMATION by Robert de Pontearch—for the salvation of King Henry [I] and William de Pontearch, his father, his lady mother, lords and ancestors, [and] of himself, his wife, children and kindred—of the gift, made by his father to the canons regular of Portchester at their foundation, of churches, chapels, lands, waters, woods, meadows, pastures, men, rents, mills, roads, paths and all appurtenances, viz: the church of Portchester (*Porcestria*) with all appurtenances; the churches of Wanstead (*Wanestede*),[2] Shalden (*Scaldedene*),[3] Candover (*Candeura*) and Swindon (*Swindona*)[4] with lands, tithes and all appurtenances; land and wood at Southwick (*Sudwica*) and a mill, meadow and pasture; the manor of Candover comprising 5 hides with wood, meadow and land at *Sumersill*[5], and all other holdings given by William. The canons will have and hold all the aforesaid ecclesiastical and secular possessions freely, in perpetuity. Witnesses: Henry, Bishop of Winchester; Ralph, Archdeacon of Winchester; Robert, Archdeacon of Surrey (*Surr'*); Albert de Summa; Herbert, son of Anketill'; Reinelm de Burhunt; Richard Capellanus; Richard, son of Dan[iel]; and many others.

1 Robert first occurs as Archdeacon of Surrey, 1155-9 (*Fasti* II, p. 94). Henry of Blois, Bishop of Winchester, died in 1171.

2 The church of Wanstead was not included in the list of churches confirmed to the priory by Pope Eugenius III in 1151-2 (I 85). It was given to the priory not by William de Pont de l'Arche but by Robert, between 1152 and 1163, after his father's death (I 112); or it may be that Robert was in fact confirming the gift made by Richard son of Daniel (I 36). Dr Mason has suggested that it was in the interests of the priory to have this confirmation worded in such a way as to give the impression that the possessions concerned were gifts made at the time of its foundation in the reign of Henry I, rather than acquired in Stephen's reign, thereby strengthening its title to them (Mason, "The King, the Chamberlain and Southwick Priory", p. 4).

3 It seems likely that William de Pont de l'Arche had granted the church of Shalden to the priory before his death *c.* 1148. The priory's possession of it was confirmed by Henry of Blois, Bishop of Winchester, at the request of both Prior Anselm and his successor, Prior Walter (I 3, 4); also by Pope Eugenius III in 1151-2, and Pope Alexander III in 1162-3 (I 85, 86). Nevertheless, William de Pont de l'Arche lacked authority to make the gift, as when Henry I divided the honour of Portchester, Shalden and Hartley Mauditt had been assigned to William Mauduit (II). His son and heir, William (III), tried unsuccessfully to recover the church of Shalden from the priory (E. Mason, *loc. cit.,* pp. 4-5). Both William Mauduit (III) in 1157-61, and his younger brother, Robert, to whom he granted the manor of Shalden *c.* 1175-6, accepted the situation and "gave" the church to the priory (I 111, 31).

4 See I 11, note 2.

5 See I 196, note 7.

Copy III 79. Variants: Pontearcharum; Wanstede; Schaldene; Swyndon'.

I 19   [*c.* 1148-50][1]

NOTIFICATION by Robert de Pontearch to Jocelin, Bishop of Salisbury, of his gift, in free alms—for the salvation of his father, who, with King Henry's consent, founded the church of regular canons at Portchester (*Porcestr'*); and for the salvation of his mother, lords and ancestors, and of himself, his wife, heirs and successors—to the aforesaid canons, of the church of Swindon (*Suwindun'*), situated in his fief, with full tithes both of his demesne and of the villeinage, together with lands, pastures and all appurtenances. Robert seeks the bishop's confirmation of this gift, made, with his father's consent, for the perpetual maintenance of the canons' guest house (*hospitalitas*). Witnesses: Richard, son of Turstun; William, brother of the same Richard; John de Medehach'; Herbert Trachewel'; Reinelm de Burh'; Richard de Burh'; Richard, son of Daniel; and many others.

1 This notification was probably made after the death of William de Pont de l'Arche, Robert's father, *c.* 1148, and before the canons' move to Southwick—if indeed they were still at Portchester. The names of the witnesses suggest a rather later date. The actual gift of the church of Swindon may have been made some time previously (see I 11, note 1).

Copy III 405. Variants: Pontearchar'; Swindon'.

I 20 [1150-9][1]

NOTIFICATION by Robert de Pontearche to Henry, Bishop of Winchester, of his gratitude for the bishop's care in transferring, with royal consent, the foundation of regular canons to Southwick owing to the convenience of the place. The foundation was first established at Portchester (*Porcestr'*) by Robert's father through King Henry [I] (*per dominum Henricum regem*).[2] Robert confirms to Southwick Priory whatever his father had given to the canons at Portchester, and all holdings, ecclesiastical and secular, he himself had given and confirmed to them. Witnesses: Ralph, Archdeacon of Winchester; Albert de Summa; M. Jordan Fantasma; Robert Elemosinarius; Turstin the sheriff; Herbert Trachevel'; Gilbert Oin; and many others.

1 The move to Southwick had taken place by early 1150. Turstin was succeeded as sheriff of Hampshire by his son Richard in 1159.
2 The wording of this reference to Henry I's part in is founding is of special interest in view of the priory's efforts to obtain recognition as a royal foundation (see I 1, notes 2 and 3).
Copy III 91. Variants: Pontearcharum; Porcestre; Suthewyk'.

I 21 [1150-79, possibly 1150-60][1]

INSPEXIMUS by Jocelin, Bishop of Salisbury, of Robert de Pontearch's charter to Southwick Priory, giving it the church of Swindon (*Suwind'*).[2] The bishop has admitted the canons of Southwick to Swindon church on presentation by Robert de Pontearch, with the reservation that Robert the priest will keep his vicarage as long as he lives and wishes to minister there.[3] After the priest's death, the canons will possess Swindon church in free alms, saving episcopal customs and reasonable maintenance for the vicar who will minister there for the bishop or his successors, and [fo. 3ᵛ] will be responsible to the canons for the temporalities, and to the bishop for the spiritualities. Witnesses: A., Dean of Lincoln (*Lincoln'*), Archdeacon [of Dorset] (*archidiaconus noster*); Archdeacon Richard; Ailard, Prior of St Denys (*Sanctus Dionisius*);[4] R., Prior of Sherborne (*Sireburn'*);[5] Osbert.

1 After the priory's move to Southwick, which had taken place by early 1150, but before the death of Adelelm, Dean of Lincoln and Archdeacon of Dorset; possibly before 1173, when he last occurs as dean (*Fasti* III, p. 8). See also note 3.
2 Probably III 404. See also I 11, 19.
3 It is impossible to be certain whether the priest referred to was Robert the elder or the younger. The priory contested the right of Robert the younger to the vicarage after he had acquired it from Robert the elder (I 12). If the above inspeximus refers to Robert the elder, it was probably made *c.* 1150-60, and the statement that the priory would possess the church after the priest's death would account for its discontent over the arrangement made between the two priests.
4 Ailard occurs as prior of St Denys, near Southampton, in 1151 (*St Denys Cartulary*, p. xix).

5 The earliest known prior of Monk Sherborne is Robert of Inglesham, who
occurs as archdeacon of Surrey from *c.* 1155-9, and as prior from *c.* 1158-9
(Knowles *Heads of Religious Houses* p. 106; *Fasti* II, p. 94.
Copy III 407. Variants: Pontearcharum; Swindon'.

I 22   [1150-79]¹

INSPEXIMUS by Jocelin, Bishop of Salisbury, at the request of Robert
de Pontearch', of Robert's charter giving to Southwick Priory the church
of Swindon (*Suwind'*). The bishop acknowledges the need for episcopal
authority to protect the pious gifts made by the faithful to religious places,
and, expecting (*attendentes*) the devotion of the canons of Southwick to
himself and his church, and their religious zeal, confirms them in possession of Swindon church. They will hold it wholly and without disturbance in perpetuity, saving episcopal customs and reasonable maintenance
for the vicar, who, on presentation by the canons, will minister there for
the bishop and his successors, and will be responsible to them for spiritual
matters and the cure of souls, and to the canons for temporalities.
Witnesses: Richard, Adelelm, Az' Archi[diaconi];² John Subdecanus;
Thomas de Cic', canon; M. Jordan; Roger Clericus.

1 See I 21, note 1.
2 Probably refers also to Archdeacons Richard and Adelelm.
Copy III 412. Variants: Joselin; Pontearcharum; Swindon'.

I 23   1st August [1177]¹

LETTER to Pope Alexander [III] to Philip, Prior of Southwick.
    Since he understands the priory to have insufficient income, and wishes
to secure it against loss in the future, so that the needs of the brethren
may be adequately met, the pope prohibits the prior, or any of his
successors, from granting the church of Swindon (*Swindona*), which
belongs to the priory, to any person other than the priest who serves
there in person and is responsible, with no intermediary, to the prior
and his successors. It is to be kept, with all its customary profits, to
provide for the needs of the canons of Southwick. No man is to infringe
or contradict this ruling, on peril of incurring the wrath of Almighty
God and his Blessed Apostles, Peter and Paul.
                    Venezia Rialto (*Venet' in rivo Alto*), Kalends of August.

1 Alexander III was at Venezia Railto June—August 1177. Holtzmann gives the
date as 1177 at the end of his calendar of the version at III 25 (*Papsturkunden in
England,* III, p. 111).
Copy I 90. Variant: Suendona.
Copy III 25. Variants: Swyndon'; Suthwycen', Suthwyn' [Southwick]; [ends,]
Venet'.

I 24   26 or 27 February [1163–81]¹

CONFIRMATION by Pope Alexander [III] to Southwick Priory of
possession of the church of Portsea (*Portesia*), the chapel of Empshott
(*Ymbesieta*), and the church of Nutley (*Nuthlega*), with all appurtenances,
and their house in Winchester adjoining the east gate granted to them,
in perpetual alms, by Robert de Sancto Pancratio.² No man is to infringe
or oppose this ruling on peril of incurring the wrath of Almighty God
and the Blessed Apostles, Peter and Paul.

Anagni (*Anag'*), 4 Kalends of March.

1 Probably this confirmation was issued after 1163, as the church of Portsea and
the chapel of Empshott were not included in the pope's privilege of 1162–63, and
had probably not yet been granted to the priory at that date (I 86, 6–9, 113).
2 In 1148 Robert de Sancto Pancratio was one of the ten richest landlords in
Winchester, holding, or drawing rent from, eleven properties: one in the High
Street, two outside the West Gate, three outside the North Gate and five in Busket
Lane (*WS I* pp. 73, 89, 91, 93–5, 117–19, 372). The tenement which he gave to
the priory was probably that described in the 1148 Survey as "next to the wall",
for which he paid 2d. to the king (*ibid.*, 692, p. 118). Robert witnessed a charter
for Henry, Duke of Normandy, in 1149, and was a canon at Sarum *c*. 1150–60
(*ibid.*, 31 note 3, p. 73).
Copy I 89. Variants: Imbesieta; Nutlega.
Copy III 5. Variants: Imbescheta; Nuthlia; Panchracio. The place of issue, day
and month are omitted.
This copy is printed in Latin by Holtzmann in *Papsturkunden in England* III,
no. 303.

I 25   [1181–2]¹

[fo. 25ᵛ]² NOTIFICATION by Augustine, Bishop of Waterford
(*Watreford*), to all sons of Holy Mother Church, that, by desire and
consent of King Henry [II] and at the request of Richard, Bishop of
Winchester, the church of Southwick has been consecrated in honour of
the Blessed Mary, Mother of God, by himself, Richard, Bishop of the
diocese, and S[effrid], Bishop of Chichester (*Cicestr'*). The bishops have
granted 100 days' indulgence from penance to all the faithful who, within
[fo. 4]² 8 days of the celebration of the anniversary of the dedication, have
honoured, visited or endowed the church with goods. The dedication,
indulgence and endowments are confirmed, to safeguard them in perpetuity, and the gifts and names of donors are recorded, viz:

John Maud'³ gave tithes of all the annual produce (*de omnibus rebus
qui ei renovantur per annum*) of his manor of East Boarhunt (*Estburhunt*)
and its appurtenances.

Reinelm de Burhunt gave whatever right he had in 2 acres in front of
the main gate of the priory adjoining the new guest house (*hospitale*) as
far as the middle of the stream which flows below (*subtus*) the priory's
courtyard down to his own mill; also whatever right he and his heirs
had in the spring of Offwell (*Affewell'*), and permission to channel it
through his fief to the priory.⁴

Peter de Cosham and his wife, Adeliz, gave a virgate, which Serichius held, and a ½ virgate adjoining it, with appurtenances.⁵

Richard de Denemeda, on behalf of himself and his heirs, gave permission to dig and carry away as much [? stone] from his quarry of Gliddon (*Gletedun'*)⁶ as was needed for building work at the priory.

Anathema pronounced upon anyone disturbing the peace of the priory, or injuring its possessions.

1 Bishop Augustine Ua Selbaig died in 1182; the dedication of the church of Southwick had taken place within the preceding year (see III 959).

2 The opening passage of this deed is missing from fo. 4, but is to be found at the bottom of fo. 25ᵛ. (For an explanation of the numbering of the folios and their original organisation, see p. xliii.) It follows similar notifications of the dedication of the church by the other presiding bishops, Richard and Seffrid (viz. I 124-6). So that variants in those notifications can be compared with the above version, they are noted below.

3 Either John Mauduit, younger son of William Mauduit II, who died after 1178, or his son, John, who died before Michaelmas, 1210 (E. Mason, *The Beauchamp Cartulary*, p. lix).

4 Reinelm had been involved with various land transactions with the priory (I 120, 103). Offwell Farm and spring are about ½ mile south-west of the site of the priory. See also I 28. Reinelm's gift was confirmed by his son, William, *c.* 1200 (I 100).

5 Peter had given this land to Thomas, son of Roger la Wayte, and at his request gave it to the priory (III 397, 336; I 26, 27). According to the Final Concord between Peter and the priory in 1187, the land was "next to Stakes" (I 27), but Thomas' quitclaim to the priory of 1½ virgates—probably the same land—describes it as "all the land of Newelonde" (III 336). Newlands Farm is about 2½ miles east of Southwick, and Stakes a further 1½ miles to the east. See also I 87, 91; III 989.

6 Gliddon is about 2 miles north of Denmead, which is about 3 miles north-east of Southwick. See the alternative spellings: "Gluddun", in a marginal note to the copy III 951; "Gleteduna" in I 87; "Cleddene" in III 2; "Cleddon" in III 670. Copy III 954. Variants: Malduit; Estburunt; Denemede.

[fo. 24ᵛ-25] I 124   [As I 25, but issued by Richard, Bishop of Winchester]. Variants: John Mald'; Hestburhunt; Denemed'.

Copy III 951 [of I 124]. Variant: Estburhunt. Marginal note alongside entry concerning Richard de Denemed': "Note concerning Gliddon quarry (*Nota pro Quarreria de Gluddu'*)".

[fo. 25] I 125   [of I 124]. Variants: Wathreford; Estburhunt; [to] anniversary of the dedication [add:] "after Easter week";
          [before list of donors add gift from Bishop Richard himself, viz:] "gift, in perpetual alms, of land first held of the priory by Swain (*Suanus*) Fustarius, in Trafalgar Street (*Garestret*), Winchester, below the castle, in the parish of St Edmund";¹

[In Reinelm de Burhunt's gift:] the stream which "flows down from the priory's mill to his own mill"; omit: "permission to channel the spring through his fief to the priory";

[after Reinelm's gift, add:] "Matthew Oisel gave the priory the annual tithe of his mill at Crofton (*Croft'*),[2] which he bought, and the tithe of his hay there";

[to description of Peter de Cosham's gift, add:] "first given by Peter to Thomas, son of Roger le Vaite, as Peter's charter testifies".[3]

1 This tenement does not appear to be identified by Dr Keene, but much of the property on the west of Trafalgar Street, between it and the castle ditch, belonged to the bishopric (*WS II* pp. 910-12, and Fig. 100). There is no St Edmund's in the list of parish churches of medieval Winchester (*ibid.*, pp. 134-5).
2 See note 4 above.
3 Probably Crofton in Titchfield, where Southwick Priory had already received various gifts from Helewise de Crofton and her son, Geoffrey Talebot, including tithes of a mill (I 41-56).
Copy III 952 [of I 125]. Variants: Estburunt; Affewelle; Denem'.
[fo. 25ᵛ] I 126   [as I 25 but issued by Seffrid [II], Bishop of Chichester].[1] Variant: Serichus.
1 Printed in full in Latin in *The Acta of the Bishop of Chichester, 1075-1207* ed. H. Mayr Harting (Canterbury and York Society, 130; 1964) pp.186-7.
Copy III 953 [of I 126]. Variants: Affewelle; Serichius.

I 26   1187

CONFIRMATION by Peter de Cosham—for the salvation of the souls of himself, his wife, Adeliz, and all their kindred and friends—of his gift, in free alms, to Southwick Priory, of 1 virgate which Sericus [rubric: Serichus] held, ½ virgate adjoining it which Walter Parvus held, and all their appurtenances. The gift was made in the presence of Bishops Richard of Winchester, S[effrid] of Chichester (*Cicestr'*), and A[ugustine] of Waterford (*Watreford'*), and many other witnesses, at the dedication of Southwick church.[1]

Peter had granted the 1½ virgates in fee simple (*in feudo et hereditate libere et quiete*) to Thomas, son of Roger, at an annual rent of 2s. for all service, except that owing to the king. At Thomas' request, he willingly agreed to give the 1½ virgates and appurtenances to the priory, and, to increase the endowment, he has quitclaimed the 2s. rent,[2] and has also given to the priory a croft called *Heortsole* adjoining the 1½ virgates.[3] Consideration, 5 marks, given to him in his great need. Witnesses: Herbert, Archdeacon of Canterbury (*Cantuar'*); Hugh Bard', William Briwar', M. Thomas de Husseb',[4] Alan de Furnell', King's Justices; Walter Walerand; Geoffrey, son of Azo;[5] Matthew de Scuris and Roger, his son; Richard de Herierd'; Henry Dacus; Rein' de Denmede; Germanus; Henry, son of Herbert; Thomas, son of Roger.

On Friday after the feast of the translation of St Swithun [17 July], in the chapter house of Southwick Priory, Peter de Cosham recieved 5 marks from the priory[6] and was admitted into confraternity (*suscepit fraternitatem ecclesie nostre*). He placed on the high altar his charter, [fo. 4ᵛ] drawn up for the priory at Winchester, concerning the 1½ virgates, croft, and 2s., in the presence of Hugh Bard', William Briware, Alan de Furnell' and M. Thomas de Husseb', King's Justices;[4] Matthew de Scuris and Roger, his son; Robert Clericus of Bere (*Bera*); Reginald de Denmede; Richard, son of Daniel; Henry, son of Herbert; Thomas de Ho; Gervase, son of Richard de North; William, son of Gilbert; William Clericus of Hambleton (*Hamel'*); Humphrey Mahumet; Clement Scriba; Robert, son of Thomas; Thomas, son of Roger; Daniel, son of Richard; William Frater; Henry Crispus; William, son of Herbert de Heis'; Hirdman; Walter Simplex; Gilbert Thaleb'; Turstin Tegulator; Alfred Pelliparius.

> 1187, when there was war between the king
> of France and our King Henry [II].

1 This took place in 1181–2 (I 25, note 1).

2 See III 397, 336; I 25 and note 5, I 26.

3 Hertesole is described *c.* 1300 as "common pasture in the priory's manor at Newlands of the fee of Drayton" (III 483). See I 25, note 5.

4 Justices Hugh Bardolf, William Briwere and Thomas de Husseburne are recorded as visiting Hampshire during the fiscal year ending Michaelmas 1188 (*Itinerary of Henry II* p. 291).

5 Geoffrey, son of Azo, was sheriff of Hampshire, 1179–89 (*ibid.*, p. 338).

6 See I 27.

Copy III 398. Variants: rubric, Cossham; Cossam; Selfridus; Aug' Watroforden'; Hertsole.

Copy in H.R.O. 4M53/B7, pp. 2–3. Variants: [after "which Walter Parvus held" add:] with wood and meadow; Cycestr'; Hehotsole; Cant'; Briwerri'; Scur'; Datus; Reginald de Denemeda; Gertuanus; [the first part only is copied, ending with the first line of witnesses].

I 27   19 June 1187

FINAL CONCORD, made in the royal court at Winchester on Thursday after the feast of St Botulf, 33 Henry II, before Hugh Bard', William Briwarus, M. Thomas de Husseborna, Alan de Furnell', King's Justices, and other barons, between Southwick Priory and Peter de Cosham, concerning 1 virgate next to Stakes (*Frendstapl'*) which Serichus held, and an adjoing ½ virgate which Walter Parvus held, and all appurtenances.[1] Thomas, son of Roger, held the above from Peter freely and by hereditary right, paying an annual rent of 2s. for all service except that owed to the king, and he gave it in free and perpetual alms—for the souls of his father and ancestors—to Southwick Priory, saving the aforesaid 2s. rent.[2] Peter, at Thomas' request, confirmed the gift to the priory, in free alms—for the salvation of himself and his—and quit-claimed the rent, adding his own gift of a croft called *Heortsole* adjoining the aforesaid land on the south side.[3] Consideration, 5 marks.

1 See I 25 and note 5, I 26.
2 III 397, 336.
3 See I 26, note 3.

I 28 [soon after 1182][1]

GIFT by Reinelm de Burhunta—for the salvation of his soul and those of his wife, ancestors, heirs and kindred—to Southwick Priory, of himself and his body for burial, and, in free alms, (i) ¼ virgate (*unum ferdingum*) which Taleuaz held, with adjoining meadow; the ¼ virgate is next to the land of the priory's mill which the canons hold of Alexander de Burhunt's fee, in front of his gate;[2] (ii) the whole moor (*mhora*) below the ploughland of Applestead (*Appelsteda*)[3] as far as the stream which flows westward below the priory's courtyard down to the land of the mill which adjoins the moor in the west, with the road and footpath; (iii) 1 acre up the hill in *Staplecroft*[4] which adjoins the priory's acre on the south; (iv) 1 acre adjoining *Widedell*, lying between the priory's acres and formerly in dispute between the donor and the priory, measuring in length and breadth the same as any other acre in the same furlong; (v) the right, which he gave to the priory at the time of its dedication, to [fo. 5] channel through his land the spring of Offwell (*fons de Affewell*).[5] The donor also grants on behalf of himself and his heirs, all tithes due to the priory, having acknowledged his sin in failing hitherto to pay his tithes, and accepted mercy. Witnesses: Robert de Limes'; Geoffrey Capellanus; Walter Clericus of Hambledon (*Hamel'*); John de Hant', canon of Chicester (*Cicestr'*); M. John de Insulis; Charles de Limesi, and Ralph, his partner (*socius eius*); Nicholas, son of Herbert; Robert Diaconus; Hubold; William, son of Pagan; Thomas de Sancta Maria; Hirdman; Ralph; Hugh; William Frater; Walter Simpl'; Richard, son of Daniel; Robert de Norm'; Gilbert Talebot; Henry de Druvall; Humphrey Mahumet.

1 The dedication of Southwick Priory's church took place in 1181–2 (I 25, note 1). In the above charter Reinelm confirms his gift made at the dedication and adds to his benefaction.

2 See I 29, 30.

3 For the location of Applestead, see I 1, note 4.

4 Staple Cross is about 1½ miles north-west of the site of Southwick Priory.

5 See I 25, note 4.

Copy III 270. Variants: Talevaz; de Limesi.

I 29 [1165–82][1]

GIFT, in free alms, by Alexander de Burhunt—for the salvation of his soul and those of his wife, father and mother, grand-parents, brothers, kindred and friends—to Southwick Priory, of (i) all his tithes; (ii) his share in the common of Applestead (*de communi de Appelstede*) between the two streams;[2] (iii) the mill in front of his gate with all land belonging to it, and the bed of rushes (*iunchera*) or island which adjoins the mill between the old waterway and the mill stream. The land belonging to the mill extends as far as Reinelm's land in the east and to the stream, and the sluice gates can be freely opened and closed (*excluse etiam molendini aperientes et claudentes in pace remaneant*). Also the priory can erect, raise and strengthen [the banks of] the mill pond to a certain mark well known in the neighbourhood where an alder used to stand, and 7 feet beyond the mark; (iv) whatever he owned adjoining *Sadewell* from the stream to the road which leads from *barra* to the bridge and the priory's fish pond. He has also made the following exchanges: 7 acres of *Dichedecroft* for 7 acres of *Gerseworde*, but the grove of *Gerseworde*, now cleared, will remain in the priory's possession; *Smithcroft* and *Uplongemore* for 7 acres up the hill on the west of the road from Southwick to Portchester (*Porcestr'*); 6 acres of *Chirchfurlang* adjoining the spinney (*spina*) for 5 acres in his two enclosures (*garstuna*) and 1 acre beyond the hill; ½ acre in *Blakefurlong* for 3 butts (*buttera*) of 3 acres south of *Wlfied'emhore*; 3 acres in Sericus Surlevoche's holding and 2 in Odo's land, for 5 acres in his close; 2 acres south of *Pantulfeslie* for Roger Sturue's ½ acre from Alexander's enclosure (*garstuna*), ½ acre on the east of the road between Wlmer's land, and a half-grove (*havedgrave*) in Alexander's marl pit (*marlicium*);[2] and the acre formerly held by Coleman for an acre of *Siouledeland*.

The priory is to have and hold all the aforesaid lands quit of all service and exaction in perpetuity. The soul of Alexander's father has been received into full confraternity, and the priory will celebrate his anniversary each year, and Alexander's after his death. Witnesses: Aelard, Prior of St Denys (*S' Dion'*);[3] Audoen de Exton', dean; Augustus and Andrew de Ferlinget', priests; Reinelm de Burhunt; Richard, his brother; Richard de Denem' and Reginald; Hamo de Midelt'; Adam de Tiggehale; Peter de Wingeh'; Richard, son of Daniel; William, son of Drog'; William Frater; Richard Ansgod; Thomas Cementarius; Roger Lancel'; Simon, son of Gerald; Hugh Wac'; Thomas de Sancta Maria; Alexander Brito and Philip; Robert and William; Walter; Ralph Hiredman.

1 This deed is for the most part a confirmation of the gifts made to the priory by Alexander de Burhunt and his father, Herbert, before 1165, and of the exchanges of land agreed between the priory and Alexander (see I 121, 122). It probably preceded the final concord made between the priory and Alexander in 1182 (I 30).

2 See the version of this exchange in I 121.

3 Aelard or Adelard occurs as prior of St Denys in 1151. He also witnessed charters *c.* 1163–8 (I 7) and *c.* 1150–60 (I 21).
Copy III 192. Variants: Borhunt'; Sadewille; Dichdecroft'; Chirchesfurlong'; Wlfiedemore; Roger Sturne; hafdgrave; prior de Sancto Dionisio.

I 30   18 November 1182

[fo. 5ᵛ] FINAL CONCORD made in the King's Court of the Exchequer, at Westminster, Michaelmas term, on Thursday before the feast of St

Edmund, 28 Hen. II, before Richard, Bishop of Winchester; G[eoffrey], Bishop of Ely (*Eliensis*); John, Bishop of Norwich (*Norewic'*); Ranulf de Glanville, King's Justice (*iusticia*); Richard, the Treasurer;[1] Godfrey de Luci; William Mauduit, Chamberlain; Roger, son of Reinfr'; Ranulf de Gedding'; Gilbert de Coleville; Gervase de Cornhull; and other barons and faithful subjects, between Southwick Priory and Alexander de Burhunt, concerning the mill in front of Alexander's house, which his father, Herbert, gave in free alms to the priory and Alexander confirmed, and the mill pond, sluices, land, boundaries and other appurtenances of the mill.[2]

Alexander acknowledged, for 10s., the priory's right to the mill and appurtenances. The mill pond can be set up, raised, mended and strengthened at the priory's convenience, as far as the boundary mark, a stone about 7 feet from an alder which formerly marked the boundary; and the water from the mill pond can overflow as necessary, up to the boundary stone, on to Alexander's meadow or land at all times of the year. The sluices can be opened and closed freely as often as desired. The mill, sluices, mill pond, land, boundaries, bed of the stream (*gista*) and overflow of water (*refullatio aque*) will belong to the priory freely, in perpetuity.

1 Richard Fitz Neal was Treasurer from ?1159 to 1196.

2 Since Herbert de Burhunt, Alexander's father, granted the mill site to the priory some time before his death, which had taken place by 1165, there had been much controversy over the new mill and damage said to be caused to Alexander's land (see I 121, 122 and 29).

I 31   [?*c.* 1175–88][1]

NOTIFICATION by Robert Mauduit [rubric: Malduit] to R[ichard], Bishop of Winchester, of his gift, in free alms, made in the Bishop's presence—for the salvation of his soul and those of all his parents, friends and heirs, and of his wife and all his ancestors—to Southwick Priory, of the church of Shalden (*Scaldedena*), as far as it belongs to him, with all appurtenances. Witnesses: M. Stephen Remen'; William de Sancta Fide; M. Ham'; Ranulf Capellanus; Thomas de Turn'; Luke Cononicus; Robert de Mara; William de Phaleisa; Rotsone de Scot'; Hugh Clericus and Henry Clericus; Roger Mon' and Robert de Lat'; William, son of Drog'; William, son of Gerold.

1 William Mauduit III granted the manor of Shalden to his younger brother, Robert, *c.* 1175–6 (*Beauchamp Cartulary* p. lv). Bishop Richard died in December 1188.

This deed is printed in full, in Latin, as Appendix IV in E. Mason, "The Mauduits and their Chamberlainship of the Exchequer", p. 18.

For the explanation as to why the priory was anxious to obtain yet another confirmation of its possession of Shalden church, see I 18 and 111 and notes; also I 3, 4 and 32.

Copy III 78. Variant: Schalden'.

I 32   [*c.* 1180–88][1]

NOTIFICATION by Richard, Bishop of Winchester, to the archdeacons, deacons, and all clergy and people of his bishopric, that he has inspected the authentic writings of his predecessor, Henry, and of William Mauduit, to whom belonged the advowson of the church of Shalden (*Scaldedena*). Inspired by divine piety, Bishop Richard has granted, in free alms, to Southwick Priory, the church of Shalden with all its appurtenances, so that the priory will receive towards its own maintenance 20s. a year from [fo. 6] the parson of that church, who is to be responsible for spiritualities to the bishop and church of Winchester, and to their successors and officials. Witnesses: Herbert, Archdeacon of Canterbury (*Cant'*); Roger, Archdeacon of Winchester; Ranulf Canonicus, chaplain to the Bishop of Winchester; Luke Canonicus; M. Stephen Rem'; M. Ham' Medicus and M. Richard Medicus; M. Walter de Aug'; M. Gervase Cicestr'; Thomas de Turnai; Richard de Lond'; Luke Capellanus; Ralph Clericus; Jocelin de Risendona; Jordan de Sancto Michaele; Richard de Bera; Geoffrey de Vei'; William, son of Drag'.

1 Roger, Archdeacon of Winchester, occurs before 1181 and until 1205. Herbert Poore or le Poer, probably the son of Richard of Ilchester, first occurs as Archdeacon of Canterbury in 1176/7, and held that office until he became Bishop of Salisbury in 1194 (*Fasti* II, p. 14). Richard of Ilchester, Bishop of Winchester, died in December 1188. Shalden was one of the churches confirmed to the priory by Henry of Blois, Bishop of Winchester, *c.* 1155–71 (I 4). William Mauduit III's grant was made *c.* 1155–61 (I 111 and note). See also III 942.
Copy III 941. Variants: Stephen Remen'; Thomas de Torn'.

I 33   [Before 1186, possibly 1185–6][1]

GIFT by Gervase de Windeshor' and his wife, Alice, to Prior Guy and Southwick Priory, of their bodies for burial, wherever they may be at the time of death. Also—for the salvation of their souls and those of their son and heir, Thomas, and his wife Agnes, and all their kindred and friends—gift, in free alms, of the entire tenement which Aldwin de Wadeden', son of Turbert', held, with messuage, garden, land, wood and all other appurtenances. Witnesses: William, Abbot of Bindon (*Binend'*) [Dorset]; Robert de Limes'; Henry Dacus, Constable of Portchester (*Porcestr'*); Geoffrey Capellanus; Herbert Capellanus; M. John de Insula; Richard de Bera; Rothlandus Rothomag'; Hamo de Midling'; Herbert de Midlinct'; Ang'us Miles; Charles de Limesi and Ralph, his partner (*socius*); Roger de Hameslap'; William Walensi; Hugh Bacun; William Frater; Thomas Cementarius; Walter Simplex; Thomas de Sancta Maria.

1 The first known dated document in which Guy occurs as prior is of the year 1185 (I 91). Gervase's gift was among the priory's lands which were taken under the protection of Pope Urban III by a privilege addressed to Prior Guy on 9 February 1186 (I 87 and note 6).
Original in H.R.O. 5M50/7. Variant: Alwin de Wadeden'.
Seal: plaited silk thread, green, white and brown or faded red, but no seal.
Endorsements: (a) Karta Gervas' de Windeshor' de sepultura eius et de terra de Wadeden' in Flexland' [13th century hand].

       (b) 58

       (c) gift of a tenement [modern hand].

       (d) VII

       (e) 6

The originals of I 33, 34 and III 366 (5M50/7-9) all appear to be in the same hand or very similar hands. Likewise the endorsements are in very similar hands.
Copy III 364. Variants: Wydesore; Alwin de Wadedene.
See also III 363; a version of the second part of I 33, possibly slightly earlier, with the rubric: Charter of Gervase de Wyndesore concerning land in *Flexlond'* and *Wadeden'*.
Flexland was in the parish of Soberton. Part of it is now represented by Ingoldfield Farm, and Wadedene possibly by Watton Lane (*VCH Hants* III, p. 260; Gover, p. 51).

I 34   [*c.* 1185-6][1]

GIFT by Thomas, son of Gervase de Windeshor', and his wife, Agnes, to Prior Guy and Southwick Priory, of their bodies for burial, wherever they may be at the time of death. Also—for the salvation of their souls and those of their fathers, mothers and all their kinsmen and friends— they have given, in free alms, the entire tenement which Alwin de Wadeden' son of Turbert held, with messuage, garden, land, wood and all other appurtenances. Witnesses: [as in I 33, variants: Rotlandus; de Midlinct'].

1 See notes to I 33.
Thomas de Windsor held land in Soberton by serjeanty of weighing money at the Exchequer (*VCH Hants* III, p. 259).
Original in H.R.O. 5M50/9. Variant: Rothlandus.
Seal: tag missing, except for detached fragment, and seal missing.
Endorsements: (a) [Carta Th]ome fil' Gervas' de Windeshor' de sepultura eius et terra [13th century hand. "Carta Th" is written on the fragment of the tag, now detached].

       (b) VII

       (c) Southwick [in pencil; modern hand].

Copy III 365. Variant: Wydesore.
See also III 366; a version of the second part of I 33, possibility slightly earlier, with the rubric: Charter of Thomas, son of Gervase de Wyndesore, concerning land in *Wadeden'* in *Flexlond'*.

I 35   [*c.* late 12th or early 13th century][1]

GRANT, in free alms, by Richard de Hoivilla—for the salvation of his
soul and those of his wife, parents, heirs and all their lords and friends—
to Southwick Priory, of the whole tithe of the fulling mill he has built in
his tenement at Funtley (*Funteleia*). Witnesses: Roger and Bartholomew,
chaplains (*capellani*); Michael de Basevill'; Richard de la Bere and his
son, Lewis (*Ludowicus*); William, son of Drog'; Richard Angod'; William
Frater; William and Clement, clerks of Southwick; Thomas, son of
Roger; Simon Forestarius; Adam Caperun; Reinalm Snelgar; Thomas
Cementarius; Richard Cocus; Walter Simplex; Robert Batt'; Nigel;
William Wise.

1 Four names in the witness list also occur in a list dated *c.* 1185-6 (I 33). In
1251 Hugh, son of Richard de Hoyvill or Hoiville, was holding a fourth of a
knight's fee in Funtley in the hundred of Titchfield as sub-tenant of the Countess
of Arundel (*Cal. Inq. p.m.* I, no. 222, p. 56). Possibly Hugh's father, or
grandfather, was the above donor.
Copy III 888. Variants: Houville, Hoyville (rubric), Hovyle; Basevile.

I 36   [2nd half of the 12th century][1]

[fo. 6ᵛ] GIFT, in free alms, by Richard, son of Daniel, and his wife,
Basilia—for the salvation of their souls and those of their sons, parents
and friends—to Southwick Priory of the church of Wanstead
(*Wanested'*), as far as they are able to give it; with a certain messuage
in the vill of Wanstead which from ancient times has belonged to the
church; and a croft of 8 acres and close belonging to the messuage; and
they have added, for the upkeep of the chapel, the acre which was Imbe's
enclosure making 9 acres in one close. Also a certain headland acre
(*havedacra*) to the west of the court belonging to John Mald' in East
Boarhunt (*Estburhunta*), at the head (*caput*) of 4 acres belonging to the
donors' fee, which headland acre adjoins the road towards the hill; and
1 acre beyond the hill adjoining the land of Wymering (*Wimeringes*),
which is the boundary acre (*mercacra*) between the lands of Wymering
and John Mald', and is east of Paulsgrove (*Palesgrava*); and 1 acre west
of (*del West de*) Godecrofte beyond the hills west of (*del West de*)
Paulsgrove in *Middelfurlonga*, which lies by itself between land belonging
to John Maud'—thus there are 12 acres belonging to Wanstead church.
Also they have granted the whole annual tithe of all things reasonably
tithable, both from their demesne and from the rest of their fee at
Wanstead.
    On account of the poverty of the place, the priory has granted, for
the maintenance of the chaplain who is to serve the aforesaid church
and reside in that vill, the whole tithe from half a hide belonging to
Drayton (*Draitona*), which is called *Mierdesmor*. Moreover, each year,
at the feast of St Lawrence [10 August], out of respect for the martyr
and for the place (*propter ipsius martyris et loci reverenciam*), the priory

shall send some of their brothers to Wanstead church so that divine service may be more honourably celebrated there, and all oblations and other obventions brought to that place will be received for the honour and use of Southwick church. The chaplain serving there is to be responsible to the bishop of Winchester and his officials for all things pertaining to himself and the aforesaid church. Witnesses: Bartholomew Capellanus of Wymering; Henry Dacus; Matthew Oisel; Thomas de Bera; Alan de Olt'; Theobald Serviens of Fareham (*Ferreha'*); Walter de Remn'; Nicholas le Bel; Robert Clericus and his brother, Reginald; Baldwin; Elias (*Helias*); Walter; Thomas; Henry de Druevall'; William Portarius; Hurricus.

1 The church of Wanstead is among the priory's possessions over which Pope Alexander III extended his protection in 1162 or 1163 (I 86). It did not occur in the list given in Pope Eugenius III's bull of 1151-2 (I 85). The gift or confirmation of that church to the priory appears to have been made between these dates by Robert de Pont de l'Arche (I 112), although in a later confirmation it is said to have been given by his father, William de Pont de l'Arche, the priory's founder (I 18).

None of these charters makes mention of any right Richard, son of Daniel, had to the church. Richard appears frequently as a witness to charters granted to the priory in the second half of the 12th century, and in particular to one dated 1165 (I 122) and another of 1187 (I 27). It may be that he is confirming Robert de Pont de l'Arche's gift of the church and adding to its endowment a gift of land from his fee.

Copy III 457 Variants: Wanstede; Estborhunt'; Wymeryng; Drayton'.

I 37 [2nd half of the 12th century, possibly before 1180][1]

GIFT, in free alms, by Michael de Basevilla—for the salvation of his soul and those of his lord, Richard de Humeto, and of his wife, Isabel (*Hysabel*), and all their kinsfolk and friends—to Southwick Priory, of 1 acre of his land, the nearest to the priory's lower ploughland (*que scilicet propinquior fuit culture illorum subteriori*) which is called *Wetecroft*. Robert, son of Alwin, Michael's man, held the land of him. Witnesses: Alexander de Burhunta; Richard de Bera; Reinelm de Burhunta; Matthew Oisel; Hugh, son of Robert de Havresh; Robert de Warewic; William de la Garde; Roger Lanceleve; Henry, son of Richard, son of Daniel; William, son of Matthew Oisel; William, son of Drogo; William Frere; Thomas de Sancta Maria; Robert de Basevilla; Gowin.

1 Michael de Baseville held land in Boarhunt of Richard de Hommet. After William de Hommet had succeeded his father, Richard, as Constable of Normandy in 1180, he gave all his property in Boarhunt to the priory with the exception of three tenements, one of which was that held by Michael de Baseville (I 138). As there is no mention of William in the above charter it seems likely that it was drawn up before he succeeded his father.

Copy III 462. Variants: Humet'; Ysabel; Alexander de Borhunt; Richard de Ber'.

24

I 38

GIFT, in free alms, by Herbert de Froill' [rubric: de Froile]—for the souls of his father and ancestors and the salvation of his soul and those [fo. 7] of his heirs—to Southwick Priory, of 1 acre lying in *Mearcfurlong* adjoining the acre which the priory exchanged with Robert de Normann'.[1] The priory has received Herbert and his father's soul into their fraternity, and will celebrate annually his father's anniversary, and his own after his death. Witnesses: Richard de Northona; Richard de Burhunt; Herbert de Heges; Peter de Heges and his brother, Alan; Robert de Molend'; Gervase de Norhton'; Andrew Capellanus; Walter Presbyter; Robert Clericus; Elias de Loventona; Walter Clericus; Henry de Druevall'; William Frater; William Simplex; Thomas; Reginald; Luwin.

1 The donor may have been the father of Sir Herbert de Froylle, who was holding ¼ knight's fee of Sir Herbert de Burhunt, probably in the first half of the 13th century (III 132). Part of that land was in Portchester, and Robert de Normannia also held land in Portchester (II 195). There was a *Mearc* or *Merkefurlong* in Portchester field (II 174, 207).
Copy III 439 Variants: Froyle; Merefurlong'; Norma'; Richard de Borhunt'.

I 39

Charter of William de Humet' concerning 2s. rent in the manor of Boarhunt (Burhunt').

GIFT, in free alms, by William de Humeto—for the salvation of his soul and those of his wife Lucy, their sons and daughters, his father and mother, and all their kinsmen (*parentes*) and friends, and for the good estate of his lord (*pro statu et conservatione domini mei*), King Henry— to Southwick Priory, of certain land, which Ralph Crabbe held of his manor of West Boarhunt (*Westburhunta*), lying between *Stapelcroft*[2] and Roger Maword's land, together with Ralph and a messuage, and with 2 acres on the hill (*super montem*), and all other appurtenances. The gift is made at the request of William's wife, Lucy, to provide a light before the crucifix in Southwick Priory church. Witnesses: Robert de la Haie; William de Piro; Roger des Mustiers; Geoffrey de Piro; William de Surevill'; Alexander de Burhunta; Robert de Ranvill'; Henry Dacus; William de Sai and his brother, Henry; William de Colevill' and his brother, Robert; Salvagius; Thomas de la Bere; Alexander de la Bere; William Frater; Hiredman; Hugh; Thomas de Sancta Maria.

1 During the reign of Henry II. The donor succeeded his father, Richard de Hommet, as Constable of Normandy in 1180. As he is not referred to here as Constable, the charter may be prior to 1180. William de Hommet, as Constable, confirmed this and other gifts to the priory after his wife's death (I 76; III 41; and see I 77).
2 Staple Cross is a mile north of Boarhunt.
Copy III 43. Variants: Stapelcrouch'; Robert de la Haye.

I 40 [Late 12th cetury][1]

GRANT, in perpetual alms, by Simon de Wahelle [rubric, de Wahilla]—for the souls of his father and his ancestors, and the reception of himself into their fraternity—to Southwick Priory, of 1 mark of silver annually at Easter from the rent of his mills of Ravenstone (*Ravenstonia*), [Bucks]. If Simon or his heirs can assign to the priory, either for the church or for other alms, this mark or more, they will keep the rent from the mills (*et si forte ego vel heredes mei possimus assignare predictos canonicos de hac marca argenti predicta aut in ecclesia aut in aliqua elemosina que tantum valeat aut magis redditus molendinorum predictorum nobis quietus remanebit*).

Witnesses: Adan de Port; John his son; William de Port; Robert de Port; William de la Bere; Seierus de Wahilla; Walter de Wahilla; Simon de Patishillia; Robert de Langeford; Nicholas de Landast; Baldwin Clericus.

[Marginal note, written vertically down right-hand margin, in a later hand:] void (*vacat*). [This seems to imply that the charter never took effect, which is borne out by the fact that there is no evidence elsewhere to suggest that the priory ever received the rent or that any alternative arrangement was made.]

1 Simon de Wahull succeeded Walter de Wahull (*fl.*1165–72), who had acquired Ravenstone from the Bolbecs. In 1212, Simon's son, John, did homage to the Bolbecs for his land (*VCH Bucks* IV, p. 440).

I 41 [1152–63][1]

GIFT, in free alms, by Helewise de Croftona—for her salvation, for the soul of her lord Talebot, and for the salvation of her sons—to Southwick Priory, of 1 virgate in Stubbington (*Stubinctuna*)[2] which Fugelere held, and the full (*plenaria*) tithe of her mill, to be held free from all exaction and service except that due for a virgate to the king or to her chief lords (*domini mei qui super me sunt*) when her land is taxed. Witnesses: Philip Talebot; Hugh, his brother; John de Insula; Gilbert Sacerdos; Fabian, son of Gilbert (*Gislebertus*); Matthew; Serlo; Anschetil Norreis.

1 This is the earliest of Helewise's many gifts to the priory. It is recorded in Pope Alexander III's bull of 1162–3 (I 86), but does not occur in Pope Eugenius III's bull of 1151–2 (I 85).

2 Crofton and Stubbington were in the hundred of Titchfield.
Copy III 159. Variants: Croftuna; Stobynton'.

I 42 [2nd half of 12th century][1]

GIFT, in free alms, by Geoffrey Talebot [rubric: Geoffrey Talebot', [fo. 7ᵛ] son of Helewise]—for the salvation of his soul and those of his wife, sons, father and mother, and of all his lords and ancestors—to Southwick Priory, of 1 virgate which Godwin Fugelere held in Stubbington, in Geoffrey's manor of Crofton.[2] Also the full (*plenaria*) tithe of his mill of Crofton. [Conditions of tenure as in I 41]. Witnesses: Ralph de Mednil'; Henry Dacus; Michael de Basevill'; M. John de Insula; Jordan de Mednil'; Robert de Mednil'; Geoffrey de Mednil'; Alexander de Burhunt; Richard de Hoivil'; Gilbert de Basevil'; Reginald and Richard de Denem'; Adam, son of Regin'; Peter de Wing'; William, son of Drog'; Elias (Helias) de Lovent'; Walter son of Roger; Walter Simplex; Elias (*Helias*) and Baldwin, sons of the donor (*filii mei*); and many others.

1 Later than I 41, probably by several years. Ralph de Mednil' had died by 1195 (*PR 7 Richard I* p. 208).

2 See I 41, note 2.
Copy III 140. Variants: Croftune, Croftuna.

I 43 [*c.* 1173–85][1]

GIFT, in free alms, by Lady Helewise of Crofton (*Croftona*)—for the salvation of the souls of her lord, John Talebot, and her sons, Elias (*Helyas*) and Philip, her father and mother, and other deceased friends and lords, and for her own salvation and that of her sons, Geoffrey and Hugh, and all her kinsmen (*parentes*), lords and friends—to Southwick Priory, of 1 virgate called *Cumed'*, from the manor of Crofton which is hers by inheritance, with meadow and pasture, marsh, ways, paths and all other appurtenances, to be held free of all exaction and secular service except that due to the king and the Earl of Richmond (*Richemont'*),[2] viz. when 20s. are required from the manor of Crofton to be paid to the ward of Richmond, the aforesaid virgate is taxed at 7½d. This gift has been made at the request of M. John de Insula, to whom Helewise had given the aforesaid virgate for his service.[3] Witnesses: Robert de Croft'; Bartholomew Capellanus of Wymering (*Wimering'*); Alexander de Burhunt; Hugh, son of John; Baldwin (*Baudewinus*), son of Geoffrey; Gilbert, son of Taleb'; Walkelin, son of Philip; Stephen, son of Hugh; William Talun'; William, son of Drog'; William Frater; Walter de Sancto Jacobo; Thomas de Sancta Maria; Clement Clericus; Walter Simplex; Andrew, son of Richard; Reinald'; Ralph Pell'; and another Ralph, son of Richard.

1 Helewise notified Richard of Ilchester, Bishop of Winchester 1173–88, of her gift to the priory, and it was recorded in Pope Lucius III's confirmation of the priory's possessions in 1184–5 (I 48, 91).

2 Crofton was probably amongst possessions granted to Alan of Brittany after the Conquest, and subsequently formed part of the honour of Richmond (*V C H Hants* III, p. 226).

3 See I 46, 45.
Copy III 153, marked *duplicata*. Variants: Helie; Coumede; Richemunt; Robert de Crofton'.

I 44[1]   *c.* 1173–85][2]

GIFT, in free alms, by Geoffrey Talebot to Southwick Priory, at the request of M. John de Insula [identical terms and gift as made by Geoffrey's mother, Helewise, in I 43]. Witnesses: Henry Dacus; Alexander de Burhunt; Robert de Croft', [and] Bartholomew de Wimering', chaplains; William Clericus; William, son of Drog'; Baldwin, son of the donor (*filius meus*); William Frere; Philip, son of Richard; Ralph Hirdman; Thomas de Sancta Maria; William, son of Osbert; William Talun; Reinald'; Thomas, son of Baldwin; Ralph Pell'; Ralph, his brother, son of Richard; Clement; Walter de Sancto Jacobo; Henry de Druvall'; Arnold (*Ernold*) Baf'.

1 On a piece of parchment 18.5 cms × 9 cms sewn between fo. 7ᵛ and fo. 8. The intended position of this charter is indicated by a rubric on fo. 7ᵛ immediately following I 43, and a symbol, which is repeated on the inserted parchment.

2 See I 43 and notes.
Copy III 146. See also another version at III 137.

I 45   [*c.* 1170][1]

GIFT by Geoffrey Talebot of Crofton (*Croft', Croftona*) to M. John de Insula, for service rendered by him to Geoffrey, and to his father and mother, of a virgate called *Cumed'*, from the manor of Crofton which is his by inheritance (*de heretagio meo*), with meadow and pasture, marsh, ways, path, and all appurtenances. John and his heirs will hold it of Geoffrey and his heirs, free from all exaction and service except that due to the king and the Earl of Richmond (*Richem'*)[2], viz. when 20s. are required to be paid from the manor of Crofton to the ward of Richmond, the aforesaid *Cumed'* with appurtenances is taxed at 7½d. Witnesses: Hugh Talebot, brother of the donor (*frater meus*), Stephen, son of Hugh; Alexander de Burhunt; Gilbert, son of Geoffrey; William, son of Talun'; William, son of Drog'; William Frater; Clement; Walter de Sancto Jacobo; Thomas de Sancta Maria; Andrew, son of Richard; Ralph Hiredman.

1 This gift, which confirmed that of Helewise, Geoffrey's mother (I 46), obviously preceded the gift of the same land by M. John de Insula to the priory, which Geoffrey and Helewise confirmed (I 43, 44), and of which notice was given by M. John to Richard of Ilchester, Bishop of Winchester (I 47).

2 See I 43, note 2.
Copy III 141. Variants: Croftuna; Richemunt.

I 46   [*c.* 1170][1]

[fo. 8] GIFT by Lady Helewise of Crofton (*Croftona*) to M. John de Insula, of a virgate called *Cumed'* [terms identical with I 45]. Witnesses:

Philip, the donor's son (*filius meus*); Ralph, son of Rand'; Hugh, his brother; William Wigemorum; William Talun'; Richard de Strat'; Simon, son of Hubert; Walter de Insula; Robert, son of Joce; and many others.

1 See I 45 and notes.

Copy III 157. Variants: Coumede; Robert, son of Rand'.

I 47   [*c.* 1173–85][1]

NOTIFICATION by M. John de Insula to Richard, Bishop of Winchester, of his gift, in free alms—for the salvation of his soul and that of his uncle, John Talebot, and for the salvation of his lady, Helewise de Croftuna, and her sons, Geoffrey Talebot and Hugh, and his other friends and lords—to Southwick Priory, of the virgate called *Cumed'* in the manor of Crofton, with meadow and pastures, marsh, ways, paths and all other appurtenances, saving service due to the king, to the Earl of Richmond (*Richem'*),[2] and to his lady, viz. when 20s. is required from the manor of Crofton to be paid to the ward of Richmond, the aforesaid virgate is taxed at $7\frac{1}{2}$d. The virgate with appurtenances was given to John for his service by his lady, Helewise, to be held by hereditary right; he has given his inheritance to the Church of the Blessed Mary of Southwick, where his uncle is buried, and where his aforesaid lady will be buried (*ubi predicta domina mea se dedit*). Witnesses: Geoffrey Talebot and Hugh; Alexander de Burhunt; William, son of Drog'; William Frere; Bartholomew de Wimering and Robert de Crofton; Thomas de Sancta Maria; Andrew, son of Richard; William Talun; Reinald'; Clement; Walter de Sancto Jacobo.

1 See I 43, note 1; I 45, 46, 48, 49.

2 See I 43, note 2.

Copy III 167. Variants: Croftuna; Coumede; Richemont.

I 48   [*c.* 1173–85][1]

NOTIFICATION by Helewise de Croft' to R[ichard], Bishop of Winchester, of her gift, in free alms—for the salvation of the souls of her lord, John Talebot, and her sons, Elias (*Helias*) and Philip, deceased; and for her salvation and that of her sons Geoffrey Talebot and Hugh, and all her kinsmen, friends and lords—to Southwick Priory, of $\frac{1}{2}$ virgate in the manor of Crofton from her inheritance. The $\frac{1}{2}$ virgate was formerly held by Alfric, son of Ailnod', and adjoins the virgate called *Cumed'* to the south (*versus austrum*).[2] It will be held free from all exaction and secular service saving that due to the king and the Earl of Richmond (*Richem'*)[3], viz. when 20s. are due from Crofton manor to the ward of Richmond, the $\frac{1}{2}$ virgate will be taxed at $3\frac{1}{4}$d. This gift was made at the request of the donor's son and heir, Geoffrey, who has given himself, living and dead, to the same church (*qui se ipsum dedit ecclesie eidem et vivum et mortuum*), and because his father, Helewise's lord, John Talebot, is buried there, and Helewise has given herself likewise (*ego me ipsam dedit similiter*). Witnesses: Henry Dacus; Alexander de Burhunt; Geoffrey Capellanus; M. John de Insula; Henry de Druevall'; William, son of Drog'; Clement Scriba; William Frater; Walter de Sancto Jacobo; Thomas de Sancta Maria; Walter Simplex; Robert Diaconus; William Talun; Arnold (Hernald) Baf; Andrew, son of Richard; Ralph Hirdman; Robert de Sancto Clero; Baldwin Talebot; William Paumer; Robert, his son; Matthew.

1 Richard of Ilchester was Bishop of Winchester from 1173 to 1188. The $\frac{1}{2}$ virgate referred to in this charter is probably included in Pope Lucius III's confirmation of the priory's possessions in 1184-5 (I 91).

2 See I 43-7. The $\frac{1}{2}$ virgate appears to have become known as Ailbricteshille (I 54).

3 See I 43, note 2.
Copy III 155. Variants: Ailfric son of Ailnold; Coumede; Richemunt.

I 49 [*c.* 1173-85][1]

NOTIFICATION by Geoffrey Talebot to R[ichard], Bishop of [fo. 8ᵛ] Winchester, of his gift to Southwick Priory of his body for burial, wherever he dies. He has been accepted into the full fraternity of the priory, so that, after his death, they will hold divine service for him as for one of their brothers (*facient servitium pro me sicut pro fratre suo*), and inscribe his name in their martyrology and keep his anniversary each year in perpetuity. Because his father, John Talebot, is buried there, and he and his mother likewise have given their bodies for burial, Geoffrey has given the priory $\frac{1}{2}$ virgate in the manor of Crofton [viz. the same holding and terms as described in I 48; the witness list is the same except that the name of Robert Diaconus occurs twice; for Matthew read Matthew de Chamus; there is one new name, Roger de Bedeh'].

1 See I 48 and notes. See also III 148 for Geoffrey's charter giving this $\frac{1}{2}$ virgate to the priory.
Copy III 138. Witnesses: Henry Dacus; Geoffrey Capellanus; M. John de Insula.

I 50 [Late 12th century, possibly after 1186][1]

GIFT, in free alms, by Lady Helewise of Crofton (*Croftona*)—for the salvation of souls [as in I 48]—to Southwick Priory, where she has chosen to be buried, of certain ploughland (*cultura*) called *Disgrave*, from the demesne of the vill of Crofton which is hers by inheritance, lying next to the virgate called *Cumed'* to the north (*versus aquilonem*), together with marsh next to that ploughland on the west towards the arm of the sea, adjoining the marsh which the donor had previously given to the priory with the virgate called *Cumed'*. Witnesses: Robert Capellanus of Crofton; Alexander de Burh'; Hugh, son of the donor (*filius meus*); Nicholas de Port; Gilbert Taleb'; Walkelin, son of Philip; Roger, son of Durand'; Hugh Franceis; Stephen and James, sons of Hugh Taleb'; Anket'; Reginald, son of Gilbert.

1 There is no mention of *Disgrave* in Pope Lucius III's confirmation in 1184–5 of the priory's possessions, nor in Pope Urban III's confirmation of 1186, although other gifts from Helewise are recorded (I 91, 87).
Copy III 154. Variants: Coumede; Borhunt'.

I 51   [Late 12th century, possibly after 1186][1]

CONFIRMATION, in free alms, by Geoffrey Talebot, at his mother's request—for the soul of his father, John Talebot, who is buried at Southwick, and the salvation of his mother, who has given her body for burial there (*se eidem ecclesie dedit sepeliendam*), and of himself and all his lords, kindred (*parentes*), and friends—to Southwick Priory, of his mother's gift of certain ploughland called *Disgreve*, from the demesne of Crofton (*Crofton'*), lying next to the virgate called *Cumed'* to the north; and marsh next to the ploughland on the west, stretching as far as the arm of the sea. Witnesses: Stephen, Prior of Taunton (*Tant'*);[2] M. John, Sub-prior; Othelmus; Richard, son of Azor; Baldwin Taleb'; [fo. 9] Gilbert Taleb'; John, son of Azor; Walter Barate; Ranulf, nephew of the prior of Taunton (*Tanton'*); Reginald, son of Gilbert.

1 See I 50 and note.
2 Stephen, Prior of Taunton, occurs between 1158 and 1188–91 (Knowles *Heads of Religious Houses* p. 185.
Copy III 144. Variants: Disgrave; [one witness only:] Bartholomew Capellanus.
Copy III 161. Variant: Coumede.

I 52   [Late 12th century, possibly after 1186][1]

GIFT, in free alms, by Lady Helewise of Crofton (*Croftona*)—for the salvation of her soul and those of her lord, John Talebot, who is buried at Southwick, her sons, kindred, friends and lords—to Southwick Priory, of a meadow called *Chercmede*, with service of mowing and carrying which the villeins of Crofton (*Croftun'*) are obliged to carry out each year. *Chercmede* lies next to the meadows called *Normede* and *Cherlemede*, and extends as far as Titchfield water (*ad aquam de Tichefeldia*). This gift was made at the request, and with the consent, of the donor's son and heir, Geoffrey Talebot. Witnesses: Robert Capellanus of Crofton; Richard de Portes' [and] Bartholomew, chaplains; Alexander de Burh'; Alexander de Benesteda; Baldwin and Gilbert de Crofton'; Stephen, son of Hugh; William Bonsergant; William Frater; Thomas de Sancta Maria; Walter Simplex; Osbert; Alfred; Hugh; Ralph Hirdman.

1 See dating evidence for I 50. *Chercmede* is not mentioned in the papal confirmations.
Copy III 163. Variants: Crofton'; Tichefelda; de Portesy.

I 53 [Late 12th century, possibly after 1186][1]

CONFIRMATION, in free alms, by Geoffrey Talebot—for the salvation of the souls of himself, his heirs, his father, who is buried at Southwick, his mother, who will be buried there (*se eidem ecclesie dedit*), and all their lords and friends—to Southwick Priory, of the gift, made at this request by his mother, Lady Helewise, of a meadow called *Chercmede*, as his mother's charter testified.[1] Witnesses: Robert de Croftun'; Richard de Portesia, Bartholomew de Wimering', chaplains; Alexander de Burhunt'; Alexander de Benesteda; Baldwin Taleb'; Gilbert Taleb'; Stephen, son of Hugh; William Bonsergant; William Frater; Thomas de Sancta Maria; Walter Simplex; Osbert; Alfred; Hugh; Ralph Hirdman.

1 See I 52 and note.
Copy III 145. Variants: Chermede; Crofton'.

I 54 [Late 12th century, possibly after 1186][1]

GIFT, in free alms, by Lady Helewise of Crofton (*Croftona*)—for the salvation of the soul of her lord, John Talebot, who is buried in the cemetery of Southwick church, where she also has given herself in sisterhood (*ubi etiam ego me ipsam dedi in sororem*) and has chosen to be buried, and for her salvation and that of her son and heir, Geoffrey Talebot, who will also be buried there, and for the souls of all her sons, kindred, friends and lords—to Southwick Priory, of 1 virgate which Godwin Fugelere held in the manor of Crofton (*Croftune*) which is hers by inheritance;[2] 1 virgate called *Cumede*, with meadow, marsh, ways, paths, and all other appurtenances;[3] and $\frac{1}{2}$ virgate called *Ailbricteshille*, which Wlward held, and which lies next to *Cumede* on the south (*versus meridiem*), with the marsh which adjoins the $\frac{1}{2}$ virgate on the west.[4] The priory will hold the land free of all service saving that owed to the king, and to her lords, and whatever is due to the ward of Richmond (*Richemunt*) from the virgate Fugelere held, from *Cumede* or from *Ailbrichteshille*.[5] She has also given a certain ploughland called *Disgrave*, from her demesne of Crofton, adjoining *Cumede* on the north, with marsh which adjoins the ploughland on the west and extends by way of the ditch (*per fossatum*) as far as the arm of the sea;[6] and a certain [fo. 9ᵛ] meadow called *Chirchmede* (*Chercmede*), to provide feed for the priory's cattle (*ad sustentationem peccorum suorum*), with service of mowing, hay-making and carrying which the villeins of Crofton are obliged to carry out each year;[7] this meadow is to be held by the priory as freely as anyone held it of the donor's ancestors (*sicut aliquis antecessorum meorum idem pratum unquam melius et liberius tenuit*). *Chercmede* lies between the meadows called *Nordmede* and *Cherlemede*, and extends as far as Titchfield water (*ad aquam de Tichefelda*). All this has been given at the request, and with the consent, of the donor's son and heir, Geoffrey Talebot. Witnesses: Robert Capellanus of Crofton (*Croftuna*); Richard de Portes'; Bartholomew Capellanus of Wymering (*Wimering'*); Alexander de Burh'; Alexander de Benested'; Baldwin and Gilbert Taleb'; Stephen, son of Hugh; William Bonsergant; William Frater; Thomas de Sancta Maria; Walter Simpl'; Osbert; Alfred; Hugh; Ralph Hirdman.

1 See dating evidence for I 50 and 52.
2 See I 41, 42.
3 See I 43-7.
4 See I 43, note 2.
5 See I 48, 49.
6 See I 50, 51.
7 See I 52, 53.
Copy III 158. Variants: Albrichteshille; Ailbrychteshille; Coumede; Crofton'; Portesy.
Copy III 162. Variants: Crofton'; Coumede; after "feed for the priory's cattle", add, "and animals"; Chermede.
Description of position and extent of Chermede is omitted. Witnesses: Robert Capellanus; Bartholomew; Alexander de Burhunt.

I 55   [Late 12th century, possibly after 1186][1]

GIFT, in free alms, by Geoffrey Talebot—for the salvation of the soul of his father, John Talebot, who is buried at Southwick; and the salvation of his mother, Helewise, and himself, who have both chosen to be buried there; and of his heir, Elias (*Helyas*), his other sons, and all kindred, friends, and lords—to Southwick Priory, of [lands as described in I 54, said to be given at the request and with the consent of Lady Helewise. Variants: Richemonte; Albricthishill', Ailbrihceshell'. The description of the situation and extent of Cherchmed' is omitted]. Witnesses: Robert Capellanus of Crofton (*Croftun'*); Richard Capellanus of Portsea (*Portes'*); Bartholomew Capellanus of Wymering (*Wimering'*); Alexander de Benested'; Baldwin Taleb'; Gilbert Taleb'; Stephen, son of Hugh; William Bonsergant; John Scach'; William Frater; Walter Simplex; Thomas de Sancta Maria; Osbert and Alfred Parmentarii; Hugh; Ralph Hirdman; Reginald, son of Gilbert.

1 See I 54 and notes.
Copy III 139. Variants: include Geoffrey's wife (*et uxor mea*) in list of those whose salvation is sought; Helias; Fugiler'; Wulwardus; Ailbryteshille; Ailbricteshell'; Chermede; Portesie.

I 56 [Late 12th century, possibly after 1186][1]

CONFIRMATION, in free alms, by Geoffrey de Furnell'[2]—for the salvation of his soul and those of his wife, heirs, father and mother, and all kindred, friends and lords—to Southwick Priory, of the gift made by Lady Helewise of Crofton (*Croftuna*), with the consent of her son [fo. 10] and heir Geoffrey, [description of lands and terms as in I 54] and the tithe of the mill and hay of Crofton, as the charters of Helewise and Geoffrey testify. This confirmation is made at the request of the aforesaid Helewise and Geoffrey. Witnesses: Ralph de Wirecestr'; William Clericus; Robert de Wirecestr'; Simon de Wirecestr'; William Frere; Henry Crispus; Hugh de Upton'; Daniel de Upford; Roger, son of Gilbert.

1 See I 54 and notes.

2 The Furneaux family held Crofton of the honour of Richmond in the 12th century and up to 1331 (*V C H Hants* III, p. 226).
Copy III 149. Variants: Croftun'; Coumede; Chermede; Wirecestre.

I 57 [*c.* 1180–90][1]

GIFT, in free alms, by William de Cumbrai [*rubric: de Cumbraio*]—for the salvation of his soul and those of his brothers and all his kindred, friends and lords—to Southwick Priory, of half the ½ hide his brother Ralph de Cumbrai gave him, from his demesne in *Preveta* for his service and homage, viz., the ¼ hide to the south adjoining Anmore (*Huius autem dimidie hyde medietatem scilicet quartam partem unius hyde versus partem australem et iuxta Henedemer'*).[2] The gift was made in the chapter house of the priory and brought to the high altar, and William was accepted into the fraternity (*et frater eorum deveni*). Witnesses: Geoffrey Taleb'; Richard, son of Bald'; Hugh Taleb'; Baldwin Taleb'; Gilbert Taleb'; Robin Clericus; William de Heges; Thomas de Sancta Maria; Hirdman; Turstan Tegul'; Alfred Pelliparius.

1 This gift was confirmed by William, Earl of Sussex, between 1186 and 1193 (I 136).

2 See III 115.
Copy III 122. Variants: rubric, Cumbray; Prevetta; Enedemere; Talebot; Richard, son of Balol'.

I 58[1] [*c.* 1180–90][2]

CONFIRMATION, in free alms, by Ralph de Cumbrai—for the salvation of his soul and those of his kindred and friends—to Southwick Priory, at the request of his brother, William de Cumbrai, of the gift of 1 virgate, viz. all that land which is west of the road that leads from Anmore (*Enedem'*) to Hinton (Hent'), together with 10 acres on the east of the same road adjoining Anmore (*Enedm'*) to make up the virgate. Ralph had given this land to William for his service and homage.[3] Witnesses: Matthew and Roger de Scur'; Alexander de Burh'; Gilbert de Basevill'; Peter de Kateringt'; William de Laber, son of Richard; H. de Druevill'; Roger de Mien'; Thomas Cementarius; Hirdman; Ralph de Labaic; Adam de Hent'; Reginald and Richard de Denemed'; Thomas, son of Roger.

1 On a piece of parchment 15 cms × 8.5 cms, sewn between fo. 9ᵛ and fo. 10.

2 See dating evidence for I 57.

3 See III 115.
Copy III 119. Variants: Enedemere; Henton'; Andemere; [two witnesses only:] Matthew de Scuris; Roger de Scuris.
Copy in H.R.O. 4M53/B7, p. 3. Variants: Cumbraii, Cumbray; Anedemere; Henton'; [the names of the following witnesses are given:] Matthew de Scures; Alexander de Burhunt; Gilbert de Basevil'; Peter de Kateryng'.

I 59   [*c.* 1180–90][1]

GIFT, in free alms, by Ralph de Cumbrai—for the salvation of his soul and those of his wife, Auda, his brothers, kindred, and friends—to Southwick Priory, of a virgate from his demesne in *Prevettus* from the east part of Anmore (*Enedem'*), i.e. adjoining on the east the ½ hide (*que scilicet proxima iacet ex orientali parte iuxta dimidiam hydam*) he gave to his brother, William de Cumbrai.[2] Witnesses: Ralph de Mesn'; Matthew de Scur'; Roger de Scur'; Robert de Mesn'; Gilbert de Basevill'; William de Cumbrai; Alexander de Burh'; Reginald and Richard de Denem'; Peter de Cateringet'; Adam de Hent'; Gilbert Oin; Roger de Menes; W. de la Bere.

1 See dating evidence for I 57.

2 See III 115.
Copy III 118. Variants: Cumbray; Ralph de Mesnill'.

I 60   [*c.* 1180–90][1]

GIFT, in free alms, by William de Cumbrai—[salvation clause as in I 57] to Southwick Priory, of half the ½ hide his brother Ralph de Cumbrai gave him for his service and homage from his demesne in *Prevettus*,[2] viz. 1 virgate [location and description as in I 58]. The gift was made in the presence, and with the assent, of William's lord and brother, Ralph. The charter was brought to the high altar and William was accepted into fraternity. Witnesses: Ralph de Mesn'; Matthew de Scur'; Roger de Scur'; Robert de Mesn'; Gilbert de Basevilla; William de Bera; Alexander de Burh'; Reginald and Richard de Denem'; Peter de Katering'; Adam de Henton'; Gilbert Oin; Roger de Menes'; Hiredman.

1 Dating evidence as for I 57. This charter is similar to I 57, but has different witnesses.

2 See III 115.

Copy III 121. Variants: Ralph de Meisenill'; Matthew de Scuris.

I 61 [*c.* 1185, before 1194][1]

GIFT, in free alms, by John de Gisorz—for the salvation of himself, his wife and all his friends—to Southwick Priory, of a messuage in his vill [fo. 10ᵛ] of Portsmouth (*in villa mea de Portesmue*) for repairing the chapel of St Thomas at Portsmouth. The messuage will be 4 perches wide and the same in length as other messuages. He has granted also to the priory 4 messuages, similar in size to neighbouring messuages, which will be held in perpetuity from him and his heirs for an annual rent of 4s., i.e. 12d. from each messuage, at Michaelmas, for all service. Witnesses: Baldwin Wac; William de Aubenni; Ralph le Bret; William le Bigot; Ralph de Breucurt'; Payne (Pagan) de Portesia; Adam, son of Payne; Henry de Burh'; Richard, son of Daniel; John de Possebroc; Gilbert de Kerebrige; Gilbert Sellarius; Roger de Monte Chanisi; Walter Clericus.

1 The chapel built in honour of Thomas Becket was probably erected soon after 1180 by Southwick Priory with the encouragement of Richard of Ilchester, Bishop of Winchester 1174–88 (I 94). In 1186 Pope Urban III included the church of Portsea and its chapel in a list of the priory's possessions over which he extended his protection (I 87). John de Gisors had donated the site (I 116), and his gift for repairing the chapel was probably made not long after its completion, and before he forfeited his English lands in 1194. For a discussion of the role of John de Gisors as the founder of Portsmouth, see M. Hoad, "The Origins of Portsmouth", pp. 18–20.

Copy III 205. Variant: Gisors.

Copy Win. Coll. Muniments 15246, fo. 11ᵛ. Variant: Portesmuth'.

I 62 [Before 1195, *c.* 1187–95][1]

GRANT in free alms, by Thomas de Windlesor'—for the soul of his lord and father, Gervase, who is buried at Southwick; and for his own salvation and that of Lady Avis (*Auica*), his mother, and Agnes, his wife, all of whom have chosen to be buried there; and for the souls of all their lords, heirs, kindred and friends—to Southwick Priory, of the whole tithe of all his demesne of Soberton (*Subertona*), both of corn and of sheep, pigs, cheese, wool and all other things annually tithable there (*de omnibus aliis rebus que mihi siue heredibus meis ibidem decimande renovantur per annum*). Both Thomas' father and his ancestors, from the time of the conquest of England, have always contributed this tithe to whomsoever they wished, when those who had it before ceased to have it (*cum eam qui prius possederant desinerent possidere*). Witnesses: Roger Capellanus; Henry de Burh'; Roger de Muntchanisi; Thomas de Sancta Maria son of Roger; Herbert de Scaldeden'; Turstan; William Waleis; Walter Simplex; Alfred; William Gardin'.

1 Gervase, Thomas and their wives had already in c. 1183-7 granted to the priory
their bodies for burial and a tenement in Soberton (I 33, 34). This grant of tithes
was made by Thomas after his father's death, but before 1195, when Godfrey de
Lucy, Bishop of Winchester, presided over the settlement of a dispute between
the priory and the vicar of Meonstoke over the tithes (III 135). In 1212 Thomas
was holding 10 marks' worth of land in Soberton by serjeanty (*Book of Fees* I,
p. 76).
Copy III 314. Variant: Wyndeshore.
Copy III 315. Variant: de Burhunt'.

I 63   [1180–93][1]

GRANT, in free alms, by William de Humeto [rubric, de Hum'], King's
Constable—for the soul of his wife, Lucy, and the salvation of himself
and all his ancestors and successors—to Southwick Priory, of the advow-
son of the church of Boarhunt (*Burh'*) with all appurtenances. Witnesses:
Jordan de Hum', Richard de Hum', William de Sai, Henry de Hum',
sons of the donor (*filiis meis*); Henry de Similli; William, his brother;
Robert de Haia; Ralph Capellanus; Ralph de Agnis; Jordan de Mesn';
Fulk (*Fulco*) Dacus; Gilbert de Valle; Oratius Pincerna; Geoffrey
Pincerna;[2] Peter and Hugh de Basevill'; William Clericus;[3] William de
Capella; Henry de Cormort.

1 William de Hommet succeeded his father, Richard, as Constable of Normandy
in 1180. If the grant was made after Lucy's death, it was probably later than
1184 (I 73 n. 1). On 4 October 1193, Godfrey de Lucy, Bishop of Winchester,
inspected and confirmed William's charter giving the church of St. Nicholas, West
Boarhunt, to Southwick Priory (I 141). See also I 140, 64, 80.

2 This name is in the lefthand margin, immediately alongside those of Peter and
Hugh de Basevill'.

3 The names of the last 3 witnesses are written downwards on the extreme lefthand
edge of the folio. Obviously the scribe had omitted some names in error. Cf.
below copy 4M53/B7.
Copy III 47. Variants: Humet'; Burhunt.
Copy III 48. Variants: Humet'; Borhunt.
Copy in H.R.O. 4M53/B7, p. 1. Variants: Humet'; Burhunt'; Say; Haya; Jordan
de Meisvill'; Datus; Orato Orato [*sic*] Pincerna; Geoffrey Pincerva; [all 19 witnesses
are given as in I 63, but the name William Clericus is written between that of
Peter de Basevill' and Hugh de Basevill'].

I 64   [1186–1200][1]

NOTIFICATION by H., Abbot of Sées (*Sagiensis*),[2] of an amicable
agreement made between his abbey and Southwick Priory concerning the
church of Boarhunt (*Burh'*), said by the priory to belong to it by right.
Having sought the truth, with the help of religious and prudent men,
and being inspired by fraternal charity, the abbey, with the consent of
its whole chapter, has renounced entirely its rights in the aforesaid church
in favour of the priory. The priory and abbey have joined in a mutual

and perpetual compact to take care of each other's interests, both in spiritualities and temporalities (*Et prescriptos canonicos Suwic' conventui nostro sub mutua et perpetua fraterne caritatis inter nos confederatione tam in spiritualibus quam in temporalibus associavimus*). The priory will celebrate divine service (*servicium facient spirituale*) for the monks of the abbey, professed and deceased, and the monks likewise for the [fo. 11] canons of the priory. Witnesses: Hugh, Bishop of Lincoln; William de Hum'; Richard de Hum', his son; Jordan de Hum'; William de Sai; Henry de Hum'; Henry de Similli; William, his brother; Walkelin, chaplain to the Bishop of Lincoln; Ralph Capellanus; Geoffrey de Sancto Edwardo; Geoffrey de Lichelad'; M. William Medicus; Ralph Hirdman; Thomas de Porc'.

1 Hugh of Avallon was consecrated Bishop of Lincoln on 21 September 1186, and died on 16 November 1200.

2 Henry de Bracqueville occurs as Abbot of Sées between 1185 and 1210 (*Gallia Christiana* XI, p. 721). See also I 63, 80, 140; III 102.

I 65 [*c*.1185–90][1]

GIFT, in free alms, by William de Hum', King's Constable—for the salvation of his soul and those of his wife, Lucy, their sons and daughters, and all their predecessors and successors—to Southwick Priory, of the whole tenement given to William de Warda for his service from the fee of Drayton (*Draiton'*),[2] for which he owed an annual rent of 3s. The gift was made at the request, and with the consent, of William de Warda. Witnesses: Richard de Hum'; William de Sai; Henry de Hum'; Baldwin Wac; William de Montignis; Ralph de Agnis; William le Moine; Ralph Capellanus; Oratius Pincerna; Peter de Basevill'; Gilbert de Valle; William de Capella.

1 William de Hommet succeeded his father as Constable of Normandy in 1180. His wife, Lucy, had died before the end of Henry II's reign (I 71), but was still alive in 1184 (I 73 n.1). The rent from William de Warda's tenement was part of the gift made by William de Hommet to the priory, to provide a perpetual light before the crucifix above his wife's tomb (I 76).

2 Drayton in Farlington.
Copy III 52. Variants: Humet'; de Saieo.

I 66 [*c*. 1185–92, or 1195][1]

GIFT, in free alms, by William de Hum'—for the soul of his wife, Lucy, and the salvation of himself, their children, and all their ancestors and kindred—to Southwick Priory, of all that land of Ketton (*Ketena*), [Rutland], which Ralph de Agnis held of him, and from which Ralph received 5 marks' annual rent.[2] He surrendered it to William with all appurtenances, except ½ mark's rent which he had given with William's consent to the monks of Aunay (*Alnetus*), [Calvados, Normandy], and another ½ mark to the nuns of the church of St Michael, Stamford (*Stanf*'), [Lincs].[3] Witnesses: John, Archbishop of Dublin (*Dubil*');[4] William, Abbot of Durford (*Dureford*'), [Sussex]; T., Abbot of Croxden (*Crokedene*), [Staffordshire];[6] Jordan de Hum'; Ralph de Mesnill'; William de Pirov; Geoffrey de Mesn'; Ralph de Agnis; Bartholomew de Mortuo Mari; Geoffrey de Auci; Hugh de Cardunvill'; William de la Faleise; Alexander de Burh'; Reginald and Richard de Denemede; German Clericus; William de Grafton', clerk; Henry Pigun; Roger de Montch'; Thomas de Sancta Maria; Alexander de Bera.

1 The land at Ketton was given to the priory for the celebration of the anniversary of William de Hommet's wife, Lucy, who had died before the end of Henry II's reign, probaly after 1184 (I 76, 71, 73 n. 1). William, Abbot of Durford, was elected c. 1183 (Knowles *Heads of Religious Houses* p. 195). Probably the fourth witness, Jordan, is the brother of William de Hommet, and he may be identified with the Constable of Sées of the same name, who died in 1192 (Powicke *Loss of Normandy* p. 336). Ralph de Mesnill' had died by 1195 (*PR 7 Richard I* p. 208).

2 See I 69.

3 See I 67–72, 76, 77.

4 John Cumin was consecrated Archbishop of Dublin in March 1182, and died c. November 1212.

5 The first abbot of Croxden, Thomas of Woodstock, held office from 1178 to 1229 (Knowles, *op. cit.*, p. 131).

I 67   [c. 1185–92 or 1195][1]

EXCHANGE between Ralph de Agnis and his lord, William de Hum', of the whole tenement given to Ralph by William in the vill of Ketton (*Ketena*), [Rutland], except ½ mark's worth of rent in lands, men and all appurtenances which Ralph gave with William's consent to the monks of Aunay (*Alnetus*), [Calvados, Normandy], and a similar ½ mark's worth to the nuns of the church of St Michael, Stamford (*Stanf*'), [Lincs]. Ralph voluntarily surrendered to William whatever right he and his heirs had in their tenement at Ketton, saving the aforesaid alms (*elemosina*) given to the monks and nuns, and William—for the souls of his wife, Lady Lucy, and all his ancestors and children—gave it, in free alms, to Southwick Priory, in Ralph's presence and with his consent. Witnesses: Jordan de Hum'; Ralph de Mesn'; Odo Pincerna; Jordan de Mesn'; Robert de Mesn'; Peter de Aupegart; William Clericus of Hambledon (*Hameledon*'); German Clericus; Thomas de Bera; Adam de Tigehale; Walter Clericus; Roger de Montech'; Thomas de Sancta Maria.

1 See dating evidence for I 66. See also I 68–72, 76, 77.
Copy III 67. Variants: Stamford'; de Humet'; de Meisenill'.

I 68 [*c.* 1185–92 or 1195][1]

[fo. 11ᵛ] RELEASE and EXCHANGE between Ralph de Agnis and his lord, William de Hum', of 4 marks' worth of rent at Ketton (*Keten'*), which William had given to Ralph for his service, for £10 worth of rent in the coin of Anjou (*redditus ad Andeg'*) given by William to Ralph at Vienne en Bessin (*Viana*), [Normandy]. Ralph surrendered to his lord the charter he had had, and William—for the salvation of his soul and those of his wife Lucy, his ancestors and successors, and at Ralph's desire and with his consent—gave, in perpetual alms, to Southwick Priory, the aforesaid 4 marks' worth of rent. Ralph confirmed the gift, lest he or any of his heirs should claim any right in the said 4 marks. Witnesses: Richard de Hum', William de Sae, Henry de Hum', sons of William de Humeto (*filii domini mei*); Silvester de Siccavill'; Hugh de Cardonisvilla; Ralph de Mesn'; Gilbert de Valle; Girelmus; Peter de Basevilla; Oratius Pincerna.

1 See dating evidence for I 66. See also I 67, 69–72, 76, 77.

2 See III 41, in which the location is described more fully: *in Normannia apud Vianam in Baiocassinam.*
Copy III 68. Variants: Ketena; Andeng'; de Saye.

I 69

[after 1180, *c.* 1180–5][1]

GIFT by William de Hum', King's Constable, to Ralph de Agnis, for his service, of 5 marks' worth of rent a year at Ketton (*Keten'*), [Rutland], in lands and men. In return Ralph has become liege man (*homo ligius*) of William and his family, saving loyalty to the king (*salva fide domini regis*). Ralph will have the aforesaid 5 marks' worth quit of all exaction, for personal service (*per serivicium sui corporis*), for as long as he lives. After his death, his heirs will hold it from William's heirs for 1/7th of the service of a knight's fee (*per septimam partem servicii feodi unius militis*). Witnesses: Richard de Hum', son of the donor; William de Sae and Henry de Hum', Richard's brothers; Geoffrey de Solign'; William de Montign'; Thomas and Richard de Grocei; John de Solign'; Haculf, his son; Ralph Capellanus; Fulk Dacus.

1 William de Hommet succeeded his father as Constable of Normandy in 1180. His gift to Ralph de Agnis must precede the subsequent exchange arranged between them, and gift of the Ketton rent to Southwick Priory (I 67, 68). See also I 66, 70–72, 76, 77.
Copy III 65. Variants: rubric, Sir William de Humet'; Ketena; de Saio.

I 70   [*c.* 1185–92 or 1195][1]

Charter of Sir W. de Hum' concerning land at Ketton (Keten'), [Rutland], giving details of the rent.

GIFT, in free alms, by William de Hum'—for the salvation of the king and his household (*et suorum*), and for the soul of William's wife Lucy, and the salvation of himself, their children, and all their ancestors and kindred—to Southwick Priory, of all that land from the manor of Ketton, with all appurtenances, which Ralph de Agnis held from William and voluntarily surrendered to him, with the exception of ½ mark's worth of rent Ralph had given, with William's consent, to the monks of Aunay (*Alnetus*), [Calvados, Normandy], and another ½ mark's worth to the nuns of St Michael, Stamford (*Stanf'*), [Lincs]. That William's alms to the priory may be more clearly defined, a description of the tenants and tenements of Ketton follows:—

John de Ghiston holds 1 virgate and ⅓ bovate with meadow from the manor of Ketton for 8s. a year.

William Prepositus pays 7s. 7½d. for a virgate; 2s. 1½d. for land held from the demesne of the aforesaid manor; and 2d. for socage (*de sochagio quod tenet*).

Roger de Ketelhistorp' pays 7s. 7½d. for a virgate, and 2s. 1½d. for demesne land.

Ralph, son of William, Ralph de Ghiston', Gilbert de Camera, and Haco de Ghiston', each hold ½ virgate for 3s. 9¾d., and demesne land for 12¾d.

Ada, widow of Roger, and her sons Stephen and Henry, pay 4s. 6d. for 1⅓ bovates in *Livestorp'*.

For the ½ bovate which Hugh del Hamel held, 20½d. are paid.

Witnesses: J., Archbishop of Dublin (*Dubil'*); William, Abbot of Durford (*Def'*), [Sussex]; Herbert, son of Herbert; Jordan de Hum'; Ralph de Mesn'; William de Pirov; Geoffrey de Mesn'; Ralph de Agnis; Bartholomew de Mortuo Mari; Geoffrey de Auci; Hugh de Cardon'vill'; W. de la Faleise; Alexander de Burh'; Reginald and Richard de D'n'; German Clericus; W. de Graft', clerk; H. Pigun; Ro. de M'ch'; A. de Bera; Thomas de Sancta Maria.

1 For dating evidence see I 66. See also I 67–9, 71, 72, 76, 77.
Copy III 69. Variants: de Humet'; Stamford; Ketehistorp'; Eda, widow of Roger; Dureford. John de Ghiston holds land for 8s. 0¼d. (*viii s. et q'*); omit "a year".

I 71   [*c.* 1185–9][1]

[fo. 12] GIFT, in free alms, by William de Hum'—for the good estate of his lord, King H[enry II], and the king's household (*pro statu et incolumitate domini mei regis H' et suorum*), and for his own salvation and for the souls of his wife Lucy, and all their ancestors and kindred— to Southwick Priory, of a bovate of land in the manor of Ketton

(*Ketena*), [Rutland], which Stephen, son of Roger, holds for 3s. 9½d. a year;[2] and land from the demesne for which he pays 10½d. a year. This 4s. 8d. William has attorned (*attornavi*) to the priory, with 2s. worth of rent which he gave them in the manor of Boarhunt (*Burhunt*),[2] to make up ½ mark to provide a light each night before the crucifix in the priory's church on the tomb of his wife, Lucy, and to provide candles for the daily service which will be held for her soul in the aforesaid church by one of the brothers in perpetuity. Witnesses: J., Archbishop of Dublin (*Dubil'*);[1] W., Abbot of Durford (*Def'*), [Sussex]; Herbert, son of Herbert; Jordan de Hum'; Ralph de Mesn'; William de Pirov; Geoffrey de Mesn'; Ralph de Agn'; Bartholomew de Mortuo Mari; Geoffrey de Auci; Hugh de Cardon'vill'; William de Faleisa; Alexander de Burh'; Reginald and Richard de Denemed'; German Clericus; William de Grafton', clerk; H. Pigun; Roger de Montech'; Alexander de Bera; Thomas de Sancta Maria.

1 William, Abbot of Durford, was elected *c.* 1183 (Knowles *Heads of Religious Houses* p. 195). The gift was evidently made during the reign of Henry II, and so before 1189. The first witness, John Cumin, was elected Archbishop of Dublin in 1181, consecrated in 1182, and died in 1212. This charter provides evidence that Lucy de Hommet had died before 1189. See also I 73 n. 1.

2 See I 39.
Copy III 66. Variant: Dereford.

I 72   [*c.* 1185–9][1]

Those present at Stamford (*Stanfordia*), [Lincs], on the feast of St Peter in chains, when seisin was given of land at Ketton (*Keten'*), [Rutland]:

Hugh de Boebi, steward of Sir Baldwin Wac; Richard de Estonia; Roger Barre; William de Marisco; David, son of Sweyn (*Suanus*), burgess of Stamford (*Stanf'*); Gilbert, chaplain of St Martin in Stamford; Adam Janitor; Landemer; Henry Pigun'; Thomas de Sancta Maria; William de Stokeis; Nicholas de Ripov; Robert le Plaur; Robert, son of Isabel; Richard Cocus.

Tenants of Southwick Priory in the vill of Ketton:
[List of tenants and description of holdings and rents as in I 70. Variants: John de Ghiston is said to hold his virgate "freely"; this holding, and those of William Prepositus, Ralph de Ghiston' and Hacho de Ghiston are said to be "in Ghiston"; Ralph, son of William, and Gilbert de Camera each hold a ½ virgate "in Ketton"; Hugh del Hamel; add: "Stephen, son of Roger, holds a bovate in Ketton for 3s. 9½d. and demesne land for 10½d., and these rents are part of the ½ mark given to provide a light before the crucifix".]

1 Dating evidence as for I 71 to which these two entries are appended, with separate rubrics, to provide supplementary information. (Cf. I 79).

I 73   [*c.* 1185–95, possibly 1188–92][1]

GRANT, in free alms, as far as he is able (*quantum ad me pertinet*), by
Robert de Bera, clerk—for the souls of his lord, Richard de Hum', who
gave him the land for his service, and Richard's wife, Agnes, and of
Robert's lady, Lucy, wife of William de Hum', who is buried at South-
wick; and for the salvation of William, his lord, and of himself and all
his lords and friends—to Southwick Priory, of 3s. worth of land which
Godwin Orpedeman holds adjoining the house of Alexander de Burh'.[2]
Robert has moreover given himself to the priory (*ego autem me ipsum
predicte ecclesie dedi*). Witnesses: William, Abbot of Durford (*Duref'*),
(Sussex]; Brother Vuiettus; Robert Capellanus of Petersfield (*Peteresfeld'*)
Thomas de Ho; Lewis (*Lodovicus*) de Bera; Roger de Montechan'.

1 William was elected Abbot of Durford *c.* 1183 (Knowles *Heads of Religious
Houses* p. 195). This grant was made after the death of Lucy de Hommet, which
is likely to have occured after 1184 (the date suggested for a charter she witnessed
(*Cal. Docs. in France* no. 779, p. 282)); but was certainly not later than 1189
(I 71), and it was probably made after the death of Richard de Hommet. According
to Robert de Torigni this occured in 1179 (*Recueil des Actes de Henri II* Introduction, p. 430), but Eyton states that Richard was still alive in September 1180,
having resigned the office of Constable of Normandy, probably the previous July,
and having retired to the Abbey of Aunay, where he became a monk (*Itinerary
of Henry II* pp. 233, 236). The date of his death is given in the Regesta as 1188
(*Regesta* III, p. xxxvii). Of the witnesses to William de Hommet's confirmation
of Robert de Bera's grant (I 74, 75), Jordan de Hommet may have died in 1192,
and Ralph de Mesnil had died by 1195 (I 66, note 1).

2 The land was in the manor of Boarhunt (I 76).
Copy III 382. Variants: Humet'; Dureford'; Brother Umatus.

I 74   [*c.* 1185–95, possibly 1188–92][1]

CONFIRMATION by William de Hum', King's Constable—for the salvation and safety (*incolumitas*) of the king, and of himself and all his
lords and friends; and for the souls of his father Richard de Hum', his
mother Agnes, his wife Lucy, and all their ancestors and children—to
Southwick Priory, of the gift, in free alms, made to it by Robert de Bera,
clerk, of land which Godwin Orpedeman held of him,[2] together with
[fo. 12ᵛ] Godwin himself and his messuage, which adjoins the land of
Alexander de Burh'. Richard de Hum' gave Robert the land for his
service, and William confirms that the priory is to hold it in free alms,
as Robert's charter testifies.[3] Witnesses: Thomas, Abbot of Valle Sancte
Marie; William, Abbot of Durford (*Deford'*), [Sussex]; Jordan de Hum',
the donor's brother (*frater meus*); Robert de la Haie; Ralph de Mesnill';
Ralph de Agnis; Odo Pincerna; Jordan de Mesn'; Peter de Aupegard';
German, son of Robert de Ranvill'; Thomas de Bera; Adam de Tigehal'.

1 For dating evidence see I 73, note 1.

2 The land pertained to the manor of Boarhunt (I 76).

3 I 73.

Copy III 59. Variants: Humet'; Borhunt; Dureford.

I 75 [*c.* 1185-95, possibly 1188-92][1]

CONFIRMATION by William de Humet', King's Constable—for the salvation of his soul and the relief of the souls (*pro remedio animarum*) of his father and mother and his wife, Lucy—to Southwick Priory, of the gift, in free alms, made by Robert de Bera, clerk to his father and himself, of all the land which Godwin Orpedeman held from William's father, Richard, and from Robert, together with Godwin himself, and the messuage adjoining the croft of Alexander de Burh' next to Alexander's house on the north (*proximo ex aquiloni' parte mansionis eiusdem Alex'*), with all appurtenances. Witnesses; Thomas, Abbot of Valle Sancte Marie; W., Abbot of Durford (*Duref'*), [Sussex]; Jordan de Hum', the donor's brother (*frater meus*); Ralph de Mesn'; Ralph de Agnis; Odo Pincerna; Jordan de Mesn'; Peter de Aupegard'; German, son of Robert Ranvill'; Thomas de Bera; Adam de Tigebaul.

1 For dating evidence see I 73, note 1. The above charter is another version of I 74.

Copy III 45. Variant: Dureford'.

I 76 [*c* 1190][1]

CONFIRMATION, in free alms, by William de Hum', King's Constable—for the salvation of his soul and those of his wife Lucy, their sons and daughters, and all their ancestors and successors—to Southwick Priory, of the church of Boarhunt (*Burh'*) and all appurtenances, for the solemn celebration of Lucy's anniversary in Southwick church in perpetuity.[2] Also all that land with appurtenances in his manor of Ketton (*Ketena*), [Rutland], which Ralph de Agnis held of him and voluntarily surrendered, except for ½ mark's worth of rent which Ralph had given with his consent to the monks of Aunay (*Alnetus*), [Calvados, Normandy], and another ½ mark's worth to the nuns of St Michael, Stamford (*Stanf'*), [Lincs].[3] Also the land which Stephen, son of Roger, held from the manor of Ketton for 4s. 8d. rent a year,[4] the land which Ralph Crabbe held in the manor of Boarhunt for 3s [*sic*][5] rent a year; and the land which William de Warda held from the manor of Drayton (*Draiton'*) for 3s. rent a year.[6] These rents are to provide a light in perpetuity before the crucifix above the tomb of the donor's wife, Lucy, in Southwick church, i.e., a lamp burning day and night, and candles for use while mass is celebrated daily for her soul by one of the brothers. Confirmation also of the gift to the priory by Robert de Bera, clerk to

William's father and himself—for the salvation of his soul—of all the land Godwin Orped' held from the manor of Boarhunt; land which Richard de Hum' gave to Robert for his service.[7] Confirmation also to [fo. 13] the priory of all land Ranulf Fresel held from the manor of Drayton, which it obtained from the nuns of Stamford in exchange for ½ mark's worth of rent which William's wife, Lucy, had given it in alms, at Stamford.[8] Witnesses: William, Abbot of Saint-Lo (*Sanctus Laudus*), [Manche, Normandy]; Richard de Hum'; Jordan de Hum'; William de Sai; Henry de Hum'; Henry de Similli; William, his brother; Robert de Haia; Ralph de Agn'; Ralph Capellanus; Gilbert de Valle; Oratio Pincerna; Geoffrey Pincerna; Peter de Besevill'; Hugh de Besevill'.

1 This charter is a confirmation of the various gifts to the priory made by William de Hommet and with his consent; it must therefore be of a later date than the charters which convey each individual gift. The similar confirmation of those gifts which was granted to the priory by William's son, Richard, was probably witnessed by William's brother, Jordan, who may have died in 1192 (I 77; I 66, note 1). See also the inspeximus and confirmation issued in 1193 by Godfrey, Bishop of Winchester (I 141); and another by Hugh, Bishop of Lincoln 1186–1200 (I 146).

2 See I 63, 64, 140, 141.

3 See I 66–70.

4 See I 71.

5 Probably a scribal error for 2s. (see rubric to I 39; I 77; III 41). The copy at III 40 has 2s. (*duos solidos*), but III 51 has 3s. (*tres solidos*).

6 See I 65.

7 See I 73–75.

8 See Appendix I; I 145; III 357, 94.
Copy III 40. Variants; Humeto, Humet'; add, "the advowson" of the church of Boarhunt (*Burhunt'*) "and that church"; Stanforde; Draitona; Godwin Horpedema'; witnesses: Richard de Hum'; William Saie; and many others. See also note 5 above.
Copy III 51. Variants: Humeto, Humet'; Burhunt', Borhunt'; Stamford'; Drayton'; Horpedema'; Ralph (*Rad'*) Fresel; first three witnesses as in I 76, "and many others". See also note 5 above.

I 77 [*c.* 1190][1]

CONFIRMATION, in free alms, by Richard de Hum', son of William de Hum', King's Constable—for the salvation of himself and his father, and the souls of his mother Lucy, and all his ancestors and successors—to Southwick Priory, of all the gifts his father gave them, viz. the church of Boarhunt (*Burh'*) with all appurtenances; 4 marks' worth of rent in land and men at Ketton (*Ketena*), [Rutland]; also land which Stephen, son of Roger, held in the manor of Ketton for 4s. 8d. annual rent; land which Ralph Crabbe held in the manor of Boarhunt (*Burhunta*) for 2s. [*sic*] annual rent; and land which William de Warda held in the manor of Drayton (*Draiton'*) for 3s. annual rent; these rents having been assigned by his father for the provision in perpetuity of a light before the crucifix above his mother's tomb. Also the gift of land in the manor of Boarhunt, made by Robert de Bera, clerk, with the consent of William de Hum'; and the land which Ranulf Fresel held in the manor of Drayton and which the priory obtained from the nuns of Stamford (*Stanf'*), [Lincs], in exchange for ½ mark's worth of rent, which Lucy, Richard's mother, had given them at Stamford. Witnesses: William de Sai, Henry de Hum', and Thomas, the donor's brothers (*fratri mei*); Jordan de Hum'; Henry de Similli; William, his brother; Ralph de Agn'; William de Redu's.

1 See I 76 and notes.
Copy III 60. Variants: Borhunt'; Ralph de Bera; Ralph Fresel; Stamford'; de Saie; de Humet'.

I 78   [1182–95, c. 1190][1]

GIFT, in free alms, by Robert de Novo Burgo—for his salvation and for the soul of his friend, Lucy, of pious memory—to Southwick Priory, of a virgate in Cottesmore (*Cotthesmhora*), [Rutland], from his demesne, viz. the third-best virgate out of the five he has there in demesne. Witnesses: J., Archbishop of Dublin (*Dubil'*); Abbot of Durford (*Def'*), [Sussex]; Abbot of Croxden (*Crokedena*), [Staffs]; William de Hum'; Jordan de Hum'; Ralph de Mesn'; William de Pirov; Geoffrey de Mesn'; Ralph de Agn'; Bartholomew de Mortuo Mari; Geoffrey de Auci; Hugh de Cardon'vill'; Herbert, son of Herbert; William de Faleisa; Peter de Aupegart'.

1 Lucy, wife of William de Hommet, for whose soul this gift was made, had died by 1189 (I 71 and note). The witness John Cumin was consecrated Archbishop of Dublin in 1182 and died *c.* 1212. William occurs as Abbot of Durford *c.* 1183–99 (Knowles *Heads of Religious Houses* p. 195).
Thomas of Woodstock was Abbot of Croxden from 1178 to 1229 (Knowles, *op. cit.*, p. 131). If the fifth witness is Jordan, brother of William de Hommet, he may have died by 1192, and the next witness, Ralph de Mesnil, had died by 1195 (I 66, note 1).
Copy III 74. Variants: Cotesmore; Dureford'; omit provision specifying the third-best virgate.

I 79   [1182–95, c. 1190][1]

Those present when seisin was given at Cottesmore (Cotthesmhora), [Rutland]:

John, son of Girold; William, parson of the church of Cottesmore; Thomas Clericus, his son; Terricus Prepositus; Simon de Gretham, the countess' serjeant; Henry, son of Gilbert; Oliver, son of Hugh; Pigot; Osbert, son of Childiung'; Gamel Rufus.

That virgate which Robert de Novo Burgo gave at Cottesmore is divided into 2 bovates, one held by Ralph, son of Ailwin, and the other by Blacwin.

1 Dating evidence as for I 78, to which this entry is appended with a separate rubric. (Cf. I 72).

I 80   [c. 1185-1200]

[fo. 13ᵛ] NOTIFICATION by H., Abbot of Sées (*Sag'*) to R., Archdeacon of Winchester, of the amicable agreement reached with Southwick Priory over Boarhunt church [as in I 64. No witness list. Ends with the word "*Valete*"].[1]

1 See I 64, note 1. The Abbot of Sées was probably Henry de Bracqueville, who occured c. 1185-1210 (I 64, note 2); and the Archdeacon of Winchester, Roger I, who occured from before 1181 to 1205, and died in 1207 or 1208 (*Fasti* II, p. 92).

I 81   [Before 1195, c. 1190][1]

GIFT, in free alms, by Ralph de Mesn' [rubric: Mesnill']—for his salvation and for the souls of his lady, Lucy de Hum', and his brother, Henry, and for the salvation of all his ancestors and successors—to Southwick Priory, of 10 acres at Soberton (*Suberton'*) which Randolph de Lega held. Witnesses: Robert, the donor's son; Jordan de Mesn'; Geoffrey de Mesn'; Ham' de Midlingeton'; Thomas de Ho; Ralph de Eth're; Philip Walensi; Henry de Burh'; Roger de Monte Chan'; John Cocus; Hugh Anglicus.

1 Lucy de Hommet had died before 1189, possibly between 1184 and 1189 (I 71, n. 1; 73 n. 1). In 1195 Ralph de Mesnill's son, Robert, paid 2 marks to succeed to his inheritance in Hampshire (*PR 7 Richard I* p. 208).
Copy III 321. Variants: rubric: de Mesenill'; de Mednille; de Humet'; Ralph de la Lye [for Randolph de Lega]; de Meisnille.

I 82   [Before 1195, c. 1190][1]

CONFIRMATION by Robert de Mesn'—for his salvation and that of all his ancestors and successors—to Southwick Priory, of the gift made by his father, Ralph de Mesn'—for his salvation and the souls of his lady, Lucy de Hum', and Henry de Mesn', Robert's uncle—viz. 10 acres at Soberton (*Suberton'*) which Randolph de Lega held. Witnesses: Jordan de Mesn'; Geoffrey de Mesn'; Ham' de Midlinget'; Thomas de Ho; Ralph Eth're; Philip Walensi; Henry de Burh'; Roger de Monte Chanisi; John Cocus; Hugh Anglicus; Pincewerra.

1 See I 81 and note 1.
Copy III 322. Variants: de Medenille, Mednille; de Humet'; Randolph de la Lye
[for de Lega]; de Mednill'.

I 83 [*c.* 1184–1205][1]

CONCESSION by Roger, Archdeacon of Winchester, to Guy, Prior of
Southwick, and the priory, that all their churches and chapels may be
quit of liability for gifts, which, by ancient custom, used to be made to
the archdeacon at Christmas and Easter: viz. from the churches of
Portchester (*Porc'*), Portsea (*Portesia*), West Boarhunt (*Westburhunt*),
Nutley (*Nuthleia*), Candover (*Candeura*), and Wanstead (*Wanested'*);
from the chapels of Empshott (*Ymbesiet'*), Wymering (*Wimering*), and
Walesworth (*Waleswrth*); and from the church of Shalden (*Scaldeden'*)
in the event of its being in their hands. Also, by virtue of its monastic
status (*gratia loci religiosi*), the parish church of Southwick will be quit
of synodal dues and the aforesaid gifts. Indulgence is granted, as far as
it lies within Roger's power to do so (*indulsi etiam quantum ad me
spectat*), to the canons of Southwick to preach freely in their parish of
Portsea, and to accept oblations both on sea and land. Consideration,
12s. a year, viz 6s. at Michaelmas and 6s. at Easter. This concession is
made, saving Roger's right to hospitality and to the provision of hospitality (*salvis hospiciis meis et hospiciorum procurationibus*), and saving
other customs in the aforesaid churches. Witnesses: Audoenus Decanus;
M. John de Hechfeld'; Ralph Clericus; William Capellanus; M. Simon
Medicus; Richard Camerarius; Henry de Heling'; Roger de Monte Chan',
clerk; Walter Clericus; Richard de Limesia; William Capellanus, the
archdeacon's chaplain; Henry de Burh'; Henry de Eling'.

1 Guy first occurs as Prior of Southwick in 1185 (I 91). Roger occurs as Archdeacon of Winchester before 1181, and lastly in 1205. He died 1207–8 (*Fasti* II,
p. 92).

[fo. 14] **Here begin copies of the priory's papal privileges.**

I 84 [June 14–October 12 1147][1]

First privilege from Eugenius in the time of Prior Anselm (*Antelmus*)
concerning the church of Portchester (*Porcestr'*) and its possessions.[2]

PRIVILEGE from Pope Eugenius [III] to Prior Anselm and the brethren
of the church of St Mary, Portchester (*Porcestria*), extending his protection, at their request, to their church and its possessions and goods justly
and canonically owned at present, or acquired in the future, including:
the church of St Mary, Portchester, with all appurtenances; the manor
of Candover (*Candeura*), which William de Pontearch', with the consent

of his wife, Constance, and his sons, gave his demesne, together with Southwick and 1 hide in Applestead (*Appelsted'*) which William bought from Ivo Pandulfus, with the consent of King Henry, for the use of the church.[3] Injunction against anyone disturbing the priory's possessions, and blessings on all observing justice there. Amen.

[Auxerre][4]

1 This date is given by Holtzmann, and the privilege is printed in Latin, collating Madden's transcript of III 11 and 29, in *Papsturkunden in England* III, no. 72.

2 Comparison of I 84 with I 85 shows that between the issue of these two privileges the priory had moved from Portchester to Southwick.

3 See I 1.

4 Place of issue from III 29.
Copy III 11. Variants: Pontearc'; Apelstede; Pondulfus. [Amen followed by:] Dat etc.
Copy III 29. Variant: [add place of issue:] Altisiodori [Auxerre].

I 85 [July 1151–October 1152][1]

Privilege from the same [pope] in the time of the same [prior], concerning the church of Southwick and its appurtenances.

PRIVILEGE from Pope Eugenius [III] to Prior Anselm and the brethren of the church of St Mary, Southwick,[2] extending his protection, at their request, to their foundation, which follows the rule of the Blessed Augustine, and to their possessions and goods owned at present or acquired in the future, including: the church of Southwick with all appurtenances; the churches of Portchester (*Porcestria*), Wymering (*Wimering*), Candover (*Candeura*), and Shalden (*Scaldedena*);[3] the manor of Candover, which William de Pontearch, with the consent of his wife Constance and his sons, gave from his demesne; Southwick, with woodland, and 1 hide in Applestead (*Apelsteda*), given by William with the [fo. 14ᵛ] consent of King Henry;[4] 1 hide in Boarhunt (*Burhunta*) and 1 hide in Westboarhunt (*Westburhunta*); 1 virgate given by Herbert, son of Anscatillus, with the consent of his heir. Burial will be allowed freely at Southwick of those who choose to be buried there, unless prevented by excommunication or interdict, saving the rights of the mother church. The liberties and reasonable customs hitherto enjoyed by the priory are confirmed. The prior and his successors are to prevent anyone from being appointed there by cunning or violence, but only those by common consent of the brethen or of the wiser among them, as provided for by the Augustinian rule. Injunction against anyone disturbing the priory or its possessions, and blessing on all observing justice there. Amen.

[Segni][5]

1 The date is given by Holtzmann, and the privilege is printed in Latin, collating Madden's transcript of III 26 with an original fragment from Essex Record Office in which the names of some of the witnesses survive; the spelling is the same as in I 85, except *Wimeringes* and *Appelesteda* (*Papsturkunden in England* III, no. 143).

2 See I 84 note 2.

3 See I 3 and note.

4 See I 1 and note.

5 Place of issue from the copy III 26.
Copy III 26. Variants: Wymerynge; Schalden'; Pontearca; Apelstede; Westborhunt'; Anschatellus. [Amen followed by:] Dat' Singnie, etc.

I 86   [10 October 1162–18 June 1163][1]

PRIVILEGE from Pope Alexander [III] to Prior Walter and Southwick Priory, following the example of his predecessor, Pope Eugenius [III] by extending his protection at their request to them and to their possessions, including: [list as in I 85. Variants: Scalderlaena; de Ponte Arcarum; Appelsteda; Anschetillus. In addition:] the church of Wanstead (*Wanesteda*), the chapels of Widley (*Widelega*), Walesworth (*Waleswrda*), Nutley, (*Nutlega*), Candover Scotland (*Candeura Scudlandi*), and the church of Swindon (*Suindona*) in the bishopric of Salisbury (*Salesburien'*); 2 hides in Fishbourne (*Fisseburna*) given by King Henry;[2] 3 hides in Stubbington (*Stubinton'*) given by Alfred de Herierd, with the consent of his lord, Richard de Humez; in the same vill,[3] a virgate given by Lady de Croftuna; lands and houses in the city of Winchester given [fo. 15] by Turstin Clericus[4] and by William, son of Roger[5]—as shown in their charters. [Provisions concerning burials, liberties and elections, and final injunction and blessing as in I 85]

[Tours][6]

1 The date is given by Holtzmann, and the copy of this privilege found at III 10 is printed in Latin in *Papsturkunden in England* III, no. 143.

2 See I 2, III 99, 989.

3 Probably this was Stubbington in Titchfield hundred, of which Crofton was part (see I 41). The 3 hides given by Alfred de Herierd may well be those which at the time of the Domesday Survey were included among the lands of Hugh de Port (*Domesday Book: Hampshire* ed J. Munby (Chichester, 1982) 23, 15). See however I 17 n.2.

4 See III 565.

5 See III 569.

6 Place of issue from the copy III 10.
Copy III 10. Variants: Wymering'; Schalden; Wansted; Wydelyeg'; Walesworth'; Nuthlye; Swyndon'; Pontearc'; Apelstede; Fyscheborna; de Humet'; Stubynton'; Crofton'. [Conclude with:] Dat' Turon' [Tours] etc.

I 87 [9 February 1186][1]

PRIVILEGE from Pope Urban III to Prior Guy and Southwick Priory, following the example of his predecessor, Pope Alexander,[2] by extending his protection at their request to them and to their possessions, including: the place in which the church of Southwick is situated, with the chapel, vill, wood, land, meadow, waters, mills, roads, paths, and all other appurtenances; the chapels of Wanstead (*Wanesteda*), Walesworth (*Waleswrd'*), Widley (*Wideleia*), and Wymering (*Wimering*) with all their appurtenances; the church of Portchester (*Porcestr'*); the church of Portsea (*Portseia*) with its chapel;[3] the church of Candover (*Candeura*) with the chapel of *Stanebiria*,[4] lands, tithes and all appurtenances; the churches of Nutley (*Nutleia*) and Shalden (*Scaldedena*) and the chapel of Empshott (*Imbeseta*); the church of Swindon with all appurtenances; the manor of Candover, with land, wood, pasture and all appurtenances; the whole ploughland (*cultura*) of Applestead (*Appelsted'*) and whatever belongs to Alexander de Burhunt's fee between the stream (*acqua*) that flows down in front of his gate and the stream which descends below the priory's court westwards towards Reinelm's mill, as Alexander's charter testifies;[5] 1 virgate adjoining *Wadenden'*, which was held by Alwin with messuage, garden, land, and all appurtenances;[6] 1 virgate at Crofton (*Croft'*) which was held by Godwin Fugelere, given by Helewise, Lady of Crofton, her son, Geoffrey, and his heir (*Galfridus filius eius et heres sui*); 1 virgate called *Cumede*, and an adjoining ½ virgate with meadow, [fo. 15ᵛ] marsh, pasture and all appurtenances from the same donors;[7] 1 virgate which was held by Serichius, and an adjoining ½ virgate with appurtenances, which Peter de Cosham and his wife gave to Southwick church at its dedication;[8] and the right, granted by Richard de Denem' at that dedication, to take freely as much stone as necessary from his quarry at Gliddon (*Gleteduna*) for building-works at the priory.[9] No one may presume to extort tithes from newly cultivated land which the priory are tilling with their own hands for food or fodder for their animals. The priory may appoint to (*ponere in*) its parish churches three or four of its brethren, according to the decree of the Lateran Council:[10] to one of whom, if he is suitable, the bishop will commit the cure of souls; and they are to be held responsible to the bishop for spiritualities, and to the priory for temporalities and observance of the Rule (de ordinis observantia).

Right of burial at Southwick is freely granted, for those who choose to be buried there, unless prevented by excommunication or inderdict— saving the rights of those churches to which the bodies of the dead are taken. When there is a general interdict on the land, the priory may celebrate divine office with hushed voice and with closed doors—the excommunicated being excluded—and with the bells silent. Churches, lands or any benefice owned by the priory may not be given to any person, or alienated in any way, without the common consent of the whole chapter, or the greater and wiser part of it. If any alienations are made otherwise, they will be invalid. No new or undue exactions, aids or burdens are to be levied on the priory's churches by archbishops, bishops, archdeacons, deacons, or other ecclesiastics, whether for the dedication of churches or for other ecclesiastical purposes (*pro aliis ecclesiasticis sacramentis*). No one may presume to build a church or oratory within the parishes of the priory's churches without the consent of the bishop of the diocese and the priory, saving the privileges of the Roman church. The religious life of the priory, based on the rule of the Blessed Augustine, and their institutions, commended in writing by their fathers, may not be altered without the advice and consent of the greater and wiser part of the chapter, lest there be detriment to their religious life or their salvation, or to the sound institutions of the fathers. Any canons or lay brethren bound by vows of obedience to the priory are prohibited from standing surety for anyone, or accepting a loan from anyone beyond an amount agreed by the chapter, without the consent and licence of the prior or of the greater and wiser part of the chapter; and if this is presumptuously attempted by anyone, it will be declared invalid by papal authority. The priory is allowed to receive and keep clerics or laymen fleeing from worldly temptations to the monastic life of the priory. Lay brethren and professed canons subject to the priory's rule must not take away any of the priory's possessions without the knowledge and consent of the prior and convent. For the sake of the peace and tranquillity of the priory, no one shall dare commit violence or theft or arson within the priory's enclosures or granges, nor arrest nor kill a man. No one in the priory or its churches may pronounce sentence of excommunication or interdict without manifest and reasonable cause. Injunction against anyone disturbing the priory or its possessions, and blessing etc.

[Verona][1]

1 Date and place of issue are given in the copy III 2, which is printed in Latin by Holtzmann in *Papsturkunden in England* III, no. 379.

2 See I 86, 24; III 3.

3 Probably this was the chapel at Portsmouth which the priory had recently built in honour of St Thomas the Martyr, with the advice and consent of Richard of Ilchester, Bishop of Winchester (I 94). The priory had another chapel in the parish of Portsea, given to it by Warin de Plaiz and dedicated to St Andrew; but this had probably not yet come into its possession, for Godfrey de Lucy, the Bishop of Winchester whom Warin notified of the gift, held that office from 1189 to 1204 (III 394).

4 The chapel of *Stanebiria* in Preston Candover was in the manor that came to be known as la Stevenbury or Horwoods. In the 16th century it appears as Horwoods *alias* Stoniburie (*V C H Hants* III, pp. 373-4). See also III 374, 375.

5 See I 121, 122, 29, 30; also I 25, 28, 120.

6 This tenement in Soberton was given to the priory by Gervase de Windeshor' and his wife, Alice. The gift was confirmed by their son, Thomas, and his wife, Agnes (I 33, 34).

7 See I 41-9.

8 See I 25 and note 5, I 26, 27.

9 See I 25 and note 6.

10 The Lateran Council of 1179 decreed that no monk or canon was to be sent on his own to serve a parish church, but was to be accompanied by other brothers (Mansi, XXII, 244, c. 10).

Copy III 2. Variants: Gwide prior; Wanstede; Walsworthe; Wyidelye; Wymeryng; Scantebiria; Nutlia; Schalden'; Imbeschete; Swyndone; Candeur'; Appulstede; Burhunta; Reynelmus; Wadendon; Godwyn Fugeler; Helewise de Crofton'; [*et heres sui* crossed through and most of following sentence, leaving:] and ½ virgate adjoining Coumede with all their appurtenances [the words *cum omnibus* and *eorumdem* are interlineated, and the alterations appear to have been made by a later 15th century hand]; [reference to Sechirus (Seridius) crossed through, leaving;] 1½ virgates which Peter de Cosham and his wife gave to Southwick church [etc.]; Denemede; Cleddene [for Gleteduna]; [add in conclusion:] Given at Verona (*Veron'*) by the hand of Transmundus, notary of the Holy Roman Church, 5 Ides of February, 4th indiction, A.D. 1185, the first year of the pontificate of Pope Urban III. [Dating by indiction was a practice adopted by Imperial Rome, and in the 12th century was still occasionally used for papal and royal documents. Indictions were calculated in 15-year cycles, beginning in 312. The year 1186 therefore represented the 4th indiction of a cycle (the 59th).]

I 88 [fo. 16–16ᵛ] Copy of I 87. Variants: Scalded'; Imbesite; Suindona; Denemeda; Gleted'.

I 89 Copy of I 24.

I 90 Copy of I 23.

I 91   15 March [1185][1]

[fo. 17] LETTER from Pope Lucius [III] to Prior Guy and Southwick Priory, confirming, at their request, their rightful possession of the chapel of Empshott (*Imbesita*) and the church of Swindon (*Swindona*), which they have acquired canonically through the diocesan bishopric on the representation of the patrons; of 1½ virgates with appurtenances at Stakes (*Frundestaple*), given by P. de Cosham and his wife at the dedication of Southwick church;[2] and of 1 virgate which Fugelere held, 1 virgate called *Cumede*, and another ½ virgate, all of which were the gifts of Helewise de Croftuna and her son, Geoffrey Talebot.[3] Injunction against anyone infringing this confirmation.

Verona (*Veron'*), the Ides of March.

1 The copy of this letter given at III 35 is printed in Latin in *Papsturkunden in England* III, no. 365. Holtzmann gives the date as 22 July 1184–25 November 1185, but as the day and month appear above, an exact date can be given.

2 See I 25 and note 5, I 26, 27.

3 See I 41–9.
Copy III 35. Variants: [omit name of prior]; Ymbeschete; Swyndon'; F. [for Fugelere]; Coumede; Halewysa de Crofton'; [omit date].

I 92   24 December [1185 or 1186]

LETTER from Pope Urban [III][1] to Prior Guy and the convent of
Southwick, informing them that he has taken up their grave complaint
that the archdeacons and deacons, against the decrees of the Lateran
Council,[2] have unashamedly sought to extort money from them for
chrism and other sacraments of the Church, and, as often as the priory
has resisted, have illegally passed sentence of suspension or interdict
against their clergy and churches. He declares that such a sentence is not
binding.

Verona (*Veron'*), 9 Kalends of January.

1 The copies of this letter given at III 4 and 33 are calendared by Holtzmann,
and the pope is idenitified as Urban III (*Papsturkunden in England* III, p. 110).

2 This appears to be a reference to the decrees of the 3rd Lateran Council of
1179 (Mansi, XXII, pp. 219–222, especially caps. 4, 7).
Copies III 4, 33. Variant: [the name of the prior is omitted in each case].

I 93   [*c.* 1185–8][1]

CONFIRMATION, in free alms, by Richard, Bishop of Winchester, to
Prior Guy and the convent of Southwick, at their request, of his
protection for the priory and its possessions, viz: the churches of Portchester (*Porcestria*), Wymering (*Wimering'*), Portsea (*Portesia*), Candover (*Candeura*) with the chapel of *Stanebiria*,[2] Nutley (*Nuthlega*),
Shalden (*Scaldedena*), and Wanstead (*Wanestede*), and the chapels of
Widley (*Wideleia*) and Walesworth (*Waleswrth*); the priory's possession
of these churches and chapels with all appurtenances had previously been
confirmed by Bishop Henry, Richard's predecessor.[3] The priory can
lawfully use all profits and revenues (*fructus et obventiones*) from them
for its upkeep and for the provision of hospitality, saving reasonable
maintenance for the vicars who minister now in those churches and
[fo. 17ᵛ] chapels by authority of (*per*) the bishop's officials, or will do so
in the future by that of his successors. Anathema pronounced upon
anyone attacking or disturbing the said churches and chapels, or any
other lawful possessions of the priory.

1 Prior Guy first occurs in 1185, and Bishop Richard died in December 1188.

2 See I 87, note 4.

3 Henry of Blois, Bishop of Winchester 1129–71 (I 3, 4).
Copy III 943. Variants: Scaldedene; Wanstede; Waleswrd.

I 94   [*c.* 1185–8][1]

CONFIRMATION by Richard, Bishop of Winchester, to Prior Guy and
the convent of Southwick, at their request, of their possession of churches
and chapels confirmed to them by his predecessor, Bishop Henry, viz:

[list as in I 93, with omission of chapel of Stanebiria and addition of the chapel of Candover Scotland (*Candeura Scudlandi*)[2]]. Bishop Richard also confirms them in possession of the chapel of Empshott (*Imbeseta*),[3] the chapel of St James-Without-the-Priory-Gate:[4] and the chapel which, with his advice and consent, they have undertaken to build in their parish of Portsea (*Portesia*), and to dedicate to the Blessed Martyr Thomas;[5] with tithes, oblations, lands, revenues and all other appurtenances belonging to the said churches and chapels. Anathema [as in I 93].

1 See I 93, note 1.

2 See I 13, 14.

3 See I 113.

4 The present parish church of Southwick.

5 This chapel was destined to become the nucleus of the cathedral of Portsmouth. Copy III 947. Marginal note opposite reference to the chapel of St Thomas: "chapel of Portsmouth (*Portusmuth'*)".

I 95   28 February 1254

DECREE of Pope Innocent [IV] concerning hardship caused by procurations incurred by reason of visitations.[1] Having received many complaints, and wishing to remove the cause of grievances, the pope has decreed that archbishops, bishops, archdeacons and other prelates carrying out visitations in person are to receive moderate procurations in the way of food and other necessities, at a cost not exceeding 4 marks for any visitation. The expenses will be calculated, within that total, in accordance with the numbers in the retinue, as limited by the Lateran Council in relation to the higher or lower rank of the prelates. But in the case of more fertile and better supplied places where there are less rents or ecclesiastical revenues, less shall be spent on procurations in accordance with the greater abundance of necessaries and shortage of revenues (*Sed in locis in quibus maior fertilitas vel copia rerum habetur, et ubi minores[2] sunt redditus seu ecclesiastice facultates, minus secundum ampliorem necessariorum ubertatem et parvitatem proventuum in ipsis, procurationibus expendatur*). The prelates will restore any excess to the use of the churches from which it has been obtained, and those who exacted it will be obliged to pay out of their own resources double that amount to the poor, and may be mulcted further if this seems fitting. Other regulations known to be laid down in relation to visitations are not to be affected. Injunction against anyone infringing this decree.

Lateran, 2 Kalends of March, 11th
year of Innocent's pontificate.

1 This decree follows a succession of attempts to set limits to the demands which could be made for procurations. The Third Lateran Council of 1197 to which reference appears to be made in the text had stipulated the numbers of mounted followers who might accompany the respective ranks of visiting prelate, ranging from forty or fifty for an archbishop to two for a deacon. This had not prevented

complaints against undue exactions, and successive papal attempts to meet these grievances. In 1246 Innocent IV had ordered that procurations be restricted to payments in kind; in 1252, following a dispute arising from Archbishop Boniface's visitation of the province of Canterbury in 1250, he had written to the bishops of Lincoln, London and Wells laying down a maximum of 4 marks. The present decree gives this letter universal application (See C. R. Cheney *Episcopal Visitation of Monasteries in the 13th Century* (Manchester, 1931) pp. 104–8; *Annales Monastici* I, pp. 300–2; *Matthaei Parisiensis, monachi sancti Albani, chronica majora* ed. H. R. Luard (7 vols., Rolls Series, London, 1872–83) VI, pp. 188–90). A summary of the decree is given by Potthast and attributed to Pope Innocent III, but according to Cheney it is "almost certainly misplaced" (Potthast *Regesta Pontificum Romanorum* II, 3312; Cheney, *op. cit.*, p. 108, n. 1). See also Potthast, *op. cit.*, 15259.

2 *Majores* in the version of the pope's letter of 1252 (above, note 1) which is printed in the "Annals of Burton". Otherwise the Burton version varies from that above only in minor scribal details. (*Annales Monastici* I, pp. 300–2).
Copy III 27. Variant: omit year of pontificate.

I 96 [*c.* 1180–90][1]

[fo. 18] GRANT in free alms, by Girard, son of Wermund, Vidame of Picquigny (*Pincomo*)—for his salvation and the souls of his father and all his ancestors and successors—to Southwick Priory, of the advowson of the chapel of Wymering (*Wimeringes*), and that chapel with 8 acres and all liberties and other appurtenances. Also the whole tithe of salt from his manor of Wymering which belongs to his demesne. Also 3 acres in his ploughlands (*in culturis meis*) at Wymering exchanged with the priory by his grandfather, Girard. Witnesses: Ingeramnus de Hedingcurt'; Warin de Bee Loi; Richard de Lahoga; Robert Presbyter of Wymering; Peter de Cosham; Henry de Burh'; Hugh de Brediport; Philip de Risford; John de Hockesore; Thomas, son of Roger; Hirdman; Peter, son of Geoffrey.

1 Four of the witnesses also witnessed dated charters of the 1180s. The donor's grandfather had probably exchanged the land with the priory *c.* 1160 (I 118, 119). The Vidame of Picquigny in 1166–7 accounted for ½ mark at Wymering (*PR 13 Henry II* p. 188). A Vidame of Picquigny, unnamed, died at Acre in August 1192 (*Itinerary of Richard I* p. 68).
The church of Wymering was among the priory's possessions taken under the protection of Pope Eugenius III in 1151 or 1152 (I 85), and subsequently occurs in papal privileges of 1162–3 and 1186 (I 86, 87).
Copy III 81. Variants: Wyrmund; Pincon'; Wymeryng'; Engerannus de Hedyngton'.

I 97 [*c.* 1180–90][1]

GIFT by Girard, son of Wermund, Vidame of Picquigny (*Pincomo*), to Southwick Priory, of all the land of *Peteford* with 10 acres pertaining to it which lie beyond the hill (*ultra montem*) towards the sea. Walter held the land of Girard and voluntarily surrendered it to him in the chapter house at Southwick. The gift is made at the request of the aforesaid Walter de Burh'.[2] The priory will hold it in perpetuity of Girard and his heirs, for 5s. annual rent at Michaelmas, for all service and custom.[3] Consideration, 20s. Witnesses: Ingelramnus de Harincurt'; Warin de Bee Loi; Richard de Lagoha; Robert Presbyter of Wymering (*Wimering'*); Peter de Cosham; Henry de Burh'; Hugh de Brediport; John de Hockesore; Thomas, son of Roger.

[Marginal note in a later hand:] Wymering (*Wymeryng'*): the land of Peteford with 10 acres.

1 See dating evidence for I 96.

2 Peteforde had been given by Girard, Vidame of Picquigny (probably the grandfather of the above donor, see I 96, 118), to Joan, wife of William, son of Roger, and her heirs (III 84). Joan's son, Simon de Burhunt, gave Peteforde with 10 acres to the priory on the occasion of the burial of his wife, Alice, and he, his mother, and his brother Walter presented to the priory the charters they had from Sir Girard and Sir Weremund concerning that land (III 82). It would appear that Walter de Burhunt surrendered his claim to the land to Girard, son of Weremund, who confirmed the gift of it to the priory.

3 Wymering apparently came into the possession of the Vidame of Picquigny through marriage with the eldest daughter of Stephen, second Count of Aumale, who died *c.* 1121–30 (*V C H Hants* III, p. 166). By 1242–3, Wymering was held of the king by the Count of Aumale (*Book of Fees* II, p. 700). In the first half of the 13th century confirmation of the priory's possession of Peteforde was given by the Count, to whom the priory was to pay the annual 5s. (III 86).
Copy III 83. Variants: Wiremund; Walter de Borhunt; Engelrannus [for Ingelramnus de Harincurt'].

I 98　　　　　　　　　　　　　　　　　　　　　　[*c.* 1200][1]

GIFT, in free alms, by Engelrannus, Vidame of Picquigny (*Pinc'*)—for the salvation of himself and his ancestors and most of all (*maxime*) for the soul of his mother, Lady Flandrina—to Southwick Priory, of land called *Adredecroft* in the manor of Wymering (*Wimeringes*). For the special celebration of his mother's anniversary in the priory in perpetuity, and for the assent of the prior and convent to his request for a cemetery in his vill of Wymering, he has given to the priory land called *Lingestoke* for which 2s. rent a year used to be paid. Witnesses: Roger de Scuris; Matthew Oisel; Matthew de Scuris; Hugh de Pagaham; Robert Bastard'; William de Cosham; Alan; Adam de Portesia; John Aurifaber; Robert Capellanus, reeve.

[Marginal notes in a later hand:]　i) Wymering: land called *Adredcroft*
　　　　　　　　　　　　　　　　　ii) land called *Langstoke*

1 See dating evidence for I 96. Possibly Engelrann was the son of Girard, son of Wermund. The witnesses occur *c.* 1187–1230. See also I 97, note 3.
Copy III 80. Variants: Engerann; Adedrecroft'; Wymeryng'; Langestoke; Roger de Scurys.

[fo. 18ᵛ blank]

I 99 1210

[fo. 19] LEASE—for 20 years from next Michaelmas, after King John comes from Ireland (*Hubernia*) with his army—by Prior G[uy] and Southwick Priory, to Stephen, son of Ralph de Bretevill', of all the land William le Faire held in the manor of West Boarhunt (*Westburhunt*), with all appurtenances. Annual rent 5s., viz. 30d. at Michaelmas and 30d. at Easter, for all except outside service (*salvo forinseco servicio*) pertaining to that amount of land. Consideration, 100s. The same Stephen swore on the Holy Gospels that neither he, nor any others on his behalf, would contrive any impediment or fraud during the aforesaid 20 years, so that at Michaelmas 20 years later the aforesaid lands and appurtenances would be given back without any argument or disturbance, and the priory will be free to do with them what it pleases. If ill befalls Stephen within the aforesaid term, the priory will grant the remainder of the lease, on the same terms and at the same rent, to the man who is chosen by Stephen to take his place and to whom he assigns this charter.

In the month of August King John returned from Ireland, and at the following Michaelmas, 1210, Stephen received this land. Witnesses: Jocelin de Monte, Constable of Portchester (*Porcestr'*); Humphrey Capellanus of Portchester (*Porc'*); Roger de Scuris; William de Bretevill'; Thomas de Ho; Alexander de Bera; Robert de Bera; Alan de Frendest'; Robert de Barra; Peter de Havunt'; Guy Clericus; and many others.

I 100 [*c.* 1200]¹

CONFIRMATION by William, son of Reinelm de Borhunt'—for the salvation of himself, his wife and heirs, and for the souls of all his kindred, lords and friends—to Southwick Priory, of gifts, in free alms, made by his father, viz. ¼ virgate (*ferlingus*) Taleuaz held with adjoining meadow; the marsh (*et de mhora*) below the ploughland (*cultura*) of Applestead (*Appelstede*) as far as the stream which flows down below the priory's court to the west as far as William's mill, which adjoins that marsh on the west, with the way and footpath; 1 acre above the hill in *Stapelcroft*, which is next to the priory's acre on the south; 1 acre adjoining *Widedelle*, which has the same measurements as other acres in the same furlong; also the gift made at the dedication of Southwick church, i.e. licence and sanction freely to channel the spring of Offwell (*Affewelle*) through his land during his lifetime and that of his heirs, as may seem most useful to the priory and profitable to his soul.² He grants also to the priory tithes which, according to the institutes of the church, ought to be paid from all annual produce; these tithes the priory will receive in full from William and his heirs without any trouble or argument. William has confirmed to the priory everything shown in his father's charter, which he has seen, handled and caused to be read in the presence of many people.[3] Witnesses: John de Hamton', canon of Chichester (*Cicestrn'*); Philip de Lestane; Herbert de Froila; Gervase de Nortun'; M. Lawrence de Rid'esfeld'; Alexander de Bera; Guy, the donor's brother (frater meus); M. William de Tanton'; William Dogestreng; Ralph Hirdman; and many others.

1.John de Hampton occurs as canon of Chichester in 1197 (*Chichester Cartulary* 198, 401, pp. 47, 104); Philip de Stane as a witness *c*. 1190-1215 (*Selborne Charters* I, pp. 1-2); and Gervase de Nortone as a witness *c*. 1200 (*Win. Cath. Cart.* 71, p. 34). The other witnesses occur in the late 12th and early 13th centuries.

2 See I 25. The dedication of the priory's church took place in 1181 or 1182.

3 See I 28, 120.

Copy III 249. Variants: Stapelcrofte; John de Hamt'.

I 101   [*c*. 1235-50]

[fo. 19ᵛ] GIFT, with warranty, by Thomas de Burhunt, son of Herbert de Burhunt, to Southwick Priory, of (i) a certain marsh (*mora*) which lies between his croft, called *Huscrofte*, and the priory's new mill, and extends eastwards from the corner of Thomas' new ditch to a cetain fertile meadow (*almum pratum*), and from there to a certain crab-apple tree, and thence by an old ditch to the stone cross. Also (ii) all the land, with the water-course, from the aforesaid corner of his new ditch westwards along the length of that ditch to certain bounds to the south (*ad certas metas versus austrum*) adjoining *le Pudduk'*, for building a mill there and setting up a mill pond in the place already provided, as seems most expedient to the priory, with free entry and exit beyond *le Pudduk*; saving rights of common in *la[sic] Pudduk* in perpetuity for the priory and Thomas and his heirs, outside the bounds of the said pond and road. The priory is obliged to repair the causeway outside Thomas' gate on both sides of the bridge (*ex utraque parte pontis forinseci*) as often as necessary, at their own reasonable cost, in perpetuity, unless it has been damaged by Thomas or his heirs. Whenever necessary the priory may raise up, erect, strengthen, improve and enlarge the said mill and mill pond on all sides from the site of the mill to the stone cross, for their profit, saving damage to Thomas' new ditch, meadows or lands. And if damage occurs through the damming of the water of the mill, amends will be made to Thomas or his heirs in the sight of mutual friends. Thomas may fish in the said mill pond with a net called *butur*, but the priory will have all the fish at the sluices. Thomas and his heirs have equal right with the priory to put swans (*oleres*) in the aforesaid mill pond when they wish, and future profit and increase will be shared equally without any argument. In exchange the priory has given Thomas the curtillage formerly held by William Horn, and 2 marks.[2] Thomas' warranty includes the whole of the aforesaid marsh with the mill, the site and pond, ways and footpaths, metes and boundaries on both sides of the water course, with all other improvements (*emendamenta*).

Witnesses: Robert de Bello Alneto; Roger de Merley; William de Cobeham; Roger Horn;[3] Herbert son of William de Burhunt; Peter de Bera.

1 The exchange was made with Matthew, who was Prior of Southwick from 1235 to 1266 (I 102). The witness Roger de Merley had died by 1250 (*Cal. Inq. p.m.* I, 221, p. 51). The first three witnesses and the last were all holding land in Hampshire in 1242–43 (*Book of Fees* II, p. 696–7, 699, 703). The donor was probably the Thomas de Burghunte who, at the time of his death in 1263, was holding two knights' fees of Sir Robert de Sancto Johanne (*Cal. Inq. p.m.* I, 536, p. 162). See also III 182.

2 See I 102.

3 Possibly a scribal error for Roger de Ho (see I 102, note 1). Copy III 195. Variants: rubric, Borhunt'; de Merlay.

I 102 [*c.* 1235–50]

GIFT by Prior Matthew and Southwick Priory to Thomas de Burhunt, son of Herbert de Burhunt, of the messuage with curtillage in ?Middle Boarhunt (*Milde Burhunt*), formerly held by William Horn, which is west of the road which runs from Southwick (*Suwik*) to Portsea (*Portesia*), in exchange, for (i) a marsh (*mora*) lying between the priory's mill-pond and Thomas' croft, and also (ii) the site of the mill and the right to make a mill-pond in which Thomas and his heirs may fish with a net called *Butur*. The priory and Thomas and his heirs have equal rights to put swans (*oleres*) in the aforesaid mill-pond, and they will share the profits equally in perpetuity. The priory is obliged to repair Thomas' causeway outside his gate on both sides of the bridge as necessary in perpetuity, unless it is wrongfully damaged at any time by Thomas or [fo. 20] his heirs. The priory is responsible for keeping Thomas' new ditch undamaged, unless the damage is done in any way by Thomas or his men. Thomas and his heirs and the priory will share rights of the common in *le Pudduk* (*del Pudduck*) in perpetuity. The priory is responsible for any damage done to Thomas' lands near the mill pond by damming the water of the mill, and if damage occurs the priory will made just amends in the sight of mutual friends. Witnesses: Robert de Bello Alneto; Roger de Merlay; William de Cobeham; Roger de Ho; Herbert, son of William de Burhunt; Peter de Bera.

1 Dating evidence as for I 101. The witnesses are the same for both charters, except Roger de Ho above, and Roger de Horn in I 101. Roger de Horn does not occur elsewhere in the cartularies, but Roger de Ho was holding Hoe as ½ knights' fee in 1242–43 (*Book of Fees* II, p. 695).

I 103 [after 1165, probably 1180s][1]

AGREEMENT between Southwick Priory and Alexander de Burhunt over a certain ¼ virgate (*ferdingus terre*) called *Horapeldre*. Alexander voluntarily recognised that he had no right to the ¼ virgate which was taken from the priory's fee (*de feudo evire*), and asked that he might hold it of the priory for annual service. Because of the benefits received from Alexander's father and himself, and in the interests of peace and mutual affection, the priory has granted the ¼ virgate to Alexander and his heirs, to be held of it for an annual rent of ½lb of incense (*dethure masculino*) at the Nativity of St Mary [8 September]. The ¼ virgate extends from the ditch on the east of the marsh—over which there was previously controversy with the priory on the part of Alexander and Reinelm concerning rights of common—to the ditch which is on the east of the ¼ virgate, between it and Alexander's land; it is also enclosed by ditches on the north and south. Alexander is obliged to maintain the ditches (*predictum ferdingum ita debet claudere*) so that neither the priory and its men nor its neighbours are disturbed from there. On the aforesaid marsh west of the ¼ virgate, the priory, Alexander and Reinelm will share rights of common, and together are obliged to demolish and fill in the new ditch made around the marsh. Alexander has sworn fealty to the prior and convent, and henceforth will serve them peacefully and faithfully as his lords, and they will esteem and support him as their tenant (*tanquam tenentem nostrum diligemus et manutenebimus*). Witnesses: Roger de Porcestr'; Andrew de Suwik'; Robert de Farham; Bartholomew Capellanus; Gervase de Windesore; Michael de Basevile; Henry Dagus, Constable of Portchester (*Porcestr'*); Baldwin de Montsorel; Matthew Oysel; Reinelm; Robert de Sancto Clero; Richard, son of Daniel; Richard de Denemede; Thomas de la Bere; Henry de Druval; Roger Clericus; Elias (*Helias*) de Lovinton'; Thomas de Sancta Maria; Turstin Tegulator; Hyrdman; Ralph Doket; Walter le Simple; Reinald'; Hubald; and many others.

1 At least 15 of the witnesses also witnessed charters that can be dated in the 1180s. Henry Dacus, Constable of Portchester, witnessed Gervase de Windeshor's charter of *c.* 1183-7 (I 33). In *c.* 1165 the ¼ virgate called Horapeldre had been granted by the priory to Alexander, after the settlement of a dispute between them over land granted to the priory by Herbert, Alexander's father (I 121). Subsequently both Alexander and Reinelm de Burhunt were in dispute with Prior Walter, who had ceased to be prior by 1177 (I 120, 122). In 1182 a Final Concord was made between Alexander and the priory concerning the mill granted to the priory by Alexander's father (I 30). For other gifts made to the priory by Alexander and Reinelm in the 1180s, see I 25, 28, 29.

I 104   [1281-91]¹

ASSIZE held at Winchester, before Sir Robert Fulc and Sir W. Brexbuf on the Friday after the feast of All Saints, in the year of the reign of King etc., to examine whether the following—Thomas de le Beche; Beatrix, widow of John Taplard; Richard, bailiff of Thomas de la Beche; Stephen de la Beche; John Taplard; John David; J. le Saucir; and Walter de Godenge—have unlawfully disseised the prior of Southwick of his freeholding in Ellisfield (*Ulsefeud*) as etc., and enquire about his being disseised of 40 acres of land and 10 acres of wood with appurtenances.

Thomas and all the others came, and all except Beatrix say that they have done no injury or disseisin, and have nothing, nor claim to have anything, in the aforesaid holdings; and on this day they take their stand.

Beatrix says she has not committed injury or disseisin, because a certain Michael de Chinnham held the aforesaid holding from her for knight service, and he enfeoffed a certain Bartholomew Peche,[2] who enfeoffed Prior Andrew of Southwick,[3] predecessor of the present prior, [fo. 20ᵛ] the plaintiff, so that the holding then passed into mortmain. And because all the aforesaid chief lords of that fee were negligent, she has taken over the holding on account of the statute, and now holds it for that reason, and not by disseisin. She therefore claims benefit of statute, and seeks judgement as to whether the case should proceed.

The prior says that his predecessor, Andrew, formerly Prior of Southwick, was enfeoffed by Bartholomew before the publication of the statute and had seisin of the holding four years before the end of his priorate;[4] after which, the king took over the holding with the other possessions of the priory, because of the vacancy, until the present prior was confirmed in office. Then the king restored all of the aforesaid holding, with other possessions, and the prior had good and peaceful seisin of it as his freehold, until unjustly disseised by the aforesaid Thomas and others. Moreover the prior says that Michael de Chinham held nothing from the aforesaid Beatrix which she can claim by reason of the statute. And on this he takes his stand. And Beatrix likewise.

The jurors say that the aforesaid holdings descended to Michael as his share of the inheritance of a certain ancestor of Beatrix, and he never held them from Beatrix, but from a certain Richard Sifrewast.[5] Andrew, predecessor of the present prior, was in possession of the holdings for a long time, having been enfeoffed by the aforesaid Bartholomew; then the king, during the vacancy; and afterwards the present prior, the plaintiff. Asked in which year the aforesaid prior was enfeoffed, they say in the 7th year of the present reign. And asked from whom Richard held them, they say from John de Sancto Johanne, who held from the king in chief. And they say that precisely on the feast of St. Lawrence this year, the prior was disseised.

Afterwards, on the feast of St Edmund, King and Martyr [20 November], before Sir John de Kirkeby, Sir Ralph de Henguham, Sir John Limetot and others present on the king's orders to hold an inquisition between the Countess de Insula[6] and the Abbot of Quarr (*Quarrarreya*),[7] it was adjudged that the priory of Southwick had been enfeoffed with the aforesaid holding before the statute, and therefore the prior should keep peaceful seisin of it; and, on more evidence, not shown, that the prior had been enfeoffed on the feast of the Purification of the Blessed Mary [2 February] 1279, and the statute was passed the following Michaelmas [29 September], as was testified by Sir J. de Kirkeby and others aforementioned.

1 Dates of John de Clere's priorate.

2 In 1272 Herbert Peche died seized of 60 acres in Ellisfield, which he held of William de Chunham. Herbert's heir was Bartholomew Peche (*VCH Hants* III, p. 360). Probably Michael de Chinham was William's heir.

3 Andrew de Winton was Prior of Southwick from 1273 to 1281.

4 As Prior Andrew was removed from office by Archbishop Pecham on 10 January 1281 (*VCH Hants* II, p. 164), he would have had seisin of the holding by January 1277, but this does not agree with the date given in the final judgement.

5 In 1255 Richard de Sifrewast was holding land in Ellisfield of Robert de Sancto Johanne (*VCH Hants* III, p. 360). Robert died in 1267, and was succeeded by his son, John, who died in 1302 (*Complete Peerage* XI, pp. 322–5).

6 Isabella, Countess of Aumale, was the widow of William de Forz, who had died in 1260. In 1263 she succeeded her brother, Baldwin de Redvers, Earl of Devon and lord of the Isle of Wight. She died in 1293 (*HBC* p. 459).

7 Adam of Arundel was Abbot of Quarr from 1274 to 1304 (Hockey *Quarr Abbey* p. 259).

I 105   12 June 1274

INQUISITION concerning rights of pasturage in dispute between (i) the Prior of Southwick and (ii) Sir Richard de Portes', the Abbot of Titchfield (*Tichefeld*), the Prior of the Domus Dei of Portsmouth (*Portesmut'*), Alan le Weyte, Henry Wade, Geoffrey Byaumund and others.

Memorandum: Richard de Portesia, Brother [ ]¹ of the Domus Dei of Portsmouth, Alan le Wayte, Reginald Kene, Richard le Kenteys, and Reginald, hayward of the Abbot of Tichfield on his manor of Walesworth (*Waleswrth*), were attached to answer Prior Andrew of Southwick's charge of trespass, viz. that on Monday before the feast of Pentecost [14 May], 1274, Richard de Portes' and the others aforenamed illegally and contrary to the king's peace and the queen's liberty in the forest of Portchester (*Porcestre*) came into the aforesaid forest, where the prior has rights of pasturage in the demesne wood of Richard de Portes', took [fo. 21²] 26 of the prior's oxen and 52 of his pigs, illegally drove them off to a certain holding of Richard's in Fratton (*Frodinton'*) outside his manor of Portsea (*Portesia*) and outside the aforesaid forest, and kept them until they were freed by the queen on Friday in the week of Pentecost, involving 100s. damage to the prior and 5 marks for outrage, and he has suit (*ad dampnum ipsius prioris Cs. et huntagium v marcarum et habet sectam*). Richard and the others aforenamed came and defended etc. And they say that on the Monday aforesaid they found the prior's beasts in Richard's wood, where the prior has no rights of common, and they impounded them legally in the aforesaid park, as Richard and his ancestors were wont to do from time immemorial; and he says that he did not take the animals in any other way as the Prior says he was prepared to prove etc. And the prior says rights of pasturage in the said wood belong to his freeholding and priory of Southwick, and have always done so from time immemorial, because he and his predecessors always used them peacefully up to the aforesaid day. Moreover the prior says Richard cannot make any enclosure for herbage in the aforesaid forest, nor can anyone else, except the foresters of the king or queen. And all enclosures ought to be made, and have been up to now, by the royal foresters within the bounds of the forest and not elsewhere, and no enclosure whatever by others. The enclosure that was made caused the greatest injury to the liberties of the queen and the inheritance of the king, and this he would undertake to prove etc.

Richard says the prior has no rights of common in the aforesaid wood. He and his ancestors have always been accustomed to impound animals which had no right of common there in their park outside the forest, and not the queen's foresters as the prior says. This is the truth and on this he takes his stand.

Inquisition held at Wanstead (*Wanstede*) before Guy de Taunton' on Tuesday, the day after the feast of St. Barnabas the Apostle [12 June] in the aforesaid year. Jurors: Peter Tureville; William de Swanemere; William Finamur; Thomas de la Bere; William de Ranvill'; Nicholas de Langerihsse; Robert de la Bere; James de Henton'; William de Chiddene, clerk; Geoffrey Wygant; Henry de Crabbeden', clerk; Nicholas de Bosco; Ralph Tannator; Hugh Maurdin; William le Provere; and Stephen Clericus. They say that right of pasturage in Sir Richard's wood belongs to the freehold of the prior and priory. Richard illegally took the aforesaid beasts and drove them to his park outside the forest, causing the greatest injury to the liberties of the queen, since no one is allowed to impound animals within the covert of the forest except the foresters of the king or queen in the royal park within the forest bounds. Therefore it was decided that Richard and the others aforenamed should make amends to the prior for the aforesaid trespass, and they are at mercy: Richard de Portesia, for his part, 5 marks; Richard Kenteys, $\frac{1}{2}$ mark; Alan le Weyte, 20s; Reginald le Kene, $\frac{1}{2}$ mark; the Prior of the Domus Dei, 20s.; Geoffrey Beaumnd for the same, and because he wrongfully took distraint from the prior's men, 20s.

1 Name erased in MS. Copy II 24 has "Brother of the Domus Dei" with no space for a name.

2 The top of fo. 21 is damaged; the missing lines have been supplied from the copy II 24.
Copy II 24. Variants: Walewrthe; de Suanemere; de Crabbedene.

I 106

[fo. 21ᵛ]¹ Com' tent . . . . . Prior de Su . . . . . iuste non att . . . . . in manerio de Ulsefe[ld] . . . . . tenet de predicto Hug' . . . . . sex denar' per annum Unde p . . . . . predictus Hug' sepius requisitus et adm . . . . . per predictum Johannem ei deliberet et quod ip . . . . . districtiones ipsi factas non deliberauit nec ipsum ?acq . . . . . Hugo recognovit cartam predictam esse factum predecessoris ?sui et teneri m . . . . . per servicium predictum Et quod districtiones factas per predictum Johannem debet deliberare et ip . . . . . ndem Johannem penitus acquietare Et predictus Prior remisit dampna.

1 The top right-hand side of this folio is missing.
Between 1279 and 1291 John de Sancto Johanne issued orders to the officials of his manor of Basing instructing them not to take distraint at Ellisfield from

the prior of Southwick for suit of court owed at Basing (I 206). The St Johns
were lords of the manor of Ellisfield and the priory had been given land there in
1279 (I 108). Possibly the Hugh referred to above was Hugh de Sancto Johanne,
grandson of the above John, who succeeded his father, John, in 1329, but did
not come of age until 1331. He had died by February 1337 (*Cal. Inq. p.m.* VIII,
82, p. 50). At the time of his death the prior of Southwick and John de Roches
were holding a knight's fee of him at Ellisfield. It seems likely that the above
fragment concerned an enquiry into distraint unlawfully taken from the prior at
Ellisfield, but too much is missing for any satisfactory calendar to be made.

I 107   23 May 1286

CONFIRMATION by Walter, Bishop of Salisbury,[1] with the consent of
his dean and chapter, to Southwick Priory, at the urgent request of
Queen Eleanor (*Alianore*), mother of the king,[2] of an annual pension of
100s. from the profits of the church of Swindon (*Swyndon'*) in his diocese
and in the patronage of the priory, owed and paid to them from of
old, conceded by his predecessors and acknowledged in law (*in judicio
recognitus*) by the rector of that church, and paid in equal portions at
the feast of the Resurrection (*Resurrectio domini*) [27 March] and at
Michaelmas [29 September] by the rector of the day, in perpetuity, to
sustain the charitable hospitality (*ad hospitalitatis gratiam . . . . susten-
tandam*) laudably practised by the priory beyond its resources (*ultra
vires*).

Ramesbury (*Remmesbur'*), [Wilts.], 10 Kal. June, A.D. 1286, the
second year of Walter's episcopate.

1 Walter Scammel was consecrated Bishop of Salisbury on 22 October 1284, and
died on 20 September 1286. The pension had been granted to the priory in 1199
by Herbert Poore, Bishop of Salisbury, 1194–1217 (I 154).

2 Eleanor of Provence, widow of Henry III and mother of Edward I, died in
1291.

Copy III 416. Variant: the date is given as, "10 Kal. July [22 June], A.D. 1286".

I 108   30 September 1303

INQUISITION held at Ellisfield (*Elsefeld*) before Henry Wyard, the
king's subsescheator in the county of Hampshire (*Sutht'*). Jurors: Philip
Walerond, Hugh de Spayne, John Lucays, Robert de la Hurne, Richard
Consail, Philip de Stepelton', Henry le Clerk, Michael Bukeberd, William
le Wyte, Nicholas Sare, Roger de Allewod and William Dureward. They
say that Prior Andrew of Southwick and the priory took over (*appropri-
are*) a carucate of land with appurtenances in Ellisfield from Bartholomew
Peche in the 7th year of King Edward's reign [20 November 1278–19

November 1279] before the Statute [of Mortmain],[1] and all other acquisitions in that vill were made before the Statute. Sealed by the jurors and Henry Wyard.

1 The priory's right to this holding had earlier been in dispute. At an inquisition held in Winchester, the date on which the priory was enfeoffed with the tenement was said to have been 2 February 1279, whereas the Statute of Mortmain had not been passed until the following Michaelmas (I 104).

I 109 [*c.* 1165][1]

[fo. 22] Charter of Robert de Pontearch' concerning land of Stubbington (Stubinton'); the gift of Alfred de Herierd'.

GIFT, in perpetual alms, by Robert de Pontearch' to Southwick Priory, of land in Stubbington (*Stubinctona*) to be held well and freely as his father held it (*ut pater meus eam melius et liberius tenuit*) in the time of King Henry [I], or as Robert held it in the time of King Henry the younger [II], saving service due for that land. Witnesses: Gilbert Oin; John de Medeheche; Richard son of Daniel; Nicholas de Medehe[che]; Peter de Stopeha'; William Caball'; William Clericus; Alexander de Burhunta and Ralph, his brother.

1 If the rubric is correct, and this charter is a confirmation by Robert de Pont de l'Arche, of Alfred de Herierd's gift to the priory, it would appear that both the de Pont de l'Arche family and the de Hommets had claims as overlords (I 110). Alfred de Herierd probably gave the land to the priory between 1153 and 1163 (I 17). The problem remains as to whether it was in Stubbington in Titchfield or Stubbington in Portsea (see I 17, note 2, I 86, note 3; II 56). The first four witnesses also witnessed other charters for Robert de Pont de l'Arche about the middle of the 12th century (I 11, 19, 20).
Copy III 108. Variant: rubric, Confirmation of Robert de Pontearcharum concerning land of Stubbington (*Stobynton'*).

I 110 [*c.* 1165][1]

Confirmation by Richard de Humeto of the same [gift].

NOTIFICATION by Richard de Hum', the King's Constable, to his steward Malg' Malc', and Henry de Maisnil, and all his men and English friends, that he has confirmed the gift made by Alfred de Herierd to Southwick Priory, of his land in Stubbington (*Stobint'*), which Alfred held of Richard. The priory is to hold the land with those quittances which Richard can lawfully make (*con quietatiis quas illi terre facere possum iuste*). Witnesses: William de Hum'; Pagan de Cardunvill'; Geoffrey de Sol'; Robert Dacus, chaplain; Walter Brito; and many others.
Le Hommet (*Humetum*), [Manche, Normandy].

1 Alfred de Herierd's gift to the priory was probably made between 1153 and 1163 (I 17, note 1). In 1165 Henry de Maisnil or Mednill' was Constable of Portchester, and Walter Brito or Bret, Steward, in the service of Richard de Hommet, then lord of Portchester (I 122, 120). See also I 109 and note, I 17 note 2.

Copy III 61. Variants: Meisenille; Herier; Stubeton'; Witnesses: William de Hum'; Robert Saio, etc.; [omit place of issue].

I 111[1] [1155-61][2]

GIFT, in perpetual alms, by William Maled' [rubric: Mauduit], the King's Chamberlain, to Southwick Priory, of the church of Shalden (*Scaldedena*),[3] with all appurtenances, viz. lands, tithes, pastures, wood and plain, and all liberties and free customs which the church had in his father's time. Richard Baligan, William's clerk, will hold the church, paying the priory $\frac{1}{2}$ mark annually at the feast of St Giles [1 September], and after his death the priory may treat it as their own property. Witnesses: Theobald, Archbishop of Canterbury and Papal Legate; Hilary, Bishop of Chichester (*Cic'*);[4] John, canon of Salisbury; John Maleductus;[5] and Hugh, son of Michael Hamesclapie.[5]

1 Printed in full, in Latin, as Appendix I, E. Mason, "The Mauduits and their Chamberlainship of the Exchequer", p. 17.

2 Between 1155-8, when William Mauduit (III) succeeded to the chamberlainship (Mason, *loc. cit.*, p. 3), and the death of Archbishop Theobald in 1161.

3 Before his death, *c.* 1148, William de Pont de l'Arche granted the church of Shalden to the priory, though it was not within his competence to do so. The gift was later confirmed by his son, Robert (I 18 and note), and the church was included among the priory's possessions in Pope Eugenius III's privilege of 1151-2 (I 85). The Mauduits did not abandon their claim, but when William (III) failed to regain the advowson, he conceded this confirmation to the priory, but ensured that his clerk would hold the church for life. See also III 942; I 31, 32.

4 Hilary was Bishop of Chichester from 1147 to 1169.

5 John Maleductus, or Mauduit, was William (III)'s younger brother, and Hugh of Hanslope was their maternal uncle (*Beauchamp Cartulary* p. lix).
Copy III 177. Variants: Schaldene, Schaldena; Cicestr'.

I 112 [1151-63][1]

NOTIFICATION by Robert de Pontearch' to Henry, Bishop of Winchester, Archdeacon Ralph, and all his officials (*ministri*) of his gift, in perpetual alms, to Southwick Priory, of the church of Wanstead (*Wanest', Wanesteda*), with lands, tithes, and all appurtenances. The priory will hold it free from all secular services. Witnesses: William Martel; Nicholas; William Peccatus; Geoffrey; Reinalm; and Richard, his brother.

This gift was made in the chapter house of Southwick on the day on which Robert de Pont' received the benefits of the fraternity (*recepit fraternitatem canonicorum*).

1 The church of Wanstead was not included among the priory's possessions confirmed by Pope Eugenius III in 1151-2 (I 85), but it does occur in Pope Alexander III's confirmation of 1162-3 (I 86). See also I 4, 18. It appears that Richard, son of Daniel, and his wife, Basilia, also had a claim to the church of Wanstead, for they gave it to the priory, "so far as they were able", with land for its upkeep from their fee of Wanstead (I 36).

I 113   [1163-81, possibly after 1174][1]

GIFT, in perpetual alms, by Ralph son of Gilbert, his wife Constance, and their son Ralph,—for the redemption of their souls and those of their ancestors—to Southwick Priory, of their chapel of Empshott (*Imbesita*), [rubric: *Imbeschete*], with tithes, oblations and all appurtenances, and 1 virgate. Half the virgate will be quit of all service; the other half will be liable for royal service, and will provide two men at harvest for each of the donors' boonworks. Witnesses: Philip, their son-in-law, with his wife Isabel and his sons, Peter and Ralph; Ralph, priest (*presbyter*) of Empshott chapel; Alexander de Burhunta; Geoffrey, Bartholomew and Richard Lachehwei, priests (*sacerdotes*); Herbert Clericus of Empshott.

The donors have requested that when the priory hears of their deaths and the deaths of their heirs, and of Philip and his wife Isabel, it will hold divine service for their souls as for the souls of special brothers and sisters.

1 The chapel of Empshott was not included in the list of the priory's possessions confirmed by Pope Alexander III in 1162-3 (I 86). It is included in another privilege granted by the same pope, c. 1163-81 (I 24), and in a bull that can possibly be dated 1170 (III 3). However, when Richard of Ilchester, Bishop of Winchester from 1174 to 1188, granted to Prior Guy confirmation of the priory's possessions, he included the chapel of Empshott "obtained by his concession and with his consent" (I 94).

The gift of the chapel and land was confirmed by Philip de Stanis, or de Stanes, and his wife Isabel, presumably the son-in-law and daughter of the above Ralph, son of Gilbert (III 275).
Copy III 274.

I 114   [1152-63][1]

NOTIFICATION by William de Venoiz to Henry, Bishop of Winchester, of his gift, in perpetual alms,—for the salvation of the souls of his father, mother and ancestors, and for the safety of himself and his family [fo. 22ᵛ] (*pro incolumitate mea et meorum*)— to Southwick Priory, of the chapel of Nutley (*Nutlega*), [rubric: *Nutleia*], with lands, tithes, and all profits pertaining to it. Witnesses: Ralph, Archdeacon and chaplain of Winchester; Robert Claford; William, son of Azo; William Escotland; Richard, son of Daniel; Ralph, son of Herbert.

1 The chapel of Nutley was among the possessions of the priory to which Pope Alexander III extended his protection in 1162 or 1163 (I 86). It was not included in Pope Eugenius III's privilege of 1151 or 1152 (I 85). The witness William Escotland was probably the donor whose gift to the priory of the chapel of Candover Scotland was of similar date and was also witnessed by Archdeacon Ralph and by Richard, son of Daniel (I 13).

William de Venoiz had died by 1197. His son, Robert, confirmed the gift of the chapel of Nutley to the priory (III 176 and note).
Copy III 175. Variants: rubric, Nuthlia; Nuthlya [marginal note]; Nutleg'.

I 115   [*c.* 1185–1200][1]

Chirograph [drawn up] by the priory with Matilda de Bochl' and Robert, son of Peter, concerning the chapel of Walesworthe.

Prior Guy acquired this charter at Buckland (Bokeland).

GIFT, in free alms, by Matilda de Bochland' and her son and heir, Robert, son of Peter—for the salvation of their souls and those of Peter de L[ ]tegarhal', Hugh de Bochland, Petronella wife of the aforesaid Robert, and all their kindred, ancestors, heirs and friends—to Southwick Priory, of the chapel of Walesworth (*Waleswrd'*), so far as it belongs to them, with tithes and all appurtenances; and, for the use of the chaplain ministering there, a messuage with its croft which is situated between the house of the donors' man, William de Waleswrd', and that of William Forestarius, who holds from the Vidame of Picquigny (*Pinkenni*); also 5 acres which the chapel used to have, of which 3 acres are beyond the hill and 2 on the near side of it. The chaplain's messuage used to be in the donors' demesne adjoining their court, and it will be quit [of services pertaining] to them and their heirs. The priory is obliged to provide a chaplain to live and minister there in perpetuity. Witnesses: William de Bocland'; Hugh, his brother; William de Etona; Geoffrey M'dac; Roger, son of Peter; Robert, son of Ranul; William, son of Arnold; Robert Clericus; William de Waleswrd'; Matefrei; William, son of Robert; William Frater; Eustace, son of William; William Diaconus; and many others.

1 On 25 January 1185, in the presence of Henry II at Melksham, a fine was levied dividing the inheritance of William de Say between his two daughters, Beatrice, wife of Geoffrey fitz Peter (later Earl of Essex) and Matilda, wife of Hugh de Bochland. On the same day the king issued a charter giving his express consent to the settlement (*Itinerary of Henry II* pp. 260–1).

It would appear that Matilda's son, Robert, predeceased her, because after her death Walesworth passed to her sister's husband, who died in 1213 (*VCH Hants* III, p. 107).

The chapel of Walesworth was first given to the priory by Henry of Blois, Bishop of Winchester, and the gift was confirmed by him, *c.* 1155–63 (I 4). It occurs among the priory's possessions in Pope Alexander III's privilege of 1162 or 1163 (I 86), but not in the earlier privilege issued by Pope Eugenius III in 1151 or 1152 (I 85).
Copy III 449. Variants: rubric: de Boklande; Lutegarhal'; de Bokland'; Walesword'.

I 116 [*c.* 1180-6][1]

GIFT, in free alms, by John de Gisorz—for the salvation of his soul, and those of his father, mother, ancestors and heirs—to Southwick Priory, of a site for the erection of a chapel in honour of the glorious martyr, Thomas of Canterbury, formerly Archbishop, on his land called *Sudeweda* on the island of Portsea (*Portesia*), west of the land which Lucas then held from him. The site is 13 perches long and 12 perches wide. John besought the priory to remember him and his kindred in their prayers in perpetuity, so that they might share in all the beneifts of the church. Witnesses: Richard Sacerdos; Fabian de Tichefeld'; Richard, his brother; Hugh Clericus; Peter de Reilli; Richard Clericus; William Aurifaber; Roger and Adam, his brothers; Roger Niger; Henry, son of Richard.

1 This is probably the earliest mention of the chapel of St Thomas, part of which is still incorporated in the cathedral of Portsmouth. When Richard of Ilchester granted to Prior Guy confirmation of the priory's possessions, *c.* 1185-8, he included the chapel, the building of which was said to have been undertaken in its parish of Portsea on his advice and with his consent (I 94). The chapel must have been in existence by February 1186, when Pope Urban III extended his protection to the priory's possessions including "the church of Portsea and its chapel" (I 87). See also I 61, 133, 134.
Copy III 207. Variant: de Gisors. A marginal note reads: "Chapel of Portsmouth (*Portesmuthe*)".

I 117 [*c.* 1165][1]

GIFT, in perpetual alms, by Henry de Mednill' [rubric: Mesnill'] and Adelidis, his wife—for their salvation and safety, and the redemption of their souls and those of their ancestors and kindred, and especially of Robert de Ruenora, and for the prosperity of their lord, Richard de Humet' and his children—to Southwick Priory, of $\frac{1}{2}$ virgate from their inheritance in Rowner (*Ruenora*), which Roger de Bedeham recently held from them, free from all except royal service or other service for which that land and theirs may be liable. These alms are given so that while the donors live the priory will remember them in its prayers, and after their deaths, in masses, vigils, alms and all the benefits of the church, and their names will be written amongst those of the brothers, and the anniversary of their deaths will be commemorated with the office due for one of the founders of the church. Witnesses: Ralph de Mednill'; William de Risford; Robert de Ramvilla; Reynalm; Richard, son of Daniel; Richard de Wimering'; Hamo Bretu'; Roger Clericus.

1 The donor and six, perhaps seven, of the witnesses occur in 1165 (I 122). At that time Richard de Hommet is referred to as "lord of Portchester", and it would appear that Henry de Mednil served him as Constable (I 120-2. See also I 110, 6, 81, 82).
Copy III 334. Variants: de Mednillis; de Reuenora; de Humez; de Risforde.

I 118   [*c.* 1160]¹

[fo. 23] GRANT, in perpetual alms, by Girard, Vidame of Picquigny
(*Pinch'*) [rubric: *Pinkeni*]—for the souls of his father and mother, his
wife, Matilda, and his ancestors, and for the salvation of himself and
his heirs—to Southwick Priory, of the tithes of salt pertaining to his
demesne at Wymering (*Wimering'*), and 3 acres adjoining the priory's
land at Wymering which he has exchanged for another 3 acres formerly
held by the priory elsewhere in his ploughlands (*culture*). Witnesses:
[ ]²audredus Sensescallus; Peter de Breisli; Thomas Canonicus; Philip
Clericus; Bartholomew Sacerdos; Alexander de Burhunta; Richard Loc'.

1 A Girard, Vidame of Picquigny, witnessed a charter of Henry II *c.* 1158–62
(*Cal. of Docs. in France* p. 64). He is probably the Vidame who was holding
Wymering in 1167 by right of his wife, the eldest daughter of Stephen, second
Count of Aumale (*VCH Hants* III, p. 166). His grandson, Girard son of Wermund,
confirmed the grant and exchange (I 96).
2 First letter missing in MS: ? Gaudredus.

I 119   [*c.* 1170–80]¹

NOTIFICATION by Bernard de Sancto Walerico to his friends, French
and English, that he has granted to Southwick Priory undisturbed
possession of the holding shown in Vidame Girard's charter, for as long
as he, Bernard, is keeper of the alms of Wymering (*Sciatis me concessisse
. . . tenendum quiete quamdiu custos ero elemosinam de Wimering*).
Witnesses: William de Braiose; Hodo de Dantmartin; Peter de Chosham;
Alermus Clericus, who drew up the charter at Tandridge (*Tenruge*),
[Surrey].

1 Presumably the charter referred to in this notification is I 118 of *c.* 1160.
Bernard de Sancto Walerico is said to have served Henry II on missions in 1165
and 1186, and occurs in the Pipe Rolls between 1172 and 1176 (*Recueil des Actes
de Henri II* Introduction, p. 357–8; *PR 18–22 Henry II*). No evidence has been
found to explain why he should have had custody of Wymering. See also I 96–8.

I 120   [1154–77, possibly 1164]¹

Chirograph between the priory and Reinelm de Burhunta under the seal
of R. de Humeto.

AGREEMENT by Prior Walter and Southwick Priory with Reinelm, son
of Henry, and his brother, Richard, concerning the acre which is south
of the mill and the claim the brothers made in the priory's vill of
Southwick. In exchange for that acre the canons gave Reinelm another,
in *Osendena*, in the midst of (*inter*) his 4 acres; the prior gave Reinelm a
palfrey [in compensation] for damage to his mill, and remitted 8s. owed

to the priory by his brother Robert and 3s. by Richard. The brothers Reinelm and Richard took up a book of the gospels (*librum evangeliorum sumpserunt*) and placed it on the altar, promising to keep faith and peace as long as they lived; thus they were received into the fraternity, and they, and the soul of their father, will be remembered in the prayers, and share in the benefits, of the church.

Peace having thus been made, it was decided by both parties that all exchanges of land made between the priory and the father [of Reinelm and Richard] in the time of King Henry[2] should be fully upheld. In the case of exchanges made after the king's death, it was agreed that the prior should choose three of Reinelm's men, and Reinelm three of the prior's men, and they would accept the sworn judgement of these men. The prior chose William Morevilla, their brother (*frater eorum*), Goding and Roger Drageleg; and Reinelm chose Roger Clericus, Ralph, son of Wulward, and Pagan. These men swore to speak the truth concerning the matters in dispute.

The prior kept 1½ acres in the east part of *Wulfgid'e* moor in exchange for 1½ acres in front of Reinelm's gate, and another acre was kept by the prior adjoining the road from *Wulfgid'e* moor and ½ acre for a right of way (*ad aissam*). The prior has the curtillage above Algar's house, and Reinelm the small meadow below the house. The prior has ½ acre below the road that leads to Wymering (*Wimering*), in exchange for ½ acre in the elder Ribout's close (*in clauso patris Ribout*) adjoining the road. The prior has the meadow which Odo holds adjoining Beckford (*Bikeford*) water, and the acre of Sancsida, in exchange for an acre for easement. The jurors divided the assart between the prior and Reinelm. It was agreed that the exchange of salt pans should stand. Reinelm claimed a small meadow and rights of common within the prior's close of *Wlgid'e* moor, but, on the advice of friends, he granted whatever right he had there to the priory. This agreement, accepted by both parties, was confirmed by Richard de Humet's lord of Portchester (*Porcestria*), and no claim is ever to be raised again between them concerning the lands, grazing, wood, roads or paths, and if anything arises from this it will be settled by neighbours by agreement and deed (*scriptum*).

Southwick, the vigil of the feast of the Assumption in the year in which King Henry sent Richard de Humet' to Normandy (*Norm'*) and to take charge of his other lands beyond the sea. Witnesses: Richard Presbyter of Wymering; Ralph Presbyter of Portsea (*Portesia*); Richard Capellanus of Southwick; William de Risford; Henry de Mednil; [fo. 23ᵛ] Alexander de Burhu'; Richard, son of Daniel; Ivo Clericus; Roger Clericus; Richard Curtillarius; Edmund; Blachem'; and other of the prior's men; Roger Molendinarius; Goding'; William [   ][3] and all Reinelm's men.

1 Between the beginning of Henry II's reign and the date by which Philip had succeeded Walter as Prior of Southwick (I 23). In 1164 the king sent Richard de Hommet, Constable of Normandy, with the Bishop of Evreux, on an embassy to Louis VII of France, and thereafter Richard was engaged in putting down disturbances, probably in the Limousin (*Itinerary of Henry II* pp. 70, 73).

2 This must refer to Henry I, so that the priory had exchanged land with Reinelm's father, Henry, before 1135, while it was still at Portchester. Probably the land involved was part of the two hides at Applestead and Southwick given to the priory by its founder, William de Pont de l'Arche, on the occasion of its foundation (I 1 and notes 2, 4).

3 The right hand edge of the folio is damaged, and this name is lost.

Copy III 271. Variants: rubric, Richard de Humaz; Osedena; Dragleg'; Wulfward; Wulfgiþ'e more; Wimeringes, Wymeringes. [After the names of the first two witnesses add:] Item, Reinelm granted to the priory (i) his part of the common of Applestead (*Apelsteda*) between the two streams; Herbert de Burhunt' and his heir, Alexander, having previously granted their share of the same common [see I 121]; (ii) a small meadow, next to Algar's house, which was from his demesne; and (iii) his share of the common of *Chalnecroft'*. For the confirmation of these alms, the prior gave Reinelm a black colt from the stud of Richard de Humez, and will provide for him and for his wife two beautiful candles for the procession on the feast of the Purification of St Mary, in recognition of the gift of their share of *Chalnecroft'*, made with the consent of Reinelm's brother, Richard, and witnessed by Richard son of Daniel and Richard de Wimeringes.

I 121   [*c.* 1160–5][1]

Chirograph between the priory and Herbert de Burhunt' under the seal of R. de H[umeto].

AGREEMENT by Prior Walter and Southwick Priory with Herbert de Burhunta concerning lands exchanged in the time of King Henry. Dispute had arisen over common pasture which ought to have been shared, but which Herbert had enclosed and occupied as his own demesne. To settle this, the justice of the lord of Portchester (*iusticia domini de Porcestrie*) and neighbours and friends of the priory met many times, but were unable to complete the business to the satisfaction of both parties. However, when Herbert had been struck down by illness that proved fatal, he gathered his friends, sent for the prior and brothers of the priory, and humbly and penitently confessed that, on bad advice, he had unjustly opposed the priory (*sua mater ecclesia*) and harassed it in many ways. Wherefore he restored to the prior whatever he had that belonged by right to the priory, or whatever he had withheld of his alms and he gave seisin to the prior by means of a green branch (*per viridem ramum*). So that peace might be safely kept between the priory and his heirs, he ordered his son and heir, Alexander, to promise to observe what he had undertaken and on no consideration to change anything, and this he did.

First Herbert acknowledged that he had given the priory long previously his tithes and chapel, and in this he rejoiced. Also he had given—for the soul of his mother—the site of a mill with land pertaining to it, and the priory had built a mill, which he wished it to hold in perpetual alms. When he had been in prison in Portchester, Herbert had vowed to God that on his release he would give a virgate in alms to the church. After being released, he gave the priory his share of the common of Applestead (*Apelstede*),[2] viz. all his part between the two streams (*aque*). With the consent of all his sons, he now gave the priory those alms, free from all the service he had retained, and they besought the prior, with many prayers, to investigate, by a jury of law-worthy neighbours, how the exhange of lands was made in the time of King Henry, and to confirm it. This the prior promised to do. Having been reconciled to the priory in this way, Herbert died. Alexander, his heir, wishing to augment his father's alms, gave the priory, for his father's soul, the land of *Sadewlla* below the road, with the consent of all his brothers, and they came with him to put the gift on the altar so that their father's anniversary might always be celebrated in the priory.

After Herbert's death, it was agreed between Alexander and the priory that the prior should choose four of Alexander's men, viz. Selingar, Sewin Ribout, Jocelin Niger and Edwin Harel; and Alexander, four of the prior's men, viz. Roger Clericus, Blachemann, Seward and Pagan; and by mutual consent both parties chose from Reinelm de Burhunta's men, William de Morvilla and Roger Sturne. These ten swore to tell the truth concerning the exchanges and pastures according to their knowledge, viz:—7 acres of *Gerseworde* were exchanged for 7 acres of *Dichedecrofta;* the grove adjoining *Gerseworde* on the west was retained by the priory and another grove by Alexander; 7 acres above the hill on the north of the road were exchanged for *Smid'crofte* and *Wlgid'emore;* 5 acres in two enclosures (*garstuna*) and an acre beyond the hill were exhanged for 6 acres from *Chirichfurlonga* to the thorn tree (*spina*). The following belong to the priory:—*La Bienhalve;* an acre adjoining Dunning's half acre in the north; 2 acres of *Sadewlla* and 5 acres of *Osden;* also 1 acre above Reinelm's 2 acres and 1 acre above the road from Wymering (*Wimeringes*); ½ acre between Alexander's two marl pits (*suos duos marliz*), and Wlmer and his park; ½ acre that was Roger Sturne's in Alexander's enclosures under *apsancre* acre which Aldwin Peche held from the priory. On the south of Alexander's marl pit, ½ acre was taken from the priory's 3½ acres. And on *Wlfied'emore* the butts of 3 acres belonging to the priory are kept by Alexander in exchange for ½ acre in *Blakefurlong'* (*Et super Wlfied'emore butieres trium acrarum de ecclesia que remanserunt Alexandro propter dimidiam acram in Blakefurlong'*); 1 acre in *Stapelcrofte* adjoining *Bruces',* and ½ acre on the hill adjoining the priory's newly broken ground (*nostra fractura*); ½ acre in Reginald's close and a small meadow and curtillage belonging to the priory and a ?jointure (*junc'tura*) which was Wlward Cnave's; in the close, Alexander has 5 acres in exchange, and the priory has 3 acres in Sericus Surlefoche's tenement and 2 with Odo's land (*In clauso Alexander v acras cambium istorum habet ecclesia iii acras in tenemento Serici Surlefoche et ii cum terra Odonis*). *Chalnecrofte* is held in common. All [   ]*odhulle* is held [fo. 24] in common, and what was taken after King Henry's death is to be restored and held in common. The land in front of Reginald Dunstanvile's house is held in common. The ditch in front of the mill westwards to the bridge, and two small meadows, belong to the priory, and *Dichedecrofte* at Colemore (*Colemere*), and a salt pan (*salina*) at Portchester (*Porc'*). On the advice of jurors and neighbours the following exchange was agreed: Alexander will keep Roger Sturne's ½ acre from his enclosure (*garstuna*), and the ½ acre east of the road between Wlmer's land and the $\frac{1}{2}$ acre between his two marl pits, in exchange for 2 acres of *Subpanteolfeslie*. When these lands were agreed, perambulated and recorded, the prior granted Alexander the right to hold them until the following Michaelmas so that he should not lose his labour and seed as they were sown; then, when harvest was in, he would release them, and what previously had been held in common would revert to common. And as Alexander agreed to this willingly and in a good spirit, the prior demised to him $\frac{1}{4}$ virgate (*feord'ingus*) at *Horeapeldre* from Pantulf's fee,[3] the corner (*angulus*) of *Pleiseiz*, and Edwin Harel, one of his bondmen. This the jurors witnessed.

At Michaelmas, however, Alexander released part of the land and retained part, so that discord arose again between him and the priory. And because the king was levying danegeld that year, Alexander wanted to make the priory chargeable for service due from the alms it had received from his father and himself (*voluit ecclesiam de elemosina patris sui et sua in servitium ponere*), so that what the priory held from his fee would be taxed at half a hide. The prior was unwilling to undertake service which had never before been the responsibility of the priory, and on the advice of friends and neighbours he came to terms with Alexander and gave him a palfrey and 1 mark so that the priory might hold from him and his heirs in perpetuity in free alms, quit of all service and aids which might be required by the king or lords. And Alexander was to exchange $2\frac{1}{2}$ acres in *Shadewlla* from Hamelin's fee with Robert de Feversham if he could, and if not he was to give the prior land of similar value in another place. Alexander agreed to all this and confirmed the present deed. Witnesses: Gilbert de Extuna and his brother; Reginald de Hamel'; William de Risfort; Osbert, his brother; Richard Presbyter of Wymering (*Wimeringes*); Richard, son of Daniel; Rein' de Burhun'; Richard; his brother; Peter de Cosham; Robert de Ho; Henry Clericus de Hamel'; Bernard; Henry and Ralph, brothers of Alexander; Selingar; Edwin Harel; Simon de Hamel'; Roger Clericus; Godwin Turneor; Osmund and Robert, his sons; Elgar'; Richard Curtill'; Edmund; Adam Cocus; Blaceman'; Seward; Pagan; Seman' Peche; Seman' Mercator; Odo.

1 The final agreement copied here was drawn up between Alexander de Burhunt and the priory, after the death of Alexander's father, Herbert, as the text shows. It probably belongs to a date not much earlier than the subsequent agreement of 1165 (I 122), and may be the same date, or slightly earlier than Reinelm de Burhunt's chirograph, also said to be under the seal of Richard de Hommet (I 120). See also I 29, 30, 103.

2 For the location of Applestead, see I 1, note 4.

3 See I 103. Alexander did eventually hold this land from the priory. It was probably part of the hide in Applestead bought by William de Pont de l'Arche from Ivo Pantulf, and given to the priory at the time of its foundation (I 1).
Copy III 194. Variants: Burhunt'; Shadewulle, Schadewella; Goselinus; Gerseworthe; Smythcroft'; Wlfiethemore, Wlfiepemore; Cherecforlonga; Wimerynges; Wulmerus; Wlfwardus; Serecus; Strodhulle; Dunstanville [no forename]; Forlingum; Gilbert (*Gisleb'*) de Exton and his brother [the names of other witnesses are not copied].

Chirograph between the priory and Alexander de Burh' under the seal of Walter Briton.[1]

AGREEMENT between Alexander, son of Herbert de Burhunta, and Southwick Priory. After the settlement made between Alexander and Prior Walter, concerning pastures, and alms given by Alexander's father, and drawn up under the seal of Richard de Humet',[2] Alexander sued the prior over the mill which, as the first chirograph testified, his father, Herbert, had given, in perpetual alms, to the priory, with land surrounding it, and whatever right he had between the two streams (*aque*) which are on either side of the prior's ploughland of Appelstead (*Apelsteda*).[3] Alexander would not allow the prior to repair his mill, but complained to the bailiffs of the lord of Portchester (*Porc'*),[4] viz. to Walter Bret, steward, and Henry, the constable, and other men, that his land had suffered great damage from certain sluices the prior had made for letting out the water, and had, so he said, unreasonably put them on his land. The prior replied that he had made them lawfully and reasonably, and had put them on land given to the priory, with the mill, by Alexander's father. To settle this dispute the lord's bailiffs and his justice and almost all neighbours and free men of the shire (*provincia*) met three times on the land, and having heard the case of each party gave judgement (*ad iuditium perrexerunt*). When however Alexander's friends, who favoured his cause, discussed the judgement amongst themselves, they asked the prior to come to another amicable agreement. The prior, on the advice of his friends, gave Alexander 1 mark, over and above the 2 marks he had given him for the first agreement. It was decided that: (i) the priory should keep in perpetuity a certain small bed of rushes (*iunchura*), which lies in front of the mill enclosed on one side by an old conduit or watercourse (*ductus vel filus aque*), and on the other by a new one which turns the mill; and should have the right to open and close the sluices in peace; (ii) Alexander cannot claim anything beyond the first water-course in the south; (iii) the prior can set up, raise and strengthen (*erigere et elevare et roborare*) the mill pond as far as a certain mark which Alexander fixed as part of the agreement viz. a small elm (*ulnus*), and, for the love of the prior (*in amore priori*) he agreed to extend the width by 8 feet (*ultra progredi concessit latitudinem viii pedum*); (iv) the roads (*vie*) made for Alexander from the priory's land at Applestead will be [fo. 24ᵛ] maintained, and the footpath giving him access to the church which should be 6 feet wide for convenience of passage (*sic in pace servetur*), and will be enclosed with a hedge or ditch as the prior wishes or as is expedient (*vel facultas ei suppeditaverit*). Witnesses: Walter Bret; Henry de Mednill'; Robert de Ramvilla; William de Risfort; Osbert, his brother; Matthew de Scuris; William de Haliwella; Richard de la Bera; Robert Clericus, his brother; Reginald de Denemeda; Reinalm; Richard, his brother; Richard, son of Daniel; Peter de Cosham; Richard de Wimering'; Roger Clericus; Robert Turnur; Robert de Ho; Henry de Hameled'; [   ][6] de Froillia; Walter, brother of Alexander; Bernard.

This exchange was made between them: Alexander will keep *Solvelede* acre adjoining the road from Wymering (*Wimeringes*), and the prior an acre in another furlong which Coleman held between 2½ acres belonging to the priory.

1 Richard de Hommet confirmed an exchange of lands in Northamptonshire between his son, Engeram, and Walter Briton in *c.* 1170–80 (*Langley Cartulary* 570, p. 116).

2 See I 121 and note.

3 See I 1, note 4.

4 At this time Richard de Hommet appears to have held the castle of Portchester (I 120).

5 Probably Henry de Mednill' or Mesnil (see second witness and I 6).

6 This name is lost on the right hand edge of the folio.
Copy III 181. Variants: de Burhunt'; de Humez; Walter Bert'; de Medenille; Wymerynges.

Transcripts of the priory's charters from the time of Prior Guy (*Incipiunt transcripta kartarum Sudwic' ecclesie de tempore Guidonis prioris*).

I 123   [1174–83, possibly December 1174]²

King Henry II's charter of protection¹

NOTIFICATION by King Henry that the church of St Mary, Southwick, is his own church, and the prior and canons, their lands, rents, men and all their possessions, are under his protection (*sunt in manu mea et custodia et protectione*); therefore they and all their affairs and possessions, secular and ecclestiastical, are to be given support and protection as the king's own property, so that no violence or harm is done to them nor allowed to be done. If any wrong is done to them, they are to receive full justice without delay. They are not to be impleaded concerning any holding they have in their demesne, except before the king. Witnesses: Richard, Bishop of Winchester; M. Walter Constanc', Archdeacon of Oxford; Godfrey de Luci.

Vaudreuil (*Vallis Rodol'*)

1 This charter is printed in full in Latin in Appendix III (Mason, "The King, the Chamberlain and Southwick Priory", p. 9).

2 Not earlier than October 1174, when Richard of Ilchester was consecrated Bishop of Winchester, nor later than May 1183, when Walter of Coutances was elected Bishop of Lincoln. December 1174 is the suggested date for a charter issued by Henry II at Vaudreuil, and witnessed, amongst others, by Richard, Bishop of Winchester. M. Walter of Coutances was in Normandy in the same month (*Itinerary of Henry II* pp. 187, 186). There is no other record in the Itinerary of the king at Vaudreuil before 1183.
Copy II 7.
Copy III 991. Variant: names of second and third witnesses only given.

I 124 [1181-2]

[fo. 25] NOTIFICATION by Richard, Bishop of Winchester, of the dedication of the church of Southwick Priory. [Similar to Bishop Augustine's notification, see I 25. Variants and copies are listed there.]

I 125 Copy of I 124, see I 25.

I 126 [1181-2]

[fo. 25ᵛ] NOTIFICATION by Seffrid [II], Bishop of Chichester, of the dedication of the church of Southwick Priory. [Similar to Bishop Augustines notification, see I 25].

[At the bottom of folio 25ᵛ, the beginning of Bishop Augustine's notification of the dedication of the church of Southwick Priory is written. The remainder is on folio 4. The notification has been calendared as I 25.]

I 127[1] [early 13th century, before *c.* 1210][2]

GIFT, with warranty, by Prior Guy (*Gwydo*) and Southwick Priory to Guy (*Guydo*) Wake, of all their land at Ketton (*Ketene*), [Rutland], with men, rents and all other appurtenances which Sir William de Humeto gave the priory for the soul of his wife, Lady Lucy; also their land at Cottesmore (*Cotesmore*), [Rutland], given them by Robert de Novo Burgo for the soul of the same Lucy. Guy and his heirs will hold these lands at fee farm, free from relief and all other service belonging to the priory, paying ½ mark annual rent[3] on the Sunday in the middle of Lent at Stamford (*Stanford*), [Lincolnshire], in the parish of St John, at the place called [ ][4] which is in Guy Wake's fee. Consideration, 40 marks, by means of which the priory has freed itself from the burden of Jewish usury which gravely oppressed it at that time. Guy and his heirs are bound to do fealty to the priory on payment of the aforesaid annual rent. Witnesses: etc. [*sic*].

1 Between fo. 25ᵛ and fo. 5; on a piece of parchment measuring 15.5 cms × 13.2 cms.

2 Guy was Prior of Southwick at least until 1210 (I 99). The priory had acquired the property in Ketton and Cottesmore in the late 12th century (I 76-8).

3 The ½ mark rent due from Sir Guy is recorded in the rental (I 182, fo. 38ᵛ). He appears to have obtained the property on very favourable terms, perhaps in view of the priory's urgent need of ready money, or the difficulty of collecting rents so far from Southwick. Sir William de Hommet's gift at Ketton was 4 marks' worth of rent and a further 4s. 8d. a year, and Robert de Novo Burgo had given a virgate at Cottesmore (I 77-8).

4 Space left blank in MS.

I 128[1]   [1186–9][2]

GIFT in free alms, with warranty so far as possible against all except
royal service, by Robert de Henton'—for the salvation of his soul and
those of all his lords, ancestors, heirs and kindred—to Southwick Priory,
of the whole ploughland (*cultura*) adjoining Ludmore (*Ledmera*), which
is said to be 7 acres; and all the land called *Aldelonde*, with part of the
grove which extends as far as the hedge between the aforesaid land and
the fee of Hambledon (*Hameledon'*). The priory will pay 3s. annual rent
at St Giles' fair, in lieu of all service; the same rent as Henry son of
Herbert de Burh' used to pay when he held the aforesaid lands. The gift
is made with the consent of the aforesaid Henry.[3]

Also Robert has given, in perpetual alms, all the land from his demesne
that lies between *Aldeland'* and the road that runs towards Hinton
(*Hent'*), and adjoins the land of Wlfric de Crabbeden' and Gilbert de
Ledmer'. The lands of *Aldeland'* and Ludmore are assessed for royal
taxation as ¼ virgate (*unum ferlingum*), and the land from Robert's
demesne between *Aldeland* and the road as ⅛ virgate. Consideration,
40s., given to Robert in his great need, and many other benefits. He was
accepted into full confraternity. Robert has chosen to be buried at the
priory, and the canons will celebrate his anniversary each year. Witnesses:
Geoffrey, son of Azo, sheriff; Matthew de Scur'; Robert Mald'; Roger
de Scur'; Roger, son of Henry; Nicholas de la Mara; Richard de Limesia;
Anketill Lupus; Reginald and Richard de Denemed'; Henry, son of
Herbert; Thomas de Ho; Richard and Alexander, chaplains; Thomas,
son of Roger; Thomas Cementarius; Hirdman; Alfred Parment'.

1 Verso of I 127, see note 1.

2 The first witness was sheriff of Hampshire from 1179 to 1189 (P.R.O. *List of
Sheriffs to 1831* (Lists and Indexes, 9; 1898) p. 54). The 7 acres at Ludmore with
Aldelonde had been given to the priory by Henry de Burhunt' not earlier than
1186 (I 135, note 1).

3 It was Henry de Burhunt', son of Herbert, who had held the land of Robert
de Henton' (I 130, III 482), and gave it to the priory (I 135). Robert's charter is
strictly a confirmation of that gift, reserving to himself the 3s. annual rent that
Henry used to pay him, although his "gift" is said to be in free, pure and
perpetual alms.
Copy III 477. Variants: Hameldon'; de Borhunt'; Aeldelond', Aldelond; Henton';
Crabden'.

I 129   [1186–9][1]

[fo. 26] GIFT, in free alms, by Robert de Hent'—for his salvation and
that of all his lords, kindred, heirs and friends—to Southwick Priory, of
all the land from his demesne that lies south of the land of Wluric de
Crabeden' and west of the road adjoining the tenements of Henry de
Burh' and Gilbert de Ledmere. The priory will be quit of all service
owing to Robert and his heirs, but when royal service is imposed on
Robert and he is unable to avoid it, the priory will be assessed at ⅛

virgate for the aforesaid alms. Witnesses: Robert Mald'; Matthew de Scur'; Roger de Scur'; Richard de la Mare; Anketill Lupus; Henry, son of Herbert; Simon; William Lupus; Richard Capellanus; Ralph Cocus; Thomas, son of Roger; Peter, son of Geoffrey.

1 The gifts recorded in this charter and I 130 both feature in another charter from Robert de Henton', which can be dated 1186-9 (I 128). I 129 and 130 probably predate I 128, but only slightly. Six of the witnesses above also witnessed I 128.
Copy III 481. Variants: rubric: Charter of Robert de Henton' concerning 9 acres assessed at ½ ferling; Wlfric de Crabbeden'; de Borhunt'; Ledemere; de Scuris.

I 130 [1186-9][1]

GIFT, in free alms, by Robert de Hent'—for the salvation of his soul and those of his lords, kindred and friends—to Southwick Priory, of the whole tenement Henry de Burh', son of Herbert, held from him at Hinton (*Hent'*), viz. the ploughland, said to be 7 acres, adjoining Ludmore (*Ledmer'*) and all the land called *Aldelond'* with appurtenances.[2] The priory will pay Robert and his heirs the same service as Henry used to pay, viz. 3s. at the feast of St Giles [1 September] for all except royal service. This gift was made by concession, and at the request, of the aforesaid Henry.[3] Witnesses: Matthew de Scur'; Roger de Scur'; Richard de Porc', Robert de Wimering', chaplains; Richard, son of Daniel; William de la Mara; Anket'; Ralph Ridel; Roger de Montchan'; Ralph Cocus.

1 See dating evidence for I 129.
2 See III 482.
3 For Henry de Burhunt's gift of this land to the priory, see I 135.
Copy III 476. Variants: de Henton'; Henry, son of Herbert; de Scuris.

I 131 [late 12th century, *c.* 1193-1200][1]

[List of tenants at Hollowell, Northamptonshire][2]

Arnold [Ernaldus] de Holewell' holds 1 virgate for 5s. rent viz. 15d. at each feast: St Peter ad Vincula [1 August], Michaelmas [29 September], Christmas and Easter.
   Anketillus, son of Levricus, holds 1 virgate for the same rent at the same terms; Alexander, son of Roger Anglicus, ditto; Hugh Pintelman, ditto; Lewin, son of Richard, ditto.
   Ralph le Kenteis holds ½ virgate for 20d. rent payable to the priory, and 10d. to Guy de Diva.
   Those present at Guilsborough (*Gildelburg'*), [Northamptonshire], where the [tenants] did fealty:—Sir Henry, deacon of Haddon (*Haddon'*);

Warnerus, chaplain of Guilsborough (*Gildesburg*); Brother Adam, brother of the hospital, then master, at Guilsborough; Baldwin de Wagrave; Buisson; Simon de Wirec'; Gupil; Alexander, son of the deacon of Haddon.

1 For dating evidence, see I 132, note 1.

2 No rubric in MS. but cf. I 71, 72, 78, 79. The first entry is in the same careful hand as the text of Guy de Diva's charter (I 132). The following entries and rubric for Guy's charter appear to be in a different, less neat, but probably contemporary hand. The list is of tenants and land, some if not all given to the priory by Guy de Diva, but it is not identical with the list in Guy's charter or in the priory's rental (I 182, fo. 38ᵛ). The total amount of land above is 5½ virgates and the rent 26s. 8d. In the charter and rental the land totals 3¼ virgates, but according to the rental the same rent of 2 marks or 26s. 8d. is paid. Hollowell is 8 miles north-north-west of Northampton; Guilsborough 1½ miles north-west of Hollowell, East Haddon 3 miles south-south-west, and West Haddon 4 miles west.

I 132   [*c.* 1193–1200][1]

GIFT, in free alms, by Guy de Diva—for the soul of his brother, William Diva, and his own salvation and that of his brother, Sir Robert, and all his kindred and friends—to Southwick Priory, of 2 marks' worth of land in Hollowell (*Holewell*), [Northamptonshire], reckoned in men and their holdings, viz: Anketillus, son of Levericus holds 2 virgates; Hugh Capellanus, 1 virgate; Ralph le Kenteis, ¼ virgate. Also Guy has given ¼ [fo. 26ᵛ] of the mill at Hollowell, of which half belongs to Philip de Diva and the other half to himself and his heirs. The priory will hold the above 3¼ virgates, the men and their households (*sequela*), with meadows, pastures and ¼ of the mill, free from all service. Witnesses: Robert de Diva; Simon de Hachingeha'; Hugh de Muscamp'; Ralph de Cha'a'meri; Simon de Sumeri; William de Muschamp'; Odo de Ponte; William de Achingeha'; Thomas de Essece; Thomas de Sancta Maria; Walter Bucel; Gupil.

1 William de Diva had died by 1193. He was buried at Southwick, and his kinsman, William, Earl of Arundel, gave the priory an annual sester of wheat for the celebration of his anniversary (III 85). Hugh of Avallon, Bishop of Lincoln, confirmed Guy's gift before 1200 (I 146). For the later history of the priory's tenements at Hollowell, see I 243, 242; II 62, 63.
Copy III 241. Variants: Livericus; de Kenteys; Holiwell'; Roger [*sic*] de Diva; Simon de Achingeham.

I 133   [1189–94][1]

Charter of John de Gisorz concerning the tithe of a water-mill in Portsea (*Portesia*).

NOTIFICATION by John de Gisorz to Sir Godfrey, Bishop of Winchester, that he has given, in free alms—for the soul of his wife,

Agnes, and the salvation of himself, his lords and heirs, and the souls of his father and mother and all his kindred, lords and friends—to Southwick Priory the whole tithe of his water mill on the arm of the sea north of his vill of Portsmouth (*Portesm'*), and has placed this gift on the high altar of Southwick church. Witnesses: Robert de la Haie; Philip de la Stane; Robert de Meisnill'; John de Rebez; William de Bello Monte; Roger de Karcenni; Gilbert de Morvile; William de Aubenni; William de Portesia; Richard Lachevei, chaplain; Richard, son of Daniel; Henry, son of Herbert; John de Possebroc; Alexander de Karcheni.

1 Godfrey de Lucy was consecrated Bishop of Winchester in October 1189. After King Richard's return to England in 1194, John de Gisors forfeited his lands, including Portsmouth, presumably because he had supported the rebellion of Richard's younger brothr, John (Hoad, "The Origins of Portsmouth", p. 19). John de Rebez was sheriff of Hampshire from Michaelmas 1190 to Michaelmas 1191. If he is the witness of that name above, not described as sheriff, it would appear that the notification was not made during his shrievalty.
Copy III 204. Variants: Portesm' [for Portesia, rubric]; de Gisors; Lestan' [for la Stane]. Marginal note: concerning the tithe of Portsmouth (*Portesmuth'*) mill.

I 134 [1189–94]¹

NOTIFICATION by John de Gisorz to Sir Godfrey, Bishop of Winchester, that he has granted, in free alms—[salvation clause as above, I 133]—to Southwick Priory, 20s. worth of rent in the parish of Portsea (*Portesia*), viz: ½ hide John de Kingeston' held, for which he used to pay 10s. annual rent and 32d. for service; together with John and all his household (*sequela*), and his messuage and croft, for which he used to pay 2s. annual rent; and 1½d. for ½ acre Fabian used to hold; and, to complete the rent, ½ virgate Richerius held in Kingston (*Kingeston'*), for which he used to pay 30d. annual rent and 8d. for service; also a small croft (*croftetta*) in front of the house of Richard Shroch', for which Richerius used to pay 12d. annual rent; and the messuage formerly held by Richard de Suwod', and afterwards by Richerius, who used to pay 16d. annual rent for it. The priory will hold all the aforesaid tenements, with the men and their households, and may improve and enlarge them as is expedient. Witnesses: Robert de la Haie; Philip de le Stane; John de Resbaco; William de Bello Monte; Ralph de Sancto Georgio; Roger de Karchenni; Gilbert de Morvil'; William de Aubenni; Peter de Sancta Maria Ecclesia; William de Portesia.

1 See dating evidence for I 133.
Copy III 203. Variants: Gisors; Kyngeston'; Sroch'; de Hai; de Stan'.

I 135 [1186–9]¹

GIFT, in free alms, by Henry, son of Herbert de Burhunta—for the salvation of his soul and those of his father and mother, kindred and

lords—to Southwick Priory, of all his land at *Aldelond'* and all his
ploughland, said to be 7 acres, adjoining Ludmore (*Ledmere*) at Hinton
(*Hentona*), which Robert de Hent' gave him for his service and confirmed
by his charter.[2] Henry gave that charter to the priory and put it, with
this one, on the high altar of Southwick church. Consideration, 6 marks,
[fo. 27] paid to Henry in his need. Witnesses: Earl William de Arundel';
[Her]bert, son of Herbert; Simon Canonicus of Chichester; Simon, son
of Richerius; Roger de Scur'; Richard de Limesi; Robert de [   ];[2]
Benedict de Haversam; Ralph de Ferri; Peter and Matthew, sons of
Herbert; Richard, son of Daniel; Audoenus Clericus; Reinald de
Denemed'; Adam de Henton'; Henry, son of Richard; Reginald Giffard;
Walter, son of Reinelm; Hugh, son of Ralph; Roger de Montechanesi.

1 Robert de Henton gave the land to Henry, son of Herbert de Burhunta, after
1177 and before 1189, probably *c.* 1185 (III 482). He confirmed Henry's gift to
the priory before 1189 (I 128). The first witness above must be William d'Aubigny,
second Earl of Arundel, who was not styled earl until 1186, and died in 1193.
His father, also named William, had died in 1176, before Robert's gift to Henry
was made.

2 The top left-hand corner of this folio is damaged.
Copy III 179. Variants: Aldelonde; Henton'; Robert de Henton'; de Arundelle;
Herbert, son of Herbert.

I 136   [1186-93][1]

Confirmation by W. Earl of Arundel concerning Anmore (*Anedmer'*),
and the land Robert de Hent' gave.

CONFIRMATION, in free alms, by William, Earl of Sussex—for the
salvation of the king and of himself and all his family (*et meorum
omnium*), and for the souls of his father and mother and all his ancestors
and heirs—to Southwick Priory, of the gift to them by Ralph de
Cumbrai of 1 virgate from his demesne in *Prevettus* adjoining Anmore
(*Anedemere*), and another virgate adjoining that which his brother
William gave, with his consent, to the priory with 10 acres; also a certain
ploughland adjoining *Aldelond'* next to the land of Wlfric de Crabbeden'
and Gilbert de Ledmere which Robert de Henton' gave to the priory.
The priory will hold all the aforesaid tenements freely as the charters of
the donors testify. Witnesses: Robert de Mortuomari; Reinerus de
Aubenni; Roger Tirel; Roger Gulafre; Ilbertus de Rachint'; Robert, son
of Geoffrey; Walkelin de Bosevile; Roger, Prior of Sherborne (*Sireburn'*);
Stephen Capellanus; Ralph de Aubenni; William de Aubenni, son of
Earl William (*filio meo*); M. Gregory; M. William; Robert de Cleies;
Andrew Capellanus; Andrew Pincerna.

1 The donor of this confirmation is almost certainly William, second Earl of
Arundel (see I 135, note 1), who died in 1193. His son, who appears as witness,
was born after 1173. Another witness, Roger, was Prior of Monk Sherborne,
c. 1170-1200 (Knowles *Heads of Religious Houses* p. 106). See also I 57-60;
I 128-30.

Copy III 114. Variants: Preuectus; Eldelond'; Crabbedene; Ledmer'; [after Robert de Henton's gift add:] also all the land of Bekewode which Ralph de Cumbrai gave in alms together with the service of Arnold (*Ernald*) Frilende; Witnesses: ?Geoffrey (Gofr') de Aubeigni, the donor's borther; William de Milliers; and others.

I 137   [1186-93][1]

CONFIRMATION, in free alms, by William, Earl of Sussex—[salvation clause as above, I 136]—to Southwick Priory, of the gift by Henry, son of Herbert, of land called *Aldelond* and 7 acres of ploughland adjoining Ludmore (*Ledmere*), which Robert de Henton had given him for his service. The priory will hold the tenements freely, as the charters of Henry and Robert testify.[2] Witnesses; Robert de Mortuomari; Rein' de Aubenni; Roger Tyrel; Roger Gulafre; Robert, son of Geoffrey; Andrew Capellanus; Roger, Prior of Sherborne (Shirebur'); Ilbertus de Rachint'; Ralph de Aubenni; William de Aubenni; Stephen Capellanus; M. Gregory; M. William; Robert de Cléés; Andrew Pincerna.

1 See I 135, 136 and notes.
2 I 135, 128-30.
Copy III 113. Variant: Adelonde.

I 138   [1180-1204, *c.* 1190][1]

Charter of William de Hum' concerning the manor of Boarhunt (Burhunt').

GIFT, in free alms, by William de Hum', the King's Constable—for the salvation of the souls of his father and mother, himself, his wife Lucy, his sons and daughters, and all his ancestors and successors—to Southwick Priory, of whatever he had at Boarhunt in the way of wood [fo. 27ᵛ]and plain, waters, roads, paths, men, demesnes, and all things and places, except the tenements of Michael de Basevill',[2] Alexander de Bera and Robert Clericus,[3] which he has kept. Witnesses: Richard de Hum', William de Saio, Henry de Hum', Jordan de Hum', [Thomas][4] de Hum', Engeramn de Hum', sons of the donor who give their consent; Ralph, the donor's chaplain; Odo Pincerna; Horatio; Henry Medicus; William de Capella; Robert de Haia; Geoffrey de Semill'; Engeramn de Cardunvilla; Robert Aurifaber; Robert Capellanus; Ralph Clericus of Airel (*Airellus*), [Manche, Normandy]; and many others.

1 William de Hommet was Constable of Normandy from 1180 until his defection to Philip Augustus of France in 1204. In 1190 his six sons (as named above, in the same order and including Thomas) gave their consent to a gift of land made by their father to the Abbey of Aunay on the occasion of the dedication of its church (*Gallia Christiana* XXIV, p. 90).

2 Michael de Baseville gave an acre of his land to the priory (I 37).

3 Possibly this is Robert de Bera, clerk to William de Hommet and to his father, Richard. Robert also gave land to the priory (I 73).

4 The edge of the folio is damaged and this name is lost, but see note 1 above and the copy in H.R.O. 4M53/B7 below. The copies of I 138 in volume III give the names of two witnesses only.
Copy III 42. Variants: de Humet'; Borhunt'; de Basevile; de Saieo.
Copy III 44. Variants: de Humet'; Bourhunt'; de Basevile; de Saieo.
Copy III 46. Variants: de Humet'; Borhunt'; de Basevyle; witnesses: Richard de Hum'; William de Saieo; "and with the consent of my sons (*et filiis meis testibus et concedentibus*); and many others".
Copy in H.R.O. 4M53/B7, p. 1. Variants: Basevilla; Humet'; Saeio, Jordan de Humet'; clerk; Thomas de Humet'; Edo Pincerva, then steward; Sir Robert de Haia.

I 139   [*c.* 1185–1210][1]

ABJURATION made in the hundred of Portsdown (*Portesdune*) on the feast of Saints Primus and Felicianus [9 June] by Walter, son of Hugh Locc,[2] and his brothers, Clement, the first born (*primogenitus*), and Richard, the younger (*natu posterior*), of whatever right they had or could have in the part appertaining to them of the land their father had held in the manor of West Boarhunt (*Westburhunt*), for which 5s. ought to be paid with other service. Quitclaim in favour of Southwick Priory. Consideration, 20s. Witnesses: Guy, Prior of Southwick; Robert Sacristanus; Alexander de Burh'; Walter and Henry, his brothers; German de Ranvill'; William de Ho; William de Warda; William de Ranvill'; Simon de Burh'; Martin; and Humphrey Mahum' and John, serjeants of the hundred. The priory paid the brothers 10s. on that day.

1 Guy occurs as Prior of Southwick between these dates (I 91, 99).

2 In the earliest surviving rental for West Boarhunt, a Hugh Loc paid 3s. rent and owed suit of court (I 175, fo. 34[v]).

I 140   [1180–93, *c.* 1190][1]

GIFT, in perpetual alms, by William de Humetis [rubric: Hum'] the King's Constable—for the salvation of his soul and those of his father and mother and his wife Lucy, of pious memory, and all his ancestors and successors—to Southwick Priory, of the church of St Nicholas, West Boarhunt (*Westburhunta*), with tithes and all appurtenances, for the upkeep of its guest-house (*ad sustentationem hospitalitatis sue*). Witnesses: William de Saio; Richard de Hum'; Henry de Hum'; Thomas de Hum'.

1 See dating evidence for I 63. See also I 141, 64, 83. Whereas by I 63 William de Hommet granted the advowson of Boarhunt church to the priory, by the above charter he appears to have given it full possession of the church (see William's charter of confirmation I 76, and the variant in the copy III 40).
Copy III 49. Variants: de Humet'; de Saieo. [The names of the first two witnesses are given in reverse order.]

I 141   4 October 1193[1]

INSPEXIMUS by Godfrey, Bishop of Winchester, of the charter of
William de Humet' giving to Southwick Priory the Church of St Nicholas,
West Boarhunt (*Westburh'*).[2] Godfrey has admitted the canons of Southwick to that church at William's presentation, but Simon Clericus will
keep his vicarage while he lives. After Simon's death the priory will have
possession of the church with all appurtenances, saving episcopal rights
and customs and reasonable maintenance for the vicar, who will minister
there for the bishop and his successors, and will be responsible to the
priory for temporalities and to the bishop for spiritualities. Witnesses:
M. A[micius], Archdeacon of Surrey (*Surr'*);[3] M. Alexander, ?Gregory
(*G'G'*), John, chaplains; Godfrey Territus, Reginald, Humphrey
(*Unfridus*), Stephen, Peter, Simon, Henry, clerks.
                        Winchester, 4th year of Godfrey's episcopate.
[Contemporary note in left hand margin:] This charter was cancelled
because of the later one (*ista confracta est propter sequentem*).[4]

1 Godfrey de Lucy was consecrated Bishop of Winchester on 22 October 1189.

2 See I 140 and I 63, 64.

3 M. Amicius occurs as Archdeacon of Surrey *c.* 1191–1215, and had died before
26 October 1216 (*Fasti* II, p. 94).

4 The words *propter sequentem* would normally mean "because of the next one";
but, although I 142 was also issued by Bishop Godfrey, it is obviously not the
document to which this reference applies. Presumably the reference is to some
subsequent charter or agreement concerning the church of West Boarhunt, but, if
so, it does not appear to have been copied into the cartularies.

I 142   12 March 1196

[fo. 28] [NOTIFICATION by Godfrey de Lucy, Bishop of Winchester].[1]
Hitherto the bodies of the dead have been carried from Portsmouth
(*Portesmue*) to the mother church of Portsea (*Portesia*) with great
difficulty and danger on account of the twisting road and gusting storms.
Therefore, at the request of King Richard and the canons of Southwick,
to whom the church of Portsea and chapel of St Thomas, Portsmouth,[2]
and their other appurtenances in the whole island of Portsea are known
by right to belong, the bishop has solemnly consecrated the cemetery of
that chapel and two altars there. Trusting in God's mercy and the merits
of Saints Peter and James and others in whose honour he has dedicated
the aforesaid altars, he has granted 20 days' indulgence to all the faithful
who, truly penitent and confessed, worship God there within 8 days of
the consecreation; to those who visit the place on the anniversary of
either of the altars, or on the feast of any of the saints in whose memory

they are consecrated, and to those who bring gifts, he has granted 7 days' indulgence for (*ad*) each altar. The consecration and grant of indulgence took place on [the above date]. The bishop wishes it to be recorded for future reference that he had dedicated the altar on the south side in honour of the Saints and brothers James and John, the Blessed Gregory and Saints Katherine and Margaret, and the altar on the north side in honour of Saints Peter the Apostle, Lawrence the Martyr, Martin and Leonard, Confessors, and the Blessed Mary Magdalene. Anathema pronounced against anyone daring to disturb the peace of that place, and peace and honour in Christ Jesus and life eternal to all serving there with due reverence. Amen.

> The feast of St Gregory, 4 Ides of
> March, A.D. 1196, 7 Richard I, the
> 7th year of [Godfrey's] episcopate.

1 The top left hand corner of folio 28 is missing. The identity of the bishop can be ascertained from the date of the charter.

2 For the origins of the chapel of St Thomas the Martyr, now incorporated into Portsmouth Cathedral, see I 116, 94, 61 and note.

I 143   1189

AGREEMENT between S[imon], Abbot of Quarr (*Quarraria*)[1] and G[uy], Prior of Southwick. The Abbot of Quarr, with the unanimous consent of his chapter, and on the advice of William de Dovera, Abbot of Savigny (*Saviniensis*),[2] granted to Southwick Priory the whole tenement called *Planta*,[3] which Baldwin de Portesia had given to the abbey, with wood, meadow, land, pasture, and buildings;[4] and a certain virgate adjoining William de Warda's land,[5] which Pagan de Portesia had exchanged for ½ virgate the abbey had in Portsea (*Portesia*) which the aforesaid Baldwin had given them. The priory will hold the aforesaid [fo. 28ᵛ] tenements in perpetuity for an annual rent of 20s., viz. 10s. at Easter and 10s. at Michaelmas. This has been mutually agreed because *Planta* is a long way from Quarr Abbey and of little use to it, whereas it is in the parish of Southwick, near and convenient to the priory. Consideration, 20s. If, however, the monks of Quarr acquire other lands or rents in that parish, the priory cannot claim them by virtue of this agreement. To draw closer the bond between the two convents, the abbey will celebrate divine service on the death of any canon of Southwick as for one of its monks, and the priory will do likewise for the monks of Quarr as for its own canons, and they will help each other in business matters when requested. Witnesses: Sefr[idus], Bishop of Chichester;[7] Jonas, Prior of Hastings;[8] Sefr[idus] Thesaur'; M. Robert de Boseham;[9] Matthew de Scur'; Roger de Scur'; Richard Presbiter of Walesworth (*Walesword'*); Anketillus Lupus; Rein' and Richard de Denemed'; William Clericus of Grafton (*Grafton'*); Thomas, son of Herbert; Henry, son of Herbert; Roger Greuesac; Roger de Montechan'; Gilbert Talebot; Thomas, son of Roger; Walter de Burhunta.

1 Simon, Abbot of Quarr, occurs 1189–95 (Hockey *Quarr Abbey* Appendix B, p. 259).

2 Quarr Abbey on the Isle of Wight near Ryde, was a daughter-house of Savigny in Normandy, and was founded by Baldwin de Redvers, probably in 1132 (Hockey, *op. cit.*, pp. 5–6).

3 Represented today by Plant Farm about 3 miles east of Southwick.

4 Baldwin's original charter has survived (P.R.O. E326/9260). It had been granted before 1144 as land given by Baldwin is mentioned in Pope Lucius II's bull of that date confirming the possessions of Quarr Abbey (Hockey, *op. cit.*, pp. 9, 85).

5 William de Warda's tenement in Drayton in Farlington was given to the priory at William's request by his lord, William de Hommet, *c.* 1180–9 (I 65 and note).

6 The top right hand corner of folio 28ᵛ is damaged; the missing words have been supplied from the copy at III 124.

7 Seffrid II was Bishop of Chichester from 1180 to 1204.

8 Jonas occurs as Prior of Hastings, *c.* 1176–89 (Knowles *Heads of Religious Houses* p. 165).

9 Canon of Chichester Cathedral, who appears as a witness *c.* 1187–1197. (*The Acta of the Bishops of Chichester, 1075–1207* ed. H. Mayr-Harting (Canterbury and York Society, 130; 1964) p. 215).
Copy III 124.
Original is in P.R.O. E326/8901. Variants: William de Douem; Self' Thesaurar'; Waleswrth'; de Graft'; de Burh'. Top cut straight through letters.

Seal: on tag; round, *c.* 4.5 cms; natural wax, damaged; device, a church; inscription missing. Counter seal: pointed oval, 4 cms × 2.8 cms; device, an eagle above a gem, classical, a human figure; inscription: . . . ITUS.EI . . .[Early seal of Southwick Priory].

Endorsements:
   a) Cirografu*m* eccle*sie* de Suwic [13th century hand].
   b) Sutwyk de planta [13th or 14th century hand].
   c) Co Southampton [modern hand].

I 144   [1189–99][1]

GIFT, in free alms, by Count Geoffrey de Perche (*de Pertico*) and his wife, Countess Matilda, niece of King Richard and daughter of Henry, Duke of Bavaria and Saxony (*Baiuer' et Saxonum*)—for the salvation of their souls and those of their heirs and all their ancestors and lords—to Southwick Priory, of 2 virgates from their manor of Aldbourne (*Aldiburn'*) [rubric, *Aldiburne*], [Wiltshire], viz. one held by Richard Anglicus and the other by Robert Heiward', with these men and their households (*sequela*), and the messuages which are in *Westret*, in wood and plain, in market place (*in foro*) and pasture, with other free customs, for the provision of wine for the celebration of mass in their church. The priory has accepted the donors and their successors into full and special confraternity and after their deaths will celebrate their anniversaries each year in perpetuity. witnesses: M. Rain' de Elemosina Nongenti; M. Robert de Losello; Philip de Nederaven'; Hugh de Vannoiso; Hugh de Tabaria; Roger de Longo Ponte; Odo de Lormeri; M. Hugh Medicus; William de Ponte Archarum; Gervase, the donor's clerk (*clericus noster*);

Elias (*Helias*); Hubert; Serlo, son of Adam; Richard de Hog'; Richard de Aldiburn', clerk; Hugh de Upham; William de Buet; Herbert de Mauritania; and many others.

1 It would appear that this gift was made during the reign of Richard I. Count Geoffrey died in 1202, while preparing to go on crusade (Powicke *Loss of Normandy* p. 246, note 212). The gift was confirmed by William Longéspee, Earl of Salisbury, *c.* 1214–26 (III 97).

2 According to the priory's rental (I 182, fo. 39), four tenants at Aldbourne each paid 5s. a year. The land was still in the priory's possession at the time of the Dissolution (*VCH Hants* II, p. 168).

Copy III 96. Variants: Aldiborne; M. Rainulphus de Elemosina Nongenti.

Copy in H.R.O. 4M53/B7, p. 7. Variants: Heyward; [omit names of witnesses 3–7]; Ponte Arche'; Gerard, the donor's clerk; Heylas; [omit names of the last 5 witnesses.]

I 145   [*c.* 1190][1]

[fo. 29][2] EXCHANGE between Southwick Priory and the convent of St Michael, Stamford, [Lincolnshire], of a virgate given to the nuns by Walter de Cardonvilla, which Ranulf Fresel held for an annual rent of ½ mark, and which is from the fee of Drayton (*Draiton'*) adjoining William de la Warda's land and near Southwick Priory,[3] in return for ½ mark's worth of rent in Bradecroft' near the nunnery, given to the priory by Lady Lucy de Hum' with the consent of her lord.[4] By mutual agreement, and with the consent of William de Hum' to whose fee both alms are known to belong, the nuns quitclaimed to the priory in perpetuity the virgate from the fee of Drayton, and handed over all the deeds (*munimenta*); and the priory quitclaimed the ½ mark's worth of rent and similarly handed over all the deeds. Sealed by both convents and Sir William de Hum'. Witnesses: Richard de Hum'; Jordan de Hum'; Baldwin Wac; Ralph de Agnis; William de Pirov; William le Moine; Bartholomew de Mortuomari; Peter de Aupegart'; William de Hastenvilla; Salvagius; William de Saie; Henry de Hum', his brother; Gilbert de Valle; Henry de Druevalle; Roger de Monte Canisi; Oratius Pincerna.

1 The latest date for Walter's gift to Stamford Priory would be 1188, but it may have been made several years earlier (III 357). Lucy de Hommet had died before 1189, (I 71, note 1), and her husband, William, confirmed Southwick Priory's possession of Ranulf Fresel's land in Drayton probably before 1192 (I 76, note 1). See also the confirmation of the exchange by Walter's son, Engelramn (I 152), and his confirmation of Ranulf's tenure of the virgate (III 285). Between 1189 and 1199 Ranulf gave the virgate to his son, John, who became responsible to the priory for the ½ mark rent (III 94, 95).

2 The top left hand corner of the folio is damaged; the missing words have been taken from the copy at III 93.

3 III 357.

4 Lucy de Hommet's original charter giving this rent to Southwick Priory has survived (B. L. Harley Charter 52A22). See Appendix I.

Copy III 93. Variants: Humet'; Bradecrofte; Stamforde.

I 146 [1186–1200][1]

INSPEXIMUS and CONFIRMATION by Hugh, Bishop of Lincoln, of the charters given to Southwick Priory by: (i) William de Hum', concerning 4 marks' worth of rent in lands and men at Ketton (*Keten'*), [Rutland];[2] (ii) Robert de Novo Burgo, concerning 2 bovates at Cottesmore (*Coteshmore*), [Rutland];[3] (iii) Guy de Diva, concerning 2 marks' worth of rent in lands and men, and part of a mill at Hollowell (*Holewel'*), [Northamptonshire], in the parish of Guilsborough (*Gildeburg'*).[4] Injunction against any man disturbing or injuring the priory's men or possessions in the diocese of Lincoln. Witnesses: M. Richard, subdeacon of the church of Lincoln; Robert Clericus, chaplain; Hugh Presbyter and M. Geoffrey de Dep', canons of Lincoln church; Hugh de Rebi, the bishop's steward; Roger Bacun; Eustace de Wilton'; and many others.

1 Hugh of Avallon was Bishop of Lincoln from 1186 to 1200.

2 I 66–72, 77, 78.

3 I 78, 79; III 72, 73.

4 I 132, 131.
Copy III 71. Variants: Ketene, Cottesmor', Holewelle [rubric]; Cotteshmor'; Robert de Capell' [for Robert Clericus].

I 147 [1189–99][1]

Confirmation by Queen Eleanor (Alyenor) concerning the land of Ketton (Ketien'), [Rutland].

[fo. 29ᵛ][2] CONFIRMATION, in free alms, by Queen Eleanor (Alienor)—for the souls of her lord, King Henry [II], and of her sons King Henry and Count Geoffrey, and her daughter, Duchess Matilda, and her other children, kindred, friends and all the faithful, and for her own salvation, and the state and welfare (*status et incolumnitas*) of her son, King Richard and his brother, Count John[3]—to Southwick Priory, of all the land, with men and all other appurtenances, which William de Humet' gave them in the manor of Ketton (*Keten'*), [Rutland], for the soul of his wife, Lucy, as his charter testifies. Witnesses: M. Walter, Abbot of Holy Cross of Waltham, [Essex];[4] [   ][2] and John, the queen's chaplains; M. Walter de Driefeld; M. William, the queen's almoner; M. [   ] de Redereffeld; Peter Cheveter; Humphrey de Hemmeston'; Nicholas, son of Richard; John de Sanford; Jordan de Pele [   ]; Engelramnus Pincerna.

Southwick.

1 Dates of the reign of Richard I. Henry, son of Henry II and Queen Eleanor, was crowned in 1170 in his father's lifetime, and died in 1183. Another son, Geoffrey, Count of Brittany, died in 1186. Henry II and his daughter, Matilda, who had married Henry the Lion, Duke of Saxony and Bavaria, both died in 1189.

2 The top right hand corner of I fo. 29ᵛ is damaged; missing words have been supplied from III 70, but this has not been possible where names of witnesses are not given in that copy.

3 John, Count of Mortain, succeeded his brother, Richard, as King in 1199.

4 Walter of Ghent was Abbot from 1184 to 1201 (Knowles *Heads of Religious Houses* p. 188).

Copy III 70. Variants: Alienor', Ketene [rubric]; Ketena. [The names of the first and fifth witnesses only are given.]

I 148	13 July 1198

GIFT, in free alms, by John, Count of Mortain (*Moret'*)[1]—for the salvation of his soul and those of his predecessors—to Southwick Priory, of Colmore (*Colemera*), which is a member of Dean (*Dene*), with all appurtenances outside Dean, viz. wood and plain, meadows, grazings, mill ponds and mills, fishponds, fields, roads, paths and all liberties and free customs pertaining to the aforesaid land. Witnesses: Peter de Pratell'; Geoffrey de Bosco; Roger de Hamundevill'; Richard de Reviers; Robert de Teill'; Adam de Sancto Martino; William de Cantelo; M. Benedict; Hubert de Burgo; Richard de Owedale.

Isle of Les Andelys (*insula Andel'*), [Normandy], by the hand of John de Gray.[2]

1 See I 147 note 3. John confirmed this gift to the priory after he became king (I 161).
2 John de Gray became Bishop of Norwich in 1200, and died in 1214.
Copy III 829.

I 149	[15 July 1198][1]

CONFIRMATION by King Richard—for the salvation of his soul and those of his predecessors—to Southwick Priory, of the gift [as in I 148] made by his brother, John, Count of Mortain (Moreton'), as John's charter testifies. Witnesses: J., Count of Mortain; R[anulph], Earl of Chester (*Cestr'*);[2] William; Earl of Salisbury (*Sar'*);[3] William, son of Ralph, Steward of Normandy (*Norm'*);[4] William de Hum', Constable of Normandy;[5] Ralph Teisson'; Warin, son of Gerold; Ralph de Arden'; Geoffrey de Say; M. Thomas de Husseburn; William, son of Richard, the king's clerk.

[By the hand of E., Bishop of Ely, Chancellor,[6] at the rock of Les Andelys.[7]]

1 The date and place of issue of this charter are taken from the copy at III 830.
2 Ranulph was Earl of Chester from *c.* 1188, and died in 1232.
3 William Longespée, illegitimate son of Henry II, was styled Earl of Salisbury in 1197, and died in 1226.

4 William fitz Ralph died in 1200 (Powicke *Loss of Normandy* p. 208).

5 William de Hommet succeeded his father as Constable of Normandy in 1180, and retained that office until 1203, when he joined the king of France. His English lands were subsequently confiscated by King John.

6 Eustace was consecrated Bishop of Ely in March 1198; he was Chancellor from May 1198 to May 1199, and died in 1215.

7 It was on the rock above Les Andelys that King Richard had the Château Gaillard built in 1197-8 (Powicke, *op. cit.*, p. 190).
Copy III 830. Variants: [names of first two witnesses only followed by:] "Given by the hand of E., Bishop of Ely, Chancellor, at the rock of Les Andelys (*apud rupem Andeliaci*), 15 July, in the 9th year of the king's reign".

I 150 [*c.* late 12th century][1]

[fo. 30][2] CONFIRMATION, in pure and perpetual alms, free of scutage, hidage and all service, by Roger Pantolf—for his salvation and that of all his lords and friends—to Southwick Priory, of [its possession of] 1 hide of land in Applestead (*Apelstede*), with all appurtenances, which William de Pontearcharum bought from Ivo Pantulf with the consent of King Henry I for the use of the same church.[3] Consideration, 4 marks, and the priory has received Roger into full confraternity. Witnesses: Ralph, canon of St Denys;[4]. . . .[5] Roger de Scuris; Robert Pantulf; Stephen Capellanus; Robert Clericus.

1 Witness Roger de Scuris is probably the son of Matthew. He occurs *c.* 1180-1210, and witnessed charters dated 1187, 1189, 1210 (I 27, 143, 98).

2 The top of I fo. 30 is badly damaged. Missing words have been supplied from III 312, but in that copy only the name of the first witness is given.

3 The hide at Applestead, just west of Southwick, was one of the earliest gifts presented by William de Pont de l'Arche when he founded the priory at Portchester (I 1 and note 4).

4 No canon named Ralph occurs in the St Denys Cartulary.

5 Probably the names of two witnesses are missing.
Copy III 312.

I 151 [*c.* late 12th century, possibly before 1193][1]

GIFT, in free alms, by Ralph de Cumbraio—for his salvation and that of his ancestors—to Southwick Priory, of ½ virgate from his demesne in *Prevetus* at Anmore (*Enedemer'*), east of the road which runs from Anmore to Hinton (*Henton'*) adjoining the priory's ploughland which Ralph had previously given them.[2] The ½ virgate lies between the virgate given to the priory by Ralph's brother, William de Cumbraio,[3] and land called *Beckewod'* held by Ralph's man Arnold (*Ernaldus*).[4] Witnesses: Roger, Archdeacon of Winchester; W. Prior of Halingh'; M. John de Hecfel'; Hugh de Forest; Thomas de Ho; Roger and Walter, clerks of the archdeacon of Winchester; William, son of Roger; William, son of Rein' de Bureh'; Walter de Sancto Martino; William Blundus; John Aurifaber.

1 Roger first occurs as Archdeacon of Winchester before 1181 and died in 1207–8 (*Fasti* II, p. 92). This gift from Ralph may be included in the confirmation granted to the priory by William, Earl of Sussex, *c.* 1186–93 (I 136).

2 See I 59; III 120; I 136; III 123.

3 See I 57, 58, 60; III 115.

4 Ralph subsequently gave *Beckewod'* or *Bekewode*, and the services of his man, Arnold, to the priory (III 116).
Copy III 117. Variants: Cumbray, Cumbrayo; Prevettus; Enedemere, Endemer'; Bickewode.

I 152   [*c.* 1190][1]

Confirmation by Englr' de Caddewl' concerning the land of Ran' Frysel

CONFIRMATION, in free alms, by Engelramn de Cardunvilla—for the souls of his father and mother, and all his ancestors and lords, and for his salvation and that of his heirs—to Southwick Priory, of possession of 1 virgate from his fee in Drayton (*Draiton'*), which Ranulf Fresel held, and which the convent of St Michael, Stamford, [Lincolnshire], exchanged for a certain meadow and rent adjoining Stamford, with the assent of Sir William de Humeto, as his charter and the chirograph drawn up between the two convents testify.[2] Engelramn and his family have been accepted into confraternity (*me et meos in plenam fraternitatem ecclesie sue susceperunt*), and the priory will celebrate his anniversary and that of his father. Witnesses: Robert de Mesnill'; Richard de Haia; Richard, son of Daniel; Henry, his son; Alan de Holt; Henry, son of Herbert; Baldwin Clericus; Ralph Hirdman; Thomas de Mesnill'; Serl', son of Adam.

1 The virgate in Drayton in Farlington had been granted to the nuns of Stamford by Walter de Cardunvilla, Engelramn's father, with the consent of Richard de Humeto before 1180 (III 357). The tenant was Ranulf Fresel, and Engelramn confirmed that Ranulf should pay the same rent to Southwick Priory as he had done to Stamford, and should not be liable for any other service (III 285). Before 1199 Ranulf had passed the virgate to his son, John, who was to pay the rent to the priory (III 94, 95).

2 See I 76, 145.
Copy III 440. Variants: Engelrannus de Cardunvill'; de Mesenille; Richard Haia.

I 153   [Late 12th century; before 1196 and possibly before 1189][1]

GRANT by Engelrannus Pincerna—for the salvation and safety (*incolumnitas*) of his lady, the queen,[2] and his own salvation—to Southwick Priory, of 1 mark in rent, to be paid each year on the feast of St Thomas the Apostle [21 December] by him and his heirs at Eaton Bray (*Eiton*), [Beds].[3] Witnesses: Henry, son of Walter, the donor's nephew; William, son of [?] the king (Reg'); Aug', Richard, John, the donor's men; Geoffrey.[4]

1 The second witness is possibly William Longespée, illegitimate son of Henry II, who married the only daughter and heiress of William fitz Patrick, Earl of Salisbury, and succeeded to the earldom after his father-in-law's death in 1196. As he is not given the title here, the charter must belong to an earlier date, provided that the list of witnesses is genuine; it must be before 1189 if Henry II was still living.

2 Probably Eleanor of Aquitaine, wife of Henry II. Engelramn Pincerna witnessed the charter which she granted to Southwick Priory in the reign of Richard I (I 147).

3 Probably Eaton Bray (spelt *Eiton* or *Eyton* in the *Book of Fees* I, p. 22; II, p. 869) near Dunstable, Beds., which was given by Queen Eleanor to Engelram, her butler (*pincerna*) (*Cal. Docs. in France* 1093, p. 388). The first witness of that undated charter was W[alter], Abbot of Waltham, who also witnessed the charter given by Queen Eleanor to Southwick Priory (I 147). In 1196 the queen confirmed Engelram's gift of half of the vill of Eaton Bray to the Abbey of St Mary, Fontevrault (*op. cit.*, 1094, p. 388).

There is no evidence elsewhere in the cartularies or rentals that Southwick Priory ever received the above rent.

4 The list of witnesses may have been continued overleaf in the MS., but the top of folio 30ᵛ is torn and the left-hand side is missing.

I 154   8 January 1199

[fo. 30ᵛ]¹ NOTIFICATION by Herbert, Bishop of Salisbury,² that— knowing the maintenance of religious houses to be pleasing to God, the rewarder of all good gifts, and recognising the burden on the canons of provision of hospitality to all and everyone making the crossing through Southwick—he has granted to Southwick Priory 100s. a year from the church of Swindon (*Swindona*),³ to be paid over by (*per manum*) Gilbert, vicar of that church, and his successors, as a pension for the priory's use in perpetuity, saving the right and authority of the bishop and his succesors, and his church. Witnesses: Roger de Winton' and Richard de Wiltesir', archdeacons; . . . ., Abraham, chaplains; John de Winton'; William de Celar', burgess; Roger de Hamptun'. . . . . .mo de ?Capella; and many others.

Southwick, by the hand of William de Winton; the 5th year of Herbert's episcopate.

1 As the top of I fo. 30ᵛ is badly damaged, the missing part of this deed has been taken from III 408, but in that copy the names of the first two witnesses only are given.

2 Herbert Poore, consecrated Bishop of Salisbury 5 June 1194, died 1217.

3 This pension is recorded in the rental (I 184). See also the confirmation granted in 1286 by Walter Scammel, Bishop of Salisbury, at the request of Queen Eleanor (I 107).

Copy III 408. Variant: [rubric:] Swyndon'.

I 155   [early 13th century, possibly before 1221][1]

Charter of Richard de Herurd, senior, concerning thirty shillings' worth
of land in Ellisfield (*Eldefeld*), which Stephen de Werewella[2] gave to the
priory (*quod habemus de dono Stephani de Werewella.*)

GIFT, with warranty, by Richard de Hereierd', with the consent of his
sons, Robert and Richard his heir, to Stephen de Cand' of 30s. worth of
land in Ellisfield (*Elsefeld'*), for his homage and service, viz. the ½ virgate
Robert, son of Stiward, held, and the ½ virgate Robert's sister, Emma,
held, with appurtenances. Stephen and his heirs will hold the land with
the service of the men (*cum servitio hominum*) paying an annual rent of
1 lb of pepper at Michaelmas for all service pertaining to Richard and
his heirs, except royal service. If Richard and his heirs are unable to
implement the warranty, they ought to give Stephen in exchange land of
equal value. Witnesses: Richard Capellanus of Wherwell (*Werewell'*);
Alan Capellanus of Herriard (*Hereird'*); Peter Parsona of Herriard; John
Clericus; Richard de Sifrewast; William de Hattingeleg'; Gilbert de Esli;
Baldwin de Bulendun'; John de Candebr'; Baldwin de Cumb'; William,
his brother; Ralph, son of Thomas; Thomas, his brother; Thomas, son
of Geoffrey Forestarius; Richard de Hinwde; Adam de Burcote; William
Sulkebiril; Serlo de Brueria; and many others.

1 A Richard de Heryerd, son of John, died in 1221, leaving as his heiress his
sister, Maud, who was married to Richard de Sifrewast (see fifth witness). If the
above donor was this de Heryerd his sons must have predeceased him (*VCH
Hants* III, p. 367). In 1255 Richard de Sifrewast was holding Ellisfield of Robert
de St John (*ibid.*, p. 360). The witness William de Haettingeleg' and two, possibly
three, of the witnesses to the confirmation by Richard, son of Richard de Herrierd,
(I 156), were jurors in 1208 (I 164). Maurice de Turvill' and William, son of
Henry, witnessed that confirmation, and a charter dated 1200 (I 156; III 550).

2 Stephen de Werewella, *alias* de Candeura, was probably steward of the Benedic-
tine nunnery at Wherwell about 10 miles north-west of Winchester (see rubric to
copy III 340 noted below).
Copy I 157. Variants: de Candeura; Werewella; Alard Capellanus of Herriard;
Cifrewast; Hattingeli; Bulendune; Cumbe; Candeu' [reverse order]; Hinewude.
Copy III 340. Variants: [rubric:] 'Charter of Richard de Herierde, which he gave
(*fecit*) to Stephen, steward of Wherwell (*Werewell*); de Candeur'; Elsefelde;
Werewelle; Alard Capellanus de Herenis.

I 156   [early 13th century, possibly before 1221][1]

Charter of Richard de Heriird, junior, concerning the same thirty shillings' worth of land.

CONFIRMATION, with warranty, by Richard, son of Richard de
Herreird'—for the salvation of his soul and those of all his ancestors
and successors—to Southwick Priory, of 30s. worth of land in Ellisfield
(*Elsefeld*): viz. ½ virgate with appurtenances which Robert, son of Stiward,
held, and ½ virgate with appurtenances which Robert's sister, Emma,
[fo. 31][3] held. The land was given to the priory by Stephen de Candewr',[2]

and the gift confirmed by Richard's father . . . . If the warranty
cannot be fulfilled, Richard ought to give [the priory in exchange] land
of equal value. Witnesses: Walter de Andeli; Roger d. . . . .;
Maurice de Turvill'; Matthew de Scrures; Henry de Ferleg'; Richard de
Cumbes; William, son of ?Henry; Richard Makerel and John and
Thomas, brothers; Gregory Wassthuce; John de Hereird', clerk; and
many others.

1 See dating evidence for I 155.

2 See I 155, note 2.

3 The top of folio 31 is damaged and most of the last part of the text of this
charter is missing. The names of the witnesses have survived except for the second
surname. It may be that this should read "de Scuris" (see the list of jurors in
I 164).

I 157 Copy of I 155.

I 158   [1210–27, possibly 1225–7][1]

GIFT by Luke, Prior of Southwick, and the priory, to Ralph Harang,
for his homage and service, of all the land given to them in Clanfield
(*Clanefeud*), [Oxon.], by Alice de Kesneto. It had been given to her by
her brother, Ralph de Kesneto, as her dowry or to dispose of as she
wished (*ad se maritandam vel consiliandam ubi vellet*):[2] viz. 6 ½-virgates,
one each held by Richard, son of Baldwin Medicus; Roger, son of
Amaurus; Fulk Blundel; Nicholas; Ralph Franceis; and Evermund. Ralph
and his heirs will hold the land with grazings and all other liberties and
men's service pertaining thereto and will pay the priory, for the upkeep
of the infirmary, 20s. a year at the Nativity of St John the Baptist [24
June], for all exaction and service, except forinsec service, for which the
whole hide of Clanfield pays 4 marks a year and is taxed at ¼ of a
knight's fee (*defendet se per servicium quarte partis unius militis*). Ralph
and his heirs are bound to pay the rent faithfully to the priory, but if
the aforesaid Alice decreases the alms (*prefatam elemosinam minuat*) for
any reason, the 20s. rent will be decreased in proportion, etc. .[3]

1 Prior Luke died in 1227. His predecessor, Prior Guy, occurs 1185–1210. Of the
charters granted by Alice de Chesneto to the priory, the earliest which can be
dated with any certainty belongs to 1225–9 (III 297).

2 See III 286–94.

3 Ralph Harang subsequently quitclaimed to the priory all his rights to this land
(III 296). His name does not appear in the rental, which may predate the grant
of the land to him (I 182, fo. 83ᵛ). Alice de Chesneto's latest charter to the priory
concerning this land is dated 1245, and the list of tenants of the 3 virgates is
identical, except for one name, with that given in her charter of 1225–9 (III 297).
There had been no diminution of her gift (III 291).

I 159 [*c.* 1190–1200][1]

[fo. 31ᵛ][2] GIFT, in free alms, by Ranulf Bulard—for the salvation of his lord, William de Hum', and William's family (*et suorum*), and his own salvation, and for the souls of Lucy de Hum' his lady, and Hawise his wife, and all his lords and heirs—to Southwick Priory, of all the land in the manor of Boarhunt (*Burh'*), which was given to him for his service by William de Hum', his lord, and which Siward held. Ranulf abjured whatever right he had in that land, its men or its rent, and touching holy things he swore that neither he nor anyone on his behalf in perpetuity would lay complaint against the priory concerning the aforesaid land (*de prefata terra questionem moneret*). Consideration, 60s. . Witnesses: Richard de Lechewai, chaplain; William, son of Henry; Richard Falconar'; Elias de Lam'a; Geoffrey, his son; Richard Ubich; Adam, his brother; Simon de Mo't'forti; Andrew de Haliwell'; Robert de la Barr'; William and William [*sic*] Wal'ns'; Ralph Hirdma'.

1 William de Hommet gave the 5s. worth of rent from the tenement in Boarhunt held by Siward *alias* Sewart to Ranulf *alias* Ralph Bolard in *c.* 1180–90 (III 54 and note). William's wife, Lucy, had died by 1189 (I 71). Ralph first granted 1s. of the annual rent to the priory (III 62) and then, by this charter, the whole rent. William de Hommet confirmed the quitclaim of the entire rent (III 56).

2 The top of this folio is badly damaged and a large part of I 159 has been taken from the copy at III 392, which only gives the name of the first witness.
Copy III 392. Variant: Borhunt'.

I 160 [early 13th century, after 1204][1]

Final (*ultima*) charter of Robert de Berleia concerning all lands of Bereleigh (*Berleia*) and Drayton (*Draitona*)

CONFIRMATION , in free alms, with warranty, by Robert de Berleia— for the soul of his father, Anketill, and his own salvation, and that of his mother, Olimpiadis, and of his children and friends—to Southwick Priory, of the gift to them, in perpetual alms, by William, son of Henry, of all the land of Bereleigh and Drayton (*Draitun'*)[2] which William bought from M. Thomas de Chalcton',[3] who had previously bought it for 8 marks from Anketill, Robert's father, and had given Robert 2 marks for his consent.[4] The priory will hold the land with all appurtenances, viz. the whole tenement with messuage which Gilbert de Draitun held from Robert, i.e. 16 acres: 2 acres adjoining Robert's mill; 4 acres in *Siepslade*; 2 acres which Richard held at the cross of *Swandene*; and 6 acres in the furlong (*quarentana*) of *Leuepute*; paying 12d. annual rent at Michaelmas to Robert and his heirs. They will be quit of all service, except royal service, for which they will be taxed for the entire tenement as for 1 virgate from the tenement of Bereleigh (*salvo servicio domini regis Quare quando evenerit tunc adquietabit se totum tenementum illud sicut una virgata terre de tenemento de Berleia se adquietat*).

Robert has also granted to the priory (i) all the land Walklin, son of Lewin de Draitun', held from him in Drayton, with Walklin himself, and all his household (*sequela*), the messuage and everything pertaining to that land, and 1 acre adjoining Robert's meadow.[5] The priory will pay 1 lb. of cummin annually at Michaelmas for all service, except forinsec service, for which it will be taxed as for a cotland (*pro uno cothsetlo*); (ii) pasturage for 8 oxen with his oxen, and 50 sheep with his [fo. 32][6] sheep in his demesne pasture, and 50 sheep in his common pasture, as shown in his father's charter, which the priory has;[7] likewise 3 acres under *Benedinche* given to the priory in free alms by his father.[8] Consideration: 1 mark paid to Robert's father, and 30s. 8d. to Robert for his confirmation and warranty. Witnesses: Roger de Scuris; Walter de Andeli; Maurice de Thurevile; Godfrey [. . . . . .] de Menes; German le Ramvile; Nicholas de Langerille; M. Laurence Medicus; Robert de Fere; Ralph Geldetop; Lewis (*Lodovicus*) de Bera; William Burh'; Peter de Havunte; Ralph Hirdeman; Reginald Gupil; William de Wint'; and many others.

1 This is probably the latest of 12 charters concerning land which was finally given to the priory by the de Berleias and William, son of Henry (III 259–63, 265–9, 284, 568). Of these the only dated charter is III 266, a confirmation given in 1204 by Godfrey by Lucy, Bishop of Winchester. But there can be little doubt that all the charters belong to the end of the 12th or early 13th centuries, and the witnesses confirm this.

2 Bereleigh is about a mile north of East Meon, and Drayton a mile north-west.

3 III 284.

4 III 261, 265.

5 III 268 and 260, 259, 266.

6 The top of the folio is badly damaged. The missing part of the charter has been taken from the copy at III 264 which only gives the names of the first two witnesses.

7 III 267.

8 III 262.
Copy III 263. Variants: Drayton'; Chalton; de Draiton'; Sepelenda.

I 161 21 July 1201

CONFIRMATION, in free alms, by King John—for the salvation of his soul and those of his predecesors—of his gift to Southwick Priory, of Colemore (*Colmera*), which is a member of Dean (*Dena*), with all its appurtenances outside Dean, as contained in the charter which he gave them when he was Count of Mortain (*Moreton'*).[1] Witnesses: Earl William Marescallus;[2] William, Earl of Salisbury (*Sar'*);[3] William de Hum', Constable of Normandy; Eustace de Vesci.

Chateau-du-Loire (castrum Lygdi), by the hand of Simon, Archdeacon of Wells (Well'). 21 July, 3 John.

1 See I 147.

2 William Marshal married Isabel, daughter and heir of Richard fitz Gilbert, Earl of Pembroke, August 1189. He received the earldom in 1199, and died in 1219.

3 William Longespée, illegitimate son of Henry II, was styled Earl of Salisbury in 1197, and died in 1226.
Copy III 828. Variants: Dene; Maresc'; Wellensis.

I 162[1]　　　　　　　　　　　　　　　　　　　　20 April [1204]

GRANT in perpetuity at fee farm by King John to Southwick Priory, of the whole land of Dean (*Dene*) with appurtenances, which was in the king's hands, and was formerly held of him by Theodorius Theutonicus. The priory will pay £7. 18s. 5d. a year at Michaelmas to the Treasury for all service, enjoying all liberties and free customs pertaining to that [fo. 32[v]] land. Witnesses: G. son of Peter, Earl of Essex; R., Earl of Chester (*Cestr'*);[2] [Warin, son of Gerold; Robert de Veteri] Ponte; Adam de P[ort]; Richard de Perti; Peter [de Stok'].
　　　　　　　　　Wallingford (*Walingeford*), [Berks], by the hand of
　　　　　　　　　S., Bishop-elect of Chichester (*Cicestr'*),[3] [5 John].

1 The top of I fo. 32[v] is badly damaged and the last lines of this charter have been supplied from the copy in the inspeximus of Edward II at II 8, with the date and those names of witnesses given above in square brackets.

2 Geoffrey FitzPeter was Earl of Essex from 1199, and died in 1213; Ranulph 'de Blundeville' was Earl of Chester from 1188, and died in 1232.

3 Simon FitzRobert was elected Bishop of Chichester 4–9 April, 1204, and consecrated 11 July. He died in 1207.
Copy in II 8. Variants: Dena; Theodoricus; de Perty; Wallyng'.
Copy III 828b.

I 163　　　　　　　　　　　　　　　　　　　　　　　　　[1208][1]

WRIT of CERTIORARI from King John to the sheriff of Hampshire (*Suhamt'*), for an inquisition to be held without delay to discover from free and law-worthy men (*liberi et legales homines*) of the neighbourhood of Colemore (*Colemera*) and Dean (*Dena*) what holdings, fees and labour services (*servicia hominum*) were alienated from the aforesaid manors of Colemore and Dean by the sheriff, bailiffs or anyone else, while they were holding them, without the assent of the king or his ancestors, and when the alienation took place. The king has granted the manors to his priory of Southwick.[2] The sheriff is to notify the king promptly when the inquisition has been held, and report the names of the jurors.

1 Dated by reference to I 164.

2 See I 147, 161, 162.

I 164   Monday, 21 July 1208

INQUISITION held in response to King John's writ to the sheriff of
Hampshire [above I 163] concerning the lands of Colemore (*Colemera,
Clemera*) and Dean (*Dena*), the first year of the interdict, 12 Kal.
August, Monday the feast of St Praxedis. Jurors: (*Hec sunt nomina militum
juratorum*) Roger de Scuris; Walter de Andeli; Roger, son of Henry;
Matthew de Scuris; William de Hattingeleia; Adam de Porteseia; Hamund
(*Hamo*) de Midlingeton'; Mansel de Sarwentone; Humphrey (*Huntfridus*)
de Dunstigeleia; John de Bradesita; Henry Wiard; German de Ramvilla;
[who say:]
(i) the wood called Doscomb (*Dossumbe*)[1] was in the king's hands and
was made over (*traditus fuit*) to Gilbert Oyn by William de Venoiz.[2]
Men of the vill used to take their estovers at Christmas as allocated by
the reeve (*per liberationem prepositi*), and now that the wood is in
Gilbert's hands they cannot take anything. (ii) The men of the vill had
rights of common in the wood called *Weitesiote*. It has come into
Gilbert's hands, and they do not know by what warrant. (iii) The field
called Snowdown (*Snaudun*)[3] is an enclosure from the common pasture
and is in Gilbert's hands. He pays nothing for it, and this was Richard
the sheriff's doing. (iv) The field called *Loddredesrigg'* is an enclosure
from the common pasture. It is in Gilbert's hands, and they do not
know by what warrant. (v) Land formerly held by Seward Seele, the
father of Godard, who is still living, is held by Gilbert. Seward, his wife
and son were violently evicted from it by Turstan the sheriff.[4] Likewise
Turstan evicted the father of William Pie from land now held by Gilbert,
[fo. 33][5] and also a certain widow Soburge. . . . . .and in these three
lands Gilbert's house is situated. . . . . . . .de Havetliga holds was in
demesne. . . . . .of the king and will contribute annually to
the king's farm. . . . . .and it was delivered to the men of
the vill by Geoffrey, son of Azo.[6] Item: the chapel of Dean is in the
king's demesne and Richard the sheriff,[7] who was parson of Alton
(*Aulton'*) and Colemore, attorned it to the church of Colemore. Item: in
the time of Turstan the sheriff, the men of Colemore and Dean used to
perform labour services on the manor of Barton (*Bertona*),[8] which is the
chief manor (*quod est capud manerii*) for Colemore and Dean. Because
they lived a long distance away, Turstan doubled their rents (*gabula*)—
except those of the father of William de Bluntesmera and the ancestors
of William de la Lode and Stephen le Hore who were too poor to pay
double—and thereafter they no longer went to Barton to work. They
held the vill at farm of the sheriff and annually provided the farm as
best they could (*et annuatim faciebant inde firmam sicut melius poterant*).
So they were creating new liberties and customs amongst themselves
when, by right, they ought to have no liberties other than those of the
men of Barton, and they owe all customs and services that the men of
Barton owe. This has all been done since the time of Turstan the sheriff.

1 Doscomb about half a mile S.E. from Priors Dean church.

2 Geoffrey de Venuz, the king's marshal, held the manor of Empshott and $\frac{1}{2}$ hide
at Nutley at the time of the Domesday Survey. His grandson, William, gave the

church of Nutley to Southwick Priory, (I 114). Presumably William had custody of Doscomb when he passed it to Gilbert Oyn. *VCH Hants* III, pp. 17, 370.

3 Snaudun or Snoudon; Snowdon near Windmill Farm, ½ mile east of Priors Dean church (Hervey *History of Colmer and Priors Dean* p. 15).

4 Turstin, sheriff of Hampshire, Michaelmas 1155—Michaelmas 1159 (*Itinerary of Henry II*).

5 The top of fo. 33 is damaged and the left hand corner missing.

6 Sheriff of Hampshire, Michaelmas 1179—Michaelmas 1189 (*Itinerary of Henry II*).

7 Richard, son of Turstin, sheriff of Hampshire, Michaelmas 1159—Easter 1170 (*Itinerary of Henry II*).

8 Colemore was in the hundred of Barton Stacey. At the time of the Domesday Survey, Barton Stacey was held by the King. The only mention of Colemore is of a hide there held by Humphrey the Chamberlain, (*VCH Hants* I, p. 500). Hervey suggests that this hide was the land that came into possession of the Kernet family (Hervey *History of Colmer and Priors Dean* p. 160). William de Kernet, lord of Colemore, appears as a witness in 1278 and 1296 to grants of land to Southwick Priory (III 843, 850). Of the many references to Dene in Hampshire Domesday, none can be clearly identified with the Dean near Colemore that became Priors Dean. The extract from Domesday copied into the cartulary does not concern Priors Dean (below, I 172). Colemore was granted to Southwick Priory by John, when Count of Mortain, in 1198 (I 148), and in 1204 King John leased at farm to them the whole land of Dean (I 162). Therefore the priory had a keen interest in recording any alienations that had taken place of the rights of the owner of Colemore and Dean. See also II 235.

I 165   21 June [1214][1]

MANDATE from King John to Sir P., Bishop of Winchester,[2] instructing him to carry out the business of Southwick Priory concerning the land of Dean (*la Dena*), as the King ordered him by word of mouth in England.
Witnessed by the King at Roche aux Moins (*Ruppula Monachi*), [Anjou],
11 Kal. July.

1 The date as given in the mandate is 21 June. The only visit of John to Roche aux Moins recorded by T. D. Hardy in the "Itinerary of King John" (*Archaeologia*, Vol. 22, 1829, p. 154) was in 1214, from 19 June to 1 July. See also I 163, 164.

2 Peter des Roches, consecrated Bishop of Winchester 25 September 1205; died 9 June 1238.

I 166   [after 21 July 1208,?1214][1]

MANDATE from King John to the Barons of the Exchequer ordering them to deliver to Southwick Priory the land of Dean (*la Dena*) with demesnes, tenements and fees according to the charter he has given them and the inquisition carried out on his instructions.

1 See above I 162-5.

I 167 [after 21 July 1208, ?1214][1]

MANDATE from King John to the sheriff of Hampshire (*Suhamt'*). After the canons of Southwick have paid the sheriff surety of 24 marks for the King's Treasury, he is to give them full seisin of the land of Dean (*la Dene*) with its appurtenances, demesnes, tenements, fees and labour services alienated, by the sheriff and bailiffs, as shown by the inquisition held on the king's orders, or held by anyone else who holds them without the consent of John or his ancestors. When he has received the surety from the priory, the sheriff is to inform the Barons of the Exchequer without delay. Witness: Sir P., Bishop of Winchester.[2]

1 See I 162–166.
2 Peter des Roches, see I 165, note 2.

I 168 14 October 1214

LETTERS PATENT of King John granting his protection to Southwick [fo. 33ᵛ][1] Priory and all their lands, men, possessions and rents. No injury, molestation or harm is to be done, or allowed to be done, to them, their possessions or men; and if any occurs, amends are to be made. They are not to be impleaded concerning any of their freeholdings, except before the king or his chief justice.
Witnessed by the King at Dartmouth (*Dertemutha*), [Devon].

1 The top of fo. 33ᵛ is badly damaged, and the last part of this entry has been supplied from the copy at III 988.
Copy III 988.

I 169[1]

. . . . to lords and friends, Barons of the Exchequer, W . . . . canons of Southwick that Gilbert de la Dene asserted before us and . . . . proved to us present in his court that the prior of Southwick paid 31s. 4d. which the aforesaid G[ilbert] used to pay to the prior.[2] And because we do not wish to hinder the priory's business, we signify to you with certainty that we have never interfered in this business and have never heard that such a proof was made in the King's court. Farewell.

1 The top of fo. 33ᵛ is damaged and the beginning of this deed is missing.

2 In 1212, Gilbert de la Dene was holding land in Dean (*Den'*) of the king, for which he paid 31s. 4d. a year to the Exchequer (*Book of Fees* I, p. 76). Because so much of I 169 is missing it is difficult to make out the meaning, but it would seem that Gilbert is asserting that the prior of Southwick is responsible for paying the 31s. 4d. to the Exchequer. See, however, the following writ, which shows that in 1238 Gilbert claimed to hold the land of the king in chief and complained that the prior was deforcing him.

I 170   6 May 1238

WRIT of PRECIPE QUOD REDDAT from King Henry [III] to the
sheriff of Hampshire (*Suhamt'*) to command the prior of Southwick justly
and without delay to render two carucates of land with appurtenances in
Dean (*la Dene*) to Gilbert de la Dene, who claims that they are his by
right and inheritance, and that he holds them of the king in chief, and
that the prior deforces him.[1] If the prior will not do so, and Gilbert has
given the sheriff security for prosecuting his claim, then the sheriff is to
summon, by good summoners, the prior before the King's justices at
Westminster (*Westm'*) on the quindene of Trinity [13 June], to show
why he has not done so; and the sheriff is to have there the summoners
and this writ. Witness: the King, at Windsor (*Winloghore*), 22 Henry
[III].

1 See I 169, note 2; 171.

I 171   12 April 1239

WRIT of PRECIPE QUOD REDDAT from King Henry [III] to the
sheriff of Hampshire (*Suhamt'*) to command the prior of Southwick justly
and without delay to render two carucates of land with appurtenances in
Dean (*la Dene*) to Richard de la Dene, who claims that they are his by
right and inheritance, he holds them of the king in chief, and that the
prior unjustly deforces him.[1] If the prior will not do so, and Richard
has given the sheriff security for prosecuting his claim, then the sheriff is
to summon, by good summoners, the prior before the King's justices at
Westminster (*Westm'*) on the morrow of Holy Trinity [23 May] to show
why he has not done so; and the sheriff is to have there the summoners
and this writ. Witness: the King, at Westminster, 23 Henry [III].

1 Probably Richard was the son of Gilbert de Dene, and succeeded him after
May 1238, when the claim was issued (I 170). By an undated grant (*c.* 1210–15),
William de Venuz had given to a Gilbert de Dene a virgate at Oakhanger for the
use of Gilbert's son, Richard, on his marriage with William's daughter, Lucy
(*Selborne Charters* I, p. 1). Oakhanger is about 4½ miles north-east of Priors
Dean.

I 172

MEMORANDUM: These are the words of Domesday concerning the
manor of Barton [Stacey] (*Berton'*): In Barton Hundred the King held
Barton [Stacey]. In the same Hundred is Dean (*Dene*) which appertains
to this manor,[1] and there is 1 plough there in the demesne, and 2 villeins
and 14 bordars (*bordelli*) with 1½ ploughs. There are 2 serfs, and 2 mills
worth 20s., and 4 acres of meadow, and woodland for 3 pigs. In the

same manor [the King] has [in]² Wallop (*Wellope*)³ 5 villeins and 1 serf,
and 1 mill worth 30d., and 2 ploughs in demesne, and freed serfs
(*coliberti*) [and boors (*et Bures*)]² as above render the accustomed services
[of the others (*aliorum*)]². Formerly the reeve had the honey and pasture
from these manors towards paying his farm (*ad firmam suam*) and timber
for building houses; now the foresters and reeves have these or 7s., the
price of the honey; 10s. worth of pasture are in the King's forest (*modo
habent hec forestarii et prepositi vel vij sol' precium mellis xs. pasture
sunt in foresta regis*).⁴

1 In Domesday Book this entry concerning Dene does not come under the heading,
"In Bertun Hundret" (*VCH Hants* I, p. 452). After "The King himself holds
Bertune" (Barton Stacey) there is an entry concerning Ordie (King's Worthy),
said to appertain to the manor of Bertune. Next is the heading, "In Odiham
Hundret"—The King holds Esseham (Lasham). . . . Then "In Brocton Hundret"
(Broughton, later Thorngate Hundred)—The King himself holds Wallope (Nether
Wallop). . . . The King holds another Wallope. . . . The King holds Brestone
(Broughton). . . . In the same hundred is Dene (East Dean) which appertains to
this manor (i.e., to Broughton, not Barton Stacey as implied by the entry in the
cartulary).

Presumably the scribe who copied the entry from Domesday Book was prompted
to look for a Dean, held by the King in Barton Stacey Hundred, as Colemore,
adjoining what became Prior's Dean, belonged to that hundred (*op. cit.*, p. 500).
He failed to see, or ignored, the intervening headings.

Three other entries in Domesday concerning Dene are all in Brocton Hundred
(*op. cit.*, p. 497), and probably refer to East Dean, none to Prior's Dean.

Domesday Book was used as a source for information concerning ancient royal
demesne, but if that was the intention, the entry copied here is misleading to say
the least, and certainly does not refer to the Dene granted at fee farm to the
priory by King John in 1204 (above, I 162). See however the reference in the next
entry, I 173, to Prior's Dean as being ancient royal demesne.

2 In D.B. but omitted in cartulary version.

3 D.B. has "Wallope".

4 In D.B. this reads: "Now the foresters have these, and the reeves nothing. The
honey and pasture in the King's forest are worth 10s. each (*Modo habent h'
forestarii et prepositi nichil Decem sol' mellis et xs. pasture sunt in foresta regis*)."

I 173   [*c.* 1267-72]¹

WRIT of King Henry [III] to the prior of Southwick. Since by common
counsel² it has been provided that fines shall not be received from anyone
for fair pleading (*pro pulcre placitando*) or for freedom from molestation,
the King commands the prior not to demand or cause to be demanded
in future fines of this kind from the priory's men of the manor of Dean
(*Dene*), which was ancient royal demesne (*quod fuit antiquum dominium
nostrum*), against the aforesaid provision. And if the prior has taken
any distraint for this reason he is to release it without delay, lest repeated
complaint reaches the king so that he is obliged to take further action
(*Ne iteratus clamor ad nos perveniat propter quod manum ad hoc aliter
apponere debeamus*). Witness: the King, etc.

1 Between the passing of the Statute of Marlborough and the death of Henry III.

2 Statute of Marlborough (1267),c. 11.
See also II 235.

I 174 [? 1291][1]

LETTER from Brother William, Sub-prior of Southwick,[2] and the canons to King Edward informing him of the death of Prior John. Lest their church should remain for long bereft of a pastor, they are sending to him their brethren William de P., one of the obedientiaries, viz., the almoner, or etc., and N. de B., precentor, or etc., to show this letter to the king, humbly beseeching him to grant them a licence to hold an election, so may his reign be long and prosperous.

The Chapter House of the priory, on such a day in the year [   ][3] [Marginal note:] Let your letter seeking a licence be sent to the king, with the common seal attached (*Fiat littera vestra directa regi pro licencia petenda aperta cum communi sigillo pendenti*).

1 If this is a genuine letter rather than a "model", then presumably the deceased Prior is John de Clere, 1281–91, and the King, Edward I. John was succeeded as prior by Robert de Henton' (Hempton), 1291–1315. There is a similar letter at I 201 giving notice of the death of Prior R.

2 In 1290 the sub-prior of Southwick was called William (III 524).

3 The corner of the folio is missing.

I 175 [*c.* 1220–30][1]

[fo. 34] RENTAL of the men of the Prior of Southwick in the vill of [?Portchester][2]

From the land of:	Michaelmas	Christmas	Easter	St John the Baptist's Day	Martinmas
William Coliz	2s.				
Thomas Cote		28d.			
William le Wise†		20d.			
Robert Randolf*		12d.		12d.	
Richard le Haye†		4d.	4d.	4d.	4d.
Hurberyn	2s. 6d.				
formerly Eustace*	2s. 0d.				
Simon Gabriel	2s. 0d.				
Widow of Pistor†	3s. 0d.				

From the land of:	Michaelmas	Christmas	Easter	St John the Baptist's Day	Martinmas
Syger* [3]	2d.				
Widow Gamel	12d.				
Walter Flemigd	8d.		8d.		
Walter Swift	8d.		8d.		
Walter Lott [4]	3s. 0d.				
William Kiggel†	8d.		8d.		
Widow Crede*	12d.				
Widow of Nigel†	2s. 0d.				
Piiun	6d.		6d.		
Felicity, daughter of Haya	18d.		18d.		
Philip, forester in Portchester [5] (*for' in Porcestrie*)	18d.		15d. for land at Paulsgrove (*Palesgrave*)		

Salt rents from the same vill.

Robert Randolf*	15 sesters (*sextaria*)
Hurberyn	15 sesters
Syger*	8 sesters
Richard le Bike†	10 sesters

Accustomed services (*consuetudines*) of the aforesaid men.

Work owed to the prior at harvest:		Churchscot
William Coliz	1 man for 2 days	
Thomas Cote	1 man for 4 days	4 hens (*Gallin'*)
William le Wise†	1 man for 4 days	4 cocks (*Gall'*)
Robert Randolf*	1 man for 4 days and for other land 1 man for 4 days	4 hens
Richard Haye†	1 man for 2 days	2 cocks
Hewrberyn	1 man for 4 days	4 cocks
The widow of Eustace*	1 man for 2 days	2 cocks
Syger*	1 man for 2 days	2 cocks
Walter Flemig'	1 man for 2 days	2 cocks
Le Beke's land used to provide	1 man for 4 days	2 cocks 4 cocks
Walter Swift	1 man for 2 days	2 cocks
Walter Lott†	1 man for 2 days	
William Keggel†	1 man for 1 day	
Widow Crede*	1 man for 1 day	
Widow of Nigel†	1 man for 2 days	

1 In this first group of rentals only one for Winchester is dated, viz. 1219. It seems likely however that all were compiled within about a decade of that date.

2 Illegible in MS, but possibly four of the tenants (indicated*) also appear in the later Portchester rental *c.* 1248 (I 193, fo. 43–4); together with the widows or descendants of several others (indicated†). Names are often differently spelt.

3 See Sigar (I 193, fo. 43ᵛ). Either his holding was afterwards greatly increased, or the 2d. rent recorded here is a scribal error. He paid 32d. for 6½ acres according to the later rental.

4 See Robert, son of Walter (I 193, fo. 44).

5 A Philip Forestarius witnessed a charter given to a Portchester man c. 1240–50 (III 383, and note 2).

I 176 [c. 1220][1]

[fo. 34ᵛ] RENTAL of the prior's men in the manor of West Boarhunt (*Westburhunt'*)

From the land of:	Michaelmas	Easter	St John the Baptist's Day	Martinmas
Basil de Hsete	2s. 6d.	15d.		
Walter Kalbel	15d.	15d.		
Geoffrey Faber	15d. and 1 lb. of cummin	15d.		
Nicholas Karectarius	15d.	15d.		
William Rand'	15d.	15d.		
Ralph de la Hale	7½	7½		
Alan de la Hale	8d.	8d.		
Richard le Wite	7½	7½		
William le Wite	7½	7½		
Roger de Mundegom'	7½	7½		
Anneys	7½	7½		
Ralph Sveyn	6d.	6d.		
Henry de la Broke	6d.	6d.		
William de la Stapele	6d.	6d.		
William Faber	7½	7½		
Roger le Sopere	18d.	18d.		
Thomas Russel	21d.	21d.		
Gilbert Alwine	7½	7½		
Richard, G[ilbert's] neighbour	7½	7½		
Basil	7½	7½		
John Crabbe	10d.	10d.		
Jordan Bissop	7½	7½		
Peter de la Bere	12d.	12d.		

	Michaelmas	Christmas	Easter
Goda de la More	6d. and 1 lb. of cummin and suit of the prior's court.		
William Syward	2s. 0d.	2s. 0d.	2s. 0d.
Richard de la Hale custodian of woodland at the lord's will.			
Roys for a mill (*ad molend'*)	12d. and suit of court.		

	Michaelmas	Christmas	Easter
Andrew Crabbe[2]	12d.		
Richard Cruse	12d.		
Philip le Franceys	8d. and 1 lb. of pepper and suit of court.		
Hugh Loc[3]	18d.		18d. and suit of court.

Accustomed services of the aforesaid men of West Boarhunt.

From the land of Basil Hsethe[4] 3 works are owed each week throughout the year with 1 man, horse and cart; during harvest the tenant will find 3 men to work every other day, but during the 12 days of Christmas and the weeks of Easter and Pentecost he will not to any work (*sed . . . . ullam operam faciet*). He will give 1½ bushels of rye for churchscot at Martinmas.

Walter Kalbel owes the same works and churchscot as Basil (*faciet omnia predicta*), except that he will find 2 men every other day at harvest.

Geoffrey Faber, Nicholas Karectarius, and William, son of Rand' owe the same services as Walter. Geoffrey pays the same churchscot; Nicholas and William each owe 1½ bushels of wheat.

All the aforesaid tenants will take turns to bake bread, using the lord's wheat and wood, for the boonworks, and whoever bakes will not do any other work that day but after he has taken the bread to the boonwork he will make *bende* for the whole day.

Ralph de la Hale will find 1 man for 1 work every week in the year, except Christmas, Easter and Pentecost, and during harvest he will find 2 men every other day. For churchscot, he will give 3 hens and 1 cock at Martinmas.

Alan de la Hale owes the same services and churchscot as Ralph. And it is known that Ralph and Alan owe the same services as Walter Kalbel, except for baking bread for boonworks.

The following owe the same services and churchscot as Ralph: Richard le Wite; William le Wite; Roger Mundegom'; Anneys; Ralph Swein.

Henry de la Broke will find 1 man every other day during harvest, and will give for churchscot 3 hens and 1 cock at Martinmas.

The following owe the same service and churchscot as Henry: William de la Stapel; William Faber; Roger le Sopere; Thomas Russel; Gilbert Alwine; Richard, Gilbert's neighbour; Basel; John Crabbe; Jordan Bissop.

[fo. 35] All the aforesaid tenants are obliged to mow, make and carry [the hay] in the lord's meadow, and they will have a good sheep (*bonus multo*) and 4d. They are obliged to dip and shear the lord's sheep and also the lambs, and they will have a cheese.

Each of the aforesaid men who holds ½ virgate is obliged to plough 2 acres for the lord prior each year, viz. 1 acre at the winter sowing and 1 acre for oats (*ad avenas*).

William Syward will find 1 man for 1 work at harvest and owes suit of the hundred and manorial courts (*debet sectam hundredi et curie*).

Andrew Crabbe and Richard Cruse will each find 1 man for 3 works at harvest, and they owe and suit of court.

All the aforenamed who do any works owe suit at the lord prior's court.

They will give pannage dues, viz: for 1 year old pig, 2d.; for ½ year old pig, 1d.; for ¼ year old piglet (*purcellus*), ½d.

If the said men do any works outside the manor of Boarhunt (*Burhunte*) it will count as 1 or 2 or more works according to the existing rate, dependant on the distance they go. If they cart to Southwick it will count as 1 work for each man, and he will have one small loaf.

All the aforesaid men, except the free men, owe aid (*auxilium*) to the lord prior each year, if he wishes to exact it.

1 See I 175, note 1; also note 3 below.

2 An agreement was reached in 1288 between the priory and the vicar of West Boarhunt over small tithes formerly due to the vicar from certain of the priory's tenants, but no longer paid after the priory had taken over the land. Amongst tenements involved were those formerly held by William Randolf, Andrew Crabbe and Hugh Lok' (III 76, 785).

3 Walter, Clement and Richard, the sons of Hugh Locc, renounced in favour of the priory any right they might have had to land their father had held in West Boarhunt (I 139). The deed was witnessed by Guy who occurs as Prior of Southwick between 1185 and 1210. If the Hugh Loc who appears in the rental died or surrendered his land during Guy's priorate, this may suggest a date for the rental slightly earlier than 1220. See also III 461, which could possibly refer to the same tenement; and note 2 above.

4 In subsequent entries it should be understood that the obligations are similarly attributed to the land rather than to its holder.

I 177   [*c.* 1220–30][1]

RENTAL of the prior of Southwick's men at Fishbourne (*Fisseburne*) [Sussex][2]

From the land of:	Michaelmas	Christmas	Easter	St John the Baptist's Day
Herbert Prepositus	13d.	13d.	13d.	13d.
Richard Todere	15d.	15d.	15d.	15d.
Ralph le Paumer	7d.	7d.	7d.	7d.
Gilbert son of Ode	11d.	11d.	11d.	11d.
Widow Seild	8d.	8d.	8d.	8d.

Accustomed services of the aforesaid men of Fishbourne:

Each will find for his lord 1 man for 3 works at harvest; and they are obliged to make the lord's hay.

The $\frac{1}{2}$ acre in the field of Chichester (*in campo Cicestr'*) which is held by Humphrey Piscator yields 12d. at the feast of Annunciation.[3]

Total 19s.

1 This is the only rental for Fishbourne, and none of the tenants recorded here appears elsewhere in the cartularies. The only dating evidence is provided by the last entry (see note 3).

2 Two hides in Fishbourne were given to the priory by Turstin, son of Engelramn, *alias* Engeler, and the gift was confirmed by King Henry II c. 1154–8 (III 99; I 2).

3 The land was given to the priory by Richard de Pagham before 1246, probably c. 1220–30 (III 308). He also gave $\frac{1}{2}$ acre in the same field to the dean and canons of Chichester, and the tenant holding it was Humphrey Pessonarius, who was to pay 12d. rent (*Chichester Cartulary* 349, p. 93).

I 178 [After 1227, c. 1230][1]

RENTAL of the Prior of Southwick's men of Priors Dean (*Den'*)[2]

From the land of:	Michaelmas	Christmas	Easter	St John the Baptist's Day
Humphrey de Golleya†[3]	$34\frac{1}{2}$	$34\frac{1}{2}$	$34\frac{1}{2}$	$34\frac{1}{2}$
Gilbert de Goll'	$17\frac{1}{4}$	$17\frac{1}{4}$	$17\frac{1}{4}$	$17\frac{1}{4}$
Ralph de Goll'	$17\frac{1}{4}$	$17\frac{1}{4}$	$17\frac{1}{4}$	$17\frac{1}{4}$
H., son of Clericus' land and the garden of H. Juvenis	22d.	22d.	22d.	22d.
Nicholas þurstan*[4]	$18\frac{3}{4}$	$18\frac{3}{4}$	$18\frac{3}{4}$	$18\frac{3}{4}$
Richard Antiquus de la Fosse[5]	$6\frac{1}{2}$	$6\frac{1}{2}$	$6\frac{1}{2}$	$6\frac{1}{2}$
William Faber	13d.	13d.	13d.	13d.
Richard Juvenis de la Fosse*[5]	$9\frac{1}{2}$	$9\frac{1}{2}$	$9\frac{1}{2}$	$9\frac{1}{2}$
Widow Hawisa*[6]	$13\frac{3}{4}$	$13\frac{3}{4}$	$13\frac{3}{4}$	$13\frac{3}{4}$
Hugh Juvenis†	$13\frac{3}{4}$	$13\frac{3}{4}$	$13\frac{3}{4}$	$13\frac{3}{4}$
Gilbert Alfrich†	15d.	15d.	15d.	15d.
William de la Lode*[7]	18d.	18d.	18d.	18d.
Stephen Juvenis*[8]	$20\frac{1}{2}$	$20\frac{1}{2}$	$20\frac{1}{2}$	$20\frac{1}{2}$
Philip, son of G. de Goll*	$19\frac{1}{2}$	$19\frac{1}{2}$	$19\frac{1}{2}$	$19\frac{1}{2}$
Walter de Dossecumbe*	$10\frac{1}{2}$	$10\frac{1}{2}$	$10\frac{1}{2}$	$10\frac{1}{2}$
Peter de Dossecumbe†[9]	$10\frac{1}{2}$	$10\frac{1}{2}$	$10\frac{1}{2}$	$10\frac{1}{2}$
Ploughland (*cultura*) de la Forde[10]	2s. 0d. and the aforesaid Walter and Peter hold that ploughland.			
From the gully (*de Guletta*)	6d.; it descends from Doscomb (*Dosscumbe*) and Peter de Dosscumbe holds it.			
Land attached to (*que est inpendenti de*) Horenfeld	2d. and the aforesaid Walter and Peter hold it.			
Hugh de la Forde*	3d.	3d.	3d.	3d.
John de la Forde*	5d.	5d.	5d.	5d.

From the land of:	Michaelmas	Christmas	Easter	St John the Baptist's Day
Hugh Hering'	8¾	8¾	8¾	8¾
Gervase*	8¾	8¾	8¾	8¾
H. le Kyng's* old holding (*de antiquo tenemento*)	4½	4½	4½	4½
H. le Kyng for *B'hamesgrave*	3d.	3d.	3d.	3d.
H. le Kyng for White Croft	3½	3½	3½	3½
H. le Juvene's former holding	7¼	7¼	7¼	7¼
Stephen Endm'	14½	14½	14½	14½
John, son of Peter*[11]	15d.	15d.	15d.	15d.
Richard Franceys*	5d.	5d.	5d.	5d.
Stephen Feliz†[12]	9d.	9d.	9d.	9d.
William de la Lane†	1½	1½	1½	1½
[fo. 35ᵛ] Alan de la Slade†[13]	19d.	19d.	19d.	19d.
Gilbert de la Slade†	19d.	19d.	19d.	19d.
Elyas de Ledeponde	2d.	2d.	2d.	2d.
William le Berker	3d.	3d.	3d.	3d.
Humphrey de Goll' and Gilbert de Goll' for land called *Heringesdun* formerly held by Peter de Hauecleye†[14]	18d.	18d.	18d.	18d.
Richard Vetus de la Fosse and Hugh Harang' for *Piperland*, formerly held by Peter de Hauecleye†[15]	2s. 0d.	2s. 0d.	2s. 0d.	2s. 0d.
Gervase,* Hugh Harang, Henry le King* and Gilbert Champeneys* for land called *Kanappe* and *Eldecumbe*[16]	2s. 0d.	2s. 0d.	2s. 0d.	2s. 0d.
Richard Vetus de la Fosse,[5] William Faber, Richard Juvenis* de la Fosse, Hawisa de Godeshell', Hugh Juvenis, Gilbert Alverich for lands called *Burnecumbe* and *Hyndecumbe* from P. de Heuecleya's lands [17]	20d.	20d.	20d.	20d.

Total £8. 0. 9½d.

RENTAL of Colmore (*Colemere*)

From the land of:	Michaelmas	Christmas	Easter	St John the Baptist's Day
Jordan de la Felde	8d.	8d.	8d.	8d.
Walter de Colemere*	26d.	26d.	26d.	26d.
Mayfolc*	26d.	26d.	26d.	26d.
Reginald de la Spine	19½	19½	19½	19½
John de Colemere[18]	20½	20½	20½	20½
William de Bluntesmere†[19]	2s. 0d.	2s. 0d.	2s. 0d.	2s. 0d.
Bikesecle	42d.	42d.	42d.	42d.
Walter Clericus*	12d.			
From the court of Colemore for common pasture with the prior's men[20]	18d. and 18d. at Hockday (*Hocheday*)			
Wunigg	12d.	12d.	12d.	12d.

CUSTUMAL of the aforesaid men of Priors Dean (*la Dene*) and Colemore (*Colemere*), when they pay half rent according to their possessions (*quando dant dimidium gabulum secundum bona eorum*).[21]

Each plough ought to plough 2 acres for the lord at the winter sowing, but the lord will sow and harrow them; at the Lent sowing it will plough 1 acre and sow it with the lord's seed and harrow it. This, they say, is to be done by each plough whether it is owned by one man or many.

Each tenant will do 2 works for his lord at harvest, and if asked as a favour (*rogati in amore*) will do a third.

Each tenant will find a man for hoeing ½ acre without food, or, if the man hoes throughout the day, the lord will provide food.

Each tenant will give 3 hens and 1 cock for churchscot; a man without a wife will give 1 cock and 1 hen, and a widow 2 hens.

Each [tenant] on the manor will pay pannage dues, viz. for a 1-year-old pig, 1d.; for a ½-year-old, ½d.; for a younger [pig] (*de minori etate*), nothing.

They say that when any tenant's daughter is married outside the manor the lord will be given 2s., and if she is married within the manor, 1s. .

If any tenant's son wishes to leave the manor of Dean he will pay a fine (*faciet finem*) to his lord as he is able.

When anyone makes cider for sale in the manor of Dean, he or she will send cider worth 1d. to the serjeant of the manor.

They say that whenever anyone dies, his widow or heir will give the lord his better ox, but she or he will not give a horse.

The last four customs will apply whether the tenants pay full rent or half (*sive sint ad plenum gabulum sive ad dimidium*).

1 Between 1227 and 1235 Peter de Haueklye, or Hauecleye, quitclaimed to Prior Walkelin all right he had to land he held of the priory (III 838).

2 Dean was granted at fee farm to the priory by King John in 1204 for £7. 18s. 5d. a year (I 162).

3 See Millesent de Gollye (I 195, fo. 50^v). Goleigh Farm is 1½ miles east of Colemore.

4 See Nicholas Hurstan (I 195, fo. 51). Also III 833, 834.

5 Probably Richard Antiquus de la Fosse is the same man as Richard Vetus below, unless three generations are involved: Antiquus, Vetus and Juvenis. In the later rental Richard Juvenis de la Fosse is probably the Richard de la Dih [sic] who paid 6s. rent (I 195, fo. 51). He probably appears as Richard de la Diche when with Nicholas þurstane he witnessed a neighbour's charter (III 833). Richard Vetus de la Fosse had apparently died before the second rental was compiled. It was the widow of Richard de la Dih who was then paying 4s. for Piperland. See also II 235.

6 See Hawise de Godeshull (I 195, fo. 51^v).

7 An inquisition held in 1208 found that when Turstin the sheriff had doubled the rents of the tenants of Dean in lieu of labour services they used to perform on the manor of Barton [Stacey], because they lived so far away, the ancestors of William de la Lode were exempted on account of their poverty (I 164). See also II 235.

8 This tenement probably represents the tenement of Stephen Juvenis recorded in the later rental (I 195, fo. 51^v).

9 See I 195, note 6. Doscomb is about ½ mile south-east of Priors Dean church.

10 Possibly Forde and the two following entries can be accounted for in the later rental by Hamme and Dulve, held by Walter de Doscumbe and Petronilla, and the extra 1s. rent paid by Petronilla (I 195, fo. 51). Ford Field was south of Doscomb, and Ham Field off Warren Lane (Hervey, *History of Colmer and Priors Dean*, p. 15). The gully or water-course probably adjoined Doscomb pond.

11 Possibly this is the John Piris of the later rental (I 195, fo. 50^v).

12 See Widow le Fiz (I 195, fo. 50^v).

13 See the tenements held by Lawrence de la Slade and by John de Burwlle with Widow Slade (I 195, fo. 50^v). Slade Farm is about ¾ mile north-west of Priors Dean church.

14 See III 838; and note 3 above. Herrings Land Copse is just south of Goleigh Farm.

15 Piperland was off Button's Lane which runs westwards off the road from Priors Dean to Goleigh, about ¼ mile south of Goleigh Farm. See also note 5 above, and III 838.

16 The Knap is ¼ mile south-west of Colemore. Eldecumbe may be the Allecumbe or Alecumbe held by Gervase de Den and others (I 195, fo. 51).

17 Hyndecumbe was on Hawkley Hanger which is ½ mile east of Priors Dean (Hervey, *op. cit.*, p. 15). Burnecumbe was later said to be held by Richard de Dih (probably Richard Juvenis de la Fosse: see note 5) and his partners, for 6s. 8d. (I 195, fo. 51).

18 John de Colemere, son of Walter de Suthuse (probably Walter de Colemera, above), gave to the priory c. 1240–50 all the land he held at Colemore (III 832). John does not appear in the later rental, but Walter does (I 195, fo. 51^v, and note 6).

19 The inquisition held in 1208 found that when rents were doubled in lieu of labour services, William de Bluntesmere's father had been exempted on account of his poverty (I 164, and note 7 above). See also I 195, fo. 50, and note 4).

20 The 3s. rent for pasture was owed by the Kernet family, who had held land at Colemore since about the middle of the 12th century (*VCH Hants* IV, p. 423). Their own land was not affected by the gift of Colemore to the priory in 1198 by John, when Count of Mortain (I 148). The pasture rent was quitclaimed to the priory by Theodoric Teutonicus, who held Dean before it was granted to the priory by John in 1204 (III 840; I 162). In the later rental Lady Cecilia de Kernet paid the 3s. rent for pasture (I 195, fo. 50ᵛ). William Kernet, as Lord of Colemore, witnessed charters for the priory between 1273 and 1296 (III 842, 843, 850).

21 Colemore, said to be a member of Dean (later Priors Dean) (I 148), was in the hundred of Barton Stacey. When Turstin, who was sheriff of Hampshire from 1155 to 1159, had charge of Colemore and Dean on behalf of the king, he doubled the rents of the tenants in lieu of labour services they used to perform at Barton (I 164). After the priory had received from John the grant of Colemore, in 1198, and Dean, in 1204, disputes arose between the tenants and their new landlords over rent and services. The inclusion among the priory's rentals of the accustomed services of the men of Barton (probably Barton Stacey), (I 185), may indicate the priory's anxiety to ensure that all services due were recorded and performed, or rent paid in lieu. The inquisition held in 1208 expressly stated that the men of Colemore and Dean owed all the same customs and services as those owed by the men of Barton (I 162). It is noteworthy that in the case of Barton alone no tenants are mentioned by name; Barton Stacey never belonged to the priory.

I 179   [*c.* 1220–30][1]

[fo. 36] RENTAL of the prior of Southwick's men of the manor of Candover[2]

	Michaelmas	Easter
Walter Lucas*[3]	10s. 0d.	
John Blundus[4]	7s. 6d.	7s. 6d.
Ralph Normaneton[4]	7s. 6d.	7s. 6d.
Philip Hunte*	5s. 0d.	
Richard Thuyd†	2s. 6d.	
Ralph le Paumer	2s. 6d.	
Hugh le Messer	2s. 6d.	
Henry Kute	2s. 6d.	
Stephen Basilus	2s. 6d.	
William Brent'*	2s. 6d.	
Richard Parvus*	2s. 6d.	
William, son of Basilus*	2s. 6d.	
Elyes Azelm	2s. 6d.	
Thomas de Puteo*	2s. 6d.	
Ralph Ruffus*	2s. 6d.	
Richard Faber*	2s. 6d.	
John de la Strode*[5]	2s. 6d.	

	Michaelmas	Easter
Thomas de la Strode*[5]	2s. 6d.	
Walter Faber†	3s. 6d.	
Robert Kate*[6]	2s. 0d.	
Isabella (*Ysabell'*)*[6]	12d.	
Widow of Yvo	6d.	
Robert Horsman	6d.	
William King	6d.	
M. Thomas	2s. 0d.	

Total £4. 10s.

CUSTUMAL of the aforesaid men of Candover (*Kandev'*)

Walter Lucas[3] will accompany the prior, if required, throughout the county at the prior's expense, and will harrow oats and barley at the prior's expense if the prior's palfrey (*palefridus*) is harrowing. He holds ½ hide and owes suit of court.

John Blundus, and likewise Ralph Normaneton,[4] holds ½ virgate and owes suit of court.

Philip Hunt' holds 1 virgate. He will give for the churchscot at Martinmas 1 quarter of wheat by the old measure (*de veteri mensura*). He will pay pannage dues, viz., for a pig more than 1 year old (*superannatus*), 1d. He will find 2 men for 6 works at harvest, will cart the lord's corn for 2 days, and will have his food and 1 sheaf of the corn. He will carry the lord's hay from *la Wildemore* for 1 day, and if it is harvest time (*si sit infra autumpnum*) he will have his food. He will twice cart (*faciet duas kariagias*) oats or barley to Southwick, and will have his food and fodder for his beast (*averus*). He will dip and shear the lord's sheep for 1 day. He will find 1 man to hoe for 2 half days. He will collect nuts for half a day. He will plough 1 acre in winter, and harrow it. He will harrow 1 acre of *Dustland*. He will carry 2 hurdles twice a year when the lord's fold is moved.

Richard Thuyd holds ½ virgate. He will give ½ quarter of wheat by the old measure for churchscot, and he will give pannage. He will plough and harrow ½ acre in winter. He will harrow 1 acre of *Dustland*. He will find 2 men for 6 works at harvest. He will carry the lord's corn for 2 days, and have his food and 1 sheaf of the corn. He will carry the lord's hay for 1 day from *la Wildemore*, and if he does this during harvest he will have his food. He will do carrying service twice a year to Southwick and have his food, and fodder for his beast. He will find 1 man to hoe for 2 half days. He will find 1 man to dip and shear sheep. He will carry 2 hurdles twice a year when the fold is moved. He will hold the lord's plough when the lord wills; he will then be quit of 1s. 6d. of his rent (*de gabulo suo*) and ½ quarter of wheat for churchscot and from all other services except 6 works by 2 men at harvest. If he serves as ploughman he will have the use of the lord's ploughs to plough 9 acres for himself, and will have 1 loaf each day from the feast of St Peter in Chains [August 1] until Michaelmas [September 29]. And if the lord's plough is held up by bad weather, the ploughman will do other work during that time; but if he ceases to be ploughman he will carry out the same services due to the lord as other men with similar holdings.

The following each hold $\frac{1}{2}$ virgate for the same service as Richard Thuyd: Ralph le Paumer; Hugh le Messer; Henry Kute; Stephen Baselus; Richard Parvus; William de Brent'; William, son of Baselus; Elias Azelm; Thomas de Puteo; Richard Ruffus.

Richard Faber holds $\frac{1}{2}$ virgate for the same service as Richard Thuyd. Alternatively he will make the ironwork for 2 of the lord's ploughs, provide at his own cost the ploughshares and coulters and whatever is necessary for them throughout the year, and will have 1 cheese and 1 cloak (*vellus*); but during harvest he will do 6 works as aforesaid and have food provided by the lord; he will be quit of all other works so long as he makes the aforesaid ironwork.

John de la Strode[5] holds $\frac{1}{2}$ virgate. He will mow the lord's meadow [fo. 36ᵛ] called *la Wildemore*, make and carry 1 cartload of hay (*levabit fenum et cariabit cum j karectata*), and will have 3d. from the lord's purse (*de bursa domini*). He will give 4 hens for churchscot at Martinmas.

Thomas de la Strode[5] holds $\frac{1}{2}$ virgate for the same services and churchscot as John.

Item: all the aforesaid men who do works will carry the lord's hay from *la Wildemore*, viz. 1 cartload each, and if they cannot carry all the hay, John and his partner (*socius suus*) will carry another load, but the lord will provide food.

Walter Faber holds 12 acres. He will pay pannage dues, and provide 2 men for 6 works at harvest (*faciet vj operas in autumpno per duos homines*). He owes suit of court.

Robert Kate[6] holds 2 acres. He will give pannage dues, provide 2 men for 6 works at harvest, and have his food and 3 loaves at dinner (*ad dinnarium*). He will hoe for 2 half days. He will dip and shear sheep. He will collect nuts for half a day. He will carry 2 hurdles twice a year when the lord's fold is moved. He will give 4 hens for churchscot at Martinmas.

Isabel[6] and the widow of Yvo each hold a messuage for the same services as Robert Kate, but while they are widows they will give 2 hens for churchscot.

Robert Horsman holds a messuage for the same services as Robert Kate, and while he is without a wife will give 2 hens for churchscot.

William King holds a messuage for the same services as Robert Kate, and will give 2 hens for churchscot.

Maurice de Turville will give 1 lb of cummin at Michaelmas, and will have rights of common for his own sheep at *Berdun'* (*habebit communionem de Berdun' ad bidentes suos proprios*).[7]

---

1 Possibly as many as 12 of the tenants of Preston Candover (indicated *) were still holding their tenements when the later rental was compiled in 1249 (I 196); in other instances heirs (marked †) had probably succeeded. This suggests that no great time had elapsed between the drawing up of the two rentals. However the inclusion of Maurice de Turville (below and note 7) points to a date earlier rather than later than 1230.

2 Five hides and 1 virgate of land at Preston Candover comprised the principal endowment granted to the priory at its foundation by William de Pont de l'Arche (I 1).

3 Woodland held by Walter Lucas was referred to in an agreement drawn up in 1239 (III 375).

4 Possibly the tenements held by John Blundus and Ralph Normaneton were at Ellisfield. William Albus and Sare de Helsefeld' each held ½ virgate there and paid 15s. for all service in 1249, and these tenements were included in the Preston Candover rental (I 196). Ellisfield is 3 miles north-east of Preston Candover. Stephen of Candover (*Candewr'*) had given the priory 30s. worth of land, viz. two ½-virgates, in Ellisfield *c.* early 13th century. A confirmation of the gift by the son of Richard de Herierd was witnessed by Maurice de Turville (I 156; also see below and note 7).

5 It seems likely that John and Thomas de la Strode appear in the later rental as John and Thomas de Somersulle (I 196).

6 Probably this is the Robert le Cute of the later rental, and the following tenant is Isabella le Cute (I 196).

7 In 1200 Maurice de Turville witnessed a charter for Godfrey de Lucy, Bishop of Winchester (III 550). He served as the bishop's steward and held ½ knight's fee of the bishop in Wield, which is about 2 miles south-east of Preston Candover (*Pontissara Register* p. 387). He witnessed other charters after the bishop's death in 1204 (I 160; III 568). There is a Barton Copse south of Upper Wield; possibly the site of *Berdun*. The later rental has no mention of Maurice (I 196).

I 180　　　　　　　　　　　　　　　　　　　　　　　　　　[*c.* 1220–30][1]

RENTAL of the prior of Southwick's men in the vill of Southwick.

From the house of:	Michael-mas	Christ-mas	Easter	St John the Bap-tist's Day	Holy Cross Day
Richard de la Pette	15d.	15d.	15d.	15d.	
Roger Fabert†	4½	4½	4½	4½	
Simon Aurifaber 1 lb. of cummin and	3d.	3d.	3d.	3d.	
Adam Swele,*[2] for his land and house except Melcroft	15d.		12d.		
Richard Capellanus[3]					½ lb. incense
Robert le Waleys*	3d.	3d.	3d.	3d.	(*olibanus*)
Richard de Peteresfeld	6d.		6d.		
Rents of Neuhestr'					
Richard Pistor	6d.		6d.		
Richard Coke[4]	1 lb. of pepper				
Thomas le Cuperet†	6d.		6d.		
John Purst†	6d.		6d.		
Osbert Harding*	6d.		6d.		
Thomas Lardiner*[5]	6d.		6d.		
Juliana Lotringham	9d.		9d.		

From the house of:	Michael-mas	Christ-mas	Easter	St John the Bap-tist's Day	Holy Cross Day
Robert Calvus	6d.		6d.		
Richard Pethit*	6d.		6d.		
William Bun[6]	6d.		6d.		
Richard Swele*[7]	6d.		6d.		
Wulwin'†	6d.		6d.		
Richard Chesun†	6d.		6d.		
Luke Brun*		6d.		6d.	

Rents of Mullecroft

	Michael-mas	Christ-mas	Easter	St John the Bap-tist's Day	Holy Cross Day
Ralph le Chapm', for his place (*placia*)		12d.		12d.	
Margar'		6d.		6d.	
Le Hoppere*		6d.		6d.	
John le Cupere*		6d.		6d.	
William Cocus		6d.		6d.	
Roger de la Helle,* for his place (*placia*)		6d.		6d.	
Peter le Harel		6d.		6d.	
Peter Buyn		6d.		6d.	
Adam Swele,* for his place (*placia*)		6d.		6d.	
Richard Swele*[7]		12d.		12d.	

usque huc

	Michael-mas	Christ-mas	Easter	St John the Bap-tist's Day	Holy Cross Day
Richard Swele,* adjoining the house of Richard le Hore*				12d.	
Richard Snelger*[8]	6d.	6d.	6d.	6d.	
Richard Cementarius*[9]	6d.	6d.	6d.	6d.	
Ralph le Frere[10]	3d.	3d.	3d.	3d.	
William le Beke*[11]	6d.	6d.	6d.	6d.	
Maria Mazre	4s. 0d.				
Reginald Gupiyl*[12]					
Richard le Hore*	3d.	3d.	3d.	3d.	
Philip Cridiho*[13]	6d.	4d.	4d.	4d.	
Henry Morin*	8d.		8d.		
Robert Peyteuin†	3d.	3d.	3d.	3d.	
Peter de la Bere*	6d.		6d.		
Reginald Gupil for Flaxlande	5s. 0d.[12]				

21s. 1½d.

[fo. 37]

From the house of:	Michaelmas	Christmas	Easter	St John the Baptist's Day
Peter de Havehunte†[14]	9d.	9d.	9d.	9d.
Lady Joan de Burhunt:[15] 1 lb. of wax at Michaelmas and	3d.	3d.	3d.	3d.
Alfred Peytevin, for his place (*placia*)	3d.	3d.	3d.	3d.
Seburyht,* next to Peter de Haueh'	3d.	3d.	3d.	3d.
Simon Capellanus: 5s. to the custodian of St Mary's altar at Annunciation, and	3d.	3d.	3d.	3d.

From the house of:	Michaelmas	Christmas	Easter	St John the Baptist's Day
John Molend'	3d.	3d.	3d.	3d.
Arnold	3d.	3d.	3d.	3d.
Alfred Peytevin; in the prior's hands	3d.	3d.	3d.	3d.
John Pistor	3d.	3d.	3d.	3d.
Farmus, and his son each pay	3d.	3d.	3d.	3d.
William le Curtyller*	3d.	3d.	3d.	3d.
Formerly Robert le Curtiler	3d.	3d.	3d.	3d.
William le Kareter*	3d.	3d.	3d.	3d.
Richard le Horseya†	3d.	3d.	3d.	3d.
Bolresford[16]	3d.	3d.	3d.	3d.
Adam, son of Hervus	3d.	3d.	3d.	3d.
Ralph Sport	3d.	3d.	3d.	3d.
William Kukehorn*	3d.	3d.	3d.	3d.
Hervus	3d.	3d.	3d.	3d.
Roger Finel	3d.	3d.	3d.	3d.
Geoffrey Hsanke*	3d.	3d.	3d.	3d.
Ralph de la Hurne†	3d.	3d.	3d.	3d.
Felicia Swift	3d.	3d.	3d.	3d.
Geoffrey Bulle[17]	3d.	3d.	3d.	3d.
Robert Burgeys*	3d.	3d.	3d.	3d.
Osbert le Syur	3d.	3d.	3d.	3d.
Adam le Karether	3d.	3d.	3d.	3d.
Widow of Richard Rotharius	3d.	3d.	3d.	3d.
Formerly le Karether	3d.	3d.	3d.	3d.
William Aywen	3d.	3d.	3d.	3d.
Robert le Rower	3d.	3d.	3d.	3d.
Richard*[18] and Adam le Lorimer	3d.	3d.	3d.	3d.
Gelus*[19]	3d.	3d.	3d.	3d.
John Swift[20]	3d.	3d.	3d.	3d.
Luke le Wise*[21]	3d.	3d.	3d.	3d.
William le Hore*	3d.	3d.	3d.	3d.
Widow W. le Bukere	4d.	4d.	4d.	4d.

Tenant (*de terra . . .*)	Michaelmas	Christmas	Easter	St John the Baptist's Day
Ralph Chobayn, for house and land,[22]	9d.		9d.	
Hugh de la Helle*[22]	4d.	4d.	4d.	3d. [*sic*]
Roger de Helle, for curtillage next to Hugh's house	3d.		3d.	
Roger de Helle*	18d.	18d.	18d.	18d.
Richard de la Durefold*	4d.	4d.	4d.	4d.
Robert de Bikeford,* for land and mill[23]	18d.	18d.	18d.	18d.
Adam Smalhoppere	8d.			
John Heyrun*	6d.	6d.	6d.	6d.
Elias (*Helyas*) de Culern',† for meadow	6d.			

Tenant (*de terra . . .*)	Michaelmas	Christmas	Easter	St John the Baptist's Day
Land called Craketayleslond	4d.	4d.	4d.	4d.
Richard de la Felde	12d.	12d.	12d.	12d.
William de la Felde	12d.	12d.	12d.	12d.
Richard de Sandfide	5d.	5d.	5d.	5d.
William de Ponte*	$3\frac{3}{4}$.	$3\frac{3}{4}$.	$3\frac{3}{4}$.	$3\frac{3}{4}$.
Geoffrey de Ponte†[24]	$3\frac{3}{4}$.	$3\frac{3}{4}$.	$3\frac{3}{4}$.	$3\frac{3}{4}$.
Thomas de la Frihe	12d.		12d.	
Richerus de la Frihe*	18d.		18d.	
Walter Freysel,† a $\frac{1}{2}$ mark payable before lunch (*ante prandium*)[25]				6s. 8d.
Randolph	$10\frac{1}{2}$.	$10\frac{1}{2}$.	$10\frac{1}{2}$.	$10\frac{1}{2}$.
John de Lingest'*	12d.	12d.	12d.	12d.
Le Sauuner	18d.		18d.	
John le Blic†	6d.		6d.	
The daughter of Hornus	3d.	3d.	3d.	3d.
The daughter of Hornus, for a croft	$6\frac{1}{2}$.	$6\frac{1}{2}$.	$6\frac{1}{2}$.	$6\frac{1}{2}$.
Adam le Syur†	4d.	4d.	4d.	4d.
William Bercharius*	3d.	3d.	3d.	3d.
Stoyleslond	$3\frac{3}{4}$.	$3\frac{3}{4}$.	$3\frac{3}{4}$.	$3\frac{3}{4}$.
The mill in front of Sir Herbert's gate[26]	5s. 0d.	5s. 0d.	5s. 0d.	5s. 0d.
The windmill	12d.		12d.	

Robert Sharp 1 stook of corn (*sok'*) at Martinmas.

Robert Novus Homo 1 stook of corn.

David* 1 stook of corn, at the same term.

Robert le Hore 2 capons (*kapuns*) at the same term; his brother Richard* is his surety (*plegius*).

Robert le Burgeys* for land called Coltesh', 12d. at the feast of the Purification of the Blessed Mary.

Total: 36s. $11\frac{1}{4}$d.

32s. $\frac{1}{4}$d.

[fo. 37ᵛ] Richard le Hore will find 1 man for 4 days' work at harvest (*operabit in autumpno iiii diebus per i hominem*). He will give pannage dues, viz. for a 1 year old pig, 2d., and a $\frac{1}{2}$ year old, 1d., and a $\frac{1}{4}$ year old, $\frac{1}{2}$d. He will give $\frac{1}{2}$d. at the mowing of the lord's meadow, and he will provide 1 man for 1 day to help at haymaking (*adiuvabit per i diem cum i homine levare pratum*). He will dip and shear the lord's sheep, and will give 4 hens for churchscot at Martinmas.

The following will do all the same services as Richard le Hore: Seburyht; Simon Capellanus; John Molendinarius; Arnold; Alfred Paytevin; Farmus; William le Curtiller; Robert le Curtyller; William le Kareter; Richard Horsi; Bolreford; Adam, son of Hervus; William Kukehoren; Hervicus Hose; Roger Finel; Geoffrey Shonke; Ralph de la Herne; Felicia Swift; Geoffrey Bulle; Robert le Burgeys; Osbert le Syur; Adam le Kartter; the widow of Richard Rocharius; the daughter of Richard le

Kareter; Robert le Roer; Richard and Adam, sons of Simon; Gelus; John Swift; Lucas le Wise; William le Hore; the widow of William le Cupere; William Aywar; Richard de la Berefold; John Heyrun; Craketayleslond; the daughter of Horen; Adam le Syur; William le Berker.

Richard de Sandfide owes the same services as Richard le Hore, and moreover at Christmas he will go to the wood with his axe for 1 day.

John Pistor will give pannage dues as the others aforesaid, will find 1 man for 4 works at harvest, and will give 1 lb. of cummin [   ].

Ralph Sport will give the same pannage dues as the others, and will find 1 man for 4 works at harvest.

Hugh de la Helle will do all the same services as Richard le Hore; moreover he is required to provide 3 hurdles and take them to the lord's fold, and to carry hay with his cart for 1 day.

Roger de la Helle will find 1 man for reaping wheat for 1 day, and oats for 1 day. He used to accompany his lord with his horse at the lord's expense throughout the county to carry the lord's clothing (*panni*) if requested; moreover was required to go in turn (*in visce*) for the lord's food (*cybum*) to Winchester, Chichester, Southampton, Titchfield (*Ticheffeld*), Christchurch (*ad Christi ecclesiam*) and also to the Isle [of Wight], and when he had been summoned in the evening to [go to] any of these places, he would go [next] morning with a man and horse at his own expense, but he would buy the fish with the lord's money. Because this service was not greatly valued by the priory it took in lieu a certain meadow which Roger formerly held, and which belonged to the land he holds. (*et quando citatus esset ad aliquem locorum vespere mane iret cum homine et equo et sumptibus ipsius Rogeri sed cum denariis domini pisces emet, sed quia istud servicium parum valuit canonicis ipsi acceperunt quoddam pratum in manua sua pro servicio ipsius Rogeri quod pratum idem Rogerus ante ea tenuit et fuit pertinens ad terram quam ipse tenet*).

Robert de Bikeford will find 2 men for 4 days' work at harvest. He will carry the lord's corn at harvest with a horse and cart for 4 days and the lord's hay for 1 day. When he carries corn, he will have his food and in the evening 1 sheaf of that corn. When he carries hay, he will have food likewise. In Lent he will harrow for 4 days, and have 1 loaf each day. At Christmas he will go to the wood with his axe, on the bailiff's instructions, for 2 days, and will have his food. He will give 4½d. at haymaking.

Richard de la Felde will reap 4 acres of corn at harvest, and will have 4 wheat and 4 barley loaves and something with them (*et companagium*) and ale. He will harrow 4 acres of oats and will have 4 loaves; and 1 acre of wheat and will have his food. At Christmas he will carry wood for 2 days. At harvest he will carry the lord's corn for 4 days, and will have his food each day and a sheaf of the corn that is carried. He will give 4½d. at the mowing of the meadow, but will find 1 man at haymaking (*ad erigendum et levandum pratum*). He will carry hay for 1 day and will have his food. He will dip and shear the lord's sheep. He will give the same pannage dues as Richard le Hore. At Christmas he will carry manure for 9 days for the lord, and will have 1 loaf each day; he will find 1 man with an axe (*secura*) to mend 1 house in the court at

Southwick; and he will provide 1 man to make 1 fence in the court for 1 day with food supplied. He is to provide (*furnire*) 3 hurdles and carry them to the fold.

William de Ponte will provide 2 men for 4 days' work at harvest (*operabit in autumpno per iiij dies cum duobus hominibus*). Moreover, from the feast of St Peter in Chains [1 August], each day during harvest except feast days, he is to mow ½ acre, and for each ¼ acre he will have 1 sheaf; but on Saturday he will not do any work. He will carry the lord's corn, but while he is carrying he will not do any other work, and when he carries corn he will have 1 sheaf of that corn. From the end of harvest to Michaelmas he will work every other day until noon, with a cart if the lord wishes, and he will have 1 loaf each day he works. From Michaelmas until Christmas he will do 1 work each week until noon with a cart, and will have 1 loaf each day he works, but at Christmas he will carry manure for 9 days until noon, and will have 1 loaf each day. And from Christmas until Purification [2 February] he will do 1 work until noon each week with a cart, and will have 1 loaf on the day he works. And from Purification until the feast of St Mary in March [25 March], when they sow oats, he will harrow every other day until noon, and will have 1 loaf each day he works. And from the feast of St Mary in March until the feast of St Peter in Chains he will do 1 work until noon each week with a cart, and will have 1 loaf each day he works. He will give the same churchscot and pannage dues as the others.

Geoffrey de Ponte will do all the same services as William de Ponte.

1 The cartulary contains two rentals for Southwick; this one is the earlier. The later can probably be dated 1248 (I 190, note 1) and must have been compiled within a lifetime of the earlier, since it contains 34 of the same names (often differently spelt), as indicated (*); there can be no reasonable doubt that a number of these names were those of the same men. In a further 14 instances (marked †) it was probably the widow or son of the earlier tenant who had taken over the holding.

2 Adam witnessed a charter (II 206) during the priorate of Walkelin (1227–35), and after his death his daughter, Lucy, gave that part of the house which she had inherited from him to Richard Marescallus, who was to pay the 6d. rent due to the priory (III 304; see also II 200).

3 This may be Richard Capellanus of Wanstead, who, with another tenant who appears in this rental, William de Ponte, was holding land near Southwick sometime between 1227 and 1235 (II 206, and note 2 above).

4 A John Cotus [*sic*] was later paying the same rent for a messuage (I 193, fo. 47ᵛ).

5 Probably the same Thomas gave a piece of land next to his house in New Street to the priory to provide a candle while daily mass was said in its church (III 1003). His son, William, subsequently gave both land and house to the priory (III 297; see also III 305).

6 Possibly this is the William Dun of the later rental (I 193, fo. 46ᵛ). Six entries probably appear in the same order in both rentals.

7 Richard acquired a messuage in Southwick from William, son of Walter de la Plante, for which he was to pay 12d. a year at two terms to the priory (III 932). Between 1235 and 1266 he sold a messuage in Southwick said to lie between those of Robert Rotarius and Gelus (III 997). See also II 168, 193, 154, 142, 199, 200.

8 Richard had died by 1275 (III 489). See also III 998, 490, 560.

9 See III 490, 506.

10 Ralph witnessed a charter sometime between 1235 and 1266 (II 206); see also III 932. His tenement was vacant when the later rental was compiled (see Ralph Frater, I 190, fo. 44^v).

11 It may have been William's son, Thomas, who gave a piece of land with two houses to the priory's almshouse by a charter witnessed by Richard and Adam Swele (III 688).

12 No rent is recorded for this tenement but 5s. rent was paid by Reginald for Flaxlande (see below and I 182, fo. 39). See also I 193, notes 15, 34.

13 See III 490, 560. After Philip's death, his daughters granted 3d. rent to the priory, sometime between 1281 and 1291 (III 197 and notes).

14 Peter appeared as a witness in 1210 and between 1227 and 1235 (I 99; II 206). He was succeeded by his son, known as William Suwyk (I 193, fo. 46^v).

15 Possibly this is the wife, or widow, of William de Burhunt and the mother of Herbert (III 253, 254).

16 See Walter Bolleford (I 193, fo. 45^v).

17 See II 181.

18 See III 779, 778.

19 See Robert Gelus (I 193, fo. 45). See also III 997.

20 John no longer held his messuage when the later rental was compiled (I 193, fo. 45). See also III 677.

21 See III 347.

22 In the later rental William Svift was holding two places in Cobayn croft (I 193, fo. 47^v). In 1255–6 Agnes, daughter of Ralph Cobayn, quitclaimed to the priory any right she had to her father's land, and in return she was to hold for life the land of her late husband, Hugh de la Hulle (III 533).

23 Beckford Bridge is about 1½ miles north of Southwick.

24 Geoffrey may have been succeeded by Richard de Ponte (I 193, fo. 43). See also II 195.

25 This may be the tenement later held by Marcha (I 193, fo. 43). In that case both Walter and Marcha may have inherited it from John Fresel, who received it from his father, Ranulf, in the reign of Richard I, 1188–99 (III 94, 95 and notes).

26 The reference is almost certainly to Sir Herbert de Burhunt's gate. One of the earliest gifts from the de Burhunt family to the priory was the site for a mill (I 121). In the 1180s this mill was described as being in front of Alexander de Burhunt's gate or house (I 28, 29, 30). Amongst many undated charters of the first half of the 13th century in which the name of Sir Herbert de Burhunt appears, one at least can be dated between 1227 and 1235 as Prior Walkelin was a witness, together with Sir Herbert, and probably three of the priory's tenants who appear in this rental (II 206).

I 181a   6 November 1219

[fo. 38] RENTAL of the canons of Southwick at Winchester.

Drawn up on the feast of St Leonard in the presence of Prior Luke; Sub-prior Andrew; Bartholomew and Nicholas, canons; Geoffrey, clerk; and many others.

In ?Buck (*Berkesir'*) Street:[1]
(i) Ralph Pogcarius held land and used to pay 6d. rent to the priory on Hock Day [2nd Tuesday after Easter], and 6d. landgavel (*landgabulum*) to the nuns of Godstow (*Godestowe*), [Oxfordshire], he increased the rent so that, apart from (*preter*) the landgavel, the priory will have 12d. This land was given to the priory by Robert Spilem and is now in the hands of the canons.

In Colebrook Street (*Colebrokestr'*)—rents due on Hock Day:
(ii) The priory used to have 2d. from land Thelarius holds, and 4d. is owed for landgavel;
(iii) from land Elyas Portarius holds, 6d.;
(iv) from land Alfred Cocus held, 3d.;
(v) from land Wilbe's wife held, 4d.[2]

In Little Minster Street (*Manstrestr'*):
(vi) from land Hugh de Kardunvil' held, the gift [to the priory] of William, son of Reymund, 4s. 2d., at Michaelmas; Hugh increased the rent by 8d. to 4s. 10d.[3]

In St Thomas' Street (*Kalpstr'*):
(vii) from land Reginald Facke held, the gift of Gilbert Oin, 3s. at Purification; it is the house on the corner where the goldsmiths are (*in angulo ubi aurifabri sedent*);[4]
(viii) from land Godwin Hor's wife held, 16d. at four annual rent-paying terms.

In Trafalgar Street (*Garstr'*):
(ix) from land Swein Fustarius held, given to the priory at its dedication by Bishop Richard, 12d. on Hock Day.[5]

In the Shambles (*Mazakerie*):
(x) from land Roger Ruffus held, 30d. at four annual terms.[6]

In St Peter's Street (*Alwarestr'*):
(xi) Osbert Mercarius held land which Hugh Tymbermangere had held, and paid 2s. at fair time (*in nundinis*); afterwards it was in the hands of John Josep.[7]
(xii) Osbert held other land, adjoining the north wall, and also land Osmund Juvenis held, and paid 2s. at fair time; afterwards John Perekine, O.'s son held them.[8]

In Parchment Street (*Flesmongerestr'*):
(xiii) the same Osbert held a small piece of land (*terrula*), adjoining Hugh Tymbermongare's house; his wife afterwards held it, paying 2s. at Michaelmas.[7]

In the High Street (*in magno vico*):
(xiv) the same Osbert held 1 seld (*selda*),[9] the gift of Brother Thomas Ruffus, paying 12d. on St Giles' Day [1 September]; afterwards it was in Guy's hands; it is in front of (*ante*) the Guildhall (*guihaud*).[10]

On St Giles' Hill:
(xv) the same Osbert held 1 seld, paying 12d. a year at fair time.

In Parchment Street:
(xvi) from land Richard Archers held, 3s. 6d. at Michaelmas.

In Upper Brook Street (*Suldwortenestr'*):
(xvii) from land formerly held by Richard Cordarius, 8d. at Michaelmas.[11]
(xviii) from land Robert Monachus held, 4d. at fair time.[12]

In Lower Brook Street (*Tannerestr'*):
(xix) from meadow held by Margaret the priory used to have 4s. 6d. at fair time; afterwards Bartholomew Tannator held it for 2s.[13]
(xx) for meadow, the gift of Simon son of Richerius, Roger son of Turoldus pays 12d. a year at Michaelmas, and the wife of Godfrey son of Alexander pays 12d. for landgavel.
(xxi) from the house and land of Lady Reginalda, 12d. paid at fair time by William de Sancta Maria.[14]

On St Giles' Hill—rents payable at fair time:
(xxii) from the seld Richard de Scotia held, 6s. paid by the aforesaid William; afterwards it was in the bishop's hands.
(xxiii) from the house Gerard held, the gift of Thomas Oysun,[15] 16d.

In the High Street:
(xxiv) from the gift of Alice, (*Aliz*), wife of Arnold Bell, and her son, Herbert, 12d. paid by Henry Bule at fair time.[16]

In Parchment Street:
(xxv) for a certain garden, the gift of the same Alice, [   ] paid at fair time by Thomas Oysun.[17]

By the Eastern gate near Ralph de Porta's house:
(xxvi) for a certain house, the gift of Henry de Tisted, clerk, 2s. paid at fair time by Richard, son of Gervase.[18]

Outside Kingsgate (*Kingate*):
(xxvii) from certain cottages (*bordelli*),[19] the gift of Simon, son of Richerius, 40d. at Michaelmas.

In *Sewinestwichene* adjoining the church of St Michael:[20]
(xxviii) for a certain orchard, the gift of the aforesaid Simon, 4s. at fair time paid by Gocelin Sumet.[21]

(xxix) for land which was held by Adam de Rehcesfeld, the gift of Guy de Vo, 12d. at fair time from the brothers of the hospital of St John.[22]

In the High Street:
(xxx) for the house he lives in, Robert le Furbur pays 12d. at
Michaelmas.[23]

Afterwards, by process of time, the rents at Winchester altered in this
way:—

I 181b   [after 1219, *c.* second quarter of the 13th century]

[SECOND RENTAL]
In St Thomas' Street:
(1) for land, the gift of Osbert [*sic*] Oyn, which is on the corner of that
street where the goldsmiths are, and which Thomas Cupere held, 3s.
at Purification paid by Eberimus Westman [cf. vii].

In the High Street:
(2) for the house he lives in, near the West gate, Robert le Furbur pays
12d. at Michaelmas [cf. xxx].
(3) for a seld, the gift of Thomas Ruffus, which is in front of the
Guildhall, Guy, son of Osbert de Burn' pays 12d. at St. Giles' Fair
[cf. xiv].

In St Peter's Street—rents payable at fair time:
(4) for land John de Burn holds, at the top [of the street] adjoining the
north wall, the gift of William, son of Roger, 12d. [cf. xii];
(5) for the land Peter, son of Osbert de Burn' held, adjoining the above
land, which is now held half by Valentine Presbyter and half by
Luke Tannator, 12d. [cf. xii].
(6) for land, in a lane in front of Elias Westman's house, which is held
by Robert Bric' and his wife Isabel, and Luke Tannator and his wife,
2s. [cf. xi].

In Parchment Street:
(7) for land given by Thurstan the sheriff which was held by Hugh le
Tymbermongare and now is held by Scolastica, widow of Osbert de
Burn', 2s. at Michaelmas [cf. xiii].

In Upper Brook Street:
(8) for land which was held by Ralph [*sic*] Cordere, and now half by
William de Bedeford, clerk, and half by Aldelm, 8d. at Michaelmas
[cf. xvii].
(9) for land Robert Monachus held, now held by William Aurifaber, 4d.
[cf. xviii].
(10) for land in front of the monastery of St. Ruald (*Rumbildus*), which
William Sheluemele and the widow of Stephen le Mercer hold,
2s. 6d. at Michaelmas.[25]

In the High Street:

(11) from the gift of Alice, wife of Maynard Bell, and her son Herbert, 12d. at St Giles' fair paid by Hugh le Noreys, who lives in front of Hugh de Bunteford's house[26] [cf. xxiv].

In Lower Brook Street:

(12) from the gift of Reginalda, from her house which is next to the house Guy Pict' had on the east, 12d. paid by Henry Silvestr' [cf. xxi].

(13) for meadow which Margaret de Broc held, 2s. paid by Bartholomew Tannator [cf. xix].

(14) for land which Adam de Retheresfeld held, the gift of Guy de Vo, 12d. at fair time paid by the brothers of the hospital of St John [cf. xxix].

In Colebrook Street:

(15) from land which Elias Pogt' held and is now held by his son, Ralph Presbyter, 4d. on Hock Day [cf. iii].

(16) from land Wilbe's wife held, 6d. on Hock Day [cf. v].

Outside Kingsgate in *Sewinestwychene*:

(17) for an orchard near St Michael's church, the gift of Simon, son of Richerius, 4s. at fair time [paid] by Goselin le Miere; and this belongs to the sacristan of Southwick [cf. xxviii].

(18) At Winchester at St Giles' fair, 1 mark, the gift of Ronaldine, [paid] by Amicia, widow of William Petit.[27]

(19) At the same fair, for 1 seld which extends from the top of one street to the top of another in the grey cloth market (*in foro grisangor'*), the gift of William, son of Henry, a rent of [   ].[28]

1 Possibly Buck Street (*Bucchestret*) now partly represented by Bucket Lane (*W S II* Fig. 81, p. 733). In 1148 Robert de Sancto Pancratio had an interest in a tenement there which was in the possession of the nuns of Godstow (*W S I* 705, p. 119). He might be the Robert Spilem of the cartulary. Pope Alexander III (1159–81) confirmed Southwick Priory in the possession of a house situated next to (*iuxta*) the East Gate of the city, given to it by Robert de Sancto Pancratio (I 24).

2 These four properties probably lay on the south side of Colebrook Street, east of a stream which ran through the grounds of St Mary's Abbey and under the Abbess' Bridge (*W S II* 544–6, Figs. 94, 95, pp. 844, 830–1). See also I 181 b (15) and (16). In 1242–44 the priory acquired an adjoining site by gift from Agnes, Abbess of St Mary's (III 552).

3 The priory had granted its land in Little Minster Street, formerly held by Matilda, daughter of Reymund, and the house which Ralph Hlachewei was holding, to M. Hugh de Cardonvilla c. 1165 (III 543). In 1148 tenements had been held in Little Minster Street by William, son of Raymond, Matilda, and by Lachewei (*W S I* 800–2, p. 125).

4 This appears to be the same land and rent as I 181 b (1). See also *W S II* 205 and Fig. 68, pp. 610, 598. A Gilbert Oin witnessed two charters between 1155 and 1159 when Turstin (*alias* Turstin Clericus) was sheriff of Hampshire (I 20; III 534). When Peter Westman, grandson of Elias Westman, was holding the tenement c. 1251, the rent was in arrears, and c. 1262 he acknowledged that an annual rent of 3s. was due to the priory (III 604, 567).

5 Richard of Ilchester, Bishop of Winchester, dedicated the priory's church in 1181–2 (I 25 and copies 124, 125). Extensive lands in Trafalgar Street pertained to the bishopric (*W S II* 672–3, 675, and Fig. 100, pp. 910–11, 860).

6 Possibly to be identified with the shop, in front of the gable of St Peter's in the Shambles, which Turstin Clericus, the sheriff, bought from Martin de Bintewerda and granted to Blithilda *c.* 1155–9. Roger Rufus and Gilbert Oin (vii above) witnessed Turstin's notification of the transaction. (III 534; *W S II* 60 and Figs. 56, 52, pp. 494–5, 464).

7 This land and the small piece in Parchment Street (I 181 (xiii)) were probably given to the priory *c.* 1148–54 by Turstin Clericus, who was sheriff of Hampshire from 1155 to 1159 (III 565; *W S II* 313 and Fig. 76, pp. 687, 676). See also I 181 b, (6) and (7).

8 These lands were probably those given to the priory by William, son of Roger, *c.* 1150–62, probably before 1154 (III 569 and notes). They are represented by two separate entries in the later rental (I 181 b (4) and (5)). See also *W S II* 300–3 and Fig. 76, pp. 675–6.

9 In this instance "seld" may be synonymous with "shop", but the term could also be used to denote a much larger property such as the rows in St Giles' Fair with many windows (*fenestre*) or booths, each let to an individual trader (*W S II* p. 138). A row of this kind is almost certainly indicated in I 181 b (19).

10 See I 181 b (3). It is certain that by the second half of the 13th century until 1361, the Guildhall, the meeting place of the city court of Winchester, occupied the first floor of a house in the High Street on the west of the passage leading into Great Minster Street (*W S II* 186 and Fig. 62, pp. 593, 548).

11 This land was later shared by two tenants (I 181 b (8)).

12 See I 181 b (9).

13 Bartholomew Tannator was still holding the meadow when the later rental was compiled (I 181 b (13)).

14 See I 181 b (12).

15 Thomas Oysun flourished by 1172; sold wine 1176–7. He was probably the first mayor of Winchester *c.* 1200 (*W S II* p. 1312).

16 For Herbert's confirmation of his mother's gift, see III 547 and note. In that confirmation and in the later rental (I 181 b (11)), Alice's husband is called Maynard.

17 See note 15 above. If this is the same Thomas Oysun, presumably he was still alive in 1219.

18 This may have been the house from which 2s. rent was due to the Abbey of St Mary, Winchester. In *c.* 1248–51, the abbess quitclaimed to the priory 12d. of the rent because Lady Joan de Tistede had remitted that amount which she was used to receive from the abbey for the house (III 555).

19 *Bordellus* is the term used in 12th century records of Winchester to denote the simplest form of dwelling-house (*W S I* p. 338). Such small houses seem also to have been described as shops (*shopa, schoppa*), having both commercial and domestic use, and after *c.* 1350 as cottages (*cotagia*). See *W S II* p. 138.

20 The lane called *Sewinestwichene* ran approximately on the line of St Michael's Road/St Michael's Passage. St Michael's church lay on the north side of it, near the entrance to Kingsgate Street (*W S II* p. 1430 and Fig. 127).

21 According to the later rental the orchard belonged to the sacristan of Southwick Priory, and the 4s. rent was paid by Goselin le Miere, probably identical with Gocelin Sumet (I 181 b (17)). In *c.* 1300–18 John Howlond and his wife, Isabel, quitclaimed to the priory any right they had in this or a neighbouring croft (III 877). See also *W S II* 851 and Fig. 127, pp. 1003, 1000.

22 This land was in Lower Brook/Tanner Street (I 181 b (14)). Guy de Vo's son, Gesekin, witnessed two charters which Adam, son of Adam de Rutherfeld', gave to the priory *c.* 1200 (III 545, 566).

23 See I 181 b (2).

24 What follows is in effect a separate rental, but it includes only a total of 19 tenements, of which three (10, 18, 19) are not comparable with any of those in the previous rental. It was evidently compiled within a lifetime of the previous one, since undoubtedly three (3, 7, 13) and probably a fourth (2) of the tenements were still held by the same persons. Where a comparable entry exists in I 180 a, its number is given at the end of the relevant entry below.

25 This was probably the land granted by the priory *c.* early 13th century to Theolus Textor for 4s. annual rent (III 879). See also *W S II* 89 and Fig. 56, pp. 509, 495. The church of St Ruald or Rumbildus, which was possibly a pre-Conquest foundation, continued as a parish church until 1528 when it was united with the church of St Mary Kalendar, and the building on the west side of Upper Brook Street on the corner with St George's Street fell into ruins (*ibid.*, Fig. 76, p. 676).

26 Hugh de Bunteford may have occupied a house on the north side of St George's Street, *alias* Felter Street (*W S II* 370 and Fig. 76, pp. 717, 676). On the opposite side of the street was a complex property which stretched as far as the High Street (*ibid.*, 91, and Fig. 56, pp. 515, 495). It seems possible that part of this property may have been occupied by Hugh le Noreys, but he is not mentioned in the account of it, nor do Maynard Bell, Alice or Herbert occur in *W S I or W S II*.

27 Amicia, widow of William Petit, had a seld on St Giles' Hill in Hereford Street which she granted to Southwick Priory *c.* 1260 (III 551). It is possible that she already paid the mark's rent, given to the priory by Ronaldina, for that seld, or it may have been for another one she held in the area of the fair. See also *W S II* 1084, p. 1096.

28 The amount of the rent is left blank in the MS. The seld was one of those granted in 1200 by Bishop Godfrey de Lucy to William, son of Henry (III 550). William gave it and other property to the priory after the bishop's death in 1204 (III 568). As it is not included in the 1219 rental, the gift may have been made after that date, or it may have been omitted in error. Grey Cloths' Street ran parallel to Fullers' Street, and the tenement lay at the east end stretching from the one to the other. See also note 9 above, and *W S II* 1083, p. 1096.

I 182 [*c.* 1220–30][1]

[fo. 38ᵛ] RENTAL of Southwick Priory's men at Clanfield (*Clenefeld*), [Oxon.]

The following tenants owe 20d. at each of four terms, viz. at Michaelmas [29 September], St Thomas the Apostle's Day [21 December], [the feast of] Mary in March (*Maria in Marcio*) [25 March], and St John the Baptist's Day [24 June]:

Richard Baldewin, Ralph Rex, Anzelm Muskat, Widow Pauia, Widow Cecilia, John and William for 1 holding, Walter Barun.

Total: 46s. 8d.

CUSTUMAL of the aforesaid men of Clanfield:

Richard Baldewin holds 18 acres 1 rood of arable in the fields of Clanfield, 3 acres 1 rood of meadow, and 1 part of *inmedwes*. He owes an aid (*auxilium*) to the prior each Christmas. He is required to give a present to his lord on ?entry to his [tenement] (*debet present facere domino suo in adventu suo*). He cannot give his daughter in marriage, nor sell the ox he has reared (*bos suus nutritus*) or his male horse [which is] more than 2 years old (*pallus suus masculus ultra duos annos*), without licence from his lord. His land owes *leyrwite*. A widow holding it cannot marry without her lord's licence, but while she lives as a widow she can hold it in peace for the aforesaid services. When any man or widow dies, the lord will have his or her best animal (*primum melius capud*).

The following tenants hold the same amount of land, meadow, and *inmedwes*, for the same service as Richard Baldewin:

Ralph Rex, Anzelm Muskat, Widow Pauia, Widow Cecilia, John and William, Walter Barun.

None of them can make a will except in the presence of the lord's bailiff or reeve, if he can be found in the vill; if not, the will is to be made in the sight and hearing of the prior's men from the same holding.

Ketton (*de Ketene*),[2] [Rutland].

Sir Guy Wac and his heirs are bound to pay to the prior, or to his messenger (*nuntius suus*) [bearing] his letters patent, ½ mark each year on Sunday in the middle of Lent, at Stamford (*Stanford*), [Lincs.], in the parish [   ][2] in the place called [   ].[3]

Hollowell (*Holewell'*),[2] [Northants].

The prior's men at Hollowell hold 3¼ virgates: Henry and M., his wife, hold 2 virgates; Widow [   ][4] 1 virgate; and [   ][4] a ¼ virgate. They are bound to pay to the prior, or to his representative, 2 marks at this place (*ad hoc destinato*), around the middle of Lent. The priory also has a quarter of the mill of Hollowell, for which it receives 4s. a year at the aforesaid time.[5] From a certain messuage south of the vill (*ex australi parte ville*) the prior receives 12d. a year. All the aforesaid tenants, except the tenant of the messuage, are serfs (*servi sunt*), and were accustomed to do the same labour services as other serfs with similar holdings in the same vill. But because they are far from all the prior's demesnes, he increased their rent to the aforesaid 2 marks in lieu of works, on the advice of the donor.

It is known that they are not allowed to give their daughters in marriage, nor to send their sons to another's fee, without the lord's licence.[6]

Total 38s. 4d.

From the lands of:—	Thomas de Giuldelande	3s.	0d.
	Jocelin Pin[7]	4s.	0d.
	Reginald le Taylur[7]		18d.
	Robert de Brodeweya[7]	3s.	0d.
From land formerly held by	Stephen		18d.
From the land of:	William Pyn[7]	3s.	4d.
	Randolph[8]	3s.	6d.
	[　　] Blike[9]		12d.
	[　　]10 adjoining Totel		12d.

Total 21s. 10d.

From Meonstoke (*Monestoke*), 2s. at the Nativity of St. Mary
[8 September][11]

[fo.39] At ?Winchester (W...estre)[12]		14s.	9½.
At Stubbington (*Stubinton*)		5s.	0d.
At ?Farlington (*F'lingt'*)[12]			12d.
At Portsea (*Portesey*): from Richard Buc for a messuage,[13]			10d.
from the land of Badde de Crofton',		4s.	0d.
At Drayton		13s.	0d.

From the land of: Elias de Cossam,[14]	4s.	4s.	
Fuhelere of Colemore,[15]	2s.	2s., and it was Adam de Retheresfeld's gift.

From Reginald Gupil's land at *Flaxlande* at Michaelmas	5s.	0d.[16]
Kilmeston (*Culmeston'*): from the land of William de Bewurche,	2s.	0d.[17]
At Rowner (*Rumenore*): from the land of William Thaun,[18]		26d.
From Gilbert de Basevile's gift for a pittance for the soul of [　　],19 his wife,[20]	5s.	0d.

From Lady Olive de Kateringet's gift[21] for a pittance for her soul.　26d. and 1 quarter of wheat and 1 lb. of pepper.

At Aldbourne (*Aldeburne*), [Wilts], from the gift of the Count and Countess.[22]

From the priory's land which Peter Lothewic holds 30d.	30d. and he holds freely by charter.
From the land of Christine, who was the daughter of the priest,	30d.	30d. and she holds by a certain deed that testifies she is a serf and her land owes service of old.
From the land W. Presbyter holds	30d.	30d. and he will hold freely for his lifetime for that service.
From land [　　]23 holds	30d.	30d. and this [　　]23 is

a serf and, if his lord wills, he is bound to do all the same labour services as his neighbours on the Count's land, according to the amount of land he holds. None of them owes suit at the Count's court by reason of land they hold from the prior. After the death of W. Presbyter his land and messuage, in entirety, will revert to the prior unconditionally.

1 Alice de Chesneto gave 3 virgates, a meadow called Inmede, and 25 acres from her demesne to the priory in the time of Priors Luke (*c.* 1219–27) and Walkelin (1227–35) (III 289, 290; and see III 286–8). She confirmed the gift at the request of Prior Matthew in 1245 (III 291). One of her charters can be dated 1225–9 (III 294), and the list of tenants it contains, whose lands and persons were to belong to the priory, includes two, possibly four, of the names given below. It seems likely that this rental was compiled not long after the priory acquired the lands (see III 290 note 1).

2 In left-hand margin.

3 The arrangement by which Sir Guy Wac or Wake was to hold all the land at Ketton which had been given to the priory by Sir William de Hommet, as well as land at Cottesmore, given by Robert de Novo Burgo, was made by Guy, who occurs as Prior of Southwick between 1185 and 1210 (I 127). The rent was fixed at ½ mark, to be paid at Stamford in the parish of St John, but the following place name was left blank as here in the rental.

4 Left blank in MS.

5 The 3¼ virgates, and ¼ of a mill, with the men and their households, were given to the priory by Guy de Diva, *c.* 1193–1200 (I 132). The list of tenants given in Guy's charter in no way agrees with the rather vague list in this rental and suggests that some time had elapsed since the original gift was made.

6 A similar arrangement had been made by Turstin the sheriff in respect of the men of Colemore and [Priors] Dean, who should have travelled to Barton [Stacey] to do their labour services (I 164). In that case confusion seems to have arisen over the status of the tenants, and it is noteworthy that here it is expressly stated that they are still serfs. The only mention of manumission which occurs in the cartularies concerns tenants of Hollowell (III 242, 243; II 62, 63).

7 It seems probable that Jocelin Pin, Reginald le Taylur, Robert de Brodewaya and William Pyn held land at Anmore (see I 193, fo. 48ᵛ).

8 In the earlier Southwick rental a certain Randolph paid this amount of rent for his land (I 180, fo. 37ᵛ).

9 The name is left blank, but see John le Blic (I 180, fo. 37), or Walter Blik' (I 193, fo. 43).

10 Blank in MS.

11 Between 1189 and 1204 Henry de Bosleye granted 2s. to the priory to be paid annually from his manor of Meonstoke (III 441).

12 Very faint and indistinct in MS.

13 See the pittance from Richard Bukke recorded in the Portsmouth rental (I 194, fo. 49).

14 See III 447.

15 See I 195, and note 8.

16 See I 180, fo. 36ᵛ, and note 12.

17 The 2s. was granted to the priory by William de Gemeges (Gymynges) early in the 13th century, and was to be paid by William, son of Gilbert de Beoworde (III 354, 355, 358, 402).

18 The land was granted to William Taun (Thaun) by Luke, who was Prior of Southwick by 1219 and died in 1227 (III 346 and notes).

19 Space left blank in MS.

20 Gilbert de Basevile granted 8s. rent to the priory from a tenement in Portsmouth, for the care of the poor. This grant, made c. 1230, was for the souls of his father and mother, and of his wife Cecilia, and for his own salvation (III 713). There may have been an earlier grant specifically to provide for the pittance.

21 The donor was the daughter of Robert de Praeres, and the widow of Sir Roger Tyrel. Her gift was made early in the 13th century (III 331-3).

22 Count Geoffrey de Perche and his wife, Countess Matilda, gave 2 virgates in Aldbourne to the priory in the reign of Richard I (I 144). The tenants were then Richard Anglicus and Robert Heiward.

23 Space left blank in MS.

I 183¹   3 November 1312

[fo. 39] FINAL CONCORD between John Prany of Winchester, plaintiff, and Clement Burgeys, deforciant, concerning 1 messuage, 80 acres of land, 10½ acres of meadow, a mill, and 18d. worth of rent, with appurtenances in Hipley (*Huppelegh*) adjoining Southwick. Clement acknowledged that the aforesaid tenements and appurtenances were John's by right, and he restored them to him in the court, except for 4 acres of land, 10½ acres of meadow and 6d. worth of rent; he also granted for himself and his heirs that (i) the aforesaid 4 acres with appurtenances, which Philip de Saneresham and his wife, Juliana, held for their joint lives,³ (ii) the 6d. worth of rent and the ½ acre of meadow with appurtenances which they held for Juliana's life-time, and (iii) the 10 acres of meadow with appurtenances which Mary, widow of Philip de Hyvuyle, and William de Hyuyle held by life tenure, from the inheritance of Clement in the said vill, on the day this concord was made,³-[all of] which had been due to revert to Clement and his heirs after the deaths of Philip and Juliana, Mary and William—should revert wholly to John and his heirs, to be held, with the aforesaid tenements which are restored to him by this fine, of the chief lords of that fee, for the services pertaining to them in perpetuity.⁴ Warranty by Clement and his heirs in perpetuity. Consideration from John to Clement, £20.

Southampton, the morrow of All Souls, 6 Edward II, father of the present [king] (*anno sexto regis E secundi patris qui nunc est*). Enrolled etc. 20-27 January, on the day assigned to them at the chief court (*Dies datus est eis de capitale curia in octabe Sancti Hillarii*). John was represented by William de Preslond', and Clement by John Fikeys.

1 This item has no connection with the rentals, but has been interpolated in a later hand.

2 Probably the croft called Coltesok', leased to Philip and his wife in 1310 (III 1010). Saneresham is probably a scribal error for Haveresham.

3 La Brodemede in Hipley was leased to Sir Philip de Hoyville, his wife, Mary, and their son, William, for their lives, on 31 October 1309 (III 788). Sir Philip had died by December 1310 (III 787, 786, 790).

4 Because John Prany was a bastard and died without an heir of his body, these lands escheated to the priory (III 678; I 187-9).

I 184

[fo. 39ᵛ] PENSIONS of the churches:[1]

From the hospital of Portsmouth (*Portesm'*):[2]	5s. 0d.	5s. 0d.	5s. 0d.	5s. 0d.
From the tithe of the mill of the same hospital:	6d.	6d.	6d.	6d.
From the vicarage of Portsea (*Porteseya*):[3]	7s. 6d.	7s. 6d.	7s. 6d.	7s. 6d.
From the vicarage of Portchester (*Porcestr'*):[4]	12s. 0d.		12s. 0d.	
From the vicarage of Wymering (*Wimering'*):[4]	15d.	15d.	15d.	15d.
From the vicarage of Widley (*Wideleya*):[5]	12s. 0d.		12s. 0d.	
From the vicarage of Walesworth (*Waleswurthe*):[6]	4s. 0d.		4s. 0d.	
From the vicarage of Shalden (*Scaldeden'*):[7]	10s. 0d.		10s. 0d.	
From the vicarage of Empshott (*Ymbesec'*):[8]	5s. 0d.			
From the church of Swindon (*Swindon'*):[9]	50s. 0d.		50s. 0d.	
From the church of Farlington (*Farlingeton'*):[10]	10s. 0d.		10s. 0d., and that pension belongs to the infirmarer.	

1 The rubric *ecclesiarum pensiones* is in the left-hand margin and is bracketed to cover items 3–10. Pensions and tithes were often the cause of disputes between the priory and the incumbents of churches which had been granted to the priory (see I 204; III 15, 18, 223). See also the list of pensions in II 230.

2 The hospital at Portsmouth for the relief of the poor, known as God's House (*Domus Dei*), was founded by Peter des Roches, Bishop of Winchester, 1205–38. It was granted a charter of confirmation by King John on 2 November, 1214 (*VCH Hants* II, pp. 206–7).

3. The church of Portsea was given to the priory by Baldwin de Portesia, and the gift was confirmed by King Henry II, probably in 1164 or 1166 (I 6–9).

4 The churches of Portchester and Wymering were among the earliest possessions of the priory, apparently held by it during the episcopate of William Giffard, Bishop of Winchester, who died *c.* January 1129 (I 3, 4). See also I 1, 85.

5 Matthew de Scuris gave the church of Widley to the priory (I 16), and Bishop Henry of Blois added his confirmation before 1163 (I 4). See also I 86.

6 The chapel of Walesworth was also among the churches confirmed to the priory by Henry of Blois before 1163, and included in Pope Alexander III's privilege (I 4, 86). See also I 115.

7 Although the church of Shalden had probably been given to the priory by its founder, William de Pont de l'Arche, before his death *c.* 1148, its possession of that church did not go undisputed, as the Mauduit family had a prior claim (I 3, 4, 18 and note, 111, 31).

8 The church of Empshott was given to the priory by Ralph, son of Gilbert, his wife Constance, and their son Ralph, before 1181, possibly before 1170 (I 113, 24).

9 The church of Swindon was another of the gifts to the priory from its founder (I 11, 12, 18–23, 86). The annual pension of 100s. was granted to the priory in 1199 by Herbert Poore, Bishop of Salisbury (I 154). It was confirmed in 1286 by Bishop Walter Scammel, at the special request of Queen Eleanor (I 107).

10 Roger, son of William de Merlay, gave the church of Farlington to the priory, *c.* 1215 (III 220). Peter des Roches, Bishop of Winchester 1205–38, confirmed his gift of the advowson of the church and granted the priory 20s. pension a year for its infirmary (III 226, 222). This pension was confirmed by Bishop William de Ralegh in 1245. It appears that the priory lost control of the advowson, because in 1346, when Edward III granted to the priory the manor of Crookhorn and Farlington, he included the advowson of the church of Farlington; both manor and advowson having been forfeited to the crown by Hugh le Despenser (I 212).

I 185

CUSTUMAL of the men of Barton (*Bertuna*);[1] what they do for their lands and what they receive.

A virgator, viz. one who holds 40 acres, will pay 7s. 6d. annual rent at four terms, and whoever holds more will pay more according to the aforesaid rate. Whoever has his own plough is required to plough 3 acres at his own expense, and 1 acre at the lord's expense. Whoever has a horse is required to harrow 2 acres, viz. 1 in winter and 1 in spring. He will hoe 1 acre, and reap and bind $\frac{1}{2}$ acre, and he will have 1 sheaf. Also he will cut and make $\frac{1}{2}$ acre of hay. He will do 3 harvest boonworks, and the lord will provide food (*ad pastum domini*); at supper each man will have a loaf and 2 herrings or the equivalent.

He is required to carry the lord's corn to the barn throughout harvest, if he has a horse, and he will receive for his wages 6 sheaves, viz. 2 of wheat, 2 of oats, and 2 of barley. Any man who does not have a horse will stack the corn and ?throw it up [on the rick] (*? pericient sursum*)[2]. Each man on the day he makes hay will carry a reasonable weight from the lord's meadow, and when the hay is made they will all likewise carry it to the lord's barn, and at the completion of haymaking each man will have a reasonable bundle of hay. The lord will hold 2 scot ales for the whole year; a man and his wife will come for 2 days bringing 2d. each day, but if his whole family comes he will bring $\frac{1}{2}$d. on the first day. On a third day the man and his wife will come bringing 1d. (*Vir etiam et uxor eius per duos dies veniet scilicet in utraque die cum duabus denariis tota si quidem familia sua in prima die cum obolo tercia die vir et mulier cum denario*). All will make malt (*brasium*) for this ale. Any one of them who brews ale or cider will pay the lord or his bailiff by custom for the right to retail it (*ad hoc atturniatis denariat' pro consuetudine solvet*), or he will be at the lord's mercy. He will have 4 oxen quit of pasture dues in the lord's pasture, and for each additional one that he has, over a year old, he will pay 6d. at 2 terms, viz. at Martinmas and on Palm Sunday. He is required to pay pannage dues for his pigs at Martinmas, viz. for a year old pig, 1d., and for others, if 6 months old or weaned, $\frac{1}{2}$d. He will give 4 hens a year for churchscot (*churryseth*) if he is a married man, but a widow will give 2 hens (*cum sint uxorati cum* *autem vidue duas gallinas*). When he pays a tithe to the lord, the lord of the church will get a second tithe. If however he does not have a tithe for his lord, he will pay 1d. for [each] 4 lambs. Whoever sells a calf before or after it is weaned, or before it is mature (*vel ante etatem bovis*), will pay 1d. He can sell an ox or horse bred from his own stock (*cum sint sibi probenti de vaccis et de equis propriis*). He cannot give his daughter [in marriage] without the lord's consent (*Item filiam suam dare non poterit nisi ad voluntatem domini*). A half-virgater or a cottar (*cottarius*) will put his sheep in the lord's fold each night from Hock Day (*Okeday*) until Martinmas, and then he will have 1 sheep by custom. All cottars dip and shear the sheep, wethers and lambs. Each man will wattle 5 hurdles for the fold, and carry them from place to place, and will carry the lord's wood on two occasions (*per duos terminos*). If the king levies tallage, the house of Southwick will do the same (*si faciat dominus rex tallagium sicut et ipse faciat domus de Suwic'*). No one can make a will except in the presence of the lord's bailiff, and the best possession will go to the lord (*et quod melius fuerit domino erit*).

Rent . . . £14. 11s. 4d.   Rents of Winchester, Portsmouth
                             (Portesm'), Southwick, ?Alresford
                             (Al . . . ford) aforesaid.

External (*forinsec'*) rents   £4. 6s. 11½d.

Grand total £56. 3s. 8½d.

Rents *resolute* and total remaining: £38. 6s. 8½d.
(*?Solutis redditibus et summa remanens*)[3]

1 Possibly this is Barton Stacey (see I 178, note 21).

2 Indistinct in MS.

3 These figures etc. are given at the bottom of the folio, and are very small and faint.

I 186   Between 10 and 17 May 1332

[fo. 40] [PROCEEDINGS for RECOVERY of property in] Portsmouth (*Portusmuth'*)

The prior of Southwick presented himself by his attorney, Thomas Stak', on the 4th day, against Joan, widow of William Gomes,[1] and her son, John, on a plea for one messuage with appurtenances in Portsmouth (*Portesmuth'*); and against William, son of Hugh, on a plea for one messuage with appurtenances in the same vill; and against William de Burhunt'[2] and his wife Alice, on a plea for 2 messuages with appurtenances in the same vill as the right of his church of St Mary, Southwick, by the king's writ *cessaverunt per biennium* etc. And the defendants did not come; they have defaulted before, namely on the quindene of Holy

Trinity. After essoin, etc. So the sheriff was then ordered to take the aforesaid messuages into the king's hands. And he set a day, etc. And he summoned them to appear on the morrow of St Martin's day next, etc. Until which day the sheriff sends word that he ordered the bailiffs of the liberty of Portsmouth to take no action, etc. So that the sheriff was then ordered to proceed by writ of *non omittas*, etc. to take the said messuages into the king's hands. And he set a day, etc. And he summoned them to appear here on this day, viz. 3 weeks after Easter, etc. And the sheriff testifies to the day of confiscation, and that he summoned them, etc. So it was decided that the prior should from this time recover his seisin from them by default, etc. And the aforesaid Joan, and the other defendants are in mercy. But because fraud was suspected in contravention of the Statute of Mortmain, the sheriff was ordered to make 12 [knights and others] come here 15 days from Holy Trinity, etc. by whom [the truth can best be known], etc. and who have no affinity with the aforesaid prior, etc. to declare [on their oath], etc. what right the prior has in the aforesaid messuages, and which of his predecessors had seisin there, etc. as by right of his priory, etc. And [the sheriff] shall inform the chief lords of that fee, both mediate and immediate, that they shall be there to hear the proceedings of that jury, etc. Meanwhile there shall be a stay of execution, etc. On that day the suit was held over until this day, viz. the morrow of Martinmas, unless John Juge should come earlier to Winchester, viz. on the Saturday after the feast of St Margaret the Virgin. On which day John was present and held an inquisition at the aforesaid place, the outcome of which he sent here in these words:—In the presence of J. Juge with John de Scures, knight, at Winchester on Saturday after the feast of St Margaret the Virgin, the prior of Southwick came by his attorney, and the sheriff sends word that the prior is mediate chief lord, and there is no other lord, mediate or immediate, of that fee. The jurors came, and say on oath that one messuage with appurtenances in Portsmouth which was held by Joan, widow of William Gomes, and her son, John, is held of the said prior for the service of 10s. annual rent; and that one messuage in the same vill which was held by William, son of Hugh, is held of the same prior for the service of 13s 4d. annual rent; and that 2 messuages with appurtenances in the same vill which were held by William de Burhunt and his wife, Alice, are held of the same prior for the service of 5s. annual rent. And they say that the prior[3] was seized of the aforesaid services, and likewise William de Winton, formerly prior, and all his predecessors from time immemorial, as of the right of Southwick Priory, from the tenants of the aforesaid tenements, and that there is no collusion between the aforesaid parties. Therefore let execution be made, etc.

Three weeks after Easter (*de tribus septimanis Pasche*) 6 Edward III.

In roll 221 (*Rotulo ccxxj*).

---

1 The name William Gomes appears among the witnesses to 18 Portsmouth charters between *c.* 1270 and 1324. In 1315 he is cited as a neighbour with a house in Portsmouth (III 920).

2 A William de Burhunt was bailiff of Portsmouth in 1319 (III 341). A charter dated 1324 concerned a tenement next to that held by William de Burhunt in Portsmouth High Street (III 711).

3 Nicholas de Cheriton was Prior of Southwick from 1316 to 1334. His immediate predecessor, William de Winton, held office for one year only, from 1315 to 1316. Copy II 23; Win. Coll. Cart., fo. 6–6ᵛ.

I 187   24 November 1318

[fo. 40ᵛ] WRIT of *certiorari* from King Edward [II] to M. Richard de Clare, escheator beyond the Trent, for an inquisition to be held concerning Hipley (*Huppele*).[1] The Prior of Southwick has shown that he entered as his escheat, according to the law and custom of the realm, the 4 acres and ½ carucate of land and 10 acres of meadow in Hipley, held of him, as of the right of his church, by John Prany, a bastard, who had died without an heir.[2] Yet M. Richard, alleging that the prior had acquired the aforesaid land and meadow after the publication of the Statute of Mortmain and contrary to its terms, has taken the holding into the king's hands and still holds it; therefore the prior has appealed to the King for redress. M. Richard is to establish the facts by inquisition and report without delay under his seal and the seals of the jurors. Witness: the King, 12th year of his reign.

York (*Eborac'*)

1 *Cal. Inq. misc.* II, 373, p. 92.

2 In November 1312, by a Final Concod, Clement Burgeys surrendered to John Prany a messuage, land and mill at Hipley, together with the reversion of other property there, to be held by him and his heirs of the chief lords of the fee (I 183). The chief lords of part at least of the property were the prior and canons of Southwick. John had died by 19 July 1313, when an inquisition was held which established that he was a bastard without an heir of his body, and that his lands had been taken by the priory as their escheat (III 678). In August 1317 the priory obtained a quitclaim from John's kinsman, Thomas Everarde, relating to the property John had acquired from Clement Burgeys in Hipley (III 676), and in September of the same year similar quitclaims were obtained both from John's mother, Eva, to whom he had given his property in Hipley, and from his brother, another John Prany (III 794, 798, 896). However the priory's right to the property evidently remained in doubt as the above writ shows, but it was confirmed by the subsequent inquisition and royal writ (I 188, 189).

I 188   21 December 1318

Inquisition held in the presence of Roger de Brieteston', subescheator.

INQUISITION before the king's escheator at Winchester, on Thursday, the feast of St Thomas the Apostle in the 12th year of the reign of King Edward, son of King Edward, into whether the prior of Southwick had entry to 4 acres and ½ carucate of land, and 10 acres of meadow, with appurtenances, in Hipley (*Huppele*), as his escheat, or in fraudulent contravention of the Statute of Mortmain.[1] Jurors: Richard Dammory, Adam de Henton', Roger de Chalghton', Peter atte Grevette, William atte Bergh', John Beaumont, Roger atte Lighe, John Horsy, Geoffrey de Brokhampton', William Aleyn, Richard Thomas and Matthew atte Hale.

They say that a certain John Prany held the aforesaid lands and meadow from the Prior of Southwick for annual service of 13s. 4d., and suit at the prior's court at West Boarhunt (*Westbourhunte*) every three weeks (*de tribus septimanis in tres septimanas*). He was a bastard and died without an heir of his body, so that after his death the prior entered the aforesaid lands and meadow as his escheat as immediate chief lord (*tanquam capitali domino immediato incumbentem ingressus est*).

Concerning the charge as to whether there was fraudulent collusion between the prior and the aforesaid John Prany during his lifetime, or, after his death, between the prior and John's rightful heirs, they say that they have certain knowledge of the manner of John Prany's birth and how he held the aforesaid land and meadow, and that no fraud or collusion was attempted in any way, but that he held the lands and meadow in the mannor aforesaid, and died a bastard without a legitimate heir of his body seised of them in his demesne as in fee (*ut de feodo*); and that the prior entered the same lands and meadow as his escheat and not in any other way. In witness whereof the jurors have appended their seals.

1 See I 187 and note 2.
Copy II 17. Variants: Dammori; Gravette; Borgh'; Beaumond; Ligh'; Horsye; Brochamton'; Alayn.

I 189   10 February 1319

WRIT from King Edward [II] to M. Richard de Clare, his escheator beyond the Trent. Since, at the prosecution of the Prior of Southwick, the escheator's inquisition,[1] returned in Chancery, found that the said John [Prany] held the aforesaid land and meadow of the prior for the service of 13s. 4d. a year, and suit of the prior's court at West Boarhunt (*Westbourhunt'*) every three weeks, and that John was a bastard and died without an heir of his body, and that, after his death, the prior entered [the land] as his escheat, without fraud or collusion in reference to the Statute [of Mortmain], and not otherwise, the escheator is to release the aforesaid land and meadow, if they have been taken into the king's hands for this reason and no other, and still remain in his hands. He is no longer to concern himself with them, saving the rights of the king and anyone else, and he should restore the profits taken in the meantime to those to whom they belong. Witness: the King, 12th year of his reign.

York (*Ebor'*)

1 See I 187 and note 2; 188.

I 190 1322–4

[fo. 41] PROCEEDINGS for RECOVERY of a tenement. The prior of Southwick, by his attorney, Geoffrey le Fauconer, made presentment of a stake (*presentatus est unum stachium*) on the place formerly held by Hugh Blak' in Tanners' Street (*Tannerestret*), Winchester,[1] on account of 20s. arrears rent for one year. Because the alderman testified that nothing was found for distraint, a stake was placed there on Wednesday before the feast of St George, 15 Edward, son of King Edward [21 April, 1322].

The prior of St Swithun's, by his attorney, made presentment of the same stake for 6s. arrears, viz. 3s. a year for two years. And they made presentment for 8 days three times and for 40 days the fourth time, after which it was said to be sequestrated for a year and a day, according to the custom of the city, on which day the priors sought judgement.

It was publicly proclaimed three times, and because no one came to pay the arrears it was decided that the aforesaid priors and their successors should recover possession of the place in perpetuity. And thereupon the prior of St Swithun's, by his attorneys Robert de Thorncombe and Robert de Cantuar', remitted to the prior of Southwick all right of action he had on that place, and for that remission the prior of Southwick acknowledged that he was bound to pay the prior of St Swithun's and his successors, for the whole of the aforesaid place, 2s. annual rent in equal portions at the four principal terms. [This was agreed] when Philip Aubyn was mayor,[2] and the tenement was recovered in the 16th year [of Edward II's reign] (*Tempore Philippi Aubyn nunc maioris Et predictum tenementum recuperatum fuit anno xvj*).

1 This was the place which Hugh Blak', *alias* Hugh atte Quabbe, acquired from William Tinctor, who gave the rent from it to the priory in 1289–90 (III 519, 523, 526; *W S II* 413, p. 747 and Figs. 81, 86). See also I 191.

2 Philip Aubyn was mayor of Winchester, in 1312–13 and 1324–25 (*WS II* p. 1150).

Copy II 20. Variants: le Francon'; Tanneristret; Thorncounbe.

I 191 1320–1

[fo. 41ᵛ] PROCEEDINGS FOR RECOVERY of a tenement. The prior of Southwick, by his attorney, Geoffrey le Fauconer, made presentment of a bolt (*presentatus est unam seruram super tenementum*) on the tenement of Nicholas de Exon' in Middle Brook Street (*Wongarestret*), Winchester, on account of arrears of 5 marks, 4s. 10d., owing for the past 5½ years, viz. 13s. a year.[1] And because nothing was found for distraint, a stake (*stachia*) was put in there by William Gailefer, the alderman of that street, and the serjeant, on Wednesday after the feast of St Luke the Evangelist, 14 Edward son of King Edward [22 October, 1320]. And presentment was made three times for 8 days, and a fourth time for 40 days, and so on for a year and a day, according to the custom, etc. And William, rector of the church of St Pancras, Winchester (*Vynton*), and the parish, took similar proceedings for arrears of 8s. 3d. owing for 5½ years, viz. 18d. a year. And presentment was made, etc. It was publicly proclaimed three times [to see] if anyone wished to acquit the aforesaid bolt (*acquietare seruram predictam*). Because no one came to pay the arrears, it was decided that the aforesaid prior and William, the rector, with the parish, and their successors, should recover the aforesaid tenement, in perpetuity.

1 This is probably the rent which had formerly been paid by Hugh atte Quabbe, *alias* Hugh Blak' (III 526, 519; *W S II* 413, p. 747, and Figs. 81, 86). Copy II 21. Variants: le Francon'; William Taillefer; Wynton'.

I 192   1343–4

PROCEEDINGS FOR RECOVERY of a burgage tenement in the city court of Winchester, on Wednesday after the feast of St Denis, 17 Edward III [15 October, 1343]. The prior of Southwick, by his attorney, Robert Giffard, made presentment of a stake on a tenement in Middle Brook Street (*Wonegarestret*) with a certain adjacent place, of which William de Exetr' is seised, on account of 18 marks' arrears of rent owing for 9 years, viz. 2 marks a year.[1] It is situated between the tenements of John de Wight, chaplain, on the north, and Thomas de Chiddene on the south, and extends as far as Tanners' Street (*Tannarestret*). Because the alderman, serjeants and neighbours testified that nothing was found there for distraint, the court decided to put in a stake, and this was done on the day aforesaid. And the procedure was followed for 8 days, and again for 8 days, and for 40 days, and thus for a year and a day (*sequatur per octo dies et iterum per octo dies et sic per quadraginta dies et sic per annum et diem*). And Alexander, Prior of St Swithun's, came, by his attorney, Brother Robert de Sancto Omero, and prosecuted the same stake on the aforesaid tenement and place for arrears of 30s. rent owing over 10 years, viz. 3s. a year.

At Winchester court held on Friday after the feast of St. Andrew the Apostle, 18 Edward III [3 December, 1344], proclamation was made according to the custom of the city, and no one came to acquit the aforesaid stake. Therefore the court decided that the priors and their successors should recover the tenement and place from the aforesaid William, his heirs and assigns, in perpetuity. William de Farnefeld, mayor;[2] William Cuppyng' and John Speg, bailiffs.

1 William de Excestre had acquired the tenement from Thomas Chudden' and his wife, Edith, in 1340 (III 529; *W S II* 413, p. 747, and Figs. 81, 86). See also I 190, 191.

In 1346 the prior of Southwick successfully contested an attempt by the parish of St Pancras to obtain arrears of rent from this tenement, on the grounds that they had not put in their claim when the stake was prosecuted and before judgement was given in favour of himself and the prior of St Swithun's. (I 207). See also III 878.

2 William de Farnefeld, *alias* le Ismongere, was mayor, 1344–5 (*WS II* p. 1272). Copy II 22. Variants: Thomas de Chidden'; William de Exetre. Copy II 27. Variants: Gyffard; William de Cycestr'; Thomas de Cheddene; Tannestret; after "again for 8 days", add "and a third time for 8 days"; by his fellow monk (*commonachum*) and attorney; Sancto Homer'; John Speeg.

I 193   ?1248[1]

[fo. 42] RENTAL and CUSTUMAL of the vill of Southwick, Portchester (*Porcestr'*), Stubbington (*Stobynt'*), Anmore (*Andem'*), Crofton (*Crofton'*), and Drayton (*Drayton'*), with the men, their lands, rents and services in the time of Prior ?Matthew, the 14th year of his priorate.

Roger de la Hulle,* juror (*juratus*), holds 1 *quadranta* of land, viz. 8 acres, and pays 6s. 8d. annual rent. He also holds a piece of purpresture (*placita de purprestura*) and pays 6d. annual rent for all service.   7s. 2d.

Hugh de la Hulle* holds ½ quadranta with 2 small groves which contain 1 acre, pays 15d. annual rent, and is obliged to find 1 man to reap at harvest for 4 days, and to give 3 hens and 1 cock for churchscot (*cheriset*). He will make 3 hurdles and carry another 3 to the sheepfold. He will not give his daughter in marriage without the lord's licence. He will dip and shear sheep, give pannage dues, and make hay.   15d.

William Longus holds 7 acres and pays 16d annual rent. He will find 1 man to reap at harvest for 4 days, and will have food (*habebit conredum*). He will give 3 hens and 1 cock for churchscot, and also pannage dues. He will dip and shear sheep, and make hay and gather it into haycocks (*levabit fenum et faciet muylum*). He owes merchet.   16d.

Richard Durevold* holds 1 *quadranta* and pays 16d. annual rent. He will do the same service as the aforesaid William Longus.   16d.

John Heyrun* holds 1 *quadranta* and pays 2s. annual rent. He will do the aforesaid service, except that he will not carry hay. He also holds 7 acres for 8s. 8d. a year on St Augustine's Day [28 August]. He owes merchet.   10s. 8d.

Wyburg holds 1 *quadranta* and pays 4s. annual rent. He will give pannage, and owes merchet.   4s. 0d.

[fo. 42ᵛ] Robert de Bikeford'* holds ½ virgate and pays 6s. annual rent. He will find 2 men to reap at harvest for 4 days, and 1 man for 1 day at boonwork, and at Christmas he will find 1 man to cut wood (*scindet in bosco*) for 2 days, and will have food (*habebit pastum*). He will give 3 hens and 1 cock for churchscot, and pannage dues. At harvest he will cart corn for 2 days, and hay for 2 days; and for 4 days in Lent he will harrow, and have 1 loaf for a day's harrowing. He will dip and shear sheep, and owes merchet.   6s. 0d.

Geoffrey de la Newelonde holds 1 *quadranta* and pays 16d. annual rent. He will find 1 man to reap for 4 days at harvest. He will dip and shear sheep, give pannage dues, and give 3 hens and 1 cock for churchscot. He will make hay, and owes merchet.   16d.

Stephen de la Feude holds ½ virgate and pays 4s. annual rent. He will reap 4 acres at harvest, and have food, and he will carry for 4 days. He

will give money at haymaking, and make and carry hay while it is being
brought in (*donec introductum fuerit*). He will harrow 4 acres in Lent.
He will carry manure for 9 days and wood for 2 days at Christmas, and,
like the priory's carter (*sicut caretarius domus*) will have food. He will
carry 4 hurdles to the sheepfold, wash and shear sheep, and shear lambs.
He will pay pannage dues, and owes merchet.   4s. 0d.

William de Ponte* holds 1 *quadranta* and pays 15d. annual rent. He
will find 2 men to reap at harvest for 4 days (*metet in autumpno iiij dies
per duos homines*), and as often as instructed he will reap ½ acre, and
have 1 sheaf. At harvest he will either carry [sheaves] every day or reap,
as instructed. He will carry manure at Christmas for 9 days, and have 1
loaf daily. He will give 3 hens and 1 cock for churchscot, and dip and
[fo. 43] shear sheep, and shear lambs. He will pay pannage dues, and
owes merchet. He will wattle (*waldabit*) 3 hurdles for 1 week's service,
and carry 3 hurdles to the fold for all the service of that week. He will
harrow 3 days a week in Lent.   15d.

Richard de Ponte†2 holds 1 *quadranta* and pays 15d. annual rent and
the same service.   15d.

Richard de la Friþe* holds land [called] Sheepwash (*de la Sipwasse*),
which Matthew de Scures gave to Southwick,3 and he pays 3s. annual
rent for all services.   3s. 0d.

Richard de Ho holds 2 acres4 and pays 2s. annual rent for all service.
                                                                 2s. 0d.

Marcha holds land which her father, John Fresel, formerly held, and
pays 6s. 8d. annual rent for all service.5   6s. 8d.

Robert de Pont' holds 3 acres and pays 4s. annual rent. He will find 1
man to reap at harvest for 4 days. He will give pannage dues, and 3
hens and 1 cock for churchscot, and he owes merchet.   4s. 0d.

John de Lengestoke* holds 15 acres and pays 4s. annual rent for all
service.   4s. 0d.

Hugh de Lengestoke holds 12 acres and pays 3s. annual rent for all
service.   3s. 0d.

Walter Blik'† holds a certain house and curtillage at *Pottewelle* and
pays 12d. annual rent for all service.   12d.

William Brun6 holds 6 acres and pays 2s. 4d. annual rent. He will find
1 man to reap at harvest for 4 days, and will give 3 hens and 1 cock for
churchscot.   2s. 4d.

Emma, widow of le Wyse,† holds 2 acres and pays 16d. annual rent,
[fo. 43ᵛ] and she will find 1 man to reap at 4 boonworks at harvest. She
will give 3 hens and 1 cock for churchscot, and owes merchet. She also
holds 1 acre for 12d. annual rent payable at Michaelmas.   2s. 4d.

Robert Ranulfus* holds 4 acres and pays 2s. annual rent. He will find
1 man to reap at 4 boonworks at harvest. He also holds 5 acres of
salterns (*v acre terre saltarne*), for which he pays annually 15 sesters,
each sester containing 5 bushels. He will give 3 hens and 1 cock for
churchscot, and owes merchet. He will find 1 man to reap for 4 days at
harvest for these 5 acres.   2s. 0d.

                                                         15 sesters of salt

Emma, widow of Richard Hay,† holds 2 acres and pays 16d. a year at
4 terms. She will find 1 man to reap for 2 days at harvest. She will give

1 hen for churchscot; if she were married she would give 1 hen and 1 cock. She owes merchet.   16d.

Sigar* holds 2½ acres and will pay annually 15 sesters of salt, each containing 5 bushels.[7] He will give 3 hens and 1 cock for churchscot. He will find 1 man to reap for 4 days at harvest. He also holds 5 acres of salterns (*v acre terre saltarie*), for which he will give 8 sesters of salt, each containing 5 bushels. He will find 1 man to reap for 2 days at harvest for these [salterns], and will give 1 cock and 1 hen for churchscot. He also holds 6½ acres for which he pays 32d. annually at Michaelmas. He owes merchet.   32d.
                                                                23 sesters of salt.

Muriel, widow of Eustace,* holds 4 acres and pays 2s. annual rent at Michaelmas. She will reap for 2 days at harvest, and will give a cock and 1 hen for churchscot.   2s. 0d.

Walter le Bike[†] holds 3½ acres of salterns and pays annually 10 sesters of salt. He will find 1 man to reap for 4 days at harvest. He gives 3 hens and 1 cock for churchscot, and owes merchet.   10 sesters of salt.

Alice, daughter of Richard Portir, holds 3 acres and pays 2s. annual [fo. 44] rent at Michaelmas. She will find 1 man to reap for 2 days at harvest. She owes merchet.   2s. 0d.

Robert, son of Walter,[†8] holds 1 acre for which he pays 3s. annually at Michaelmas. He will find 1 man to reap at 2 boonworks at harvest.
                                                                      3s. 0d.

John Pistor[†] holds 3 acres for which he pays 3s. 4d. annually at Michaelmas. He will find 1 man to reap for 4 days at harvest. He will give 3 hens and 1 cock for churchscot, and owes merchet.   3s. 4d.

Yvo holds 1 acre for which he pays 16d. annually. He will find 1 man to reap for 2 days at harvest. He will give 1 hen and 1 cock for churchscot, and owes merchet.   16d.

William Nigellus[†] holds 2 acres for which he pays 2s. annually at Michaelmas. He will find 1 man to reap for 2 days at harvest. He owes merchet.   2s. 0d.

Agnes, widow of Crede,* pays 12d. annual rent at Michaelmas. She will find 1 man to reap at harvest for 1 day, and owes merchet.   12d.

Matilda, widow of Kiggel,[†] pays 8d. annual rent at Michaelmas. She will find 1 man to reap at harvest for 1 day, and owes merchet.   8d.

Total 26s. 0d.[9]

Richard Barre,[10] for a certain holding with curtillage, pays 5s. annually, for all service.   5s. 0d.

Christine, widow of Roger Faber,[†] holds a messuage and pays 12d. annually, for all service.   12d.

She also holds a place for which she pays 6d.   6d.

Richard Lormarius* holds a messuage for 12d. a year. He also holds a place for which he pays 1 lb. of cummin annually, for all service. 12d.
                                                                 1 lb. cummin

[fo. 44ᵛ] Adam Swele* holds a messuage for which he pays 1s. annually. He also holds a [   ][11] which he bought from Yvo, and pays 1s. annually. He also holds a place at Mulecrofte for which he pays 1s. annually, and 1 acre for which he pays 4d.,[12] for all service. 3s. 3d.[12]

William Digun holds a messuage for which he pays 32d. annually, for all service.   32d.

Margery, widow of Simon Fode, holds a place for which she pays 4s. annually, for all service.   4s. 0d.

Robert Walens'* holds a place for which he pays 12d. annually, for all service.   12d.

Richard Snelgar*[13] holds a place for which he pays 2s. annually, for all service.   2s. 0d.

M. Richard Cementarius* holds a place for which he pays 2s. annually, for all service.   2s. 0d.

The land formerly held by Ralph Frater* lies vacant; he used to pay 12d.   12d.

William le Beke* holds a place for which he pays 2s. annually, for all service.   2s. 0d.

William le Hore* holds a place for which he pays 12d. annually. He will find 1 man to reap for 4 days at harvest, and will give 3 hens and a cock for churchscot, and pannage dues. He will give ½d. when the hay is mown (*ad falcandum fenum*) and will make hay. He will dip and shear sheep, and owes merchet.   12d.

Luke le Wyse* holds a messuage for which he pays 12d. annually, and [fo. 45] he will do the same service as the aforesaid William le Hore.
                                                                                                                12d.

Roger Gupil[15] holds a messuage for which he pays 1 lb. of cummin annually, for all service.   1 lb. cummin

Philip Crideho* holds a place for which he pays 18d. annually, for all service.   18d.

Seburg* holds a place for which he pays 16d. annually, for all service.
                                                                                                                16d.

A messuage was formerly held by John Swift,* who paid 12d. annually and did the same service as W. le Hore.   12d.

Robert Gelus* holds a messuage for which he pays 12d. annually, and he will do the same service as W. le Hore.   12d.

Walkelin and Richard Cooperari hold a place for which they pay 12d., and they will do the same service as W. le Hore.   12d.

Robert Carpentar' holds a messuage and pays 12d. a year. He will do the same service as W. le Hore.   12d.

Alice Caretar'—the same.[16]   12d.

Roger le Clekere—the same.   12d.

Alice, widow of Caretar'—the same.   12d.

Osbert le Syur†—the same.   12d.

Robert le Burgens'*[17]—the same.   12d.

Geoffrey le Kete—the same.   12d.

[fo. 45ᵛ] Peter de la Bera* pays 6d. a year for Osbert Strech's messuage, for all service.[18]   6d.

Richard Hoymoy and Alice hold a place for 4s. a year, and these two will do 1 service, the same as William le Hore.   4s. 0d.

Richard le þrel holds a messuage for which he pays 2s., and he will do the same service as W. le Hore.   2s. 0d.

Felic' de la Hurne† holds a place for which she pays 12d. She will find 1 man to reap for 2 days at harvest. She will give 1 hen and 1 cock for churchscot, and pannage dues. She will dip and shear sheep, and make hay. She owes merchet.   12d.

Matilda, daughter of Petevin, holds a place for 12d. for all service.
                                                                             12d.

Geoffrey Sonke*[19] holds a place for 12d. and the same service as William le Hore.   12d.

Agnes, widow of le Duyt, holds a place for 12d. and the same service.
                                                                             12d.

Adam Hersi holds 2 acres with a messuage for 20d. and the same service.   20d.

William Kukhorn* holds a messuage for 12d. and the same service.
                                                                             12d.

Hugelina, widow of Sprot, holds a messuage for 2d. [*sic*] and the same service.   12d.

Adam Hersi holds a place for 12d. and the same service.   12d.

Walter Bolleford*[20] holds a messuage for 12d. and the same service.
                                                                             12d.

[fo. 46] Lucy, widow of Horsi,—the same.[16]   12d.
William Caretarius*—the same.   12d.
William Curcellarius*—the same.   12d.
Robert Sonke—the same.   12d.
William Faremus—the same.   12d.
Walkelin Faremus [holds] 1 perch for 12d. annually for all service.
                                                                             12d.

Item: ?the same[21] [holds] a place for 6s. 8d. a year. He will find 1 man to reap for 4 days at harvest. He will give churchscot. He will give ½d. at mowing.   6s. 8d.

Stephen le Scoldare and Philip hold a place for 6s. a year and the same service as William le Hore.   6s. 0d.

Arnold Porcar' holds a place for 12d. and the same service.   12d.
Robert Molendinar' holds a place for 12d. and the same service. 12d.
Henry Morin* holds a messuage for 16d. for all service.   16d.

Reginald [and] John, son[?s] (*fil'*) of Hudelin', hold a place for which they pay 12d., and they will do the same service.   12d.

[fo. 46ᵛ] Seburg* holds a messuage for 12d. and the same service. 12d.

William Suwyk'†[22] holds a messuage, 5 acres and 1 croft, and will pay 2s. [*sic*] for all service.   1 lb pepper and 3s. 0d.

William le Vilur holds 3 acres and 1 mesuage. He pays [4s.] annually at Michaelmas for all service.   4s. 0d.

Richard le Hore* holds a messuage for 12d. and the same service as W. le Hore.   12d.

Alice, widow of Petevin,† holds a messuage for 12d. for all service.
                                                                             12d.

Thomas Dun holds a messuage for 5s.   5s. 0d.
Olimpias holds a messuage for 12d. for all service.   12d.
David* holds a messuage for 18d. for all service.   18d.
Muriel holds a messuage for 12d. for all service.   12d.
Wymund Sagiere—the same.[16]   12d.
Richard Petit*—the same.   12d.
William Dun*[23]—the same.   12d.

Richard Swele*—the same.	12d.
The widow of Wlwyn†—the same.	12d.
[fo. 47] Matilda, widow of Tessun,†24—the same.	12d.
Luke le Brun*—the same.	12d.
Ralph Tapenarius25—the same.	12d.
Johanna, daughter of William Prute,26—the same.	12d.
Walter Molendinar'27—the same.	12d.
Roger le Hoppar'—the same.	12d.
John le Cupare—the same.	12d.
Margery, daughter of Olimpias,—the same.	12d.
Walter Molendinar'—the same.	12d.
Peter þrul—the same.	12d.
Ralph le Buyng—the same.	12d.
Richard Dun holds a messuage for 5s. for all service.	5s. 0d.
Thomas Lardeneir* holds a messuage for 12d. for all service.	12d.
Osbert Harding*—the same.16	12d.
[fo. 47ᵛ] Johanna, widow of Purs,†—the same.	12d.
The widow of Thomas Cuparius†—the same.	12d.
Joan, widow of Philip Cementarius,—the same.	12d.

John Cotus holds†28 a messuage and pays 1 lb. of pepper for all service.

1 lb. of pepper.

Higun holds a messuage for 12d. for all service.	12d.
Anicia de Peteresfeld—the same.	12d.

William Svift holds 2 places in Cobayn croft for 4s. for all service.

4s. 0d.

John Astil holds a messuage for 2s. for all service.	2s. 0d.
Henry Finel—the same.	2s. 0d.
William Papilim—the same.	2s. 0d.
Richard Crabbe—the same.	2s. 0d.

Hugh de la Hulle* holds a messuage for 2s. 6d. for all service.

2s. 6d.

The same Hugh holds another place for 2s. 6d. for the same (*pro simili*). 2s. 6d.

Richard Worde holds a messuage for 2s. 6d. for the same. 2s. 6d.

[fo. 48] William Bercarius* holds 2 messuages for 5s. for all service.

5s. 0d.

Edith, widow of Hoppare, holds a place (*platita*) for 2s. 6d. for the same. 2s. 6d.

William Chipman holds a place (*platita*) for 2s. 6d. for the same.

2s. 6d.

Adam le Hoppere holds land, which was formerly Richard Koterel's,29 for 8d. for all service. 8d.

Lawrence Serviens pays 12d. from Richard Koterel's gift.29 12d.

The widow of Elias de Culerne† holds a small piece (*pars*) of meadow for 6d. 6d.

William Bercar'* holds 1 acre with a messuage for 12d., and he will do the same service as William le Hore. 12d.

Total receipts £10. 5s.30

Stubbington (*Stubinton'*).

Henry de Kingestone holds 2 acres for which he pays 2s.[31] He will find 1 man to reap at harvest for 8 days. He gives 2 hens for churchscot, and pannage dues, and owes merchet. 2s. 0d.

Warin, son of John, holds 1½ acres for 2s. and the same service as Henry. 2s. 0d.

William Metehol holds [   ].[32] 3s. 8d.

William Norens' holds 3½ acres for 4s. at Michaelmas for all service.
4s. 0d.

Henry Gupil holds land at Flexland' for 5s.[33] He also holds a place for 12d. for all service. 5s. 12d.

[fo. 48ᵛ] Hwyton de Bera holds a messuage with curtillage and pays 2s. 2s. 0d.

Robert le Burgeis holds a place at *Coltesstok'* and pays 2s. for all service.[34] 2s. 0d.

Total 22s. 8d.

Anmore (*Anedemere*).

Jocelin holds 2½ acres for which he pays 4s. [*sic*] for all services.[35]
3s. 0d.

Reginald Capelain holds 1 acre with a messuage for 18d. He also holds a croft called *la Hildelond* at farm for 16 years, for which he pays 16s. annually for all service. 17s. 6d.

John le Taylur holds 1 acre with a messuage for 18d. for all service.[35]
18d.

Robert de Brodeweye holds 2 acres with a messuage for 3s. for all service.[35] 3s. 0d.

William Pin holds 2 acres with a messuage for 3s. 4d. for all service.[35]
3s. 4d.

Total 29s. 4d.

Crofton

Cecilia, widow of Wlward', holds ½ virgate for which she pays 4s. for all service.[36] 4s. 0d.

Drayton

The tenants of Drayton pay 13s. 4d.[37] [13s. 4d.]

Rowner

John de Fortun' pays 4s. for land which was from Taun's tenement at Rowner (*que fuit Taun de tenemento de Drugenor'*).[38] 4s. 0d.

1 The top of this folio is damaged and part of the heading is indistinct. The name of the prior ([ ]*thi*) cannot be read with certainty, but Matthew seems possible, and is in accord with other dating evidence (see notes 18, 22). Matthew was prior from 1235 to 1266.

Names (often differently spelt), which also occur in the earlier Southwick and Portchester rentals (I 180 and 175) have been indicated (*), as have those of possible widows or heirs of earlier tenants (†).

The obligation to obtain the lord's permission for the marriage of a daughter occurs in the case of most tenants (*Non maritabit* (or *non potest maritare*) *filiam suam licentia domini*). After the first occasion this has been rendered as "He/She owes merchet".

2 See Geoffrey de Ponte (I 180, fo. 37, note 24).

3 See Richer de la Frihe (I 180, fo. 37). Sheepwash Farm is 2 miles east of Southwick. For Matthew de Scures' charter, see I 16.

4 One of Richard's acres lay in Blakefurlong in Southwick field (II 142, 168).

5 See Walter Fresel (I 180, fo. 37, note 25).

6 This may be the William Brun to whom Thomas de Borhunt gave ½ acre at Portchester (II 170).

The next 13 entries refer to Portchester tenants, and 11 of them can be traced in the earlier rental (I 175).

7 Sigar (*Syger*) appears to have taken over the salterns previously held by Hurberyn (I 175), in addition to his own holding for which he still owed 8 sesters of salt. The total salt rent (48 sesters) is the same in both rentals.

8 Walter Lot (I 175).

9 This is the total rent owed by the preceding 14 Portchester tenants.

The following entries again concern Southwick, and comparison should be made with I 180.

10 This may be the Richard Barry of III 779.

11 Word omitted in Ms.

12 *Sic* in MS.

13 Richard had died by 1275 (see I 180, note 8).

14 See Ralph le Frere (I 180, fo. 36ᵛ).

15 Henry, son of Reginald Gopyl, gave a messuage in Southwick, next to Luke le Wyse's messuage, to Adam le Copere and his wife. The messuage had been given to Reginald Gopyl by the priory, to which the new tenants were to pay 1 lb of cummin and 1d. a year (III 347).

16 In each case a messuage is held for 12d. a year and the same service as the immediately preceding tenant.

17 This may be the Robert le Burgeys who acquired various tenements in and around Hipley (III 677, 679, 682-4, 792, 797, 899). He also appears below on fo. 48ᵛ; see note 34.

18 Peter de la Bera quitclaimed to the priory, *c.* 1250, a messuage and curtillage, half of which had been held by Osbert Streche (III 359).

19 See Geoffrey Hsanke (I 180, fo. 37).

20 See Bolresford (I 180, fo. 37).

21 "*Ide*" followed by a space in MS.

22 William Suwyk' was the son of Peter de Havehunte (I 180, fo. 37, note 14). In 1255-56 William quitclaimed to the priory any right he had to a house in Southwick situated between the house of William le Vilur and that of Seburg (III 505, and see III 504, 496).

23 See William Bun (I 180, fo. 36ᵛ).

24 See Richard Chesun (I 180, fo. 36ᵛ).

25 Ralph was succeeded by his son, John de Suthewyk', *alias* Tapenarius. John gave the house in Southwick, which was next to Luke Brun's, to the priory in return for a new loom and 5s. (III 494).

26 See III 1005, 1004, 1002.

27 See III 182, 999.

28 John may have succeeded Richard Coke (I 180, fo. 36ᵛ).

29 Richard Coterel gave 12d. rent to the priory *c.* 1230 to provide a pittance of wine on his anniversary. The rent, from 6 acres, was to be paid by his nephew, Lawrence Hubold (III 352, 356, 401).

30 It appears that this is meant to be the total of all rents so far, excluding those for the 14 Portchester tenements which amount to 26s.

31 See III 633 and note.

32 Space left blank in MS. In the 1270s a William Metehol' had land in fields near Stubbington (III 748, 768, 802, 808, 820). In 1280 William and his fellow tenants held land from the demesne at Stubbington for 19s. 4d. rent (Stubbington Account Roll, 1280-1).

33 In the earlier Southwick rental, Henry's father, Reginald Gupil, paid 5s. for Flaxland (I 180, fo. 36ᵛ; and I 182, fo. 39). See also note 15 above.

34 This tenement appears to have been included in the earlier Southwick rental (I 180, fo. 37). See also note 17 above.

35 See rents given for the lands of Jocelin Pin, Reginald le Taylur, Robert le Brodewaya, and William Pyn (I 182, fo. 38ᵛ).

36 In the late 12th century, Lady Helewise, widow of John Talebot, gave to the priory ½ virgate called *Ailbricteshille* from her manor of Crofton (I 54-6). It was held by Wlward, possibly the father of Cecilia's husband.

37 See I 182, fo. 39.

38 Before 1227 Prior Luke gave ½ virgate called *Purselond,* in Rowner, to William Taun (III 346). Prior Matthew (1235-66) granted the land to William's daughter, Alice (III 343). See also I 182, fo. 39.

I 194 [*c.* 1248][1]

[fo. 49] RENTAL of Portsmouth (*Portesmota*)

John, son of Sacerdos,[2] at Michaelmas	46d.
Matilda de Murivelde, at Michaelmas	8d.
Joan, daughter of William Russellus, at Michaelmas	12d.
The widow of Peps, at Michaelmas	8d.
Diliota	16d.
John Pistor[3]	2s. 6d.
Baldwin Attewatere	18d.
Luke Cemetarius	10d.
John Kuluert	10d.
The widow of Simon Fode	6d.
The son of Cumbe	6d.
Richard Lainte	12d.
Randolph Peliparius	12d.
William Kok	12d.
Matilda, daughter of Kingestune	12d.
William Richerius	3s. 10d.
The heirs of Robert Stuherus	3s. 10d.
De la Flicte	9d.

Thomas Cruk	9d.
Philip, son of Reginalda	12d.
The widow of Thomas Piscator	12d.
Osanna, wife of William de Molend'[4]	14d.
John le Bekke, at the feast of St Thomas the Apostle	13s. 4d.
Walter Molendinar; at Michaelmas 12d. and at Easter 12d.	2s. 0d.
Robert le Barbur	10s. 0d.
Thomas	20d.
William Seindenis	20d.
Goda	20d.
Ralph Strode	22d.
Robert [?]Tussnnel	2s. 0d.
William Seindenis	12d.
Thomas Raggi[5]	4s. 0½
Richard Cooperator, attorney of Richard Cupar'[6]	12d.
Thomas Tral	12d.
Thomas de Nortintun'	12d.
Prior of the Domus Dei, at 4 terms[7]	24s. 0d.

For the Altar of the Blessed Mary:—

Stephen Clericus	3s. 0d.
Richard Sevogel	4s. 0d.
Walter Aynolf'	14d.
Matilda Petevin	12d.
Robert Scipwrthe	8d.
Joan, daughter of Russellus	12d.
Henry de Grangia	12d.
Hersus Rufus	16d.
Geoffrey Saltar'	18d.
Robert Spurie	12d.
Ydecosa, daughter of William Rusel	12d.
Simon, son of Eve	12d.
Robert Renewhe	12d.

For the infirmary:—

Simon Beandehors[8]	8d.
From 3 windwills	6s. 0d.

For pittances for the priory:—(*de pitantia conventus*)

From Ralph Clericus' will[9]	2s. 0d.
Richard Bukke[10]	10d.
From John Truk's house[11]	5s. 0d.
Widow Fraunces	12d.
Ralph Scipwrte	12d.
William de la Arewe	6d.
William Pam	6d.
From the house given to the priory by Alan le Tannor[12]	6s. 0d.
[fo. 49ᵛ] John de la Crofte[13]	6d.
Peter de Mechinge[13]	6d.
Ragenilda, widow of H... Burg'	12d.

John Kewe	11d.
Matilda, widow of Geoffrey	6d.
Stephen Grice	6d.
Lucy, daughter of Cuparius	8d.
Robert Strokehose	6d.
Roger Rufus	6d.
William Russel	1 lb. of cummin

Thomas Grey, for ½ acre from Hamund de Brokhurst's holding[14]

26d.

Christine, wife of Henry de Brokhurst, 16¼d. from Hamund's holding and 1 pair of gloves[15]   16¼.

The hospital of St Mary Magdalene (*de Magdalena*) for a curtillage inside the bar (*infra barram*)   1d.

Total: £6. 16s. 4¾d.

Total for the altar of St Mary, the
infirmary and pittance: 13s.

Grand Total: £7. 9s. 4¾d.

---

1 It seems likely that this rental was compiled about the same time as the preceding rentals, which can probably be dated 1248 (I 193, note 1). See notes 4, 5, 10, 11 below.

2 A John, son of the priest (*Sacerdos*), witnessed the quitclaim of a site in Portsmouth to Augustine, who was Abbot of Quarr from 1239 to 1249 (P.R.O. E 315/31/248; Hockey *Quarr Abbey* Appendix B, p. 259). Possibly John, son of Presbyter, was the same man; he witnessed in 1257 a record of Portsmouth rents due to Quarr Abbey (P.R.O. E 326/9366), and was bailiff of Portsmouth *c*. 1265-8 (III 626).

3 An exchange of land took place between John Pistor of Portsmouth and the priory *c*. 1250-70 (III 213). John was dead by *c*. 1270, when his son, Henry, sold ½ acre to the priory (III 704).

4 A William Molendinarius was reeve of Portsmouth in 1241 (III 611), and appeared as a witness in 1247 (P.R.O. E 210/154; E 315/34/182).

5 Thomas Raggi or Raggy appears in the Stubbington Account Rolls of 1247-52, and witnessed undated charters for Hugh Raggy between 1234 and 1266 (probably in *c*. 1240 and 1252) (III 696; P.R.O. E 326/2942).

6 Before 1238 Richard Cuparius of Portsmouth and his brother, Thomas, were granted land by Philip, Abbot of Quarr, for which they were to pay 15s. rent a year (P.R.O. E 326/890; E 315/40/228; Hockey, *op.cit.*, Appendix B, p. 259). Richard Cooperator or le Coveror appears in the Stubbington Account Rolls of 1249-69, and in 1272 he gave to Southwick Priory 6 acres in various fields near Portsmouth; he had acquired these acres over several years (III 733 and 734-46).

7 See I 184, note 2. The Stubbington Account Roll for 1252 records the payment of 24s. annual rent from the Domus Dei of Portsmouth.

8 William Richer of Portsmouth gave the priory, *c*. 1240, 8d. annual rent to be paid by Simon Bendehors. William de Molendinis (Molendarius) as reeve witnessed the charter (III 717).

9 A Ralph Clericus had died by 1247, in which year Quarr Abbey leased a house and burgage in Portsmouth to his widow, Mabel (P.R.O. E 210/154).

10 See Richard Buc (I 182, fo. 39).

11 Early in the 13th century Simon de Hampton, son of Odo, granted 4s. annual rent at Portsmouth to the priory. This rent was to be paid by John Truc and his heirs for the celebration in the priory of the anniversary of Simon's uncle, Peter Caballus (III 722).

12 Alan le Tannor was reeve of Portsmouth in 1247 (P.R.O. E 210/154). He appears in the cartularies from 1241 to c. 1270. He gave a shop (*selda*) in Portsmouth to the priory c. 1250; the rent from it was to provide a pittance on the obit day of himself and his wife, Joan (III 720, 721). Similarly he gave a shop in Portsmouth to Quarr Abbey; the witnesses to both charters are the same, but in the latter Alan's wife is called Mabel (P.R.O. E 315/44/262).

13 John's house adjoined that of Peter de Mechinge (next entry). Peter sold half a house to Henry Garite, who was to pay 6d. a year to the priory (III 825).

14 When c. 1240-7 Hamund de Brokhurst (Brochurste) gave and quitclaimed land and rents to the priory, they included 26d. to be paid by Thomas Grey and his heirs for a messuage and ½ acre (III 279–83). The Stubbington Account Rolls of 1249 and 1250 record Thomas' payment of 2s. 2d. By 1270 the payment was in default because the land was in the priory's demesne (Stubbington Account Roll, 1270).

15 According to Hamund de Brokhurst's charters cited above (III 279, 283), the heirs of Henry de Brochurste were to pay the priory 17¼d. for 11 acres. In 1250 Christine de Brochurste, Henry's widow, paid 16¼d. (Stubbington Account Roll, 1250). See also III 813 and note; 819 and note.

I 195　　　　　　　　　　　　　　　　　　　　　[c. 1240–50][1]

[fo. 50] RENTAL [and CUSTUMAL] of Priors Dean (*la Dene*) and Colemore (*Colemere*)

Adam de Bukesetle,[2] juror, says he pays 4s. for his 7 acres. He cannot give his daughter in marriage without the lord's licence.[3]　　　4s. 0d.

Henry de Bukesetle holds 10 acres and 4 of woodland, and pays 10s. a year. He owes merchet.　　　　　　　　　　　　　10s. 0d.

Isabella de Bluntesmere[†] holds 44 acres and 20 of woodland, and pays 8s. a year.[4] She will plough 2 acres in winter, if she has a plough, and 1 acre in Lent. She will pay pannage dues, if she has pigs, and give 3 hens and 1 cock for churchscot if she has a husband, if not, 2 hens. She owes merchet. And she is obliged to find 1 man to reap for 3 days at harvest.
　　　　　　　　　　　　　　　　　　　　　　　　　　　8s. 0d.

Walter Clericus* holds 3 acres and pays 12d. a year for all service, according to the charter (*per cartam*).　　　　　　　　12d.

Oselia de Spina holds 34 acres and 20 of woodland, and pays 4s. 10d. a year. She owes merchet.　　　　　　　　　　4s. 10d.

Thomas de Spina holds land called *Puppellebere*[5] and 1 curtillage, and pays 3s. a year. He owes merchet.　　　　　　　　　3s. 0d.

John de Gardino holds 32 acres and 20 of woodland, and pays 10s. 10d. a year.[6] He owes merchet.　　　　　　　　　10s. 10d.

Gilbert de Campo holds 16 acres and 4 of woodland, and pays 2s. a year. He owes merchet.　　　　　　　　　　　　2s. 0d.

Ralph de Campo holds 13 acres and pays 5s. a year. He owes merchet.
　　　　　　　　　　　　　　　　　　　　　　　　　　　5s. 0d.

Walter de Colemere* holds 40 acres and 12 of woodland, and pays 8s. 8d. a year.[7] He owes merchet. 8s. 8d.

[fo. 50ᵛ] William Maifolc* holds 40 acres and 12 of woodland, and pays 8s. 8d. a year.[7] He owes merchet. 8s. 8d.

Lady Cecilia de Kernet' pays 3s. a year for herbage dues.[8] 3s. 0d.

Robert de Fogelere pays 4s. a year for all service, according to the charter.[9] 4s. 0d.

Dean (*La Dene*)

Millisent de Gollye[†] pays 11s. 6d. a year for 52 acres, 11s. 6d. and 6s. for *Heringesdone*.[10] She owes merchet. 6s. 0d.

Peter de Gollye holds 26 acres for 5s. 9d. a year. He owes merchet.[11] 5s. 9d.

Lawrence de la Slad' holds 24 acres and 6 of woodland, and pays 6s. 3½d. a year.[12] He owes merchet. [*sic*] 6s. 3d.

John de Burwlle and the widow of Slade[†] hold 24 acres and 6 of woodland for 6s. 3½d. a year.[12] They owe merchet. 6s. 3½

Widow le Fiz[†] holds 9 acres for 3s. a year.[13] She will pay pannage dues if she has pigs, and 1 cock and 1 hen for churchscot if she has a husband, if not, 1 hen. She will dip and shear sheep; will carry 5 hurdles when the fold is moved, and have 1 loaf; and will collect withies (*virge*) for the cattle-shed and sheep-fold, and have food (*victus*). She owes merchet, and she is obliged to find 1 man to reap for 4 days each week at harvest, who will have food. 3s. 0d.

John Piris* holds 11 acres for 5s. a year, and he will do the same service as the aforesaid widow.[14] Moreover he is obliged to find 7 men to reap each week at harvest, who will have food. And he will give 1 cock and 3 hens for churchscot. 5s. 0d.

Richard Fransesius* holds 10 acres for 3s. a year. He owes merchet. 3s. 0d.

[fo. 51] Henry le King* holds 6 acres for 3s. a year, and he is obliged to find 1 man to reap for 3 days at harvest. He owes merchet. 3s. 0d. Also for *Allecumbe* [he pays] 2s.

Henry le Cove holds 14 acres for 4s. 9d. a year. He owes merchet. 4s. 9d.

Gilbert Champeneis* pays 2s. annual rent for *Alecumbe*.[16] He owes merchet. 2s. 0d.

Gervase de Den'* holds 7 acres for 2s. 10½d. a year. He owes merchet. And he pays 2s. for *Alecumbe*.[16] 4s.10½

Henry Carpentarius holds 20 acres for 8s. a year. He owes merchet.[17] 8s. 0d.

Nicholas Hurstan* holds 20 acres and 7 of woodland, and he pays 6s. 3d. a year.[16] He owes merchet. 6s. 3d.

Thomas Clericus[19] holds 7 acres for 2s. 10½d. a year, and he pays 2s. for *Allecumbe*; 4s. for *Piperlonde*; 2s. 5[d.] for a croft at *Churesburg'*. He is obliged to find 1 man to reap for 3 days each week at harvest for that croft, who will have food. He will give 1 cock and 1 hen for churchscot. He owes merchet. 11s. 3½

Richard de la Dih*[20] holds 20 acres and 4 acres of woodland, and he pays 6s. a year. He owes merchet. 6s. 0d.

The same Richard*[20] with his partners (*socii sui*), pays for Burnecumbe 6s. 8d.   6s. 8d.

Jocelin Faber holds 18 acres and 4 of woodland for 4s. 4d. a year. He owes merchet. He also holds 6 acres for which he makes the ironwork (*feramenta*) for 3 ploughs.   4s. 4d.

Robert de la Lan'[†] holds ?½ acre (*alva*) of land for 8d a year. And he is obliged to find 1 man to reap for 4 days at harvest. He will give 1 cock and 1 hen for churchscot. He owes merchet.   8d.

[fo. 51ᵛ] The widow of Richard de Dih[†21] pays 4s. a year for *Piperlonde*. She owes merchet.   4s. 0d.

Hawise de Godeshull'* pays 4s. 6d. a year for 18 acres and 4 of woodland. She owes merchet. She is obliged to find 1 man to reap for 3 days at harvest, who will have food. For churchscot, [she will give] 1 cock (*gall'*).   4s. 6d.

Richard Juven'[†] holds the same as Hawise for the same rent, service and dues.[22]   4s. 6d.

John Alfricus[†] holds 10 acres for 5s. a year. He will do the same service as John Piris.   5s. 0d.

William de la Lode*[23] pays 6s. 1d. a year for 24 acres and 7 of woodland. He will plough 2 acres in winter if he has a plough, and will have his oxen in the lord's pasture. In Lent he will plough 1 acre and harrow it. He will give 3 hens and 1 cock for churchscot. He owes merchet, and will give pannage dues if he has pigs.   6s. 1d.

Philip de Gollye* holds 18 acres and 5 of woodland for 6s. 8d. a year. He owes merchet.   6s. 8d.

Stephen Iuven'* holds 19 acres and 5 of woodland for 8s. a year. He owes merchet.   8s. 0d.

Walter de Doscumbe*[24] pays 3s. 6d. a year for 13 acres and 2 of woodland. He also pays 1s. at Michaelmas for *Hamme*; and 1d. for *Dulve*. He owes merchet.   [*sic*] 3s. 6d.

Petronilla de Doscumbe[†24] pays 3s. a year for 14 acres and 2 of woodland. She also pays 1s. at Michaelmas for *Hamme*; and 1d. for *Dulve*. She owes merchet.   [*sic*] 5s. 1d.

John de Ford'* holds 3 acres for 20d. a year. He is obliged to find 1 man to reap for 18 days at harvest, who will have food. For churchscot [he will give] 3 hens and 1 cock. He owes merchet. He will give pannage dues if he has pigs.   20d.

[fo. 52] Hugh de Ford* holds 1 acre for 12d. a year. He is obliged to find 1 man to reap for 12 days at harvest, who will have food. He owes merchet, and will give pannage dues if he has pigs.   12d.

Hugh Slade holds 7 acres for 2s. a year. And he is obliged to find 1 man to reap for 3 days each week at harvest, who will have food. He will carry 3 hurdles when the sheepfold is moved, and have food. He is obliged to collect withies (*virge*) for 1 day for the sheepfold, and another day for the cattleshed, and will have food. He will pay pannage dues if he has pigs, and 1 hen and 1 cock for churchscot. He is obliged to dip and shear the lord's sheep, and he and the other shearers will have a cheese [in return] for shearing.   2s. 0d.

Total £11. 18s. 2d.

1 This rental was drawn up not long after the earlier rental (I 178) as possibly 18 of the tenants (indicated*) were still holding the same tenements; in at least three instances widows had succeeded their late husbands, and in other instances probably sons or heirs had taken over the tenements (indicated †). By 1266 at the latest two tenements had been surrendered (see notes 4 and 6 below).

2 Beckseddle Farm is about ¼ mile south-west of Colemore. See also III 848, 851.

3 The provision concerning the marriage of a tenant's daughter is hereafter rendered as "He (or She) owes merchet".

4 Isabella was the widow of William de Bluntesmere and had succeeded to his tenement (I 178, fo. 35ᵛ and note 19). She appears to have remarried, and with her second husband, Hamund de Northampton, quitclaimed to the priory all the land they held at Bluntesmere (III 853). The quitclaim is undated, but was probably given at the same time as a similar quitclaim made by William de Bluntesmere's daughter, Alice, to Matthew, who was prior of Southwick from 1235 to 1266 (III 849).

5 Probably Rumpleberry Wood (O.S., 6″ map; Gover, p. 89).

6 John's son, John, gave to the priory all the land in Colemore which was formerly held by his father (III 844). Matilda, John senior's widow, quitclaimed to Prior Matthew, between 1235 and 1266, any right she might have to the land. In return the priory undertook to provide food for her in their almshouse, where she was to look after the inmates (III 835).

7 Walter de la Suthehuse (probably Walter de Colemere) and William Maifolc (see next entry) quitclaimed to the priory any right they had to land which includes 2 acres, one held by Petronilla de Doscumbe and the other by Walter de Doscumbe (see below). In return the priory reduced their rents from 8s. 8d. to 5s. (III 833, 834).

8 See I 178, note 20.

9 The character is probably that by which *c.* 1230 Adam de Redheresfelde or Rutheresfeld gave to the priory the tenement which Roger Fugheler held of him in Colemore. Roger and his heirs were to continue to hold it, and were to pay 4s. rent to the priory (III 836). See also III 837 and I 182, fo. 39.

10 See I 178, note 14.

11 In 1266 a Peter de Golle was one of those involved in a successful lawsuit against the priory to prevent it from exacting additional services from its tenants at Priors Dean (II 235). The list of plaintiffs also included four other names, or variants thereof, that occur in the above rental: Lawrence atte Slade, Henry le Carpent', Richard le Yonge [Juvenis], and William atte Lode.

12 See Alan and Gilbert de la Slade (I 178, fo. 35ᵛ, and note 13). Between 1273 and 1281 Lawrence de la Slade and his wife, Edith, quitclaimed to the priory all their tenement in Priors Dean (III 842).

13 Possibly this is the widow of Stephen Feliz (I 178, fo. 35).

14 See the entry concerning John, son of Peter (I 178, fo. 35). In 1278 Henry, son of John Peres, quitclaimed to the priory all the land he held of it in Priors Dean (III 843).

15 Omitted in MS.

16 See I 178, note 16.

17 See note 11 above.

18 See I 178, note 4.

19 Thomas appears to have succeeded to the tenements of Hugh Harang (I 178, notes 15, 16).

20 This is probably the Richard Juvenis de la Fosse who appears in the earlier rental (I 178, notes 5, 17).

21 This is probably the widow of Richard Vetus de la Fosse (I 178, notes 5, 15).

22 See note 11 above.

23 See I 178, note 7.

24 See note 7 above, and I 178, note 10.

I 196   31 March 1249[1]

[RENTAL and CUSTUMAL of] Moundsmere (*Moundesmere*) [in Preston Candover].[2]

Court of Candover (*Candefre*), Wednesday after the feast of the Annuciation of the Blessed Mary, 33 H[enry III]

Robert le Thuit[†], juror, says that he holds ½ [virgate] of land (*dimidia terre*). Annual rent at Michaelmas, 2s. 6d. He gives 3 bushels of wheat for churchscot at Martinmas. He gives pannage dues if he has pigs, viz. 1d. for a pig over a year old; ½d. for a half year old. He will plough and harrow ½ acre in winter, and have his draught animals (*avaritia sua*) in the lord's pasture from Martinmas until the feast of the Purification. And after Martinmas he will plough 1 acre, as it lies, at each ploughing (*et arabit de qualibet caruc' j acram sicut iacet*). He will do carrying service from Candover to Southwick (*apud* [sic] *Candeure apud Suwike*) twice a year, and have food: viz. he will carry 4 bushels of wheat or barley, and have food and fodder there, and 6 bushels of oats. Before the day of St Peter in Chains [1 August] they [sic] can sell pigs without a licence, but not after that day. They will harrow 1 acre in Lent, and are obliged to carry seed from the barn to the field which they are harrowing. They are obliged to dip and shear the lord's sheep; Robert (*ipse*) and the other shearers [will have] one cheese made that day. He [sic] will find 1 man to hoe for 2 days before noon without food, and he will carry a cartload of hay from *Somersulle* to Candover; if [he carries it] before Lammas Day (*ante ad Vincula*) he will not have food, if after, he will have food. He will carry for 2 days at harvest, and have food and 1 sheaf. He will find 2 men to reap for 6 days at harvest, and have food at noon, viz., barley bread and 2 helpings of something with it (*ij mod' conpanag' et panem ord'*). When he binds 1 acre, he will have a [fo. 52ᵛ] sheaf. He will find 1 man to collect nuts before dinner. He is obliged to carry 2 hurdles when the lord's sheepfold is moved. At one boonwork he will have wheaten bread, ale and meat.   2s. 6d.

Nicholas, son of Lucy, holds ½ virgate for 2s. 6d. a year. He will do the same service as the said Robert.   [sic] 2s. 0d.

Hugh de Axore[3] [pays] 2s. 6d. and the same service (*ad eundem servitium*).   2s. 6d.

Philip le Honte* holds 1 virgate. Annual rent, 5s. Churchscot, 6 bushels of wheat. He will plough and harrow 1 acre in winter, and do the same service as the others (*sicut alius*).   5s. 0d.

Walter Blundus holds ½ virgate for 2s. 6d. and the same service as the said Robert.   2s. 6d.

William le Bedel holds 2 acres with 1 messuage, paying 2s. a year for all service.   2s. 0d.

Robert le Cute*[4] pays 2s. a year for 2 acres with 1 messuage. Church-scot, 3 hens and 1 cock. He will find 2 men to reap for 6 days, and they will have breakfast (*iantaculum*) on 3 days, viz. 3 loaves. He will find 1 man to dip and shear sheep for 3 days. He will hoe for 1 day before dinner (*prandium*), and have nothing. He will collect nuts before dinner, and have nothing. He will carry hurdles like the said Robert.   2s. 0d.

Isabella le Cute*[4] holds a messuage. Annual rent, 12d. Churchscot, 1 cock and 1 hen. She will find 1 man to reap for 6 days, and do other services [like] Robert le Cute.   12d.

Stephen de Linche holds 1 acre. Annual rent, 9d. He will do the same service as Isabella.   9d.

Jordan Berc' holds 1 acre with a messuage. Annual rent, 9d. and the same service as Isabella.   9d.

Widow Alice holds a messuage. Annual rent, 6d. and the same service as Isabella.   6d.

Peter le Fader holds a messuage. Annual rent, 8d. and the same service.   8d.

[fo. 53] Moundsmere (*Moundesmere*)

Widow Matilda holds a messuage. Rent, 6d. and the same service. 6d.

Walter Caretar' holds 1 acre with messuage. Rent, 8d. and the same service.   8d.

John Purchas holds 4½ acres. Annual rent, 15d. for all service.   15d.

Richard Faber holds ½ virgate. Rent, 2s. 6d. and the same service as R. le Thuit.   2s. 6d.

John Faber[†] holds 11 acres. Rent, 3s. 6d. He is obliged to find 1 man to reap for 8 days at harvest, and will have food; and he will do nothing more.   3s. 6d.

Ralph Rufus holds ½ virgate. Rent, 2s. 6d. and the same service as R. le Thuit.   2s. 6d.

Henry le Bailif holds ½ virgate. Rent, 2s. 6d. and the same service as R. le Thuit   2s. 6d.

Thomas de Puteo* holds ½ virgate. Rent, 2s. 6d. and the same service.   2s. 6d.

William de Brante* holds ½ virgate. Rent, 2s. 8d. and the same service.   2s. 8d.

Richard Petit* holds ½ virgate. Rent, 2s. 6d. and the same service.
                                                                  2s. 6d.

William, son of Baselie*, holds ½ virgate for 2s. 6d. a year and the same service.   2s. 6d.

Walter Lucas*[5] holds ½ virgate. Rent, 10s. for all service, but his palfrey (*palefridus*) will harrow with the prior's palfrey, and he will have food and fodder. He will accompany with the lord wherever the lord wishes at the lord's expense, but on the first day at his own expense.
                                                                  10s. 0d.

Ellisfield (*Hulsefelde*)

William Albus holds ½ virgate.[6] Rent, 15s., viz. 7s. 6d. at Michaelmas and 7s. 6d. at Easter, for all service. 15s. 0d.

Sare de Helsefeld' holds ½ virgate.[6] Rent, 15s. at the same terms, for all service. 15s. 0d.

[fo. 53ᵛ] (*Somersulle*)

Thomas de Somersulle*[7] holds ½ virgate. Annual rent, 2s. 6d., and, for churchscot, 5 hens and 1 cock. He will look after the lord's barley-meadow (*custodiet pratum domini bere*) and mow the meadow and make hay. He is obliged to take 2 cartloads of hay to Candover (*Kandevere*), and will have 6d. or 2 bushels of barley. 2s. 6d.

John de Somersulle*[7] holds ½ virgate. Annual rent, 2s. 6d. and the same service as Thomas. 2s. 6d.

Alresford (*Alrisforde*)[8]

Alice, widow of Ralph, holds 1 messuage. Rent, 3s. for all service.
3s. 0d.

Stephen Rotarius[8] holds 1 messuage. Rent, 3s. for all service. 3s. 0d.

From increase (*de incremento*) 2s. 3d.

Total £5. 0s. 2d.

1 The date given for this rental must refer to the reign of Henry III. The priory did not acquire the rents at Alresford until after 1204 (III 568).

2 Moundsmere is a little over a mile north-east of Preston Candover.

3 Axford is 1 mile north of Preston Candover.

4 See I 179, note 6.

5 A tenant of the same name was paying the same rent when the earlier rental was compiled, but there the tenement is described as ½ hide, which seems correct in view of the amount of the rent (I 179).

6 See I 179, note 4.

7 See I 179, note 5; also I 18. According to *V C H Hants* IV, p. 114, Somershill was in Basingstoke hundred, probably near Bramshill and Stratfield Turgis. This would be about 15 miles north-east of Preston Candover.

8 Between 1204 and 1228 William, son of Henry, gave the rents of four houses in Alresford to the priory (III 568). One of these houses was then held by a Stephen Rotarius for 21d. rent.

I 197 [1281–91, probably 1289–91][1]

EXCHANGE by Richard de Burh' with Prior John and Southwick Priory. The priory will hold of Richard and his heirs in perpetuity all his land called *Fordham*, which lies south of the road which runs from Southwick to Wanstead (*Wanstede*), and is bounded by a ditch and hedge, from *la Norhtcrofte* as far as the field called *Schadewelle*, and the site of a mill called *Cuperesmulle* with a small adjoining meadow called *Mulemede* for the construction of a mill, with their appurtenances, viz. ways, paths, ponds, waters, moors, hedges, meadows, feeding (*pascua*), pastures, liberties and easements, in exchange for a mill called *la Niwemulne*, land called *Cokkesdelle*, and a croft called *Mulecrofte* which lies between Henry Brun's holding and land called *la Pudduke*. Witnesses: Sir Hugh de Rupibus, Sir Philip, son of Peter, Sir Baldwin de Bello Alneto, knights; Roger de Hoo; Roger de Moletone; John de la Grange; Roger de Wanstede; John le Burgeis; John de Colemere; and others.

1 John de Clere was Prior of Southwick from 1281 to 1291. In November 1289 Richard de Burhunt' obtained a licence from the king to alienate in mortmain to the priory the site for a mill and 50 acres in Southwick, in exchange for a mill and 15 acres in the same vill (III 983). Assuming that Richard obtained his licence before making the exchange, his brother, Herbert, must have quitclaimed his right to *Cuperesmulle* to the priory before the exchange took place (I 198).
Copy III 198. Variants: Borhunt; Northcrofte; Shadewulle; Cuperesmylle; Newemelle; Pudduk'.
Copy in H.R.O. 4M53/B7, p. 6. Variants: Burhunt'; Couperesmelle; la Nywemelne; [after the name of the 2nd witness add:] Roger Launceleveye; Molton'; [omit the names of the last 4 witnesses.]

I 198 16 June 1286

QUITCLAIM by Herbert de Burh' to Southwick Priory, of all right and claim he and his heirs have or could have in the site of a certain mill [fo. 54] called *Cuperesmulne*, with adjoining meadow called *la Mulemede* and all appurtenances, which formerly he held as a gift from his brother, Richard de Burh'.[1] Witnesses: Sir Hugh de Rupibus, Sir Roger Lancelevee, Sir Philip de Esteneye, Sir Baldwin de Bello Alneto, Sir Richard de Burh', knights; Roger de Hoo; John de Grangia; and many others.

Southwick; Sunday, the feast of the translation of St Richard, 14 Edward, son of King Henry.

1 See I 197 and note.
Copy III 187. Variants: rubric: Borhunt', Cuparesmulle; Burhunt'; Cuperesmulle; Mulmede; Launceleve; Estenye. Location and dating omitted.

I 199 [*c.* 1290][1]

LETTERS PATENT from John de Sancto Johanne[2] taking note of the exchange between Richard de Burh' and Southwick Priory of 50 acres of land and the site of a mill in Southwick, for a mill and 15 acres in the same vill. The priory is to hold the 50 acres and site from John and his heirs without opposition, as they formerly held the mill and 15 acres.

1 See I 197 and note; 198.

2 Probably Sir John de Sancto Johanne, who succeeded his father, Sir Robert, in 1267 and died in 1302. He was active in the king's service and a notable landowner in Hampshire (*Complete Peerage* XI, pp. 322–4; *Knights of Edward I*). He was probably Richard de Burhunt's overlord. When Thomas de Burhunt died before June 1263, he was holding two knights' fees of Sir Robert de Sancto Johanne; he was succeeded by his 15 year old son, Richard (*Cal. Inq. p.m.* I, 536, p. 162).
Copy III 186. Variant: Burhunt. Marginal note: Licence of Sir John de Sancto Johanne concerning the exchange of Fordham.

I 200 28 December 1291

[fo. 54ᵛ] WRIT of CERTIORARI from King Edward [I] to Malculinus de Harley, his escheator beyond Trent. The prior-elect[1] and convent of Southwick have shown that, since their church was founded by the alms of William de Pundelarge, the King and his ancestors, from the time of the foundation, have had no right of custody over the priory during a vacancy, so that nothing might be taken for royal use unless by chance the said priory, at the request of the prior-elect and convent, was taken into the hands of the King or his ancestors for its protection and that of its goods and possessions.[2] The escheator, believing the profits of the aforesaid priory to belong to the crown on the occasion of a vacancy, has taken them for the King's use and unjustly retained them, causing no small loss to the prior-elect and convent. Therefore the escheator is to establish the facts by inquisition, and meanwhile to take charge of the fixed rents and aforesaid profits as trustee, without sale or distraint, having deducted the necessary expenses of the prior-elect and convent, until the rights of the case are known. Witness: the King.

Westminster, 20 Edward [I]

1 The prior-elect was Robert de Henton' or Hempton, who succeeded John de Clere in 1291.

2 This writ throws revealing light upon the question of the priory's founder, and the ambivalent attitude of the priory according to whether its interests were better served by posing as a royal foundation or otherwise. See introduction, pp. xii, xv–xvi.
Copy II 65.

I 201 9 January 1292

INQUISITION carried out in the presence of the King's escheator at Southwick on Wednesday after the feast of the Epiphany in the 20th year of King Edward's reign, according to the royal brief, to discover whether Southwick Priory was founded by alms of the progenitors of William de Pundelarche, and whether custody of the priory belongs to the King during a vacancy so that something is received for the King's use, or has been recieved from the time of the foundation by the King or his progenitors.[1] The jurors, Thomas Stak', Gilbert le Rus, and others, say on oath that the said church was founded by alms of the progenitors of William de Pundelarche. The King has custody during a vacancy through his officers for reasons of security and defence of the church and its possessions, at the request of the canons, so that the King takes and levies nothing except food and drink for one man during the vacancy. Neither the present King nor his progenitors received anything during a vacancy from the time of the foundation of the said church. Sealed by the jurors.

1 See I 200 and note.
Copy II 66.

I 202 [1315][1]

LETTER from R., Subprior of the monastery of Southwick, and the canons, to King Edward notifying him of the death of R. their prior.[1] Lest their church remain destitute of the care of a pastor, they are sending their brothers N. and A., bearers of these letters, to request a licence to hold an election, if it please the King generously to grant it, and may his reign be long and prosperous.
                                   Given etc.

1 Prior Robert de Henton died in 1315, and the king was therefore Edward II. No other prior with a name beginning with R. died while an Edward was on the throne. For a similar letter see I 174 and note.

I 203 13 May 1314

MEMORANDUM: Thomas de Burh', with the consent of his lady, spontaneously paid 3 dove chicks (*pulli columbarum*) by way of tithe from his newly built dovecote. They were handed over in the refectory at Southwick by his serjeant to John de Lavintone, then sacristan, on Monday before the feast of St Dunstan.

I 204 30 April 1369

[fo. 55] AGREEMENT between William Powel, Vicar of Wymering (*Wymeryng*), and the prior and convent of Southwick.

Brother Richard Bromden', Prior of Southwick, pursued a writ before the King's justice against Sir William Powel, Vicar of Wymering, for unjustly taking and retaining a horse valued at 40s. and more, which the prior claimed as belonging to the priory by way of mortuary fee for a

certain gentleman from outside the parish (*generosus extraneus*) who died
there; and he said that from ancient times to the present, mortuary fees
from lords of Wymering and from all gentlemen from outside who bore
arms, belonged to the priory, because it owned the parsonage of Wymering (*causa parsonatus de Wymeryng'*); and from any other parishoners
outside whose mortuary fees were worth 40s. or more.[1]

And the aforesaid William came to the court and rejected the prior's
claim on every count, and said that all cases specified above and other
unspecified mortuary fees from those who died within his parish had
belonged from time immemorial, and still belong, to his church of
Wymering.

When the suit had been strongly contested for a long time, William's
case appearing the weaker, he arranged through a certain worthy man
(*probus homo*), Peter atte Yerd', a day on which to treat with the prior
concerning the aforesaid complaint. On the day assigned, Monday before
the feast of the Apostles Philip and James, 43 Edward III, both the
prior and William, the vicar, appeared in the hall of the guest house at
Southwick with friends and counsel for both parties who amicably agreed
that the prior and convent and their successors, by reason of the
aforesaid parsonage and the right of their church, will receive and possess
henceforth in perpetuity, without any hindrance from William or his
successors, all mortuary fees whatever their value of lords of Wymering
and any gentleman bearing arms from outside the parish who happen to
die within the parish, and also of anyone else who dies in the parish if
the fee is worth 40s. or more. Moreover William and his successors, as
the right of their church, will receive and possess in perpetuity without
hindrance from the prior and convent and their successors, mortuary
fees of all other parishoners and outsiders who die there and whose fee
is worth less than 40s. For future reference these letters are inserted in
the register of Southwick Priory.

1 For a dispute, *c*. 1260–70, between the priory and the vicar of Wymering over
tithes, see III 687. In 1310 Henry Woodlock, Bishop of Winchester, had intervened
in another dispute over mortuary dues. Sir John le Botiler had requested burial
at Wymering Church, and his horse and horse-armour, which preceded his body
to the church, were claimed both by the priory and by the Vicar of Wymering.
The bishop wrote to the vicar of Boarhunt ordering him to prevail upon Sir
John's heir to hand over the horse and armour to the priory, which was to have
custody of them—without prejudicing the issue—until the matter was resolved
(*Woodlock Register* p. 429).

I 205   2 April 1289

[fo. 55ᵛ][1] AGREEMENT made on Saturday before the Lord's Passion,
1289, between the priory and Roger de Bradeli, then custodian of the
tannery. To make up arrears for clothing, then £4, the priory would
provide the following portions, viz. from the pension of Swindon
(*Swindone*), [Wilts] at next . . . 50s.;[2] from rent of Clanfield (*Clanefeud*),
[Oxon.], 14s. 4d;[3] from William Long, 10.; from John le Burgeis, 6s.
8d., and the cellarer will keep the surplus 1s. . . . . After the aforesaid

term, it is agreed that the £4 will be found from the pension of Swindon without the other contributions named above, and the aforesaid £4 will be taken from the said pension when it is evident from the amount available for allocation that the [profits of] the tannery are insufficient to provide for the priory's clothing, and then the deficiency will be made up from the pension. When the tannery is able to provide enough, no money will be found from the pension or any other source.

1 This folio is damaged and some words are illegible or missing.

2 A pension of 100s. a year from the church of Swindon had been granted to the priory by Herbert Poore, Bishop of Salisbury, in 1199 (I 154). It was confirmed by Walter Scammel, Bishop of Salisbury, at the request of Queen Eleanor, in 1286 (I 107).

3 Land at Clanfield was given to the priory by Alice de Chesnefo before 1227 (I 158; III 289–94). According to an early 13th century rental, it brought in 46s. 8d. a year (I 182).

I 206   [1279–91][1]

LETTERS PATENT from John de Sancto Johanne[2] to his steward, bailiffs and officers (*ministri*) of his manor of Basing (*Basing'*), ordering them not to take any distraint from the prior and canons of Southwick on his manor of Ellisfield (*Elfeld*) by reason of suit owed to him for the aforesaid manor, until they receive other instructions from him, because Richard de Enfrewast and his heirs are bound to acquit the suit[3] even though (*tamen*) the heir is a minor and in the custody of the illustrious Lady Eleanor (*Alienor*), mother of their lord, King Edward.

1 After 1279 when the priory acquired land in Ellisfield (I 108), and not later than 1291, the date of the death of Eleanor of Provence, widow of Henry III and mother of Edward.

2 John de Sancto Johanne succeeded his father, Robert, who died in March 1267. John died in 1302 (*Complete Peerage* XI, pp. 322–4).

3 In 1255 Richard de Sifrewast was holding land in Ellisfield of Robert de Sancto Johanne, and owed suit at the courts of Basing and Sherborne (*VCH Hants* III, p. 360). The land in Ellisfield given to the priory by Bartholomew Peche in February 1279 was held of Richard Sifrewast, who held it of John de Sancto Johanne (I 104).

I 207[1]   4 October 1346

[PROCEEDINGS against DISTRAINT.] At the court held at Winchester on Wednesday after Michaelmas, 20 (F. 7) Edward III, the prior of Southwick came and accused the parish of St. Pancras, Winchester, of unjustly distraining on his place in Middle Brook Street (*Wonegarestrete*), of which William de Excestre was formerly seised (*que quondam fuit in seisina Willelmi . . .*), and he sought that the parish should show at the next court why they took the aforesaid distraint.[1] At that court the parish

came and showed that the aforesaid place owed them an annual rent of
18d., and they took distraint for arrears of that rent. On this, the prior
alleged that the place was held of him for an annual rent of 2 marks,
and, because the rent was 9 years in arrears, according to the custom of
the city of Winchester and on the decision of the court there, he had put
in a stake, and prosecuted that stake for a year and a day. And on
account of this, the prior of St. Swithun's had come and had entered his
claim on the aforesaid place for 3s. annual rent, 10 years in arrears.
And because after a year and a day, the proclamation having been made
thrice, no one had come to acquit the stake or claim rent (*nec aliquem
redd' calumniand'*), therefore, on the decision of the city court, the
aforesaid priors had recovered [the place] for their churches and their
successors in perpetuity. On account of this, [the prior] sought judgement
whether or not, as no one had come on behalf of the parishioners before
judgement was given to claim rent, the aforesaid place ought to be
charged with the rent after the judgement, against the custom of the
city, without a special deed; and the aforesaid parish likewise [sought
judgement]. And afterwards judgement was given that the parish had no
claim in future on the place by reason of the rent, but for unjustly taking
the distraint were at mercy, etc.
In the time of John le Lyndraper, mayor of the city; Stephen le Fox and
Ralph atte Church, bailiffs.

1 This item is almost illegible and has been calendared from the copy in volume
II. See also III 529; I 192; III 878; *W S II* 413, p. 747 and Figs. 81, 86.
Copy II 19, and II 25.

I 208　　　　　　　　　　　　　　　　　　　　28 June 1346

[fo. 56] LETTERS PATENT [of King Edward III] to his Chancellor,
M. John Efford,[1] Dean of Lincoln (*Nichole*).

Out of compassion for Southwick Priory, which was founded by the
king's progenitors, and has been impoverished both by fire and robbery
carried out by the king's enemies and by the many charges sustained on
account of the passage of the king and other faithful subjects to Brittany
(*Bretaigne*) and Gascony (*Gascoyne*), M. John is instructed to draw up
letters[2] in due form under the great seal granting to the priory (i) the
reversion of all the lands and holdings, with their appurtenances, which
belonged to Hugh le Despensir in Crookhorn (*Crouker*) and Farlington
(*Farlyngton'*), and were among those [lands] forfeited by Hugh which
came as escheat into the king's hands. The king granted them to John
de Mont Gomery for life, with reversion to the king and his heirs, and
they are valued at not more than £12 a year.[3] The priory is to have and
hold them in perpetuity, after the said John's death, from the king and
his heirs and from other lords of the fee, for accustomed services. Also
(ii) the advowson of the church of Farlington, which was similarly
forfeited by Hugh to the king.

　　　　　　　　　　　　　　Portsmouth (*Portesmuth'*), 20 [Edward III].

1 John Offord, Dean of Lincoln, Keeper of the Privy Seal, 1342–4; Chancellor, 1345–9; Archbishop-elect of Canterbury, 1348–9; died 20 May 1349.

2 *Crouker* is no longer in existence, but its location was almost certainly represented by Crookhorn Farm and Wood on the 1810 O.S. map (approximately SU 6907).

3 See below, I 212

4 See I 209, 210.

Copy II 13. Variants: Offord; Despenser.

I 209   1331

MEMORANDUM: the King by Letters Patent of 5 July 1329 committed to John de Monte Gomere, *dilectus vallettus suus*, custody of the manors of Crookhorn (*Crouker*)[1] and Farlington (*Farlyngton'*), with appurtenances in the county of Hampshire (*Suthant'*), to be held at the King's pleasure, returning to the royal exchequer an annual [amount in accordance with] the extent drawn up by chosen and faithful subjects specially selected: half at Michaelmas and half at Easter.

John de Scures and John de Tycchebourne were chosen by Letters Patent of the Exchequer, dater 28 February 1331 (*hoc anno quinto*),[1] to survey the aforesaid manors.

On 13 July they delivered, under their seals, the extent of the manors drawn up in their presence on Monday after the feast of the Ascension [13 May] by jurors John Beaumont, Richard de Hoghton', John Carbonel, Simon le Rous and others named in the extent, which is among inquisitions and extents for this year in the custody of this remembrancer. The extent states that Crookhorn (*Crouker*) and Farlington are one and are worth £7.19s. 11d. a year, which includes all profits except accustomed services (*servicia inde debita*), as shown in detail [fo. 56ᵛ] in the extent.[3] The Barons [of the Exchequer], having considered that extent, decided that John de Monte Gomery should pay the King £7. 19s. 11d. a year for the aforesaid manors from 5 July 1329 for as long as they remain in the King's hands and in John's custody.

1 See I 208 note 2.

2 Presumably 5 Edward III, hence 1331.

3 See I 210.

Copy II 14. Variant: Monte Gomeri.

I 210   13 May 1331

[fo. 56ᵛ] EXTENT of the manor of Crookhorn (*Creuker*)[1] and Farlington (*Farlyngton'*) drawn up in the presence of John de Scures and John de Tyccheborne on Monday after the feast of the Ascension, 5 Edward III. Jurors: John Beaumond', Richard de Hoghton', John Carbonel, Simon le Rous, John Stake, Geoffrey de Brokhampton', Richard Thomas, John de Horsy, John le Longe, William de Lengestok', John atte Hulle and

German le Tayllour who say on oath that Crookhorn and Farlington are
one [manor] and are worth 6s. 8d. a year in demesne easements of houses
(*in dominicis aysyamentis domorum*), having allowed for repair of the
barn, which has two rotten posts (*ultra reprisam ita quod grangia ibidem
reparetur in qua dirruti sunt duo posti*). Item: 166 acres of arable worth
41s. 6d. a year at 3d. an acre and no more, because the land lies in the
common field and is common after wheat harvest for the rest of the
year. Item: 17 acres of separable pasture (*pastura separalis*) worth 5s.
8d. a year, at 4d. an acre. Item: a certain pasture called *Benny* worth
13s. 4d. a year. Item: a certain pasture called *Asschy* worth 9s. a year.
Item: 5 acres of pasture at *Leyntheye* and *Todwell'* worth 15d. a year,
at 3d. an acre. Item: 2 acres of meadow worth 2s. a year. Item: the
pasture in the park worth 2s. 8d. a year; there is no underwood in the
aforesaid park, nor wood for pannage. Item: 55s. 4d. rent from free
men. Item: 7 cottars, whose services are worth 15s. 6d. a year. Item:
pleas and perquisites of the court worth 2s. a year.

Total: £7. 19s. 11d.[2]

Sealed by the jurors, Winchester.

Among extents and inquisitions returned to the Exchequer by different
people in 1331–2 kept in a certain canvas bag (*Baga de Canabo*) in the
custody of Reinemer', treasurer.

1 See I 208, note 2.

2 The total of the amounts given in the extent comes to £7. 14s. 11d., but see
I 211, note 2.

Copy II 15. Variant: Baga de Canalo.

I 211   [1331]

The rolls of your exchequer having been scrutinized concerning the matter
in your brief,[1] it was found that John de Scures and John de Tyccheborne
were lately assigned, by commission under the seal of the said exchequer,
to the manors of Crookhorn (*Crouker*) and Farlington (*Farlongton*) with
appurtenances in the county of Hampshire (*Sutht'*)—custody of which
from 5 July 1329 was granted by Letters Patent under your Great Seal
to John de Monte Gomery, to be held during your pleasure—returning
annually to the aforesaid exchequer the amount then assessed or amounts
subsequently assessed by our expressly chosen representatives with law-
worthy jurors from the neighbourhood of the aforesaid manors, [show-
ing] what the manors include (*extendend' quid*) and how much they are
worth annually in all profits according to their true value, so that the
exchequer will have extents clearly and openly drawn up.

[fo. 57] On Monday after the feast of the Ascension in the 5th year of
your reign [13 May 1331], John de Scures and John de Tycchebourne
returned to the exchequer an extent [of those manors] (*quorum*), and on
the basis of that extent the said John de Monte Gomery can be charged,
etc. It was found that Crookhorn (*Creuker*) and Farlington (*Farlyngton'*)
are one [manor].

[There follows a copy of the extent, above, I 210. Variants: omit reference to allowance for repair of the barn; *Asschi*; 10s. [value of *Asschi*]; *Lentheye*; 6s. 8d. [value of pasture in the park].[2]

In accordance with this extent, the aforesaid John de Monte Gomery is charged, on the decision of the then Treasurer and Barons of the Exchequer, for custody from the time at which [the manors] passed into his hands as a result of the aforesaid grant.

1 This would appear to be a report to the king of the action taken concerning the manor of Crookhorn and Farlington as shown above in I 209, 210.

2 The altered values given here for *Asschi* and the pasture in the park bring the final total of £7. 19s. 11d. Possibly a surcharge has been added at the Exchequer. See above I 211, note 1.

Copy II 15. Variants: Todewell [in copy of extent].

I 212   10 July 1356

[fo. 57ᵛ] LETTERS PATENT of King Edward [III]. Owing to damage and loss suffered by Southwick Priory, founded by the king's progenitors, both from fire and destruction inflicted on their manors, benefices and other possessions near the sea in the county of Hampshire (*Suthamptonia*) by foreign enemies making frequent raids during the war, and also from the cost and burden which the frequent coming of the king, his household, magnates and others for the purpose of crossing the sea brought to the priory, its manors and other places over a long period, the king wishes to bring relief to the priory, which is greatly impoverished for the aforesaid and other reasons. Therefore he has granted in perpetuity to the priory all the lands and holdings with appurtenances which belonged to Hugh le Despenser in Crookhorn (*Crouker*) and Farlington (*Farlyngton*), worth £7. 19s. 11d. a year, as certified by the Treasurers and Barons of the King's Exchequer in his Chancery. The lands had been forfeited by Hugh and had come into the king's hands as his escheat, and the king had granted them to John de Monte Gomery for life, with reversion to himself and his heirs. After John's death, they will pass into the possession of the priory, which will hold them from the king and his heirs and other chief lords of that fee for accustomed services. The king grants moreover to the priory the advowson of the church of Farlington, which was similarly forfeited by Hugh and fell into the king's hands as escheat. They will hold it from him and his successors and other chief lords of that fee for accustomed services in perpetuity.[1] Witness: Lionel, the King's most dear son, Custodian of England.

Windsor (*Wyndesore*)10 July, 20 (F. 7) Edward [III].

1 See I 208–11.
Copy II 16. Variant: Wydesor'.
Copy III 224, and in inspeximus of Richard II, III 971.

I 213   13 July 1346

GRANT by John de Mount Gomery to Southwick Priory, of warranty
of the reversion of all the lands and holdings with appurtenances which
belonged to Hugh le Despenser in Crookhorn (*Crouker*) and Farlington
(*Farlyngton*'), and were granted to John for life by the king without any
charge of rent and, thereafter, with reversion to Southwick Priory.[1]
London, Thursday before the feast of St Margaret, 20 (F. 7)
[Edward III].

1 See I 208–12. In August 1347 Sir John de Montgomery leased the manor of
Crookhorn and Farlington to the priory for one year on payment of £30 (III 234,
236). Sir John died on 14 October 1347, only a week after arranging to surrender
the manor permanently to the priory in return for £30 a year for life (*Cal. Inq.
p.m.* IX, 17, p. 7; III 237). Sir John's executors sold the corn and livestock on
the manor to the priory for £50, but there is no record that the priory paid more
than £10 (III 238, 240, 239).
Copy III 235. Variant: Mont'Gomyry.

I 214   1360

[fo. 58][1] SETTLEMENT of a dispute between Southwick Priory, owner
of the manors of Southwick and West Boarhunt (*Westburhunte*), and
Sir Bernard Brocas and his wife, Lady Mary, tenants of the manor of
Boarhunt Herberd (*Burhunte herberd*) by right of the said Mary, over
the taking by Bernard's officials (*ministri*) of the prior's beasts in three
pastures, viz. in Creech (*Crich*), Walton Heath (*Walkenhethe*) and *Strodhulle*, and over the taking of Bernard's beasts in the pasture of the
priory's manor of West Boarhunt.[2] Arbitration at Southwick on Sunday
in the middle of Lent, 1360, was committed to Sir Robert Markaunt,
knight, Robert de Hoo, Roger Engelfeld, Richard Dannvers and Thomas
Bealmond on Sir Bernard's side, and Sir Lawrence de Pageham, knight,
John Buteler, Thomas de Wallop, Thomas Everard' and Thomas Stake
on the prior's side. The arbitrators decided that (i) the aforesaid prior
and his successors and the tenants of their land of Southwick have rights
of common in perpetuity in the said pasture called *Crihc* [*sic*] with all
kinds of beasts at all times of the year (*omni tempore anni*) without
hindrance, as they used and ought to have from time immemorial, and
the prior has greater right of common because he has, and his predecessors
had, a certain piece of land of their own there (*in predicta placia
quandam parcellam soli propri*) in which he ought and is wont to pasture
his beasts. (ii) The tenants of the said prior and the aforesaid Sir Bernard
and his wife, Lady Mary, ought and are wont to have rights of common
for all their beasts, just as the prior and his tenants ought and are wont
to have, in the whole of the rest of the pasture of Creech. (iii) The prior
and his tenants at Southwick will henceforth have rights of common for
all their beasts in Walton Heath and *Strudhulle* as they used and ought
to have from ancient times without hindrance.

1 This folio is slightly damaged. Missing words have been supplied from II 12.

2 Creech Farm is about 1½ miles north-east of Southwick; Walton Heath 1 mile north-west. Possibly Strodhulle or Strudhulle is now represented by Stroud Copse ½ mile south-west of Southwick.

For a memorandum setting out the priory's complaints against Sir Bernard Brocas and Lady Mary, see II 118, and another version at II 124. The above settlement was not the end of the matter; see II 117, 119.

Copy II 12. Variants: John le Boteler; de Wollep; Everarde; cum [sic] tempore anni.

Copy II 231. Variants: Crych'; Walkynheth; Stroudhull'; Marcaunt; Ingelfelde; Beaumond; Wolhop; [add:] (iv) The lords of the manor of Boarhunt Herberd cannot claim, and must not in future exercise, right of common in the prior's separable pasture of *la Stroude*, nor in the fields of West Boarhunt except for pasture reasonably pertaining to two acres which they have there.

II 1　　　　　　　　　　　　　　　　　　　　　12 July 1357

[fo. 1] GRANT by Robert, Bishop of Salisburty (*Sar'*), to Southwick Priory, of the fruits, rents and profits of the parish church of Swindon (*Swyndon'*) in his diocese, over and above the advowson[1] and annual pension of 100s.[2] which belonged to the priory.

The bishop acknowledged that his pastoral office required him to care for the religious who have devoted themselves to the service of God, and to relieve their wants and poverty. Since the priory was endowed for the most part with lands and temporal possessions from of old, and now, on account of the infertility of the lands and fall in rents caused by the poverty of the tenants; arrears of rent; the fall in the number [of tenants] through a recent attack of plague; the destruction by fire of various buildings, which has happened by chance in the manors of Southwick and West Boarhunt (*Westborhunte*), and by enemy action, occasioned by war between England and France, in the vills of Portsmouth (*Portesmuthe*) and Southampton (*Suthampton'*) on the coast, in which are to be found a great part of the priory's rents; and moreover the loss of various other possessions by the shore through continuing erosion, and the great cost to the priory of sea defences (*propter maris custodiam*); also costly repairs made as necessary to the church and houses of the priory built both inside and outside its enclosures (*septa*) and various other burdens inevitably more usual (*plus solito*) these days, the priory is so poverty stricken that its resources are insufficient to provide for its customary hospitality and other works of charity, and it cannot be maintained without help. Therefore, having considered the priory's petition, the bishop has made over the aforesaid profits, over and above the pension, which do not exceed 20 marks according to the assessment of [fo. 1ᵛ] the tithe, and he has granted possession to the priory in perpetuity to relieve in part its needs. The bishop's action was based on information confirmed by inquisition and followed discussion by the chapter of Salisbury as to what was required for the perpetual granting of churches in this manner, the archdeacon of Wiltshire being present and giving his consent. Having seen the licence granted by the king to the priory,[3] the bishop has decided to assign the church of Swindon to the priory, saving sufficient portions for the vicarage and the perpetual vicar appointed there, and assessed and ordained by the bishop and his successors. When the present rector of the said church retires or dies, or for any other reason the church is vacant, the priory or its proctor may take possession of that church by the authority of these presents and hold it, disposing of its rents and profits as they please.

So that provision may be made from the aforesaid grant for the church of Salisbury, the bishop, his successors, the chapter of his church, and the aforesaid archdeacon of Wiltshire, the bishop, with the express consent of his chapter and the priory, has reserved the following annual [fo. 2] pensions to be paid on the feast of the Annunciation in lieu of accustomed profits during a vacancy: (i) for himself and his successors, 13s. 4d. to be paid in the church of Salisbury; (ii) for the archdeacon of Wiltshire and his successors, 6s. 8d. to be paid in Swindon church; (iii) to the chapter of Salisbury, 6s. 8d. to be paid in that church. Failure to pay these pensions or any part of them will involve sequestration of the profits of Swindon church until they are fully paid, with any damages and expenses incurred.

The bishop, moreover, with the express consent of the priory, has reserved a suitable portion of the profits of Swindon church for the perpetual vicar who has the cure of the parish, from which episcopal dues and other incumbent charges can be paid. The priory, henceforth in perpetuity, will present a suitable parson to that vicarage, to be admitted and instituted by the bishop and his successors if there is no canonical [fo. 2ᵛ] objection, saving to the bishop and his chapter all right, suzerainty, law and jurisdiction, ordinary and diocesan, and the jurisdiction of the said archdeacon over the said church, which the bishop does not in any way intend to prejudge or derogate by these presents. Sealed by the bishop, chapter and archdeacon.

The Chapter House, [Salisbury], 28th year of Robert's episcopate.[4]

1 The church of Swindon was first granted to the priory by its founder, William de Pont de l'Arche. According to the priory this grant was made in the reign of Henry I (I 12). It was confirmed by William's son, Robert (I 11, 18, 19); by Bishop Jocelin of Salisbury (I 21, 22); Pope Alexander III (I 23, 86); Pope Urban III (I 87) and Pope Lucius (I 92).

2 The pension of 100s. was granted to the priory by Herbert Poore, Bishop of Salisbury, in 1199 (I 154), and was confirmed by Walter Scammel, Bishop of Salisbury, in 1286, at the request of Queen Eleanor, widow of Henry III (I 107). That is the amount recorded as the pension from Swindon church in the rental (I 184).

3 See III 982, 403.

4 Rober Wyvil was consecrated Bishop of Salisbury on 15 July 1330. He died in 1375.

II 1a 14 September 1357

RATIFICATION by Southwick Priory [of II 1]. The priory bound itself and the church of Swindon to observe in perpetuity all the bishop's ordinances therein, so far as they concern them.

The Chapter House, Southwick.

Copy III 409. Variant: rubric, Appropriation of the church of Swindon (*Swyndon'*) in the time of Richard, the 17th prior. [Richard Bromdene was prior, 1349–81. If he was the 17th prior, the names of two priors are unknown, See list of priors p. lxiv].

II 2 27 July 1359

NOTIFICATON by Robert, Bishop of Salisbury, that Nicholas Haughman, rector of the parish church of Swindon (*Swyndone*) in his diocese, has voluntarily and absolutely surrendered his church. The bishop has approved and accepted Nicholas' resignation, absolved him from the cure of souls and care of the aforesaid church, and declared it vacant. He has informed the prior and convent of Southwick in the diocese of Winchester, to whom the church is appropriated, that they may enter into possession of it, receive the fruits, rents and profits, and dispose of them freely.

[fo. 3] The manor of Woodford (*Wodeforde*), [Wilts], the 30th year of Robert's episcopate.[1]

1 See II 1, note 4.
Copy III 410.

II 3 25 July 1359

NOTIFICATION by Robert, Bishop of Salisbury. Since by his lawful authority he has annexed in perpetuity the parish church of Swindon (*Swyndone*) in his diocese to the Priory of Southwick in the diocese of Winchester, as needful for certain legitimate reasons, saving the right of himself and his successors to assign to the perpetual vicar, installed there by him and his successors at the presentation of the priory, a suitable portion of the fruits and profits of the said church, and also to specify the amount to be paid for the suitable maintenance of episcopal and archidiaconal rights and to support other incumbent debts—wishing to specify fairly the portions and obligations of the aforesaid vicarate, he ordered a careful inquisition to be made of the rents, profits and whatever oblations belong to the said church of Swindon. After which, Brother Adam, concanon of the priory and its proctor, and William Matthew, vicar of the said church of Swindon, in person, appeared before the bishop, and all matters were considered concerning the rights of the vicarate. The portions and charges were laid down initially by the priory and the bishop, and subsequently agreed by the priory and the said vicar as follows:—the vicar and his successors will have (i) for their dwelling, the houses situated in the rectory of that [fo. 3ᵛ] church, viz.,the granary and the whole house under that roof; (ii) the kitchen and all adjoining houses, also the curtillage and the small garden with the little gate leading to the church; (iii) all the meadows which once belonged to the demesne of that church, and half the arable, and common and separable (*separabilis*) pasture belonging to the church from ancient times; (iv) all tithes, oblations and obventions and every emolument pertaining to that church.

Tithes of corn of any kind, and hay, and the other half of the arable and common and separable pasture of the said church, and also mortuary fees from those living within the said parish (*necnon mortuariis viviis infra dictam parochiam provenientibus*), and from a certain tenement outside the bounds of the said church and belonging to it, and other houses, buildings, gardens and places of the said rectory or in any way pertaining to it, and not specifically assigned above to said vicar or vicarage, remain, and ought to remain, the property of the priory by the aforesaid annexation.

The bishop orders that the vicar of Swindon and his successors should (a) serve the church suitably and perform divine service as in times past at their own expense; (b) pay archidiaconal fees and other accustomed annual rents to the archdeacon of Wiltshire; (c) provide two processional candles and incense (*thura*); (d) provide, repair and maintain the books, vestments and all other ornaments in the chancel of the said church; build and repair houses, buildings, walls, partitions (*parietes*), closes and whatever places belong to the said vicar, and [undertake] all other ordinary charges which used to pertain to the rector of that place before the appropriation of the church.

The building and repair of the chancel, as often as necessary, and the maintenance of charity and all other extraordinary payments (*prestaciones*) and charges will be the responsibility of the aforesaid priory.

[fo. 4] The bishop's ordinances are to be observed in perpetuity saving his full power (*potestas libera*), and that of his successors, to declare, interpret, increase and change them; saving also the rights of the benefactor, episcopal rights and customs, and the dignity of the church of Salisbury.

Woodford, [Wilts], 30th year of Robert's episcopate.[1]

1 See II 1, note 4.
Copy III 411.

[fo. 4ᵛ] Blank.

[fo. 5] **II 4** Copy of I 1.

II 5 Copy of I 2.

[fo. 5ᵛ] II 6 Copy of I 9.

II 7 Copy of I 123.

II 8   20 February 1353

[fo.6] INSPEXIMUS and CONFIRMATION by King Edward III of:—
(i) confirmation granted by his father, Edward II, to Southwick Priory
following inspeximus [fo. 6ᵛ] of (a) and (b), two charters of King John
[I 160, 161;] [fo. 7] (c) Henry III's confirmation [of I 161] and grant to
the priory of quittance in perpetuity from tallage on that land: witnesses:
William [*sic*], Bishop of Carlisle (*Kareol'*);[1] R., Earl of Cornwall, the
King's brother;[2] Ralph, son of Nicholas; John, son of Philip; Godfrey
de Craucumbe; Geoffrey Dispens'; Bartholomew Peche; Geoffrey de
Chauz; Richard, son of Hugh; Henry de Capella; and others: given by
the hand of R., Bishop of Chichester, the King's Chancellor,[3] at Ashley
(*Esleg'*), 28 December, 1231; (d) Henry III's inspeximus and confirmation
of the charter of his great-great-grandfather (*abavus*), Henry I,[4] viz:—
Grant to Portchester Priory of the church of St. Mary, Portchester,
founded by him (*deo et ecclesie beate Marie de Porcestra et canonicis
regularibus ibidem servientibus ipsam ecclesiam Sancte Marie ibidem a
me fundatam*), with lands, tithes and all appurtenances, haybote and
housebote (*heybod' et husbot'*) from his wood of *Kyngesden'*, right of
pasturage both in the wood and on the plain (*planus*), and reasonable
maintenance for their hearth (*focum*) from his forest in his lifetime and
that of all his successors without contradiction or vexation; also the
manor of Candover (*Candeura*) containing 5 hides, 1 virgate, which
William de Pontearch gave the priory in alms from his demesne; 1 hide
in Southwick and 1 hide in Applestead (*Appelstede*),[5] which William
bought from Ivo Pantulf for the use of the church, with the king's
consent. For the souls of his father, his brother William, his mother,
ancestors and successors, the king will maintain and defend the priory
and all its appurtenances free from all secular service, exaction and
charge, and will give it his protection against all men, as his own alms
(*sicut meam propriam elemosinam*). The canons, their officials (*ministri*)
and serjeants are to hold their possessions and alms with soke and
sake, toll and team (*soca et sacha et thol et theam*), infangetheof and
utfangenethef [*sic*], and all liberties, free customs and quittances in wood,
plain, meadows, grazings, waters, mills, ways, paths, marshes, fisheries
(*piscaria*), granges, and virgates (*virgulta*), within the borough and without, in all places and matters free and quit of [the jurisidiction of] the
shire and hundred [courts], and all manner of suits, pleas, claims and
charges for murder, larceny, house-breaking (*hamsoken*), forest, scutage,

hidage geld and Danegeld, horngeld (*hornguld*), assarts, assizes, gifts
(*dona*), aids, service of carriage by pack animals (*summagium*), ward-
penny (*war pani*), ?carrying-service-penny (*aver pani*), hundred-penny
(*hundredes peni*), miskenning (*meskenninge*) and blood-wite (*blodwite*).
And they are quit in perpetuity, both on land and water, of tolls,
transport dues (*passagium*), pontage and tallage, and all custom and
cause, except jurisdiction over life and limb (*justicia mortis et membro-
rum*). Injunction agaisnt anyone molesting the canons or their property,
or attempting to lay any charge against them except in the presence of
the king or his heirs. [Witnesses and location as in I 1]. Witnesses [to
Henry III's confirmation]: N., Bishop of Winchester;[6] Roger de Mortuo
Mari; William de [fo. 7ᵛ] Wintreshull; Stephen de Eddwrth'; Roger de
Wanton'; Peter Everard'; William Ernaud'; and others.
Given by the King's hand at Waltham (*Wautham*), [Essex], 10 August
1269.

Witnesses [to Edward II's confirmation of (a), (b), (c), (d)]: R., Bishop
of London;[7] W., Bishop of Worcester (*Wygorn'*);[8] Gilbert de Clare, Earl
of Gloucester (*Glouc'*) and Hertford (*Herford'*); John de Britannia,
Earl of Richmond (*Richemund'*); Hugh le Despenser; Bartholomew de
Badelesmere; Nicholas de Segrave; and others.
Given by the King's hand at Westminister, 21 February 1313.

(ii) Grant by King Henry [III], his great-grandfather (*proavus*), to Southwick Priory, of a weekly market each Friday in perpetuity, and an annual
fair lasting for two days, viz. on the eve and feast of the Assumption of
the Blessed Mary [14th and 15th August], on condition that no injury is
done to neighbouring markets or fairs; with this proviso the priory will
have all liberties and free customs pertaining to a market and a fair of
this kind. Witnesses: W. Bishop of Carlisle (*Karleol*);[9] H. de Burg', Earl
of Kent (*Kanc'*);[10] Ralph, son of Nicholas; Godfrey de Craucumbe;
Amaurus de Sancto Amando; John, son of Philip; William de Picheford';
Geoffrey Dispens'; Geoffrey de Cauz; and others.
Given by the hand of R., Bishop of Chichester, the King's
Chancellor,[3] at Westminister, 18 April 1235.

(iii) Grant by King Edward [II] his father (*proavus*)[11] to Southwick
Priory, of free warren in all its demesne at Southwick, West Boarhunt
(*Westbourhunt*), *Basevil'*, Hipley (*Hippeleye*), Crofton, Stubbington near
Portsea (*Stebynton' iuxta Porteseye*), Newlands (*Nova terra*), Anmore
(*Anedemere*), [fo. 8] Moundsmere (*Mundesmere*) [in Preston Candover],
Ellisfield (*Elsefeld'*), Priorys Dean (*Dene*) and Colemore (*Colemere*) in
the county of Southampton; Fishbourne (*Fisscheburne*) in the county of
Sussex; and Clanfield in the county of Oxfordshire, so long as those
lands are not within the bounds of royal forest. No one may enter these
lands to hunt or take anything pertaining to warren without priory's
licence, on penalty of £10 fine (*super forisfacturam nostram decem
librarum*). Witnesses: W., Archbishop of Canterbury;[12] J., Bishop of
Norwich, the King's Chancellor;[13] W., Bishop of Exeter, Treasurer;[14]
Aymer (*Adomarus*) de Valencia, Earl of Pembroke (*Pembroch'*) Hugh

le Despenser, the elder; Hugh le Despenser, the younger; Bartholomew de Badelesmere, Steward of the Royal Household (*senescallus hospicii nostri*); and others.

By the King's hand at Westminister, 7 October 1320.

(iv) Letters Patent by which he [Edward III] granted to Southwick Priory all the lands and holdings which belonged to Hugh le Despenser in Crookhorn (*Crouker*) and Farlington (*Farlyngton'*) [I 212].

[fo. 8] The King confirms all the aforesaid charters and letters, and, wishing to make a more fruitful gift (*uberiorem gratiam facere*) to the priory, he has granted them any liberties or quittances in these charters and letters which for any reason they have not so far used. They can enjoy and use them without action or impediment by the king of his heirs, justices, escheators, sheriffs or other baliffs or officials whatever, in perpetuity. Also he has granted to the priory, in perpetuity, free warren in all their demesne land of Crookhorn and Farlington, so long as they are not within the bounds of the royal forest. No one may enter those lands to hunt or take anything pertaining to warren without the priory's licence, on penalty of £10 fine. Witnesses: S., Archbishop of Canterbury, Primate of all England;[15] J., Archbishop-elect of York (*electus Ebor' confirmatus*), the King's Chancellor;[16] W., Bishop of Winchester, the King's Treasurer;[17] Henry, Duke of Lancaster; Richard, Earl of Arundel; Bartholomew de Burgherssh'; John de Gray, Steward of the Royal Household; and others.

Given by the King's hand at Westminister.

1 Will' in MS., but Walter Mauclerc was Bishop of Carlisle, 1223–46.

2 Richard, Earl of Cornwall, was the second son of King John; born, 1209, created Earl, 1227; died, 1272 (*HBC* p. 422).

3 Ralph Neville, Bishop of Chichester, 1222–44; Chancellor 1226–38 (*HBC* pp. 216, 83).

4 This charter, the original of which is in the Hampshire Record Office (4M53/1), was printed by Dugdale (*Monasticon Anglicanum* VI, 1, 244, no. 1). It has been shown to be a forgery (see I 1, note 3).

5 For the location of Appelstead, see I 1, note 4.

6 Nicholas of Ely, Bishop of Winchester, 1268–80.

7 Ralph Baldock, Bishop of London, 1304–13.

8 Walter Reynolds, Bishop of Worcester, 1308–13.

9 Walter Mauclerc, Bishop of Carlisle, 1223–46.

10 Hubert de Burgh, Earl of Kent; created, 1227; deprived, 1232; restored, 1234; died, 1243 (*HBC* p. 433).

11 *Sic* in MS., but this must be a mistake. It is evident from the witnesses that the grant was made by Edward II.

12 Walter Reynolds, Archbishop of Canterbury, 1313–27.

13 John Salmon, Bishop of Norwich, 1299–1325; Chancellor, 1320–3 (*HBC* pp. 243, 84).

14 Walter Stapeldon, Bishop of Exeter, 1308–26; Treasurer, 1320–5 (*HBC* pp. 225, 101).

15 Simon Islip, Archbishop of Canterbury, 1349–66.

16 John Thoresby, translated from the bishopric of Worcester 1352, restitution of temporalities 8 February 1353, died 1373. He was Chancellor from 1349 to 1356 (*HBC* pp. 264, 84).

17 William Edington, Bishop of Winchester, 1346–66; Treasurer, 1344–56 (*HBC* 258, 84).
Copy III 992.

II 9   4 May 1336

[fo. 9] WRIT of CERTIORARI from King Edward [III] to John de Roches, William de Harudone and Robert de Hoo. The Prior of South-wick has appealed to the king [on the ground] that his house ought, and was wont, to be charged with the maintenance of only one of the king's servants at a time, as requested. Lately the prior admitted on request the king's servant, Simon Bacoun, during the lifetime of another royal servant, John le Veneour, to whom he had previously granted mainten-ance at the king's request. Wishing to provide protection for the prior and his successors lest his house be charged in this way in the future, because of the admission of the aforesaid Simon, and so that justice might be done to the prior, the king has appointed them [John, William and Robert], or two of them, to establish by inquisition whether the priory was wont in times past to be charged with maintenance for two royal servants at a time or one, and if two, then from what time and in what way; and how, and by whom, the priory was founded; and from other relevant circumstances to discover more fully the truth of the aforesaid matters. Having held the inquisition, they are to report without delay to his chancellery under their seals and those of the jurors. And the king ordered them to notify his sheriff of the county of Hampshire to summon jurors from his bailiwick to appear before them on the day and at the place appointed by them for the inquisition.

By [the hand of] Peter Cons', Westminister, 4 May, 10 Edward [III].

II 10   9 July 1336

INQUISITION held at Southwick before William de Haruedone and Robert de Hoo [in response to writ II 9]. Jurors: John de Molyns, [fo. 9ᵛ] William Brutoun, Ralph Strut, John de Bradelegh', William de Wanstede, Richard Abraham, Roger atte Ligh', Richard Thomas, William Alayn, John de Horsy, Richard Roget and John de Porteseie, who say that (i) the house of Southwick was wont to be charged in times past with the maintenance of one man only on the orders or at the request of the king or his predecessors; (ii) the priory does not hold anything of the king [given] at the time of its foundation, but only holds of him the manor of [Priors] Dean, at fee farm, paying £7. 18s. 5½d. to the royal exchequer by the hand of the sheriff of Hampshire; (iii) the priory was founded by Sir William de Pondelarg'. Sealed by the jurors. Tuesday after the feast of the Translation of St Thomas the Martyr, 10 Edward III.

II 11   2 October 1336

LETTERS PATENT from King Edward [III] repeating the writ of certiorari and findings of the subsequent inquisition [II 9 and 10], in [fo. 10] consideration of which he concedes that the admission of Simon [Bacoun] into the priory will not count as a precedent in the future, and after Simon's death the priory will be quit in perpetuity of the charge of admitting and maintaining two men at the same time, saving the right of the king and his heirs to maintenance for one servant there, after the deaths of John and Simon.

Witnessed by the King at Leicester (*Lecestr'*), 2 October, 10 Edward III.

Copy III 975. Variants: William de Pountlarge; Leycestr'.

II 12   Copy of I 214.

[fo. 10ᵛ] **II 13**   Copy of I 208.

[fo. 11] **II 14**   Copy of I 209.

[fo. 11–11ᵛ] **II 15**   Copy of I 210, 211.

[fo. 12] **II 16**   Copy of I 212.

[fo. 12ᵛ] **II 17**   Copy of I 188.

II 18   19 July 1313

[fo. 13] INQUISITION held before the King's Escheator at Southwick. Jurors: Richard, son of Thomas de Porteseye; Robert le Eyr; Roger atte Legh'; Henry Odo; Richard Stak'; Matthew atte Hale; William le Frenche; Adam atte Spense; William Aleyn; William Pynkenye; William de Longestok'; Thomas de Colemere; and William Dorynal. They say on oath that Clement le Burgeys formerly held a messuage, $\frac{1}{2}$ carucate, 12 acres of meadow, and a water mill, with appurtenances, at Hipley (*Huppelegh'*), of Southwick Priory in chief, for 13s. 7d. annual rent and suit of court three-weekly at the prior's court at West Boarhunt (*Westbourhunte*), for all service. Clement leased 12 acres of meadow to Mary de Hoyvile and her son, William, for their lives;[1] 3 acres to Philip de Haversham and his wife, Juliana, for their lives;[2] and 4 acres to Mary de Hoyvill', for 4 years.[3] Afterwards Clement enfeoffed at farm a certain John Prany, clerk, of the remainder of that messuage and mill, with reversion of the lands leased as above, for John and his heirs to hold in perpetuity of the chief lords of that fee, for the accustomed service.[4] Mary, William, Philip and Juliana did fealty to John Prany. As John Prany was a bastard and died without a legitimate heir of his body, the prior and convent, as chief lords of that messuage, land and mill, with reversion of the said farms, took them into their hands as their escheat, and are now holding them as such.[5] Sealed by the jurors.

Southwick, 7 Edward [II].

1 The lease, drawn up on 31 October 1309, was for the lives of Sir Philip de Hoyville, his wife Mary, and his son William. Sir Philip had died by December 1310 (III 785, 787, 786, 790).

2 Probably this was the croft called *Coltesok'* which was leased to Philip and Juliana on 15 August 1311 (III 1010).

3 See III 788, 794.

4 The Final Concord between Clement and John was drawn up on 3 November 1312 (I 183).

5 This inquisition did not settle the matter of the priory's right to John Prany's lands. The King's Escheator took them into the hands of the crown on the ground that they had been acquired by the priory in violation of the Statute of Mortmain, and the King ordered another inquisition. Among the jurors who met on 21 December 1318, three names occur that are also on the list above, and the evidence given was substantially the same. The King then ordered the Escheator to restore the lands to the priory (I 187–189; see also III 676, 798, 896).

Copy III 678. Variants: Portesie; Stake; French'; Lengestoke; Westburhunt'; Hoyville; Haveresham.

[fo. 13ᵛ] **II 19**   Copy of I 207.

II 20   Copy of I 190.

[fo. 14] **II 21**   Copy of I 191.

II 22   Copy of I 192.

[fo. 14ᵛ] **II 23**   Copy of I 186.

[fo. 15] **II 24**   Copy of I 105.

[fo. 16] **II 25**   Copy of II 19.

II 26   1356–7

[fo. 16ᵛ] PROCEEDINGS for RECOVERY of a tenement. John, Prior of the Cathedral Church of St. Swithun, Winchester,[1] prosecuted a stake on the tenement formerly of Henry le Brewere in Gold Street (*Goldstrete*), Winchester, for arrears of rent owed to the office of sacristan of the said church, etc. And Richard, Prior of Southwick,[2] entered his claim on the said tenement for arrears of rent owed to the priory, etc.[3] And the third proclamation was made on Wednesday after the feast of St. Dunstan, 31 Edward III [24 May, 1357]. Because no one came to acquit the said stake, it was decided by the court of the city that the priors should recover the tenement in proportion to the rent owed them, and hold it in perpetuity.

1 John Merlawe was Prior of St. Swithun's, 1349–61 (*Fasti* IV, p. 47).

2 Richard Bromdene was Prior of Southwick, 1349–81.

3 Southwick Priory's claim derived from the gift made to them in 1256–8 by Walter le Chamberlayn, son of John, who had been chamberlain to the prior of St. Swithun's (III 560 and note 2). William de Wyntonia, clerk, acquired the house and tenement from Prior Peter of Southwick (1266–73), for a payment of 5s. annual rent to the priory and 20d. to Romsey Abbey (III 562).
See also *WS II* 638, p. 893, and Fig. 100.

II 27   Copy of I 192, and of II 22.

II 28   28 May 1319

[fo. 17] WRIT of CERTIORARI from King Edward [II] to M. Richard de Clare, Escheator South of Trent.[1] The prior of Southwick has shown that a certain predecessor of his acquired, before the publication of the

Statute of Mortmain, 13s. 4d. worth of rent with appurtenances in the fee of William le Dighere in Winchester.[2] M. Richard, however, asserting that the aforesaid prior acquired that rent after the publication of the Statute, without having obtained a licence from King Edward I or the present king, took it into the king's hands, causing no little loss and injury to the prior, who has sought redress from the king. Because he does not wish the prior to be injured in this way, the king has ordered M. Richard to establish the facts by inquisition, and report without delay, under his seal and those of the jurors.

York (*Ebor'*), 28 May, 12 Edward [II].

1 *Cal, Inq. misc.* II, no. 367, p. 91.

2 See below, II 30, note 1.

II 29 [Shortly after 7 November 1319]

NOTIFICATION by Ricahrd de Clare, Escheator South of Trent, to John de Ledrede, Subescheator in the county of Hampshire (*Sutht'*), of the king's mandate, viz. the inquisition [below, II 30, held in response to the king's writ, II 28], returned in Chancery, ascertained that William le Dighere enfeoffed the then prior of Southwick with 13s. 4d. worth of rent eleven years before the publication of the Statute of Mortmain, by reason of which the priory has always up to now received the rent freely, and it is not held of the king. Wishing justice to be done to the prior, the king has ordered his escheator to release the rent and concern himself no further with it. If anything has been taken from it for the king's use, it is to be restored to the prior without delay.

Witnessed by the King at York (*Ebor'*), 7 November, 13 Edward [II].

II 30 17 September 1319

[fo. 17ᵛ] INQUISITION held before the King's Escheator at Winchester, jurors: Adam de Cheriton', Ralph de Mallyngg', Bartholomew de Tytingg', John de Wyght, Richard le Forestir, Simon le Drapier, Robert Dymaunde, William de Farham, William le Coupere, Henry le Caneuacyr, Adam de Portreyue, William le Pouletyr.[1] They say that the 13s. 4d. worth of rent with appurtenances in Winchester, with which William le Dyghere at some time enfeoffed the priory of Southwick, was acquired eleven years before the publication of the Statute of Mortmain. And they say that the rent is not by itself held of any lord, because it is a certain rent-seck (*sictus redditus*), issuing from the tenement in Winchester of the same William, and granted ot the priory for devotion as aforesaid, from which time the priory has always received and held it freely. Sealed by the jurors. Monday before the feast of St Matthew the Apostle,

13 Edward [II].

1 With the possible exception of Richard le Forestir and Simon le Drapier, all the jurors appear in Dr. Keene's Biographical Register (*WS* II, p. 1133 sqq). William le Dyghere cannot be identified in the Register with certainty, but if his grant was made to the priory in 1268, it is possible that he is the same man as William Tinctor, or the Dyer, whose son was a canon at Southwick, and who was granted various rents in Winchester to the priory before his death in 1290 (III 519–525).

II 31 [after 1349, *c.* 1360][1]

Benedict in le Hale had two wives[2]

[MEMORANDUM:] The first wife begat Robert, the firstborn, Peter, John, Adam, Geoffrey and Thomas and two daughters; Robert begat Robert, to whom the right descended, etc. Robert begat John Beneit of *la Leghe* in the parish of Havant (*Havonte*), now the claimant, etc.

The second wife, Agnes, begat Robert, Stephen, Hugh and Richard and daughters, Isabella, Agatha and Alice. Hugh, son of the said Benedict and his wife Agnes, acquired (*perquisivit*) a messuage with garden and 5 acres with appurtenances in *le Waitestrete*, in the parish of Farlington (*Farlyngton'*), of the holding of John le Waite; and a messuage, 4 crofts, 1 meadow and 1 grove with appurtenances at *Lengestoke*, from John de Portesye, of the fee of the prior of Southwick. Hugh died without an heir of his body (*de se*), and after his death for want of an heir the aforesaid messuage with garden and 5 acres came into the possession of John le Wayte, as his escheat, etc.; who held them while he lived. After his death, the right descended to Clarice and Johanna, his daughters and heiresses, who were unjustly disseised by the aforesaid John Beneit, the claimant, etc. Also, after Hugh's death, for want of an heir the aforesaid messuage, 4 crofts, meadow and grove with [fo. 18] appurtenances at *Lengestok'* came into the possession of Southwick Priory, as its escheat, etc., and are so held, etc., until, etc..

[Marginal note in a later hand:] The land called Lengstok' came into the prior's hands as escheat, for lack of an heir (*pro defectu sanguinis*).

1 Hugh, son of Benedict and Agnes, *alias* Hugh Beneyt, acquired the land at *Lengestoke* in the parish of Southwick from John de Portesye in 1349 (III 448). He had been involved in other land transactions between 1340 and 1343 (III 351, 672, 681, 685, 889, 890, 894). In 1343 he had obtained a licence from the king for the alienation in mortmain to the priory of land worth 60s. a year (III 981, 897). There is no mention of Hugh later than 1349; the above memorandum was probably drawn up some years after his death, as the claimant, John Beneit, was his step-great-nephew.

2 Contemporary rubric in left-hand margin.

II 32 1381

[fo.18] (a) INQUISITION held on 4 May 1381 (4 Richard II) at South-wick before Thomas Illeston', Royal Escheator in the county of

Hampshire, on account of the vacancy caused by the death of Richard Bromden', lately Prior of Southwick. Jurors: Richard Upham, Peter atte Zerd, John Russhemere, Robert Cutte, Robert Bruwere, John Horsye, William Barbour of Hawkley (*Haukelegh'*), John atte Hale, William Okschete, Robert le Frye, William atte Frethe, and Richard Tralle, who say on oath that the late prior held, in free alms, on the day he died, as by right of his church—the priory having been founded by the king's progenitors (*qui quidem prioratus est de fundacione progenitorum domini Regis*)—the following manors:—

(i) Southwick, given in free alms to the canons by William de Ponte Arcarum: £10 rent from free and bond [tenants], paid in equal portions at Christmas, Easter, the Nativity of St John the Baptist and Michaelmas; 153 acres of arable worth 32s. 2d. a year, i.e., 2d. an acre; 41 acres of pasture worth 3s. 7d. a year, i.e., 1d. an acre; 22 acres of meadow worth 7s. 4d. after deductions (*ultra reprisam*), i.e., 4d. an acre; woodland and under-wood worth nothing after deductions; easement of houses (*aisiament' domorum*) with profits of the garden there worth 1s. a year after deductions; the perquisites of the court with two views of frank-pledge worth in normal years 3s. 4d.; recognition paid by customary tenants worth 6s. 8d. a year; a watermill which is worth nothing after deductions.

(ii) West Boarhunt (*Westburhunte*) with *Coumede* given in free alms to the canons with appurtenances by William de Humet': 111 acres of arable worth 18s. 6d. a year after deductions, i.e., 2d. an acre; 110 acres of pasture worth 9s. 2d. a year after deductions, i.e., 1d. an acre; 10 acres of meadow worth 3s. 4d. a year after deductions, i.e., 4d. an acre; underwood with pasture in it worth 6d. a year after deductions; easement of houses with profits of the garden there worth 6d. a year; rents of free and customary tenants, 40s. 3d., paid at the aforesaid terms; perquisites of the court, 16d., in normal years; a watermill worth 10s. 6d. a year after deductions.

(iii) Newlands (*Newelond'*) held of the abbot and convent of Quarr (*Quarrer'*), [Isle of Wight], for service of 20s.: 80 acres of arable worth [fo. 18ᵛ] 13s. 4d. a year after deductions, i.e., 2d. an acre; 102 acres of pasture worth 8s. 6d. a year, i.e., 1d. an acre; 4 acres of meadow worth 16d. a year; underwood with moors worth 8d. a year; easement of houses with profits of the garden worth nothing after deductions.

(iv) A place called Anmore (*Andemere*), held of John Andemere, but the jurors do not know by what service: 20 acres of arable worth 3s. 4d. a year after deductions, i.e., 2d. an acre; 20 acres of pasture worth 20d. a year after deductions, i.e., 1d. an acre; underwood worth 3d. a year.

(v) The manor of Stubbington (*Stubbyngton'*) held, in free alms, of Alfred Heriarda: £4 rent of assize paid at the aforesaid terms; 60 acres of arable worth 15s. a year after deductions, i.e., 3d. an acre; 56 acres of pasture worth 9s. 4d. a year after deductions, i.e., 2d. an acre.

(vi) The manor of [Priors] Dean (*Dene*) held of the king at fee farm: £15 rent of assize paid by free and customary tenants at the aforesaid terms from which £7. 18s. 5½d. is paid annually to the royal exchequer for fee farm at Michaelmas; 103 acres of arable worth 17s. 2d. a year after deductions, i. e., 2d. an acre; 200 acres of pasture worth 16s. 8d. a year after deductions, i.e., 1d. an acre; underwood worth 9s. 6d. a year after deductions; easement of houses with profits of the garden worth nothing after deductions; perquisites of the court with two views of frankpledge worth 18d. a year.

(vii) The manor of [Preston] Candover (*Candevere*) held, in free alms, of William de Pontearcharum: 42s. 4d. rent from free and customary tenants paid at the aforesaid terms; 60 acres of arable worth 10s. a year after deductions, i.e., 2d. an acre; 80 acres of pasture worth 6s. 8d. a year, i.e., 1d. an acre; perquisites of the court worth 12d. in normal years; a dovecote worth 2s. a year after deductions; easements of houses with profits of the garden worth 6d. a year after deductions.

(viii) The manor of Farlington (*Farlyngton'*) and Crookhorn (*Croukern*), held, in free alms, of John de Monte Acuto: 14s. 2d. rent from free and customary tenants paid at the aforesaid terms; 105 acres of arable worth 26d. 3d. a year, i.e., 3d. an acre; certain pastures called *Bynny* and *Asshy* worth 8s. a year after deductions; 2 acres of meadow worth 8d. a year, i.e., 4d an acre; pasture in the park worth 12d. a year after deductions; in the demesne letting of houses with profits of the garden worth 2s. a year after deductions.

The said prior and his predecessors had and held no land, tenement, rent or service, in demesne or in villeinage, acquired in the same county before or after the Statute of Mortmain, other than the aforesaid. The prior died on 28 April, i.e., Saturday after the feast of St Mark the Evangelist, in the aforesaid year. Inquisition indented and sealed by the jurors.

Total rent: £12. 7s. 6d.,[1] whence 20s. 7½d., i.e., 8¼d. a day to the king for 30 days' vacancy as aforesaid from 28 April to 27 May, according to the proportion of the aforesaid total (*iuxta ratam extent' predicte*).

[fo. 19] (b) INQUISITION held on 1 May 1381 (4 Richard II) at Salisbury (*Novum Sarum*), in the county of Wiltshire (*Wilts'*), in the presence of the Escheator. Jurors: Thomas Forde and others, who say on oath that Richard Bromden', the aforesaid prior, did not hold on the day of his death lands or tenements, in demesne or in villeinage (*in dominico nec servicio*), of the king in chief in the said county, other than 23s. rent with appurtenances derived from certain land and tenements in Aldbourne (*Aldeborn'*), and paid at Michaelmas to the office of sacristan of the same priory to buy wine for the administration of the sacrament (*pro ministracione ad altare*) there. Neither the prior nor his predecessors had any other possessions in the county, acquired before or after the Statute of Mortmain, except the aforesaid, as far as they can discover. Witnessed, etc.

(c)[2] INQUISITION has not revealed that the priory holds in Sussex any gift other than that held in free alms of the king or his progenitors, i.e. 40s. rent in Fishbourne (*Fyssheborn'*), payable at Michaelmas.

(d) INQUISITION has not revealed that the priory holds in Oxfordshire (*Oxon'*) any gift other than that held in free alms of the king or his progenitors, i.e. 56s. 8d. rent in Clanfield (*Clanefeld*), payable at Michaelmas.

1 This total does not agree with the sum of the rents quoted as payable on the Hampshire manors, viz. £25. 18s. 3½d., not including the £7. 18s. 5½d. paid to

the king from Priors Dean. The annual value of the lands etc. in Hampshire
amounts to £12. 4s. 3d., and the rents from Wiltshire, Sussex and Oxfordshire to
£6. 19s. 8d. The total value of rents and lands etc. of all the estates therefore
amounts to £45. 12s. 2½d..

2 Rubric in right-hand margin: "Concerning the same vacancy".

II 33   **27 May 1381**

COPY OF LETTERS PATENT from the King to the Escheator of
Hampshire (*Sutht'*), directing him to deliver the afore-written
temporalities.[1]

   King Richard [II] to Thomas Illeston', his Escheator in the counties
of Hampshire and Wiltshire (*Wiltes'*): William, Bishop of Winchester,
lately held the election, in the convent church of Southwick, of Brother
Richard Nowell, canon of the same house, as prior of that place,
having previously received the royal assent (*cui prius regium assensum
adhibimus*); and he confirmed the choice, as shown in his letters patent
to the king.[2] Having accepted that confirmation, the king has received
the fealty of the elected [prior], and has restored the temporalities of the
priory to him as in customary. Therefore the king orders [his escheator]
to deliver to the prior the aforesaid temporalities with appurtenances in
his bailiwick, saving rights pertaining to anyone (*salvo iure cuiuslibet*).

                                             Westminster, 4 Richard [II].

By virtue of this mandate, the same escheator delivered to Richard
Nowell, Prior of the aforesaid church, all the aforesaid temporalities
with appurtenances in his bailiwick.

1 *Cal. Pat. R., 1381–5*, p. 15.
2 *Wykeham Register* I, p. 116.

II 34   **[c. 1243–54]**[1]

[fo. 19v] CLAIM (*petitio*) of Thomas de Burhunte for land and tenements in the manor of Belney (*Belany*),[2] on account of the death of
Robert de Belany and the minority of his son and heir, both of the
demesne of the fee of Belney and of Boarhunt (*Burghunt'*), representing
¼ of a knight's fee, viz.: (i) the greater part of the court of Belney and
also two gardens called *Greynepark* and *Wynerd*, and another called
Bonbelesparyk' marking the bounds between his fee and the fee of
William de Bellony (*aceciam ÷ bunde posite inter feodum suum et feodum
Willelmi de Bellony condonant duos gardinos*); (ii) a place called *Ywem-
arl*; (iii) a place called *le Lytlemede*; (iv) another grove called *Hasillemor*;
(v) another place called *Wudafeld'*; (vi) 40½ acres of arable lying in the
field of Belney; (vii) a croft of arable lying south of the court; (viii) a
grove called *le Halselhoke*;[3] (ix) a meadow called *Estmede*; (x) another

acre called *le Westmede*; (xi) all the land at *le Frythe* with meadow, moor and grove; (xii) all the waste ground on which a windmill is now built; (xiii) all free and bond tenants belonging to the said manor of Belney. He says the aforesaid Richard de Belony[4] and his predecessors paid 5s. annually at Michaelmas to the said manor of Boarhunt for the said ¼ knight's fee, and owed suit of court three-weekly, and scutage when it occurred.

1 Robert de Belany (Bello Alneto) was holding ½ hide in East Boarhunt of William Mauduit in 1242–3 (*Book of Fees* II, p. 696). William de Belany was his son (III 460). Presumably this claim by Thomas de Burhunte preceded the inquisition held in 1254–55, by which time William de Belany had succeeded to his father's ¼ fee and was paying 5s. a year to the manor of Boarhunt (below, II 35). William had died by 6 May 1262, when a writ *de custodia* was issued concerning his son Baldwin (*Cal. Inq. p.m.* I, p. 145, no. 514). When custody of Baldwin was granted to William Maudit, 10 April 1263, it was said that William de Bello Alneto held of him ½ fee in Belney and Boarhunt, and ¼ fee of Thomas de Boarhunt, whose son was in the wardship of Robert de Sancto Johanne (*op. cit.*, p. 170, no. 560). Thomas had died by 15 June 1263, when a writ for an inquisition was issued; it was subsequently found that Thomas held 2 knight's fees of Sir Robert de Sancto Johanne, and his son and heir, Richard, was 15 years old (*Cal. Inq. p.m.* I, p. 162, no. 536).

2 Now represented by Belney farm, about 1½ miles E.N.E. of Southwick.

3 Hazelhook copse occurs in the Tithe Award.

4 *Sic* in MS. This would seem to be an error for Robert de Belany, but see below, II 37.

II 35

Free Tenants[1]

Adam atte Frithe holds 1 messuage and 12 acres and owes 3s. 7d. a year, viz. at Michaelmas 3s., and at Easter 7d., and scutage when it occurs.

Richard le Comp' holds 4 acres of arable and 1 meadow and owes 5s. a year, viz. equal amounts at Michaelmas and Easter, and scutage when it occurs.

John le Schepurde holds a messuage with curtillage and owes ½d. a year at the feast of St John the Baptist.

William Joye holds 1 acre and owes 14d. a year in equal amounts at 4 terms, and scutage when it occurs.

William Jolyf holds a messuage and 7 acres and owes 5s. a year in equal amounts at 4 terms, and scutage when it occurs.

Ralph de Kent holds a messuage and curtillage and owes 2s. a year in equal amounts at 4 terms.

Robert Lenkestoke holds 2 acres and owes 1 lb. of cummin a year at Michaelmas.

William Boll holds 1 place and owes 1 lb. of cummin a year at Michaelmas.

Richard Comyn holds 1 messuage and curtillage and owes 1 lb. of cummin a year at Michaelmas.

Robert de Hoo holds 8 acres and owes 1 pair of gloves worth ¾d. a year at Michaelmas.

Bond men (*Nativi*)

John Davy holds 4 acres and owes 4s. 8d. a year at 4 terms, scutage when it occurs, and 1 cock and 1 hen a year for churchscot.

Geoffrey [   ]² holds 4 acres and owes 4s. 8d. a year at Michaelmas, and 1 cock and 1 hen a year for churchscot.

William atte Compe holds 1 messuage and curtillage and 8 acres and owes 9s. 4½d. a year, viz. at Michaelmas and Easter in equal amounts; 1 cock and 3 hens a year for churchscot; he is also obliged to reap for ½ day at his own expense at harvest, and to give pannage dues.

Inquisition was held into the customs and rents pertaining to the manor of Boarhunt (*Bourghunte*) in the time of Thomas de Bourghunte, on the oath of law-worthy men (*legales homines*) in 39 Henry [III, 28 October 1254–27 October 1255], which said that William de Bello Alneto holds ¼ of 1 fee and pays annually 5s. at Michaelmas to the said manor of Boarhunt, and royal service and suit of court.

1 A marginal note reads: "de Belany." Presumably these are the free and bond tenants claimed by Thomas de Burhunte during the minority of William, son and heir of Robert de Bello Alneto (above, II 34 and note).

2 Blank in MS.

II 36   [1st half of the 13th century, probably before 1242]¹

Copy of Robert de Bello Alneto's charter

GRANT by Robert de Bello Alneto for his lifetime and that of his heirs (*tempore meo vel heredum meorum*) to his lord, Herbert de Burghunte, and his lord's heirs, of the same obligations per head from the men of his fee as [are due] from Herbert's men, viz. concerning amercements of Martinmas and Hocke, murder, and all those matters pertaining to the tithingman (*ad Thethyngmannum*). Witnesses: Sir Adam de Portesye; Elias de Falayse; William, his brother; Roger de Merlay; William de Hoo; Thomas de la Bere; Stephen Roget; Robert de Horsy; John de Crych; and others.

1 Sir Adam de Portesia occurs between 1208 and 1230 (I 164; *Cal. Chart. R., 1226–57* p. 119). By 1242–3, his son, Andrew, was holding a fee in Fratton of Sir Robert de Sancto Johanne (*Book of Fees* II, p. 695). Herbert de Burghunt was the father of Thomas (I 101—this deed, a gift by Thomas to Southwick Priory, was witnessed by Robert de Bello Alneto, and by Roger de Merlay, who had died by November 1250 (*Cal. Inq. p.m.* I, no. 221, p. 51)). See also II 34 and 37.

II 37 [c. 1334–40]¹

ITEM: Thomas de Burhunte claims all lands called *Crychlond*² which Richard de Belany held for ⅛ part of 1 knight's fee and all the following tenants:—

Richard atte Stokke holds 1 messuage with curtillage and 8 acres, and he owes 9s. 4½d. a year in equal amounts at Michaelmas and Easter, and 1 cock annually for churchscot.

Johanna Joye holds 1 acre and owes 14d. a year in equal amounts at 4 terms, and scutage when it occurs.³

1 This appears to be a later claim than II 34, and was possibly made by Thomas son of Gilbert de Burhunte following the death of Richard de Belany, which took place between those dates (see II 131, 78, 148).

2 Possibly now represented by Creech Farm, about 1½ miles N.E. of Southwick (Gover, p. 22).

3 This entry appears to have been added in a different hand.

II 38

Folios 20–44 consist of two indexes of the priory's charters (see p. xliv). The earlier list (*c.* 1220–60) is contained in folios 36–43; the later precedes it in folios 20–35, and is headed:

"Register of all papal privileges, charters of protection from king's of England, and deeds of covenant concerning churches, liberties, land, rents, tenements and all other possessions and matters, wherever they exist, pertaining to the priory of Southwick, as they are collected in each box in the priory's treasury. A.D. 1366, in the time of Sir Richard de Bromdene, then Prior."

These lists have not been included in this calendar, but any additional information found in the description of a charter or spelling of names has been noted where that charter occurs in the cartularies.

II 39 27 July 1334

[fo. 44ᵛ] INQUISITION, held at Southwick, 27 July, 8 Edward III, before Robert Selyman, Royal Escheator in the county of Hampshire according to the writ appointing it. Jurors: William de Wanstede; John de Kenelworth'; John de Fostebury; Robert Whitehors; Roger atte Leghe; Richard Petefyn; Richard Thom'; William Lynkestok'; John de Longe; John Horsy; John atte Hull'; and Guy de la Shipewasshe who say:

On the day he died, Gilbert de Borhunt' held the manor of Boarhunt Herbelyn with appurtenances in his demesne as in fee (*ut de feodo*) of the King in chief for the service of providing 1 man, armed with a padded tunic (*acuton'*), hauberk, basnet, mailed gloves and lance, to guard the east gate of Portchester (*Porcestr'*) for 15 days in time of war at his own cost. In [the manor] is:—a chief messuage with adjoining close worth 12d. a year; 80 acres of arable worth 20s. 3d. a year, i.e., 3d. per acre; 7 acres of meadow worth 10s. 6d. a year, i.e., 18d. per acre; no separable pasture (*pastura separabilis*); 1 acre of wood with no underwood because it was laid waste in Gilbert's time; 1 water-mill, worn out and broken down, worth 20s. a year and let at farm to Richard le Leche for that amount a year (*et sic dimittitur ad firmam Ricardo le Leche per annum*); 37s. 4d. rent from free tenants, viz:—4s. 11d. at Christmas, 7s. 7d. at Easter, 8s. 5d. at the Nativity of St John the Baptist, and 16s. 5d. at Michaelmas; pleas and perquisites of the court worth 12d. a year. Thomas de Borhunt', son of the aforesaid Gilbert, is the next heir and was 15 years of age on the feast of the Nativity of the Blessed Mary [8 September] last. Sealed by the jurors.

1 *Cal. Inq. p.m.* VII, no. 616, p. 417. Writ dated 28 May, 8 Edward III. Inquisition dated 27 June [*sic*], 8 Edward III. The extent of the manor is not given.

II 40   [?1303][1]

[fo. 45] [MEMORANDUM:] Thomas Whyting holds 3½ acres with a salt-pan and 20 lb. of lead at the lord's will. Annual rent at Martinmas 5 quarters 5 bushels of salt, valued at 5s. 7½d. And he will have, by custom, 1 cart-load of wood for the upkeep of the said salt-pan.

Richard Knave and William Rhuter each hold, pay and do the same as the aforesaid Thomas.

Nicholas Chappe, holds, pays and does the same as Thomas, except that he pays 7½ quarters of salt and it is valued at 7s. 6d., and he has 11 lbs. of lead.

John le Werghte holds 3½ acres with a salt-pan, and pays 5 quarters 5 bushels of salt at Martinmas, valued at 5s. 7½d.

1 Probably these 5 men are the 5 customary tenants of Portchester referred to in the inquisition held there on 9 December 1303 (II 40a). They paid the rent called *le Salterne*, but according to the inquisition it was paid at Michaelmas, not Martinmas. On fo. 45 there is a space between the above list and the start of the inquisition, but the two are connected by a bracket in the left-hand margin.

II 40a   9 December 1303

INQUISITION at Portchester (*Porcestria*) in the county of Hampshire, 9 December 32 Edward [II], concerning the true value of the castle of Portchester with appurtenances, viz. how much all the revenues (*exitus*) are worth a year. Jurors: Thomas Stake, Reginald Stasy, Guy de Horsy, Robert de Erly, Matthew atte Hale, John Taylefer, Robert le Eyr, John

Schouke, Henry de Borhunt', Thomas Whyting', Thomas le Ray, and Roger de Wanstede; who say there are:—

Annual rents of 110s. 11d. from 77 free tenants and 9 customary tenants, viz., 55s. 5½d. at Michaelmas, 55s. 5½d. at Easter, 30 quarters of salt a year at Michaelmas from 5 customary tenants[1]—that rent is called *le Salterne*, and is worth 12d. per quarter; 1 water-mill worth 20s. a year; pasture at Wicor (*Wycor'*)[2] and Kingston (*Kyngeston'*) worth 10s. a year; a wood called *Kyngesden*[3] containing 12 acres, [in which] 1 acre of the underwood, worth 2s., can be sold per year without causing devastation (*sine vasto*); a forest called *la Bere* and *le Rode* containing 100 acres of big timber—the annual revenues of the forest are worth nothing after the new perambulation;[4] the perquisites of the courts of Portchester and the forest are worth 24s. a year; there is a perquisite of one wild-fowl marsh on the shore (*Est ibi qued' perquisit' in mari unius volatilis*) worth 12d. a year; there are 7 customary tenants paying 2 quarters of wheat at Martinmas, worth 4s. per quarter; there are 2 customary tenants paying 2 cocks and 6 hens at the same feast, worth 1d. per cock; there is a certain ?park meadow (*parcum pratum*) worth 2s. a year. Total, £10. 8s. 7d.

1 See II 40, and note 1.

2 Near the coast, a little over a mile west of Portchester castle. The manor of Wyker in Portchester was included among the possessions of Titchfield Abbey at the time of the Dissolution (*V C H Hants* II, p. 186; III, p. 159).

3 In 1233 the Constable of Porchester had been ordered to allow the men of Portchester to have common pasture for their animals in *Kingesden* wood, as had been customary before the king took the wood into his own hands (*Cal. Close R., 1231–4* p. 21. See also II 8(d).

4 See the copy of the perambulation of 1300 (II 54, 55).

A 16th century copy of this inquisition, on paper, is in H.R.O. 5M50/1367.
Endorsements:
   a) 56
   b) Inquisition on Portchester Castle [19th century hand].

II 41   1300–1

Perambulations made of all the forests in the county of Hampshire, 29 Edward, son of King Henry

[fo. 45ᵛ] LETTERS PATENT of King Edward [I]. Since the commonalty of the realm has granted the king 1/15 of all movable goods, to be collected at Michaelmas next, he desires and concedes for himself and his heirs that the bounds of his forests in the county of Hampshire be observed as ascertained by perambulations made on his orders, viz.:

WRIT of King Edward [I] to his chosen and faithful John de Berewyk', Walter de Glouc', Walter de Pauely, and John de Crokesle. Desiring that the charter of his father, King Henry [III], concerning the forest be observed inviolate, the king has appointed them to assemble before them the Justice of his Forest this side of Trent, or his *locum tenens*, and all foresters of the fee and verderers of his forests in the counties of Hampshire and Wiltshire, for a true perambulation to be made by jurors, both knights and other law-worthy men, from the same counties; full authority is given to them to carry it out. If any one of those appointed by the king is prevented, through death or infirmity, from attending, a suitable replacement is to be chosen from the aforesaid counties. They are to summon the sheriffs of the counties to attend them, at the times and places they specify, together with the jurors, and the results of the perambulation are to be reported to the king under their seals and those of the jurors.

Witnessed by the King at Westminster, 1 April 1300.

[fo. 46] On the authority of this writ, John de Berewyce and his associates summoned the sheriff of Hampshire, who, with knights and law-worthy men of the county, with John de Romeseye, *locum tenens* of the Justice of the Forest, and with the foresters and verderers, came before them at Winchester on the day after Ascension Day, 28 Edward, son of King Henry [20 May 1300].

Those assembled chose the following jurors: John de Basynges, John de Popham, Hugh de Chikenhulle, Baldwin de Bello Alneto, John Romyn, Hugh de Escote, John de Dommere, Edmund de Sutton', Thomas de Levynton', Valentine Bek', Robert de Clere, John de Audely, Philip de Denmede, John de Thedden', Alan de Sutton', Ralph de Godeworth', Nicholas de Ichene, Henry de Berton', Philip de Heyford, William Strecche, William de Tygenhale, Thomas Stake, Robert Totteforde, Richard de Suttone, and Richard de Tystede.

The jurors made the following perambulations:

II 42

(i) The forest of ALICE HOLT and WOOLMER (*Alsesholt' et Woluemere*)[1]—in the bailiwick of Adam Gurdon, chief forester,[2] in his presence and that of Richard de Westcote and Peter de Heeches, verderers—

To the ford of Ameresford;[3] thence as far as Isingtonhatch (*Isyngtoneshacche*); to *Aldewyk'*, and through the middle of a small marshy thicket (*strouda*) to the top of the hill above *Grymeshamme*; thence to the old marl pit in *Brockareslonde*; to *Bonhommesponde*; and so by the edge (*per costeram*) of the said hill to John de Popham's wood[4] above *la Sturtelemede*, by the same edge to *la Brodehacche* at *la Vuere*, and by the same edge as far as the headland of John de Bienstede's combe (*Cumbe*);[5] thence by the hedge adjoining *la Sarstrete* on the east to *la Playstowe* of Wheatley (*Wately*), and by the east hedge the length of *la Shorstrete* as far as the foot of the bailiff of Wheatley's marl pit; thence to the top of *Ameresputte*; over the top of *Randolfesclyve* to *Modiesputte*; as far as the ash tree of South Hay (*Suthheghes*) and a little to the north, still by the edge of the hill, to *Wolstones Wolle*; straight down to

Godesmulle; to Wyck (*Wyk'*), and through John de Lynche's middle gate towards *Schorcheswelle*; ascending to the east corner of Nicholas de Corly's garden; by the hedge of the field as far as the hedge between *la Rude* and *Poghewell*; directly to *Godeswelle*; through the middle of the field of *Houk'* of *Wyk'*; through the middle of the field which is called *Poghewellestrete*; through the middle of *Berecroft* as far as the corner of the garden of *Fernhulle*; descending by *la Stanbrigge* outside John le Venutz's park[6] to *Curesdiche*; by the hedge of the said park to *Stanrigge* by the ditch of the park to *Dansiesmersche*; beyond the ditch of *Dansiesmersche* as far as *Manduteshacche*;[7] by the stream[8] descending to below Doget's house, and to *la Holelane*; through the middle of Oakhanger (*Hokhangre*) following (*iuxta*) the east hedge as far as the main road which leads to *Hethgate*; around a certain marsh, which is called Oakwood Ponds (*Houcwode*), to *la Hethlak'* under *la Honne*; to *la Borghurn'*; and descending by the stream as far as the aforesaid *Hethgate*; by the main road which leads to Blackmoor (*Blakemere*), and by the road which runs to Tealbridge (*la Thelebrigg'*),[9] and so descending by [fo. 46ᵛ] Redwater (*la Ricdewatere*) to Cuppynge's house;[10] thence as far as the long ford; down Longmere (*Longemere*) as far as the high road which leads from Woolmer (*Wolluemere*) to Midhurst,[11] and by the same road to *Bokereswelle*; thence by *Thevenepathe* as far as *Oulethorn*; and by the same *Thevenepathe* to Conford (*Querneforde*); thence descending by the stream[12] to *Southeles*, to *Bradebrigg'*, to the ford called *Durneford*, to *Lingfordbrigge*, and on as far as the bridge of *Brockesheved'*, to *Hutenesford*, to the monks' mill of Dockenfield (*Dockenesfeld*), and as far as the stream which descends from *Coppehacche*; and so ascending by the same stream between the land of James le Beel[13] in the county of Surrey and of Dockenfield in the county of Hampshire as far as *Bouthelerespulle*; thence by the boundary dividing the aforesaid counties as far as *Kynewardeshatte* and *Udeshacche*, and ascending the stream to Rowledge (*la Rowediche*), and following the county boundary as far as *Hommengesmere*; thence ascending by the bank of the stream to the aforesaid ford of *Ameresforde*.

And the jurors say that the whole forest of Alice Holt and Woolmer was enclosed within the aforesaid metes and bounds before the coronation of King Henry [II], great-grandfather of the present king.[14] The same King Henry afforested the wood of Chasehurst beyond these metes and bounds; it was his demesne wood. It is now in the hands of the king, and he has no other wood outside the aforesaid metes and bounds adjoining the aforesaid forest. The officials of the present king's father [Henry III] afforested the vill of Colemore (*Colemere*) together with the woods of the vills of Faringdon (*Faryndon'*) and Chawton (*Chauton'*), and a certain part of the vill of *Colride*, with lands, groves, meadows and pastures of *Colride* to the forks (*furce*) of Wely, viz. from the king's highway which leads towards Farnham to the watercourse of the Wey (*Waye*). And all the other woods, groves, lands, and places of the aforesaid appropriated forest which are disafforested by this perambulation were afforested by the officials of King Henry [II], and by those of King Richard and King John;[15] but what and how much in each individual reign no one can now show.

1 I am indebted to Mr Edward Yates for the identification of placenames.

A copy of this perambulation is given in full in Latin as Appendix I to the 6th Report of the Woods and Land Revenue Commission, 1790 (*House of Commons Journal* 45, p. 136). There is considerable variation in the spelling of placenames.

2 John de Venuz held the bailiwick of the forests of Alice Holt and Woolmer in fee from the king. In 1257, because of age and infirmity, he obtained the king's permission to grant it for life to Adam Gurdon, his son-in-law (*Cal. Pat. R., 1247-58*, p. 547). John died in 1260 leaving an infant son, John, as his heir. After Adam's death in 1305, the bailiwick reverted to John le Venuz the younger, then said to be more than 40 years old. (*Cal. Inq. p.m.* I, no. 458, p. 126; IV, no. 273, p. 188).

3 Ameresford is unidentified, but was on the River Wey near Farnham.

4 John de Popham held Binsted about ¾ mile south of Isington (*VCH Hants* II, p. 484).

5 This John de Benstede, or possibly his son of the same name, died on 29 June 1358. He was then holding the manor of Binsted from Sir John de Popham (*Cal. Inq. p.m.* X, no. 468, p. 372).

6 The park was in East Worldham, which was held by the Venuz family (*VCH Hants* II, p. 518).

7 Probably the hatch or gate of Hartley Mauditt.

8 Oakhanger Stream.

9 The road would have run roughly on the line of the A325.

10 Now Kippences, north-east of West Liss.

11 Probably the Roman road (to Silchester).

12 The eastern branch of the River Wey.

13 Now represented by Bealeswood.

14 i.e. before 19 December 1154.

15 There is an account of the bounds of Alice Holt and Woolmer forests in the reign of King John in the *Pontissara Register* II, p. 450.

II 43

(ii) The forest of BERE (*la Bere*) by WINCHESTER—in the presence of John de Berewyk' and his associates; John de Romesye, *locum tenens* of the Justice of the Forest; John de Farlyngton', forester of the fee; and Richard le Port of Sparsholt and Adam de Kyngesbrigg', verderers of the aforesaid forest—

First to *Edrichestapel*; thence keeping to the road from *Langeley*, to *la Whyteflode*; thence as far as the north gate of *Haselye*; thence to *Merkeweye*; to *Heggesflod*; to *Lypsedecroft*; to *Twyseledewaterhoc*; to *Wuderherlenepath*; to the road (*via*) called *Burgate*; thence by the new clearing (*trenchia*) below Hambledon (*Hameledon*) to Hambledon; to Flexland (*Flexlond'*), and thence as far as the aforesaid *Edrichestapel*.

The jurors say that these metes and bounds used to enclose the whole forest of Bere before the coronation of King Henry [II]. The king has no demesne wood adjoining these bounds, and all woods, lands and places outside them, which are disafforested by this perambulation, were appropriated to the forest after the coronation of King Henry [II], but which ones, and how much, in each individual reign, no one can be sure.

1 Also known as West Bere or Bere Ashley. The custody of this forest was held by the lord of the manor of Ashley, about 6 miles west of Winchester.

A copy of this perambulation is given in full in Latin as Appendix I to the 13th Report of the Woods, Lands and Revenues Commission (*House of Commons Journal* 47, p. 1038). There is some variation in the spelling of placenames: *Haselye* appears as *Asscheley*.

2 John de Farlington's mother, Joan, had inherited the manor of Ashley and bailiwick from her mother, whose father, William Briwere, had frequently entertained King John there. When Joan died in widowhood in 1275, the bailiwick was said to be worth 40s. and to be held of the king in chief for keeping the vert and venison for the king's use (*Cal. Inq. p.m.* II, no. 107, p. 73). John succeeded his mother and held the manor and bailiwick until 1312, when he granted them to Hugh le Despenser the elder, in return for 20 marks a year for life (*VCH Hants* IV, p. 440).

II 44

[fo. 47] (iii) The bailiwick of BAGSHOT (*Baggehurst*)—in the presence of John de Berewyk' and his associates; John de Romesye, *locum tenens* of the Justice of the Forest; John de London', keeper of the forest; and William de Bynteworthe, verderer. The jurors for that bailiwick say that that part of the forest of Windsor (*Wyndesouere*) which is in the county of Hampshire, called the bailiwick of Bagshot, begins where it adjoins the forest of Alice Holt (Alsesholte), viz.:

At *Houvyggwere*; thence by the boundary dividing the counties of Hampshire and Surrey to *Wlueputte*; thence to *Warebrave*; to *Gloreneye*; to *Langebrigg'*; to *Lynesiesford*; to *Coleford*; to *Bradnesford*; and by the edge of the bailiwick of Eversley (*Everley*) to Winchester.

It was afforested after the coronation of King Henry [II]; so that before that date, so far as the bailiwick of Bagshot (*Baggeshete*) was concerned, [only] the wood called *Whytmondesley* was the king's demesne wood; it still is, and it pertains to the manor of Odiham, so no other royal official concerns himself therein.

1 The bailiwick of Bagshot ran from the Blackwater River, which formed the boundary between Hampshire and Surrey, south-westwards to Winchester. It shared a common boundary with Eversley (II 46) in the west and with Alice Holt and Woolmer (II 42) in the south-east.

2 Before his death, which had taken place by 3 April 1306, John de London had granted to Edward, Prince of Wales, 126 acres of arable purpresture in Windsor forest, which he had held of the king for an annual rent of 6d. and acre. The prince had re-enfeoffed John for life, with reversion to himself and his heirs (*Cal. Inq. p.m.* IV, no. 382, p. 250-1).

II 45

(iv) NEW FOREST (*Nova Foresta*)—in the presence of John de Berewyk'
and his associates; John de Romesye, *locum tenens* of the Justice of the
Forest; John Randolf, then steward (*senescallus*) of the aforesaid forest;
and Gilbert de Teye, John de Cauce, and William de Buttesthon,
verderers—

The forest begins at *Tyntebrok';*[1] then [continues] by the road to
Shortescrouche; to *Bradeneswell'*; to *Cherchestyele*; to *Holeweye*;[2] to
Horewhytheghe; to *Heggesflode*;[3] to *Cuttedelane*;[4] to *la Brigge*;[5] to
Burnford Bridge (*Borneford'*),[6] and keeping along the stream to *Burde-
ford';*[7] thence as far as the place called *Cuttedehok'*; to *Riedeclynesford*;[8]
to *Cerkeford*[9]; to *Horemore*,[10] and so by the marshy thicket (*stroda*) as
far as the stream which comes from *Gaywyldeslonde,* and by the hedge
of the same croft directly to *Chekegrove*; thence descending to Bartley
Bourne (*Alsiesbourne*),[11] and along the hedge to *la Heggelane*; thence to
Otereslane,[12] and along the same to *Pynthorneshurne,*[13] to *Mangeford',*[14]
and by the same to *Terndehulle*; to *Potteresforde*;[15] to *Fleteswodes-
westende*;[16] thence by the road to Dykes Beach (*Dykedebech'*), and as
far as the new ditch of *Langeley*;[17] thence by the king's highway[18] between
the land of the prior of Breamore (*Brommore*) and the land of John de
Faudon' as far as the corner of *Ypelyngescrofte,*[19] and by the main
road to Applemoor Hill (*Dounshamele*);[20] thence to Horestone Hill
(*Stonyehupe*)[21]; to *Bothehaghe*;[22] to *Northewell'*; to *la Hacche* of *la
Stonyelonde*; to *Butebrigge*;[23] by *Wamelemore* as far as the sea,[24] and
by the sea to *Roggesflete*;[25] to *Oslakeford*; to *Crokeslonde,* and to the
street (*vicus*) called *Nutleghesdych'*; thence descending by a small ditch
to *Narkydelwell';*[26] to *Mekestake*; by the edge of Langley (*Langeley*)
Wood[27] to the west corner of *la Wodecrofte,* and by the same croft to
the other *Merkyngstake,* [and by the marshy Dark Water (*Derkewatere*)
Stream[28] to the sea; thence by the sea to the *Merkyngstake*] of Sharpricks
(*Scharperisse*);[29] thence to the ditch called *Dereclausum,* and by the same
ditch from the north as far as Ralph le Hurt's house;[30] thence westwards
as far as the street to *la Dereligh,* and along it to *Prattesstyghele*;
thence by the road to *Coppesstyghele*; by the ditch of *Cockeslonde* to
Gaugerescroft; to *Pecchegrove,* and from the south of the same to
Terwestighele; thence by *Dereligh* to *Goudichestighele*; to *Pratteshok',*
and by the long ditch between the lands of Adam Stegg' and *Depemanton'*
to the king's highway[31] which leads from Walhampton (*Wolhampton*)
towards Beaulieu (*Bellus Locus*); thence to Vicar's Hill (*Wykeneshulee*)
of Warborne (*Wereborne*),[32] and thence descending by the ditch to Boldre
(*Bolre*); thence directly beyond the water through the middle of two
crofts to *Gervesburgh'*; thence to the tall (*longus*) oak,[34] and by the
king's highway to *Baterhammesdich'*[35] as far as the corner of *la Stinelond*;
thence to *Brokebrigg',*[36] and ascending by the stream to the ditch at the
back of Fetmore Pond (*Fettemere*);[37] thence by the great ditch as far as
the mound (*Hoga*) of *Northweye,*[38] and by the ditch to the head of
the great ditch west of Durnstown (*Stanforde*);[39] by the stream to
Stanfordeshende; thence to *Whitedicheswesthende,*[40] and by the same to
Hoggeleye and to *Stapeldene*; thence by the stream to *Gerenesladeford';*[41]

through *Fernycroft*; by the ditch bordering the king's highway from *Crokesfordescrofte* and ascending by *Whiterden'* as far as the marlpit of *Beaurepeyr*;[42] by the hedge to Rowditch (*Roughedich'*);[43] thence to Blackditch (*Blakedich'*); to *Haghethornneslade*; to Devil's Den (*Develden'*);[44] thence ascending as far as *Hogham Everlonesmere*; to *Whythindesburgh*; to *la Combaresdich'*, and along it as far as the road which leads to Shirley (*Schirligh*) towards *Everleiescrouch'*; thence to Lugden Barrow (*Lokedenesburgh'*),[45] and to the road by the west of *Thurleden'*; directly to Alisborough (*Hayllardeburgh*); to Knaves Ash (*Knaveneburgh'*),[46] and descending as far as the hedge which divides William de Butesthorn's croft from William Giles' land; thence to *Merkyngstake* next to *la Hyde*; to *Greneslade* of Burcombe (*Buricumbe*);[47] to Linford (*Lymford*);[48] to Whickens Stake (*Wykeneslade*);[49] to *Rodene-shened'*;[50] thence descending to Dockens Water (*Bokeneswater*)[51] and by Dockens Water to la *Merkyngstak'*; to *Whitladdeslak'*; to *Kyngburgh'*[52] above Goreley Hill (*Gorlynggesdoune*), and directly to *la Putte* in *Merkyngeslade*;[53] to *Berlyght*; to Shallowford (*Colyeresford*);[54] to Abbots Well (*Albitewelle*);[55] to *Goseleye*;[56] to Blissford (*Byseford*);[57] thence ascending the stream to Robert Ernys' court;[58] through the middle of his court and garden, coming out on the king's highway which runs between Fritham and Fordingbridge (*Forthyngebrigge*); thence to *Butine*,[59] and as far as *la Haccheghate*;[60] to *la Hulle*; to Giles' Well (*Gelewelle*);[61] along the stream which runs down into the River Avon (*Avene*);[62] thence following the same river to Milton (*Muletone*),[63] and ascending by the ditch of the canons of Breamore to the hedge of Hale (*la Hale*);[64] ascending by that hedge to the top (*capud*) of *Suthulle*; thence by the king's highway to Millersford (*Medenesford'*)[65] northwards by *Wellemereslak'*[66] to Woolmer Post (*Wolnedeneshende*),[67] which ascends by (*in*) *Markeweye* to *Goreshende*; thence along the king's highway to *Tytebrok'*.

The jurors say that these metes and bounds used to enclose the whole New Forest before the coronation of King Henry [II]. The present king has no demesne wood outside the same bounds adjoining the said forest. All woods, lands, and places outside these metes and bounds appropriated to the aforesaid forest, which are disafforested by this perambulation, were appropriated after the said coronation, but which ones, and how much, in each individual reign, no one can now be sure.

This perambulation is printed in full in Latin as Appendix 3 to the Fifth Report of the Woods and Land Commission, 1789 (*House of Commons Journal* 44, pp. 574–5). There are again considerable variations in the spelling.

I have followed the identification of place-names made by Mr David Stagg in his translation of a perambulation of the bounds of the New Forest carried out in 1217–18 (*Report of the Hampshire Field Club and Archaeological Society, New Forest Section* 13, January 1974, pp. 26–7). See also his translation of the perambulation made in 1670 (*A Calendar of New Forest Documents 15th–17th Centuries* (Hampshire Record Series, 5; 1983) pp. 233–4).

I am also indebted to Mr Arthur Clark, who has shared with me the results to date of his field studies of the bounds. This has enabled me to include the following grid references of various boundary sites which he has identified, either with certainty or with a reasonable degree of probability:

1 Probably Leburn Gutter,
  SU 242163
2 SU 259177
3 SU 265172
4 SU 265168
5 SU 269166
6 SU 270155
7 SU 276136
8 Probably Wittensford,
  SU 283137
9 SU 293137
10 SU 295136
11 SU 306128
12 SU 137117
13 SU 319114
14 SU 323112
15 SU 327109
16 SU 334108
17 SU 353096
18 SU 364085
19 SU 384077
20 SU 397076
21 SU 403065
22 SU 418055
23 SU 422066
24 SU 431073
25 SU 451050
26 SU 432046
27 SU 448015
28 SZ 452992
   The passage in square brackets is
   omitted from the cartulary copy.
29 SZ 358952
30 Now Pilewell House,
   SZ 353958
31 SZ 336971
32 SZ 326974
33 SZ 322974

34 SZ 316973
35 SZ 313975
36 SZ 305979
37 SZ 292983
38 SZ 287983
39 SZ 282985
40 SZ 269992
41 SZ 266985
42 SZ 225984
43 SZ 215983
44 SZ 204998
45 SU 189009
46 SU 184040
47 SU 181061
48 SU 179068
49 SU 179083
50 SU 178092
51 SU 182100
52 SU 182109
53 SU 181114
54 SU 179123
55 SU 178129
56 SU 173133
57 SU 170135
58 Now Arniss Farm,
   SU 175144
59 SU 170144
60 Probably Sandy Balls Gate,
   SU 169145
61 SU 169157
62 SU 164162
63 SU 162175
64 SU 175176
65 SU 192169
66 SU 200176
67 SU 210179

II 46

[fo. 48] (v) The bailiwick of EVERSLEY (*Evereslye*)[1]—in the presence
of John de Berewyk' and his associates; Thomas Paynel, forester of the
fee;[2] Henry de Maneto and John de Hereyerd', verderers.

The bailiwick begins at the stream which flows from *Doddebrok'* between the land of the prior of St Swithun's, Winchester,[3] and the land of John Hagheman; thence to *Haughtesford'* above the Blackwater (*Blakewatere*), and by that stream as far as *Smythesford'*; thence to *Thursterford'*, and to the bank of *Sualeweye*; thence to the corner of John Bruton's croft, and directly by the county boundary to *Hayweye*; to *Fouelegate*, and by the north side of the wood called *Graundesgrove*; thence by the hedge which divides the counties of Hampshire and Wiltshire,[4] keeping to the north side of the croft called *Graundeslond'*, directly by the county boundary to Stanford End (*Stanford'*);[5] thence by the side of the bailiwick of Pamber (*Pambere*) to the vill of Headbourne Worthy (*Wordi Mortymer*).

The jurors say that all this bailiwick of Eversley was afforested after the coronation of King Henry [II], and that there was no forest within the aforesaid metes and bounds before that time.

1 Eversley Forest lay between the Forests of Pamber to the west and Bagshot to the east; very narrow at its southern end near Winchester, and broadening out as it ran north-eastwards to the county boundary between Hampshire and Berkshire.

2 Probably this was the Thomas Paynel who died in 1314, and was then holding the manor of Oakhanger from the king in chief for keeping the forest of Woolmer, and 2 assarts in Pamber forest for 11s. (*Cal. Inq. p.m.* V, no. 456, p. 254).

3 St Swithun's Priory held a large amount of land in north-east Hampshire, from Long Sutton and Crondall northwards to Yateley.

4 Probably a scribal error for Berkshire.

5 The starting place for the perambulation of Pamber forest, at its north-eastern extremity (II 47).

II 47

(vi) The bailiwick of PAMBER (*Pambere*)[1]—in the presence of John de Berewyk' and his associates; Thomas Paynel, forester of the fee;[2] and Nicholas de la Berton'and Hugh de Shirefeld, verderers.

The bailiwick begins at Stanford End (*Stamford'*) and ascends the Loddon (*Lodene*) stream as far as the stream called *Blakewatere*[3] which descends from the Loddon, ascending by the same stream to Houndsmill (*Hundeswelle*) above the *Blakewatere*; thence by the same stream, [and] as far as Nicholas de Stanwode's house to the west;[4] thence keeping on beyond (*super*) to the stream which runs down to Axmansford (*Anadesford*) as far as the *Frenburne*, which joins the stream from Axmansford; from the *Frenburne* to the *Haleburne*; thence by the road which leads to *Trehages*[5] on the county boundary between Hampshire and Berkshire; thence to Impstone (*Ingeston'*); to *Uppetruwe*; to *Hoddeston'*, and by the said county boundary to Stanford End.

The jurors say that the bailiwick does not exceed these metes and bounds; any [lands and woods] outside them, which are disafforested by this perambulation, were afforested after the coronation of King Henry [II], but which ones, and how much, in individual reigns, no one can now be sure.

1 I am indebted to Dr Paul Stamper for the identification of placenames in this perambulation. He has described the forest as occupying, roughly speaking, the central part of the Hampshire woodlands, adjoining the boundary with Berkshire, and stretching approximately 9 miles from east to west, and a maximum of 6 miles from north to south. The overall area subject to forest law amounting to something like 43 square miles (P. A.Stamper, "The Medieval Forest of Pamber, Hampshire", *Landscape History* 5 (1983) pp. 41–52). To the west of Pamber lay the bailiwick of Freemantle, and to the east, Eversley.

2 See II 46, note 2.

3 Blackwater was an old name for the River Loddon.

4 The western most part of the bounds lay through Sandford wood.

5 i.e. the three barrows on the county boundary (SU 579627).

II 48

(vii) The bailiwick of FREEMANTLE (*Freomantel*)[1]—in the presence of John de Berewyk' and his associates; John de Keniggeworth', forester of the fee; Robert de la Sale and John de Lovers, verderers.

Beginning at the hedge of the park of Freemantle[2] on the west; descending by the boundary between the pastures of the dean and chapter of Rouen (*Rokomagen'*), [Normandy][3], and the combes of Freemantle, to *Whytedelle* adjoining *la Stoynyestrete*; thence to *Uthaghesdelle*; to *la Pyk'*, which is the boundary between the pasture of North Oakley (*Northokle*) and the combes of Freemantle; thence ascending northwards to the aforesaid hedge of the park.

[fo. 48ᵛ] The jurors say that these metes and bounds enclose the whole of the aforesaid forest. Outside those bounds the manor of Polhampton with adjoining woods was afforested in the time of King Henry [III], father of the present king, while it was in the hands of the Countess of Aumale (*Albe Marle*); now it is in the king's hands.[4] All other woods, lands and places appropriated to the aforesaid bailiwick, which are disafforested by this perambulation, were afforested by royal officials after the coronation of King Henry [II], but which [lands], and how much, in individual reigns, no one can be sure.

1 The bailiwick of Freemantle lay between those of Finkley (II 49) and Doiley (II 51) in the west, and Pamber (II 47) in the east. The name is still preserved in Freemantle Farm, less than ½ mile south-east of North Oakley.

2 A reference to the royal estate of Freemantle, which comprised a manor, houses and park. King John was a frequent visitor to Freemantle. Freemantle Farm is said to be the site of his house (*VCH Hants* IV, p. 252).

3 In 1107 Henry I had granted Kingsclere, about 4 miles north-north-east of North Oakley, to the church of St Mary, Rouen. The grant was confirmed by Henry III in 1227, following his grant to the dean and chapter of the wood of *Witingelegh,* to be held in free alms quit of forest law (*Cal. Chart. R., 1226-57* pp. 44, 46). In 1331 an inquisition was held into a claim by the royal foresters of Pamber that 100 acres of wood and 300 acres of pasture held by the dean and chapter of Rouen were within the bounds of the forest. In 1335 the link with Rouen ended when the dean and chapter obtained a royal licence to grant these possessions to the archbishop of York (*VCH Hants* IV, p. 251).

4 In 1205 King John granted land in Polhampton to Baldwin de Béthune, Count of Aumale, and in 1225 the remainder of the manor was granted by Henry III to Baldwin's step-son and heir, William de Forz. The manor passed to William's son, William, and then to his grandson, Thomas (*VCH Hants* IV, p. 213); he died in 1269 and was succeeded by his sister, Aveline de Forz, as Countess of Aumale. In the same year she married Edmund, Earl of Lancaster; she died without issue on 10 November 1274 (*HBC* p. 416).

The name Polhampton survives in Polhampton Lodge 1½ miles west of North Oakley.

II 49

(viii) The bailiwick of the forest of FINKLEY (*Fynkeley*)[1]—in the presence of John Berewyk' and his associates; John de Romeseye, *locum tenens* of the Justice of the Forest; John de Insula, forester of the fee;[2] Roger Lecford' and Thomas Spireboc, verderers.

Beginning at *Durerdeshord'*; keeping to the edge of the wood as far as the road which runs from Stoke (*Crockerestok'*) to Andover (*Andevere*); thence to the corner of the hedge called *Burghegge*; ascending as far as *Scotfordelangeshegge*; to the hedge of *Blomescrofte*, and by that hedge to Woodhouse Lane (*la Wodehoselane*);[3] to the corner of *Wysecrofte*, and ascending by that croft to *Whithondesden'*; ascending by the hedge as far as the ditch of *Basywelonde*, and by that ditch to *Blakedeneshende*; ascending by the hedge of *Appelcroft* to the road from *Mayesgrove*, and directly by the hedge as far as the corner of *Mayesgrove*; by the road which leads between the pasture of Charlton (*Cherleton'*) and *Knythenelese* to *Chilegrove*; by the edge of *Bilegrove* as far as the ditch which separates the lands of Charlton and Knights Enham (*Knythteshenham*); descending by that ditch to *la Bruyl*[4] of Charlton, and keeping to the same ditch, between the land of Charlton and the aforesaid *Bruyl*, to the road which leads from Charlton towards [   ]; keeping to the ditch bordering the king's highway as far as the ditch at the east corner of *Langhanger*; thence by the ditch of *Lawedelonde* as far as the cross in *la Heghestrete*; by the road which leads to *Northwodedelle*; by the hedge to *Ryngat*, and ascending to *la Ricdesherde* by the hedge and by the road which leads to *Penmere*; and so from the east (*a parte orientali*) by the hedge which runs to *la Wolhouse*, and by that hedge to the east corner of the croft of *Penemere*; directly by the path to St Andrew's croft; by the hedge of *la Knolledich'* as far as *Knolledich'southende*; ascending as far as the clearing (*trenchia*) which separates the wood of the abbess of Tarrant (*Tarente*)[5] from that of the prior of St Swithun's, Winchester,[6] and so keeping on the north (*a parte boriali*) of that clearing as far as *Ridehord'*; thence by the clearing on the west (*a parte occidentali*) between the woods of the king and of the prior of St Swithun's as far as the road which runs from Stoke to Andover; thence by the boundary separating the king's wood from the prior's, to the road from Chapmansford (*Chapmannesford'*) to Andover, and by that road to *Fastendich'*; thence descending by the small ditch to the aforesaid *Durerdeshorde*.

The jurors say that these metes and bounds used to enclose the whole of the forest of Finkley, before the coronation of King Henry [II]. The [fo. 49] King has no demesne wood adjoining the bounds of that forest. All woods, lands and places outside these metes and bounds, which are disafforested by this perambulation, were appropriated after the coronation of King Henry [II]; but which ones, and how much, in each individual reign, no one can be sure.

1 Finkley, Chute (II 50) and Doiley (II 51) together comprised the fee of John de Insula and shared the same verderers. In the thirteenth century the whole area of northern Hampshire from Hurstbourne Tarrant in the east to the Wiltshire border in the west had been included in the great forest of Chute, which also extended into Wiltshire. As defined by this perambulation, Finkley covered an area extending about 6 miles to the west from Hurstbourne Tarrant and about 3 miles from north to south. To the north lay the bailiwick of Doiley, and to the west, Chute.

Finkley survives as the name of a house and two farms just north-east of Andover.

2 John de Insula and his wife Nichola were granted the bailiwick of the forest of Chute and the heaths of Andover by Nichola's uncle, Matthew de Columbariis, to be held of the king in chief for 10s. a year. On 4 November 1281 the king instructed his barons of the exchequer to acquit Matthew of the 10s. rent and charge it to John and Nichola (*Cal. Close R., 1279–88* p. 104). When he died in 1304, John still held the bailiwick of Chute by grand serjeanty of keeping that forest and paying 10s. a year to the king. He also held several manors on the Isle of Wight and other property in Hampshire (*Cal. Inq. p.m.* IV, no. 232, p. 153).

3 Besides the bailiwick of the forest of Chute, John de Insula held at the time of his death "a ruinous house at *la Wodehouse* where the foresters are received" (*ibid.*).

4 Probably heath-land.

5 In 1266 Henry III had granted Hurstbourne, later known as Hurstbourne Tarrant to the abbey of Tarrant Crawford in Dorset. The woodland thus acquired proved a valuable source of revenue to the abbey. In 1292 Edward I granted a licence to the abbess to sell 40 oaks from her wood at Hurstbourne within the forest of Finkley for the settlement of the abbey's debts (*VCH Hants* IV, p. 319). A similar licence for the sale of 40 acres of wood was obtained in 1302 (*Cal. Pat. R., 1303–7* p. 68). In 1343, following the destruction of some of the abbey's property in Dorset by enemy action, the king gave permission for 200 acres of its demesne woodland in the forest of Chute to be felled at the rate of 20 acres a year, and for the land to be enclosed (*Cal. Pat. R., 1343–5* p. 127).

6 The priory of St Swithun's held Stoke, 1½ miles south-east of Hurstbourne Tarrant, as a tithing of its manor of Hurstbourne Priors. Many of the tenants of that manor held pieces of woodland in *Crokkereswode* at an annual rent of 1s. 6d. an acre, (K. A. Hanna, "An Edition of the Custumal of St Swithun's Priory", unpublished University of London M.A. thesis, 1954, I, pp. 288–340).

II 50

(ix) The forest of CHUTE[1]—in the presence of John de Berewyk' and his associates; John de Insula, forester of the fee;[2] Roger de Lecford and Thomas Spirecok, verderers.

Beginning at *Grymesdich'ende* which separates the woods of the king and Ralph Walke; thence, keeping to the road which leads towards (*iuxta*) *Frith'*, as far as *la Dikedeheghe*; continuing along the boundary between the king's wood and the pasture of *Marrays*; thence by the edge of the wood as far as the corner of *Durdantescrofte*; by the hedge to *Burchecrofte,* and by that croft to Tangley Bottom (*Capyedene*); along Tangley Bottom as far as *Okwaye*; thence ascending by the same *Okewaye* to *Grymesdicheswestende,* and by *Grymesdich'* as far as *Grymesdichesestende* aforesaid.

The jurors say that these metes and bounds used to enclose the forest of Chute before the coronation of King Henry [II], and that the king has no demesne wood adjoining that forest. All woods, lands and places appropriated to the aforesaid forest, outside these metes and bounds, and disafforested by this perambulation, were appropriated after the coronation of King Henry [II], but which ones, and how much, in each particular reign, no one can be sure.

1 See II 49, note 1. For a map and explanation of the bounds of the forests of Chute in Wiltshire in the time of Henry III, and in 1300, see *VCH Wilts* IV, pp. 452-3. *Capydene* is identified as Tangley Bottom, and Grim's Ditch as Chute Causeway.

2 See II 49, note 2.

II 51

(x) The forest of DOILEY (*Dygherley*)[1]—in the presence of John de Berewyk' and his associates; John de Insula, forester of the fee;[2] Roger de Lecford' and Thomas Spirecok', verderers.

Beginning at *Falkestapel*; thence keeping to the king's highway as far as the corner of the wood; to the edge of the wood as far as the ditch of *Medenedon',* and by that ditch as far as the ditch of Faccombe (*Faccumbe*);[3] thence by the boundary between the king's wood and Faccombe wood to the main road which runs from *Bolkeputte* and separates the king's wood from that of the prior of St Swithun's, Winchester;[4] [thence] as far as the aforesaid *Falkestapel*.

The jurors say that these metes and bounds used to enclose the whole forest of Doiley before the coronation of King Henry [II]. The king has no demesne wood outside them adjoining the forest. All woods, lands and places appropriated to the said forest, outside these metes and bounds, and disafforested by this perambulation, were appropriated to the forest after the coronation of King Henry [II]; but which ones, and how much, in the reign of each individual king, no one can now be sure.

1 See II 49, note 1. Doiley manor is a little over a mile north of Hurstbourne Tarrant.

2 See II 49, note 2.

3 Faccombe is a mile south of the county boundary between Hampshire and Berkshire and less than 2 miles north of Doiley manor; between the two lies Faccombe wood.

4 Possibly this was the eastern boundary; the priory of St Swithun's held Binley and Stoke as tithings of its large manor of Hurstbourne Priors.

II 52

(xi) The forest of BUCKHOLT (*Bocholte)* PUTTON'[1]—in the presence of John de Berewyk', etc.; John de Vyene, bailiff of Clarendon (*Clarindon);*[2] John de Putton', forester of the fee;[3] Benedict de Galrogg' and John de Molendinis, verderers.

Beginning at *Stonyedene*; thence as far as *Whitheweye*; to *Thorngate*; following the ditch by *Kyngrode* to *Merkeweye*; thence by *Merkeweye* as far as the corner of Oliver de la Suche's hedge; to *Primedene*; to *Pippemere*; to *Ykeneldestrete*; thence by the boundary between the king's wood and the aforesaid Oliver's to *Portweye*; thence to the aforesaid *Stonyedene.*

Note: there is another piece of forest called *Haywode* in this bailiwick: it begins at *Merkeweye* and proceeds as far as the grove of *Basyngestok'*; thence to *la Hulle,* and so to *Merkeweye* along the hedge of Bentley (*Benetley).*

The jurors say that these metes and bounds used to enclose that [fo. 49ᵛ] bailiwick before the coronation of King Henry [II]. The king has no demesne wood adjoining that bailiwick outside these bounds. All woods, lands, and places outside these metes and bounds, which are disafforested by this perambulation, were appropriated to the bailiwick after the coronation of King Henry [II]; but which ones, and how much, in each individual reign, no one can now be sure.

1 The forest of Buckholt lay south of that part of the forest of Chute which was in Hampshire. On the west it was divided by the county boundary from the Wiltshire forest of Clarendon to which it was closely linked; this western boundary, as determined by a perambulation made in 1327, is shown on a map of Clarendon and Melchet forests in *VCH Wilts* IV, p. 454.

2 On 3 March 1291 John de Vienne was appointed to take custody of the bailiwick of the forest of Clarendon during the king's pleasure. He was succeeded in 1308 by William de Beauchamp (*Cal. Pat. R., 1281–92* p. 424; *Cal. Pat. R., 1307–13* p. 67).

3 The east bailiwick of Buckholt, together with responsibilities in Clarendon forest, had been held by the Putton family for at least three generations. Inquisitions held in 1255 after the death of James de Putton, John's grandfather, found that he had held a virgate of the king in Wiltshire for keeping Clarendon forest, and another in Hampshire for keeping the bailiwick of Buckholt; doing service himself on horseback, providing a man on foot at his own expense, and paying 20s. a year to the warden of Clarendon forest, who was evidently receiving it for the king (*Cal. Inq. p.m.* I, no. 330, p. 88). James was succeeded by son William, who died in 1297. William's holding in Hampshire was described as 40 acres with pasture at Broughton *ibid.,* III, no. 442, p. 339). William's son, John, succeeded him; when John died in 1320 he was holding 50½ acres in Broughton of the king for keeping the forest of Buckholt, and a messuage with 20 acres in Pitton, Wiltshire, for keeping the king's park of Clarendon. He was succeeded by his son, William (*ibid.,* VI, no. 253, p. 149).

II 53

(xii) The forest of BUCKHOLT (*Bocholte*) LOVERAZ[1]—in the presence of John de Berewyk', [etc.]; Stephen Loveraz, forester of the fee;[2] Benedict de Galrogg', and John de Molendinis, verderers.

Beginning at *Denweye,* which runs from Richard Beauchief's house to the cross [of] *Dubbet;* thence, keeping to the boundary between the counties of Hampshire and Wiltshire, to *Ykenildestrete;* by that street to *la Pulle;* and so by the same way (*via*) to *la Holeweye;* thence to *Wyntcroft;* to *Stomede;* thence by the north of *Lo* . . . . *osthorn*[3] as far as *Thornhurst',* and to the meadow [at] *Deneweye.*

The jurors say that these metes and bounds used to enclose that bailiwick before the coronation of King Henry [II]. The king has no demesne wood adjoining the bailiwick outside these bounds. All woods, lands, and places outside these bounds, which are disafforested by this perambulation, were appropriated after the coronation of King Henry [II]; but which ones, and how much, in each individual reign, no one can now be sure.

1 See II 52, note 1. This was the western bailiwick of the forest of Buckholt.

2 Stephen succeeded his nephew, Richard de Loveraz, in 1297. Richard had held of the king 5s. rent at Cowsfield for the service of hunting the wolf at the king's expense if one was found in Hampshire, and the keepership of Buckholt wood in the forest of Clarendon for 20s. a year to be paid to the king by the hand of the bailiff of Clarendon (*Cal. Inq. p.m.* III, no. 388, p. 258).

Stephen obtained a licence from the king in 1334 to grant to Roger Normand, his wife Joan, and his heirs, the bailiwick of Buckholt forest, and 18d. rent in Lockerley, to be re-granted to him for life. The fine for the licence was only $\frac{1}{2}$ mark as the bailiwick was found to be worth nothing (*Cal. Pat. R., 1330–4* p. 542). When Roger Normand died on 1 April 1349, the 18d. rent at Lockerley was said to be held of the king by grand serjeanty of keeping the forest of Buckholt, and his land at *Couelesfeldeloveras,* held of the king by knight service, had been leased for 20 years at the rent of 1 rose; it included 20 acres of underwood, but they were worthless as no buyers could be found on account of the Black Death (*Cal. Inq. p.m.* IX, no. 233, p. 231).

3 Stained and partly illegible in MS.

II 54

(xiii) The forest of PORTCHESTER (*Porcestre*)[1]—in the presence of John de Berewyk', [etc.]; Adam de Rypplyng', steward of John de Sancto Johanne, forester of the fee;[2] Roger de Launceleveye and Thomas Stak', verderers.

Beginning at Mislingford (*Maselyngesford*);[3] continuing eastwards as far as the corner of Simon de la Beere's grove, by the ditch of that grove to Robert de la Beere's grove; thence by the ditch of that grove to *Hameleweye;* by *Hameleweye* to the head of *Horlareslak';* thence to the main road which runs from Soberton (*Subertone*) to Fareham (*Farham*), and by that road to *Haseley,* which separates the king's wood from that of Richard de Wallop'; thence by the boundary between the king's wood and Wickham (*Wycham*), towards *Bedenesheued*; descending by the ditch between the king's wood and *Bedenesheuedstrete* to the Meon Stream (Munestreym), and by that stream to the aforesaid Mislingford (*Maselyngesford'*).

1 Also known as the forest of South or East Bere. The forest extended eastwards from the Meon River and northwards from Portsdown Hill. Its custody was in the same hands as that of Portchester castle. A copy of a perambulation carried out in 1688 is printed as Appendix 2 to the 13th Report of the Woods, Lands and Revenues Commission (*House of Commons Journal* 47, p. 1038).

2 Sir John de St John spent a lifetime in royal service at home and abroad (*Knights of Edward I*). He was first granted custody of Portchester castle during the king's pleasure in 1267 in succession to his father, Robert; but the following year it was granted to Isabel, Countess of Arundel (*Cal. Pat. R., 1266–72* pp. 67, 204). It subsequently passed through various hands before being returned to Sir John. He died in October 1302 (*Cal. Inq. p.m.* IV, no. 96, p. 62).

3 Mislingford is on the west of the River Meon about 2 miles above Wickham and across the river from Bere Farm.

II 55

(xiv) *LA RODE*—another piece of the same bailiwick.

Beginning at *Pottereshurne*; thence to the road which leads south of (*a parte australi de*) *Foxholes*, and by the road to *Malet'cheslake*; thence to *Cricheslak'*; to *Hulnesuthelak'*; and thence keeping to the stream, ascending as far as *la Steypole*; then ascending by *la Muleweye* to *Palmard'hurn'*; to *Colyer'slaneshende*, and thence ascending by the road alongside the hedge to the aforesaid *Pottereshurne*.

The jurors say that these metes and bounds used to enclose the whole forest of Portchester before the coronation of King Henry [II]. The king has no demesne wood adjoining the said forest outside the bounds. All woods, lands, and places outside these metes and bounds, which are disafforested by this perambulation, were appropriated to the forest after the coronation of King Henry [II]; but which ones, and how much, in each individual reign, no one can now be sure.

Whatever is placed outside the forest by these perambulations will remain outside the forest, and the rest will be forest in perpetuity. In testimony whereof the king has caused these letters patent to be drawn up.

　　　　　　　　　Witnessed by the King at Lincoln, 14 February,
　　　　　　　　　　　　in the 29th year of his reign [1301].

[Marginal note in the left-hand margin beginning alongside the heading *La Rode*:]

　Lords in the East Bailey of the forest (*Domini in Estbayly foreste*)
　Earl of Salisbury (*Comes Sarum*)
　Prior of God's House (*Godushous*)
　Prior of Southwick (*Suthewyk'*)

Richard Beamund
Abbot of Titchfield (*Tichefelde*)
Lord of Belny (*Dominus de Belleney*)
Roger Wanstede
Prior of Southwick
Pageham

Lords in the West Bailey (*Domini in Westbayle*)
Prior of Southwick
Abbot of Titchfield
Uvedale
Wallop
Prior of Southwick (*Suthwik'*)
Pageham
Faukon'
Prior of Southwick

II 56   26 October 1389

[fo. 50] INQUISITION at Southwick, in the county of Hampshire, before Richard Horn', Royal Escheator, 26 October, 13 Richard II. Jurors: Simon Jurdan', Roger Upham, Thomas Stake, Roger Ingelfeld', John Russhemre, John Beamond', Robert Cut', Thomas Chidyngfelde, Thomas Mayle, Philip Honnte, John Wanstede, and John Frye; who say that Richard Nowell', late prior of Southwick, died on Thursday before Michaelmas [23 September], causing a vacancy, and the priory and its temporalities were taken into the king's hands and there remain. The priory is held of the king in chief, having been founded by his progenitors and the king is the true patron.[1] On the day he died, the prior held: (i) the manor of Southwick with appurtenances, in free alms, the gift of William de Pontearcharum,[2] which is worth in all £11 a year; (ii) the manor of West Boarhunt (*Westbourhunte*) with appurtenances, in free alms, the gift of William de Humet,[3] which is worth in all 66s. a year; (iii) a place called Newlands (*Newelond'*) with appurtenances, from the abbot and convent of Quarr (*Quarrera*) for service of 20s. a year at Michaelmas[4]—it is worth in all, after deductions, 22s. a year; (iv) a place called Anmore (*Andemere*), in free alms, with 20 acres of arable and 20 acres of pasture worth, with appurtenances, 5s. a year, the gift of John Andemere, but by what service they do not know;[5] (v) the manor of Stubbington (*Stubynton'*) with appurtenances, in free alms, the gift of Alfred Heriardus, which is held of the king in chief, except 45 acres within the same manor held of William Fifhyde,[6] and the manor with the aforesaid 45 acres and other appurtenances is worth, after deductions, 100s. a year; (vi) the manor of [Priors] Dean (*Dene*) with appurtenances, held in free alms, of the king in chief for service of £7. 18s. 5½d. annual rent at Michaelmas paid to the king's exchequer as fee farm,[7]—it is worth, after deductions and payment, £8. a year; (vii) the manor of Moundsmere (*Moundesmere*) and [Preston] Candover (*Candevere*), in free alms, the gift of William de Pontearcharum[2] worth in all after

deductions, 58s.; (viii) the manor of Farlington (*Farlyngton'*) with Crook-horn (*Cruquer*) and other appurtenances, in free alms, the gift of the king's progenitors, but it is held of John de Monte Acuto, knight (*chivaler*), of his manor of Warblington (*Warblynton'*) for service of [fo. 50ᵛ] 3 barbed arrows a year on the 1st August;[8]—it is worth in all 40s. a year. The prior did not hold or have, by right of the priory, any other land, or tenement, or service in the said county.
In testimony etc.

27 October 1389

INQUISITION at Marlborough (*Marleburgh*), in the county of Wiltshire, before Richard Horn', Royal Escheator, 27 October, 13 Richard II. Jurors: John Wyly; Hugh Pipard; William Hoppegraas; John Colyn; William Perschut; William Chamberlayn; John Stamford'; John Hame-lyn; Simon Michel; John Gibon'; Richard Calf, and John Kepenhull', who say that Richard Nowell', late prior of Southwick, held on the day he died, in free alms, by right of the priory, 23s. annual rent with appurtenances, from certain tenements in Aldbourne (*Aldeborn'*) in the aforesaid county,[9] paid to the sacristy at Michaelmas to provide wine for the administration of the sacrament in the priory. The prior died on Thursday before Michaelmas last [23 September]. In testimony etc.

1 For the true identity of the priory's founder see Introduction, p. xii and I 1 note 2. Other juries, and the priory, when circumstances made it advantageous, stated that William de Pont de l'Arche was the founder (II 10, 11, 76, 77, 84. See also III 100). But at inquisitions post mortem held in 1381 and 1398 Southwick Priory is said to be a royal foundation (II 32, 75).

2 See I 1. Land given to the priory in Applestead became incorporated into the manor of Southwick. Moundsmere became the focal point for lands in and around Preston Candover, that were the gift not only of William de Pont de l'Arche but of many later benefactors.

3 See I 138, the culmination of various gifts relating to West Boarhunt (I 39, 63).

4 Obviously Newlands here incorporates the tenement called *Planta* and the adjoining virgate, which were the subject of an agreement made between Southwick Priory and Quarr Abbey in 1189. The rent, then fixed at 20s. remained unchanged in 1389 (I 143), and at the Dissolution (P.R.O. SC6/Hen VIII/3340) Newlands and Plant farms lie between two and three miles E. of Southwick.

5 The only mentions of John de Andemere are here and in the inquisition following the death of Prior Richard Bromdean in 1381 (II 32). However, the priory had received land at Anmore from the brothers Ralph and William de Cumbrai, probably in the late 12th century (I 57, 59, 151).

6 For Alfred de Heriard's gift and the problem of distinguishing between Stubbing-ton in Titchfield and Stubbington in Portsea, see I 17, 86 and notes. Land given to the priory by William Fifhyde was definitely in Portsea (III 468–75).

7 [Priors] Dean was granted at fee farm to the priory by King John in 1204 (I 162). It is hardly appropriate to say, as in the MS., that it was held in 'pure' and perpetual alms.

8 Margaret, wife of Sir John Montagu, inherited Warblington from her mother, Margaret, widow of Thomas Monthermer. It passed to her son, John, who became Earl of Salisbury (*VCH Hants* III, p. 135). The priory was granted the reversion

of the manor of Farlington and Crookhorn by King Edward III after the death of John Montgomery, which took place in 1347 (I 208, 211, 212). But the connection between Farlington and Warblington is not clear.

9 Land at Aldbourne, Wilts., was given to the priory by Count Geoffrey de Perche, who died *c.* 1202 (I 144).

II 57   4 November 1389

MANDATE from King Richard [II] to Richard Horn', his Escheator in the county of Hampshire.[1] Since he has been informed that Southwick Priory, founded by his progenitors and under his patronage, is impoverished and in debt because of frequent attacks and arson by his enemies, owing to its situation on the coast, and because of various plagues, and murrain affecting its beasts, and many vacancies, he has granted to the prior and convent, to relieve their condition, all revenues and profits which pertain or could pertain to him from the priory's temporalities after the death of the late prior, Richard Nowell', as fully shown in his letters patent. He orders [the escheator] to send in nothing from the revenues and profits of the aforesaid temporalities or any part of them, and if he has taken or levied anything to return it freely and without delay to the prior and convent. The escheator is to be entirely relieved of any responsibility to the King for the aforesaid revenues and profits.[1]

Westminister, 4 November, 13 Richard [II].

1 By contrast, during the vacancy in 1381, caused by the death of Richard Nowell's predecessor, 20s. 7½d. was paid to the king being 8¼d. a day for 30 days (II 32). This took place despite the fact that in 1308 and in 1315-16 it had been ascertained by inquisitions appointed by Edward II that the priory was not a royal foundation, and the king was not entitled to its revenues during a vacancy (II 77, 76, 84).

II 58   [1302-29][1]

PROCEEDINGS produced before the lord Constable of Winchester: evidence was produced by the proctor appointed by the prior and convent of Southwick, to whom the church of Southwick canonically belongs, against Richard de Bello Alneto, one of the parishioners, and whomsoever he appoints to act for him, viz.: all tithes and oblations within the titheable area of Southwick church belong, and have for a long time belonged, to that church and the priory by common right, and parishioners of the church, for as long as the parish has existed, have been, and still are, bound by papal decree to attend and hear mass and divine service there on Sundays and festal days, and to offer accustomed oblations due to the parish church. However, in 1302 the said Richard withheld, and caused to be withheld, for the past term the just tithes of goats, pigs and geese and of his dove-cot, and also the tithes due from his mill, known to be within the titheable area of the church, and the accustomed oblations he owed to the parish church as a parishioner.

Also, for as long as can be remebered, he has failed to attend the parish church on Sundays and festal days, and has refused and still refuses to pay the tithes and oblations due to the church and priory, violating the oath on the Gospels he voluntarily took concerning faithful and full payment of tithes due from all titheable annual produce. Richard has caused divine offices and masses to be celebrated on Sundays and festal days in his private houses and profane places within the parish bounds of Southwick every year that he has been a parishioner, and sacraments to be administered to parishioners of the church each Easter, without any authority whatever or licence required by law, but rather by his own temerity, to the grave danger of his soul and loss to the parish church and priory, and incurring the risk of damnation, the penalty of the perjurer.[2]

[fo. 51ᵛ] All these things are well known in Southwick and the neighbourhood, and public outcry has been raised against them. The proctor sought a declaration from the judge that the aforesaid tithes belonged to the church and priory, and that Richard was bound to attend the parish church of Southwick on Sundays and festal days and to offer the accustomed oblations due from a parishioner; and he sought condemnation of Richard for failure to pay. If there was legitimate dispute over the amount to be paid, he ought nevertheless to pay what is in arrears, and he should be punished for making provision for sacraments to be administered in his houses and for spiritual matters pertaining to the parish, and made to understand the law.

1 The case against Richard must have been heard after 1302 when he failed to pay his tithes, and before the agreement reached in 1329 (II 71). See also III 451–6.

2 Sometime between 1238 and 1242, the priory had granted permission to Richard's great-grandfather, Robert de Bello Alneto, to have a chapel within his property at Belney. Strict conditions had been laid down for the protection of the rights of the parish church of Southwick (III 668).

II 59   30 May 1310

MANDATE from King [Edward II] to Hugh le Despenser, Justice of his Forest South of Trent. The king has inspected the charter of his ancestor, King Henry, shown to him by the prior of Southwick, conceding to Southwick Priory the manor of Candover (*Candevere*) with appurtenances quit of all manner of suits, pleas, claims and forest laws,[1] by virtue of which the prior and his predecessors were always wont to be exempt from attendance at the swainmote in the forest and from providing maintenance for forest officials.

Nevertheless, Hugh and his officials in the royal forest of Windsor recently took surety from the prior for his attendance at the king's swainmote in that forest, and provision of maintenance for forest officials, by virtue of his dwelling at Moundesmere situated in the aforesaid manor, and have unjustly troubled him many times and caused him harm, against the purport of the aforesaid charter. If this is the case, the king orders

Hugh to desist, and allow the prior to be exempt as heretofore, and to restore to him any surety taken for the above reason.

Witnessed by the King at Windsor, the third year of his reign.

1 See II 8(d), and note 4. This is the charter the forged original of which is in the Hampshire Record Office (4M53/1).

II 60 30 October 1325

MANDATE from William de Cleydon', *locum tenens* for Lord Hugh le Despens', Earl of Winchester, Justice of the Forest South of Trent, to Ralph de Camoys, Keeper of the Forest of Woolmer (*Woluemere*), or his deputy. Since he has inspected the charters of the progenitors of the kings of England, by which the prior and canons of Southwick were granted perpetual exemption from forest law and all things pertaining thereto in their manors of Colmore and Dean (*Colmere et Dene*), and, nevertheless, Ralph and his subordinates compel the prior and canons and their men to have their dogs there expeditated, exacting from them [fo. 52] a heavy fine and causing no slight injury and grievance to them and their men, he orders Ralph to desist, and make his subordinates desist, from troubling them in this way, and to leave them in peace in the aforesaid manor. If Ralph has taken surety from them on that account, he is to release it to them without delay. Given under his official seal.

Southwick, 30 October, 19 Edward [II]

II 61 20 March ?1336

MANDATE of King [Edward III] to the Constable of his castle of Portchester (*Porcestr'*) or his *locum tenens*. Since King Henry, his progenitor, by his charter,[1] which King Edward, his father, confirmed, granted to the prior and convent of Southwick quittance in perpetuity from all manner of suits, and since he [Edward III] has accepted that the present prior and his predecessors up to now have always enjoyed this quittance, but nevertheless [the Constable] has many times unjustly troubled the prior to make suit three-weekly at the king's court at Portchester, causing him no little inconvenience by this innovation, against the tenor of the aforesaid charter—the king, not wishing the prior to be troubled in this way, orders the Constable, if this be the case, to desist, to allow the prior quittance as heretofore, and to release without delay any distraint taken from him for these reasons.

Westminster, 20 March, the 10th year of the King's reign.

1 Probably this is a reference to the charter of Henry I to Southwick Priory, which was the subject of an inspeximus and confirmation by Henry III in 1269. That inspeximus was confirmed by Edward II in 1313 (II 8(d); *Cal. Chart. R., 1257–1300* p. 124; *Cal. Chart. R., 1300–26* p. 209). I have not found any reference in the *Calendars of Charter Rolls* to any confirmation by Edward I. Presumably this mandate was sent by Edward III.

II 62   13 May 1325

WRIT of CERTIORARI from King [Edward II][1] to Matthew Broun, his
Escheator in the counties of Northampton (*Northt'*), Rutland (*Rotel'*),
and Lincoln. The king has been given to understand that various lands
and holdings in Hollowell (*Hollewelle*),[2] [Northamptonshire], held of his
progenitors, former kings of England, and given in alms to the priors of
Southwick, were alienated by the priors without licence of the king or
his progenitors; and that bondmen, who held those lands of the priors
in villeinage, were manumitted by the same priors, without action being
taken by the king's escheator and those of his progenitors as their office
required; therefore he orders the escheator to ascertain by inquisition[3]
which lands and tenements were alienated by the aforesaid priors in the
vill of Hollowell; and which, and how many, bondmen were manumitted,
at what time, by which priors, and in what way; and whether the lands
and tenements were held of the king's progenitors at the time of alienation
and manumission, or of someone else; and if of the king's progenitors,
[fo. 52ᵛ] then of whom, and by what service, and in what way; and if of
someone else, then of whom, and by what service, and in what way;
and how much the lands and tenements are worth annually in all
outgoings according to their true value; and who gave the said tenements
to the priors, and which, and in what way. Having carried out the
inquisition, the escheator is to report without delay under his seal and
those of the jurors.

> Witnessed by the King at Portchester,
> 13 May in the 18th year [of his reign].[1]

1 The king, and therefore the date, is identified in II 63.
2 In the right-hand margin: *Holewulle*.
3 See below, II 63.

II 63   20 June 1325

INQUISITION at Northampton before Matthew Broun, the King's Esche-
ator in the counties of Lincoln, Northampton, and Rutland (*Rotol'*),
20 June, 18 Edward son of King Edward. Jurors: Adam de Nanesby;
John, son of Simon de Creton'; William Clericus of Hollowell
(*Holewell'*); Hugh de Boresworth; Robert le Warde; Simon Freman of
Cottesbrooke (*Cotesbrok'*); William, son of Simon; William le Hayward';
William le Clerc' of Naseby (Nanesby); Roland, son of John; Stephen
Randolf'; and John, son of Roger Molendinar'; who say that John de
Clere, formerly prior of Southwick, and the convent, held in Hollowell
4 messuages, 3¼ virgates, 12d. rent and ¼ of a mill with appurtenances,
as a gift in free alms from Guy de Dyva,[1] who enfeoffed the prior's
predecessors. The following bondmen were alienated and manumitted to
Adam de Castello of Rothwell (*Rowell'*), clerk, on the feast of St Michael
in the 12th year of the reign of King Edward, son of King Henry and
father of the present King [29 September 1284]: Roger de Holewell' with

William and Henry, his brothers, sons of William son of Susan, with all their chattels and households, and 1½ virgates which Beatrix, mother of the aforesaid Roger, William and Henry, held of the prior and convent in villeinage.[2] The aforesaid Adam, having seisin, granted the 1½ virgates to Roger de Holewell', and Roger alienated the land with appurtenances to Henry, son of Hugh de Boresworth' when he married Roger's daughter, Agnes. Henry now holds that land.

Item: the prior and convent, on the feast of Purification, 13 Edward son of King Henry [2 February 1285], alienated without royal licence to the aforesaid Roger, William, and Henry and the heirs of their bodies lawfully procreated, the aforesaid 4 messuages, 1¾ [*sic*] virgates, and 12d. rent, with appurtenances in Hollowell, for an annual rent of 40s., saving to the priory wardships, reliefs and escheats as they occur. Item: the aforesaid Guy held all the aforesaid tenements with appurtenances, which he gave to the priory, of the bishop of Lincoln for knight service,[3] and the bishop held them of the king in chief as part of the barony pertaining to the bishopric, and the priory held them, in perpetual alms, at the time of the alienation and manumission. Item: the aforesaid lands were alienated, and the tenants manumitted, without royal licence. Item: all the aforesaid tenements with appurtenances are worth 53s. 4d. a year in all outgoings, according to their true value.

1 See I 132.

2 See III 243

3 Hugh of Avallon, Bishop of Lincoln 1186–1200, inspected and confirmed Guy's charter to the priory (I 146).

II 64   10 July 1294

[fo. 53] MANDATE of King Edward [I] to the Sheriff of Sussex. The Prior of Southwick has appointed as his attorneys Brother William de Wynton' and Reginald de la Stone, to appear, for better or worse (*ad lucrandum vel perdendum*), in the sheriff's county according to the King's brief, in the suit between the prior and Richard, son of Alan, Earl of Arundel,[1] concerning Richard's payment to the prior of 26 quarters 2 bushels of wheat, which the prior says are in arrears from an annual rent of 2 quarters 5 bushels. The King orders the sheriff to receive William and Reginald in place of the prior, or either of them if both are not able to be present.

Witnessed by the King at Portsmouth, 10 July, 22nd year of his reign.

[Marginal note:] Evidence concerning wheat in the manor of Westbourne (*de Burne*), [Sussex].

1 Richard fitz Alan, born 1267, styled Earl 1291, died 1302 (*HBC* p. 415). See also III 85.
Copy III 88.

II 65   Copy of I 200

II 66   Copy of I 201.

II 67   8 August 1374[1]

[fo.53ᵛ] ASSIZE OF NOVEL DISSEISIN at Winchester before William
Tauk' and Henry Pernehay, the King's Justices of assize in the county
of Hampshire. The assize comes to declare whether Robert Kangevylle
of Drayton, carpenter; John Southenere; John Clerk' of Bordean
(*Borden'*); John Saundre; John, vicar of the church of East Meon
(*Estmeone*); Roger Gouldyng; Thomas Willes; Nicholas Thecchere; and
John Somenour; unjustly disseised the prior of Southwick of his free
tenement in Drayton[2] after the first (*post primam*), etc., whereon he
complains that they have disseised him of a messuage, 24 acres and 2
acres of meadow with appurtenances, etc. The aforesaid Robert came in
person, and the others did not come, but a certain John atte Dale spoke
for them as their bailiff, and says that they have not injured or disseised
the prior, and thereon they put themselves on assize. And the prior
likewise. And the aforesaid Robert says that the tenements in question
are held of the bishop of Winchester, as of his manor of East Meon[3]
which is of the ancient demesne of the English crown, pleadable in the
bishop's court there by the king's little writ of right close, wherefore he
seeks judgement that he need not sue out this writ of assize at common
law, etc. And the prior says his writ ought not to be quashed in this way
because the tenements in view are held of the bishop of Winchester as
of his manor of Bereleigh (*Burle*),[3] pleadable in the king's court by writ
of assize of novel disseisin at common law, and not by the king's little
writ of right close in the bishop's court of East Meon, as Robert alleges.
And he claims that inquiry into this should be made by assize. And
Robert likewise. And so the assize is taken on the agreement of the
aforesaid parties who have elected for trial, and the jurors say that the
tenements in view are pleadable in the king's court by assize writ of
novel disseisin at common law, and not by the king's little writ of right
close in the bishop's court of East Meon. And they say that the prior
was seised of the tenements with appurtenances as a free tenement, until
the aforesaid Robert, John Southner, John Clerk', and John Saundre
unjustly and unlawfully disseised him, at a loss to the prior of 60s.; and
they say that the other defendants named in the writ were not involved
in the disseisin. Concerning the prior's right in the aforesaid tenements,
they say that the tenements in view belong to the prior as of the right of
his church of Southwick, and he and his predecessors were thereby seised
of the tenements from time immemorial. So it was agreed that the prior
should recover seisin of the tenenments with appurtenances and the
aforesaid damages, and Robert, John Southenere, John Clerk' and John

Saundre are in mercy; and likewise the prior is in mercy for a false
[fo. 54] claim against the others who are acquitted of the aforesaid
disseisin etc.
[Marginal note:] Evidence concerning Drayton (Draytun), viz. Bereleigh
(Burly).

1 Tuesday before the feast of St Lawrence, 48 Edward III. Lawrence the Martyr's
feast day is 10 August, and the previous Tuesday in 1374 is the 8th; Lawrence
the Archbishop's feast day is 3 February, and the previous Tuesday would be 31
January.

2 Drayton is about 1½ miles N.W. of East Meon.

3 East Meon was among the possessions of the bishopric of Winchester seized by
William I after the death of Stigand. It was restored by Henry II between 1154
and 1161. Bereleigh was a sub-manor dependent on East Meon (*VCH Hants* IV,
p. 417).
Copy III 264.

II 68   4 September 1316

MANDATE from the Official of Winchester, the see being vacant, to
the Dean of Droxford (*Drok'*). It has been reported to the Official, on
behalf of the prior and convent of Southwick, rectors of the parish
church of Southwick, that certain lay parishioners of Southwick and
others have sacrilegiously conspired together to collect, detain, and
convert to their own use, oblations and obventions brought to a certain
cross in the nave of the parish church, and to the altars of St Anastasius
and St Thomas the Martyr. This has been done against the will of the
rectors and their officers, and in contempt of their ecclesiastical liberty,
setting a pernicious example and incurring the risk of damnation and
sentence of major excommunication.

Wherefore the dean is ordered publicly and solemnly to denounce, and
cause to be denounced, every conspirator and everyone party to the
aforesaid [misdemeanours] who have incurred the sentence of excommunication. They are to be excommunicated in the parish church of Southwick
and in neighbouring churches on Sundays and festal days during masses,
when the greatest number of people are present, with bells rung, candles
lit and then extinguished, and the cross raised. The dean is diligently to
enquire the names of these malefactors, and to summon, or cause to be
summoned, those who are found to be involved, to appear before the
Official, or whoever presides over the consistory of Winchester, in the
cathedral on Monday nearest Michaelmas, so that justice may be done;
and he is to inform, by his letters patent, the Official or president of the
court, on the said day at Winchester, what he has done in the matter.[1]

Winchester, 2 Non. September, 1316.

1 For the response to this mandate, see below II 80.

II 69   20 December 1314

INQUISITION concerning knights' fees[1] held before Sir James de Norton' and Sir Richard de Burhunte, justices. Jurors: Thomas Stak'; John Beamond; Richard, son of Thomas de Portesye; Richard Stak'; Robert le Eyr; Roger atte Legh'; Henry Ude; Adam atte Spense; William Pynkeneye; John Lung'; Richard, son of Thomas Andreu; and Walter atte Wytecrowe; who say that:

Thomas de Stannford holds ⅛ of a knight's fee in Drayton of the king in chief.[2]

Hugh le Despens' holds Bedhampton of the abbot of Hyde for 2 knights' fees;[3] and Brockhampton of Sir John de Sancto Johanne for ½ knight's fee.[4]

Richard de Portesye holds Portsea (*Portesye*) of John de Sancto Johanne for 1 knight's fee;[4] and Copnor (*Coppenore*) of the Earl of Lincoln (*Lyncoln'*) for ½ knight's fee.

Richard de Borhunt' holds Boarhunt Herberd of John de Sancto Johanne for 1 knight's fee.[4]

John de Scures hold Widley (*Wydele*) of John de Sancto Johanne for ½ knight's fee.[4]

[fo. 54ᵛ] Richard de Belanne holds Belney (*Belanne*) of the Earl of Warwick (*Warewyk'*) for ½ knight's fee;[5] and of Richard de Burhunt a ¼ knight's fee in Belney.

The abbot of Titchfield holds Wellsworth (*Walesworth*) for 1 knight's fee by the gift of Peter de Roches, former Bishop of Winchester, who bought it from Geoffrey de Luci.[6]

The prior of God's House, Portsmouth (*Portesmuth'*) holds Fratton (*Frodyton'*) of Hugh de Plaecy for 1 knight's fee.[7]

[   ]

The said prior holds land that was Gilbert de Basevyle's of the manor of West Boarhunt (*Westburhunt'*) for ⅓ knight's fee.[8]

John de Beamound hold in Drayton ⅛ knight's fee of the Earl of Arundel (*Arundell'*).[2]

John le Butelyr holds Wymering (*Wymeryng*) of the king in chief for 1d. a year.[9]

Concerning archbishoprics, bishoprics, the honour of Wallingford (*Walyngsford*) or of Nottingham (*Notyngham*), the jurors say they know nothing. Sealed by the jurors.

Winchester, Friday the eve of the feast of St Thomas the Apostle,
8 Edward II son of King Edward.

1 The names of holders of vills and hamlets in the hundred of Portsdown recorded in 1316 agree with those in the above list, except in the case of Richard de Borhunt, who had been succeeded by his son, Thomas. (*Feudal Aids* II, p. 320). For West Boarhunt see below, note 8.

2 Thomas Sanford and John Beumunde were holding the hamlet of Drayton in Farlington in 1316. In 1346 Thomas' former holding, described as ⅛ fee, was held by Lawrence de Pageham, and John's, also ⅛ fee, by Thomas Beaumond (*Feudal Aids* II, pp. 320, 336).

3 Bedhampton was already held by the Abbot of Hyde in 1236. In 1314 Joan, widow of Reginald, brother of Herbert fitz Peter, died seised of the manor, which then passed to Hugh le Despenser, the elder, who had been enfeoffed by Reginald and Joan in 1305 (*VCH Hants* III, p. 142).

4 The St Johns, as descendents of the de Ports, succeeded to the overlordship of Brockhampton, Portsea, Boarhunt and Widley (*op. cit.,* pp. 123, 192, 145, 171).

5 On his death in 1262, William de Bello Alneto was holding ½ fee of William Mauduit, and ¼ fee of Thomas de Burhunt', whose son was in the wardship of Sir Robert de Sancto Johanne. William was succeeded by his son, Baldwin, (*Cal. Inq. p.m.* I, no. 514, p. 145; no. 560, p. 170). Richard de Belanney was probably Baldwin's son. William Mauduit V became Earl of Warwick in 1263, and when he died without issue in 1268 the title passed to his sister's son, William Beauchamp *Beauchamp Cartulary* p. lix; *HBC* p. 453). Richard de Burhunt was 15 years old when he succeeded his father, Thomas, in 1262, (*Cal. Inq. p.m.* I, no. 536, p. 162).

6 Bishop Peter de Roches founded the abbey of Titchfield in 1232. Wellsworth, in the parish of Chalton, was one of his many endowment gifts (H.M. Colvin *The White Canons in England* (Oxford, 1951) pp. 184, 186; *VCH Hants* III, p. 107; *Book of Fees* II, p. 705). Probably the reference is to Wellsworth, not Walesworth (see I 4, note 2).

7 *Book of Fees* II, p. 705.

8 A space is left blank after the entry concerning Fratton. It seems likely that some reference to Southwick was to have been included, because in the next entry the "said prior" is probably the prior of Southwick, rather than the aforementioned prior of God's house, Portsmouth. Southwick Priory received land in West Boarhunt as the gift of William de Hommet (I 138). In 1242-3 the prior was said to hold ½ knight's fee there of the Earl of Arundel, who held it of the king (*Book of Fees* II, p. 697). Gilbert, son of Gilbert de Basevile, quitclaimed to the priory in 1259 the £10 annual rent which the priory used to pay him for land at West Boarhunt, let to them at fee farm by the elder Gilbert (III 133). In the list of 1316, the prior of Southwick is recorded as holding both Southwick and West Boarhunt (*Feudal Aids* II, p. 319).

9 Wymering, with Blandford in Dorset, was acquired by John's father, John le Botiller, from the crown in 1281 in exchange for the manor of Ringwood. On the death of John, senior, in 1309, it passed to his wife, Joan, in dower, but had evidently to be passed to his son, John, by 1314 (*VCH Hants* III, p. 166; *Cal. Pat. R., 1271-81* p. 426; *Cal. Inq. p.m.* V, no. 217, p. 117).

II 70   30 July 1319

MANDATE from Robert de Wambreg', Official of Winchester, Commissioner General, to the Dean of Droxford (*Drok'*) and the vicars of Fareham (*Farham*), Portchester (*Porcestr'*), and Boarhunt (*Burghunt'*). The case was pending for some time before the Official in the consistory of Winchester, between the prior and convent of Southwick, who hold the church of Wymering for their own use, and John le Boteler,[1] parishioner of the aforesaid church, concerning tithes of John's mill and salterns, awaiting John's reply to the charge put forward by the priory, and for him to show, by the judgement day next following the feast of the Blessed Mary Magdalene, if he had reason why he should not be compelled to pay the aforesaid just tithes. By that day, John's counsel had proposed exemption from major excommunication, against [the claim] of the priory, on the ground that [the priory's charges] might be refuted in deeds; and after lengthy investigation, the exemption having been in the meantime conceded, counsel for the priory informed both the Official and John's counsel of their judicial vindication (*absolutio*) by letters and mandates of Sir J., Bishop of Winchester.[2]

The Official decided that exemption had been proposed by malice of counsel to delay the case; notwithstanding that exemption, nothing effective had been put forward on behalf of John le Botelyr, layman, that ought to exclude the priory from receiving the tithes of the said mill and salterns within the bounds of the parish of Wymering. Warning was to be given that the tithes are in future to be paid, if necessary under compulsion.

Wherefore the Official orders the dean and vicars, jointly and severally, to warn and effectively induce John to pay the tithes to the priory as they occur from day to day in future. Otherwise, if he fails, they are to compel him by united ecclesiastical censure.

[fo. 55] On receipt of this mandate, and when the warning has been given, they are to notify the Official, or his Commissioner, of what they have done in the matter, as requested by the priory's counsel, by letters under the seal of the dean of Droxford.

Winchester, 3 Kal. August, 1319.

1 See II 69, note 9.

2 John de Sandale, Bishop of Winchester 1316 to November 1319.

II 71   17 March 1329

MEMORANDUM of an agreement between the prior of Southwick and Richard de Bellennay, concerning a dispute which had arisen over guarantee (*prestatio*) of tithes from the profits of the mill, goats, geese, pigs, doves, and sheaves, withheld by Richard.[1] By the intervention of mutual friends and entreaty of those actually present—viz: Brother Nicholas de Cheryton', then prior; Brother Henry de Dene; Brother John de Glocestr'; and M. Hugh Prany; Simon Stak'; John Stak'; Geoffrey de Brokamton'; and Thomas Stak'; Sir John, Richard's chaplain; and William de Wanstede—Richard voluntarily granted to the prior 3 bushels of wheat for arrears of tithes from his mill; also he promised to pay 12 goats for 13 years' arrears of tithes from his goats; also 6 sheaves from 1 acre from which wheat had been carried and not assessed for tithe; and 100 doves for 7 years' arrears of tithe from his dovecot. Richard in the chapter house of Southwick priory, in the actual presence of those named above and others, viz. John Armigerus and Thomas Beamond, took the following oath on the Holy Gospels: I, Richard de Bellennay will pay faithfully to the prior and convent of Southwick in future, for as long as I live, true and just tithes from all and each of my titheable possessions

which accrue to me annually in my manor of Belney (*Bellenay*), East
Boarhunt (*Estburhunt'*) and Paulsgrove (*Palesgrave*), without any diminution or withdrawal, so help me God. 6 Kal. April, 1329.

1 See II 58 for details of the dispute.

II 72 ? 20 September 1309[1]

GIFT, with warranty, by William de Horewode and his wife, Christine,
to John Lucas, his heirs and assigns, of 1 acre with appurtenances in
Preston Candover (Prestone Candeuere), lying between the land of
Walter, son of the late Ralph Ipnus,[2] on either side, in the field called *le
Suthfeld'*. 1 headland of the aforesaid acre extends to the ditch of the
croft of Robert, son of the late Ralph, and the other headland to the
[fo. 55ᵛ] donor's land. The donees will hold the aforesaid acre, by
hereditary right in perpetuity, of the chief lords of that fee. In consideration, John has given William, all his part of a certain marl-pit (*marlera*)
in Preston Candover on *la Longedon'*, in exchange for the aforesaid
marl-pit and his charter, as is contained in the charter of feoffment
drawn up for William. Witnesses: Roger Daundely; William le Butel';
and others.

Preston Candover, Saturday after the feast
of St Matthew the Apostle, 3 Edward.

[Marginal note:] Evidence for the information of the assize against
William de Horwude concerning common at Moundsmere (*Mundusmer'*).
[See below, II 73].

1 The date is given as the 3rd year of the reign of King Edward. It seems likely
that this refers to Edward II, i.e., 1309. A John Lucays was a juror at an
inquisition held at Ellisfield in 1303 (I 108). A Roger Daundely presented Thomas
de Warbleton for the rectory of Chilton Candover in 1303 (*Pontissara Register*
p. 163). The Butler or Botiller family was holding land in Candover from the
early 13th century and in 1310 a William le Botiller and his wife Alice held 11
messuages, 2 carucates, 20 acres of wood and 30s. rent in Preston Candover
(*VCH Hants* III, p. 374). In 1322 William de Horwood held the manor of
Stevenbury or Horwoods in Preston Candover, consisting of 2 carucates. He died
seised of it in 1349, and his heir was his grandson, William, aged 7 (*op. cit.*,
p. 373).

2 Possibly Ipin.

The rest of fo. 55ᵛ is blank.

II 73 Easter Term 1400

[PROCEEDINGS OF THE ASSIZE COURT]. Roll 236, Southampton.

[fo. 56] William Horewode,[1] in mercy for many defaults, etc:—
    William was attached to answer the prior of Southwick on a plea that
he took by force and arms, without reasonable cause, 300 sheep belonging

to the prior at Preston Candover (*Preston' Candaver*), impounded and kept them there, against the law and custom of the realm, for so long that 40, valued at £4, died of starvation, and the remainder suffered serious harm; and he carried out other outrages to the grave injury of the prior, and against the peace of Richard II, lately King of England.

The prior, through his attorney, Thomas Emory, complained that the aforesaid William, on Friday after the feast of Saints Fabian and Sebastian in the 22nd year of the reign of the late king [24 January 1399], by force and by men armed with swords, bows and arrows, took 300 sheep [as above] and impounded them for 6 days [with the aforesaid results]. And he says damage has been incurred to the value of £100.[2] And he produces suit, etc.

And the aforesaid William, through his attorney, John Sutton', came and denied force and injury, etc., or that he came with arms or did anything contrary to the king's peace, so that he was in no way blameworthy, and thereon he put himself on [the verdict of] the country. And the prior likewise.

To the charge, William said that on the aforesaid Friday, he found the sheep in his separable pasture at Preston Candover eating his grass and doing damage, therefore he took and impounded them, as he was entitled to do. And he said that afterwards the sheep were all delivered to the prior, and 40 did not die of starvation through his fault as the prior falsely claimed. And this he was prepared to prove, whence he sought judgement whether the prior could attribute injury to him in this [fo. 56ᵛ] case, etc. And the prior maintained his charge and denied William's allegations. This he was prepared to prove, and on that he sought judgement, etc. William repeated his allegation and sought [the verdict of] the country. And the prior likewise.

Therefore the sheriff was ordered to make 12 men come in the octave of Holy Trinity, etc. by whom, etc. And who, etc. to declare, etc.. Because, etc. Afterwards the action continued between the parties and so on to this day, i.e., the quindene of Easter, I Henry IV [between 2 and 9 May. 1400], except that the king's justices at assize in the aforesaid county, taking the assize according to the form of the statute, came earlier to Winchester, viz. on Monday before the feast of St. Peter's Chair last [21 February]. And so the prior came on that day through his attorney. And the justices of assize sent this report:— both the prior of Southwick and William Horewode came through their attorneys, and likewise the jurors chosen for the trial, who say on oath that William Horewode took the aforementioned sheep from the prior's common pasture at Preston Candover and not from his own separable pasture; they were impounded illegally and retained so long that 12 died of starvation through William's fault, and the rest suffered serious harm, as the prior alleged in his plea, and they assess the damage occasioned to the prior by this trespass at 100s. And so it was decided that the prior recovers from William Horewode his damages assessed at 100s. And the aforesaid William is taken, etc.

1 Possibly the grandson and heir of William Horewode, who succeeded his grandfather in 1349 at the age of 7 (II 72, note 1).

2 This is probably a scribal error for 100s.; cf. below.
Copy III 372.

II 74 16 October 1432[1]

LETTER of King Henry [VI] to the Prior and Convent of Southwick.
As they are bound, by reason of the creation (*creatio*) of a new prior, to
provide a certain annual pension from their house for one of the king's
clerks, named by him, and the king has chosen his servant, Thomas
Pocke, his larderer, being cordially disposed to him on account of his
merits, and having obtained the advice and consent of the priory, the
king requests them to grant to Thomas such annual pension as he is
worthy to receive at their hands. And, so that he will be more bounden
to them, they should provide him with their letters patent, sealed with
their capitular seal. And they should write back to the king, by the
present bearer (*portitor*), concerning their response to his request.

Witnessed by the King at Westminister,
16 October, the 11th year of his reign.

[Marginal note:]—Note concerning the king's pension granted when
Edward Dene was newly created prior of Southwick.

1 Fortunately the marginal note gives the name of the new prior. Edward Dene
was prior of Southwick 1432-55, so King Henry must be Henry VI, and the 11th
year of his reign, 1432.
Copy III 372.

II 75 24 July 1398

[fo. 57] INQUISITION at Southwick before John Tauk', Royal Escheator in the county of Hampshire, on account of the vacancy of Southwick
Priory, founded by the king and his progenitors, through the death of
the late prior, William Hursele, who held of the king in chief. Jurors:
Richard Beumond; Thomas Swagge, Thomas Bernham, John atte Halle,
Thomas Petrusfeld, William atte Hulle, Richard Tasshon', Walter Daubeney, John Spyser, William Polere, John atte Hulle, and Michael
Neuyle; who say that (i) the manor of Southwick, which is of the prior's
portion, [has belonged to the priory since its] foundation by the king
and his progenitors (*quod est de porcione prioris ibidem est de fundacione
domini regis et progenitorum suorum*). In the manor are various houses
worth nothing after deduction (*ultra reprisam*); a garden full of thorns
and brambles, the pasture of which is worth nothing over and above the
enclosing of it (*cuius pastura nichil valet ultra claus' eiusdem*); a dovecot,
old and dilapidated, worth 18d. a year, after deductions; 103 acres of
arable, of which two parts are sown each year and are worth 3d. an
acre, and a third part is worth nothing because it lies fallow and in
common; 21 acres of dry meadow held in severalty (*xxj acre sicci prati*

separal') from the feast of the Purification of the Blessed Mary until haymaking is finished, and they are worth 6d. an acre for that time, and nothing afterwards because they lie open and in common; pasture for 300 sheep and other large animals (*grossa animalia*) worth 10s. 6d. a year; about 20 acres of wood and underwood, the latter worth nothing and the pasture there worth nothing because it lies open and in common; £9 rent from free tenants and bondmen paid in equal amounts at Christmas, Easter, the feast of the Nativity of St John the Baptist and Michaelmas; pleas and perquisites of the court, worth nothing over and above (*ultra*) the fee of the steward and his expenses.

The aforesaid prior held, as by right of his church for the support of the priory (*ut de iure ecclesie sue pertinente ad portionem supradicti prioratus*): (ii) the manor of West Boarhunt (*Westbourhunt'*) with *Cowmede* and appurtenances, in which are several houses and a garden, worth nothing annually after deductions and upkeep; 2 carucates containing 90 acres of arable, of which ⅔ are ploughed each year and are worth 3d. an acre and ⅓ is worth nothing because it lies fallow and in common; 9 acres of rushy meadow in severalty from the feast of the Purification of the Blessed Mary until haymaking is finished, worth 5d. an acre for that time, and afterwards worth nothing because it is in common; 131 acres of common pasture for large animals and sheep, worth 11s. a year; a certain grove containing 5 acres of underwood, which, with pasture, is worth 8d. a year; a broken-down water-mill, worth nothing annually after deductions; £8 rent from free tenants and bondmen, paid in equal amounts at the aforesaid terms; pleas and perquisites of the court, worth 12d. a year.

(iii) Also the manor of Newlands (*Newelond'*) with appurtenances, in which are several houses worth nothing annually after deductions; 60 acres of arable, of which ⅔ are sown each year, worth 3d. an acre, and ⅓ is worth nothing because it lies open (*in communi*) and fallow; 122 acres of pasture for large animals and sheep, worth 10s. a year; 4 acres of dry meadow in severalty from Purification until after haymaking, worth 6d. an acre for that time, and afterwards worth nothing because it lies open; 3 acres of underwood and moor (*mora*) lying open, of which the underwood is worth 6d. a year.

(iv) Also a certain place called Anmore (*Andemere*) with 12 acres of arable worth 40d. a year after deductions; pasture for 60 sheep worth 2s. 4d. a year; a small piece of underwood containing 1 acre, worth 4d. over and above the enclosing of it (*ultra claus' euisdem*).

(v) Also the manor of Stubbington (*Stubyngton'*), with appurtenances, in which are several houses worth nothing annually after deductions; 105 acres of arable, both at Fifhide and in the said manor, of which ⅔ are sown each year and are worth 2½d. an acre, and ⅓ is worth nothing because it lies open and fallow; 60 acres of common pasture worth 4s. a year; a dilapidated dovecot worth 6d. a year; £4, from rents and services of various tenants, free and bond, on the said manor and Fifhydes, paid in equal amounts at Christmas, Easter, the Nativity of St John the Baptist and Michaelmas; pleas and perquisites of the court there worth nothing over and above the fee of the steward and the wages of the hayward.

(vi) Also the manor of Priors Dean (*Prioresden'*), held of the king at fee farm for an annual rent £8. 18s. 5½d. paid to the royal exchequer at Michaelmas by the hand of the sheriff of Hampshire of the time. In this manor there are various houses worth nothing annually after deductions; 83 acres of arable of which ⅔ are sown each year and are worth 3d. an acre, and ⅓ is worth nothing because it lies open and fallow; 220 acres of common pasture, for large animals and sheep, worth 16s. a year; 6 acres of common underwood, which, with pasture, is worth nothing annually; rent and services of various tenants, free and bond, worth £7. 18d. a year at Michaelmas after payment of the fee farm owed annually to the king; pleas and perquisites of the court, worth nothing annually over and above the fee of the steward and the wages of the hayward.

(vii) Also the manor of Moundesmere and Preston Candover (*Candevere parsonat'*) in which are several houses worth nothing annually after deductions; 60 acres of arable, very stony (*valde petros'*), of which ⅔ are sown each year and are worth 2½d. an acre, and ⅓ is worth nothing because it lies open and fallow; 80 acres of pasture worth 13s. 4d. a year; various tenants, free and bond, whose rents and services are worth 44s. a year, payable in equal amounts at Christmas, Easter, the Nativity of St John the Baptist and Michaelmas; perquisites of the court worth 6d. a year over and above the fee of the steward and the wages of the hayward.

[fo. 58] (viii) Also the manor of Farlington (*Farlyngton*) and Crookhorn (*Croukerne*) with appurtenances, in which are several houses worth nothing annually after deductions; a garden worth nothing annually, over and above the enclosing of it (*ultra claus' euisdem*); 70 acres of arable of which ⅔ are sown each year and are worth 2d. an acre, and ⅓ is worth nothing because it lies fallow and open; a certain acre of meadow worth 4d. a year; 52 acres of pasture worth nothing annually because they lie open; a certain pasture for large animals called *Bynny* and *Asshy*, worth 4s. a year; various tenants, free and bond, whose rents and services are worth 13s. 4d., payable in equal portions at the aforesaid four terms; pleas and perquisites of the court worth nothing annually.

(ix) Also the manor of East Hoe (*Hoo*) with appurtenances in which are various buildings worth nothing after deductions; 60 acres of arable of which ⅔ are sown each year and are worth 2½d. an acre, and ⅓ is worth nothing because it lies fallow and open; 20 acres of common pasture worth 20d. a year; 6 acres of wood, of which the underwood and pasture are worth nothing on account of the shade of the trees and because they lie in coverts and in common (*quia iacent coopert' et in communi*); 100s. from the rents and services of various free and bond tenants, paid in equal amounts at the aforesaid four terms. Pleas and perquisites of the court are worth 12d. a year.

(x) Also the manor of Hannington (*Hanyton'*) with appurtenances, which is worth nothing annually after deductions.[2]

(xi) Also the manors of Boarhunt (*Bourhunt'*), Herbelyn and Damnverse, which are worth nothing annually after deductions because they are assigned by royal licence to the chantry of William of Wykeham, Bishop of Winchester.[3]

And they say that there are no more manors, lands, tenements, rents or temporal services pertaining to the priory, apart from those aforenamed. And the late prior, William Hursele, died on 23 June 1398. And they say that all the above manors, lands, tenements, rents and services with appurtenances are held in free alms of the king and his progenitors, founders of the said priory.

> Sealed by the jurors at the place and on
> the day aforesaid [24 July, 22 Ric. II]

1 Cf. inquisitions *post mortem* held in 1381 and 1389, after the deaths of Priors Richard Bromdene and Richard Nowell (II 32, 56 and notes).

2 The manors of East Hoe and Hannington were given to the priory by Sir Bernard Brocas, in return for a perpetual chantry and for other works of piety (III 427 and notes).

3 These manors were acquired in 1396 (II 111, 112, III 972).
A contemporary copy of the above inquisition is on a roll of parchment in H.R.O. 5M50/28. The top is rubbed and worn, and part of the right-hand edge is missing. So far as it can be checked, the text appears to be identical with the cartulary copy except for the spelling of certain names, viz. John Spyce; Fiffides; Damverse; Hursle.

II 76　　　　　　　　　　　　　　　　　　　12 June 1315

WRIT of CERTIORARI from King Edward [II] to John Walewayn, Royal Escheator South of Trent,[1] and forwarded by him to his sub-escheator in the county of Hampshire. The prior-elect and canons of Southwick have pointed out to the king that their church was founded by the progenitors of William de Poundelarge, and the king's progenitors, patrons (*advocati*) of the aforesaid church, did not have custody of it during a vacancy, nor did they take anything from it for their own use, except that it was wont to be taken into their hands for the protection and safeguarding of its goods and possessions during a vacancy without anything being taken. The escheator, however, asserting that the outgoings and profits of the priory on the occasion of a vacancy ought to belong to the king, has taken them for the king's use and kept them unjustly from the prior-elect and canons, to whom it has caused no small injury and wrong according to the complaint accepted by the king. Therefore, that justice may be done, the king orders the escheator, together with John de Insula of the Isle of Wight, to hold an inquisition into whether or not his progenitors were wont to have custody of the priory during a vacancy, and if so how and in what way; and whether or not they received anything, and if so what, how much, and in what way; and other circumstances in any way concerning the matter,[2] and to send the findings and this brief to him without delay under their seals and those of the jurors, keeping in safe custody meanwhile the outgoings and other goods and profits of the priory, having deducted the necessary expenses of the prior-elect and canons and their servants, without sale, distraint or other alienation.

> Witnessed by the King at Thundersley
> (*Thunderle*), [Essex] 12 June 8 Edward.[1]

1 M. John Walewayn was Escheator south of Trent from 19 February 1315 until 1318 (PRO *List of escheators for England and Wales* (List and Index Society, 72; 1971) p. 1). King Edward must therefore be Edward II.

2 The inquisition called for by this writ named the "progenitors" of William de Pundelarge [Pont de l'Arche] as founders of the priory, and the king subsequently ordered his Barons of the Exchequer to look up their records and ascertain what if anything had been received by his predecessors from the revenues of the priory during a vacancy (II 84).
Copy II 83.

II 77 25 January 1308

INQUISITION concerning Portsdown (*Portesdoun'*) and Bosmere (*Bosbur'*), held at Meonstoke (*Munestok'*) on Tuesday before the feast of the Conversion of St Paul, 1 Edward [II],[1] before Alexander de Halghton', the King's Sub-Escheator in the county of Hampshire, concerning knight's fees and other holdings in accordance with the King's brief. Jurors: John Beamond; Richard, son of Thomas de Porteseye; Guy de Hors'; Henry Odon'; William de Langestok'; and Geoffrey de Brokhampton'; who say on oath that:

Sir John le Butelir, knight, holds the manor of Wymering (*Wymeryng'*) with appurtenances from the king in chief, whether by knight service or serjeanty they do not know, and he pays 1d. a year into the hands of the sheriff for all service, and the manor is worth £40 a year in all outgoings.

Thomas de Sta*n*ford' holds a tenement in Drayton' from the king in chief for ⅛ of a knight's fee, and it is worth 100s. a year with (*cum*) all outgoings.[1]

The Abbot of Jumièges (*de Gemitico*) has a daughter house (*cella*) with church on Hayling Island (*insula de Halyng'*), [held] in free alms, the gift of William the Conqueror, and it is worth £100 a year in all outgoings.[2]

The church of Southwick was founded by alms of the progenitors of William de Pontelargh' (*fundata est de elemosina progenitorum Willelmi de Pontelargh'*), and the king does not levy or take anything from its goods or possessions during a vacancy.[3]

Matthew, son of John, holds the manor of Warblington with appurtenances in soke from the king for service of fealty, and it is worth £40 a year.[4]

And they say that they know nothing else. In witness whereof they have put their seals.

Meonstoke, the day and year aforesaid.

1 Thomas de Sanford, on the death of his father, Richard, inherited, in 1289, 12 acres in Drayton in Farlington, which Richard had held as the gift of the king. Thomas died in 1327. (*Cal. Inq. p.m.* II, no. 751, p. 460; VII, no. 69, p. 36). As Thomas was holding the land when this list of fees was compiled, the king referred to must be Edward II.

2 When, in 1294, as a result of war between England and France, Edward I ordered the seizure of all alien priories, the annual value of the lands and

possessions of the priory of Hayling, including the church worth £80, was found
to be £144. 8s. 3½d. Subsequently the priory suffered severely from encroachments
by the sea on its lands, culminating in the disaster of 1324–5 when much of
Hayling Island, including the priory buildings, was submerged. An inquisition
held in 1325 estimated the annual value of the lost possessions at £42. 7s. 4d., and
the remaining possessions and church at £48. 8s. 5d. (*VCH Hants* II, pp. 217–18).

3 This is supported in the findings of an inquisition held in 1316 (II 84), but in
1381, 20s. 7½d. was paid to the king during a vacancy of 30 days (II 32), and in
1389, Richard II ordered his escheator to restore any revenues taken from the
priory during the vacancy caused by the death of Prior Richard Nowell, because
he understood that the priory was impoverished and in debt (II 57).

4 Matthew, son of John Ude, quitclaimed his right in the manor of Warblington
to Henry III and Queen Eleanor, receiving in return the grant of the manor for
life. He died before 1309. (*VCH Hants* III, p. 135).

II 78   3 February 1340

[fo. 59] NOTIFICATION by Brother John de Gloucestria, Prior of
Southwick, that Thomas de Borhunte, son and heir of the late Gilbert
de Borhunte, has granted to the priory 10 acres of arable with a certain
grove, together with William le Grey, Thomas atte Berne, and John
Davy, tenants of the late Richard de Belenay, and their services,—[all
of] which came into his hands as custodian of the heir of the said Richard
during his minority,[1]—for the priory to hold in accordance with Thomas'
deed, drawn up for them; and Thomas is bound to the priory in £10.
Therefore [the prior gives notice that], if the priory and their successors
remain in peaceful possession of the said land and tenants and are not
impleaded or troubled in any way by the heir of the said Richard or his
heirs, nor suffer any other ill by reason of their custody of the aforesaid
land and tenants, Thomas' bond to the priory will be null and void after
Richard's heir, or the heir's heir, comes of age.
    Indenture sealed by the priory and Thomas.

Southwick, Thursday after the feast of the
Purification of the Blessed Mary, 14 Edward III.

1 See II 35–37, and notes; II 148; III 451, and note.

II 79   [1273–81][1]

GIFT by Prior Andrew and the convent of Southwick to Geoffrey Corbet,
of all that land with appurtenances in Stubbington (*Stubbintone*) in
the parish of Titchfield (*Tichefeld'*) which Roger Forst' formerly held.
Geoffrey, his heirs or assigns, will hold the land from the priory by
hereditary right in perpetuity, and may give or assign it to whom they
wish, except religious houses or Jews, paying to the priory 6s. 8d. a year,
viz. 3s. 4d. at Easter and 3s. 4d. at Michaelmas, for all service, exaction,
and other secular demand; saving suit of the priory's court at Boarhunt

(*Burhunta*) on two lawdays a year, i.e., Hock Day and Martinmas, and that amount of royal service and of any other outside (*forincetus*) service which pertains to such a tenement. Consideration, 100s. Witnesses: Sir John de Bottele, knight; Richard Wygaunt'; and many others.

1 Andrew de Winton was Prior of Southwick, 1273–81.
Copy III 170.

II 80   3 October 1316

[fo. 59ᵛ] REPLY from the Dean of Droxford (*Dork', Drokensford'*) to the Official of Winchester, or other person presiding over the consistory of Winchester, the see being vacant, in response to the Official's mandate of 4 September [as above II 68], informing him that, according to the mandate received on 9 September (5 Id. September), he has denounced, and caused to be denounced, in the parish church of Southwick and neighbouring churches on Sundays and festal days—when the greatest number of people come together—each and every conspirator who, having received canonical warning in advance, is liable to have incurred the penalty of excommunication, and to be publicly and solemnly excommunicated. He has made diligent enquiry concerning the names of the malefactors, and has found Walter le Bedel and Richard le Ros of Southwick guilty and noted for the aforesaid misdeeds, and he has peremptorily ordered them to appear before the Official or other person presiding over the consistory, on the day and at the place named in the mandate, to be further answerable as required, and thus he has carried out the mandate.

Southwick, 5 Non. October, 1316.

II 81   26 July 1319

[fo. 60] MANDATE from Robert de Wamberg', Official of Winchester, Commissioner General, to the Dean of Droxford (*Drokenesford*), the rectors of the churches of Walesworth, Widley and Wanstead, the vicars of the churches of Fareham, Titchfield, Wymering, Portsea, Portsmouth and Boarhunt, and the parish chaplains of Havant, Farlington[1] and Southwick. Complaint has been made to the Official on behalf of the prior and convent of Southwick, who hold the churches of Wymering and Portchester (*Porcestr'*) for their own use, that, though for some time the priory has justly taken tithes from the salterns of certain parishioners of the said churches of Wymering and Portchester, lately they sought judgement before the Official because the aforesaid parishioners—their indignation aroused against the priory over payment of tithes of any grain whatever, which, they assert, are heavy and troublesome, and over the priory's desire for the old method and custom of tithing at harvest [to be adhered to] in future—frequently and seriously threaten to ruin the wheat and other titheable [crops], leaving the tithe sheaves untied on the baulks and openly hindering the priory and its servants from recovering its possessions and collecting those tithes, causing all possible loss—so the priory tells the Official—to the prejudice of the priory and no little danger to their own souls, [setting] a pernicious example to others, and infringing the rights and liberties of the church so far as they can. Wherefore there is no doubt, if this is so, that those parishioners actually attempting the aforesaid, or any part of it, or those giving approval or support to them, have incurred, *ipso facto*, the penalty of major excommunication for infringement of ecclesiastical liberties laid down by the holy fathers. On account of which, the Official commits the matter to them, jointly and severally, and, firmly enjoining obedience, orders them—meeting in person in the churches of Wymering and Portchester, or, if through the heat of anger aroused, the parishioners of those churches will not permit a meeting there without plotting evil and causing danger to life and limb, in a field or place where the method of tithing is perverted or the priory hindered from collecting their due tithes, or other place safe from injury by the parishioners—to warn those present, and prevail upon them to desist from this presumption and temerity. Any of them who has attempted anything aforesaid is to make just amends as far he can, otherwise, after being warned, all who have incurred the penalty of excommunication by contravening ecclesiastical liberties in this way, or supporting those who do, are to be excommunicated.

All [those to whom this mandate is addressed], having put on sacred vestments, will make public denunciation in English, intelligible to all, [fo. 60ᵛ] with bells rung, candles lit and extinguished, and the cross raised, in the churches of Wymering, Southwick and Boarhunt, and each in his own church on Sundays and festal days when the greatest number of people come together.

And the dean will have the announcement made by others, notwithstanding any counter-claim made, unless he has had other orders from the Official.

And lest those parishioners should resist and hinder the dean in the execution of the present mandate with impunity because of the obstinacy and rebellion of their advisers and supporters, and should thereby give encouragement to others to do wrong, the dean is to notify the Official, or his Commissioner, by his letters patent, as properly requested by the priory, what he has done in the matter.

Winchester, 7 Kal. August, 1319.

1 Spellings in MS: Wydele, Wanstede, Farham, Tychefeld', Wymeryng', Portesye, Portesmuth', Burghunte, Havonte, Farlyngton.

II 82   Between 9 and 16 July 1234

FINAL CONCORD made before Robert de Lexintone, William de Ebor', Ralph de Norwic', William de Insula and Adam son of William, the King's Justices, and others faithful to the King then present; between

Walkelin, Prior of Southwick, plaintiff, and Roger de Merley, defendant, concerning 1 carucate with appurtenances in *La Plante*.[1]

Roger acknowledged that all the aforesaid land with appurtenances belonged to the prior and his church by right. In consideration, the prior has granted Roger, for life, from the same land, all that part with appurtenances which is north of the king's highway running from the court of Newlands (*la Newelond'*) towards the king's highway from *la Trenche* to Portsmouth (*Portesmuwe*), except the chapel of *la Plante* with appurtenances, which is situated in the same land. Roger will pay 1 mark a year at Michaelmas for all service and exaction, and he is not allowed to give, sell, mortgage, or alienate in any way, anything from that land and appurtenances, all of which will revert to the priory after his death.

And if in future Roger or his heirs bring forward any charters or deeds against this fine, they will be null and void.

Westminster, 3 weeks from Trinity, 18 Henry son of King John.

1 For Roger de Merley's quitclaim of this land to the priory see III 215. The priory first acquired land at *Planta* by agreement with Quarr Abbey (II 56, note 4).

Copy III 216. Variants: Norwyc'; Walkelyn; Niwelonde.

II 83   [fo. 61] Copy of II 76.

II 84   4 April 1316

MANDATE from King Edward [II] to M. John Walewayn, Escheator South of Trent[1], forwarded by him to Robert Selyman, Sub-escheator in the county of Hampshire. Lately, during the vacancy of Southwick Priory, at the suit of William the prior-elect[2] and the canons, the king ascertained, through an inquisition held by the escheator and recorded in chancery, that the church of Southwick was founded by the progenitors of William de Pundelarge, and that the king's progenitors did not have custody there during any vacancy from the time of the foundation, except that, at the request of the canons, for the protection of their possessions, one man used to be placed there who would have food and drink during that time, and that the king's progenitors received no other profits from the priory's possessions for their own use during a vacancy. So the king has ordered his Treasurers and Barons of the Exchequer to scrutinise the Exchequer rolls and notify him without delay, under the Exchequer seal, whether or not any escheators of his progenitors had had their accounts at the Exchequer debited for profits levied from the goods and possessions of the priory during any vacancy, for the use of the aforesaid progenitors, and if so, what profits were levied and for whom. The Treasurers and Barons have not yet replied. The king, therefore, orders the escheator to [fo. 61ᵛ] deliver without delay to Brother Nicholas Chiriton', now prior,[2] all outgoings and profits of the priory he has collected, both during the last vacancy and the preceding one, having received sufficient surety for repayment of those profits to the King before the feast of St. John the Baptist, next, if they ought to belong to him.

Witnessed by the King at King's Langley (*Langelee*), [Herts],
4 April in the 9th year of his reign.[1]

1 M. John Walewayn was Escheator South of Trent between 1315 and 1318 (PRO *List of escheators for England and Wales* (List and Index Society, 72; 1971) p. 1). C.f. *Cal. Fine R., 1307–19* p. 274.

2 William de Winton was Prior of Southwick from 1315 to 1316, and was succeeded by Nicholas de Cheriton, Prior from 1316 to 1334.

II 85		3 November 1354

MANDATE from King Edward [III] to Richard, Earl of Arundel,[1] custodian of the King's castle of Portchester (*Porcestr'*), or his *locum tenens*. The King's great-grandfather, King Henry [III], by his charter,[2] granted to Southwick Priory, in perpetuity, haybote and housebote from his wood of *Kyngesden'*, and common pasture both in the wood and on the plain, and a reasonable supply of firewood from his forest. King Edward has confirmed that charter, and moreover has granted, for himself and his heirs, so far as he is able, permission to the priory to enjoy and use in future any of the liberties contained therein, if for any reason they have not done so hitherto, without interference from the King or his heirs, justices, escheators, sheriffs or other bailiffs or officials. He therefore orders [the custodian] to allow the priory to have haybote and housebote, rights of common pasture in *Kyngesden'* wood, and firewood from the forest of Bere (*la Bere*) adjoining Portchester, without hindrance, according to the tenor of his aforesaid charter.

Witnessed by the King at Westminster, 28 Edward [III].

1 Richard fitz Alan, born 1313; restored in 1330 to the earldom which had been forfeited on the execution of his father, Edmund, in 1326; died 1376 (*HBC* p. 415).

2 See inspeximus II 8(d).

A 16th century copy, on paper, of II 85 is in H.R.O. 4M53/B2. The same manuscript contains a copy of II 86, and of a further mandate from Edward III, which is not in the Southwick cartularies, addressed to the custodian of his forest of Bere-by-Portchester (*Bere iuxta Porcestr'*), similarly ordering him to allow the prior of Southwick to have housebote and haybote in *Kyngesden* Wood and rights of common pasture in the forest. The date of this mandate, witnessed by the King at Westminster, is given as 15 November 30 Edward [III], i.e. 1356.

II 86		4 November [1354]

LETTERS from Richard, Earl of Arundel (*Darundell'*),[1] to Philip Daundele, his deputy (*lieu tenaunt*) in the office of Constable of Portchester Castle. Because he has received from the Chancery a mandate for delivery to the prior of Southwick, of wood and fuel (*fouwayle*) for housebote and haybote in the wood of *Kyngesdene*, and also for allowing him right of common (*commune en menies*) in the wood according to the king's grant, as shown in the enclosed mandate, Earl Richard therefore desires his deputy to make delivery to the prior of those things aforesaid which, according to the king's charter, they were always wont to have for that purpose. So that the king will not find fault with the earl over carrying out his grant, the earl has sent a copy of the charter to his deputy which, with the said mandate, will serve as warranty that he has informed him (*facetz saluement gard' pur le garaunt' pur nos a deu qe vous garni*).

Kennington (*Kenyngton'*).

French.

1 See II 85 and notes.

II 87   [1291–1315][1]

[fo. 62] GRANT, with warranty, by Brother Robert, Prior of Southwick, and the convent, to Sir Geoffrey Spyryng', of custody of all the lands and tenements with appurtenances which Alice de Porselond' held of them in *Porselond'* in the parish of Rowner (*Roghenore*), and of the marriage of John, son of John de Porselond', Alice's heir, until he is of age. If he dies before he is of age, then Sir Geoffrey will have custody of the aforesaid lands and marriage of successive heirs until any of them comes of age, paying the priory 5s. a year from the aforesaid tenements during the wardship. Consideration, 2 marks. Witnesses: Sir Philip de Hoyvill';[2] Sir Payne, Rector of the church of Hursley (*Hurselee*); and others.

[Marginal note:] Evidence concerning *Purselonde* at Rowner (*Ruwynor*) in the parish of Titchfield (*Tycchefelde*).

1 Robert de Henton was Prior of Southwick from 1291 to 1315.

2 Sir Philip de Hoyvill' was active in royal service 1279–1309 (*Knights of Edward I* p. 238). He had died by 1316, when his widow, Mary, was holding land in Soberton (*Feudal Aids* II, p. 307; *VCH Hants* III, p. 260). See also III 346, 343. The rest of folio 62 is blank.

II 88   14 July 1364

[fo. 62ᵛ][1] LETTERS PATENT of King Edward [III][2] granting pardon to John de Scures, knight; Peter de Hoo, chaplain; Roger Ingelfeld; Simon Stake; William Daubenye; and Simon atte Mede; on payment of £8, for failure to obtain royal licence to acquire, and enter into possession of, the manor of Boarhunt (*Burhunte*) Herbelyn with appurtenances, which Richard Dannvers held of the king in chief.[3] The manor, which has been taken into the king's hands on account of this transgression, will be restored to Sir John and the others, to hold of the king and his heirs for the accustomed service in perpetuity, without interference or hindrance by them or their justices, escheators, sheriffs, bailiffs or other officials.

Witnessed by the King at Westminster, 14 July, 38 Edward [III].

1 Alternate folios from 62ᵛ to 97 are headed as follows:

    Bourhunt   xvj   herberd (fo. 62ᵛ)
    herbelyn   xvj   henton (fo. 63)

  Probably the charters copied onto these folios came into the hands of the priory as a result of its acquisition of lands from William of Wykeham for the endowment of his chantry at Southwick (II 111); they were evidently stored in box 16.

2 *Cal. Pat. R., 1364–7* p. 8.

3 See II 89, and note.

II 89   18 October 1361

GIFT, with warranty, by Richard Danvers to Sir John de Scures, knight; Sir Peter de Hoo, chaplain; Roger Ingelfeld; Simon Stake; William Daubenye; and Simon atte Mede, of his whole manor of Boarhunt Herblyn with all appurtenances, and all lands and tenements he has in the parish of Southwick, West Boarhunt (*Westborhunt'*) and Porchester (*Porcestria*).[1] The donees, their heirs and assigns will hold the aforesaid manor, lands, and tenements, with meadows, pastures, paths, woods, plains, hedges, ditches, moors, waters, ponds, stews, gardens, curtillages, wards, reliefs, rents, escheats, reversions and all other things pertaining to the said manor, in fee, and by inheritance, in perpetuity, of the chief lords, for the accustomed services. Witnesses: Sir Robert Markaunt; John le Boteler; and many others.

    Southwick, the feast of St Luke the Evangelist, 35 Edward III.

1 According to the Inquisition *post mortem* held at Meonstoke on 24 September, 36 Edward III (1362), Richard Danvers died on Wednesday before the feast of St Luke, 35 Edward III, i.e., 13 October 1361, and it was stated that two days before his death he had made a conditional feoffment to Sir John Scures, Roger Ingelfeld, Thomas de Walhop, Simon atte Mede, and others, of his land in Boarhunt Herebelyn by Southwick so that they could appropriate it to Southwick Priory. It seems likely that the date of death should be the Wednesday after the feast of St Luke, i.e., 20 October 1361, which would be two days after the above gift was made, and the day before II 94. The inquisition declared that the feoffment was made without royal licence (see II 88), and that the land was held by grand serjeanty of providing an armed man for 40 days in time of war to defend Portchester castle (see II 111). *Cal. Inq. p. m.* XI, no. 244, p. 200. See also II 94.

Original in H.R.O. 5M 50/21. Variants: Daubenee; Westburhunte; Porcestre. To witness list add: Thomas Wallop; Eliseus Daubonee; William Ramuyle; Thomas Stake.

Seal: on tag c. 12 cms., red wax, fragment.

Endorsements: (a) 61
               (b) xvl
               (c) buruntherbylynd
               (d) M. 12

II 90   12 January 1364

QUITCLAIM by John de Scures, knight, to Simon atte Mede, his heirs and assigns, of the manor of Boarhunt Herebelyn with all appurtenances.[1]

Neither Sir John, his heirs, nor anyone in their name, can exercise any right or claim in the aforesaid manor, but hereby are perpetually excluded from any action in law. Witnesses: John le Boteler; Simon Stake; and others.

Wickham (*Wykham*), 12 January, 37 Edward III.

1 This deed and the two following form part of the process by which Southwick Priory acquired Boarhunt Herbelyn. By II 91 and 92, Simon Stake and William Daubeneye, two of the trustees to whom Richard Danvers had made over the manor (II 89), surrendered their claims to Sir John de Scures, who, in II 90, surrendered his claim to Simon atte Mede. Simon duly quitclaimed his rights to Bishop William of Wykeham (II 115), who made the final grant to Southwick Priory (II 111).

II 91   5 January 1364

[fo. 63] QUITCLAIM by Simon Stake of the county of Hampshire to Sir John de Scures, knight, and Simon atte Mede, of all right and claim he had, has, or could have in future in the manor of Boarhunt Herbelyn (*Burhunt' Herblyn*) or appurtenances. Neither Simon, his heirs nor anyone in their name will be able to exercise any claim in the said manor, but will be hereby permanently excluded from any action in law.

Fareham (*Farham*), the vigil of Epiphany, 37 Edward III.

See II 90 and note.

II 92   5 January 1364

QUITCLAIM by William Daubeneye to Sir John de Scures, knight, and Simon atte Mede, of all right and claim he had, has, or could have in future in the manor of Boarhunt Herbelyn or appurtenances, so that neither William, nor his heirs, nor anyone in their name can exercise any claim in the said manor, but will be perpetually excluded hereby from any action in law therein.

Southwick, the vigil of Epiphany, 37 Edward III.

See II 90 and note.

II 93   30 November 1363

QUITCLAIM by John Grete, executor of the will of Sir William de Overton', knight,[1] to Sir Bernard Brocas, knight, and his wife, Mary; Sir John de Scures, knight; Sir Peter de Hoo, clerk; Michael Skillyng; Valentine atte Mede; Simon atte Mede; their heirs and executors; and to the prior and convent of Southwick, of all manner of personal actions for debt and other matters which he has, or could have, against them on account of any bonds etc. made between Sir John de Borhunte and Sir

William de Overton' or others, concerning the land and tenements which belonged to the said Sir John.[2] Neither John Grete nor his executors can make any claim against the aforesaid Sir Bernard and the others. Witnesses: Lawrence Seint Martin; Robert Markaunt and others.

> Westminster, Thursday, the feast of
> St Andrew the Apostle, 37 Edward III.

[Marginal note:] Aquittance of John Grete, executor of Sir William Overton, given to several men for lands and bonds of John Burhunt' in Burhunt' herberd. [This note is in Latin, but the deed is in French.]

1 Sir William de Overton died on 13 October 1361 (*Cal. Inq. p. m.* XI, no. 153, p. 149).

2 Sir John de Borhunte had died on 10 November 1358 (*Cal. Inq. p. m.* X, no. 466, p. 371). His widow, Mary de Roches, subsequently married Sir Bernard Brocas. For Sir John de Borhunte's dealings with Sir William de Overton, see II 109, 95, 121, 122. See also II 120 and 97.

II 94   19 October 1361

[fo. 63ᵛ] GRANT by Richard Danvers to Sir John de Scures, knight; Roger Ingelfeld; Simon Stake; William Daubeney; and Simon atte Mede, of £40 annual rent which Sir John de Borhunt', knight, gave him in the manor of Boarhunt Herbert (*Borhunt' Herbert*) for his service, as fully shown in Sir John's charter. The grantees, their heirs and assigns, will hold the aforesaid rent in perpetuity. Witnesses: Sir Roger Markuant, knight; and many others.

> Southwick, the morrow of the feast of
> St Luke the Evangelist, 35 Edward III.

See also II 89.

II 95   2 January 1352

GRANT, with warranty, by Sir John de Borhunt', knight, to William Overton' and his heirs, of £10 annual rent from his manor of Hinton (*Henton'*) and all his lands and tenements in Hinton, Catherington (*Cateryngton'*) and Denmead (*Denemede*). The rent is to be paid at Hinton in equal portions at the four principal terms, viz., Easter, the Nativity of St John the Baptist, Michaelmas and Christmas. The donor binds himself, his heirs and whoever may hold the aforesaid manor and lands, to faithful payment of the rent at the place and times above, and William and his heirs will have right of distraint and coercion. They may enter the manor and lands if the rent is wholly or partly in arrears, distrain, and keep the distraint until the rent and any arrears are fully paid. Witnesses: Sir Robert Markaunt, Sir Philip Daundele, knights: and others.

> Hinton, 2 January, 25 Edward III.

See also II 109, 121, 122, 209.

II 96 10 January 1364

NOTIFICATION by Thomas de Hampton', Sheriff of Hampshire, of receipt of 40s. from Richard, Prior of Southwick,[1] on behalf of Peter de Hoo, clerk, Michael Skyllyng', Valentine atte Mede, and Simon atte Mede, for licensing the agreement (*pro lic' con'*) with John, son of Herbert de Borhunte concerning the priory's plea with regard to the manor of Boarhunt Herberd, Hinton (*Henton'*) and Hannington (*Hanyton*). The sheriff is satisfied with the above sum and gives quittance to the prior of any claim against him by the king or any others whatever.

Winchester castle, 10 January, 37th year.[1]

1 Richard Bromdene was Prior of Southwick, 1349–81. Presumably the 37th year refers to the reign of Edward III, i.e., 1364.
See also II 104, 100, 103.

II 97 11 November 1363

NOTIFICATION by John Greyte, executor of the will of the late Sir William de Overton', knight, and administrator of his property, of receipt of 120 marks from Sir Bernard Brokas, in payment of all debts owed by Sir John de Borhunt' to the aforesaid Sir William for bonds made according to the Statute of Merchants or otherwise, or any annual pension or contract existing between them up to the date of Sir William's death.[1] [The executor] has handed over to Sir Bernard all bonds and statutes, made by Sir John during his lifetime, which have come into his hands and those of his co-excutors. He has given quittance to Sir Bernard and all others, into whose hands any lands and tenements have passed, or may pass, that were formerly Sir John's. They are hereby absolved in perpetuity from any responsibility for bonds, pensions or debts. Witnesses: Sir Lawrence de Sancto Martino, Sir John de Scures, knights; and many others.

Alresford, the feast of St Martin the Bishop, 37 Edward III.

1 See II 121, 122. See also II 93 and notes.

II 98 25 November 1378

[fo. 64] LEASE, with warranty, for life in survivorship, by Elias Daubenye to Alice Carpenter and her son, John, of 20 acres of arable in Hinton (*Henton'*) field: viz. 2 acres which lie together in the west field adjoining *le Redehelde* between the lands of Robert Markaunt and de Borhunt'; 3 acres together adjoining *Nodena* between the lands of John Putlygh and John Cole; 3 acres together at *le Combeforlong'* between Emmory's land on either side; 1 acre at *Roudene* which abuts on to *Tebaldeslynch'*; 1 acre at *le Benne* between Robert Markaunt's land and Emmory's; 2 acres together in the east field, between the lands of Robert Markaunt and de Borhunt', which abut on to *le Denewey*; 3 acres together east of *le Denewey*, between Robert Markaunt's land on either side, which abut on to *Markfourlong'*; 1 acre, between de Borhunt' land on either side, which abuts on to *le Denewey*; 1 acre, between the lands of de Putlygh' and de Morell', which abuts on to *le Denewey*; and 3 acres together between the lands of Robert Markaunt and de Borhunt'. The lessees will hold the aforesaid land with common pasture pertaining thereto and all appurtenances, for an annual rent of a red rose at the feast of the Nativity of St John the Baptist for all service, secular exaction and demand. Witnesses: Sir Robert Markaunt, knight; John Tyrel; and others.

Hinton, Thursday, the feast of St. Katerine the Virgin, 2 Richard II. [Marginal note:] Evidence that Hinton appertains to the manor of Boarhunt Herberd (*Evidencia q' Henton' pertinens ad manerium de Burhunt' Herberd*).[1]

1 According to the inquisition held at Southwick on 18 February 1359, following the death of Sir John de Borhunt', Sir John was enfeoffed jointly with his wife, Mary, of the manor of Henton—presumably Hinton Burrant—which he held of Ellis Daubeney by fealty and the service of 1d. yearly. The only other land he held at Henton was a croft called Pakeday containing 1 acre which was of old escheat and rendered 2s. 6d. yearly to the Exchequer (*Cal. Inq. p. m.* X, no. 466, p. 371).
See also II 109 which refers to Sir John's lands in Hinton Daubenay.

The manors of Hinton Daubnay, Hinton Markaunt and Hinton Burrant all lay in the parish of Catherington, and this deed suggests that their lands were intermingled in crofts and openfield. All were destined to pass into the hands of the Priory of St Swithun's, Winchester (*VCH Hants* III, pp. 96–7). In the Southwick cartularies members of the neighbouring Daubenye, Markaunt and Borhunt families are frequently found as witnesses to each other's charters.

II 99   Between 6 and 13 October 1305

FINAL CONCORD made in the King's court before Ralph de Hengham, William de Bereford', Elyas de Bekyngham, Peter Malorr', William Howard, and Lambert de Trikynham, Justices; and others; between Richard de Borhunt', querent, and Thomas de Borhunt', deforciant, concerning the manor of Boarhunt (*Borhunt'*) with appurtenances,[1] and 1 messuage with 1 carucate of land in Hinton next Catherington (*Cateryngton'*), by which it was agreed that Richard recognised Thomas' right to the tenement with appurtenances, and in return Thomas granted it for life to Richard, and handed it over in the court. Richard will hold it from Thomas and his heirs, paying them annually a rose at the feast of the Nativity of St John the Baptist, for all service, custom and exaction pertaining to them, and performing, on their behalf, all other services due to the chief lords of that fee. Reversion, after Richard's death, to Thomas and his heirs, who will hold the tenement of the chief lords of that fee for the accustomed services in perpetuity.

Westminster, the octave of St Michael,
33 Edward son of King Henry.

[Marginal note:] Final concord concerning a messuage and carucate of land with appurtenances in Hinton next Catherington (*Henton' iuxta Kateryngton'*).

1 Richard de Borhunt was probably Thomas' father. Richard was still holding Boarhunt Herberd in 1314, but by 1316 it had passed to Thomas. (II 69; *Feudal Aids* II, p. 319).

II 100   12 November 1361

[fo. 64ᵛ] FINAL CONCORD made in the King's court before Robert de Thorp', John Moubray, and John Knyvet, Justices; and afterwards conceded and recorded before the same justices in the quindene of St Martin 37 Edward III [between 25 November and 2 December, 1363], between John de Scures, knight; Peter de Hoo, clerk; Michael Skillyng; Valentine atte Mede; and Simon atte Mede, querents, and John, son of Herbert de Borhunt', deforciant, concerning the manors of Boarhunt Herberd (*Borhunt' herbert*), Hinton (*Henton'*) and Hannington (*Hanyton*) with appurtenances, which Bernard Brocas, knight, and his wife, Mary, hold for Mary's life. It was agreed that the aforesaid John, son of Herbert, recognised Valentine's right to the manor with appurtenances, which was held of John's inheritance by Bernard and Mary at the time of the concord and which after Mary's death should have reverted to John, but will pass in entirety to the querents and Valentine's heirs.[1] They will hold them in perpetuity of the chief lords of that fee for the accustomed services, and John and his heirs will provide warranty in perpetuity.[2] Consideration, 200 marks. The concord was made in the presence, and with the consent, of Bernard and Mary, who did fealty to the querents in court.

         Westminster, the day after Martinmas, 35 Edward III.

[Marginal note:] Note concerning the feoffment of the manors of Boarhunt Herberd, Hinton, and Hannington (*Burhunt' Herbard, Henton' et Hanytun*).

1 The reversion of the manors after Mary's death was first granted to Sir John de Scures, Sir Peter de Hoo, Valentine ate Mede and Simon atte Mede, by John, son of Herbert, on 31 October 1361 (II 104).

2 See the bond for warranty, II 106.

II 101   [1288–1304][1]

QUITCLAIM, with warranty against both Jews and Christians, by John Daubeney to Sir Richard de Borhunt', knight, of all right and claim he had or could have in (i) 20s. annual rent, which he used to receive from a tenement Roger de Molthene gave Sir Richard in Hinton (*Henton'*) next Catherington (*Kateringtone*). Roger was given the tenement by Rose

(*Roysa*), daughter and heir of the late Adam de Henton'.[2] Also (ii) 2 acres at *la Wydedelle*. Sir Richard, his heirs or assigns, will hold the aforesaid rent and land in perpetuity, paying 1d. annual rent at Hinton at Michaelmas for all services, customs, exaction, suits of court, hidage, scutage, reliefs, heriots, aids—viz., at the knighting of a son or marriage of a daughter—escheats, and all other secular demands. Witnesses: Richard de Portesye, Philip, son of Peter, Baldwin de Bello Alneto, knights; and many others.

1 In 1288 Roger de Molton quitclaimed to Richard de Boarhunt and his wife, Maud, a tenement at Hinton comprising a messuage and 1½ carucates of land (*V C H Hants* III, p. 97). Sir Richard made it over to his son, Thomas, in 1305 (II 99). John Daubeney had died by March 1304; his son and heir John, was 12 years of age (*Cal. Inq. p. m.* IV, no. 224, p. 146).

2 Rose quitclaimed the tenement, described as a messuage and 80 acres at Hinton next Catherington, to Roger in 1283 (*V C H Hants* III, p. 97).

In 1327 John Daubeney, son of John Daubney, quitclaimed rent and land in Hinton to Thomas de Borhunt, son of Sir Richard, and his wife, Margaret (II 125).

II 102   31 October 1361

[fo. 65] GRANT by John Herbert, cousin and heir of Sir John de Burhunt', to Sir John de Scures, Sir Peter de Hoo, Valentine atte Mede, and Simon atte Mede, of £200 (*liuers*) sterling annual rent at Michaelmas, from his manors of Boarhunt, Hinton, and Hannington (*Borhunt', Henton', Hanynton*), whoever is holding them.[1] If the rent is in arrears, wholly or in part, the grantees and their heirs may distrain, and keep the distraint until fully paid. Witnesses: Sir Robert Markaunt, John le Boteler, and others.

Southwick, the vigil of All Saints, 35 Edward III. French.

1 This is the earliest of the many transactions between John, son of Herbert de Borhunt, and Sir John de Scures and the others. The manors were held by Mary de Roches, who had married Sir Bernard Brocas after the death of her first husband, Sir John de Burhunt'. See II 104, 100, 117, 106, 105.

II 103   21 December 1362

NOTIFICATION by John de Borhunt', son of Herbert de Borhunte, that he will cancel the charter by which the prior and convent of Southwick owe him a corrody for life, viz. 2 white conventual loaves; 2 *justes* of conventual ale; 2 ordinary conventual dishes (*generals mes conventuals*) with 2 pittances; 2 cartloads of hay; 4 cartloads of firewood (*buche pour fouayle*); 1 cartload of litter; 1 gown a year, similar to that received by the esquires of the priory; and 40s. a year in equal portions at the Nativity of St John the Baptist and Christmas, if Sir John de Scures, knight; Sir Peter de Hoo, chaplain; Michael Skillyng'; Simon atte Mede; and Valentine atte Mede, re-enfeoff him with the reversion of the manors of Boarhunt Herberd, Hannington, and Hinton (Borhunt' Herbert, Hanyton' et Henton') with appurtenances, of which he enfeoffed them; and he will acquit the priory in perpetuity of all other actions, burdens and escheats.[1]

Southwick, the feast of St Thomas the Apostle, 36 Edward III. French.

1 Of the manors, the reversion of which John, son of Herbert de Borhunt, made over to Sir John de Scures and the others and to the heirs of Valentine atte Mede, Boarhunt Herberd and Hannington were ultimately destined for Southwick Priory. This would provide the reason for the priory's grant of a corrody to John, and John's promise to cancel that grant if he recovered the reversion of the manors. Boarhunt Herberd was quitclaimed by Valentine atte Mede to Bishop William of Wykeham, who obtain a royal licence to grant it to Southwick Priory (II 114, 112, 111). Hannington was given to the priory by Sir Bernard Brocas (III 427).

II 104   31 October 1361

[fo. 65ᵛ] GRANT, with warranty, by John Herbert, cousin and heir of Sir John de Borhunt', to Sir (*Mons'*) John de Scures, Sir (*Sire*) Peter de Hoo, Valentine atte Mede, and Simon atte Mede, of the reversion of the manors of Boarhunt, Hinton and Hannington (*Borhunt', Henton' et Hanyton'*), after the death of Mary, who was the wife of Sir John de Borhunt'.[1] She holds them for life of the grantor's inheritance, and they are due to revert to him and his heirs after her death. Witnesses: Sir (Mons.) Robert Markaunt; John le Boteler, and many others.

Southwick, the vigil of All Saints, 35 Edward III. French.

1 See final concord with regard to this reversion (II 100).

II 105   29 November 1363

NOTIFICATION[1] by John de Scures, knight; Peter de Hoo, clerk; Michael Skillyng'; Valentine atte Mede; and Simon atte Mede. Since John, son of Herbert de Borhunt', cousin and heir of Sir John de Borhunt', knight, has granted them, by a fine levied in the king's court, the reversion of the manors of Boarhunt [and] Hinton (*Borhunt' henton'*) with their appurtenances, for them and the heirs of Valentine to hold after the death of Mary, wife of Bernard Brokas.[2] They have therefore granted to the aforesaid Bernard and Mary, and Mary's assigns, quittance and discharge for any waste committed on the said manors.

Westminster, Wednesday, the vigil of the feast of St Andrew, 37 Edward III. French.

1 Sealed, but no witnesses.
2 See II 100.

II 106 28 October 1363

BOND in £1,000 by John Herbert, son of Herbert de Borhunt', to Sir John de Scures, knight; Sir Peter de Hoo, chaplain; and William Daubeneye, to be paid to them or their assigns whenever required by them or any one of them [for warranty]. He has bound himself, his heirs and executors to make this payment together with all right and claim he has or could have by inheritance in the manor[s] of Boarhunt Herberd, Hinton, and Hannington (*Borhunt' Herbert, Hentone et Hanyton*), with their appurtenances, who ever happens to hold them; and all his goods, moveable and immoveable, for distraint by any king's justice, or bailiff, or ecclesiastical judge.

Southwick, the feast of Sts Simon and Jude, 37 Edward III.

[Marginal note:] Bond drawn up guaranteeing the manors, viz. Boarhunt Herberd, Hinton and Hannington (*Nota obligacionem factam ad warantisand' maneria viz' Burhunt' Herbard, Henton' et Hanytne*).

See II 104, 100.

II 107 Between 6 and 13 October 1344

[fo. 66] FINAL CONCORD made in the King's Court before John de Stonore, Roger Hillary, Richard de Kelleshulle, and Richard de Wylughby, Justices; and others; between John de Borhunt' and his wife Mary, querents, and William Danvers and his wife Margaret, deforciants, concerning the manors of Boarhunt (*Borhunte*) and Hinton (*Henton'*) with appurtenances. William and Margaret acknowledge the right of John to the aforesaid manors and appurtenances, given by them to him and Mary. John and Mary, and John's heirs, will hold the aforesaid manor of Hinton of the chief lords of that fee, [for the accustomed services] which pertain to that manor in perpetuity.[1] In return John and Mary have granted to William and Margaret, for Margaret's life, the manor of Boarhunt with appurtenances, and handed it over in court. William and Margaret will hold the manor of John and Mary and John's heirs, paying annually a rose at the Nativity of St John the Baptist for all service, custom, and exaction due to them, and performing all services due to the chief lords of that fee. Reversion after Margaret's death, to John, Mary, and John's heirs, who will hold the manor of the chief lords of that fee for the accustomed services in perpetuity.

Westminster, the octave of St Michael, 18 Edward III.

[Marginal note:] Mark well re. Hinton as shown here.

1 Margaret was the widow of Thomas de Borhunt, who died in 1339, and the mother of John de Borhunt. She afterwards married William Danvers. Already in 1342 John had granted William for life 100s. annual rent from his manor of Hinton with right of distraint. (*Cal. Close R., 1341-3* p. 646). After Margaret's

death, the manors passed to John and Mary, and were held by them when John died in 1358 (*V C H Hants* III, p. 145; *Cal. Inq. p.m.* X, no. 466, p. 371).

II 108   Between 16 and 23 June 1314

FINAL CONCORD made in the King's Court before William de Bere-ford', Lambert de Trikyngham, John de Wenstede, Henry le Scrop', William Inge and John Bacun, Justices; and others; between Richard de Borhunt', querent, and Thomas de Borhunt' and his wife, Margaret, deforciants, concerning the manor of Boarhunt (*Borhunt*) with appurten-ances. Thomas and Margaret have acknowledged Richard's right to the manor and appurtenances; in return, Richard has granted the manor to Thomas and Margaret, and has handed it over to them in the court. Thomas, Margaret, and Thomas' heirs by Margaret, will hold the manor in perpetuity of Richard and his heirs, paying Richard, during his lifetime, £20 annual rent, half at Michaelmas and half at Easter; and to Richard's heirs, a rose at the Nativity of St John the Baptist, for all service, custom and exaction owing to them; and performing all other services due to the chief lords of that fee in perpetuity. If Thomas dies without heirs by Margaret, reversion after their deaths will be to Richard and his heirs, regardless of other heirs of Thomas and of Margaret; and Richard and his heirs will hold [the manor] of the chief lords of that fee for the accustomed service in perpetuity.

Westminster, the quindene of Holy Trinity,
7 Edward, son of King Edward.

See also II 99.
Copy II 140. Variants: William de Gereford'; John de Benstede.

II 109   4 October 1351

[fo. 66ᵛ] GRANT, with warranty, by John de Borhunt', knight, to William de Overton', his heirs and assigns, of £10 annual rent in all his lands and tenements with appurtenances in Hinton Daubenay (*Henton' Daubeneye*), to be received in equal portions at Easter and Michaelmas. William, his heirs and assigns, will hold the rent of John and his heirs in perpetuity. If the said rent is wholly or partly in arrears, the grantees may enter and distrain on all goods and cattle (*catalla*) found in the aforesaid lands and tenements, and take, drive away and impound them at will until the rent is fully paid. Sir John has delivered full seisin to William in all the aforesaid lands and tenements with the acknowledge-ment of the tenants there. Witnesses: Philip Daundelye, Robert Mar-kaunt, knights; and others.

Hinton, 4 October, 25 Edward III.

See also II 95, 121, 122; and II 98, marginal note.
The remainder of fo. 66ᵛ is blank.

II 110[1]

CORRODY: these are the particulars of the corrody John Burhunt has from Southwick Priory, with the price at which hitherto all corrodies have been sold,[2] viz., the said John has:

		£.	s.	d.
(i)	2 conventual loaves a day worth	21.	0.	0.
(ii)	2 measures (*justes*) of ale at the same price as the loaves	21.	0.	0.
(iii)	2 conventual dishes worth the same as the loaves	21.	0.	0.
(iv)	2 pittances, exactly the same as a canon has, worth the same as a dish	21.	0.	0.
(v)	2 cartloads of hay, 4 of logs, 1 of litter worth 13s. 4d. a year	[6.	13.	4.][3]
(vi)	for shoes, 40s. a year	[20.	0.	0.][3]
(vii)	a gown with fur, of the sort worn by gentlemen, worth 16s. a year	8.	0.	0.
(viii)	a place to live within the priory with a garden	5.	0.	0.
(ix)	a tenement in the vill for [his] life and [the life of] his daughter, Joan, worth 20s. a year, costing	10.	0.	0.

Total £122. 13s. 4d.

Outside expenses (*Expens' forinsec'*) incurred for the manors of Boarhunt Herberd and Herbelyn:—

		£.	s.	d.
(i)	lodging for 20 days in London (*Loundr'*) for Sir John de Scures with the other feofees for levying the fine and for the said fine (40s.)[4]	8. 2.	0. 0.	0. 0.
(ii)	for prosecution of the writ *quid iuris clamat* several times against Sir Bernard Brocas and his wife, Lady Mary, to discover their claim to the aforesaid fiefs (*en pursuite par deuers M. Bernard Brocas et dame Marie sa femme a atorner par brief quid iuris clamat a les avanditz feoffetz par diverses foith'*)	12.	0.	0.
(iii)	for the deeds purchased concerning Sir William de Overton's release of the manor of Hannington (*Hanyton'*)—value unknown; and also costs of the case of battery and trespass done to my [the prior's] people by Sir Bernard and his people, with lodging for 20 days in London[5]	20.	0.	0.
(iv)	expenses incurred for the profession of the daughter of Sir John de Bourh' at Romsey (*Romesey*) with various gifts to the said nunnery and others[6]—(20 marks)	13.	6.	8.
(v)	for a bond for £100 on the said manor[?] held by (*vers*) a burgess of London[7]	20.	0.	0.
(vi)	various expenses incurred for the manor of Boarhunt Herbelyn in the lifetime of (*vivant*) Richard Danvers—viz. sowing his land for 3 years and the said Richard taking the profit—with various other			

costs involved in the purchase of the said manor
out of the hands of the king[8]   60. 0. 0.

(vii) £10 paid to the said Richard Danvers, for which
we have received wood sold from the manor   10. 0. 0.

Total: £145. 6. 8.

Grand total: £268. 0. 0.

[*verso*] These are some of the deficiencies found on the manor of Boarhunt Herberd, viz:

(i) Everything removed from the great chamber (*la grande chambre*) and taken to Fareham (*Farham*); the hall unroofed (*descovert*) and virtually destroyed (*et ou ponit destr' perdu*); the kitchen unroofed, and all the houses of the court tiled with stone unroofed, and the stone taken to Fareham.

(ii) an old hall [?] given by Philepot de Hoo and entirely removed (*un veile sale done par Philepot de Hoo et entierment oustre*).

(iii) 65 ash trees (*keynes*) of the size of big oaks, felled in a grove called Noreys Grove belonging to the said manor.

(iv) in another grove at least 90 small ash trees felled.

(v) in another small grove, which John Wyot holds, 36 small ash trees [? felled].

(vi) in another grove of mature and young ash trees (*de keynes et freynes*) called *La Lithe*, the greater part felled and carried away.

(vii) in the big wood called *Le Plaschette*, 200 and more mature and young ash trees felled and carried away.

(viii) in the wood sold [called] *Southboys*, much enclosure and trampling by animals, so that a total of 12 acres is for the most part destroyed.

(ix) Sir Bernard Brocas' fold, which should have been on the land of the said manor, has for a long time been removed onto other land, causing great damage to the said manor.

This total, together with the aforesaid manors, we put at the disposal of our right honourable lord, so that they, and the manor of Belney, can be appropriated by our priory of Southwick, drawing up such charters for our lord as he shall ordain and our poor house can well support (*fesaunt pour ycels tiels charges a nostre avandit Seigneur come la gratiouse Seigneurie de lui vendra ordeni' et nostre pouer' meson pourra bonement porter*).

1 French. On a separate piece of parchment 25.5 cms × 22 cms, sewn on to the left-hand margin of fo. 66[v].

2 The corrody was probably granted to John, son of Herbert de Borhunt, in 1361 when he surrendered his right to the reversion of the manors of Boarhunt Herberd, Hinton, and Hannington (II 104; see also II 103). The corrody and the following list of expenses appear to have been incurred in making available the manors of Boarhunt Herberd and Herbelyn for transfer to Southwick Priory by Bishop William of Wykeham (II 111).

3 These amounts are left blank, so that the sums given add up to £96, which is £26. 13s. 4d. short of the given total. It would appear from items vii and ix, that in each case the annual value is multiplied by 10 to ascertain the overall value

given in the right hand column. If the same principle is applied to items v and vi, the amounts £6. 13s. 4d. and £20 respectively can be added, and the total will then be £122. 13s. 4d., as given. This total, therefore, appears to represent the value of the corrody over 10 years.

4 See II 100, 96.

5 See II 117, 118, 124.

6 Probably this reference is to Sir John de Burhunt, who died seised of the manor of Boarhunt Herberd in 1358. In that case, provision was presumably made for his daughter, and any future claim by her on the manor would thus be avoided.

7 See II 200.

8 Richard Danvers had acquired Boarhunt Herebelyn from Thomas, son of Gilbert de Burhunt, before Thomas' death *c.* 1344 (II 163; *VCH Hants* III, p. 146). Before Richard died in 1361, he made over the manor to Sir John de Scures and others as trustees, but they failed to get the requisite royal licence before entering into possession, and had to pay £8 to retrieve the manor from the hands of the King (*Cal. Inq. p. m.* XI, no. 244, p. 200; II 89, 88).

II 111   1 October 1369

[fo. 67] GIFT, with warranty, by William de Wykeham to Southwick Priory. The king, by special grace, has granted a licence to the bishop[1] to give to the priory, founded by the king's progenitors and in his patronage (*qui de fundacione progenitorum ipsius domini et de suo patronatu existit*), the manor of Boarhunt Herberd (*Bourhunt' Herberd*) with appurtenances, and all lands and tenements with appurtenances in Southwick, Wanstead, Portchester, West Boarhunt, and Wymering (*Wanstede, Porchestre, Westburghunte, Wymeryng'*) which were [in the possession] of Sir John de Bourhunt', son and heir of Thomas de Bourhunte, and were not held of the king; and the manor of Boarhunt Herbelyn and all lands and tenements with appurtenances in the vills aforesaid, which were [in the possession] of Richard Danvers and were held of the king in chief. Therefore the priory is to hold them in perpetuity: viz. the manor of Boarhunt Herberd, lands and tenements of the chief lords of the fee for the accustomed service, and the manor of Boarhunt Herbelyn, lands and tenements of the king and his heirs for the accustomed service of providing one armed man at the king's castle of Portchester for 15 days in time of war, for homage and all other secular services, exactions and demands.

The bishop's gift is made in order to provide upkeep in perpetuity for certain chantries, pious works and other divine services to be performed by the priory according to an ordinance which he will cause to be drawn up concerning the method and form of the chantries, [etc.,][2] and the monetary or other penalties and securities due to him at will, and to his successors or other persons, if at any time the chantries, [etc.,] are allowed to lapse.

So that the priory can receive and hold the lands aforesaid for the maintenance of the chantries, [etc.,] the bishop has given it the special licence from the king as contained in letters patent;[1] and so that the chantries, [etc.,] may be perpetually established, he has laid down, with the consent of the priory, the method by which they will be carried out, and this will be fully contained in an indenture drawn up between them.[2]

[fo. 67ᵛ] Moreover, the bishop has granted the priory 158 marks to buy corn and livestock for the manors, lands and tenements, and not for any other use: i.e., 33 marks for seed corn of different kinds; 9 marks for 6 cart-horses each worth 20s.; 40 marks for 32 oxen for the ploughs, each worth 16s. 8d.; 75 marks for 500 sheep, each worth 2s. It is the bishop's will that this amount of corn and livestock remain there in perpetuity, so that no prior will be allowed to alienate, diminish, or transfer that stock, to the detriment of the said manors, lands and tenements.

So that the priory does not have to be excused or exonerated through poverty from supporting the burden of the chantries and other things expressly specified in the above agreement, and is not excessively oppressed by that burden during the first year, before it can receive the profits of the aforesaid manors, etc., nor have its other possessions impaired for that reason; but in order that it always has a sufficient sum each year in advance for the suitable support of the said burdens, the bishop has given the prior and convent 125½ marks as full maintenance for those burdens, viz., 50 marks for the first year, and the remaining 75½ marks for their relief and the support of those burdens in future.

It is the bishop's will that, after the second year following this gift, such a sum, i.e., 75½ marks, be put into the priory's treasury at the beginning of each successive year, from the profits of the manors and stock, so that the said sum will remain there in hand, for the upkeep of the said chantries or maintenance of 5 canons, and for distributions laid down in the said ordinance, and not for conversion to any other use.

One part of this indenture was sealed by the bishop; the other, kept by him, was sealed with the common seal of the priory, the prior and canons giving unanimous consent to everything contained therein. Witnesses: John de Lisle de Wodeton', Bernard Brocas, Ralph de Norton', knights; Nicholas Wodelok'; Henry Popham; John de Warbelton; Thomas Wodelok'; John de Scures; and others.

The vill of Southwick.

[Marginal note:] 300 marks
Westburhunt, Porchest', Wymeryng, b't herberd and herbelyne danvers with appurtenances in Suthwyk and Wansted. Item 12 copes. [In a later hand.]

1 II 112; III 972.

2 This intention was carried out the next day, 2 October 1369, and the original of the statutes which the bishop laid down on that date is preserved in H.R.O. (4M53/A4). A fine impression of the bishop's seal is appended.

These statutes made detailed arrangements for the appointment of five canons, in addition to those already in the priory, to celebrate daily masses for the souls of John and Sibil, the founder's parents, who were buried at Southwick. They made provision for the replacement of any canon who, through infirmity, death or apostasy, could no longer fulfil his duties. They laid down the amount of the allowances to be given to each of the five canons and to be distributed as pittances to other members of the priory. The form of service, with or without music, was prescribed for each occasion, with special celebrations on the obit days of those for whom the chantries were founded; and after the bishop's death a prayer was to be said daily for his soul by all the convent after complin.

Another document (4M53/A5), also sealed by the bishop, is an indenture drawn up on 9 August 1370, in the form of an inspeximus and confirmation by Prior Richard Bromdene, reciting both the statutes and the charter itself, together with the penalties to be incurred by the priory for any failure to carry out its obligations.

See also Introduction p. xxxiv, with reference to the marginal note above.

Original in H.R.O., 4M53/A3

Indented along the top. On the bottom fold: pro sigillo Ep[iscop]i [contemporary hand].

Seal: on tag 30 cms, very fine impression of William of Wykeham's seal: red on dark green wax; pointed oval 9 cms × 5 cms; device: bishop standing in the centre of 3 elaborate architectural niches; crosier in left hand, right hand raised in blessing; shields of arms to right and left. Inscription: S' WILLELMI DE WYKEHAM DEI GRACIA WINTON EPI

Endorsements: (a) William of Wickham gives the manors of Burrant Herbert and Herbelyn to this priory for maintenance of singers in ye church [*c.* late 17th-century hand].

      (b) XVI

      (c) (44)

      (d) AA

      (e) (N 27)

A small piece of parchment is sewn onto the left-hand corner of the charter and is endorsed:

No. 3. [red ink]

Grant of the Manors of Burhunt Herberd and Herbelyn to the Prior etc. of Suthwyk.

43 Edw. 3 [in the hand of W. T. Alchin].

Also in H.R.O. there is a late 17th or early 18th-century copy (4M53/A3a), on paper, of the above charter.

Endorsements: (a) dated 1 Octr 43 E. 1 [*sic*].

        [(b)–(e) as (a)–(d) above]

        (f) Copy. Examined. [All endorsements in the same hand as the text]

II 112   6 February 1368

[fo. 68] LETTERS PATENT of King Edward III granting special licence to William de Wykeham, Bishop of Winchester, for the alienation in mortmain to Southwick Priory of (i) the manor of Boarhunt Herberd (*Bourhunte Herberd*) with appurtenances, and all lands and tenements with appurtenances in Southwick, Wanstead, Portchester, West Boarhunt and Wymering (*Suthewyk' Wanstede Porcestre Westburghunte et Wymerynge*) which were [in the possession] of Sir John de Bourhunte, son and heir of Thomas de Bourhunte, and were not held of the king, as is said; and (ii) the manor of Boarhunt Herbelyn with appurtenances, and all lands and tenements in the said vills of Southwick, Portchester, Wymering and West Boarhunt which were [in the possession] of Richard Danvers, and were held of the king in chief, as is said. In accordance with certain conditions determined by the bishop,[1] the priory will hold in perpetuity the said manor of Boarhunt Herberd, lands and tenements, of the chief lords of the fee for the accustomed services; and the said manor of Boarhunt Herbelyn, lands and tenements, of the king and his heirs for the accustomed services; paying annually 6s. 8d. to the royal exchequer in equal portions at Easter and Michaelmas, for all other secular demands, wards, marriages, reliefs, suits of leet courts, lawdays (*lawedays*), rights, profits, emoluments, and easements, due to the king or his heirs, or which could for any reason accrue to them in the future.[2]

Witnessed by the King at Westminster.

1 See II 111.

2 The accustomed service which the priory owed to the king for Boarhunt Herbelyn and the other lands formerly held by Richard Danvers consisted of the provision of an armed man in Portchester Castle for 15 days in time of war (as quoted in II 111 and III 972); the priory had also undertaken to pay to the king an annual rent of 6s. 8d. in return for an assurance of undisturbed possession of all the lands granted to it by William of Wykeham in accordance with the king's licence.

In H.R.O. (5M50/23) there is a copy of an entry from the Pipe Roll of 1371-2, which records that the 6s. 8d. annual rent was due from 18 June 1369 (the date of issue of the king's second licence (III 972)); so far 13s. 4d. had been paid and 6s. 8d. was owing. The prior's obligation to provide an armed man is also noted, and interlineated in different ink, possibly by a different hand, is a description of the arms to be provided, viz. a helmet, habergeon, dagger, pole-axe, sword and spear (*cum capello ferreo haberion dagger pollax opera swerd et schere sper*).

Original in H.R.O. 4M53/A1. The text appears to be identical with the cartulary copy, but some words are missing where the parchment has worn into holes on the folds. In small writing under the bottom lines: *per brevem de privato sigillo tripplicat' Woll'*

Seal: on blue and green plaited silk thread, dark green wax with fragment of the Great Seal of Edward III as on 4M53/A2 (see below).

Endorsements: (a) Lice*n*cia re*gis* Edwardi impetrar' Burhu*n*t' et Suthwyke per manu*m* mortua*m*

        (b) 27

        (c) Burhunte Suthwyk'

A small piece of parchment is sewn onto the right-hand corner of the charter and endorsed:

No. 1 [red ink].

License to W. of Wykeh' to alien'

See the Book, pag. 358

42 Edw. 3 [in the hand of W. T. Alchin. The book referred to is his Suthwyk Record (H.R.O., 4M53/Alchin)].

Also H.R.O. 4M53/A2. Perfect condition and text identical with cartulary copy, except for the addition in very small writing below bottom line: *per brevem de privato sigillo Wollore*

Seal: on plaited purple and green/brown silk thread; dark green wax; nearly perfect impression of Great Seal, but chipped on bottom and right-hand edge; round, 11 cms diameter;

Obverse: The king enthroned in the centre of 3 architectural niches, with orb and sceptre; identical shields of arms on left and right.

    Legend: EDWARD .... NIE ET ACQUITANNIE

Reverse: In a cusped circle, the king in armour, wearing great helm, mounted on caparisoned horse; shield, with royal arms; sword raised in right hand.

Legend: EDWARDUS DEI GRAC .... TANNIE
Endorsements: (a) bourhunte
            (b) 6 Feb   42 Ed 3 [16th century hand]
            (c) 42
            (d) Notatur fac' post castyll' [?]rope [?]forisfac...: [note, done
                 after the forfeiture of castle rape [?]]
            (e) A A
            (f) Licence of Edw. [16th or 17th-century hand]
            (g) Burhunt herbert et herbelyn' alias vocat' Damvers per manum
                 mortuam
       (h) XVI
A small piece of parchment is sewn to the left-hand corner of the charter and is
endorsed:
No. 2. [red ink].
Duplicate of License to alien.
42 Edw. 3 [in the hand of W. T. Alchin].

II 113   10 July 1369
[fo. 68ᵛ] NOTIFICATION by Luke de Ponynges and his wife, Isabella,
that, since religious men and others are not allowed entry to any fee on
terms contrary to the Statute of Mortmain without licence from the
king,[1] and from the chief lord of whom it is held without intermediary;
at the request of Sir William de Wykeham, Bishop of Winchester, they
have granted licence to the bishop, for themselves and their heirs, so far
as it is in their power, to give to the prior and convent of Southwick his
manor of Boarhunt Herberd (*Burhunte Herberd*), which is held of them,
as of the inheritance of the aforesaid Isabella,[2] for knight service. The
priory is to hold it in perpetuity on certain terms drawn up by the
bishop, without impediment from Luke and Isabella, or their heirs,
notwithstanding the aforesaid Statute.

                 Southwick, 10 July, 43 Edward III.

1 Licence from the king had already been obtained (II 112).

2 The manor of Boarhunt Herberd was held of the St Johns, descendants of the
de Ports. Isabella de St John succeeded to the inheritance on the death of her
brother, Edmund, in 1347. After 1348 she married Luke de Poynings, as her
second husband. Luke died in 1376, and Isabella in 1393 (*VCH Hants* III, p. 145;
Complete Peerage XI, p. 327).

II 114   7 January 1368

QUITCLAIM,[1] with warranty, by Valentine atte Mede of Bramdean
(*Bromden'*) to Sir William de Wykeham, Bishop of Winchester, of all
his rights in the manor of Boarhunt Herberd (*Bourhunte Herberd'*), and
all other lands, tenements, rents, meadows, woods, grazings, pastures,
and services of both free and bond tenants, with all appurtenances,
which were formerly [in the possession] of John de Borhunt, knight, in

Southwick, Wanstead, Wymering, Sheepwash,[2] Portchester, West Boarhunt, Fareham and Hambledon (*Wanstede, Wymeryng', Shepewasshe,
Porchestr', Westbourhunt', Farham, Hameldon').*[3] The bishop, his heirs
and assigns, will hold all the aforesaid lands of the chief lords of that
fee for the accustomed service in perpetuity, free from any claim or
action by Valentine or his heirs. Witnesses: John de Warbleton'; Henry
de Popham; Peter de Bruges; Walter Haywode; Thomas Warn'; Richard
Pauncefote; Stephen Haym; and others.

Southwark (*Suthwerk'*) in the suburb of London, Friday, the
day after the feast of the Epiphany, 41 Edward III.

1 *Cal. Close R., 1364–8* p. 406.

2 Sheepwash is a little over 2 miles E.N.E. of Southwick.

3 John, son of Herbert de Borhunt, made over the reversion of the manor of
Boarhunt Herberd and other lands, formerly held by Sir John de Borhunt, to
feoffees including Valentine atte Mede, and to Valentine's heirs (II 104, 100). This
quitclaim by Valentine enabled William of Wykeham to give the lands to Southwick
Priory, having obtained licence from the king and from the chief lords (II 111,
112, 113).

II 115   7 February 1368

[fo. 69] GIFT, with warranty, by Simon atte Mede of Bramdean
(*Bromden'*) to Sir William de Wykeham, Bishop of Winchester, of his
manor of Boarhunt Herbelyn (*Bourhunt herbelyn*) with all appurtenances,
and also all other lands and tenements with appurtenances which were
formerly [in the possession] of Richard Danveres, in Southwick, West
Boarhunt, Portchester, Wanstead and Wymering (*Westbourhunt' Porchestre, Wanstede, Wymeryng'*).[1] The bishop, his heirs and assigns, will
hold all the aforesaid lands, with all liberties and profits pertaining
thereto, and rights of common, woods, warrens, fisheries, fishponds,
meadows, grazings, pastures, mills, dovecots, wards, marriages, reliefs,
homages, escheats, rents, and services of both free and bond tenants,
reversions of lands, tenements and rents pertaining in any way to the
said manor, lands and tenements, suits of court, and other appurtenances,
of the chief lords of that fee for the accustomed service in perpetuity.
Witnesses: John de Warbelton'; Henry de Popham; and others.

Southwick, Monday after the feast of the
Purification of the Blessed Mary, 42 Edward III.

1 Richard Danvers made over the manor of Boarhunt Herbelyn and other lands
to feoffees, including Simon atte Mede, in 1361. No mention was then made of
Wymering or Wanstead, though the latter may have been included in lands in the
parish of Southwick (II 89). Quitclaims by some of the feoffees seem to have left
Simon in possession, so that he was able to give the manor and lands to William
of Wykeham, and they subsequently formed part of the bishop's gift to Southwick
Priory (II 89, 91, 92, 90, 88, 111).

[fo. 69ᵛ] **II 116** Copy of II 115. Variants: omit Wymering and insert Belney (*Beleney*) and Beckford (*Beckeforde*); John de Warbleton'. Omit place of issue and date.
[Marginal note:] this charter agrees word for word with the immediately preceding charter.

The marginal note is not entirely accurate; see variants above. There is no mention of Belney and Beckford in the deed by which Richard Danvers made over his lands to feoffees (II 89), but both may have been included in the reference to lands in the parish of Southwick. Belney farm is about 1½ miles N.E. of Southwick, and Upper and Lower Beckford just over a mile N. of Southwick. See also note to II 115.

II 117   18 March 1362

AGREEMENT between the Prior of Southwick; Sir John de Scures, knight; Peter de Hoo, clerk; Michael Skyllyng'; Valentine atte Mede; and Simon atte Mede; on the one part; and Sir Bernard Brocas, knight, and his wife, Mary, on the other; touching all manner of disputes between them, or between the servants of the said prior and Sir Bernard. Because John Herberd'—son of Herbert de Bourhunt and cousin and heir of Sir¹ John de Borhunt'—granted in perpetuity, by a fine levied in the king's court, to the said Sir John de Scures, Peter, Michael, Valentine, Simon, and the heirs of Valentine, the reversion of his manors of Boarhunt Herberd, Hinton, and Hannington (*Borhunt Herberd, Henton', et Hanyton'*), which Sir Bernard and Mary hold for Mary's life, and which they attorned to Sir John and the others according to the fine,² and because Sir Bernard and Mary will take steps to deliver, at their own expense, to the said Prior and the others, all bonds according to the Statute of Merchants, and all annuities (*tous les Estatuz Marchauntz et annuyetes*), which Sir John de Borhunt' made over to Sir William de Overton³—therefore Sir John de Scures, Peter, Michael, Valentine and Simon will surrender in perpetuity to Sir Bernard and his heirs all right they have in the manor of Hannington with appurtenances. And the said prior will cause those who were beaten (*fra le gentz q' furent batutz*) by Sir Bernard's people to relinquish their claim against Sir Bernard and his people, and Sir Bernard will do likewise in the case of those who were beaten by the prior's people.⁴ And the £20 (*lyveres*) which Sir Bernard and Mary are due to pay to the prior and those people will be held over (*seront mys en respit*) until the Nativity of St John the Baptist next, and then what they owe according to the judgement of the Bishop of Winchester and the Earl of Arundel is to be paid unconditionally (*et a donqe sur lagard levesqe de Wyncestr' et le Counte Darundell' le quel ils devient estre payetz ou ne mye*). And the prior will do the best he can, without damage to himself, or incurring costs, to see that Sir Bernard obtains from Sir William de Overton's executors all the bonds according to the Statute of Merchants aforesaid, touching Sir John de Burhunt'. This identure was sealed by both parties.

                              Westminster, 18 March, 36 Edward III.

French.

1 *Mens'* in MS.; elsewhere *Sir'*, *Syr'*.

2 See II 100.

3 See II 121, 122, 97, 93.

4 See II 119.

II 118[1] [1360][2]

MEMORANDUM: injuries done to Southwick Priory by Sir Bernard
Brocas and Lady Mary, his wife:— (i) The present prior of Southwick
and all his predecessors and their tenants have, ever since the foundation
of the priory, enjoyed continually and peacefully rights of common for
all kinds of animals each season of the year, in pastures called *Crich*'[3]
and *Walkeneheth*,[3] until officials of the aforesaid Sir Bernard and Lady
Mary took and wrongfully impounded (*ont enparkes*) the prior's animals,
which were grazing in the aforesaid pasture as they were wont to do by
right, and took and wrongfully detained sureties from his shepherds (*ont
pris et torteuosement et ses pastours desgages et lurs gages detenuz*)
causing great loss to the prior and the priory.
(ii) The said prior, his predecessors and their tenants, have always had,
and made use of, rights of common for all their animals in the pasture
called *Stroudhulle*,[3] and that right was confirmed in the time of King
Henry by an agreement made between Walter, formerly prior of Southwick, and Herbert, formerly lord of the manor of Boarhunt Herberd
(*Bourhonte Herberd'*).[4] The officials of Sir Bernard and Lady Mary took
and wrongfully impounded the prior's animals grazing there causing loss
to the prior and priory.
(iii) The manor of West Boarhunt (*Westbourhonte*) is in the hands of
the said prior and is held of the king in chief, in which manor Sir Bernard
and Lady Mary have only 2 acres, which Thomas, father of Sir John de
Bourhonte, bought from Gilbert de Bourhonte. The said Sir Bernard and
Lady Mary, by virtue of these 2 acres, claim overlordship (*une sovereynte
de seignurye*) of the manor of West Boarhunt, after the prior's corn is
cut and carried, hindering the prior from pasturing his beasts on his own
demesne, and causing beasts from their manor of Boarhunt Herberd to
be driven there, where they had no right of common; seizing the pasture
by force and grazing it at will as sovereign lords. Besides which, the
prior had in his demesne in the manor of West Boarhunt a separable
pasture (*une pasture severale*) called *la Stroude*, in which no man had
grazing rights except the prior and his tenants. Sir Bernard and Lady
Mary illegally drove their animals from Boarhunt Herberd to graze there
at will throughout the season of the year, without the consent of the
prior, causing loss to him and the priory.
(iv) The prior is parson of the parish church of Southwick, in which
parish Sir Bernard and Lady Mary have several meadows, from which
they do not allow any tithe to be given to the church, but keep all the
hay exclusively for their own use. Likewise they retain the tithes of their

wool each year until agreement is made concerning a sum of money for shearing, against the law of Holy Church.

Concerning these grievances the prior appeals that amends be made in good faith, and all disputes settled for the future.

[*Verso*⁵] On behalf of Sir Bernard:— Sir Robert Markaunt; Sir Lawrence Pageham;⁶ Robert de Ho; Roger Ingelfeld; Richard [Danv]ers; Thomas Bealmond.

On behalf of the prior:— [Sir] Lawrence [Pageham]; John [le Boteler]; Thomas Wallop; Thomas Everard; Thomas Stake.

French.

1 On a separate piece of parchment 20.5 cms × 27 cms sewn at right angles to the top of fo. 70 and also numbered 70.

2 The complaints detailed in this memorandum were settled by an agreement made in 1360 (I 214).

3 Creech farm, Walton Heath and Stroud copse—all within a short distance of Southwick (I 214, note 2).

4 See I 121.

5 Dark, worn, and the list of names sometimes illegible, but see the names of the arbitrators in I 214.

6 This name is crossed through. Almost certainly it is the first name in the list of those appearing on behalf of the prior.

II 119   24 June 1363

[fo. 70] QUITTANCE and PARDON in perpetuity by John Bealmound, son and heir of Thomas Bealmound', to Sir (*Mens'*) Bernard Brokas and his people of all manner of claim and demand he has, or could have, against them because he was beaten by them on 12 February, the 30th year of [the reign of] the present king [1356].¹

Southwick, the feast of the Nativity of St John the Baptist, 37 Edward III.

French.

1 1 See the undertaking given by the prior of Southwick that he would endeavour to get people beaten by Sir Bernard's people to relinquish their claims (II 117).

II 120   18 July 1351

BOND in £100 by John Boront, knight, of the county of Hampshire, to Thomas Perle, citizen of London, for merchandise bought from him, to be paid to Thomas, his attorney who produces this letter, his heirs or executors, on the feast of the Purification of the Blessed Mary next following [2 February 1352]. If this is not carried out, John concedes that distraint and the penalty provided by the Statute of Westminster concerning merchants, drawn up in the time of King Edward I, be imposed upon him, his heirs and executors.

London, 18 July 25 (F. 12) Edward III.

See II 93 and 97.

II 121 6 March 1352

BOND in £1,000 by John de Borhunt', knight and merchant of the [fo.70ᵛ] county of Hampshire, to William Overton', merchant, for merchandise of various kinds bought from him, to be paid to William, or his attorney who produces this deed, at Southampton at Michaelmas next. If this is not done, John concedes that distraint and the penalty provided by [the Statutes of] Acton Burnel and Westminster concerning merchants, drawn up in the time of King Edward I, be imposed upon him, his heirs and executors. This recognizance was made before John Goseden', the King's Clerk, and John Forst, Keeper of the larger piece (*maioris pecij*) of the royal seal for the recognizance of debts at Southampton. Sealed by Sir John and with the said royal seal.

Southampton, 6 March, 26 (F. 13) Edward III.

See II 97 and 93; also II 109 and 122.
    I am most grateful to Miss Sheila Thomson, the Southampton City Archivist, for searching her archives with reference to this bond, and for calling my attention to similarly worded documents preserved there. John Forst or Frost was mayor of Southampton in 1352, but there appears to be no surviving record of John Goseden, unless he was the same man as John de Vyenna, who occurred in February 1329 as the King's Clerk of Recognizances (Southampton City Record Office SC4/2/42).

II 122 28 June 1355

GRANT, with warranty, by John Bourhunt', knight, to William de Overton', of an annual rent of £40 from his manor of Boarhunt Herberd, to be paid in equal portions at Michaelmas, Christmas, Easter and the Nativity of St John the Baptist. The rent will be held by William, his heirs and assigns, by hereditary right in perpetuity. If this rent is wholly or partly in arrears, the grantee may enter the manor, distrain, and keep the distraint until the rent is fully paid. Witnesses: Lawrence de Pageham, knight; Walter de Haywode; Thomas de Overton'; Nicholas de Overton'; Lawrence de Andevere; Nicholas Stake; Thomas Stake; Richard Danvers; and others.

Boarhunt Herberd, Sunday after the Nativity of St John the Baptist,
29 Edw. III.

See II 97 and 93; also II 109, 121, 209.

Original in H.R.O., 5M50/20:
Seal: on tag *c.* 12 cms, Bourhunt seal,[1] left-hand edge missing; round, 2.2 cms
diameter; device: in a cusped circle, the Bourhunt shield of arms: a fesse between
six martlets; legend: IOHIS D..O.....
Endorsements: (a) XVI
　　　　　　　(b) Ouert'n
　　　　　　　(c) Rent out of Burhunt Herbert of £40 per an' given by Sr John
　　　　　　　　　Burhunt to Wm Overton
1 Illustrated in *VCH Hants* III, p. 145.

II 123

NOTIFICATION by William de Wykeham, Bishop of Winchester, that,
for the honour of Almighty God and the increase of His worship in the
priory of Southwick of the order of St Augustine, founded and established
in perpetuity in the diocese of Winchester, and for the use and succour
of the aforesaid priory, etc.. This deed is to be found in box 16 as
enrolled separately (*Quam invenies scriptam cophino xvj ut iritulatur
extra*).[1]

1 Each folio in this volume from 62^v to 97 is headed xvj; these contain charters
II 88 to II 210. The above notification is not amongst those charters, nor is it
copied into Vol. I or Vol. III. Vol. I is not divided into boxes, and Vol. III goes
only up to box 15.
　　In the index of charters in Vol. II, 15 charters are listed as being in box 16,
but the notification is not one of them (II fo. 43).

II 124[1]

[MEMORANDUM of grievances] .... newly suffered by the house of
Southwick .... peaceably seised, and their tenants to pasture and have
rights of common .... the pasture called *Crich'* for all kinds of
animals for the whole season of the year. The officials [of] Sir Bernard
[Brocas] and Lady Mary wrongfully [took] the prior's animals grazing
in that pasture, causing loss to the house of Southwick.
　　There is another pasture called *Walkeneheth* in which the said prior,
his predecessors and their tenants, have, and make use of, rights of
common in the manner aforesaid. The officials of Sir Bernard and Lady
Mary wrongfully took and impounded the prior's animals, took surety
from his shepherds, and wilfully detained those sureties, causing loss to
the prior and priory.
　　There is a pasture called *Stroudhull'* where the Prior, his predecessors
and their tenants, have, and make use of, rights of common for their
animals in the aforesaid manner, and their rights were confirmed by an
agreement made between Walter, predecessor of the present prior, and
Herbert, ancestor of Sir John de Bourhunte, in the time of King Henry,
as appears in the said agreement. The officials of the said Sir Bernard
and Lady Mary wrongfully impounded the prior's animals grazing in
that pasture, causing loss to the priory.

Thomas, father of Sir John de Bourhonte purchased, for himself and his heirs in perpetuity, two acres with appurtenances from Gilbert de Bourhonte, which are held of the said prior as of his manor of West Boarhunt (*Westbourhonte*), ?lying in a field called *Estfeld'*. The aforesaid Sir Bernard and Lady Mary, claiming overlordship (*une seignurye*) in the said manor of West Boarhunt, which is held of the king in chief, had all the animals driven from the manor of Boarhunt Herberd to the manor of West Boarhunt, where they had no rights of common, and at stubble time (*en temps de stouple*) and other open seasons wrongfully occupied the prior's pasture and grazed it continually, causing great damage and loss to the priory.

[*Verso*[2]] There is a separable (*several*) pasture which is the prior's demesne of his manor of West Boarhunt .... *Stroude,* in which no man has rights of common except by consent of the p[rior] .... of the said Sir Bernard and Lady Mary grazed the said pasture with animals .... Herberd without the prior's consent, causing damage and loss to the priory.

The said prior is parson of the parish church of Southwick in which [parish] Sir Bernard and Lady Mary have several meadows from which they do not allow tithe to be given, but keep the hay entirely for their own use, contrary to the law of God and Holy Church, causing great loss to the said prior.

French.

1 On a separate piece of parchment, 21 cms × 16 cms; sewn on to the top left-hand margin of fo. 70[v]. The top left-hand corner is missing. This is a version of the list of grievances of the prior of Southwick against Sir Bernard Brocas and Lady Mary, formerly the wife of Sir John de Burhunt, which appears in II 118. See also the settlement reached in 1360 (I 214).

2 Similarly affected by the missing portion as explained in note 1.

II 125   1 August 1327

[fo. 71] QUITCLAIM, with warranty, by John Daubeney (Dawbeney), son and heir of John Daubeney, to Thomas de Bourhunt' and his wife, Margaret,[1] of: (i) all right and claim he had or could have to 2s. annual rent which he used to receive from lands and tenements formerly Richard le Dibere's in the vill of Hinton (*Henton'*); also (ii) a piece of land (*placea terre*) which lies inside the field pertaining to the court (*infra campum curie*) on the west side adjoining the garden, stretching north to south, and called *Letherslond';* and (iii) a piece of land (*pecia terre*), adjoining *la Redehullde,* from the former holding of Adam Ayward', lying within the close of the same field which is called *Nedenham.* Thomas and Margaret, their heirs or assigns, will hold all the aforesaid rent, land, and appurtenances, by hereditary right in perpetuity, of the chief lord of the fee, for the accustomed service. Witnesses: Adam de Henton'; Richard de Hengelton'; John de Lorde; Peter Grevette; Richard Emory; John Tirell'; Robert Tornton; and many others.

Hinton, Saturday, the feast of St Peter in Chains, 1 Edward III.

1 See II 101 in which John Daubeney, the elder, quitclaimed rent and land in Hinton to Thomas de Bourhunt's father, Sir Richard. The rest of fo. 71 is blank.

II 126¹   [*c.* 1369]²

MEMORANDUM concerning money received from (*ressu de*) the Bishop of Winchester in part payment of £400 for the costs of the purchase of Boarhunt Herberd (*Burhunte Herbard*) and Herbelyn, viz:

		£.	s.	d.
(i)	at Windsor (*Wyndesore*) from (*par les maynes*) Valentin atte Mede	20.	0.	0.
(ii)	at Wickham (*Wykham*) from Sir John Wallop	46.	0.	0.
(iii)	at London (*Loundr'*) from N. Quernby	13.	6.	8.
(iv)	at Winchester (*Wyncestr'*) from the treasurer of Wolvesey (*Wulvesy*)	10.	0.	0.
(v)	from John Melbryg and John atte Seler, farmers of Boarhunt Herberd	13.	6.	8.
	Total	102.	13.	4.

And £297. 6s. 8d. is owing.

French.

1 On a small piece of parchment 13.8 cms × 9.5 cms, sewn on to the left-hand margin of fo. 71ᵛ. Verso, blank.

2 The manors of Boarhunt Herberd and Herbelyn were given to Southwick Priory, with other lands, by William of Wykeham, Bishop of Winchester, in 1369 (II 111). See also the list of expenses incurred by the priory (II 110). Folios 71ᵛ, 72 and 72ᵛ are blank.

II 127¹   25 January 1373–24 January 1374

[MEMORANDUM:] property acquired by Southwick Priory in 47 Edward III:²

(i)   from Walter Hayne, 3 messuages with curtillages, 33 acres, and 2 acres of meadow of the priory's fee in (*de*) the manor of Boarhunt Herberd (*Burhunte Herberd'*), worth 30s. a year;

(ii)   from the aforesaid Walter, 9 cottages (*cotag'*) with curtillages in the vill of Southwick, of the priory's fee in the manor of Southwick, worth 16s. 6d. a year;³

(iii)   from Andrew Hurt, a croft called *Strodecroft* containing 6 acres,⁴ and 2 [acres] in the common field of Boarhunt Herberd, of the priory's fee in the manor of Boarhunt Herberd, worth 5s. a year;

(iv)   from the aforesaid Andrew, a cottage with curtillage of the priory's fee in the manor of Southwick, worth 18d. a year;

(v)   from the aforesaid Andrew, a garden with grove, containing in all 1 acre, and 1 acre or arable, of the priory's fee in the manor of Boarhunt Herbelyn (*de manerio de Danverses*),⁵ worth 3s. a year;

(vi)   from Richard Stenyng', a messuage with garden, 10 acres, with 2 acres of meadow, of the priory's fee in the manor of Boarhunt Herbelyn (*de manerio de Dannverses*), worth 10s. a year;

(vii) from Richard Duyt, a cottage with curtillage, of the priory's fee in the manor of Southwick, worth 3s. a year;[6]

(viii) from Simon atte Mede, 3 cottages with a curtillage, of the priory's fee in the manor of Southwick, worth 6s. 8d. a year;

(ix)   from Valentine atte Mede, a meadow at Beckford (*Bikeford'*) containing 1 acre, of the priory's fee in the manor of Southwick, worth 12d. a year;

(x)   from Elias Daubeney, 2s. worth of rent a year at Hinton (*Henton'*), of the fee of Hinton Daubnay (*Henton' Daubeney*);[7]

(xi)   from William Gyffard', 3 shops (*schoppe*) in the city of Winchester, worth 3s.[8]

Total value of the said lands and tenements: £4. 20d.

1 On a separate piece of parchment 24.5 cms × 21 cms, sewn at right angles along the left-hand margin of fo. 72ᵛ. Verso, blank.

2 In 1318, Edward II granted a licence to the priory enabling it to acquire property to the value of £20 a year, notwithstanding the Statute of Mortmain (II 977). It seems likely that the above lands were acquired under that licence. See also III 978–981.

3 See Appendix V (a), (b).

4 Andrew Hurt quitclaimed Strodecroft to the priory on 7 March, 1373 (III 515). See also III 516–517, 272, 174.

5 This was the manor which Richard Danvers had acquired by 1343 (III 176, 163, 145). In 1361 he made it over to feoffees (II 89), who transferred it to Bishop William of Wykeham in 1368 (II 115). It was part of the bishop's gift to Southwick Priory in 1369, for the endowment of his chantry (II 111).

6 See III 171, 172.

7 See III 258, 257.

8 It has not been possible to trace William Gyffard in Dr Keene's Biographical Register (*WS II* p. 1143 sqq.), but he may well belong to the same family as Robert Gyffard, who died in 1349 and bequeathed to the priory two shops at the entrance to Middle Brook Street, Winchester (III 572 and notes 3, 4).

II 128   [1305]

[fo. 73] LEASE, with warranty, from Michaelmas, 33 Edward [I], when John, son of Richard de Colerne, was 5 years old, until he comes of age. The lease is by Henry de Bourhunte, to Lawrence de Bynstede and his wife Isabella, of the tenement which was formerly held by Richard de Colerne and which Henry held in wardship for Richard's son, John. The lessees or their assigns, or anyone to whom they wish to give, bequeath, or sell it, will hold the aforesaid tenement with all appurtenances, viz. houses, gardens, crofts, commons, ways, footpaths, growing hedges (*haie vive*), and all other appurtenances, of Henry, his heirs or assigns, paying 8s. rent, viz. 4s. at Michaelmas and 4s. at Easter, for all accustomed services and other secular demands; except 2s. which they owe annually at Michaelmas from the aforesaid tenement, to be paid by Henry to John de Knolle. The lessees are obliged to supply, at their own expense, all the said John [de Colerne's] needs, viz. in food, drink, clothing, [and] shoe repairs, from Michaelmas of the year aforesaid [29 September 1305] until he is of age. Also they are obliged to hold and maintain, for the aforesaid term, the houses built on the said tenement, viz. the hall with chamber and grange; and, at the end of the term, they are to return them to Henry in the same or a better state of repair. Henry also grants to the lessees whatever [wood] is necessary to repair the houses or fences of the tenement, from its groves, and housebote and haybote, under the supervision of his hayward. Drawn up as a chirograph with the seals of both parties appended. Witnesses: Sir Richard de Burhunt', Sir Baldwin de Bello Alneto, knights; and many others. And there was a small dilapidated house on the said tenement which Henry did not wish to have repaired; it was valued by the neighbours at 2s. and sold, and Henry will be responsible to the heir, when he comes of age, for the 2s.

II 129 [*c*. 1314–34][1]

[fo. 73ᵛ] GIFT, with warranty, by Adam le Tailur to his son, John, of all his land with garden which lies enclosed outside the bridge called *Brodebrugg'*,[2] between the king's highway which runs from Southwick to Winchester and the tenement of Henry Pippe. John, his heirs or assigns, will hold all the aforesaid tenement with appurtenances of the chief lord of the fee in perpetuity, paying annually to Adam's lord, Thomas de Burhunte, and his heirs, 2s., viz. 12d. at Easter and 12d. at Michaelmas, for all services and secular demand, as is shown in the charter given to Adam by his lord, Sir Richard de Burhunte.[3] Consideration, 13s. 4d. Witnesses: Thomas de Saunford'; Gilbert de Burhunte; and many others.

1 Thomas de Burhunte was the son of Sir Richard, and succeeded his father between 1314 and 1316; he died in 1339 (II 69, note 1; *Cal. Inq. p.m.* VIII, no. 242, p. 177). Gilbert de Burhunte was probably Thomas' cousin, who had died by 1334 (II 39).

2 See the reference to *Brodebrigge* in Southwick (II 162).

3 Probably Sir Richard gave the land to Adam early in the 14th century, before 1310 (II 158).

II 130 22 November 1354

GIFT, with warranty, by John de Bourhunte, knight, to Adam le Muleward' of Southwick and his wife, Joan, of all the messuage and curtillage, next to that formerly held by Dulcia la Smythes in Southwick, which is situated between John Tirel's tenement on the south and that formerly held by Simon le Muleward' on the north, and the stream on the west. Adam and Joan, and Adam's heirs or assigns, will hold the messuage and curtillage, with all appurtenances, of Sir John and his heirs, by hereditary right in perpetuity, paying 3s. a year in equal portions at Michaelmas and Easter for all secular services or demands, except suit of Sir John's court and heriot. Witnesses: Robert de Hoo; Richard Danvers; and others.

Southwick, Saturday after the feast of St Edmund the Martyr, 28 Edward III

Original in H.R.O. 5M50/19. [Very faded and some words illegible] Variants: [to witness list add:] John le ?Hute; John Mulebrigge; William Barbo*ur;* Olivo W . . . Not indented. Tag, *c.* 11 cms, but seal missing.
Endorsement: XVI
See also II 133, 138.

II 131   24 February 1334

[fo. 74] AGREEMENT between Gilbert de Bourhunte and Joan, widow of John Mulebrigge of Southwick, viz., Gilbert has quitclaimed the right which he derived from a certain tenement at *Mulebrigge* in Southwick, to the wardship and marriage of John, son and heir of the late John Mulebrigge, who is a minor. For this quitclaim, Joan has paid Gilbert 5s., and will pay 12d. a year until John is of age, and the accustomed service due for the said tenement. And if John dies before coming of age, and the right to the said tenement descends to any brother or sister of his, Gilbert concedes that the brother of sister may hold the tenement without charge for wardship or marriage for the aforesaid 12d. a year, until of age. Indenture sealed by both parties. Witnesses: Thomas de Bourhunte; Richard de Belanney; and others.
Southwick, Thursday, the feast of St Mathias the Apostle, 8 Edward III.

II 132   8 May 1345

GRANT by John de Burhunte to John le Hunte and his wife Juliana, of the reversion of a messuage with curtillage and adjoining meadow from his inheritance, which is held by Joan la Hore. It lies between the said John le Hunte's messuage on the south, and John Tirel's messuage on the north.[1] The grantees and the lawful heirs of their bodies will hold the messuage, curtillage, and meadow, with all appurtenances, after Joan la Hore's death, of John de Burhunte and his heirs, for 20d. a year at the terms fixed by ancient custom, and suit of John's court at Boarhunt every three weeks (*de tribus septimanis in tres septimanas*), for all except outside (*forinsec*) service when it occurs. Witnesses: Robert de Hoo; John de Kenylworth; and others.

Southwick, Sunday after Ascension, 19 Edward III.

1 John de Burhunt, son and heir of Thomas de Burhunt who had died in 1339, had quitclaimed to John le Honte [*sic*] and his wife, Juliana, the above tenement, described as having frontage on the king's highway running from the chapel of St James [Southwick] towards Fareham, and having ?Cuttemulle at the rear; and also 8½ acres at Paulsgrove; all of which were held for life by Joan le Hor (H.R.O. 5M50/17). This original charter has several holes, so that some words are lost. The date appears as: *Anno regni Regis E. tercii a conquestu octa* .... Probably, in view of the date of II 132 above, the ending should read *octavo decimo,* i.e. 1344.

See also II 176 and 145.

II 133   30 November 1351

[fo. 74ᵛ] GIFT, with warranty, by John Bourhunte, knight, to Adam le Muleward and his wife, Joan, their heirs or assigns, of his croft called *Broundecroft* in the parish of Southwick; it lies lengthwise between a lane running from Southwick to Wickham (*Wykham*) and the land of the almoner of Southwick Priory, and breadthwise between the prior of Southwick's land and the land of John le Hunte. The donees will hold the croft, with hedges, fences and ditches enclosing it, rights of common, and other appurtenances, by hereditary right in perpetuity, paying 5s. annual rent at Michaelmas for all secular services or demands, except suit of the donor's court twice a year. Witnesses: Robert de Hoo; Richard Danvers; and others.

Southwick, the feast of St Andrew the Apostle, 25 Edward III.

See also II 130, 138.

II 134   [*c.* late 13th century][1]

GIFT, with warranty, by Herbert de Burhunt' to Alice le Frensse, of one part of a certain house in the vill of Southwick south (*in australi parte*) of the cemetery of St James', Southwick, between the houses of John Cissor and his brother Henry Cissor, which Herbert bought from John Cissor, and which, with part of a site pertaining to it, is 13½ feet in breadth and in length extends from west to east from the front (*a fronte*) of the aforesaid house to the ditch of Southwick Priory. Alice, her heirs, or anyone to whom she wishes to give, sell, bequeath, assign or mortgage it, in sickness or in health, will hold the whole part of the aforesaid house, with the site and appurtenances, by hereditary right in perpetuity, paying Herbert, his heirs or assigns, 14d., viz. at Michaelmas, 7d., and at Easter, 7d., for all service and secular extraction, except as much royal service as pertains to it. Consideration, 8s. Witnesses: William Gileberd'; Ralph Tannator; and many others.

1 Witnesses and John and Henry Cissor occur between 1271 and 1295.

II 135 [*c*. 1300, before 1305][1]

[fo. 75] GIFT, with warranty, by Richard de Burhunta to Joan Hurt and her brother Andrew, their heirs or assigns, of all that tenement with appurtenances which Robert le Hoppere formerly held of him in the vill of Southwick. The tenement is situated between those formerly held by Emma, the donor's mother, on the one side, and by William Faber, on the other, and extends in length from the king's highway which runs from Southwick to Fareham (*Farham*) as far as the stream between *la Hamme* and the aforesaid tenement. The donees will hold all the tenement with appurtenances by hereditary right in perpetuity, paying Richard and his heirs 2s. 6d. a year, viz. at Michaelmas, 12d., at Christmas, 3d., at Easter, 12d. and at the Nativity of St John the Baptist, 3d., for all services and other secular demands, except suit of the donor's court, and as much royal service as pertains to a holding of that size from the same demesne. Consideration, 40s. Witnesses: Sir William de Pageham, Sir John le Butiler, knights; and many others.

1 Sir William de Pageham had died by January 1305 (*Cal. Inq. p.m.*, IV, no. 290, p. 196).

II 136 Late 13th century, before 1303[1]

[fo. 75ᵛ] GIFT, with warranty, by William Gilbert to John de Kenelleworth' of all his land in *Luckecrofte* which lies between land given to John by Henry Snelgar and land given to him by Henry Pippe. John, his heirs or assigns, will hold it of Sir Richard de Burhunte, chief lord of that fee, by hereditary right in perpetuity, paying to William and his heirs 1 clove (*unus clavus gariophili*) a year at Easter for all service, and to the chief lord the accustomed service of 9s. a year, viz. at Christmas, 4s. 6d., and at the Nativity of St John the Baptist, 4s. 6d., for all service and secular demand, except as much royal service as pertains to that amount of land from the same fee. Consideration, 4 marks. Witnesses: Sir Richard de Burhunt'; Sir Baldwin de Bello Alneto; and others.

1 William Gilbert or Gileberd occurs between 1271 and 1295 (II 173, 171). In 1287 Henry Snelgar acknowledged a debt to John de Kenilworth of 100s. (*Cal. Close R., 1279–88* p. 484). John had died by 1303 (III 247).

II 137 24 January 1340

LEASE, with warranty, by Thomas de Burhunt', son and heir of Gilbert de Burhunt',[1] to William le Asse and his wife Isabella, of all that piece of land called *le Bundesorchard'*, enclosed with hedges, which Adam le Asse, William's late father, held for life. The lessees will hold the land with all appurtenances while they live, and for one full year after the death of either of them, without contest by Thomas and his heirs, paying 6d. a year in equal portions at Michaelmas and Easter for all except royal service. Consideration, 13s. 4d. This bipartite deed has been sealed by Thomas and by William and Isabella. Witnesses: Sir John, Prior of Southwick; Thomas Beamont; and many others.

Southwick, Monday after the feast of St Vincent, 13 Edward III.

1 Thomas de Burhunt' inherited the manor of Boarhunt Herbelyn from his father, Gilbert, who had died by May 1334 (*Cal. Inq. p.m.* VII, no. 616, p. 417; *VCH Hants* III, p. 146). See also III 686, 796, 895.

II 138   11 November 1354

[fo. 76] GIFT, with warranty, by John de Bourhunte, knight, to Adam Muleward' and his wife Joan, of the whole messuage which was formerly Juliana Tirel's; also a croft called *le Holecroft* next to the messuage. The messuage and croft are situated beyond the bridge called *Kuttebrigge* in the parish of Southwick: viz. between the king's highway that leads from Southwick to Portchester on the east, and the heath (*bruera*) called *Stroude* on the west. Adam and Joan, their heirs or assigns, will hold the messuage and croft with all other appurtenances, by hereditary right in perpetuity, paying Sir John and his heirs 2s. a year in equal portions at Christmas and Easter for all secular service or demand due to Sir John, except suit of his court. Witnesses: Robert de Hoo; Richard Dannvers; and others.

Southwick, Tuesday, the feast of St Martin, 28 Edward III.

See also II 133, 130.

II 139   [1320–34]¹

LEASE, with warranty, for life in survivorship, by Gilbert de Burhunte, son and heir of Henry de Burhunte, to Nicholas Wlwyne and his wife Elena, of 1 acre of *la Blakeforlonge,* lying lengthwise between the prior's land in the west, and Richard de Belanne's on the east, and breadthwise between John Hurt's land in the north and Nicholas Wlwyne's in the south. Also another acre, lying breadthwise between Richard Stake's land in the north and the land of Gilbert de Burhunt' called *Roselinche* in the [fo. 76ᵛ] south, and lengthwise between an acre called *Holaker* and the prior's land called *Coppelond'*. The lessees will hold the 2 acres with all appurtenances, of Gilbert, his heirs and assigns, paying 9d. a year at Easter for all services and secular demands. Consideration, 6s. 8d. Chirograph sealed alternately by both parties. Witnesses: Thomas de Burhunt'; Richard Stake; and many others.

1 Henry de Burhunte died in 1320, and the manor of Boarhunt Herbelyn passed to his son, Gilbert. Gilbert had died by May 1334 (*Brocas* p. 337; *Cal. Inq. p.m.* VII, no. 616, p. 417; and see II 177).

2 This acre had previously been leased to Nicholas and Elena by Gilbert's father, Henry de Burhunte (II 184).

II 140   Copy of II 108.

II 141   ?29 January 1335[1]

[fo. 77] GIFT, with warranty, by John de Pulberghe and Peter de Hou, clerks, to Thomas de Bourhunte and his wife, Margaret, of their manor of Boarhunt (*Bourhunt'*) with all appurtenances; also the reversion of all rents, lands, and tenements, in Portchester (*Porcestr'*), which Roger de Bourhunte, brother of Thomas, holds for life from Thomas' inheritance. Thomas and Margaret will hold for their lives the aforesaid manor, with messuages, mills, lands, woods, meadows, grazings, pastures, fishponds, ponds (*stangna*), ways, footpaths, rents, services of free men, customs and other services of villeins, with all appurtenances, and with the reversion of all rents, lands, and tenements, in Portchester. After the deaths of Thomas and Margaret, the aforesaid manor and reversion will pass to their son, John, and his wife, Mary, and the lawful heirs of their bodies.[2] If John and Mary die without an heir of their bodies, the aforesaid manor and reversion will pass to the rightful heirs of Thomas de Bourhunte and their assigns, [to be held] of the chief lords of that fee for the accustomed service. Warranty is granted for life, successively to Thomas and Margaret, John and Mary, and the heirs of their bodies. Witnesses: John de Scures; Robert de Popham; and others.
                              Southwick, Sunday before the feast of
                              the Purification of the Blessed Mary,
                              [?]9 Edward III (*anno . . . octavo finiente*)

1 The eighth year of Edward III's reign ran from 25 January 1334 to 24 January 1335. The Sunday before Purification (30 January) would therefore be at the beginning, not the end, of that year, but it is reasonable to conjecture that the scribe intended 29 January 1335, at the very beginning of the ninth year of the reign.

2 Richard de Burhunt had made over the manor to Thomas and Margaret in 1314 (II 108), and Thomas was holding it in 1316 (*Feudal Aids* II, p. 319). It would appear that Thomas and Margaret made over their lands to trustees (though that deed is not in the cartularies), to facilitate the arrangement by which they would hold them for life, with reversion to their son and daughter-in-law.

II 142   [c. mid 13th century, before 1262][1]

[fo. 77ᵛ] GIFT, with warranty, by Richard Blundus, ward (*alumpnus*) of M. Ralph de Suwike, to John Hurt' of Southwick, of: (i) a messuage with appurtenances in the vill of Southwick, formerly Richard Suele's, situated between the house of William Gust and the messuage of Ralph Bulle, and extending from the king's highway which runs to Winchester, as far as mid-stream (*filum aque*) to the west; also (ii) 17½ acres, viz. (a) ½ acre which lies in the north part of Portsdown (*Portesdune*), between the prior of Southwick's land extending from the east towards *Oselden'*; (b) 4 acres lying in Southwick field from the north part of the hill, of which 1 acre lies in the furlong called *Blakefurlang'* which Richard de Hoo formerly held, and 1 acre lies next to *Blakefurlang'* to the east, and 2 acres lie near *Oseldene* between the prior of Southwick's land and that of Herbert (*Horebert*), son of William de Bourhunte; (c) 8 contiguous acres in the furlong (*quarentena*) called *Langemarle,* adjoining an acre which Andrew le Sym held of Thomas de Burhunte from the same fee, extending from the west of that acre northwards as far as the road which runs from Southwick towards *la Barre*—the place where it joins the road was of old called *Wuksemor*—and extending southwards as far as the land of Herbert, son of William de Bourhunt; and (d) 5 acres lie at Portchester, of which 1 acre is in the vill of Porchester between the land of Richard Sueles and [that of] Robert Guldenere; 2 acres lie in the same field east of the said acre; 1 acre lies south of the granges of Southwick Priory, extending to the nearest royal highway, and was formerly held by Geoffrey Suy; and 1 acre lies between the grange of Southwick Priory and the hill of Portsdown, extending as far as the king's highway which runs from Southwick to Portchester, and was formerly held by Richard de Hoo.

John and his heirs of assigns, or anyone to whom he wishes to give, bequeath, sell or assign the messuage and lands, will hold them free from any recovery, reclaim, or charge, on behalf of the donor or his heirs (*mei vel meorum*), in perpetuity, paying annually to the chief lords 3s. 6d., viz. at Michaelmas, 18d., at Easter, 12d., and at the feast of St John the Baptist, 12d., for all service or secular demand, except the king's scutage, i.e. what was due from that amount of land in the same fee. Consideration, 11 marks. Witnesses: Sir Martin de Rupibus; William de Bello Alneto; and many others.

1 William de Bello Alneto had died by May 1262 (*Cal. Inq. p.m.* I, no. 514, p. 145). See also II 168 and 154, which show how this property had changed hands and had grown in size from a messuage and 3½ acres, by the subsequent addition of 6 acres, and then a further 8 acres.

II 143   [*c.* early 14th century, before 1316][1]

[fo. 78] GRANT and DEMISE, with warranty, by Henry de Burhunt' to Joan Hurt', sister of the late John Hurt', her heirs or assigns, of custody of John's houses and two parts of a garden, which have fallen to Henry as guardian of John, son and heir of the aforesaid John. Joan, her heirs or assigns, will have custody of the aforesaid property with all appurtenances, profits and esplees (*explecie*) which in any way can derive from them, free from any contest by Henry, his heirs or assigns, until the heir is of age. Joan will hold and maintain the houses in the state in which she received them, and for their upkeep Henry has granted her sufficient housebote and haybote on (*super*) the same tenement. And if the heir dies before coming of age, Joan will have custody of the next succeeding heir (*volo et concedo quod in etate proximi succedent' hered' defectus etatis precendentis hered' supleatur et dicte Johanne allocetur*). Consideration, 15s. Warranty until the heir is of age, and, if he dies a minor, until [the next heir] comes of age. Witnesses: Sir Richard de Borhunt', Sir Baldwin de Bello Alneto, knights; John Beamund; and others.

1 Richard de Bello Alneto (Bellaney) had succeeded his father, Sir Baldwin, by 1316 (*Feudal Aids* II, p. 319). Joan and her brother, Andrew Hurt, had received land from Richard de Burhunt before 1305 (II 135). Joan's deceased brother, John, had both father and son of the same name (II 149).

II 144 [*c.* early 14th century, before 1311][1]

LEASE for life, with warranty, by Henry de Burhunte to John Gude of Wallop (*Wollop*) of his croft called *Bondescroft,* lying at *la Hulle* between Stephen le Ropere's land in the west and John de Kenyngeworthe's in the east, and extending in length from the croft of the almoner of Southwick Priory to the king's highway which runs from the bridge called *Stonybrygge* towards Wickham (*Wykham*). John will hold the croft, with hedges and ditches and all appurtenances, of Henry, his heirs or assigns, paying annually 1 rose at the feast of the Nativity of St John the Baptist for all services, suits of court, heriots, and all other secular demands. Consideration, 60s. Witnesses: Sir Richard de Portesye, Sir Baldwin de Bello Alneto, knights; and others.

1 This lease must have been made before 1311, as in that year Henry, son of Henry de Burhunte, gave *Bondescroft* to Thomas, son of Sir Richard de Burhunte (II 189).

II 145 16 February 1344

[fo. 78ᵛ] QUITCLAIM, with warranty, by Joan, sister of Thomas de Bourhunt', to Richard, son of Thomas Damvers, knight, of all right and claim she had or could have in all lands, tenements, and reversions, with all appurtenances, which formerly belonged to her father, Gilbert Bourhunte, in Boarhunt Herbelyn, Boarhunt Herberd (*Harbard*) and Southwick.[1] Joan has also granted and released to Richard and his heirs in perpetuity, reversion of all lands and tenements which Joan, widow of Gilbert de Bourhunte, her father, holds in dower in the aforesaid vills and hamlets; and reversion of all lands and tenements which John le

Hunte and his wife, Juliana, hold for life.[2] Witnesses: John le Boteler, the younger; Valentine Bekke; and others.

Southwick, Monday before the feast of St Peter's Chair, 18 Edward III.

1 It would seem that Thomas de Burhunt, son and heir of Gilbert who died in 1334, made over his lands to Richard Danvers in or before 1343, as in August of that year his sister, Alice, quitclaimed to Richard any rights she might have therein (II 176). In May 1344, Thomas' widow, Hawise, similarly quitclaimed her rights to Richard Danvers (II 163).

2 See II 132 and note.

II 146 [probably late 13th century; before 1316][1]

[fo. 79] GIFT, with warranty, by John de Wordy, son and heir of Richard de Wordy, to William Gileberd' and his wife Claricia, of 1½ acres lying between land formerly [held by] Sir John de Burhunt' and land formerly [held by] Roger de la Hulle, which William de Plassot formerly held of Herbert, son of Walter de Burhunt'. The acres extend in length from the prior of Southwick's land called *Coppelond'* in the east, to the land of Henry de Burhunt' in the west as far as a certain acre called *Holaker*. The donees, their heirs, or anyone except religious men or Jews, to whom they wish to give, sell, bequeath, assign, or mortgage the land with appurtenances, in sickness or in health, will hold it by hereditary right in perpetuity, paying annually to John, his heirs or assigns, 1 rose at the feast of the Nativity of St John the Baptist, in the cemetery of the chapel of St James the Apostle, Southwick, and not elsewhere; and paying to Sir Richard de Burhunt' and his heirs 12d.— viz. 6d. at Christmas, and 6d. at the aforesaid feast of St John—for all other services, customs, suits of court and secular exactions, saving as much royal service as pertains to 1½ acres from the same fee. Because the donor concedes that no suit of court be done for the aforesaid land, those, whoever they may be, who hold, or ought to hold, a certain acre called *le Weyaker* are bound to do that suit. Consideration, 20s. Witnesses: Sir Baldwin de Belammey; Richard Wygaunt; and many others.

1 William Gileberd occurs 1271–95 (II 173, 193). Sir Baldwin de Belammey had been succeeded by his son, Richard, by 1316 (*Feudal Aids* II, p. 319).

Original in H.R.O. 5M50/10. Variants: Plasset; la Holaker; a certain acre *and a half* called le Weyaker; [to witness list add:] John de la Yurd; John de Colemere; John le Burgeis; William Maurdin; Richard Marscall'; Alexander de Rammesber'; Nicholas le Di[t]; William Faber; Richard de Krihc; Henry Snelgar; Stephen Clericus.

Slits for tag, but tag and seal missing.

Endorsements (a) Coppelonde
          (b) XVI

II 147 25 January 1351–24 January 1352

GIFT, with warranty, by Sir John de Bourhunte, knight, and his wife, Mary, to Thomas Estfelde, his heirs or assigns, of 1 arable croft called *Swelescroft'*, with hedges and ditches enclosing it, and other appurtenances, extending in length between Sir John's croft called *Astelesfeld* and a lane called *Dragheleggeslane,* and in breadth from the stream in the north to Sir John's land in the south. The donees will pay 6s. 8d. annual rent to Sir John and his heirs, viz. 20d. at next Christmas and 20d. at Michaelmas, for all secular service or demand, except suit of Sir John's court. Consideration, 6s. 8d. Witnesses: Richard Damvers; Robert de Hoo; and many others. 25 Edward III.

II 148 [*c.* 1334–40][1]

[fo. 79ᵛ] INDENTURE testifying that Thomas de Bourhunt', custodian of part of the lands and tenements which were held by his tenant, Richard de Bellanye, and also custodian for the king of part of the lands of Gilbert de Bourghunt', has delivered to Elizabeth, widow of the said Richard, by way of dower, the following (*stouthesrites*) lands, tenements, rents and tenants: viz. (i) a third of *Cryhlond* with a toft called *le Morghyne;* (ii) a third of *Frythecrofte* and the meadows and woods there, with free access; (iii) a third of *Bromfeld'* and *Echengrof;* (iv) a third of *Estmede* and *Westmede.*

Also Thomas has assigned to Elizabeth of his own sense of duty (*de sun sie deuenie*): Richard le Coupere with his service; 13d. to be received from (*a prendre par le mein*) Richard de Kent; 13¼d. from John Joeye; William Compe with all his suit (*sa seute*) and service; 19d. from Geoffrey Kokerel; and a ?contribution (*ket*) for churchscot and allowances from the lands, tenements, and tenants of the same places (*des mennelesluez*). Also, from Boarhunt Herbelyn, John Davy with all his services, except (*forpris*) churchscot which Thomas will keep; 3s. 6½d. from William Grey; and 1 lb. of cummin (*conmyn*) from Robert Lenkestok for the lands and tenements he holds of Thomas.

It should be noted that Elizabeth has claim to dower (*c' a doer de chif mys*) from *le Homfeld* and *Brodefeld'* and from two groves called *Haselhok'* and *Alrenemor,* which she has not received because of the dispute between the Earl of Lancaster and the said Thomas; together with a croft called *Stywemarl, Wondewepirk,* and a grant of the garden near *Alrenemor,* which have not been handed over (*qe demurt*) for the same reason.

Also Thomas has assigned to Elizabeth a third of the profits of his own mill of *Crih.*

Sealed alternately by Thomas and Hugh de Croft, Elizabeth's attorney.

Belney (*Belanye*), Thursday after the feast of the Assumption of Our Lady,[?] Edward III.

[Marginal note:] Evidence that half of Belney is held of the lord of Boarhunt (*Nota evidencia q' Bellany my parte tenetur de domino de Burhunte*). French.

1 Richard de Bellany had died some time between 1334 and 1340 (II 131, 78). By February 1340, Thomas, son and heir of Gilbert de Burhunt, had granted to Southwick Priory certain land which was in his custody during the minority of Richard's heir, together with three tenants and their services, two of whom were John Davy and William Grey (II 78). Possibly Richard's widow had died before this grant was made to the priory, and the above indenture had ceased to be valid. Otherwise it would appear that Thomas granted away two tenants who had already been assigned to the widow by way of dower, in which case the priory did well to obtain a bond for £10 from Thomas for peaceful possession of the lands and tenants during the minority. See also II 35.

II 149　　　　　　　　　　　　　　　　　　　　13 March 1323

[fo. 80] GRANT, with warranty, by John Hurt, son and heir of John Hurt, to Thomas de Bourhunt' and his wife Margaret, of ½ mark annual rent from Henry de la Warde and his heirs, which Henry paid to John Hurt, grandfather of the grantor, and his wife Alice (*Alesya*) as the gift of Richard Cocus and his wife Joan: viz. 3s. 4d. at Michaelmas and 3s. 4d. at Easter. Herbert de Burghunte, knight, gave Richard Swele that ½ mark, as is shown in Herbert's charter.[1] The grantees, and Thomas' heirs or assigns, will hold the rent with all appurtenances by hereditary right in perpetuity, paying the accustomed service to the chief lords of that fee. Consideration, 6 marks. Witnesses: John le Botelir; Richard de Belanney; John le Beaumond'; Gilbert de Burghunt'; William de Wanstede; John de la Bere; John Stak', son of Richard Stak'; and others. Southwick, Sunday before Palm Sunday, 16 Edward son of King Edward.

1 See II 193. Richard Swele's niece, Joan, and her husband, Richard Cocus, inherited a claim to this rent from Joan's uncle, and quitclaimed it to John Hurt and Alice (II 199). There is a similar quitclaim from another niece, Lucy (II 200).

II 150　　　　　　　　　　　　　　　　　　　　7 March 1354

LEASE for life from Easter 1354, with warranty, by Sir John de Bourhunt', knight, to William Perote, esquire, of his 3 acres with appurtenances in Southwick fields, all lying (*iacent' consimiles*) in the field called *Langemarle*, next to the field called *Risham* on the west, and the land called *Wolwynslonde* on the east. Annual rent to Sir John and his heirs, a gallon of wine at Christmas; and the accustomed service due to them as chief lords. Reversion to Sir John and his heirs. Witnesses: Sir Lawrence Pagham; Robert de Hoo; Thomas Beaumont; Richard Damverse; John Hunt; and others.

　　　　　　　　Southwick, Friday before the feast of St Gregory the Pope,
　　　　　　　　　　　　　　　　　　　　　　　28 Edward III.

II 151   [early 14th century]¹

[fo. 80ᵛ] LEASE for life, with warranty, by Henry de Burhunt' to John le Hay, son of John le Hay of Portchester (*Porcestre*), of 1¼ acres in the vill of Portchester lying between the land of Robert Blanchard' in the south and that of William Marescallus in the north. Annual rent to Henry, his heirs and assigns, 6d. at Michaelmas, for all services, customs, and secular demands. Consideration, 16s. Sealed by both parties. Witnesses: Richard Stak'; Richard de Stenninge; John Sandre; Thomas le Wite; Robert Blanchard; and others.

1 Witnesses occur 1308–19 (II 202, 152; III 509).

II 152   5 April 1312

AGREEMENT, with warranty, between Richard de Bourhunte, knight, and Henry de Bourhunt', concerning a water mill called *Cuttemulle,* 3 acres called *Cuttecroft,* in Southwick, and John de Kenginggewrthe's messuage in the same vill,¹ with the service of ¼ knight's fee, scutage when it occurs, 6d. rent, and 4 capons.

On the advice of mutual friends the claims were settled as follows: Richard, for himself, his heirs and assigns, quitclaimed in perpetuity to Henry, his heirs and assigns, all right he had or could have in all the aforesaid, and all action already taken in the matter. Also he granted to Henry and his wife Matilda, for their lives, a messuage with garden and 2 crofts, formerly held by Panya Scoyht² and Matilda, widow of Exton (*Relicta Extone*), with all hedges and ditches, surrounding the corn crop growing therein, and all appurtenances; and he granted to Henry each year for life a fur-lined gown (*una roba cum furfura*) of the kind he gives to his esquires on his manor of Boarhunt. In return, Henry has given in perpetuity with warranty, to Richard, his heirs and assigns, his bondman, William Dragheleg', with all his household and chattels (*cum tota sequela et catallis suis*), [fo. 81] and the tenement and all the land William held of him in villeinage, with the site of the mill called *Dragheleggesmulle,* and reversion of a croft called *Swelecroft* which Richard de Stenigges held from Henry for life.¹ Richard and Henry have bound themselves on oath to keep this agreement faithfully, and have put their seals to this bipartite deed. Witnesses: Sir John de Scures, Sir Richard de Portesye, knights; John de Seincler; Richard de Midling-tone; Richard de Denemede; Richard Stak'; John de Beaumond; and many others.

Southwick, Wednesday after the feast of St Richard the Bishop, 5 Edward son of King Edward.

1 See II 203, 202.
2 See II 198.
Copy II 196. Variants: Burhunt'; Cutemille; Cutecroft; Kenninggewrthe; Pania Scoych'; *una roba cum pelura;* William Draweleg' [omit reference to his household and chattels]; Drawelegg'mulle; de Ceynt Kler; [omit Richard Stak and add] Thomas Stak'.

II 153   4 August[1] 1353

GIFT, with warranty, by John de Bourhunt', knight, to Adam Borgeys
and his wife Joan, of all his messuage with the adjoining lands called
Asselond, in the parish of Southwick. The messuage and land are situated
near *Staleworthesahsshe* between the land of Southwick Priory and that
of Sir Lawrence de Pagheham, knight. The donees will hold all the
aforesaid messuage and land, with rights of common and all other
appurtenances, by hereditary right in perpetuity, paying 2s. annual rent
in equal portions at Michaelmas, Christmas, Easter and the Nativity of
St John the Baptist, for all other secular service, except royal service
and suit of Sir John's court. Witnesses: Sir Lawrence de Pagham, knight;
Robert de Hoo; Thomas Beaumond; Thomas Stake; John le Hunte;
William Wanstede; and others.

Southwick, Sunday before the feast of St Lawrence,[1] 27 Edward III.

1 The feast day of St Lawrence the Martyr is 10 August. If, however, the reference
is to St Lawrence the Archbishop, the feast day is 3 February, and the date of
the deed would by 27 January, 1353.

II 154   [*c.* 1243–50][1]

[fo. 81ᵛ] INSPEXIMUS by Thomas de Burhunt', son and heir of Herbert
de Bourhunt', of the charter Richard Swele gave Richard, ward
(*Alumpnus*) of M. Ralph de Suthwica, viz.

GIFT, with warranty, by Richard Swele (*Suwel*) of Southwick to
Richard Blundel, ward of M. Ralph de Suwik', of (i) a messuage with
houses built thereon in Southwick, which was given to him by Geoffrey
de la Hyde. The messuage lies between those of William le Gust and Ralph
Bulle, and extends from the king's highway which runs to Winchester, as
far as the middle of the stream (*ad filum aque*) in the west. And (ii) 9½
acres of arable with all appurtenances, from the fee of Thomas de
Burhunt, with his consent, of which 1 acre lies in Portchester (*Porcestria*)
between the donor's land and that of Robert Guludeneye; 2 acres lie in
the same field, east of the aforesaid acre; ½ acre lies in the north part of
Portsdown (*Portesdun'*), between the land of the prior of Southwick,
and extends from the east towards *Osedelle;* 1 acre, which Richard de
Ho formerly held, lies between the granges of Southwick Priory and
Portsdown hill, and extends towards the king's highway that runs from
Southwick to Portchester; 1 acre, which Geoffrey Suy formerly held, lies
south of the granges of Southwick Priory, and extends likewise to the
king's highway; and 4 acres lie in Southwick field north of the hill, of
which 1 acre, which Richard de Ho formerly held, lies in the furlong
called *Blakeforlang',* 1 acre lies in the next furlong to the east, and 2
acres lie near *Oselden',* between the land of Robert de Belanney and
Herbert, son of William de Burhunt'.

The donee and his heirs will hold all the aforesaid messuage and land
of the donor and his heirs by hereditary right in perpetuity, with free

access, and, in sickness or in health, can bequeath or give it to whomsoever he wishes, except religious houses and Jews, paying to the chief lord, Thomas de Burhunta, and his heirs, 3s. a year: viz. 12d. at Michaelmas, 12d. at Easter, and 12d. at the feast of St John the Baptist; and to Geoffrey de la Hide, a pair of gloves worth 1d., at Easter, for all [fo. 82] accustomed service, except as much royal service as pertains to that amount of land in the same fee. Consideration, 10 marks. Witnesses: Sir Robert de Bello Aunoto; Sir Roger de Merley; Herbert, son of William de Burhunt; William de Burhunt; Geoffrey de Bello Monte; Peter de la Bere; Thomas la Wayte; Adam de Wanstede; John de la Yerde; Herbert de la Barre; Richard Snelgar; Robert de Bourhunt; and many others.

Approved and sealed by Thomas de Burhunt; witnesses as above.

1 Thomas de Burhunt succeeded his father, Herbert, after 1243 (*Book of Fees* II, p. 695). Sir Roger de Merley died in 1250 (*Cal. Inq. p.m.* I, no. 221, p. 55). See also II 168, which precedes the charter quoted in this inspeximus, and II 142, which follows it.

II 155   [*c.* 1200][1]

CONFIRMATION by Walter de Borhunt to William de Ho, husband of his sister Basilia, for his service and homage, of the gift of ½ virgate from his brother, Alexander, to William for service and homage,[2] i.e. land called *Sandecroft* with all appurtenances; an acre on the near side of the hills (*citra montes*) in *Blakefurlanga;* and another acre beyond the hills (*ultra montes*) in *Chercheferlanga,* which is next to the canons' ploughland in the north part of their grange. Annual rent of 1 lb. of pepper at the feast of St Giles [1 September] for all except the royal service that pertains to that amount of land. Consideration, ½ mark. Witnesses: William de Faleise; William de Burhunt; Ralph Senescallus; Elias, son of William de Faleise; Walkelin, son of Walter; Thomas de Ho; William, his son.

1 Probably shortly after II 156.
2 See II 156.

II 156   [*c.* late 12th century][1]

GIFT by Alexander de Burhunta to William de Ho, husband of his sister Basilia, of ½ virgate for his service: viz. land called *Sandecroft* with all appurtenances, and an acre on the near side of the hills in *Blacafurlanga,* and another acre beyond the hills in *Chirchefurlanga,* which is next to the canons' ploughland in the north part of their grange. Annual rent: 1 lb. of pepper at the feast of St Giles [1 September] for all except royal service and service to his lords for ½ virgate. Witnesses: Guy, Prior of Southwick; Reinelm de Burunt; Hugh, son of Robert; Herbert de Froile; Richard de Denem'; Richard, son of Daniel, and Daniel his son; Richard

Koterel; William Dogestreng'; Matthew, nephew of Margaret, wife of
the donor; Henry de Rampen'; Jocelin Niger; Simon de Estburunta.

1 Guy occurs as Prior of Southwick between 1185 and 1210. Most of the witnesses
occur in the 1180s. See also confirmation of this gift by Alexander's brother,
Walter (II 155).

II 157   [*c*. mid 13th century][1]

[fo. 82ᵛ] QUITCLAIM in perpetuity by Clarice, widow of William le
Beke, in independent widowhood, to Herbert, son of William de Burhunt', of the whole house which she and her husband gave to Herbert,
and all the land with appurtenances called *Cuttecroft,* lying north of the
mill, which her father, Wymund Caretarius, held by charter from Herbert
for service. Consideration, 1 mark. Witnesses: Richer Mauncel, then
Constable of the town (*opidum*) of Portchester (*Porcest'*); Geoffrey de
Bello Monte; Peter de Cossam; Peter de Bera; Adam de Wanstede;
Andrew de Horsye; Adam de Lamer; Philip Clericus; and many others.

1 Most witnesses occur 1240s–60s.

II 158   [*c*. early 14th century, before 1310][1]

GIFT, with warranty, by Richard de Burhunte to Adam le Tailur of
Southwick and his heirs, of a certain tenement beyond the bridge called
Brodebrigge, formerly held by Henry Pippe and afterwards by Henry
Snelgar, lying between William Lerwite's tenement and the king's highway
which runs from Southwick to Winchester. The donees will hold the
tenement with all appurtenances of the donor and his heirs by hereditary
right in perpetuity, paying 2s. annual rent: viz. 12d. at Easter and 12d.
at Michaelmas, for all service and secular demand pertaining to the
donors. Consideration, ½ mark. Witnesses: Sir Baldwin de Bello Alneto,
[Sir] John le Butiler, knights; Roger de Wanstede; Ralph de Kenilleworth';
John de Colemere; Henry Costard; and many others.

1 Sir John le Butiler had died by 11 January 1310. His son and heir, John, had
respite from knighthood until 1324 (*Cal Inq. p.m.* V, no. 217, p. 117; *Knights of
Edward I* p. 117). See also II 134.

II 159   [*c*. mid 13th century][1]

[fo. 83] GIFT, with warranty, by Herbert de Burhunt', son of William
de Burhunt', to John Hurt, son of Baldwin, of all the land with
appurtenances which Lawrence, son of Hutbold, uncle of the aforesaid
John, held of Herbert;[2] and 1 acre which lies in Robert Ailwin's croft.

The donee, his heirs or assigns, will hold the land of the donor and his heirs for homage and service, free from all exaction and service owing to them, except as much royal service as pertains to that amount of land, paying 2d. annual rent at Michaelmas. Herbert has also granted to John, his heirs or assigns, pasture for 50 sheep in his common pasture. Consideration, 2½ marks. If Herbert, his heirs or assigns, cannot fulfil the warranty, they will exchange the land for other of similar value, in the sight of worthy neighbours. Witnesses: Matthew Oysel; Hugh Camus; Andrew de Horsya; Martin de Roches; Peter de Bera; Walter de Wimering'; Thomas de Wecces; William, son of Alan; Peter de Cossham; William de Horsya; and many others.

1 Most witnesses occur at this date as in II 157.

2 See II 172.

II 160 [*c.* 1270][1]

GIFT, with warranty, by Juliana, widow of Nicholas Pyctor, in independent widowhood, to John Hurt of Southwick and his wife Alice (*Allesya*), of 1 acre, from Richard de Burhunte's fee, lying in the east field of Portchester (*Porcestr'*) in *la Wetelond'*, between Richard le Whyte's land and Jordan le Say's and extending eastwards to the headland on the prior of Southwick's land (*versus orientem in capite super terram prioris de Suwik'*), and westwards to the headland on Henry de Burhunt's land. The acre will be held by hereditary right in perpetuity by the donees, their heirs, or anyone to whom they wish to give, sell, bequeath, assign or mortgage it in sickness or in health, paying Richard and his heirs 12d. [fo. 83ᵛ] a year, viz. 6d. at Michaelmas and 6d. at Easter, for all service and secular demand. Consideration, ½ mark. Witnesses: John Launceleve, Richard de Portesye, knights; Henry de Burhunt'; Peter de la Ber'; Walter de Belinges; William Stake; John de la Yurd; Richard Wygaunt; William Smalhach; Richard de Culerne; Richard Snelgar;[1] Stephen Clericus; and many others.

1 A Richard Snelgar had died by 1275 (III 489). See also II 199, 200.

II 161 [20 November 1285–19 November 1286][1]

GIFT, with warranty, by Alice (*Alleysia*) de Bayuse, in independent widowhood, to her daughter Matilda, for her service, of all the tenement she bought from Richard de Burhunt' at *La Strode,* viz. that which William de la Strode formerly held of the aforesaid Richard. Matilda and the legitimate heirs of her body will hold the tenement, with all appurtenances, by hereditary right in perpetuity, paying 1d. annual rent at Christmas to the donor and her heirs, and ½ lb. of cummin for the use of (*ad opus*) the said Richard and his heirs, for all services, customs, exactions and other secular demands, except as much royal service as pertains to that amount of land in the same fee. If Matilda dies without a legitimate heir of her body, reversion will be granted successively to her brother Andrew, if he survives her, and the heirs of his body, and her sister Agnes, and the legitimate heirs of her body; and if all three die without heirs, to Alice's son, John, who will inherit the whole tenement without any alienation or diminution. Witnesses: Richard de Portesye; Philip, son of Peter; Baldwin de Belanney; Peter de la Bere; John de Colemere; William Gileberd; Richard le Marescall'; William Faber; Nicholas le Dut; Adam Russel; Richard de Krihc; Stephen Clericus; and many others.

1 Date given in copy III 514.
Copy III 514. Variants: Alesia; Borhunta; La Stroude; William de la Stroude; Sir Richard de Portesia; Sir Philip, son of Peter, knights.
Dated: 14 Edward, son of King Henry.

II 162						[*c.* 1270, probably before 1275][1]

GIFT, with warranty, by Clemencia, daughter of Ralph Bulle, to William Gileberd' and his wife Clarice, of all her part of a house formerly held by her father, with a piece of land there, inherited from her father, situated on the near side of (*infra*) the bridge called *Brodebrigge* in Southwick; and all her half-share of 6d. rent a year which John Hurt used to pay her father, viz. 1½d. at Michaelmas and 1½d. at Easter; likewise half of the 4d. rent which Nicholas le Duc used to pay her father at the aforesaid terms. The half-house and rents will be held by hereditary right in perpetuity by the donees, their heirs or assigns, or anyone to whom they wish to give, sell, bequeath or mortgage them in sickness or in health, except religious men or Jews. Annual rent of 28d. will be paid to Richard de Burhunt' and his heirs, viz. 14d. at Michaelmas and 14d. at Easter, for all services, exactions, and secular demands, except as much royal service as pertains to half such a house in the same fee. Consideration, 6s. Witnesses: Baldwin de Belanney; Henry de Burhunt'; Peter de la Bere; Richard Snelgar;[1] Richard Wygaunt; William Maurdin; William Smalhach; William Faber; William de Hoo; John de la Yerde; Robert de la Lye; Stephen Clericus; and many others.

1 A Richard Snelgar had died by 1275 (III 489).
See also II 146.

II 163						29 May 1344

QUITCLAIM by Hawise (*Hawysya*), widow of Thomas de Bourhunt',[1] in independent widowhood, to Richard Danvers, of all right of claim she had or could have by way of dower in all lands, tenements, and rents, with appurtenances, formerly her husband's, in Boarhunt Herbelyn, Southwick and Portchester (*Portchestre*). Witnesses: Nicholas Haywode;

Walter Haywode; John Kenne; John Scoteneye; Thomas Polayn; and others.

Pittleworth (*Puttelworthe*), Saturday in the week of Pentecost, 18 Edward III.

1 In *Brocas* p. 334, and in *VCH Hants* III, p. 146, it is incorrectly stated that Thomas died unmarried. See also II 145, note 1.

II 164[1]   31 July 1302

EXCHANGE between Richard de Burhunte and Henry de Burhunte of 2 acres with appurtenances in Southwick, lying at *Esttnghurst'*, and adjoining lengthwise 2 acres which John de Kenylworth' holds there from Richard, for the quitclaim by Henry of all right and claim he had in 2 acres with appurtenances in West Boarhunt (*Westburhunte*): viz. the 2 acres which were taken into the king's hands by his escheator. Witnesses: Sir Roger Launceleweye, Sir Baldwin de Belloalneto, knights; Richard de Porteseye; John de Bello Monte; Guy de Horsye; John de Kenylleworth'; Robert Longus; and others.

Southwick, Tuesday, the eve of the feast of St Peter in Chains, 30 Edward I.

1 II 191 is another version of this deed.

II 165   [1320–34][1]

LEASE, for their joint lives and one year, with warranty, by Gilbert de Burhunte, son and heir of Henry de Burhunte, to Geoffrey Cokerel of Southwick and his wife, Alice, of ½ acre (*helva*) of arable in the field called *Eldeperk'*, lying lengthwise between land formerly held by John atte Brigge on both sides; of which one headland abuts onto land formerly held by Nicholas atte Barr' in the north, and the other headland abuts [fo. 85] on to a grassy ditch (*super viridem fossatum*) in the south. Annual rent, 2d. at Michaelmas for all services, customs, exactions, secular demands, heriots, and suits of court. Consideration, 2s. Chirograph sealed by both parties. Witnesses: Thomas de Burhunte; Richard de Bellanney; John de Beamond'; Richard Stak'; John Hurt; Walter atte Wytecrowe; Philip Clericus; and others.

1 Henry de Burhunte had died by 1320 (*Brocas*, p. 334; *VCH Hants* III, p. 146). His son Gilbert died in 1334 (*Cal. Inq. p.m.* VII, no. 616, p. 417).

II 166   [c. 1250–60, before 1262][1]

QUITCLAIM by William Drunivell' to John Hurt, his heirs or assigns, of all right or claim he had or could have in ¼ virgate (*in un ferlingie*), with appurtenances, in the tenement of Burhunte, from the fee of Herbert de Burhunte, son of William de Burhunt', which Henry Finel formerly held. Consideration, 16s. Witnesses: Sir Martin de Rupibus, Sir John de Lancelevee, knights; William de Bello Alneto; Herbert de Burhunt'; Peter de Bera; Walter de Bellinges; John de la Hyrd; Andrew de Horsye; John de Essebury, then Constable of Portchester (*Porcestria*); and others.

1 William de Bello Alneto died in 1262 (*Cal. Inq. p.m.* I, no. 514, p. 145).

II 167   [*c.* 1270, probably before 1275][1]

GIFT, with warranty, by Richard de Burhunt' to Osbert Souke and his wife, Emma, of ½ acre in Portchester (*Porcestr'*) field, lying between the land of Thomas Sygar and that of Cecilia, daughter of Roger Trayss, in *le Istrefurlonge*, east of a messuage formerly held by Herbert Leky, and extending from east to west. The donees, their heirs or anyone to whom they wish to give, sell, bequeath, assign or mortgage the aforesaid ½ acre with appurtenances, in sickness or in health, except religious men or [fo. 85ᵛ] Jews, will hold it by hereditary right in perpetuity, paying Richard and his heirs 6d. a year, viz. 3d. at Michaelmas and 3d. at Easter, for all services, exactions, and secular demands, except as much royal service as pertains to ½ acre in the same fee. Consideration, 2s. Witnesses: Henry de Burhunt'; Peter de la Bere; Richard Wygaunt; William Maurdin; William Gileberd'; Richard Snelgar; William Smalhach; William Faber; Nicholas le Duc; Simon Tranchem'; Stephen Clericus; and many others.

1 Dating evidence by witnesses as for II 162.

II 168   [1st half of 13th century][1]

GIFT, with warranty, by Geoffrey de la Hide to Richard Swele, for his homage and service, of a messuage with houses built thereon in the vill of Southwick, which he held of Sir Herbert de Burhunt', and which lies between the messuage of William le Gull' and that of Ralph Bulle, and extends from the king's highway running to Winchester, as far as the middle of the stream; also 3½ acres with appurtenances, of which 1 acre lies in the vill of Portchester (*Porcestre*) between the land of Richard Swele and that of Robert Guldenege, 2 acres lie in the same field east of the aforesaid acre, and ½ acre lies in the north part of Portsdown (*Portesdune*) between the lands of the prior of Southwick, extending eastwards towards *Osedelle*. Richard, his heirs or assigns, except religious houses or Jews, will hold the aforesaid messuage and land from Geoffrey and his heirs, paying 2s. annual rent—viz. 12d. at Michaelmas and 12d. at Easter—and a pair of gloves worth 1d., for all service, secular exaction and demand, except as much royal service as pertains to that amount of land in the same fee. Consideration, 8 marks 4 shillings. Witnesses: [fo. 86] Herbert de Burhunte, the younger;[2] Richard de Ho; Richer Mansel; Thomas la Wnce; Adam de Lomere; Robert le Hore; Adam de Wanstede; Peter de la Bere; Thomas Grenelief'; and many others.

1 Herbert de Burhunt was holding two knights' fees in Boarhunt, of Robert de Sancto Johanne, in 1242–43 (*Book of Fees* II, p. 695). He was succeeded by his son, Thomas, who died in 1263.

2 It seems likely that Herbert was a younger son, or predeceased his father (see note 1).
See also II 154 and 142.

II 169   25 March 1333

LEASE, for 16 years, with warranty, by Gilbert de Burhunte to John le Taylur of Southwick and his wife Juliana, of all his land at *Longhemarle,* extending in breadth between the prior of Southwick's land called *Russham* in the west and land belonging to the almonry of Southwick Priory in the east, and in length extending from the king's highway in the south as far northwards as the said land belonging to the almonry. Annual rent, 2s., viz. 12d. at Michaelmas and 12d. at Easter, for all service. Witnesses: Thomas de Burhunte; Robert Moysent; Richard Peytevyn; Roger Oysel; Richard Galioth'; John de Mullebrigge; and many others. Southwick, Thursday, the feast of the Annunciation of the Blessed Mary,
7 Edward III.

II 170   [*c.* 1250–60][1]

GIFT, with warranty, by Thomas de Borhunt' to William Brun, for his homage and service, of ½ acre (*helva*) in the vill of Portchester (*Porcestre*), which Geoffrey Soys formerly held, lying between Thomas' land and that of Herbert de Borhunta and extending from the road which runs from Fareham (*Farham*) to Wymering (*Wimeringa*) northwards to Robert Blegg's land. The donee, his heirs or assigns, will hold the said ½ acre in perpetuity, paying the donor and his heirs 9d. annual rent, viz. 4½d. at Easter and 4½d. at Michaelmas, for all services, custom and demand, except as much royal service as pertains to that amount of land in the [fo. 86ᵛ] same fee. Consideration, 3s. and ½ sester of wine. Warranty in perpetuity to the donee, his heirs or anyone to whom he wishes to give, bequeath or sell the aforesaid ½ acre, except religious houses or Jews. Witnesses: Richard de Ho; Walkelin de Felda; William Faber; Thomas Chark'; William Tredegold'; and many others.

1 The donor is probably Thomas, son of Sir Herbert de Burhunt, who died in 1263 (*Cal. Inq. p.m.* I, no. 536, p. 162). The Herbert mentioned may be his younger brother (see II 168).

II 171　　　　　　　　　　　　　　29 September 1295

AGREEMENT between Henry de Burhunt' and William Gileberd' and
his wife, Christine, by which Henry, his heirs or assigns, have leased at
farm (*ad firmam traditit*) for 6 years, with warranty, to William and
Christine, their heirs or assigns, 1 acre with appurtenances lying below
Roselinche across the road (*subtus Roselinche extransverso vie*) which
runs from Southwick to Portchester (*Porcestr'*).[1] Witnesses: John de
Kenylleworth'; John de Colemere; Roger de Wansted'; Robert de la
Yerde; Henry Snelgar; and many others.
　　　　　　　　　　　　　　Michaelmas, 23 Edward son of King Henry.

1 Cf. II 186.

II 172　　　　　　　　　　　　　　　[*c.* 1220–30][1]

GIFT by Lawrence, son of Hubold, to Baldwin, son of Walter ?Heirim,
on his marriage to Matilda, Lawrence's sister, of land formerly
Tumberel's—which Lawrence held of the fee of William de Burhunt'
and which is taxed at ¼ virgate (*ferlingus*)—except the house (*masuagium*)
which he built there (*quod super illam feci*) and will retain as agreed.
Annual rent to Lawrence and his heirs, 31d., viz. 15½d. at Easter and
15½d. at the feast of the Nativity of St Mary [8 September], for all
service and exaction, except royal service pertaining to that amount of
land. Witnesses: Richard Capellanus of Wanstead (*Wanest'*); William de
Burhunt'; Richard Coterel; Henry de Wanested'; Peter de Havunth';
Guy, son of Reinelm; Henry, son of Hubold; Bartholomew Canonicus,
who drew up this charter; and many others.

1 Precedes II 159. William de Burhunt and Henry de Wanested were holding land
by serjeanty in Boarhunt and Wanstead in 1219 (*Book of Fees* I, p. 258).

II 173　　　　　　　　　　　　　　26 November 1271

AGREEMENT between Richard de Burhunt' and Henry de Osspring'
and his wife, Isabella, whereby Richard has leased at farm for 7 years,
with warranty, to Henry and Isabella, a mill called *Buresmulle*. The mill,
with appurtenances, will be held for the aforesaid term, free from all
service, exaction, or secular demand, by Henry and Isabella, their heirs,
or anyone to whom they wish to give, sell, bequeath, assign or mortgage
it, in sickness or in health. After the completion of the term they will
have the stone from the mill and can take away unchallenged what they
have put there, because they are obliged to find at least as good a
millstone as they saw fit to provide for their use (*a dicto molendino cum*

eis petram habebunt et sine calumpnia asportare bene possunt que illuc imposuerunt quia ibidem tam bonam molam invenire debent sicut ad opus eorumdem melius viderint expedire). Richard, his heirs or assigns, are bound to find all the timber, large and small, reasonably required during the whole 7 years, to make and repair the said mill with appurtenances inside and out, and they will cart the timber and enough clay and gravel for the maintenance of the mill pond, so that repairs can be made anywhere without delay; and Henry and Isabella and their heirs will bear the cost. If the lessees fail to carry out maintenance and repair of the mill and appurtenances, after 3 or 4 days' warning, Richard, if he is in the country, or, if not, his bailiff or other attorney, in the sight of his friends, will do what is necessary (*que pertinent ad omnia prenotata faciet*). And if any loss is incurred through default of warranty of the said lease, then Richard, his heirs or assigns, are bound to make good to the lessees all loss and expenses, in the sight of upright, law-worthy men, without any contradiction, before the end of the term: either from his chattels (*catall'*), or by lengthening the lease on the same terms year by year, as he may decide (*vel in elongacione terminorum et per talem convencionem ut prius habuerunt sicut per annum evenir' vellet*). And if, at the end of the said term, Richard wishes to lease the mill for a further term, or to sell it in perpetuity, and Henry and Isabella are [fo. 87ᵛ] willing to give as much for it as anyone else, they will have the first option. Consideration, 8½ marks. Both parties have sworn to keep faith, and have attached their seals to this chirograph. Witnesses: Henry de Burhunt'; Richard Wygaunt; Peter de la Bere; Roger Giffard, then bailiff of Portchester forest; William Maurdin; Philip de Biensted'; Henry, his son; Gervase de Farham, clerk; William Gileberd'; William de la Strode; William Smalhach; William de Ho; William Faber; Richard Marescallus; Simon Tranchem'; Stephen Clericus; and many others.

The morrow of the feast of St. Katherine, Virgin and Martyr,
56 Henry III.

II 174 29 January 1322

LEASE, with warranty, for their joint lives, by Gilbert, son and heir of Henry de Burhunt', to Robert de Lyngestok' and his wife, Isabella, of one acre in the field of Portchester (*Porcestre*), lying breadth-wise between Thomas Comyn's land on the south and the lessor's land on the north, of which one headland (*capud*) abuts onto the furlong called *Merkforlang'* in the east, and the other headland abuts onto Thomas de Hoo's land in the west. Robert and Isabella will hold the said land with appurtenances, of Gilbert and his heirs, paying 6d. annual rent, viz. 3d. at Easter and 3d. at Michaelmas, for all services, suits of court and secular demands. Witnesses: Thomas de Borhunte; Richard de Bellanney; John de Beaumond; John Hurt; John Sygar; John de Palesgrave; and others.
Friday after the Conversion of St. Paul, 15 Edward son of King Edward.

II 175   [early 14th century, before 1318]¹

GIFT, with warranty, by Adam Smalhach to Thomas de Burhunte, son
of Sir Richard de Burhunt', of all his land and appurtenances with the
adjoining meadow outside the vill of Southwick, which formerly he held
of the said Thomas. It lies breadthwise between Thomas de Colemere's
land on one side and William Bardolf's on the other, and lengthwise
extends from Philip de la Newlonde's land to the prior of Southwick's
land called *Menelond'*. Thomas and his heirs will hold all the said land
of the chief lord of the fee, by hereditary right in perpetuity, for the
accustomed services. Consideration, £10, paid to Adam in his urgent
need. Witnesses: Sir John de Scures and Sir Richard de Portesye, knights;
Richard de Bello Alneto; John le Botelyr; Philip de Denemede; Thomas
Stak'; John Beaumond; Richard Stak'; and others.

1 The first four witnesses and John Beaumond were holding land in the hundred
of Portsdown in 1314 (*Feudal Aids* II, pp. 319–20). Sir Richard de Portesye had
died by 23 October 1318 (*Cal. Inq. p. m.* VI, no. 178, p. 106).

II 176   1 August 1343

[fo. 88] GIFT, with warranty, by Alice, sister of Thomas de Burhunte,
daughter and heir of Gilbert de Burhunte, to Richard, son of the
late Thomas Danvers, knight, of all lands, tenements and rents, with
appurtenances, which belonged to her father, Gilbert, in Boarhunt Herbelyn (*Burhunteherbelyn*), Southwick, Boarhunt Herberd, and within the
liberties of Portchester (*Porcestre*), together with the reversion of the
dower which Joan widow of Gilbert holds for life, and of 2 mills with 2
crofts, and all their appurtenances, which John le Honte and his wife
Juliana hold for life. Richard, his heirs or assigns, will hold the aforesaid
land and rents of the chief lords of the fee for the accustomed services.
Witnesses: Robert de Hoo; John le Boteler, junior; Valentine Becke;
John Scoteneye; Lawrence Pageham; William Wanstede; John Le Longe;
John Hurt; and many others.
                Southwick, the feast of St. Peter in Chains, 17 Edward III.

See II 145 and note.

II 177   6 March 1335

GIFT, with warranty, by Joan, widow of Gilbert de Burhunt' of the
parish of Southwick, for her lifetime, to Richard le Leche of the same
parish, of 1 acre called *Weyacre*, lying next to *Blatforlong'* and extending
length-wise between the king's highway leading from Southwick to
Wymering (*Wymeryng'*) on one side, and the land of John de Wansted'

on the other. Richard, his heirs or assigns, will hold the acre with appurtenances of the chief lord of the fee for the accustomed services. Consideration, 40d. Witnesses: Thomas de Burhunt'; Robert de Hoo; Henry, son of the said Gilbert de Burh'; Richard Peytevyn; Richard Galyoth; John Gilberd'; Philip de Huppelygh'; and others.

Southwick, Monday before the feast of St. Gregory the Pope,
9 Edward III.

II 178 12 June 1346

[fo. 88ᵛ] LETTERS PATENT of William Damvers, granting to Richard Damvers wardship and marriage of John, son and heir of John le Hort. Richard and his assigns will hold the aforesaid wardship and marriage, with appurtenances and profits pertaining to them, until John, or one of successive heirs, comes of age.

Southwick, Sunday after Trinity, 20 Edward III.
French

II 179 17 September 1347

GRANT, in perpetuity, by Thomas de Keng*n*gwerthe and his wife Joan,[1] to Richard Damvers and his heirs, of all the claim (*lestat*) they have in the third part of the manor of Boarhunt Herbelyn (*Bourhunte Herbelyn*), with appurtenances, as Joan's dower from the inheritance of the said Richard. Witnesses: Robert Popham and Lawrence Pageham, knights; Thomas Aspall'; William de Overton'; John le Boteler; Robert de Hoo; Nicholas atte Beere; Thomas de Whelton; Richard de Byenham; William le Wayte; Peter (*Peris*) Persshete; John Kenne; William Markes; and others.

Southwick, Monday before the feast of St. Matthew the Apostle,
21 Edward III.
French

1 Joan was the widow of Gilbert de Burhunt, and had subsequently married Thomas de Kengngwerthe. Gilbert's son, Thomas, who died not later than May 1344, made over Boarhunt Herbelyn and other lands to Richard Danvers (*Brocas* p. 334; II 163, 176, 145; *VCH Hants* III, p. 146).

II 180 12 January 1356

GIFT, with warranty, by John de Burhunt', knight, to Thomas Wyot, of two parts of a messuage with adjoining curtillage, which Peter Fraunceys formerly held in Sheepwash (*la Shepwasshe*),[1] and which fell to John by escheat. Thomas, his heirs or assigns, will hold the two parts of John and his heirs, by hereditary right in perpetuity, paying 2d. annual rent at Michaelmas for all secular services or demands. The warranty will cover the grant, with rights of common and all other appurtenances. Witnesses: Peter atte Yerde; William atte Futhe; William le Kantisshe; John Shonke; John le Couk; and others.

Sheepwash, Tuesday before the feast of St. Hillary, 29 Edward III.

1 Sheepwash farm is about 2 miles E.N.E. of Southwick.

II 181 [*c.* 1230–40][1]

[fo. 89] GIFT, with warranty, by Herbert de Burhunt' to Robert le Welleis and his wife, Margaret, of five pieces (*placee*) of land in *Luckecroft,* each 4 perches wide, which lie between the lands of Richard Snelgar and Geoffrey Bulle, extending from the road which runs from Southwick to Winchester as far as Wimund le Bunde's land. Robert and Margaret, their heirs or assigns, except religious men or Jews, will hold the land of Herbert and his heirs by hereditary right, paying 9s. annual rent, viz. 4s. 6d. at the feast of St. John the Baptist, and 4s. 6d. at Christmas, for all service, secular exaction and demand, except royal service pertaining to that amount of land from the same tenement. Consideration, 10s. Witnesses: Matthew Oisel; Herbert, son of William de Burhunt'; Adam de Wanstede; Herbert de la Rigge; Robert de Burhunt'; Adam de Lom*ere*; Adam Swele; Richard de Hoo; Thomas Grenelief; and many others.

1 For dating evidence see II 206, 154.

II 182 31 May 1309

LEASE, for their joint lives, with warranty, by Gilbert de Burhunt' to Thomas le Swon of Portchester (*Porcestr'*) and his wife, Anne (*Annes*), of 3 acres of land in Portchester field, which lie together between the lands of Robert de Lengestok' and Richard le Hay, extending from a butt (*un but*) on the west to another butt on the east. Thomas and Anne will hold the aforesaid 3 acres, with all profit accruing therefrom, paying 3s. rent a year, viz. 18d. at Christmas and 18d. at the feast of St. John the Baptist, for all services and demands, except suit of court and as much royal service as is due from that land. Witnesses: William de Wanstede; John de Kenylworth'; Robert Langestok'; Nicholas Bolle; William Bolle; John le Hay; and many others.

Southwick, Saturday the feast of St. Petronilla,
2 Edward son of King Edward.

French.

II 183 25 December 1279

[fo. 89ᵛ] AGREEMENT, with warranty, made between Henry de Burhunt' and Osbert Soulee, whereby Henry has leased to Osbert, at farm for 6 years, a croft which was formerly William Dragheley's, and which lies on the north of the mill called *Draghelegges melne,* and east of the road running northwards from the mill. The croft extends lengthwise from the land in the south formerly held by Ralph Reynham to the land of Geoffrey de la Nywelond' in the north. Osbert has paid 14s. in advance, for all service, custom, secular exaction, and demand; and the croft with appurtenances will be held during the aforesaid term by him, his heirs, or anyone to whom he wishes to give, sell, bequeath, assign or mortgage it, in sickness or in health. Chirograph sealed by both parties. Witnesses: John de Colmer'; Peter de Culle; Nicholas Duc; Richard le Marchal; John Bardulf; and many others.

Christmas, 8 Edward son of King Henry.

II 184   [c. early 14th century, before 1320][1]

LEASE, for their joint lives, with warranty, by Henry de Burhunt', son and heir of Henry de Burhunte, to Nicholas Wolwyne and his wife Ellen (*Elena*), of 1 acre which abuts lengthwise onto an acre called *le Holaker* in the west, and onto land called *Coppelonde* in the east. Nicholas and Ellen will hold the said acre of Henry, his heirs or assigns, paying 4d. annual rent at Michaelmas for all services, exactions and secular demands. Consideration, 1 mark. Chirograph sealed alternately. Witnesses: Sir Richard de Burhunt', knight; John de Kenelworth'; Richard Stake; Thomas de Colemere; Richard Rous; Henry Vox; and many others.

1 The lessor is probably Henry, father of Gilbert de Burhunte, who died in 1320, see II 139 note.

II 185   [c. early 14th century, before 1320][1]

[fo. 90] LEASE, for their joint lives, with warranty, by Henry de Burhunte, son and heir of Henry de Burhunt', to Nicholas Wolwyne and his wife, Ellen (*Elena*), of 1 acre called *Holaker,* which lies between land formerly held by William Gileberd' on the east and west, and abuts onto the prior of Southwick's land in the north and onto Thomas de Colemere's land in the south. Nicholas and Ellen will hold the said acre of Henry, his heirs or assigns, paying 4d. annual rent at Michaelmas for all services, exactions and hereditary demands. Consideration, 1 mark. Chirograph sealed alternately. Witnesses: Sir Richard de Burhunt', knight; John de Kenelwerthe; Richard Stake; Thomas de Colemere; Richard Rous; Henry Vox; John le Bakare; and many others.

1 For dating evidence see II 184.

II 186   25 December 1279

AGREEMENT, with warranty, between Henry de Burhunte and William le Hwite, whereby Henry has leased at farm for 8 years, to William and

his heirs or assigns, 1 acre with appurtenances below *Roselinche* across
the road which runs from Southwick to Portchester (*Porcestr'*).[1] Consideration, 8s. Bipartite deed sealed alternately. Witnesses: Sir Richard
de Portesia, Sir Philip son of Peter; Sir Richard de Burhunte, knights;
Richard Wygaunt; John de Colemere; Richard Marescallus; and many
others.

Christmas, 8 Edward son of King Henry.

1 Cf II 171.

II 187   12 May 1350

LEASE, for 16 years, with warranty, by John de Burhunt', knight, to
Brother Richard de Bromden', Prior of Southwick, and the convent, of
a meadow called *Kokelychesmede* and all appurtenances. Reversion to
[fo. 90ᵛ] John and his heirs. Indenture sealed alternately.
Southwick, Wednesday after the feast of St. John before the Latin Gate,
24 Edward [III].

II 188   [*c*. 1240][1]

GIFT by Herbert de Burhunt', son of Walter de Borhunte, to John le
Crich, of (i) that little piece (*particula*) of land with appurtenances which
lies outside *Plassiz* on the north, next to the road which leads from
Southwick to Creech (*Crich*)[2] in the west; also (ii) as much of the
purpresture above Creech as belongs to Herbert. Consideration, ½ mark.
Sealed by Herbert, lest he, or any of his heirs, should contest this gift in
the future. Witnesses: Gilbert de Basewile; William de Ho; Robert de
Bello Alneto; Herbert de Burhunte, son of William de Burhunt'; Stephen
de Site; Robert Horsye; Henry de Wansted', and his brother, Adam;
Robert de Burhunt'; Peter Dun; John de Sancto Laudo, who wrote this
deed; and many others.
[Marginal note:] Cryche.

1 See II 192 and dating evidence.
2 Creech Farm is just over a mile N.N.E. of Southwick.

II 189   28 October 1311

GIFT, with warranty, by Henry de Burhunt', son and heir of Henry de
Burhunte, to Thomas de Burhunt', son of Sir Richard de Burhunt', of a
croft called *Boundescroft,* enclosed by hedges and ditches, in the parish
of Southwick, and extending lengthwise from the king's highway leading
from Southwick to Wickham (*Wycham*) as far as the land called *Swystes-
croft,* and breadthwise from the land of John de Kenilworth' to that of

Stephen le Ropare. Thomas, his heirs or assigns, will hold all the aforesaid croft with appurtenances and with free access, of the chief lord of the fee by hereditary right in perpetuity, for the accustomed services. Consideration, £4. Witnesses: Richard de Bellanney; John le Botiler; Richard de Denemede; John de Beaumond; Richard Stak'; Matthew atte Hale; and others.

> The feast of the Apostles Simon and Jude,
> 5 Edward son of King Edward.

See also II 144 and note.

II 190   16 April 1329

[fo. 91] LEASE (*dedi concessi*), for their joint lives, with warranty, by Gilbert de Burhunt' to William Gosselyn of Overton and his wife Joan, of 2½ acres (*due acre et una helva*) in the east field of Portchester (*Porcestr'*), of which 1 acre lies between John le Hay's land on the north and the lessor's on the south; ½ acre lies between William Bolle's land on the north and Isabella Bolle's on the south; and 1 acre lies between John Sygar's land on the north and the prior of Southwick's on the south. William and Joan will hold the aforesaid 2½ acres with all appurtenances, paying 2s. annual rent to Gilbert and his heirs, viz. 12d. at the feast of St. John the Baptist and 12d. at Michaelmas, for all services, except service due to the king and suit of Gilbert's court. Chirograph sealed alternately. Witnesses: John Sygar; Robert de Ramuyle; William de Wanstede; Jordan Kutte; John atte Lyghe; and many others.

> Southwick, 16 April, 3 Edward III.

[Marginal note:] 2½ acres (*due acre et dimidia*) in the east field of Portchester.

II 191   31 July 1302

NOTIFICATION by Henry de Burhunt' that he has given to Sir Richard de Burhunt' 2 acres with appurtenances in West Boarhunt (*Westbourhunte*), formerly taken into the king's hands by escheat. Sir Richard and his heirs will hold them by hereditary right in perpetuity, in exchange for 2 acres with appurtenances lying at *Estngherst* in Southwick and adjoining lengthwise 2 acres which John de Kenilleworth holds there of Sir Richard. Witnesses: Sir Roger Launcelevee, Sir Baldwin de Bello Alneto, knights; Richard de Porteseye; John de Bellomonte; Guy (*Gwydo*) de Horsey; John de Kenilworth'; Robert Longus; and others.

> Southwick, Tuesday, the vigil of the feast of
> St. Peter in Chains, 30 Edward [I].

See also II 164 for another version of this deed.

II 192 [*c.* 1230-40]¹

GIFT, with warranty, by Gilbert de Basevill' to Herbert de Burhunt', son of William de Burhunt', of his sister Felicia, in frank-marriage, and [fo. 91ᵛ] of (i) all the land with appurtenances Richard Cokelig held of him, together with Richard and all his household; (ii) the land with appurtenances which Ralph ?Renneamne² formerly held of him, together with Ralph and all his household; (iii) all the meadow lying between Herbert's meadow and the stream flowing from Southwick to *Bukare* mill; and (iv) agistment for Herbert's own pigs in Gilbert's wood outside [his demesne] (*in forinseco bosco meo*). Herbert, and his heirs by Felicia, will hold [the aforesaid] of Gilbert and his heirs by hereditary right, quit of all service and exaction, except as much royal service as is due from that amount of land in the same vill. Witnesses: the Prior of Southwick; Adam de Portes'; Herbert de Burhunt'; William de Hoo; Robert de Bello Alneto; Andrew de Portesia; Thomas de Bera; Richard Coterel; Robert de Horsia; Henry de Wansted'; and many others.

1 Sir Adam de Portesia occurs 1208–30; his eldest son, Andrew, 1230–43, and a younger son, Adam, 1235–*c.* 1247 (I 164; *Cal. Chart. R., 1226–57* p. 119; *Book of Fees* II, p. 695; III 615, 637).

2 See the reference to *Reynhameslond'* in II 197.

II 193 [*c.* 1240, before 1250]¹

GRANT, with warranty, by Herbert de Burhunte, knight, to Richard Swele, for his homage and service, of ½ mark annual rent from Beckford (*Bekeford*),² which he will receive from Henry, son of Henry de la Warde, and his heirs, viz. 40d. at Michaelmas and 40d. at Easter. The rent will be held by hereditary right by Richard, his heirs or anyone to whom he wishes to give, assign, alienate or bequeath it, in sickness [or in health],³ except religious houses. Annual rent, 1 lb. of pepper at Michaelmas for all service, custom, and demand, pertaining to Herbert or his heirs. If Herbert and his heirs are unable to fulfil the warranty of the aforesaid rent, they will make reasonable exchange in the same fee in the sight of law-worthy men. Witnesses: Gilbert de Basevile, William de Ho, Robert de Belanney, Roger de Merley, knights; M. Ralph, then clerk of Southwick; Herbert, son of William de Burhunt'; John de Crich; Thomas la Wayte; Geoffrey Pulein [and] Richard, his son; Guy de Burhunt'; and many others.

1 Sir Roger de Merley died in 1250 (*Cal. Inq. p.m.* I, no. 221, p. 51).

2 Beckford is about 1½ miles N.N.E. of Southwick.
See also II 149 and note; II 199 and 200.

3 Omitted in MS.

II 194 18 February 1331

[fo. 92] GRANT, with warranty, by Felicia atte Warde, daughter and one of the heirs of Henry atte Warde of Beckford (*Bykeford*),[1] to Thomas de Bourhunt', her lord, of 6d. annual rent at Michaelmas from her share by inheritance of a certain meadow called *Boriemede*. Thomas, his heirs and assigns, will hold the aforesaid rent by hereditary right in perpetuity. Witnesses: Gilbert de Bourhunte; Robert de Hoo; John de Beaumot'; Philip de Huppelygh'; John de Longe; and others.

Beckford, 18 February, 5 Edward III.

1 See II 193 and note 2.

II 195 [*c.* 1200][1]

GIFT by William, son of Reinelm de Burhunt', to Roald, son of Ludus, for his service, of (i) a messuage with orchard in Portchester (*Porcestr'*), which Robert de Normannia held, and (ii) 6 acres in Portchester fields. Roald will hold [the above] of William, his heirs and their heirs, paying 3s. annual rent, viz. 18d. at Easter and 18d. at Michaelmas, quit of all exaction and service, except service due to the king. Of the 6 acres, 3 lie between *Baggeweie* and *Hildelieweie* where they are crossed by the road from Portchester to East Boarhunt (*Estburhunte*); a 4th acre lies between the prior of Southwick's grange and the marl pit, and adjoins Adam Coc's acre; a 5th lies above *Langedell';* the 6th adjoins Geoffrey de Ponte's land.

William has also given Roald (iii) 3 acres from his fee adjoining Alan de Sancto Georgio's acre, which lies near the road running between Portchester and Paulsgrove (*Palesgrave*). Roald will hold the 3 acres of William and his heirs for an annual rent of 1 lb. of pepper at the feast of St. Giles [1 September], for all service and exaction. Witnesses: Walter de Burh'; Alexander de Bera; Henry de Wansted'; Walter Paie; William Doggestreng'; Richard Coterell'; Jocelin Niger; Robert de Barra; William de Denemede, son of Walter; William de Ramvill'; Randolf Rufus; William Charc; Robert Brangrant; and many others.

1 Reinelm de Burhunt was a benefactor of Southwick Priory at the dedication of its church in 1181-2 (I 25). A William de Borhunt was holding a carucate in Boarhunt in 1212, and, at the same date, Henry de Wansted was holding 5s. worth of land in Wanstead (*Book of Fees* I, p. 74).

II 196 [fo. 92ᵛ] Copy of II 152.

II 197 10 January 1295

AGREEMENT made between Henry de Burhunt' on the one part, and Thomas le Sayghere and his wife Agnes on the other part, whereby Henry will lease for 3 years from the feast of Purification [2 February], 1295, with warranty, to Thomas and Agnes, a croft called *Reynhameslond'* with meadow and appurtenances, as enclosed by a hedge in the parish of West Boarhunt (*Westburhunt'*). They lie near the mill called *Draygheleggesmille* in Southwick parish. Thomas, Agnes, their heirs and assigns, will hold the said croft with free access, and during the term Henry cannot sell, give or assign it to anyone, in fee. Consideration, 60s. Chirograph sealed alternately by Henry and Thomas. Witnesses: [fo. 93] Baldwin de Bello Alneto, knight; Roger de Wansted'; John de Colemere; Robert de la Leghe; William Gilberd'; Clement de Ely, clerk; and others.

Monday after Epiphany, 23 Edward [I].

[Marginal note:] *Dralegges mille.*

II 198 [*c.* 1280][1]

GIFT, with warranty, by Richard de Burhunt' to Richard Marescallus, of all the messuage and land which John Skohe and his wife Panya formerly held, situated west of the king's highway which runs from north of the bridge called *Cuttebrigge* southwards to Portchester (*Porcestr'*). The messuage and land will be held by hereditary right in perpetuity by Richard Marescallus, his heirs, or anyone to whom he wishes to give, sell, bequeath, assign or alienate them in sickness or in health, except religious men or Jews. Annual rent, 12d. at Michaelmas, and one ploughshare, one coulter, and one ?attachment (*unum sulso*) for the donor's ox-plough. They will make, repair and maintain the said ironwork at their own cost, and will have two days' ploughing annually in perpetuity with that plough, without contest from the donor and his heirs. If that plough only ploughs for half the year, Richard Marescallus, his heirs or assigns, are bound to pay 2s. at Michaelmas by way of annual rent; but if it ploughs for more than half the year they will pay 12d. as aforesaid. And at the end of the year's, or half year's, ploughing, the said plough should be laid up until the time comes to plough again, and soon after it is laid up the said iron-work should be carried back, by one of the donor's servants (*famulus*), to the house of Richard Marescallus, his heirs or assigns, without contest from the donor, his heirs or assigns, because it must not be used except in the aforesaid plough, so that it will be promptly available when required, and ploughing will not be delayed. [The above rent and obligations are] for all service, custom, secular exaction, and demand, except suit of court twice a year. Witnesses: Baldwin de Belanney; Henry de Burhunt'; Peter de la Bere; John de la Yurde; Robert de la Lye; Robert Wygaunt; Ralph Tannator; William Gileberd; William de Hoo; John de Colemere; William Maurdyn; William Faber; Nicholas Dut; Stephen Clericus; and many others.

1 Dating evidence from witnesses, and from Richard Marescallus, who occurs 1271-86 (II 173, 161).

II 199 [*c.* 1280][1]

[fo. 93ᵛ] QUITCLAIM, with warranty, by Richard Cocus and his wife Joan, to John Hurt of Southwick and his wife, Alice (*Allesia*), of all right and claim they have or could have in all tenements, messuages and lands, with rents, which Richard Swele, Joan's uncle, formerly held, and all that can accrue to Richard and Joan by inheritance from Richard Swele: viz. (i) ½ mark which Henry de la Warde used to pay to Richard, i.e. 3s. 4d. at Michaelmas and 3s. 4d. at Easter;[2] (ii) 1½ acres in *Blakefurlonge;* (iii) 12d. rent, payable at the aforesaid terms by William de Ponte, for 2 acres at *la Longemarle;* and (iv) a messuage in New Street, Southwick (*in novo vico de Suwik*). All the above will be held by hereditary right in perpetuity by John and Alice, their heirs or assigns, or anyone to whom they wish to give, sell, bequeath or alienate it in sickness or in health, paying annually: for (i), 1 lb. of pepper to the lord of the fee, viz. the heirs of Thomas de Burhunt', for all accustomed services; for (ii), 12d., viz. 6d. at Michaelmas and 6d. at Easter, to the same lord of the fee; for (iii), 12d. at the said terms to the aforesaid lord of the fee of Burhunte; and for (iv), 12d. at the said terms to the prior and convent of Southwick, for all services, exactions and other secular demands. Consideration, 20s. Witnesses: Sir John Launceleve, knight; Richard de Portesye; Richard de Burhunt'; Peter de la Bere; Walter de Belling'; Richard Wygaunt; William Stake; Geoffrey de Bello Monte; Henry de Burhunt'; John de la Yurde; Richard de Culerne; Stephen Clericus; and many others.

1 Dating evidence from witnesses.

2 John Hurt's grandson, John, granted the ½ mark of rent, payable by Henry de la Warde, to Thomas de Bourhunt' in 1323 (II 149 and note). See also II 193, 200.

II 200 [*c.* 1280][1]

[fo. 94] QUITCLAIM, with warranty, by Lucy, daughter of Adam Swele, in independent widowhood, to John Hurt of Southwick and his wife Alice (*Allesya*), their heirs or assigns, of all right and claim she had or could have in all tenements, messuages, land and rents which her uncle, Richard Swele, formerly held, and which can accrue to her or her heirs or assigns by inheritance from Richard: viz [(i), (ii), (iii) and (iv), with conditions of tenure and payments to lords of the fees as in II 199].

John and Alice will give 1 rose at the feast of St. John the Baptist to Lucy, her heirs or assigns, for all services, customs, secular exactions and demands pertaining to them. Consideration, 20s. Witnesses: Sir John Launceleve, knight; Richard de Portesye; Richard de Burhunt'; Peter de la Bere; Walter de Belling'; Richard Wygaunt; William Stake; Geoffrey de Bello Monte; Henry de Burhunt'; Stephen Clericus; and many others.

1 Dating as for II 199.
See also II 193, 199, 149.

II 201   6 May 1373

[fo. 94ᵛ] GIFT, with warranty, by Andrew Hurt of Southwick to the elder John le Spicer of Portchester (*Porcestria*), his wife Matilda, and their son John, of 3 acres of arable in the east field of Portchester, which extend lengthwise from east to west above (*super*) the king's highway running from Portchester to Southwick, and of which 1 acre lies south of Southwick Priory's barns, and the other 2 north of them. John, Matilda, their son John, and their heirs or assigns, will hold the 3 acres of the chief lords of that fee for 2s. annual rent and the other accustomed services in perpetuity. They will give annually to Andrew and his heirs, for the next 40 years, a red rose on the feast of St. John the Baptist, for all services, exactions and demands; and after 40 years, they will pay 13s. 4d. a year in equal portions at the four principal terms. And if, after the 40 years, the said rent is in arrears for 3 weeks after any of the principal terms, Andrew, his heirs or assigns, may seize the 3 acres and keep them in perpetuity, without any contest. Witnesses: Thomas Stake; John Upham; Roger Upham; Valentine atte Mede; John atte Selere; and many others.

Southwick, the feast of St. John before the Latin Gate, 47 Edward III.

II 202   Friday, 18 October 1308

[fo. 95] INQUISITION,[1] held at Southwick in the presence of the King's Escheator for the county of Hampshire, concerning lands and tenements dismembered or alienated by Henry de Burhunt' without royal licence. Jurors: Thomas Stake, John Beaumond, Reginald Stacy, Richard Stake, Geoffrey de Brochampton', Gilbert le Rous, Adam de Putlye, Peter de la Grauette, Thomas atte Wode, John Sygar, Thomas Wyhtyng' and Robert Blaunchard', who say on oath that (i) the enclosure containing the spring is not in the fee of Henry de Burhunt' held of the king, but is in the land of the prior and convent of Southwick, who own the course of the same spring as far as the priory, outside Henry's land, by gift of Henry and his predecessors.[2] (ii) The meadow, which was alienated to

Beaulieu (*Bellus Locus*) Abbey, is not from land held by serjeanty, but from the fee of Sir Gilbert de Basevill'.[3] (iii) Henry de Burhunt', father of the aforesaid Henry, was formerly seised of a messuage outside the vill of Southwick and held it by serjeanty; he gave it in fee to John de Kenyngworth, for the accustomed service. John de Kenyngworthe, son and heir of the aforesaid John, now holds the messuage, but whether by royal licence or not they do not know. (iv) The land and tenement which Richard de Stenyng' holds were not from the serjeanty of Henry de Burhunt', but from the fee of Gilbert de Basevill'.[4] They do not know of any more tenants of Henry's serjeanty in spite of their enquiries. In testimony of which, etc.

Southwick, the feast of St. Luke the Evangelist, 2 Edward [II].

1 The inquisition was held in response to II 203.

2 See II 203; III 250, 450; also I 25, 28 for the original gift of the spring to the priory by Reinelm de Burhunt in 1181–2.

3 The Beaulieu Cartulary records the gift by Herbert, son of William de Burhunt, to Beaulieu Abbey, of meadows north of the Wallington River, but has no mention of any gift by Henry de Burhunt', or of the fee of Sir Gilbert de Basevill' (*Beaulieu Cartulary* no. 71, p. 61). See III 132 (b), 986.

4 See II 152, 196.

II 203   12 October 1308

MANDATE from W. de Glocestre, the King's Escheator South of Trent,[1] to Alexander de Halghton, Sub-Escheator in the county of Hampshire. Because by the inquisition lately held by Alexander, on the escheator's instructions, [it was shown] that Henry de Burhunt' holds his lands and tenements of the king in chief by serjeanty, keeping guard in Portchester castle in time of war, and that Henry dismembered the lands and tenements and alienated them without royal licence—viz.: to the prior and convent of Southwick, a close containing a spring with its course flowing into the priory; to the abbot of Beaulieu (*Bellus Locus*), a meadow; to John Kenyngworth', a tenement next Southwick; to Richard Stenyng', certain lands and tenements; and to others not named in this brief—and because, as the escheator has learnt by many reports, Alexander has been suborned by entreaty and bribes (*vos prece et precio doni subornati*), so that in contempt of the king's orders he has not taken care to intervene, the escheator orders him to hold an inquisition to discover the lands and tenements thus alienated, to take them into the king's hands and keep them intact until ordered otherwise, and to report to him without delay, sending this brief with the findings.[2]

12 October, 2 Edward son of King Edward.

1 Walter de Gloucestre was Escheator South of Trent from May 1299 to April 1311 (PRO *List of escheators for England and Wales* (List and Index Society, 72; 1971) p. 1).

2 For the findings of the inquisition held in response to this mandate see II 202.

II 204 7 February 1369

[fo. 95ᵛ] GIFT, with warranty, by Robert Markaunt, knight, to Geoffrey de Ramvile, clerk, of 3 acres of arable with salt pans (*saline*) in the parish of Portchester (*Porchestre*);[1] Robert formerly held them of the fee of John de Bourhunt', knight. 1 acre lies south of the king's highway which runs from Portchester to Wymering (*Wymerynges*), east of John le Hay's land in the prior of Southwick's fee, and west of Henry le Hay's land, formerly in the fee of Gilbert de Bourhunt'; the salt pans adjoining that acre to the south; 1 acre extends lengthwise from land, formerly of Sir John de Bourhunte's fee, in the north, abuts onto the aforesaid highway in the south, and lies breadthwise between John le Hay's land of the prior of Southwick's fee in the east, and John Jolyf's land formerly of the fee of Gilbert de Bourhunt' in the west;[2] and 1 acre lies in *Baggeweyforlang'* adjoining *la Greynelynche*, viz. between Robert Nel's land formerly of Sir John de Bourhunte's fee in the south, and the prior of Southwick's land in the north. Geoffrey, his heirs and assigns, will hold the 3 acres and salt pans, with hedges, ditches, roads, paths, pastures, commons, and all other appurtenances, of the chief lords of that fee, for the accustomed services in perpetuity. Witnesses: John Bruton'; William de Ramvile; Oliver Cutte; Richard Abreham; Thomas atte Leghe; John Horsy.

South Fareham (*Suthfarham*), Wednesday after Purification, 43 Edward III.

1 Sir Robert's letter of attorney, dated 1 February 1368/9, appointed William Poul, clerk, and William atte Hale of Southwick, to deliver seisin of all the above lands. The original is in H.R.O. (5 M 50/22); it is extensively damaged; tag and seal are missing.

2 The above 2 acres and salt pans were subsequently given by Geoffrey to John le Hay (II 205).

II 205 13 May 1369

GIFT, with warranty, by Geoffrey Ramvyle, clerk, to John le Hay of Portchester (*Porchestre*) and his wife, Joan, of 2 acres of arable with salt pans, in the parish of Portchester, which he had by gift and feoffment from Robert Markaunt, knight, and which were formerly of the fee of John de Bourhunt', knight. [Situation of land and salt pans as given for the first two acres described in II 204.] John and Joan, their heirs and assigns, will hold them, with hedges, ditches, roads, paths, pastures, commons, and all other appurtenances, of the chief lords of that fee, for the accustomed services in perpetuity. Witnesses: Richard Abraham; Thomas atte Leghe; John le Eyr; John Upham; Robert Whyteby; William Chappe; William Lengestoke; and others.

Southwick, Sunday after the feast of St. John before the Latin Gate, 43 Edward III.

II 206 [1227–35][1]

[fo. 96] GIFT, with warranty, by Herbert, son of William de Burhunt', to Herbert, son of Osmund de Barra, of his sister, Isabella, in frank-marriage, together with 6 acres from his demesne. 2 acres lie within *Barra* (*infra barram*) between the lands of Richard Capellanus of Wanstead (*Wansted'*) and William de Ponte, and abut on to the *Shadewelle* road which runs from *Barra* to Southwick; 2 acres lie next to Sir Robert de Bello Alneto's land on one side and below the croft of Robert de Borhunt' on the other; 1½ acres lie in *Hechinge*, above *Rughedella;* and ½ acre lies in *Oseldene,* above the ditch of *Longamarla.* Herbert, son of Osmund, and his heirs by Isabella, will hold the aforesaid 6 acres with all appurtenances, of Herbert de Burhunte and his heirs by hereditary right, quit of service, exaction, custom, and secular demand. Witnesses: Walkelin, Prior of Southwick; Gilbert de Basevill'; Herbert de Burhunt', knight; Robert de Barra; John de Chich; Peter de Havonte [and] John, his son; Guy de Burhunt'; William de Bera; Brother Lawrence of Southwick; Brother Ralph; Andrew de Horsia; Adam Swele; and many others.

1 Dates of Walkelin's priorate.

II 207 [?late 13th century][1]

[fo. 96ᵛ] AGREEMENT, with warranty, between Henry de Burhunt' and Robert Faber of Portchester (*Porchestre*), whereby Henry has leased for life to Robert 2 acres in Portchester field, one called *la Ludeacre* and the other lying in *la Merkeforlong';* in return Robert, for as long as he lives, will make and mend the ironwork of the ploughs as often as necessary, using Henry's iron, for all secular service, except suit of Henry's court once a year. And if Robert dies during the lifetime of his wife, Rose (*Rosea, Rosye*), Henry concedes that Rose may hold the aforesaid 2 acres for two whole years after Robert's death, paying 2s. annual rent, viz. 12d. at Easter and 12d. at Michaelmas, for all service. Chirograph, bipartite, sealed alternately by Henry and Robert. Witnesses: [blank].

1 Possibly the lessor is the Henry de Burhunt who leases land in 1279 and 1295 (II 183, 197). Cf. II 198.

II 208 1324

NOTIFICATION by Thomas de Harpeden',[1] the King's Sub-Escheator in the county of Hampshire, that he has received from Richard de Burhunt', knight, 2s. rent for lands which were Pageday's, in Hinton, for Michaelmas term, 1324 (*de reddit' pro terr' que fuerunt Pageday in Henton' de termino Sancti Michaelis anno r' r' E. xvij*).

1 Thomas de Harpeden was escheator for Hampshire and other counties in 1326 (PRO *List of escheators for England and Wales* (List and Index Society, 72; 1971) p. 143), therefore the reign must be that of Edward II.

II 209

15 March 1366

[fo. 97] QUITCLAIM by Thomas Overton', son and heir of William de Overton', knight, to Sir William Wykham, Archdeacon of Lincoln (*Lyncoln'*), his heirs and assigns, of all right and claim he has, had, or could have, in £40 annual rent owed to him, having been lately granted to William de Overton' and his heirs by John de Bourhunte, knight, from the manor of Boarhunt;[1] also in £20 annual rent similarly granted by Sir John from the manor of Hinton (*Henton'*);[2] and in any other rent from, or right and claim in, the said manors. Witnesses: Bernard Brocas, John de Insula, knights; Walter Haywode; Nicholas Wodeloc; John Boteler; Thomas le Warenner; Thomas Everard; and others.

Southwick, Sunday after the feast of St. Gregory the Pope, 40 Edward III.

1 See II 122.
2 See II 95, 109.

II 210

6 July 1369

GIFT, with warranty, by Valentine atte Mede to Sir William de Wykham, Bishop of Winchester, of the manor of Hinton (*Henton'*) with appurtenances. Sir William, his heirs and assigns, will hold the manor with woods, meadows, grazings (*pascua*), pastures, waters, pools (*stagna*), fish ponds, fisheries, rents, and all other appurtenances, of the chief lords of that fee for the accustomed services in perpetuity. Witnesses: Sir Bernard Brocas, Sir Robert Markaunt, knights; John Romyn; Simon atte Grevette; Thomas Stake; and others.

Westminster (*Westmonasterium*), 43 (F. 30) Edward III.

II 211

12 April 1402

[fo. 97ᵛ] LETTER of ATTORNEY from William de Wykeham, Bishop of Winchester, appointing John Devenyssh' and John Shyre, jointly and severally, to deliver seisin in his manor of Hinton (*Henton'*), with appurtenances, which Valentine atte Mede formerly gave him,[1] to the following—Nicholas Wykeham; John Eylmer; John Campeden'; John Wykeham, rector of the church of Mapeldurham (*Mapulderham*); Thomas Ayleward', and William Norton, clerks—according to his charter drawn up for them.[2]

South Waltham (*Suth Waltham*), 12 April, 3 Henry IV.

1 See II 210.
2 See II 212.

II 212 12 April 1402

GIFT by William de Wykeham, Bishop of Winchester, to the following—
Nicholas Wykeham; John Eylmer; John Campeden'; John Wykeham,
rector of the church of Mapeldurham (*Mapulderham*); Thomas Ayleward'
and William Norton', clerks—of his manor of Hinton (*Hentone*) with
appurtenances.[1] The donees, their heirs and assigns, will hold the manor,
with woods, meadows, grazings, waters, pools, fishponds, fisheries, rents
and all other appurtenances, of the chief lords of that fee, for the
accustomed services in perpetuity. Witnesses: Henry Popham; John
Uvedale; John Tychebourne; William Ryngebourne; John Chamflour;
and others.

South Waltham (*Suth Waltham*), 12 April, 3 Henry IV.

1 Bishop William de Wykeham had acquired the manor of Hinton from Valentine
atte Mede in 1369 (II 210).
See also II 211 and 215.

II 213 13 April 1406

LETTER of ATTORNEY from Nicholas Wykeham, [etc. as in II 212]
appointing John atte Rythe, Andrew Dene and John Colmer', jointly
and severally, to deliver seisin of the manor of Hinton (*Henton'*) with
appurtenances to John Fromond, esquire, according to their charter
drawn up for the said John Fromond.[1]

13 April, 7 Henry IV.

1 See II 214, and II 210–12, 215.
John Fromond of Sparsholt was descended from Stephen Fromond, a
Winchester merchant and mayor of the city from 1264 to 1266. He was bailiff of
several episcopal manors and steward of the manors of Winchester College in
Hampshire and Wiltshire from 1408 to 1420. Before his death in November 1420
he had had a chantry chapel erected in the cloister of Winchester College, where
it stands to this day. By his will he made provision for a chaplain to sing masses
daily in that chapel for the souls of the Fromonds, and gave other benefactions
to the college. He also endowed a chantry in Sparsholt church (T. F. Kirby *Annals
of Winchester College* (London, 1892) pp. 157, 164–5; R. Custance *Winchester
College, Sixth-Centenary Essays* (Oxford, 1982 p. 63).

II 214 12 April 1406

GIFT by Nicholas Wykeham, [etc., as in II 212, 213] to John Fromonde,
esquire, of the manor of Hinton (*Henton'*) with appurtenances. John,
his heirs and assigns, will hold the manor, with woods, meadows,
grazings, waters, pools, fishponds, fisheries, rents, and all other appurtenances, of the chief lords of that fee for the accustomed services in
perpetuity. Witnesses: Henry Popham; John Uvedale; John Tycheborne,
sheriff; John Chamflour; William Ryngebourne; and others.

12 April, 7 Henry IV.

See II 213 and II 210–212, 215.

II 215   13 April 1402

[fo. 98]   LETTER OF ATTORNEY from Nicholas Wykeham, [etc., as
in II 212–214] appointing Henry Abraham and John Compton', jointly
and severally, to receive seisin of the manor of Hinton (*Henton'*) with
appurtenances, in accordance with the charter which William de
Wykeham, Bishop of Winchester, gave them.[1]
          South Waltham (SuthWaltham), 13 April, 3 Henry IV.

1 See II 212.

II 216   2 January 1423

GIFT, with warranty, by John atte Mede, son and heir of Valentine atte
Mede, to the following—John Styward, knight; John Tyrell', Bernard
Brocas, William Wayte, Richard Holte, and John Norton' the younger,
esquires—of his manor of Hinton Burrant (*Henton' Burhunte*) next
Catherington (*Kateryngton'*). The donees, their heirs and assigns, will
hold the manor, with all appurtenances, of the chief lords of that fee,
for the accustomed rents and services. Witnesses: Walter Sandys, knight;
William Brocas; John Banastrs; Richard Spycer; John Estens; Roger
Ingelfeld; Edward Klyne; and others.
     Hinton, Saturday, the day after the feast of Circumcision, 1 Henry VI.

II 217   2 March 1425

NOTIFICATION by Richard Wallop, John Harryes, and Richard Seman,
feoffees of the late John Fromond; Robert Thurbern, Warden of the
College of the Blessed Mary, Winchester, and John Halle of Burgate,
John Fromond's executors. Whereas John Roger the elder, John Roger
the younger, John Stork, and Peter Cursy, clerk, hold divers manors,
lands and tenements in the county of Hampshire, which belonged to the
said John Fromond, by virtue of a charter drawn up by them and
enrolled in the king's chancery, in which, amongst others, the manor of
Hinton Burrant (*Henton' Burhunt*) with appurtenances in the said county
is named, and by that charter Bernard Brocas, Richard Holte, and John
Norton the younger, now possessors of the same manor, and their heirs
and assigns in the future, can be expelled and harassed. It is therefore
manifestly just and right that everything be done to cut short future
discord and openly declare the truth; for which reason they make known
what the said John Roger the elder, [etc.] have no possession or seisin
whatever in the said manor of Hinton Burrant by virtue of the said
charter or by any other action of theirs. Immediately after the drawing
up of their charter, and before any seisin was delivered to the said John
Roger the elder, [etc.] of any parcel of land by virtue of that charter,
John Valentyn, as son and heir of the late Valentine atte Mede, entered

the said manor of Hinton Burrant, on 2 January 1423 (the day after Circumcision, 1 Henry VI), and enfeoffed Bernard Brocas, Richard Holte and John Norton the younger;[1] against whom, and others, a suit of novel disseisin was brought by Richard Wallopp, John Harryes and Richard Seman before John Martyn and John Ectisinore at Winchester. Afterwards, by the intervention of mutual friends, and for a large sum of money paid to the aforesaid executors,[2] the feoffees, with consent of the executors, have quitclaimed to Bernard Brocas, Richard Holte and John Norton the younger, all their right and claim in the aforesaid manor with appurtenances.[3] Indentures sealed alternately by the feoffees, the executors, and Bernard, Richard and John.

2 March, 3 Henry VI.

1 See II 216.

2 See II 219.

3 See II 218.

Valentine atte Mede had granted in perpetuity the manor of Hinton (*Burrant*) to Bishop William de Wykeham in 1369 (II 210). The Bishop granted it to feoffees in 1402 (II 212), and they granted it to John Fromond in 1406 (II 214). Bernard Brocas, Richard Holte and John Norton the younger paid 100 marks to the executors to retain the manor (II 219).

None of this complicated story appears in *VCH*, which states that "from Valentine atte Mede the manor appears to have passed to Sir Robert Markaunt" (*VCH Hants* III, p. 98). But it seems very unlikely that the charter on which this statement is based refers to Hinton Burrant, rather than to Hinton Markaunt (P.R.O. E 326/2543).

II 218   1 March 1425

[fo. 98ᵛ] QUITCLAIM by John Halle of Burgate and John Harryes, esquires; Richard Wallop; and Richard Seman; to Bernard Brocas, esquire; Richard Holte; and John Norton the younger; their heirs and assigns: of all right and claim they have, had, or could have, in the manor of Hinton Burrant (*Henton' Bourhunte*) with appurtenances, which Bernard, Richard and John now hold by gift from John atte Mede, *alias* John Valentyn, son and heir of Valentine atte Mede; and which lately belonged to John Fromond, esquire.[1]

1 March, 3 Henry VI.

1 See II 216, 217 and note.

II 219   1 March 1425

[fo. 99] NOTIFICATION by Robert Thurbern, clerk; John Halle, esquire; and Richard Seman; executors of the will of the late John Fromond, esquire, of receipt of 100 marks from Bernard Brocas, Richard

Holte, and John Norton the younger, in full payment of all money owed to them for the manor of Hinton Burrant (*Henton' Burhunte*) with appurtenances.[1] They acknowledge that they have been paid, and that Bernard, Richard and John, their heirs and executors, are quit.

1 March, 3 Henry VI.

1 See II 217 and note.

The rest of fo. 99 and fo. 99ᵛ are blank.

II 220   30 May 1439

[fo. 100] LETTER of ATTORNEY from the following—Reginald West, Lord la Warre; Reginald Dalyngrygge; Nicholas Uvedale; Thomas de Haydock; Hugh Combe, chaplain; and William Knolle—appointing John Uvedale, esquire, and Richard Holte, jointly and severally, to deliver seisin to Edward, Prior of Southwick,[1] and the convent, in all their messuages, cottages (*cotagia*), tofts, lands, meadows, grazings (*pascua*), pastures, rents, reversions and services, with apputenances, in Southwick, Boarhunt Herberd (*Bourhonte Herberd*) and West Boarhunt (*Westbourghunt*), according to the donors' charter drawn up for the prior and convent and their successors in perpetuity.[2]

30 May, 17 Henry VI.

1 Edward Dene, Prior of Southwick from 1432 to 1455.

2 See II 221.

Original in H.R.O. 5M50/32. Variant: Westbourghonte. Damaged and repaired, most of right-hand edge missing. Probably in the same hand as 5M50/30 and 32.

Seals: on 6 tags, each *c.* 12 cms; 3 complete seals and 3 fragments; all of dark red wax.
   (1) Tiny fragment.
   (2) Round, 1.3 cms diameter; device: in a beeded circle, a seated unicorn with ?scroll on its back; no legend.
   (3) Octagonal, 1 cm × 1 cm; device: a seated deer; legend indistinct.
   (4) Round, 1 cm diameter; device: in a beaded circle, a bird; legend: [?] PU..MEMO.RE [indistinct].
   (5) Fragment.
   (6) Fragment.
Endorsement: none.

II 221   30 May 1439

GIFT by Reginald West, Lord la Warre; [etc., as in II 220] to Edward, Prior of Southwick, and the convent, of 4 messuages, 12 cottages (*cotagia*), 7 tofts, 70 acres of land, 5 acres of meadow, 2 acres of wood, and 15s. rent, with appurtenances, in Southwick, Boarhunt Herberd (*Bourhont Herberde*), and West Boarhunt (*Westbourhunt*).[1] The prior and convent, and their successors, will hold all the above of the chief lords of those fees, for the accustomed services. Witnesses: William Wayte, Richard Newport, Nicholas Banastar and John Wayte, esquires; Robert Snokeshylle; John Wanstede; Baldwin Farle; and others.

Southwick, 17 Henry VI.

1 See II 223-5, and Appendix V(c).
Original in H.R.O. 5M50/31. Variants: Bourhonte Herberd; Westbourghonte; Neuport; Banastr'; Snokeshull'.
Seals: on 7 tags, each 12-13 cms; 6 seals, all of dark red wax, and 1 missing.
(1) Missing, trace of wax only.
(2) Round, 3 cms diameter; Uvedale's seal, chipped top and bottom, otherwise clear; device: in a circle, a shield of arms; legend: SIGILLUM .... UVEDALE
(3) [As (2) on 5M50/32; see above II 220.]
(4) [As (3) on 5M50/32.]
(5) Fragment only.
(6) Round, 1 cm diameter; device: in a circle, a monogram with crown over the top; no legend.
(7) Octagonal, 1.1 cms across; device: within a cusped frame, a shield of arms with two chevrons; no legend.
Endorsement: [press mark only].
Copy II 222. Variants: Haydok'; [omit numbers of messuages etc. and amounts of land and rent; add after rent:] reversions and services; Banstr'.

II 222 [fo. 100ᵛ]   Copy of II 221.

Original in H.R.O. 5M50/30.
Seals: on 7 tags, each *c.* 12-13 cms; 2 complete seals, 4 broken pieces, 1 fragment, all in dark red wax.
(1) Round, 1 cm diameter; device: a fleur-de-lys; no legend. Wax broken and nearly half missing, but impression almost intact.
(2) [As (2) on 5M50/31; see above II 221. Part of left side and edge missing; legend survives as:] SIGIL .... OHANN ....
(3) [Piece of (2) as on 5M50/32; see above II 220.]
(4) [As (3) on 5M50/32; complete.]
(5) [Piece of (4) as on 5M50/32.]
(6) [As (6) on 5M50/31.]
(7) [Fragment of (7) as on 5M50/31.]
Endorsement: [press mark only].

II 223   3 June 1439

QUITCLAIM by John Uvedale, esquire, and his son Nicholas, to Edward, Prior of Southwick, the convent, and their successors in perpetuity, of all right and claim they have, had, of could have, in all those messuages, cottages, tofts, lands, meadows, woods, and rents, with appurtenances, in Southwick, Boarhunt Herberd, and West Boarhunt, which the donors together with the following—Reginald West, Lord la Warre; Richard Dalyngrigg'; Thomas de Haydok'; Hugh Combe, chaplain; and William Knolle—lately gave to the priory. Neither John nor Nicholas, nor either of them, nor the heirs of both or either of them, can exercise any right in the aforesaid [property], but will be permanently excluded by these presents from any action, title or claim. Witnesses: William Wayte, Richard Neuport, Nicholas Banastr' and John Wayte, esquires; Robert Snokeshyll'; John Wanstede; Baldwin Farle; and others. 3 June, 17 Henry VI.

See II 221, 224, 225. In 1434 John Uvedale had made over all his property in Southwick and Boarhunt to Reginald West and others (Appendix V(c)).

Original in H.R.O. 5M50/33. Variant: Snokeshull'.

Seals: 1 tag missing; on another, *c.* 12 cms, a broken piece of red wax with part of the impression of an octagonal seal, 1 cm across [possibly as (3) on 5M50/32, see above II 220].

Endorsement: [press mark only].

II 224   13 October 1439

[fo. 101] INQUISITION held at Southwick in the presence of John Thornebery, the King's Escheator in the county of Hampshire. Jurors: Robert Snokeshyll'; Simon atte Hale; John Wanstede; John Eyre; Edward [ ]utherle; John Gryme; John Corfe; William atte Heth'; Roger Erle; John Fleccher; Richard Leche; and John Rycher the elder. They say on oath that it will not be damaging or prejudicial to the king or others if the king allows the following—Reginald West, knight; John Uvedale; Richard Dalyngrygg'; Nicholas Uvedale; Thomas de Haydok; Hugh Combe, chaplain; and William Knolle—to give to Prior Edward of Southwick and to the convent: 4 messuages, 19 tofts, 70 acres of land, 5 acres of meadow, 2 acres of wood, and 15s. rent, with appurtenances, in Boarhunt Herberd and West Boarhunt, as specified in the king's writ.[1] The priory will hold the aforesaid [property] in perpetuity in part satisfaction of an annual £20 worth of land, tenements and rents [for the acquisition of] which King Edward [II], progenitor of the present king, granted [a licence] to the same priory by letters patent.[2] The aforesaid messuages, etc. are held of the priory in socage for an annual rent of 40s. 7d. and 3-weekly suit of court, for all service; their true value is 60s. a year over and above (*ultra*) the said rent and services. There are no other mesne lords of these tenements between the king and the donors. Over and above this gift, the donors have land and tenements in Barton Peverell, Wickham, Limborne, Greywell and Rotherwick (*Berton' Peverell', Wykham, Lymborne, Greywell', Rotherwyk'*) in the aforesaid county, sufficient to cover custom and service, owed both for the gift and for lands and tenements retained by them, and for all other burdens they are accustomed to sustain, such as suits of court, views of frankpledge, aids, tallages, watch and ward (*vigilia*), fines, redemptions, amercements, contributions and anything else arising. [The lands retained] are not held of the king, but the jurors do not know of whom they are held, or by what service. And the aforesaid Reginald, John, Richard, Nicholas, Thomas, William, and the heirs of Hugh are eligible to serve as jurors at assize or any other examinations (*recognitiones*) whatever, as they were wont to serve before making the aforesaid gift, so that the local people (*patria*) will not be burdened more heavily than before as a result of the gift.

In testimony of which, the jurors have appended their seals.

13 October, 18 Henry VI.

1 See II 225, and 221, 223.

2 III 977; *Cal Pat R, 1317-21* p. 109.
There is a contemporary copy of the above inquisition: H.R.O. 5M50/34. It is extensively damaged and, though it has been repaired, it is only partly legible.
Endorsements: (a) [a list in a 16th century hand of the names of 19 tenants who attorned to Edward, Prior of Southwick].
(b) .... John Uvedale to the Prior of Southwick .... Burrant ... [? 19th century hand].

II 225   8 November 1439

[fo. 101ᵛ] LETTERS PATENT of King Henry [VI] confirming the licence granted by his predecessor, King Edward [II], to the prior and convent of Southwick, to acquire lands, tenements and rents, with appurtenances, to the value of £20 a year, both of his own and other fees, notwithstanding the Statute of Mortmain, over and above the land, tenements, and rents held of him in chief. Wishing the aforesaid concession to be carried into effect, the king, by his special grace and in consideration of £10 paid into his hanaper, has granted licence on behalf of himself and his heirs, so far as he is able, to the following—Reginald West, knight; John Uvedale; Richard Dalyngrigge; Nicholas Uvedale; Thomas de Haydok'; Hugh Combe, chaplain; and William Knolle—to give to Southwick Priory: 4 messuages, 19 tofts, 70 acres of land, 5 acres of meadow, 2 acres of wood, and 15s. rent, with appurtenances, in Southwick, Boarhunt Herberd (*Bourghunt Herberd'*), and West Boarhunt (*Westbourghunt*). These are held of the king and others, and are worth 60s. a year according to the inquisition held on the king's orders before John Thornbery, lately his escheator in the county of Hampshire, and returned to his chancery.¹ Saving the accustomed services due to the chief lords of that fee, the priory will hold the aforesaid [property], to count as 5 marks a year, as part satisfaction of the £20 worth of land, tenements, and rents; and the donors and priory are not to be prosecuted or harassed in any way by the king, his heirs, or their justices, escheators, sheriffs, bailiffs, or officers, by reason of the aforesaid Statute. Witnessed by the King.²

Westminster, 8 November, 18 Henry VI.

1 Se II 224

2 *Cal. Pat. R., 1436-41* p. 343.

II 226   8 July 1390

[fo. 102] GRANT, with warranty, by William Bonelith' to the prior and convent of Southwick, of 1d. annual rent at Michaelmas from his messuage and curtillage at *la Brodewey*; also suit of court at two court leets a year at Southwick, viz. at Martinmas and Hocke. And if the annual rent, or suit at either court, is in arrears, the prior and covent and their successors may enter the said messuage and curtillage, distrain, and keep the distraint until full satisfaction is given. Witnesses: John le Lorde; Adam in le Lane; Nicholas de Henton'; Peter Longe; John Gyllour the younger; and many others.[1]

Le Brodeweye, 8 July, 14 Richard II.

1 In small letters at the end of the last line: G. Eyre—possibly the name of the scribe.
Copy III 929. Variants: Bonelithe; omit G. Eyre.
The rest of folio 102ᵛ is blank.

II 227 [*c.* 1300]

[fo. 103] GIFT with warranty, by Richard de Merley to Thomas Stake of Stakes (*Frendestaple*) and his wife Isabella, of 1 messuage and curtillage lying between Thomas' messuage and Geoffrey Poleyn's garden in the vill of Stakes, which is in the parish of Farlington (*Farlyngton'*); and the whole farm (*Bertomum*) extending from the east gate to the field in the west, and to the heath in the south; and all the land he had, together with a certain wood, in the vill of Stakes, lying between the park of Sir Reginald, son of Peter, and Lewyn de Fredestaple's land south of Thomas' own house. Thomas and Isabella, their heirs or assigns, will hold the aforesaid messuage, curtillage and farm, with appurtenances, of Richard and his heirs by hereditary right in perpetuity, paying to them 7s. annual rent at Michaelmas, and to the lords of the fee, whoever they may be at the time, 3 arrows, barbed and fletched, for all service, exaction, custom, suit of court and secular demand. Consideration, 8 marks. Witnesses: Sir Richard de Portsey, Sir Richard de Burhunt, Sir John le Jankeney, Sir Baldwin de Bello Augneto, knights; Roger de Multon'; Simon Stake; John Colmere; Wyot de Horley; William Alyn'; and many others.

II 228 3 February 1434

GIFT by the following—Peter Beneroo, clerk, of Winchester; Robert Monkeston', rector of the church of Farlington (*Farlyngton'*); and John Norton of Nutley (*Nuttlee*), late of Southwick—to Robert Snokeshull' [fo. 103ᵛ] and his wife Agnes, of 2 burgages in Fareham (*Farham*), and all their lands, tenements, rents, reversions, and services, with appurtenances, in Stakes (*Frendestaple*) and Farlington, which Geoffrey Hore of Lovedean (*Lovedene*) lately surrendered to them. Robert and Agnes, and the lawful heirs of their bodies, will hold the above of the chief lords of those fees, for the accustomed rent and service. If Robert and Agnes die without a lawful heir of their bodies, reversion will be on the same terms, successively, to Robert's brothers: Henry, John, Richard, Thomas, and Emoric, and the lawful heirs of their bodies. If Emoric dies without a lawful heir of his body, reversion will be to the right (*recti*) heirs of Henry Snokeshulle, on the same terms. Witnesses: John Wanstede the younger; Richard Wanstede; John Barbour of Havant (*Havont*); John Scryveyn; John Truslove; Peter Faye; John [fo. 104] Corffe; and others.

Stakes, Wednesday, the day after the feast of the Purification of the Blessed Virgin Mary, 12 Henry VI.

The rest of folio 104 and folio 104ᵛ are blank.

II 229   19 October 1438

[fo. 105¹] MEMORANDUM: (i) on Sunday, 19 October, 17 Henry VI, Robert Snokeshull did homage to Edward Dene, Prior of Southwick, in the chamber (*camera*) of the priory, for lands and tenements he holds of the prior [in] Stakes (*Frendestaple*) and Farlington (*Farlyngton'*), for knight service. The following were present: Richard Holte, then steward of the prior's land; Brother Philip Stool; Brother Henry Wranne; Brother John Soberton; John [Gold]smyth; John Wanstede; Thomas Boteler, clerk of account (*clericus compoti*) there; Thomas [...]le; and others. And the said Robert paid the prior's chamberlain 6s. [?8d.] for his fee, of which 5s. was remitted (*unde pardonatur vs.*).
(ii) On the same day, Robert Fowell' came and did homage to the prior for lands, formerly Breweres', which he holds of the prior in Stakes and Farlington, for knight service. The following were present: Richard Holte, then [steward] of the prior's land; Brother Philip Stool; Brother Henry Wranne; Brother John [Sobe]rton; Robert Snokeshull'; John Goldsmyth; John Wanstede; Richard [...] ?de Estone; Thomas Boteler, clerk of account there; and others. And Robert Fowell' paid the prior's chamberlain 6s. 8d. for his fee, of which 5s. was remitted.

1 The left-hand edge of this folio is stained and illegible. As the two entries are similar, it has been possible to supply some missing words by comparing one with the other.

II 230   [c. 1369-85]¹

[fo. 105ᵛ] TAXATION OF ALL CHURCHES AND MANORS, RENTS AND PENSIONS OF THE PRIORY OF SOUTHWICK WHEREVER THEY ARE.

The churches are assessed (*taxantur*) as follows:

Southwick   at 15 marks, of which the tenth is   20s.   0d.

Portchester	at 14 marks, of which the tenth is	18s.	8d.
Wymering	at 12 marks, of which the tenth is	16s.	0d.
Boarhunt	at 11 marks, of which the tenth is	14s.	8d.
Portsea	at 45 marks, of which the tenth is	40s.	0d.
Preston Candover	at 16 marks, of which the tenth is	21s.	4d.
Nutley	at 10 marks, of which the tenth is	13s.	4d.
Swindon [Wilts]	at 20 marks, of which the tenth is	26s.	8d.
Empshott	at 10 marks, of which the tenth is	13s.	4d.
	Total 153 marks, of which the tenth is £10.	4s.	0d.

The manors of the priory are assessed as follows:

Southwick	at	£ 7.	4s.	11d.
Westboarhunt	at	£ 6.	8s.	1d.
Crofton	at		8s.	9d.
Newlands	at		32s.	2d.
Anmore	at		10s.	2d.
Stubbington	at		46s.	0d.
Candover	at		71s.	8d.
Ellisfield	at		15s.	11d.
Priors Dean	at		60s.	0d.
Old Fishborne [Sussex]	at		40s.	4d.
	Total for all manors and lands	£27	19s.	0d.
	of which the tenth is 55s. 10½			

The manors of Farlington, Boarhunt Herberd, and Boarhunt Herbelyn are not included in this clerical taxation, but contribute with the laity.

Assessment (*taxatio*) of the rents of the priory:

at Winchester	40s.	0d.
at Aldbourne [Wilts]	23s.	4d.
at Clanfield [Oxon]	56s.	8d.
Total £ 6. 0s. 0d., of which the tenth is 12s.		

Assessment (*taxatio*) of all the pensions of the priory:

from the rectory of Shalden	20s. 0d., of which the tenth is	2s.	0d.
from the rectory of Widley	24s. 0d., of which the tenth is	2s.	5d.
from the rectory of Walesworth	8s. 0d., of which the tenth is		9¾
from the vicarage of Portsea	30s. 0d., of which the tenth is	3s.	0d.
from the vicarage of Wymering	6s. 8d., of which the tenth is		[8d.]
from the vicarage of Portchester	24s. 0d., of which the tenth is	2s.	5d.
from the ancient pension of Swindon [Wilts]	100s. 0d., of which the tenth is 10s.		0d.
Total £10. 12s. 8d., of which the tenth is 21s.			3¾

Total of all assessment for taxation of all churches, manors, rents and pensions of the priory £146. 12s. 8d., of which the tenth paid to the king, when granted by the clergy is: £14. 13s. 2¼d.

N.B. the priory only pays £11. 15s. 1½d. for its tenth in the diocese of Winchester, but the rectors and vicars themselves pay the tenths of their pensions, and this is allowed to them in their annual pensions.

Spellings of place names in the above lists are as follows: Porcest'; Wymeringe; Burhunt; Portesey; Prestoncandevere; Nutteley; Swyndon; Imbeschete; Westburhunt; Croftone; Nova terra; Andemere; Stobinton'; Candevere; Elsefeld; Dene; Fyscheborne; Farlyngton'; Aldborne; Clanefeld'; Schaldene; Wydeley; Wallesworth'.

1 These lists must have been drawn up after 1369, when the priory acquired Boarhunt Herberd and Boarhunt Herbelyn (II 111), but there is no mention of the manors of Hannington and East Hoe acquired, in 1385 (III 427).

II 231   [fo. 106]   Copy of I 214.

II 232   20 October 1415

[fo. 106^vl] MEMORANDUM: On Sunday after the feast of St. Luke the Evangelist, 3 Henry V—in the presence of Sir Nicholas Rigge, Henry Zeng', Robert Landwath and Richard [...]¹—Simon Jopp' of Cosham, brother of Thomas Jopp', came to Southwick and did homage to Sir Thomas Courtais, Prior of Southwick, for a [?]toft¹ containing 1 acre in Farlington (*Farlyngton*).

1 This folio is badly stained on the right-hand side, and some words are blotted out or almost illegible.

II 233   22 June 1418

MEMORANDUM: On the feast of St. Alban the Martyr, 6 Henry V— in the presence of M. [?]William [...]¹, the prior's chaplain, Robert Landwath and William Man—John Kentyssh came [to Southwick]¹ at

supper-time (*hora cene*) and did homage to Sir Thomas Courteys, the
prior, for ....²
[Marginal note:] Farlington.

1 See note to II 232.
2 Space left blank in MS.

II 234   8 October 1422

MEMORANDUM: On Thursday after the feast of St. Faith the Virgin,
1 Henry VI—in the presence of William, [?]the prior's hordarian,¹ and
William Man—John Bayken came to Southwick at supper-time and did
[homage to]¹ Sir Thomas ?Curteys.¹
[Marginal note:] Farlington.

1 See note to II 232.
Further evidence of the leasing of land from the priory's holdings is contained
in a memorandum drawn up on 23 October 1421, when Prior Thomas Courteys
leased numerous crofts and acres to tenants at Stubbington-in-Portsea (Win. Coll.
Muniments 15264A).

II 235   [? 13 January] 1266

PLEA at Winchester before Roger Seyton and his colleagues, Justices,
[.....] of St. Hillary, 50 Henry, son of King John, [........] Richard le
Bel, Henry le Carpent', William le Gervays, [.....] atte dych', Richard le
Yonge, William atte Lode, Hugh le Carpent', Stephen [.....], William de
Dosecombe, Lawrence atte Slade, Henry atte Slade, Gilbert [.....], Peter
de Golle, the prior of Southwick's men, [came and] put themselves [on
the verdict of] the justices [.....] against the prior, as to whether the
aforesaid Richard and the others, and their ancestors when the manor
of Dean (Dene) was in the hands of King John and his predecessors,
held their tenements there for certain services—viz. One [.....] for the
service of 7s. and collecting the rents of the vill [.....] and that they pay
tallage when the king tallages [.....] doubling their rents after the death
of their ancestors for all [?service] due for one virgate, and less according
to the size [..... as] Richard and the others say; or whether Richard and
the others, and their ancestors, [hold] their tenements for certain money
services [and] for all manner of villein [obligations] (*per omnimodas
villanas ..... villana*), [.....] as the prior says.
     The jurors chosen with the consent of the parties say on oath that
Richard and the others, and their ancestors when the aforesaid manor
was in the hands of King John, did not do [services] other than those
they now acknowledge to be due to the prior, and that the prior unjustly
exacts from them services other than those they were wont to do in the
time of King John. So it was decided that Richard and the others and

their heirs are to hold their lands in Dean of the prior and his successors for the aforesaid services, which they acknowledge to be due to him, and the prior cannot exact other services from them or their heirs in perpetuity. And the prior is at mercy, etc² .....

1 See note to II 232.

2 Dean, later known as Priors Dean, was granted to the priory by King John in 1204 (I 162). In 1208 the king ordered an inquisition to be held into the alienation of lands and labour services at Dean, which was alleged to have taken place before the manor was granted to the priory (I 163, 164).

See also the rentals for Priors Dean and Colemore (I 178, 195). Names similar to those five of the above plaintiffs occur in the later rental. Another name, that of Richard le Bel, occurs as a witness to a charter concerning Priors Dean in 1278 and again in 1296 (III 843, 850).

II 236   13 January 1351

STATUTE [5]:[1] It is agreed and established that no purveyor of wood or timber for the king's use, for building or any other purpose, shall cut or fell any man's trees growing around or enclosed by (*dedeins*) his house; on penalty of having to give satisfaction to the extent of three times the amount of the damages, being imprisoned for a year, and forfeiting his office (*et soit foriugge de son effice*).

Westminister, the feast of St Hillary,
25 Edward III, cap. 6.

French

1 *Statutes of the Realm* I, p. 321.